Balance and Boundaries in Creating Meaningful Relationships in Online Higher Education

Sarah H. Jarvie
Colorado Christian University, USA

Cara Metz
The University of Arizona Global Campus, USA

A volume in the Advances in Higher Education and Professional Development (AHEPD) Book Series

Published in the United States of America by
IGI Global
Information Science Reference (an imprint of IGI Global)
701 E. Chocolate Avenue
Hershey PA, USA 17033
Tel: 717-533-8845
Fax: 717-533-8661
E-mail: cust@igi-global.com
Web site: http://www.igi-global.com

Copyright © 2024 by IGI Global. All rights reserved. No part of this publication may be reproduced, stored or distributed in any form or by any means, electronic or mechanical, including photocopying, without written permission from the publisher. Product or company names used in this set are for identification purposes only. Inclusion of the names of the products or companies does not indicate a claim of ownership by IGI Global of the trademark or registered trademark.

Library of Congress Cataloging-in-Publication Data

Names: Jarvie, Sarah H., 1984- editor. | Metz, Cara, 1982- editor.
Title: Balance and boundaries in creating meaningful relationships in
   online higher education / edited by Sarah H. Jarvie, and Cara Metz.
Description: Hershey, PA : Information Science Reference, [2024] | Includes
   bibliographical references and index. | Summary: "The objective of this
   book is to help people who are new to or people looking to improve their
   online classroom relationships. There is currently very little
   literature, especially books, that talk about online relationship
   building. It is well documented that relationships impact the learning
   of students in positive ways, and when students enter into an online
   world, this need does not go away. As COVID has accelerated the need for
   quality online instructors, there is a lack of references and resources
   available to understand the nuances of teaching a class online and
   building a connection with students"-- Provided by publisher.
Identifiers: LCCN 2023029605 (print) | LCCN 2023029606 (ebook) | ISBN
   9781668489086 (h/c) | ISBN 9781668489123 (s/c) | ISBN 9781668489093
   (eISBN)
Subjects: LCSH: Education, Higher--Computer-assisted instruction--Social
   aspects. | Distance education--Computer-assisted instruction--Social
   aspects. | Universities and colleges--Computer network resources. |
   Web-based instruction--Social aspects. | Internet in higher
   education--Social aspects. | Teacher-student relationships--Social
   aspects. | COVID-19 Pandemic, 2020---Influence. | Teachers--In-service
   training.
Classification: LCC LB2395.7 .B35 2023 (print) | LCC LB2395.7 (ebook) |
   DDC 378.1/7344678--dc23/eng/20230808
LC record available at https://lccn.loc.gov/2023029605
LC ebook record available at https://lccn.loc.gov/2023029606

This book is published in the IGI Global book series Advances in Higher Education and Professional Development (AHEPD) (ISSN: 2327-6983; eISSN: 2327-6991)

British Cataloguing in Publication Data
A Cataloguing in Publication record for this book is available from the British Library.

All work contributed to this book is new, previously-unpublished material. The views expressed in this book are those of the authors, but not necessarily of the publisher.

For electronic access to this publication, please contact: eresources@igi-global.com.

Advances in Higher Education and Professional Development (AHEPD) Book Series

Jared Keengwe
University of North Dakota, USA

ISSN:2327-6983
EISSN:2327-6991

Mission

As world economies continue to shift and change in response to global financial situations, job markets have begun to demand a more highly-skilled workforce. In many industries a college degree is the minimum requirement and further educational development is expected to advance. With these current trends in mind, the **Advances in Higher Education & Professional Development (AHEPD) Book Series** provides an outlet for researchers and academics to publish their research in these areas and to distribute these works to practitioners and other researchers.

AHEPD encompasses all research dealing with higher education pedagogy, development, and curriculum design, as well as all areas of professional development, regardless of focus.

Coverage

- Adult Education
- Assessment in Higher Education
- Career Training
- Coaching and Mentoring
- Continuing Professional Development
- Governance in Higher Education
- Higher Education Policy
- Pedagogy of Teaching Higher Education
- Vocational Education

IGI Global is currently accepting manuscripts for publication within this series. To submit a proposal for a volume in this series, please contact our Acquisition Editors at Acquisitions@igi-global.com or visit: http://www.igi-global.com/publish/.

The Advances in Higher Education and Professional Development (AHEPD) Book Series (ISSN 2327-6983) is published by IGI Global, 701 E. Chocolate Avenue, Hershey, PA 17033-1240, USA, www.igi-global.com. This series is composed of titles available for purchase individually; each title is edited to be contextually exclusive from any other title within the series. For pricing and ordering information please visit http://www.igi-global.com/book-series/advances-higher-education-professional-development/73681. Postmaster: Send all address changes to above address. Copyright © 2024 IGI Global. All rights, including translation in other languages reserved by the publisher. No part of this series may be reproduced or used in any form or by any means – graphics, electronic, or mechanical, including photocopying, recording, taping, or information and retrieval systems – without written permission from the publisher, except for non commercial, educational use, including classroom teaching purposes. The views expressed in this series are those of the authors, but not necessarily of IGI Global.

Titles in this Series

For a list of additional titles in this series, please visit: http://www.igi-global.com/book-series/advances-higher-education-professional-development/73681

Creating Diverse Experiences for Rural Appalachian Pre-Service Teachers
Kimberly Dianne Cassidy (Shawnee State University, USA)
Information Science Reference • © 2024 • 300pp • H/C (ISBN: 9781668443699) • US $215.00

Best Practices to Prepare Writers for Their Professional Paths
Carissa A. Barker-Stucky (Carnegie Writers, Inc., USA) and Kemi Elufiede (Carnegie Writers, Inc., USA)
Information Science Reference • © 2024 • 300pp • H/C (ISBN: 9781668490242) • US $225.00

Accessibility of Digital Higher Education in the Global South
Pfano Mashau (University of KwaZulu-Natal, South Africa) and Tshililo Ruddy Farisani (University of KwaZulu-Natal, South Africa)
Information Science Reference • © 2024 • 371pp • H/C (ISBN: 9781668491799) • US $215.00

Mental Health Crisis in Higher Education
Peter J. O. Aloka (University of the Witwatersrand, South Africa)
Information Science Reference • © 2024 • 400pp • H/C (ISBN: 9798369328330) • US $300.00

Teaching Humanities With Cultural Responsiveness at HBCUs and HSIs
DuEwa M. Frazier (Coppin State University, USA)
Information Science Reference • © 2024 • 270pp • H/C (ISBN: 9781668497821) • US $230.00

Stabilizing and Empowering Women in Higher Education Realigning, Recentering, and Rebuilding
Heidi L. Schnackenberg (SUNY Plattsburgh, USA) and Denise A. Simard (SUNY Plattsburgh, USA)
Information Science Reference • © 2023 • 303pp • H/C (ISBN: 9781668485972) • US $215.00

Promoting Intercultural Agility and Leadership Development at Home and Abroad for First-Year Students
Jon Stauff (South Dakota State University, USA) and Jill E. Blondin (Virginia Commonwealth University, USA)
Information Science Reference • © 2024 • 320pp • H/C (ISBN: 9781668488324) • US $215.00

Practices and Perspectives of Teaching and Teacher Education in Africa
Gideon Boadu (RMIT University, Melbourne, Australia) George Odhiambo (United Arab Emirates University, Al Ain, UAE) and Pegah Marandi (Excelsia College, Australia)
Information Science Reference • © 2023 • 284pp • H/C (ISBN: 9781668477229) • US $270.00

701 East Chocolate Avenue, Hershey, PA 17033, USA
Tel: 717-533-8845 x100 • Fax: 717-533-8661
E-Mail: cust@igi-global.com • www.igi-global.com

Editorial Advisory Board

Daniel Bates, *Truman University, USA*
Kathleen Boothe, *Southeastern Oklahoma State University, USA*
Crystal A. Brashear, *Colorado Christian University, USA*
Elizabeth Brokamp, *Gwynedd Mercy University, USA*
Dickson K. W. Chiu, *The University of Hong Kong, Hong Kong*
Kim Cowan, *University of Arizona Global Campus, USA*
Carrie Grimes, *Vanderbilt University, USA*
Ariel Harrison, *Walden University, USA*
Donna Hickman, *University of North Texas, USA*
Yvonne Ho, *Fortis College, USA*
Elodie Jones, *Fort Hays State University, USA*
Apple H. C. Lam, *The University of Hong Kong, Hong Kong*
Marla Lohmann, *Colorado Christian University, USA*
Shalini Mathew, *Northern State University, USA*
Rebecca Mathews, *University of North Carolina at Greensboro, USA*
Paula McMahon, *Montana State University Billings, USA*
Rosina Mete, *Yorkville University, Canada*
Yuanjun Ni, *The University of Hong Kong, Hong Kong*
Heather Pederson, *University of Arizona Global Campus, USA*
Selin Philip, *Colorado Christian University, USA*
Fatma Ouled Salem, *Walden University, USA*
Jessica Snedker, *Colorado Christian University, USA*
Rebecca Taylor, *Colorado Christian University, USA*
Whitney Walters-Sachs, *Vanderbilt University, USA*
Sara Wood, *Colorado Christian University, USA*

Table of Contents

Preface xvi

Acknowledgment xix

Chapter 1
Are You Okay? Examining the Role of Student Mental Health in the Online Classroom 1
Sarah H. Jarvie, Colorado Christian University, USA
Cara L. Metz, The University of Arizona Global Campus, USA

Chapter 2
Building an Adult Learning Community While Converting an In-Person Degree Program to an
Online Format: A Case Study in Strategies and Lessons Learned 16
Carrie Grimes, Vanderbilt University, USA
Whitney Walters-Sachs, Vanderbilt University, USA

Chapter 3
Building Relationship Through Discussion: Innovative Ideas to Connect and Empower 55
Crystal Ann Brashear, Colorado Christian University, USA

Chapter 4
Challenges With Sensitivity and Boundaries in an Imperfect, Ever-Changing World: Online
Counselor Education 74
Rosina E. Mete, Yorkville University, Canada
Alyssa Weiss, Yorkville University, Canada

Chapter 5
Creating Care in the Online Classroom 90
Kim Cowan, The University of Arizona Global Campus, USA
William G. Davis, The University of Arizona Global Campus, USA
Stephanie Stubbs, The University of Arizona Global Campus, USA

Chapter 6
Cultivating Cultural Competence and Meaningful Bonds in the Virtual Classroom Using a
Narrative Approach 111
    Selin Philip, Colorado Christian University, USA
    Shalini Mathew, Northern State University, USA

Chapter 7
Cultural Competency and Meaningful Online Relationships: Creating Safe Spaces for BIPOC
Students 128
    Ariel Harrison, Walden University, USA

Chapter 8
Cultural Sensitivity in the Distance Learning Sphere 149
    Nancy Thomas, Colorado Christian University, USA
    Crystal A. Brashear, Colorado Christian University, USA
    Rebecca Mathews, University of North Carolina at Greensboro, USA
    Donna Hickman, University of North Texas, USA

Chapter 9
Enhancing Online Adult Learning Communities Through the Lens of Social Climate Theory 164
    Carrie M. Grimes, Vanderbilt University, USA

Chapter 10
Fostering Connections in the Online Learning Environment: Using Intentionality, Empathy,
Creativity, and Accessibility as Tools for Connection 193
    Fatma Ouled Salem, Walden University, USA
    Corinne W. Bridges, Walden University, USA

Chapter 11
Going Viral: Using Social Media to Build Relationships in Online Courses 214
    Marla J. Lohmann, Colorado Christian University, USA
    Kathleen A. Boothe, Southeastern Oklahoma State University, USA

Chapter 12
Hello, Is Anyone There? Strategies for Building Relationships in the Online Classroom 237
    Heather Pederson, The University of Arizona Global Campus, USA
    Stephanie Stubbs, The University of Arizona Global Campus, USA

Chapter 13
Keeping It Compliant: ADA in the Online Classroom 252
    Cara L. Metz, The University of Arizona Global Campus, USA
    Sarah H. Jarvie, Colorado Christian University, USA

Chapter 14
Leveraging Online Communities for Building Social Capital in University Libraries: A Case Study of Fudan University Medical Library 266
    Yuanjun Ni, The University of Hong Kong, Hong Kong
    Apple Hiu Ching Lam, The University of Hong Kong, Hong Kong
    Dickson K. W. Chiu, The University of Hong Kong, Hong Kong

Chapter 15
Making the Connection: Engaging and Impacting Student Outcomes by Building Self-Efficacy 290
    Paula Louise McMahon, Montana State University, Billings, USA

Chapter 16
Not Another Discussion Board: One Online Instructor's Reflective Practices to Create Effective Student Engagement 314
    Elodie J. Jones, Fort Hays State University, USA

Chapter 17
Supporting Male Students in Female-Dominated Virtual Classrooms 328
    Daniel Bates, Truman State University, USA

Chapter 18
The Role of the Instructor in the Online Classroom 350
    Nurul Naimah Rose, Universiti Malaysia Perlis, Malaysia
    Aida Shakila Ishak, Universiti Malaysia Perlis, Malaysia
    Nazifah Hamidun, Universiti Malaysia Perlis, Malaysia
    Faten Khalida Khalid, Universiti Malaysia Perlis, Malaysia
    Nur Farhinaa Othman, Universiti Malaysia Perlis, Malaysia

Compilation of References 370

About the Contributors 441

Index 449

Detailed Table of Contents

Preface xvi

Acknowledgment xix

Chapter 1
Are You Okay? Examining the Role of Student Mental Health in the Online Classroom 1
    Sarah H. Jarvie, Colorado Christian University, USA
    Cara L. Metz, The University of Arizona Global Campus, USA

As faculty, our ultimate goal is student success. Higher education is often fast-paced, and students are juggling multiple roles and responsibilities. Many students learning online have children, careers, and are older than traditional college-age students. Adding college to an already full plate can create symptoms of burnout or due to the added stress may impact the well-being of students. By exploring how to identify various mental health issues and illnesses that students may present, the chapter will give knowledge, language, and understanding. This chapter presents common mental health issues that students may experience. Information will also be presented on how faculty can help students grow to reach their full potential as students while providing a supportive online classroom environment.

Chapter 2
Building an Adult Learning Community While Converting an In-Person Degree Program to an Online Format: A Case Study in Strategies and Lessons Learned 16
    Carrie Grimes, Vanderbilt University, USA
    Whitney Walters-Sachs, Vanderbilt University, USA

This case study examines the transition of a residential professional graduate degree program in educational leadership at a major research university to an online learning model. The case incorporates the observations and field notes of the program director and the inaugural online course instructor, along with survey data collected from students, investigating the opportunities and challenges of converting an established, community-rich, in-person professional degree program to an online model, with a focus on maintaining a strong sense of community. The theoretical framework and relevant scholarship are initially considered, followed by the case. Specific instructional strategies for building a sense of community and the affiliated evidence of the case are also discussed. The chapter concludes with key recommendations for how instructors and university program administrators can partner to design effective environments that foster engagement and meaningful learning experiences for online professional graduate students, contributing to long-term benefits for the institution.

Chapter 3
Building Relationship Through Discussion: Innovative Ideas to Connect and Empower 55
    Crystal Ann Brashear, Colorado Christian University, USA

Distance education programs have proliferated, sometimes growing faster than instructors can innovate. A problem plaguing educators for decades is how to translate the synergism flowing naturally through in-seat discussion into an online environment. This chapter begins with an overview of the various purposes for class discussion and an exploration of best practices for facilitating transformative conversation. It examines the benefits and challenges of synchronous and asynchronous online discussion, offering practical, creative solutions for each approach. The ultimate goals are fostering generative conversation and genuine connection. Strategies to accomplish this include setting clear expectation, adopting a consistent, probing co-participant stance, and teaching students self-facilitation. Out-of-the-box ideas include social annotation and simulation activities.

Chapter 4
Challenges With Sensitivity and Boundaries in an Imperfect, Ever-Changing World: Online Counselor Education 74
    Rosina E. Mete, Yorkville University, Canada
    Alyssa Weiss, Yorkville University, Canada

This chapter provides an overview of the online educational environment and its context and outlines two realistic examples with suggested responses for counselor educators. The reflect, prepare, and respond approach was explained in detail for both examples. The historical context of societal changes was briefly explained within the chapter to further highlight how quickly the world may change as opposed to written resources for students. Schlossberg's research on coping with transitions enhances the chapter to provide counselor educators with an evidence-based framework to better address the challenges and inquiries that arise within an imperfect, ever-changing world in online education.

Chapter 5
Creating Care in the Online Classroom 90
    Kim Cowan, The University of Arizona Global Campus, USA
    William G. Davis, The University of Arizona Global Campus, USA
    Stephanie Stubbs, The University of Arizona Global Campus, USA

This chapter explores care with respect to theoretical concepts including belonging and mattering. The authors utilize feedback from the academic resolution process and draw from faculty experiences to illustrate the unique challenges of the adult online learner and those who work with them. They highlight data from a study that aimed to give voice to the student as well, identifying elements of perceived care that may be particularly impactful in the online environment. Warm, inviting communication and recognition of individuality were particularly valued, suggesting a desire for connection. Finally, the authors identify clear strategies for practical actions to develop meaningful online relationships which may enhance student persistence.

Chapter 6
Cultivating Cultural Competence and Meaningful Bonds in the Virtual Classroom Using a
Narrative Approach..111
Selin Philip, Colorado Christian University, USA
Shalini Mathew, Northern State University, USA

The narrative theoretical approach to content delivery is a powerful tool for educators and students to cultivate their cultural competencies and meaningful connections in the virtual classroom. By utilizing this approach, students can gain a deeper understanding and appreciation for their peers' diverse perspectives and experiences while nurturing community and belonging among themselves. Drawing upon current research, the chapter focuses on exploring the significance of cultural competence and fluency in establishing meaningful connections in online education. It introduces a novel approach to cultivating cultural competence and meaningful connections in the virtual classroom by providing practical examples of narratives and cultural content. It also includes a range of assignments and a case study that highlight different cultural perspectives and experiences, further reinforcing the importance of cultural understanding and empathy in virtual educational settings.

Chapter 7
Cultural Competency and Meaningful Online Relationships: Creating Safe Spaces for BIPOC
Students...128
Ariel Harrison, Walden University, USA

Since their creation, online and distance-learning programs have afforded traditional and non-traditional students access to learning. Black, Indigenous, and People of Color (BIPOC) students represent many enrollments each year in online and distance-learning undergraduate, master's, and doctoral programs. While the absence of in-person and synchronous learning can impact the connections made by all students, this learning modality has also amplified some existing challenges for BIPOC students in these higher educational settings. This chapter will describe themes of isolation, a sense of belonging, and the quest for safe spaces amongst BIPOC students. This chapter will also discuss the role and responsibilities of mentorship; the importance of fostering meaningful relationships that combat isolation linked to BIPOC students' perception of support, safety, and belonging; and the position of culturally specific virtual affinity spaces in uncovering links to connectedness in online programs.

Chapter 8
Cultural Sensitivity in the Distance Learning Sphere..149
Nancy Thomas, Colorado Christian University, USA
Crystal A. Brashear, Colorado Christian University, USA
Rebecca Mathews, University of North Carolina at Greensboro, USA
Donna Hickman, University of North Texas, USA

As the old adage states, "With great power comes great responsibility." Distance education is a double-edged sword – one with great power and also great responsibility. It can impact millions more than the average brick-and-mortar program, which increases the need for sensitivity to those receiving the learning. The need for competence related to multicultural factors in distance education is greater now with the sharp rise in popularity. In 2016, there were over 6 million students in the United States utilizing distance education, half of whom were fully remote. This begets the need for awareness and training at an institutional level to combat the lack of sensitivity and effectively equip students of all backgrounds to adjust to the virtual world. Students, instructors, and institutions will be best equipped to carry the load with careful attention to the three core components of professional training, professional development, and professional identity. This is an ethical and professional responsibility.

Chapter 9
Enhancing Online Adult Learning Communities Through the Lens of Social Climate Theory 164
Carrie M. Grimes, Vanderbilt University, USA

The dramatic expansion of online learning programs for adult degree-seeking professionals has opened significant access and opportunity for institutions of higher education, as well as for the adult learners they serve. However, this recent dramatic increase in online graduate degree offerings has posed challenges to educators and students. One of the most significant challenges is building and maintaining strong connections, and a sense of community, among the participants within the online setting. Social climate theory provides a useful lens for a reconsideration of the social climate of an online learning environment (synchronous and asynchronous) as embodying a "personality" that iteratively shapes the learning community and the experience of participants, and is shaped in return. This chapter presents an in-depth analysis of how educators can strategically enhance online classroom communities for adult degree-seeking professionals through the application of social climate theory principles and a proposed conceptual framework.

Chapter 10
Fostering Connections in the Online Learning Environment: Using Intentionality, Empathy, Creativity, and Accessibility as Tools for Connection 193
Fatma Ouled Salem, Walden University, USA
Corinne W. Bridges, Walden University, USA

Student retention and success in online programs seems to be closely related to their perceived sense of connection with their faculty, peers, and institution. Using activities that create opportunities for interactions and communal learning reduces attrition rates and enhances the learner's experience. In fact, Ouled Salem identified four critical strategies that distance educators can use to foster meaningful connections in the online learning environment: intentionality, creativity, empathy, and accessibility. This chapter will go into detail about each of the four skills and outline evidence-based activities that can be used in the online classroom to create and maintain meaningful relationships.

Chapter 11
Going Viral: Using Social Media to Build Relationships in Online Courses 214
Marla J. Lohmann, Colorado Christian University, USA
Kathleen A. Boothe, Southeastern Oklahoma State University, USA

The number of students wanting an online education is on the rise, thus the need for higher education faculty to ensure they are meeting the needs of their students in a way that is familiar to them. One way to do this is through the use of social media. Research is limited on the impact of social media in the remote classroom. However, the use of social media may support and enhance relationship-building in the online classroom, as well as students' perceptions of social presence in learning. This chapter provides faculty with an overview of the current research on relationship building in learning and social media for educational purposes, as well as offers practical examples of how faculty might use social media in their online coursework.

Chapter 12
Hello, Is Anyone There? Strategies for Building Relationships in the Online Classroom 237
    Heather Pederson, The University of Arizona Global Campus, USA
    Stephanie Stubbs, The University of Arizona Global Campus, USA

It is well known that the online classroom structure can cause students to feel isolated and unsupported. Asynchronous discussion boards and digitally submitted assignments as well as not seeing the instructor or classmates face to face make for an impersonal learning experience. Knowing how to effectively connect with all students and working to build caring, authentic relationships can improve the online education experience for both the faculty member and the student. This chapter includes a review of evidence-based existing literature on building faculty-student relationships and making caring connections in the online environment. In this chapter, two online doctoral faculty members who have a combined 34 years of experience teaching in online classrooms provide practical strategies for building faculty-student relationships with the hope that current and future online educators can implement these strategies to better support student well-being and success while simultaneously promoting faculty satisfaction.

Chapter 13
Keeping It Compliant: ADA in the Online Classroom 252
    Cara L. Metz, The University of Arizona Global Campus, USA
    Sarah H. Jarvie, Colorado Christian University, USA

This chapter will discuss what disabilities are, how they can impact students in an online classroom, and what it means to be ADA compliant. In addition, this chapter will provide some examples of practical applications for designing ADA compliant online classrooms with the purpose of creating relationships. Higher education faculty are at the frontline, making online classrooms accessible and setting the tone for the learning environment. They can engage in relationships with all students and work actively to come alongside those who may need additional support in the classroom. It is in creating relationships with students that barriers are broken and more opportunities for access arise.

Chapter 14
Leveraging Online Communities for Building Social Capital in University Libraries: A Case
Study of Fudan University Medical Library 266
    Yuanjun Ni, The University of Hong Kong, Hong Kong
    Apple Hiu Ching Lam, The University of Hong Kong, Hong Kong
    Dickson K. W. Chiu, The University of Hong Kong, Hong Kong

This study investigates the development of social capital in university libraries using the Fudan University Medical Library (FUML) as the case. The authors first use the SWOT matrix to analyze the FUML based on librarian interviews, official websites, and previous literature. Next, they construct a social capital evaluation framework for university libraries with four dimensions (degree of user demand, level of trust, visibility, and status in users' minds). Guided by the framework, our findings indicate that FUML's user demands in recent years are optimistic, though trust, visibility, and library status vary in users' minds. Thus, they suggest some strategies to help improve patron-library relations through online communities, such as using social media, multi-online channel user feedback, and improving related employee training. This study provides insights into how university libraries can build online relations from social capital concepts. Scant studies have applied social capital to investigate the relationship between university libraries and students, especially in East Asia.

Chapter 15
Making the Connection: Engaging and Impacting Student Outcomes by Building Self-Efficacy 290
Paula Louise McMahon, Montana State University, Billings, USA

Self-efficacy refers to a person's belief in their ability to execute behaviors necessary to produce specific performance outcomes. Bandura explained that there are four main sources of efficacy: performance accomplishments, vicarious experiences, social persuasion, and physiological reactions. Adapting a class structure and creating scaffolding that supports students does not mean that the content is less rigorous; it means how they meet these challenges is supported and developed with faculty guidance and input. Creating online learning environments that nurture students, motivate them, and engage them requires intentional practice and planning, using techniques to build student self-efficacy can assist in this process. This chapter will address how to identify tools and strategies to develop these skills.

Chapter 16
Not Another Discussion Board: One Online Instructor's Reflective Practices to Create Effective Student Engagement 314
Elodie J. Jones, Fort Hays State University, USA

This chapter sheds light on the journey of one online instructor's self-examination and purposeful approaches to engaging and eliciting robust student interactions in online graduate asynchronous settings. Centered on Knowles' Principles of Andragogy and Vygotsky's Social Constructivism, the researcher utilized an ongoing formal reflection process to gather student responses, alter course materials, and strived to create an environment that supported growth mindset, learner autonomy and the online graduate experience.

Chapter 17
Supporting Male Students in Female-Dominated Virtual Classrooms 328
Daniel Bates, Truman State University, USA

In female-dominated academic disciplines, male college students face distinct challenges, such as lagging admission and graduation rates when compared to their female counterparts. To address this concerning trend and enhance support for male students, online educators should embrace a gender-adapted, culturally responsive teaching approach. This approach enables instructors to understand and support male student academic performance and tailor their educational strategies to enhance a male student's sense of belonging and engagement in the course. By adopting this approach, online educators can help male students cultivate a pro-social, strengths-based self-perception, fostering a positive sense of identity as learners, men, and future professionals. This approach emphasizes how their masculinity can be a source of strength, enabling them to derive maximum benefit from their educational journey and make meaningful contributions to their academic pursuits.

Chapter 18
The Role of the Instructor in the Online Classroom 350
    Nurul Naimah Rose, Universiti Malaysia Perlis, Malaysia
    Aida Shakila Ishak, Universiti Malaysia Perlis, Malaysia
    Nazifah Hamidun, Universiti Malaysia Perlis, Malaysia
    Faten Khalida Khalid, Universiti Malaysia Perlis, Malaysia
    Nur Farhinaa Othman, Universiti Malaysia Perlis, Malaysia

This chapter is about the role of instructors in the online classroom particularly in Malaysian higher education. This chapter will focus on two important points, which are the redefining instructors in virtual education and the four main role of instructors in virtual education: the pedagogical role, the social role, the managerial role, and the technical role. Understanding the true role of the instructor in online classes aids in the transition between the classroom and online learning. Instructors play a more significant role in online courses than they do in traditional ones in many ways. They can adjust more easily and settle into a new environment by being aware of what the students and the online environment expect from the teachers. The requirement for instructors to facilitate an online course through a wide range of perspectives or roles is highlighted by the complexity of the online environment.

Compilation of References 370

About the Contributors 441

Index 449

Preface

Distance education is not a new concept. It has been around since the 18th century with parcel post correspondence which transitioned to radio, then to television, and finally to the computer and our current online education (Kentnor, 2015). However, the advent of the COVID-19 crisis sent many programs that were on-ground to online formats, with numerous programs at least adopting a partially online format in addition to their on-ground program permanently. For learners, online programs can be appealing because they can complete schoolwork in their own time, not have to travel to get to class, and could provide a solution for those who want to further their education while balancing a full-time job and/or a family.

Regardless of the mode of teaching, one thing remains important, the value of relationships in education. When we see our students in person, it is easy to form relationships as we see, interact, and get to know our students each class session. In an online environment, we do not see our students in person, and sometimes we do not see our students at all if education is asynchronous. Although the format of our relationship changes, the importance does not. Trying to apply a similar format to teaching and relationship building online as you did on-ground will not work in the same way. Relationship building has to be done with more intentionality when working in an online classroom.

When an educator works to build relationships with students, students can begin to feel a sense of belonging in a format that could be more isolating (Santa-Ramirez et al., 2022). Feeling more connected can lead to more participation and motivation, as well as positive emotions (Schwartz, 2019), which can in turn lead to more positive connection (Fredrickson, 2001). As an educator builds a positive relationship with a student, trust begins to form (Tormey, 2021). With great trust comes better communication with educators as the students can feel supported and trust their instructors want the best for them. Building relationships with students also helps students feel as though they are not just another student in the class, but that they are an individual who has their own unique needs and learning styles. These relationships and feeling seen by the educator can also lead to an increased sense of self-worth, mattering (Schwartz, 2019), and hope, which can improve overall grades (Snyder et al., 2002).

To help students feel seen, feel connected with their online educator, higher education faculty must implement creativity and intentionality. Faculty can not just participate in online discussions and grade papers, but must find different ways to connect with students. Throughout this book, the chapters' authors describe ways in which they have found success building relationships at a distance to support and enhance the learning and sense of community with their students. This book provides the reader with ideas they can implement in their own distance or online classroom.

This book was developed to help higher educators understand the diverse needs of online students and provide insights and ideas in order to connect more with their students. The title of the book includes the words balance and boundaries, which sets the stage to discuss not only how we can balance

Preface

meaningful relationships in online learning, but also that we also have our own limits. It is important that we are there for our students, empathize with them, and help to use the relationships we have with them to set them up for success. At the same time, online education can often blur the boundaries of work and personal life. We have to understand our role with students as educators. Although we need to understand the experiences of our students, we also need to know when to ask the students to seek out further or other help. As many people who are providing education online, work might be done at home. This work setup can easily allow for our work to begin to interfere with our home life. Being able to be fully present when working with students, but also being able to separate yourself to be fully present at home is important.

ORGANIZATION OF THE BOOK

This book is organized into 18 chapters. A brief description of each of the chapters follows:

Chapter 1 examines the impact of mental health on a student, how a student who might be struggling with mental health issues might appear in an online classroom, as well as how to best support the student given your role as an instructor.

Chapter 2 looks at how an in-person degree program converted themselves into an online program, all while supporting students through creating an adult learning community. Emphasizing how an authentic community can be built in both synchronous and asynchronous manners.

Chapter 3 discusses the importance of discussions in online classrooms. There are best practices to be used in online discussions to create intentionality in affirmation, rigor, and support, which can be use in both synchronous and asynchronous discussions.

Chapter 4 explores infusing social justice and cultural sensitivity into an online classroom, how to work with a diverse student population, and uses examples to exemplify how to handle online student situations using reflect, prepare, and respond.

Chapter 5 uses a culture of care to create personal relationships with students with students to help them feel heard, overcome barriers, and improve retention.

Chapter 6 examines the use of storytelling to engage learners and help students to understand diverse perspectives and experiences. The end results ends up being improved cultural competence and the cultivation of meaningful relationships.

Chapter 7 addresses the challenges BIPOC students may encounter that impact feelings of support, safety, and belonging. Further, the chapter looks at the power of mentorship and virtual connection spaces can help improve these areas.

Chapter 8 discusses how to a culturally responsive higher educator when teaching online. Case studies are used to help exemplify the concepts discussed.

Chapter 9 uses the social climate theory to understand how to construct an adult learning community.

Chapter 10 applies the concepts of intentionality, creativity, empathy, accessibility, and multicultural awareness to the online classroom to promote positive connections.

Chapter 11 explores how to use social media in an online classroom to improve communication and relationships between the students, faculty, and community.

Chapter 12 looks at how to use caring connections to create support for the well-being of students and faculty satisfaction.

Chapter 13 uses ADA compliance and the concept of Universal Design to help break down barriers and provide a welcoming environment for all learners to improve communication, social presence, and collaboration.

Chapter 14 examines the use of university libraries as a way to build social capital, specifically looking at the demand by users, trust, visibility, and how people regard the library. The chapter provides insights into how to gain connections and maintain relationships using social media.

Chapter 15 provides tools and insights to help online students reach their full potential through self-efficacy through environments that motivate students, engage them, and provide nurtuting.

Chapter 16 addresses the importance of genuineness and peer sharing to create connection and a sense of safety in the online environment.

Chapter 17 discusses the importance of gender-adapted, culturally responsive education when teaching male students in a female-dominated discipline. This can lead to improved sense of identity and a strengths-based self perception.

Chapter 18 informs the reader of the four main roles of online instructors, which include the pedagogical role, social role, managerial role, and technical role.

Sarah H. Jarvie
Colorado Christian University, USA

Cara L. Metz
The University of Arizona Global Campus, USA

REFERENCES

Fredrickson, B. L. (2001). The role of positive emotions in positive psychology. The broaden-and-build theory of positive emotions. *The American Psychologist*, *56*(3), 218–226. doi:10.1037/0003-066X.56.3.218 PMID:11315248

Kentor, H. E. (2015). Distance education and the evolution of online learning in the United States. *Curriculum and Teaching Dialogue*, *17*(1 & 2), 21–34.

Santa-Ramirez, S., Block, S., Vargas, A., Muralidhar, K., & Ikegwuonu, C. (2022). "It was rough": The experiences of first-generation collegians transitioning into higher education amid COVID-19. *New Directions for Higher Education*, *2022*(199), 41–56. doi:10.1002/he.20451

Schwartz, H. L. (2019). Connected teaching: Relationships, power, and mattering in higher education. *Stylus (Rio de Janeiro)*.

Snyder, C. R., Shorey, H. S., Cheavens, J., Pulvers, K. M., Adams, V. H., & Wiklund, C. (2002). Hope and academic success in college. *Journal of Educational Psychology*, *94*(4), 820–826. doi:10.1037/0022-0663.94.4.820

Tormey, R. (2021). Rethinking student-teacher relationships in higher education: a multidimensional approach. *Higher Education*, *82*(5), 993–1011. doi:10.1007/s10734-021-00711-w

Acknowledgment

This book stands as a testament to the collaborative efforts and unwavering support of many individuals who have contributed their time, expertise, and encouragement to bring this project to fruition.

As editors, we extend deepest gratitude to the authors whose dedication and creativity have shaped the content of this book. Your commitment to excellence and willingness to refine your work have been instrumental in crafting a valuable resource for helping further our knowledge and understanding of how to develop relationships and teach online.

We also wish to acknowledge the valuable contributions of the reviewers regarding the improvement of quality, coherence, and content presentation of chapters. Most of the authors also served as referees; we highly appreciate their double task. A special thanks to Dr. Rebecca Taylor and Dr. Sara Wood who served as external reviewers.

Lastly, we want to express our deepest thanks to our families, friends, and colleagues for their understanding, encouragement, and unwavering support throughout this journey.

This book is the culmination of collective dedication and collaborative effort. To everyone who has played a part, your involvement has been deeply appreciated and has made this endeavor possible.

Thank you.

Sarah H. Jarvie
Colorado Christian University, USA

Cara L. Metz
The University of Arizona Global Campus, USA

Chapter 1
Are You Okay?
Examining the Role of Student Mental Health in the Online Classroom

Sarah H. Jarvie
https://orcid.org/0000-0001-9401-4275
Colorado Christian University, USA

Cara L. Metz
https://orcid.org/0000-0002-2447-2665
The University of Arizona Global Campus, USA

ABSTRACT

As faculty, our ultimate goal is student success. Higher education is often fast-paced, and students are juggling multiple roles and responsibilities. Many students learning online have children, careers, and are older than traditional college-age students. Adding college to an already full plate can create symptoms of burnout or due to the added stress may impact the well-being of students. By exploring how to identify various mental health issues and illnesses that students may present, the chapter will give knowledge, language, and understanding. This chapter presents common mental health issues that students may experience. Information will also be presented on how faculty can help students grow to reach their full potential as students while providing a supportive online classroom environment.

INTRODUCTION

Mental health issues continue to plague our nation with the Substance Abuse and Mental Health Services Administration (SAMSHA) (2021) reporting one in five adults (ages 18 or older) experience mental illness each year. In 2021, 57.8 million people or 22.8 percent of adults in the United States experienced mental illness (SAMSHA, 2021). The 2021 National Survey on Drug Use and Health found that many adults (36.1 million people) perceived a negative effect of the COVID-19 pandemic on their overall mental health (SAMSHA, 2021). These numbers show that mental health is a serious concern.

DOI: 10.4018/978-1-6684-8908-6.ch001

The number of students in higher education stating they have a mental health disorder has increased, and the severity of the disorder has increased too (Parizeau, 2022). Students do not struggle with only one disorder, but often are diagnosed with co-occurring mental health issues. Many enter higher education without a diagnosis and are later diagnosed during their degree program (Arachchige & Wijesekara, 2022). Mental health can improve and degrade without predictability, which complicates education for the student and requires understanding from the instructor.

The purpose of this chapter is to provide an overview of common mental health issues that an online educator might encounter in the classroom. It not meant to be used as a tool for diagosis rather it is meant to be informational. The chapter will address the symptoms and possible classroom behaviors of the following disorders that are likely to be seen in an online classroom setting: depression, anxiety, bipolar disorder, post-traumatic stress disorder, and attention deficit hyperactivity disorder. While not exhaustive, this list will provide a context for common mental health issues. It is especially important for online instructors who are not in physical contact with their students to be aware of these signs and symptoms because students might not know to ask for accommodations or have a fear of stigma and avoid seeking the help needed to successfully complete courses. This chapter will then discuss why relationships are important in helping students who have been diagnosed with a mental health issue and ways higher educators can design their online classroom to enable the success of all students.

BACKGROUND OF MENTAL ILLNESS IN THE CLASSROOM/ COMMON MENTAL HEALTH ISSUES

Online education can be a preferred mode of learning for people with mental health disabilities. An online classroom often allows students to coordinate schoolwork around their disability, work, and family commitments (McManus et al., 2017). The flexibility of the online classroom was cited as an advantage by students who noted the positive impact on their overall learning experience (Turan et al., 2022). Yet, Sniatecki et al. (2015) found that faculty often have more negative attitudes towards students with mental health issues above other disabilities. This can create attitudinal barriers to education for those who are diagnosed with a mental health disorder.

People with mental illness can struggle in online education. Part of the criteria of a mental health diagnosis is that it must significantly impair day to day function (American Psychiatric Association, 2022), which includes school. Mental health issues can limit students' self-perceived ability to finish assignments, and the stress from assignments can often trigger mental health symptoms. When this happens students will often put off assignments until their mental health feels more under control, which can create a scenario where their work will be late, as well as increase anxiety and stress due to the looming deadline (McManus et al., 2017). Students who have been diagnosed with a mental health disorder are less likely to successfully complete their education than their peers who have no diagnoses (McEwan & Downie, 2013).

Students who are struggling with mental health issues often have a very loud self-critic. At times this critic can create stress and be harmful to the student; other times it pushes them to survive, get things done, and succeed (Marszalek et al., 2021). Although this push could be a driving factor for success in life and a coping mechanism that allows for some success in school, it can also create internal stress and prevent the ability to receive feedback. It creates a lot of negative self-talk, which can inhibit completing assignments and finishing school. When a faculty member does not try to exemplify empathy, students with mental illness can face greater barriers to learning and a reinforced stigma around their mental disability (McMannus et al., 2017).

DEPRESSION

What Is It?

Depression is one of the most common mental health disorders. Depression symptoms can be seen in about 34 percent of students in higher education (Deng et al., 2021). Rates of depression have increased due to COVID-19 and the stress that accompanied the pandemic; one study found depression rates in graduate and professional students were two times higher in 2020 than 2019 (Chirikov et al., 2020). The growing rate of depression is having an overall significant impact on individual functioning (Chirikov et al., 2020).

According to the DSM-5-TR, major depressive disorder (MDD) is a mental health mood disorder in which a person experiences a low mood or negative emotions almost all day, continuously, for at least two weeks. Low mood or sadness is only one of the symptoms. A person who has been diagnosed with major depressive disorder might also struggle with hopelessness, not being interested in activities or people they used to enjoy, feeling tired all of the time, weight gain or loss, getting too much sleep or struggling to sleep, having self-guilt or feeling worthless, struggling to concentrate, having thoughts about harming themselves, and thinking or moving slower than normal. Depression does not present itself the same in each person—not every person has every symptom. There are also varying levels of depression; it can range from mild to severe and severe with psychotic symptoms, which means the person might experience delusions and hallucinations. To be diagnosed, symptoms must have a significant negative impact on a person's day to day functioning (American Psychiatric Association, 2022).

Persistent depressive disorder (PDD) is another mood disorder. This disorder has the same symptoms of MDD, but they are not as intense, do not disappear for more than two months at a time, and can fluctuate in their intensity (American Psychiatric Association, 2022). Persistent depressive disorder lasts at least two years, if not more with one episode (American Psychiatric Association, 2022). Because of its long-term nature, persistent depressive disorder can be viewed as chronic depression. It is typically characterized by a sad or dark mood most days; other symptoms are similar to MMD (American Psychiatric Association, 2022).

What Does It Look Like in the Classroom?

Depression can affect an individual's performance in the classroom in a variety of ways. Medications used to treat depression can often leave students struggling to concentrate in class or recall information (McManus et al., 2017). Depression stifles the ability to synthesize thoughts and actions to work toward a goal (Miller & Wallis, 2009). MDD can affect one's input of effort, focus, time management skills, communicative thoughts, goal setting, problem solving, memory, and social interactions (Mohammed et al., 2022). It can create a scenario where a good student does not turn in their best work, which can then exacerbate depression even more. This situation grows more complicated when the online work is accelerated (Mohammed et al., 2022). Students who have MDD often struggle with procrastination, self-esteem, and stress (Cuijpers et al., 2021). Students experiencing a depressive episode may fall behind in their course reading, discussion posts and participation, and assignment completion. Students struggle to start activities. Sometimes simply getting out of bed is overwhelming, so reading several chapters or completing a five-page paper can feel impossible at times. Because MDD causes students to want to isolate more, there might be a noticeable difference in the frequency and depth of their interactions during online synchronous and asynchronous discussions. Finally, students might be absent from the online classroom all together. This can be due to many of the symptoms of depression that make participating in school an insurmountable feat.

ANXIETY

What Is It?

Anxiety symptoms can be seen in about 32 percent of higher education students (Deng et al., 2021). According to the American Psychiatric Association (2022) anxiety disorder is a general term for a group of disorders. Anxiety disorders include generalized anxiety disorder, panic disorder, social anxiety disorder, agoraphobia, as well as other phobias. Overall, anxiety disorders encompass the anticipation of future events or threats that create worry, fear, and sometimes panic in individuals. These symptoms can be experienced as an overall feeling through most of the day or triggered by specific causes like separation from certain people, a fear of heights, or a sense of confinement. Symptoms of anxiety can include uncontrollable worry, tension, a struggle to concentrate, restlessness, problems falling and staying asleep, muscle tension, being on edge, and feeling tired (American Psychiatric Association, 2022).

Sometimes anxiety turns into panic, which is called a panic attack. During a panic attack, someone's heart might race so quickly that it feels like it is pounding out of their chest. Other symptoms of a panic attack include sweating, shaking, trouble breathing, tightness in the chest, dizziness, numbness or tingling, hot or cold flashes, upset stomach, disorientation, and feeling a loss of control or sanity. Symptoms can become so intense that a person might feel like they are dying (American Psychiatric Association, 2022). People sometimes mistake having a panic attack with a heart attack.

Anxiety is reported to be experienced more often by women than men (Alshammari et al., 2022; American Psychiatric Association, 2022; Mohammed et al., 2021), students who are not stable financially, and students who struggle with depression (Mohammed et al., 2021). Comparing 2020 to 2019, rates of generalized anxiety disorder increased in graduate and professional students (Chirikov et al., 2020), which is an important factor for faculty to keep in mind.

What Does It Look Like in the Classroom?

Alshammari et al. (2022) found that those who have high anxiety tend to have poorer coping skills and that anxiety will negatively impact students' preparation and performance in class. Anxiety in the classroom can cause students to be underprepared for tests because they feel paralyzed by their symptoms (McManus et al., 2017). Additionally, time management becomes difficult to control (Duraku & Hoxha, 2021).

Low self-esteem is one factor associated with generalized anxiety disorder (Cuijpers et al., 2021). Low self-esteem can create a feedback loop that then increases anxiety. A student might struggle to believe they can finish their degree or even an assignment, or they might worry about saying the wrong answer in a discussion post, which holds them back from finishing a task. The more they put off the task, the more anxious they become. This may also result in an increase in emails or communication to the instructor without exhibiting critical thinking skills to ask questions about assignments or the class. Other symptoms that might coincide with self-esteem include procrastination, perfectionism, self-esteem, and stress (Cuijpers et al., 2021).

BIPOLAR DISORDER

What Is It?

Bipolar disorder is a mood disorder that includes emotional highs and lows. The high is often referred to as mania or hypomania and the low is depression (American Psychiatric Association, 2022). Bipolar disorder used to be called manic depression because it includes both mania and depression (American Psychiatric Association, 2022). Intense emotions are a hallmark of bipolar disorder and include changes in sleep and activity levels (NAMI, 2023). A person who is diagnosed with bipolar disorder will experience major depression symptoms, like those described earlier in this chapter, which usually occur after a period called mania (American Psychiatric Association, 2022). During mania, a person will have an elevated mood or be extremely irritable. They will often start multiple tasks without finishing them, feel an elevated self-esteem, not sleep or get little sleep for days, have rapid speech, experience racing thoughts, and become easily distracted. They might do things that have negative consequences without thought like steal, binge shop, and increase sexual activity (American Psychiatric Association, 2022).

Bipolar disorder affects about 1.7 percent of the higher education population, and this number is rising (Pedersen, 2020). This number might be undervalued; the average age of the first manic or hypomanic episode ranges from 18 to the mid-20s (American Psychiatric Association, 2022), so the data are likely excluding some students who struggle with symptoms but are not diagnosed until after they graduate.

What Does It Look Like in the Classroom?

Students might start their discussions, assignments, activities, or readings when in a manic or hypomanic state and then not finish them. This can cause missed due dates or incomplete work. A once overly involved student may stop participating in the class or they may be attentive in class activities such as online discussions but fail to turn in assignments. Assignment procrastination and test anxiety are common ways bipolar disorder presents in the classroom (Cuijpers et al., 2021). Students may have maladaptive coping strategies like giving up and self-blame that significantly impact their ability to engage in and complete their coursework (Nitzberg et al., 2016). In fact, studies have shown that many are not even completing their education due to these factors (Kruse & Oswel, 2018; Nitzberg et al., 2016). Increased stress whether in a student's personal life or as part of school may further exacerbate symptomology (Cuijpers et al., 2021). The episodic nature of bipolar creates fluctuating moods and possibly changing symptoms (for example, changes in sleep schedule), which have an impact on everyday life and academic performance (Brancati et al, 2021).

POSTTRAUMATIC STRESS DISORDER

What Is It?

Posttraumatic stress disorder (PTSD) is a mental health disorder that can occur after a person witnesses or experiences an event in person where death is threatened or happens, there is serious injury, or sexual violence takes place. With PTSD, people will have intrusive memories of the traumatizing event, might have dreams related to the event, see flashbacks where they feel they are back in the traumatic situation, or experience physical reactions to thoughts and objects that represent the event. Additionally, people with PTSD will actively avoid reminders of the traumatic event. Their mood and thoughts will become more negative; for example, they might have excessive negative thoughts about themselves or the world or the inability to feel positive emotions. Also, their reactivity to things associated with trauma becomes exaggerated; for example, they may become hyper aware of their surroundings, excessively jumpy, or angry without being provoked (American Psychiatric Association, 2022).

It is estimated that 66 percent of college students have experienced a traumatic event prior to enrolling in college, and 9 percent of those people meet the criteria for a PTSD diagnosis (Read et al., 2011). Post-traumatic stress disorder is seen more often in populations and careers that are more likely to be exposed to violence like the military, law enforcement, firefighters, and paramedics. Incidences of PTSD are estimated to be as high as 20 percent in the returning veteran population (Roehr, 2007). Females are more likely to develop PTSD and have it for longer periods of time than males. PTSD is also associated with more struggles in education (American Psychiatric Association, 2022). To complicate matters, there is comorbidity of PTSD with traumatic brain injuries, depression (Morissette et al., 2021), and substance use (Barry et al., 2012; Morissette et al., 2021), which can further affect the student and their ability to succeed in a classroom (Morissette et al., 2021).

What Does It Look Like in the Classroom?

People with PTSD might not be as engaged in classroom discussions as those without; because they can struggle to accept feedback, criticism, and praise, they may be more hypervigilant to responses from faculty and peers and choose to disengage. PTSD also impacts one's sense of fitting in (Smith et al., 2017). Additionally, a higher rate of absenteeism or difficulty focusing and staying on task may be a result of PTSD (Cory, 2011). Although many veterans are used to working under pressure to get a job done, they may now face physical or psychological limitations (Cory, 2011).

Students might have decreased motivation or struggle to complete assignments due to experiencing symptoms like difficulty sleeping, headaches, hopelessness, and loss of concentration (Barry et al., 2012). Students might fail to complete assignments thoroughly or on time. Ness & Vroman (2014) found students' belief in themselves and their abilities are strongly related to college performance for those who have PTSD.

ATTENTION DEFICIT HYPERACTIVITY DISORDER

What Is It?

Attention Deficit Hyperactivity Disorder (ADHD) refers to attention difficulty, hyperactivity, and impulsiveness. It is characterized by a persistent pattern of inattention and hyperactivity-impulsivity that interferes with development or daily functioning. Symptoms of inattention include not paying attention to details, having a hard time focusing on tasks, seemingly not listening, lacking follow through, struggling with task organization, not liking tasks that need continued effort mentally, losing things needed to complete tasks, being easily distracted, and being forgetful. Symptoms of hyperactivity or impulsivity include squirming, having a hard time sitting still, feeling restless, struggling with quiet activities, excessive talking, and interrupting (American Psychiatric Association, 2022).

ADHD is typically diagnosed in children because diagnostic criteria focus on symptoms presenting prior to the age of 12 years (American Psychiatric Association, 2022); however, there is more evidence of ADHD symptoms carrying into adulthood (Prakash et al., 2021). According to Prakash et al. (2021) ADHD should be considered a disorder across the lifespan citing an increased prevalence in adult symptomology and high comorbidity with other psychiatric and medical conditions. Academic impairment is often a result of ADHD.

What Does It Look Like in the Classroom?

ADHD can impact learning, stress, and self-efficacy. When a student who has ADHD is feeling more academic stress and has lower self-efficacy, they will tend to procrastinate in their academic endeavors (Niazov et al., 2022). In a study exploring postsecondary student experiences with ADHD, Lagacé-Leblanc et al. (2022) found participants reported academic impairments or difficulties in relation to seven themes: 1) attention, 2) motivation, 3) time management, 4) inhibition, 5) working memory, 6) organization, and 7) planning. These seven barriers affect overall learning and studying strategies resulting in a negative impact on academic performance. Emotional regulation issues and poor emotional management might also affect other areas such as time management, attention, and memory (Lagacé-Leblanc et al., 2022).

Students with ADHD might not disclose their disability due to diagnosis-related stigma or embarrassment (Lagacé-Leblanc et al., 2022; Lefler, 2016). Although some students might function well, an underlying layer of distress may inhibit one's performance (Lagacé-Leblanc et al., 2022). In fact, some students reported their ADHD diagnosis negatively affected their self-confidence, self-esteem, and overall academic performance. Stress and anxiety related to taking tests or exams can exacerbate symptoms.

Appropriate medication management might also affect one's classroom experience. Although medication often is used to treat ADHD, it cannot eliminate all academic shortfalls. If a student is not taking the medication that helps them concentrate and focus, there may be negative consequences in terms of activities that require their concentration and focus, such as reading or engaging in an online discussion (Lagacé-Leblanc et al., 2022).

WHAT CAN WE DO/THE IMPORTANCE OF THE RELATIONSHIP

People who struggle with mental health issues need the support of faculty for information, clarification, and supportive relationships. Many report that this does not happen (McManus et al., 2017; Parizeau, 2022). By focusing on building relationships with students, we can begin to create a supportive environment that lessens anxiety and demonstrates understanding of the student and their struggles. As faculty, it is important to believe the student when they discuss their struggle. It is important that instructors have boundaries. Our job is to help students learn the material and succeed in our class and in college or graduate school. Our job is not to be a therapist of the student. Faculty should know how building relationships can help students feel supported and also know when they need to refer a student to seek out more help from a professional, such as a mental health therapist. You do not need to pry into diagnoses or treatments a student could try, rather offer support, empathy, and flexibility.

One way to begin to break down barriers to this relationship is for faculty to have a greater understanding of mental health disorders and their impact on students in a classroom. Understanding the reasons for certain behaviors and not attributing them to negative aspects of a student can start to open up lines of communication, understanding, and empathy. Having a greater understanding of the signs of possible mental health issues, can also help open up the conversation with students about their struggles.

It is important to note that many times students who struggle with mental health issues might not reach out for help (Lowenthal et al., 2020). This could be due to the symptoms of the mental health issue, but it could also be because of the stigma they have received in their lives. This means that the faculty might be the first ones to offer support to students. If a faculty member sees a student struggling to complete their work or submit assignments on time, they might attempt to reach out to see if the student is OK (Terras et al., 2015); this is an effective way to open up the conversation and build trust with the student. It helps the student feel seen, which is important in an online classroom.

Without a physical classroom, students can feel disconnected from their instructors and isolated (McManus et al., 2017). Instructors should find ways to connect students with one another in an online environment (Salimi et al., 2023). Connectedness among students is not only associated with improved mental health, but with improved academic performance (Di Malta et al., 2022).

Faculty can mitigate feelings of disconnection by offering video conferences and virtual office hours (Mohammed et al., 2021), creating videos for lectures and discussion responses, and providing recorded feedback to students. These techniques allow students to feel more connected to instructors. Building a solid relationship with instructors and feeling safe to ask questions improves symptoms of depression (Gin et al., 2021; Mohammed et al., 2022), which can spike when students experience a loss of in-person routine and interaction with their peers (Mohammed et al., 2022).

Mohammed et al. (2022) found that 100 percent of surveyed students believe developing relationships with instructors and peers helped impact their depression in a positive way. Additionally, instructors must have empathy and understand the needs of the student, especially their unique mental health situation (Mohammed et al., 2021). Instructors should not only communicate in the classroom with students but strive to create a one-on-one connection through personal emails, phone calls, and video calls because students who struggle find more satisfaction in these types of communications (Di Malta et al., 2022).

For students with mental illness, finding ways to connect meaningfully with their instructor is important, and the virtual classroom can offer opportunities for them to build relationships with faculty and other students. For example, faculty might facilitate a "Getting To Know You" discussion to allow students to share and discover similarities with each another. Something as simple as connecting with another student in the same state or time zone can be helpful in an online setting. Also, giving students an optional discussion forum to ask and answer questions provides further opportunities for engagement among faculty and fellow students.

Coping skills are a big factor in helping to manage stress and anxiety, which are both prevalent in students, especially those who are struggling with mental health issues. Students who have more flexible coping strategies and self-efficacy tend to handle stress better. Instructors can help students understand that having a variety of coping strategies improves coping skills. For example, if a person tends to rely on social support only for coping, they might not handle stress as well as a person who focuses on social support, planning, and reappraisal. Having flexible coping skills can also improve self-efficacy. Taking time to create a video, write an announcement, or send emails discussing coping flexibility can help students create more of a balanced view and management of stress, especially those dealing with mental health symptoms.

Transparency in the classroom can be very important for those who struggle with mental illness; it is a way to help students minimize stress and anxiety. Ensure that the classroom is organized and structured (Mohammed et al., 2021). Have a clear syllabus that is easy to find and outlines all due dates and assignments. Students should know what expectations the instructors have of them from day one so they can begin to establish a schedule that works for them. Structure and accountability can create an environment that helps those who struggle with mental health succeed (Mohammed et al., 2022; Terras et al., 2015).

Designing an organized classroom that has open access to lecture materials can also create transparency and reduce student anxiety and stress. Even when the online classroom has a synchronous component, providing recorded lectures to students might help decrease anxiety (Mohammed et al., 2021) because they can review the material again if they need time to process and take notes. When instructors allow the flexibility (Gin et al., 2021) for students to submit work throughout the week, they create more opportunities for self-care to improve mental health. Proactively creating a classroom environment that promotes student wellbeing and productivity (Salimi et al., 2023) ensures an environment that fosters mental health.

Breaking down material or evaluations of the material into smaller chunks can help when people are struggling with anxiety or ADHD. Weekly quizzes or check-ins allow students to monitor their progress and ensure they are keeping up with the course structure (Edwards et al., 2022). These ongoing assessments might also ease the stress of a final exam. Including more opportunities to earn points and structuring individual assignments to be worth fewer points can help reduce anxiety in students (Mohammed et al., 2021; Terras, 2015). Additionally, being flexible about when quizzes must be submitted can help remove anxiety (Mohammed et al., 2021). For example, an instructor might keep a quiz open for a week so students can take the test when they feel mentally prepared. Providing flexibility with different assessment modalities allows students to demonstrate their knowledge in various ways (Lowenthal et al., 2020), which can help alleviate anxiety with high-stakes assessments.

There are no quick fixes for mental health symptoms, negative self-talk, and self-criticism (Marszalek, 2021). At the university level, counseling services should be free and available for all students to use in a comprehensive and confidential manner. Faculty might make these resources known in their syllabus, announcements, and throughout the class. By sharing this information up front, a faculty member makes it known that they understand how mental health can affect a student's experience of school. From a student's perspective, this approach demonstrates understanding and empathy.

Students might not recognize their need for mental health services. They may grow more receptive after building relationships with faculty and having more conversations about mental health. Students who struggle with mental health issues might try to keep faculty and other students at a distance because they feel they are a burden and shy away from vulnerability. While connection can help, faculty should understand that the relationship they build with a student must be genuine and open (Marszalek, 2021). Such a relationship goes beyond consistently following-up with students to demonstrating an investment in students' educational achievement and emotional wellbeing (Schwartz, 2019). This comes back to the tenets of person-centered theory, where you respond with empathy, genuineness, and unconditional positive regard for the client (Rogers, 1961).

Finally, faculty should also focus on themselves and their own mental health. A variety of stress factors accompany higher education instruction. It is important that faculty keep their limitations and boundaries in mind. They want to help students and provide them an environment for success, but this can be emotionally taxing. Social support might not be as readily available in an online environment as on a physical campus. Faculty must know the signs of burnout and ask for help when needed. If they do not take care of themselves or create healthy boundaries for their own emotional wellbeing, they might see the negative impacts on their personal lives, health, wellbeing, and students. Faculty can stay psychologically and emotionally healthy by monitoring themselves, asking for help when needed, and taking breaks. They must prioritize their mental health and wellbeing to help students and make meaningful connections that are positive for both parties.

FUTURE RESEARCH

Helping students who are diagnosed with a mental health disorder is important for creating an equitable environment. More research exists with respect to diagnoses like ADHD and anxiety over other commonly seen diagnoses like PTSD. As mental health concerns are diagnosed more frequently, more research is needed to examine the impact of diagnoses on higher education work, especially in the online environment. Current research discusses how academics affect mental health, and much research has been completed on children, mental health, and school, mainly focusing on ADHD. However, there is a lack of research completed with adults, higher education, and the impacts of mental health on students. Because mental health is stigmatized, it is often underreported. Faculty might misinterpret the results of a mental health disorder as a student's ability or effort level when it is more serious and not representative of the student's aptitude. By recognizing the symptoms and impacts of mental health, faculty can better understand how to help the student reach their potential. Mental illness is one of the leading causes of disability (Chaudhury et al., 2006), but many students may not realize that they are eligible for accommodations.

Much of the research on online education and mental health was completed because of the COVID-19 pandemic. During this time, other factors significantly affected a student's mental health. Online education was often not a choice, but rather forced upon students due to the need to minimize time spent around others to stop the spread of the infection. Because of these compounding factors, it cannot be certain that the symptoms and impact seen were due solely to the mental health disorder or how much the stress of the pandemic contributed to them. More research should be conducted to ensure the results seen can be attributed to the mental health symptoms, and the solutions work for students in both a time of global crisis and beyond.

CONCLUSION

The ever-growing world of online education provides more access for all types of students. As access to education grows, so do students' needs. Recent events that have had an overall impact on mental health such as the global pandemic are further confirmation of the connection between mental health and one's overall health and well-being; they are intertwined. By understanding how various mental health issues may present in the classroom, faculty can be better equipped with knowledge and understanding to best help and support students. It is important to also keep in mind one's role as a faculty member and the importance of student privacy and confidentiality. While we may recognize the need for help, it is vital to remember that faculty cannot ask students directly about their mental health. Luckily, many universities have systems built in place that flag when a student may be at risk. For example, when a student has not turned in assignments, has not participated in class, and as well as processes when an instructor is concerned. All of these may help bring the necessary attention to an issue which may warrant more support for the student.

Ultimately, through conscious efforts to build strong, empathetic relationships with students, faculty can improve the chances of success in the classroom for students who have been diagnosed with a mental health disorder.

REFERENCES

Alshammari, T., Alseraye, S., Alqasim, R., Rogowska, A., Alrasheed, N., & Alshammari, M. (2022). Examining anxiety and stress regarding virtual learning in colleges of health sciences: A cross-sectional study in the era of the COVID-19 pandemic in Saudi Arabia. *Saudi Pharmaceutical Journal*, *30*(3), 256–264. doi:10.1016/j.jsps.2022.01.010 PMID:35498216

American Psychiatric Association. (2022). *Diagnostic and statistical manual of mental disorders* (5th ed., text rev.). doi:10.1176/appi.books.9780890425787

Arachchige, P., & Wijesekara, D. S. N. (2022). A study in University of Ruhuna for investigating prevalence, risk factors and remedies for psychiatric illnesses among students. *Scientific Reports*, *12*. PMID:35896566

Barry, A. E., Whiteman, S. D., & MacDermid Wadsworth, S. M. (2012). Implications of posttraumatic stress among military-affiliated and civilian students. *Journal of American College Health*, *60*(8), 562–573. doi:10.1080/07448481.2012.721427 PMID:23157198

Brancati, G. E., Perugi, G., Milone, A., Masi, G., & Sesso, G. (2021). Development of bipolar disorder in patients with attention-deficit/hyperactivity disorder: A systematic review and meta-analysis of prospective studies. *Journal of Affective Disorders*, *293*, 186–196. doi:10.1016/j.jad.2021.06.033 PMID:34217137

Chaudhury, P. K., Deka, K., & Chetia, D. (2006). Disability associated with mental disorders. *Indian Journal of Psychiatry*, *48*(2), 95–101. doi:10.4103/0019-5545.31597 PMID:20703393

Chirikov, I., Soria, K. M., Horgos, B., & Jones-White, D. (2020). *Undergraduate and graduate students' mental health during the COVID-19 pandemic*. UC Berkeley: Center for Studies in Higher Education. Retrieved from https://escholarship.org/uc/item/80k5d5hw

Cuijpers, P., Smit, F., Aalten, P., Batelaan, N., Klein, A., Salemink, E., Spinhoven, P., Struijs, S., Vonk, P., Wiers, R. W., deWit, L., Gentili, C., Ebert, D. D., Bruffaerts, R., Kessler, R. C., & Karyotaki, E. (2021). The associations of common psychological problems with mental disorders among college students. *Frontiers in Psychiatry*, *12*, 573637. Advance online publication. doi:10.3389/fpsyt.2021.573637 PMID:34646167

Deng, J., Zhou, F., Hou, W., Silver, Z., Wong, C. Y., Chang, O., Drakos, A., Zuo, Q. K., & Huang, E. (2021). The prevalence of depressive symptoms, anxiety symptoms and sleep disturbance in higher education students during the COVID-19 pandemic: A systematic review and meta-analysis. *Psychiatry Research*, *301*, 113863. doi:10.1016/j.psychres.2021.113863 PMID:33984824

Di Malta, G., Bond, J., Conroy, D., Smith, K., & Moller, N. (2022). Distance education students' mental health, connectedness and academic performance during COVID-19: A mixed methods study. *Distance Education*, *43*(1), 97–118. doi:10.1080/01587919.2022.2029352

Duraku, Z. H., & Hoxha, L. (2021). The impact of COVID-19 on higher education: A study of interaction among Kosovar students' mental health, attitudes toward online learning, study skills, and lifestyle changes. In Z.H. Duraku (Ed.) Impact of the COVID-19 pandemic on education and wellbeing: Implications for practice and lessons for the future (pp. 46-63). University of Prishtina "Hasan Prishtina" Faculty of Philosophy, Department of Psychology.

Edwards, M., Poes, S., Al-Nawab, H., & Penna, O. (2022). Academic accommodations for university students living with disability and the potential of universal design to address their needs. *Higher Education*, *84*(4), 779–799. doi:10.100710734-021-00800-w PMID:35079174

Freire, C., Ferradás, M. D. M., Regueiro, B., Rodríguez, S., Valle, A., & Núñez, J. C. (2020). Coping strategies and self-efficacy in university students: A person-centered approach. *Frontiers in Psychology*, *11*, 841. doi:10.3389/fpsyg.2020.00841 PMID:32508707

Gin, L. E., Wiesenthal, N. J., Ferreira, I., & Cooper, K. M. (2021). PhDepression: Examining how graduate research and teaching affect depression in life sciences PhD students. *CBE Life Sciences Education*, *20*(3), ar41. Advance online publication. doi:10.1187/cbe.21-03-0077 PMID:34309412

Karatekin, C., & Ahluwalia, R. (2020). Effects of adverse childhood experiences, stress, and social support on the health of college students. *Journal of Interpersonal Violence*, *35*(1-2), 150–172. doi:10.1177/0886260516681880 PMID:27920360

Lefler, E. K., Sacchetti, G. M., & Del Carlo, D. I. (2016). ADHD in college: A qualitative analysis. *Attention Deficit and Hyperactivity Disorders*, *8*(2), 79–93. doi:10.100712402-016-0190-9 PMID:26825556

Lowenthal, P. R., Humphrey, M., Conley, Q., Dunlap, J. C., Greear, K., Lowenthal, A., & Giacumo, L. A. (2020). Creating accessible and inclusive online learning: Moving beyond compliance and broadening the discussion. *Quarterly Review of Distance Education*, *21*(2), 1–21.

Marszalek, M. A., Faksvåg, H., Frøystadvåg, T. H., Ness, O., & Veseth, M. (2021). A mismatch between what is happening on the inside and going on, on the outside: A qualitative study of therapists' perspectives on student mental health. *International Journal of Mental Health Systems*, *15*(1), 87. doi:10.118613033-021-00508-5 PMID:34930381

McEwan, R. C., & Downie, R. (2013). College success of students with psychiatric disabilities: Barriers of access and distraction. *Journal of Postsecondary Education and Disability*, *26*(3), 233–248.

McManus, D., Dryer, R., & Henning, M. (2017). Barriers to learning online experienced by students with a mental health disability. *Distance Education*, *38*(3), 336–352. doi:10.1080/01587919.2017.1369348

Mohammed, T. F., Gin, L. E., Wiesenthal, N. J., & Cooper, K. M. (2022). The experiences of undergraduates with depression in online science learning environments. *CME – Life. CBE Life Sciences Education*, *21*(2), ar18. Advance online publication. doi:10.1187/cbe.21-09-0228 PMID:35294254

Mohammed, T. F., Nadile, E. M., Busch, C. A., Brister, D., Brownell, S. E., Claiborne, C. T., Edwards, B. A., Wolf, J. G., Lunt, C., Tran, M., Vargas, C., Walker, K. M., Warkina, T. D., Witt, M., Zheng, Y., & Cooper, K. M. (2021). Aspects of large-enrollment online college science courses that exacerbate and alleviate student anxiety. *CBE Life Sciences Education*, *20*(4), ar69. Advance online publication. doi:10.1187/cbe.21-05-0132 PMID:34806910

Morissette, S. B., Ryan-Gonzalez, C., Yufik, T., DeBeer, B. B., Kimbrel, N. A., Sorrells, A. M., Holleran-Steiker, L., Penk, W. E., Gulliver, S. B., & Meyer, E. C. (2021). The effects of posttraumatic stress disorder symptoms on educational functioning in student veterans. *Psychological Services*, *18*(1), 124–133. doi:10.1037er0000356 PMID:31192672

Ness, B. M., & Vroman, K. (2014). Preliminary examination of the impact of traumatic brain injury and posttraumatic stress disorder on self-regulated learning and academic achievement among military service members enrolled in postsecondary education. *The Journal of Head Trauma Rehabilitation*, *29*(1), 33–43. doi:10.1097/HTR.0b013e3182a1cd4e PMID:23982790

Niazov, Z., Hen, M., & Ferrari, J. R. (2022). Online and academic procrastination in students with learning disabilities: The impact of academic stress and self-efficacy. *Psychological Reports*, *125*(2), 890–912. doi:10.1177/0033294120988113 PMID:33573501

Nitzburg, G. C., Russo, M., Cuesta-Diaz, A., Ospina, L., Shanahan, M., Perez-Rodriguez, M., McGrath, M., & Burdick, K. E. (2016). Coping strategies and real-world functioning in bipolar disorder. *Journal of Affective Disorders*, *198*, 185–188. doi:10.1016/j.jad.2016.03.028 PMID:27017375

Parizeau, K. (2022). Instructor perspectives on student mental health. *Canadian Journal of Higher Education*, *52*(2), 67–80. doi:10.47678/cjhe.v52i2.189391

Pedersen, D. E. (2020). Bipolar disorder and the college student: A review and implications for universities. *Journal of American College Health*, *68*(4), 341–346. doi:10.1080/07448481.2019.1573173 PMID:30908152

Prakash, J., Chatterjee, K., Guha, S., Srivastava, K., & Chauhan, V. S. (2021). Adult attention-deficit hyperactivity disorder: From clinical reality toward conceptual clarity. *Industrial Psychiatry Journal*, *30*(1), 23–28. doi:10.4103/ipj.ipj_7_21 PMID:34483520

Read, J. P., Ouimette, P., White, J., Colder, C., & Farrow, S. (2011). Rates of *DSM–IV–TR* trauma exposure and posttraumatic stress disorder among newly matriculated college students. *Psychological Trauma: Theory, Research, Practice, and Policy*, *3*(2), 148–156. doi:10.1037/a0021260 PMID:25621098

Rogers, C. R. (1961). *On becoming a person: A therapist's view of psychotherapy*. Robinson.

Saadé, R. G., Kira, D., Mak, T., & Nebebe, F. (2017). *Anxiety and performance in online learning. In Proceedings of the Informing Science and Information Technology Education Conference*. Informing Science Institute. https://www.informingscience.org/Publications/3736

Salim, N., Gere, B., Talley, W., & Irioogbe, B. (2023). College students mental health challenges: Concerns and considerations in the COVID-19 pandemic. *Journal of College Student Psychotherapy, 37*(1), 39–51. doi:10.1080/87568225.2021.1890298

Schwartz, H. L. (2019). *Connected teaching: Relationship, power, and mattering in higher education*. Stylus Publishing.

Smith, J. G., Vilhauer, R. P., & Chafos, V. (2017). Do military veteran and civilian students function differently in college? *Journal of American College Health, 65*(1), 76–79. doi:10.1080/07448481.2016.1245193 PMID:27723430

Sniatecki, J. L., Perry, H. B., & Snell, L. H. (2015). Faculty attitudes and knowledge regarding college students with disabilities. *Journal of Postsecondary Education and Disability, 28*(3), 259–275.

Substance Abuse and Mental Health Services Administration. (2021). *Key substance use and mental health indicators in the United States: Results from the 2020 National Survey on Drug Use and Health* (HHS Publication No. PEP21-07-01-003, NSDUH Series H-56). Rockville, MD: Center for Behavioral Health Statistics and Quality, Substance Abuse and Mental Health Services Administration. Retrieved from https://www.samhsa.gov/data/

Terras, K., Phillips, A., & Leggio, J. (2015). Disability accommodations in online courses: The graduate student experience. *Journal of Postsecondary Education and Disability, 28*(3), 329–340.

Turan, Z., Kucuk, S., & Cilligol Karabey, S. (2022). The university students' self-regulated effort, flexibility and satisfaction in distance education. *International Journal of Educational Technology in Higher Education, 19*(35), 1–19. doi:10.118641239-022-00342-w PMID:35891707

ADDITIONAL READING

Di Malta, G., Bond, J., Conroy, D., Smith, K., & Moller, N. (2022). Distance education students' mental health, connectedness and academic performance during COVID-19: A mixed methods study. *Distance Education, 43*(1), 97–118. doi:10.1080/01587919.2022.2029352

Rogers, C. R., Lyon, H. C., Jr., & Tausch, R. (2014). *On becoming an effective teacher: Person-centered teaching, psychology, philosophy, and dialogues with Carl R. Roger and Harold Lyon*. Routledge/Taylor & Francis Group.

Schwartz, H. L. (2019). Connected teaching: Relationship. power, and mattering in higher education. *Stylus (Rio de Janeiro)*.

KEY TERMS AND DEFINITIONS

Anxiety: A mental health classification; its hallmark is the feelings of worry, fear, and possibly panic.

Attention Deficit Hyperactivity Disorder (ADHD): A mental health disorder characterized by impulsivity, attention difficulty, and hyperactivity. Commonly diagnosed in childhood but lasts into adulthood.

Bipolar: A mental health disorder in which a person's mood shifts from highs and lows, sometimes extreme highs and lows, which impacts a person's ability to function throughout the day for weeks to months on end.

Depression: A mental health disorder classified as a mood disorder, in which its main symptom is feeling sadness, which impacts a person's ability to function day-to-day.

Mental Health: A state of being that involves a person's psychological, emotional, and social wellbeing.

Posttraumatic Stress Disorder: (PTSD): A mental health disorder that can develop after a person has experienced or witnessed a traumatic event; often characterized by flashbacks and attempts to avoid trauma related situations.

Chapter 2
Building an Adult Learning Community While Converting an In-Person Degree Program to an Online Format:
A Case Study in Strategies and Lessons Learned

Carrie Grimes
https://orcid.org/0009-0007-5937-0048
Vanderbilt University, USA

Whitney Walters-Sachs
https://orcid.org/0009-0004-4702-8040
Vanderbilt University, USA

ABSTRACT

This case study examines the transition of a residential professional graduate degree program in educational leadership at a major research university to an online learning model. The case incorporates the observations and field notes of the program director and the inaugural online course instructor, along with survey data collected from students, investigating the opportunities and challenges of converting an established, community-rich, in-person professional degree program to an online model, with a focus on maintaining a strong sense of community. The theoretical framework and relevant scholarship are initially considered, followed by the case. Specific instructional strategies for building a sense of community and the affiliated evidence of the case are also discussed. The chapter concludes with key recommendations for how instructors and university program administrators can partner to design effective environments that foster engagement and meaningful learning experiences for online professional graduate students, contributing to long-term benefits for the institution.

DOI: 10.4018/978-1-6684-8908-6.ch002

INTRODUCTION

The field of online graduate education has demonstrated significant growth in recent years, offering adult learners access to an ever-growing number of professional degree programs unbounded by geography. In the wake of COVID-19, college and university administrators rapidly wisened to the benefits of expanding online professional degree offerings, given the potential for increased revenue generation through scalability. Adjacent prospective benefits such as enhanced student diversity, institutional brand amplification, and expanded applicant pools have also served as significant motivating forces in institutions' efforts to increase online professional degree offerings. These initiatives have been reinforced by the fact that the immersive global experiment of remote learning amidst the pandemic accelerated the normalization of virtual learning, diminishing the stigma associated with earning a professional degree online and increasing the marketability of such programs. Despite these overall benefits, challenges and tensions are emergent as institutions of higher education continue to weigh the affordances and constraints of programmatic changes from in-person to online modalities against a complex backdrop of limited instructional design/faculty resources, multifaceted student needs, ethical phenomena, and broader institutional values and objectives.

When adult learners participate in online degree programs, their sense of community can play a crucial role in shaping their learning experiences; developing their sense of institutional loyalty and belonging; and promoting their academic and professional outcomes. As more higher education institutions develop and launch online professional graduate programs, providing a sense of community should be a top priority. Our primary objective in this study was to investigate the various ways in which community can be built relatively rapidly, yet authentically, in an online professional degree program for adult learners. While our study focuses primarily on interactions that occurred in synchronous settings, when all participants were present simultaneously on the Zoom platform, we discuss asynchronous activities and strategies as well. We consider the intentional, improvisational, and ritualistic techniques that were deployed with the first online cohort of eighteen adult learners (in an eight-year-old formerly residential program) to cultivate a sense of community over the course of fourteen weeks. Our aim is to understand the key inputs that facilitated the shift from an initial online synchronous gathering of a diverse collection of strangers to a cohesive group characterized by acts of trust, humor, support, and camaraderie and exemplifying a powerful sense of community. We also seek to establish that an online graduate degree program model, which is inherently accessible to more people, has the capacity to result in greater cohort diversity over time, and therefore, enhanced learning outcomes. Finally, we aim to explore the perceived quality and salience of the new online cohort's sense of their capacity to establish community as adult online learners.

THEORETICAL FRAMEWORK: COMMUNITY OF INQUIRY THEORY

This study is grounded in a constructivist perspective in which learning is viewed as an active, social enterprise of ongoing, collective meaning-making (Bada & Olusegun, 2015; Tam, 2000). The community of inquiry theoretical framework focuses on the intentional development of a learning community. This kind of learning community is characterized as a group of individuals who engage in collaborative critical discourse and reflective practices with the aim of constructing personal meaning and confirming mutual understanding (Garrison et al., 2001). This framework revolves around intentionally cultivating three interdependent presences—social, cognitive, and teaching—which are in an ongoing state of interaction that contributes to creating deep and meaningful learning experiences.

Figure 1. Conceptual frame of community of inquiry theory
Note: Conceptual Frame of Community of Inquiry Theory. Garrison et al., 2001. Reprinted with permission from the Community of Inquiry website and licensed under the CC-BY-SA International 4.0 license (https://creativecommons.org/licenses/by-sa/4.0/).

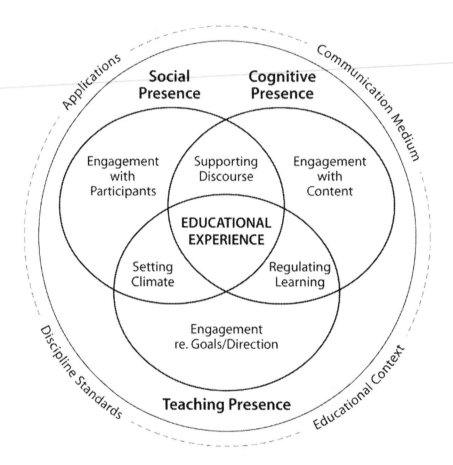

Cognitive presence refers to the ways in which members of a community of inquiry (CoI) engage in ongoing communication in order to co-construct meaning. Social presence is "the ability of participants to identify with the community, communicate purposefully in a trusting environment, and develop interpersonal relationships by way of projecting their individual personalities" (Garrison, 2009, p. 352). This presence directly impacts the success of the educational experience and can also serve as a scaffolding for cognitive presence, indirectly facilitating the processes of critical thinking carried on by the community of learners. Teaching presence encompasses the design of the learning experience (content, lesson plans, activities, and assessments) and the facilitation of cognitive and social processes that bring about learning outcomes (Garrison et al., 2001). As we both participated in knitting together this new online cohort of adult learners, we noticed that the mysterious "becoming" of the community was a phenomenon whereby each individual participant had a part to play. The notion of shifting amongst the three CoI presences became a useful tool for making sense of the evolutive and collaborative nature of creating community amidst the requisite design and facilitation of essential cognitive processes.

REVIEW OF RELATED LITERATURE

A portrait of the relevant literature is provided to facilitate an understanding of the focal phenomenon. Highlighted scholarship includes peer-reviewed articles and chapters, along with research studies conducted by educational think tanks and government agencies. Intersecting issues of classroom community, adult learning, online learning, the cohort model, higher education factors, and the proven benefits of a sense of community for individuals and institutions are explored. This synthesis of the literature empowers us to better understand the relevant tools, theories, structures, and strategies instructors may deploy in their efforts to effectively build a sense of community for adults enrolled in online professional degree programs.

Community in Learning Environments

The notion of community has long been the subject of diverse definitions and interpretations within academic discourse. The seminal contribution of McMillian and Chavis (1986) provides a useful theory for understanding the meaning of a sense of community as a social force. Their framework highlights four fundamental attributes of a sense of community: membership, influence, integration and fulfillment of needs, and shared emotional connection (McMillian & Chavis, 1986). McMillian and Chavis' notion of "membership" describes an individual's perception of belonging or interconnectedness within a specific group, distinguished by a sense of personal identification and investment. These scholars conceptualize the term "influence" as the perception of members' abilities to impact the group, coupled with the notion of the group being valued by its members. The "integration and fulfillment of needs" attribute describes the ways in which resources that are furnished to the members of a group will satisfy certain needs. Meeting individual needs within a community reinforces loyalty to the group, which inspires ongoing engagement. Elements that drive need fulfillment within the community include shared values, the competence of fellow members, and the success and status of the community. Finally, a sense of community is made more salient by a shared emotional bond that is manifested through ongoing social contact and community spirit, along with shared history, environments, and beliefs in the value of the investment of time spent together among members (McMillan & Chavis, 1986).

The construct of community within learning spaces advances the work of McMillan and Chavis and is a multidimensional concept encompassing both cognitive and emotional dimensions and shaping the holistic experiences of adult learners. A student's experience of community bears significance in adult online learning environments and directly influences outcomes such as retention, perceptions of curricular/program quality, feelings of affiliation with the university, and a sense of belonging within the learning environment and larger university community (Boyd, 2022; Kauffman, 2015; Ruey, 2010; Tinto, 1993; Yamauchi et al., 2016).

Cognitive experiences contributing to a sense of community within learning environments include intellectual engagement, knowledge sharing, and collaborative learning. Adult learners in online environments who participate in critical discussions, knowledge co-construction, and problem-solving activities facilitated by interactions with peers and instructors express a more salient sense of community (Palloff

& Pratt, 2013; Price et al., 2021). These social and cognitive experiences contribute to deeper learning and interpersonal connection, as learners participate in meaningful discourse, witness diverse perspectives, and participate in acts of metacognition and reflection (Jiang & Koo, 2020; Rovai & Jordan, 2004). Research about online learning community building by Conrad (2005), Diep et al. (2017), and LaPointe & Reisetter (2008) further emphasizes that a sense of community in online learning spaces is correlated with higher levels of belonging, cognitive engagement, and the development of critical thinking skills among adult learners. Regardless of an in-person or online learning modality, scholars concur that a sense of community is a major contributor to an adult learner's overall academic success; when adult learners feel connected to their peers and instructors, they are more likely to actively engage in the learning process, participate meaningfully in the activities of the learning community, and experience positive learning outcomes (Jiang & Koo, 2020; Rovai, 2002; Swan 2002).

The socio-emotional characteristics of a learning environment, whether online or in-person, are closely linked to the emotional experiences individuals have within a learning community. According to Rovai (2002), adult learners seek feelings of affiliation, partnership, and engagement with their peers and instructors. Garrison and colleagues (2001) claim that an atmosphere of emotional support within a learning community has the potential to enhance the overall perceptions of the learning environment, boost students' motivation, and minimize disengagement. Woods and Ebersole (2002) highlight the broader institutional value of community, contending that the establishment of a sense of community is a significant factor in enhancing learner satisfaction and emotional well-being, which consequently contribute to increased retention rates among adult learners in professional degree programs. Interestingly, adult learners may sometimes conflate their perceptions of a strong communal atmosphere within their learning environment with their assessment of a graduate program's curricular quality (Conrad, 2005). Hewitt's (2003) scholarship echoes Conrad, affirming that adult learners are motivated to persist and invest in their educational journey due to the conviction that a supportive and engaging community equates with high-quality learning experiences. It follows that a robust sense of community is a crucial factor in determining the effectiveness of a learning experience, and it is also considered to be a reliable predictor of students' assessments of individual courses and the overall degree program quality (Rovai, 2002).

A student's sense of community is also tightly coupled with their feelings of belonging within the learning environment and the larger university community. Numerous scholars (Bean & Eaton, 2000; Stebleton et al., 2014; Strayhorn, 2008, 2012) underscore the importance of students' capacity to develop a sense of belonging and membership within their academic community. Feelings of belongingness and membership are directly facilitated by a student's ability to recognize the value of their contributions to the community in conjunction with possessing an understanding of their role and place amongst faculty and fellow students (Jones & Wijeyesinghe, 2011; Maunder, 2018; Tinto, 2017). A student's understanding of their role and place within the learning environment may be moderated by their identity and the "many social structures that influence their options and opportunities" (Jones & Wijeyesinghe, 2011, p. 12). This is of particular importance when considering fostering a sense of community membership for individuals from historically marginalized groups (Jones & Wijeyesinghe, 2011; Kelly & Zakrajsek, 2023). From a persistence perspective, Tinto articulates the outcome of this kind of membership as a cohesive force that unites the learner with the community, despite obstacles that may emerge (Tinto, 1987). Through his theory of student persistence, Tinto (1993) further claims that a sense of belonging and social connection is essential for student retention and academic success. Ashar and Skenes (1993) advance Tinto's theory by specifically investigating adult learners' experiences and persistence outcomes, finding that both the social environment and one's sense of social integration have a significant and positive effect on persistence. Those who feel a strong sense of community and belonging are more likely to persist in their studies, actively engage in the learning process, and seek out opportunities for involvement and collaboration. In both in-person and online settings, these kinds of positive outcomes have cascading effects across the learning community and broader institution during a student's enrollment and into their alumni experience (Drezner, 2020; Jiang & Koo, 2020; Maulana, 2022).

Shea and colleagues (2005) emphasize that a strong sense of community significantly influences adult learners' feelings of affiliation with the university or the professional graduate program. When adult learners perceive a supportive and engaging community, they develop a sense of connection and social identification with the educational institution, which strengthens their loyalty and commitment (Ashforth & Mael, 2004; Tajfel, 1974; Tajfel & Turner, 2004). This sense of affiliation enhances the overall learning experience and fosters a positive relationship between the adult learner and the university. Junco and Mastrodicasa (2007) suggest that adult learners who feel a strong sense of community are more likely to engage in campus activities, seek out campus resources, and develop meaningful relationships with faculty and staff. This integration into the broader university community contributes to a more holistic educational experience and enhances the adult learner's overall satisfaction with their graduate program. In turn, it also benefits the institution, as feelings of loyalty toward one's alma mater are correlated with positive alumni relations behaviors such as financial contributions, volunteer engagement, and a willingness to advise others to attend the institution (Mael & Ashforth, 1992).

Growth in Online Graduate Education

Over the last decade, there has been a dramatic surge in online professional graduate program enrollments, signaling an enhanced appetite for online education among adult learners. The enrollment of students in online graduate programs in the United States increased by 17.1% between 2012 and 2016, while the overall enrollment rate of residential graduate students declined by 8.4% during the same period (Allen & Seaman, 2017). This increase in interest in online graduate programs is likely due to multiple factors, such as improvements in technology and online delivery platforms, the widespread recognition of the flexible nature of online learning, and the shifting perception of employers and universities of online degrees as legitimate and credible.

COVID-19 compounded the implementation of virtual learning within the landscape of higher education. The imperative for social distancing and the shuttering of brick-and-mortar campuses prompted academic institutions to rapidly convert all of their programs to digital formats. Consequently, many adult learners who previously resisted online education have shifted their perceptions of online degree programs from inferior to respectable. Bayview Analytics' 2021 annual report on the state of online learning in the United States revealed that 72% of graduate program administrators reported a surge in the demand for online graduate programs amidst the pandemic. The proliferation of web-based postgraduate programs has also been observed internationally. According to a 2021 report by the World Economic Forum, there has been a global surge in the popularity of online education, with a growing number of universities and institutions launching online graduate programs across diverse fields of study. This can be attributed to the growing awareness of the adaptability and convenience that online education offers adult learners, in particular, along with a forced acceptance of online teaching in the wake of the pandemic (Aslanian & Fischer, 2021).

The quantity of online graduate degree programs has not outpaced their quality. A recent study revealed that 86% of graduate online learners feel that the quality of their instructional experience online is the same or better than in-person instruction, and 84% agree or strongly agree that their online educational experience is worth the cost (Aslanian & Fischer, 2021). For adult professionals who seek to advance their academic experience, online programs have emerged as a high-quality, convenient method of learning, which allows them to effectively manage their work and personal obligations while pursuing their graduate studies.

The rise in enrollment and corresponding growth of online graduate programs underscore the need for educators and institutions to explore effective strategies for creating supportive and engaging online learning communities. In particular, faculty teaching adults in synchronous learning environments must be equipped with practices and strategies that contribute to a shared sense of community, given the numerous positive outcomes of community creation outlined above. By leveraging the unique affordances of online learning and fostering a strong sense of community, educators can maximize the potential of online graduate programs for learners and institutions while meeting pressing institutional needs related to fiscal and enrollment management.

Rationale for Change From In-Person to Online Modality

Multiple factors may contribute to the decision of a higher education institution to shift from a traditional face-to-face postgraduate curriculum to a virtual program. A notable factor is the heightened accessibility to academic programs through the online modality of delivery. Jaggars and Xu (2016) emphasize the value proposition of online programs to expand institutional reach to a wider and more diverse audience compared to conventional face-to-face programs. Access is significantly increased by eliminating geographic barriers and offering a feasible alternative for individuals who cannot relocate or travel long distances to participate in a graduate program. Borup and colleagues (2018) advance the construct of access by underscoring the capacity of online learning programs to mitigate educational inequities and increase accessibility for groups that have been historically marginalized. This includes adults from varied racial and ethnic backgrounds, persons with disabilities, and individuals representing a wider range of socioeconomic categories. The findings of a 2019 study of an online master's program indicate a steady increase in representation of female learners compared with conventional graduate programs that are conducted in physical classroom settings (Joyner & Isbell, 2019). These findings align with a report by the U.S. Department of Education (2017), which revealed that online programs are particularly attractive to adults who may need to balance their education with work or caregiving responsibilities. Expansion of access through an online modality contributes to the diversity of the graduate learning community by increasing the probability that individuals from different backgrounds, regions, and professional experiences have the opportunity to enroll in online programs. This expanded access, in turn, can enrich the learning community by offering a wider range of perspectives for faculty and students to engage with throughout the course of study.

The increased demand for online graduate programs also provides institutions of higher education with attractive incentives affiliated with meeting the educational needs of a larger pool of prospective students. Transitioning an in-person program to an online format can yield significant financial and enrollment management benefits for universities. Bates and Sangrà (2011) found that online programs can be more cost-effective, especially in terms of infrastructure, facilities maintenance, and administrative expenses. Online programs also have the advantage of scalability, allowing universities to accommodate a larger number of students without the constraints imposed by physical classroom sizes. This scalability can lead to increased revenue streams for the institution, contributing to the financial health of the university.

From an enrollment management perspective, the utilization of online education has the potential to enable institutions to broaden their scope, augment diversity, amplify their reputation, and enhance student retention and persistence. By expanding educational offerings beyond their physical confines and accessing a significantly larger pool of potential students (Aslanian & Fischer, 2021), universities can mine previously untapped markets of potential students, both domestically and abroad. In addition, by developing an initial repertoire of online degree offerings, institutions can establish internal systems, templates, and resource repositories that can be repurposed in the promotion, design, and execution of future programs. The strategic enrollment management and scaling of online programs can optimize the financial standing of institutions of higher education and help secure the sustainability of their academic programs.

Adult Learners as a Distinctive Category

Adult learners in professional graduate degree programs are a distinctive category of learners with unique needs and motivations, which have important implications for online learning environments. Cercone (2008) asserts that adult learners have significant personal and professional responsibilities (e.g., childcare, work) that interfere with and/or influence their learning experiences. Typically, adults electively enroll in graduate educational programs and juggle their classes and coursework around these responsibilities. Adult learners are also more likely to be highly motivated and focused (Merriam & Caffarella, 1999). For adults, the learning process involves learning about oneself and transforming not just what one learns, but also how one learns (Cercone, 2008). Understanding these distinctive features is essential for designing effective learning experiences. Key conceptual frameworks, including Knowles' theory of andragogy and transformative learning theory (both of which support the utilization of self-directed and experiential learning methods) shed light on the specific needs and motivations of adult learners in context.

Andragogy provides a useful window into better understanding the specific characteristics and learning preferences of adult learners (Knowles, 1984). A fundamental aspect of andragogy is the concept of self-directed learning. Typically, adult learners are intrinsically motivated and have a strong desire to take ownership of their learning journey, electing to engage in learning that is relevant and applicable to their personal and professional lives (Merriam & Caffarella, 1999). Thus, providing clear learning objectives and guidance promotes a self-directed learning process for adults in line with their learning preferences, while still allowing flexibility for learners to pursue their specific interests and goals.

Another key principle of andragogy is the emphasis on the learners' prior experiences. Adult learners bring their life experiences and pre-existing knowledge into the learning process, which shapes their perspectives and contributes to their understanding of course material. Andragogy also emphasizes the importance of practical application; adult learners are motivated by the immediate relevance and applicability of what they learn (Cercone, 2008; Knowles, 1984). By integrating practical, job-related applications into the learning experience, such as case studies, simulations, and authentic assessments that bridge the gap between theory and practice, educators can enhance the motivation and engagement of adult learners. In the specific context of professional graduate degree programs, adult learners have a strong appetite for applying newly acquired knowledge and skills directly to their professional contexts, fostering deeper learning and skills transfer.

Transformative learning theory complements andragogy by emphasizing the transformative process that adult learners undergo as they engage in the learning process (Mezirow, 1997). Adult learners in professional graduate programs often seek opportunities for critical reflection to challenge their existing assumptions and beliefs. They are likely to feel their needs are being more effectively met if learning experiences incorporate reflection, dialogue, and the exploration of diverse points of view.

Attributes of High-Quality Online Instruction for Adult Learning Communities

Online instructors who are highly competent in communication and facilitation can best satisfy the needs of adult learners by fostering feelings of connection within the learning community and ensuring that instructions, expectations, and feedback are effectively communicated to students (Palloff & Pratt, 2007). Creating a friendly and supportive environment for learners that supports their active involvement, encourages their participation in conversations, inspires an ongoing exchange of ideas, and capitalizes on peer-to-peer learning are all evidence-based ingredients for instructional success.

According to scholars, effective online education for adult learning communities requires specific characteristics and approaches to adapt to the unique demands and preferences of adult learners (Johnson, 2018; Thompson & Porto, 2014). The alignment of online instruction with previously discussed andragogical principles (Knowles, 1980) has the potential to amplify the motivation and engagement of adult learners. According to Li and Pei (2023) and Merriam and Bierema (2013), the integration of learner autonomy, relevancy, and problem-centeredness into online instruction is conducive to the cultivation of active participation and self-directed learning for adults. Utilizing authentic and experiential learning methodologies in online educational settings also allows adult learners to apply new knowledge and competencies to practical settings (Bonk & Khoo, 2014). Establishing connections between theoretical concepts and real-world contexts is another highly effective instructional practice to deploy with adult online learners, as it promotes reflective practice and enhances the utility of course material. Rovai and Downey (2010) advance the construct of learning-by-doing with their emphasis on the efficacy of collaborative activities for adults learning in virtual environments. Team projects, peer-to-peer role plays, and small group case examinations are all proven means of promoting both engagement and academic success for adult learners online.

Palloff and Pratt (2013) posit that an effective online instructor is someone "who is open to giving up control of the learning process" by making students active participants in their learning process (p. 24). A learner-centered approach acknowledges what students bring to the online classroom—their backgrounds, needs, professional roles, and interests—and what they take away as relevant and meaningful outcomes. With the instructor serving as a facilitator rather than a lecturer, students are given more control and responsibility around how they learn, including the opportunity to actively engage in inquiry and to teach one another through collaboration and personal interactions (Palloff & Pratt, 2013). Effective online instruction for adults also allows students to reflect upon their learning experiences and practice metacognition (Bransford et al., 2000). In synchronous learning environments, metacognition may be supported through facilitated reflective practice, small group discussions, and the utilization of multiple technical features of the virtual classroom during instruction, such as digital polls, mind maps, and collaborative shared documents (Berry, 2019; Khudhair et al., 2023).

The smooth integration of technology plays an important role in delivering effective online instruction for adult learners, who generally seek a low-friction virtual learning experience. Leveraging the expertise of instructional designers to build a learning management system (LMS) that is both user-friendly and intuitive has been shown to significantly reduce the cognitive load for online learners and enhance the overall learning experience (Sweller et al., 2011). Offering easy access to educational materials and delivering opportunities for learner interaction and collaboration have been emphasized by Dabbagh and Kitsantas (2012) as elemental to the learner's positive perceptions of online learning that occurs both asynchronously and synchronously. By integrating multimedia and interactive elements in online instruction, such as videos, graphics, and interactive simulations, the potential to enhance comprehension and retention of information among adult learners is also optimized (Mayer, 2014).

The Cohort Model

Cohort models, which involve a group of learners navigating through a program together, have perpetuated in the domain of professional graduate degree programs because of their propensity to enhance individual learning outcomes, promote feelings of community, and inspire collaboration and relationship-building. Evidence maintains that students enrolled in cohort models benefit through the mitigation of isolation, the development of valuable social bonds (Hill, 1995), and the sharing of a common purpose (Leithwood et al., 1995). Bratlien (1992) observed that camaraderie among cohort members provides support and inspires a sense of motivation for students to accomplish significant academic goals. Barnett and Muse (1993) studied the benefits and challenges of cohort groups in educational administration graduate programs and found that cohort communities are auspicious for learners academically and socially due to their impact on students' perceptions of improved academic self-efficacy and promotion of feelings of support and connection.

Pemberton and Akkary (2010) advanced another argument for the utilization of cohort models in graduate educational leadership programs, finding that feelings of trust and support within a cohort community elevate students' integration of learning experiences and capacity for team learning and perspective-taking. Learners are also more likely to experience a sense of belonging and commitment to the program and institution when they move forward as a cohesive group, as doing so results in more active peer involvement that facilitates knowledge sharing, deeper discussion, and increased support and networking (Teittel, 1997). The sense of belonging within a cohort of online students is underscored as a pivotal factor in the learning experiences of these students because it may be more challenging for them to assert their social presence in a virtual environment (Barber et al., 2015; Joksimovic et al., 2015). Finally, the professional benefits derived from networking within a cohort community are enhanced by the valuable impact of cohort experiences on building essential, transferable workplace skills related to managing group dynamics and real-world interpersonal challenges (Horn, 2000, 2001; McPhail, 2000).

THE DESCRIPTIVE CASE: SCHOOL LEADERSHIP PROGRAM (SLP) AT WC

Through this single-case study of a school leadership program, we sought to better understand the following question: What are the key factors in an online learning environment that transformed a diverse group of strangers into a cohesive group of adult learners characterized by a powerful sense of community? Drawing on college artifacts, student survey data, and the lived experiences, observations, and field notes of the program director and the inaugural online course instructor, we examine below the various opportunities and challenges of converting an established, community-rich, in-person professional degree program to an online model, with a focus on maintaining a strong sense of community. After describing the case, we will draw from insights gained from the literature and the case study itself to make several evidence-based recommendations for designing online programs that foster meaningful experiences and community for online graduate students, thereby contributing to long-term gains for the institution.

WC's Decision to Transition to an Online Learning Model

In 2021, WC, a private college of education situated at a major research university recognized for excellence in undergraduate and graduate study, made the decision to shift its in-person, cohort-based school leadership master's program (SLP) to a predominantly online learning format. School leadership viewed the reimagination of this program as having many potential upsides, including the heightened flexibility and accessibility that an online model would offer students and WC's corresponding ability to expand its institutional reach by inviting a more diverse group of students into its learning spaces. The new model would also enable students to maintain their current employment while pursuing this degree. From past experience launching another fully online graduate program, WC administrators understood that this transition had the capacity to attract a larger pool of prospective students (domestically and internationally), expand the reach of the WC brand, and enrich the learning community with a broader range of perspectives and experiences. An added benefit perceived by WC administration was that a transition online would offer various cost efficiencies and economies of scale for the college.

By the time the decision was made to change the format of this program, many of the college's faculty members had gained experience teaching remotely (either in other online programs or during closures associated with the pandemic), which helped to normalize the virtual learning experience and quell concerns related to the academic quality of online professional degree programs. Moreover, WC leadership had already examined the relative affordances and challenges of online modalities in connection with a prior roll-out of a fully online graduate program. Although WC and its faculty had prior experience delivering online instruction and launching a fully online graduate program, this was the first time the college would reimagine the format of a long-standing residential program. In addition, unlike the prior fully online program launched by the college, this launch would not leverage the resources or expertise of an external third party. Declining to do so came with a host of benefits, as well as its own set of complexities.

The pre-existing SLP was a 12-week incubatory summer residency hosted on the university's campus over the course of two summers. During its prior eight years of operations, SLP had amassed an active base of approximately 150 students and alumni who shared tremendous affinity for the existing program in its then-current form. When the decision was made to convert SLP to a predominantly online format, 18 students were midway through the program. These students strongly advocated that they be permitted to finish the program in person on campus, as they understood the program would function when they first enrolled. Leadership agreed, and arrangements were made for this cohort to complete their program in residence during the summer of 2022, while simultaneously transitioning the new cohort just beginning the program to an online environment consisting of synchronous and asynchronous online classes and coursework.

Perhaps not surprisingly, news of the decision brought divergent perspectives on the change. Some stakeholders (including students currently enrolled in SLP and alumni of the program) were vocal about their discontent, particularly regarding the perceived capacity of an online model to effectively perpetuate a sense of community. They felt strongly that without the unique bonding opportunities associated with an immersive residential experience, SLP students and faculty would be unable to generate feelings of belonging, community, or affiliation with the program or the university. At the same time, a significant group of stakeholders (including various administrators, faculty members, and prospective students) lauded the accessibility of the new program and the attendant removal of various barriers to entry. These constituencies felt just as strongly (but in the other direction) that the new model was essential to WC's ability to attract and serve a more robust range of students.

On balance, WC leadership was persuaded that a digitally distanced learning program could be developed in accordance with the college's pedagogical standards to provide significant value and increased flexibility to its graduate students. At WC, the redesign was viewed as an overwhelmingly favorable equity move designed to meet the needs of working professionals, remove the barriers of temporary geographic relocation, and facilitate learning throughout the academic year—all of which would lead to more diverse opportunities for students to apply their learning in real-time.

The university administration dedicated itself to the success of the online program in a number of ways. One way was by engaging a new program director with decades of subject-matter expertise, a background in admission and enrollment management, branding and marketing training, and applicable experience as an adult learner (and later, as an instructor) in an online graduate program. Other ways involved the dedication of human and financial resources to the support of the program and the program director in her new capacity, which included numerous resources furnished by the college to aid in the design and launch of the online program. Given her relevant background and the valuable support provided by the leadership team, the new director was well-positioned to leverage her experience and skill set during the ensuing development and roll-out of the reimagined program.

Redesigning SLP as an Online Program

Drawing on the pre-existing curricular assets as well as her past experience learning and working in various online graduate programs), the new program director and key faculty colleagues developed an online curriculum for a 15-month, part-time leadership program geared toward a niche group of school professionals. One key goal in the redesign was to cover the same span of calendar time (approximately 15 months from start to finish) in transitioning the program online. The program design was synergistic. Student learning and growth provided the core foundation for planning, and appropriate consideration was given to what was essential for students and faculty and sustainable for the institution.

With instructional design input from WC's Center for Teaching (CFT), courses were intentionally scaffolded and spaced to ensure that each course connected to the next as part of an overall program, with common themes and content recurring throughout. Great attention was paid to unfolding a program that was not only thoughtfully designed to deliver professionally relevant content, but also tailored to meet the unique needs of online adult learners. The redesigned curriculum was vetted and approved by the appropriate faculty and departmental committees at the university.

The prescribed curriculum for the online SLP was anchored in foundational knowledge and core competencies centered around various themes tied directly to leadership and learning. To help facilitate community within the cohort and continue to promote access, equity, diversity, and inclusivity, the curriculum also incorporated coursework focused on intercultural competence, socio-emotional learning, innovations in pedagogy and andragogy, and community-based learning.

Under the new model, the curriculum is delivered over four consecutive semesters, primarily through a series of three-credit online courses and a self-directed action research project. Each course combines synchronous meetings, along with asynchronous work and assignments that can be completed more independently. The synchronous (or so-called "live") aspects of required courses occur in online sessions held once a week for 90 minutes, which all students are expected to attend. In these sessions, students can see one another's faces through the Zoom platform and engage in collaborative learning with their peers in small and large groups. These opportunities help to create an interactive online learning community that fosters student engagement and connection among all participants. Students spend additional time between live sessions working independently on asynchronous content, participating in self-directed group work with cohort mates, and working on assignments and projects.

A standard learning management system (LMS) is utilized as an interface for all courses and remote learning components. The program director aimed to create something easy to use and aesthetically pleasing, while also durable and sound in terms of communicating the content and curriculum in a way that makes sense for adult learners. The roadmap for each course on the LMS includes the syllabus, class list, relevant dates and deadlines, weekly readings and assignments, asynchronous modules, announcements, and information on where to obtain help. Having course materials cohesively organized and easily accessible—and creating a schema by which learners can remotely navigate the program—optimizes the learning experience by providing a more frictionless experience and helping students reduce their cognitive load as they navigate through each course in the program.

The decision to adopt a central structure and design for the LMS across the entire program was also viewed as a way to promote a sense of belonging among the students by enabling them to feel part of one program and one community rather than subject to piecemeal courses. Another objective was to build the WC brand and the students' identification with the institution; key university and program branding visuals and language were visible across the LMS to provide students with ongoing reminders of their membership within the community. The program director believed (based on her experience and knowledge of the scholarship) that these efforts would yield outcomes that would be particularly beneficial for adults learning remotely.

With the new program design and learning management system in hand, the program director began thinking about her networks inside and outside the program to bring the faculty to life. For a program catering to mid-career professionals, the director appreciated the need to draw on the subject-matter expertise of scholars on the WC faculty, as well as the perspectives of scholar-practitioners who would help contextualize the scholarship with practical applications to the field. Her stated objective was to secure a faculty illustrative of the outstanding teaching and learning community at WC whose backgrounds matched the program curricula. Recognizing that people sit at the heart of effective programs, the program director knew that the faculty she selected to engage in the inaugural year of the online program would be instrumental in helping her build this learning community and making the content career-embedded and relevant to a cross-section of professionals with diverse backgrounds.

Over the course of months, the program director hand-picked an intentional mix of world-class specialists from across the university and renowned expert practitioners to collectively draw on their decades of research, practice, and leadership development. Each professor selected has a terminal degree, subject matter expertise, and direct experience with adult learners and their online instruction and engagement. The inaugural online course instructor, in particular, was chosen based on her work in the field as a scholar-practitioner, her prior affiliation with SLP as a guest lecturer, and her years of experience as an adult learner in another one of WC's online graduate programs.

To facilitate a smooth online transition, all of the SLP professors engaged to teach during the first year of the online program committed to designing the curriculum and delivering the instruction (asynchronously and synchronously during the live sessions). These steps were taken to underscore that SLP online students would have high-quality opportunities to form relationships and engage with a strong, dedicated program faculty.

Curating a faculty customized for SLP to ensure that the content and instruction were high-quality and specifically geared to adult learners in an online setting was another aspect of the decision-making that was intentionally designed to establish trust and connection with the students. The program (including the inaugural online course) was also designed to be iterative and subject to continuous improvement, which served as another strategic way of incorporating student voices. This insight into the intentions behind these choices is not meant to suggest that the approach was perfect, only that it was thoughtful, deliberate, and intended to build students' sense of community and identification with the program.

During the entire re-design process, the university evidenced its ongoing investment in creating a high-level online program by making financial and human resources readily available to the program director. The program director credits the collaboration, camaraderie, and generosity of time and resources she received from university leadership and faculty as central to her ability to animate critical pieces of the redesign and make an aspirational vision for an online program come to life.

Developing the New Cohort

While engaged in the technical aspects of the program redesign and transition online, the program director was also executing her responsibility to develop the new (online) cohort. With the intention of building a cohort of individuals with diverse backgrounds, perspectives, and experiences firmly in mind, the program director engaged in a high-touch admission process in which she got to know the applicants personally. Listening to the students' stories helped the program director understand more about the students' professional aspirations and individual learning objectives. She described the process as "putting a family together," which is emblematic of the high value she placed on building community within this dedicated learning environment.

Attention was also paid to growing an online brand for the program to help WC raise awareness of SLP and recruit students from far and wide. Posts to social media during the transition stage included information about the online format and program design and testimonials from alumni graduates, faculty members, and senior leaders affiliated with the program. In addition, the program director held multiple online information sessions for prospective students, which were followed by additional online sessions customized for admitted students. All of these sessions were structured not only as informational, but also as opportunities to establish meaningful touchpoints and connections with SLP. They were meant to serve as stepping stones in the process of building the students' sense of belonging in the community. A website for admitted students was also created to provide one central location where students could find information related to the program and community, again reinforcing concern for the student experience and a desire to engender affiliation with the program and university.

Prospective and admitted students who wanted additional perspectives were connected with current or former members of the SLP community to enable students to ask questions and hear personal reflections on the impressions and experiences of other program participants. The practice of pairing students with an ambassador from a prior cohort served as an additional form of community building within SLP. Financial aid was also made available to promote accessibility for students from a range of backgrounds.

Numerous individuals who expressed interest in the new model reported that they had previously looked at SLP but only considered applying once the format changed. They explained they could not afford (for many different reasons) to be away from work and family for six weeks at a time, two summers in a row. Students hindered by these constraints pinpointed the online program's flexibility as the determining factor in their decision to apply. Moreover, when admitted students were asked what motivated their decision to enroll in SLP, many cited the sense of community they experienced during the admission process as a leading factor.

Designing the First Course in the Online Program

The inaugural online course instructor worked in close partnership with the program director to imagine and design the curriculum for the first course in the online program—collaborating on the syllabus, course materials, and assessments with a focus on delivering high-level content, along with consistent opportunities for experiential learning, engagement, and community-building.

The course materials assembled were rooted in meaningful consideration of evidence-based research, as well as the realities of everyday professional practice to which the adult learners in the program could directly connect their experiences. From the time they spent working and learning in professional graduate programs, the program director and inaugural online instructor both understood the large extent to which adult learners seek opportunities for critical reflection to challenge their existing assumptions and beliefs. Knowing this, they intentionally integrated course content featuring a range of voices that would represent many different perspectives and challenge students to explore diverse points of view, consider issues from multiple angles, and engage in respectful dialogue with one another. A central objective was for the students to feel seen, valued, and reflected in the curriculum.

Another key focal area in terms of engagement and community building was the course's emphasis on opportunities for student engagement in identity work and reflective practice to help learners sharpen their own identities and synthesize those identities with personal and professional aspirations. Along these lines, the course design included weekly opportunities for individual reflection, expanded writing assignments, and oral presentations as culminating learning experiences. Through these experiential activities, students could learn more about themselves and develop a professional plan rooted in their core values and individual identities.

Active participation was positioned as another essential component of the curriculum. The syllabus made clear that students in this distance learning course were expected to engage just as if they were learning in a face-to-face, in-person environment. This expectation meant that students must complete all tasks/assignments on time and come to the synchronous sessions ready to actively dialogue and collaborate with others, having reflected upon all assigned course materials sufficiently in advance of the class time together. Facilitating active participation and robust dialogue in this manner served as a form of climate and norm-setting for the class.

The value placed on feedback and ongoing improvement was also embedded in the design of the inaugural course. Growth-focused feedback was positioned as something students should expect the professor to provide as an essential source of their learning. Moreover, the inaugural instructor continuously invited suggestions on the subject matter or contexts students wanted to explore, recognizing that students may have emerging questions and concerns not covered by the course content. On the more practical side, asynchronous content was released approximately two weeks before the corresponding "live" session to provide flexibility to those managing professional demands along with their graduate studies.

Collectively, the various elements of the course design positively contributed to the instructor's ability to establish from the outset some of the cognitive, socio-emotional, and teaching characteristics of the learning environment.

Norm Setting and Values Clarification Within SLP

Importantly, the program director and inaugural instructor of the first online course emphasized the importance of norm-setting right from the start. Program norms were consistently communicated on the LMS and the admitted students' website, in program materials sent to students, and in the syllabus for the first class. These norms recognized diversity as a core institutional value to be celebrated through conversations, events, and programs. From a big-picture perspective, SLP students were encouraged to relate the course readings and class discussions to their own personal and professional experiences whenever possible, while demonstrating respect for the diverse views, perspectives, and analyses of other members of the cohort.

The established expectations included student and faculty engagement consistent with the university's honor code and the college's statement on equity and inclusivity, as well as adherence to various conventions specifically established for SLP and tailored to an online setting. The college's norms underscored the need for all campus members to experience a sense of belonging, along with empowerment to discover and live out their truth. To achieve these objectives, the college and its faculty expressed and enacted a commitment to providing students with opportunities to explore their identities, both individually and collectively.

These values and commitments were echoed in the SLP core values and norms of engagement, which the program director and inaugural online professor co-constructed in the spirit of the college's core practices and beliefs and with the benefit of input from students in prior cohorts. For example, the SLP core values emphasized the program's commitment to honoring and celebrating a wide range of backgrounds, talents, perspectives, roles, experiences, and opinions—with the stated goal of creating a sense of belonging and community through active listening. Relationships were held out as central to the SLP community and the community's desire to establish a collaborative culture that fosters personal and professional growth through vulnerability. Curiosity, reflective practice, experiential and student-centered learning, process and effort, and appreciation for different contexts were all overtly articulated as values fundamental to the SLP learning experience.

The SLP norms of engagement highlighted certain expected behaviors stemming from and consistent with this value system, including: conscious and purposeful speech; active listening; collaboration; curiosity; respect for different perspectives; vulnerability; authentic and inclusive discourse; and present and productive engagement in the learning environment. With respect to online engagement in particular (including posting and interacting on Zoom), SLP students were asked to adhere to various best practices (commonly referred to as "netiquette"). These online practices included keeping cameras on as a sign of respect and engagement; not saying or posting anything online that would not be shared in person/public; responding to others promptly and thoughtfully; demonstrating respect for individual privacy by not sharing class discussions outside of the virtual classroom; and exhibiting respect the opinions of others in all aspects of online engagement.

Notably, SLP students were invited to contribute to the core programmatic values and norms of engagement to incorporate the cohort's particular belief systems and experiences. Students were also encouraged to come forward for assistance if they were uncomfortable with any post, language, or interaction in the program.

The college and program's core values and norms of engagement worked together to establish a healthy climate for the learning environment and provide a foundation for rich and meaningful discussions and interactions among students and faculty affiliated with SLP.

Instructional Methods Engaged in the First Online Course

The inaugural instructor incorporated various instructional strategies to build community in the SLP's synchronous virtual spaces. Beyond simply promoting learning, each strategy described below was explored as a way of cultivating trust; fostering peer-to-peer rapport and engagement; and establishing a psychologically safe learning community conducive to ongoing growth and high-quality learning. Every attempt was made to structure activities to make the online learning platform and spaces feel welcoming, engaging, collaborative, and productive for each learner.

Before the 90-minute "live" virtual session held each week, students engaged asynchronously with readings and an online lesson facilitated by the instructor. The asynchronous lessons consisted of different instructional components designed to help students make sense of their professional environments and connect the curriculum with real-life experiences. The modalities utilized varied by week depending on the content covered. These modalities included recorded lectures or interviews conducted by the instructor; TED Talks and other recordings to watch or listen to; short articles to read; prompts based on course content to respond to; and questions to ponder. Students completed this work individually before the weekly synchronous sessions, applying course content to their own experiences and noticing how it related to their individual identities. Because the pre-class preparation invited learners into a space of deep learning and reflection on topics covered that week, the time when students came together online was rich in discourse and personal connection.

The instructor began each virtual session with a ritualized opportunity for interaction on an emotional level. At the onset of every class, all eighteen students were asked to "check in" with two words to describe their current mindset. By taking notice of how they and their peers were feeling, learners built their core competencies around emotional intelligence while getting to know one another on a more personal level. In the first few weeks of the course, the students strictly adhered to the "two-word" aspect of the exercise. However, as time passed (and their connection grew), the check-ins became longer, more involved, and more personal. The instructor remained flexible regarding how much class time to devote to this exercise, gauging the room's temperature in light of what was being discussed to determine what the students needed in the moment. At times, the class spent over twenty minutes connecting in this ritualized space; other times, when the mood permitted, students were asked to simply post their check-in using the online "chat" waterfall function.

Following the class check-ins, synchronous class time featured a range of opportunities for students to individually and collectively grapple with the context-based implications of the course content. Instructional tools and methods engaged included: guest speakers; reflective practice; small and large group discussions; and activities to facilitate experiential learning, tackle real-life problems of practice, and apply theory to practice. These participatory, pedagogical methods invited learners into relationship with the course material, creating an atmosphere where students could go beyond shallow interaction with the curriculum to explore their individual curiosities and belief systems and, ultimately, open their minds to broader ways of thinking. In this sense, the virtual classroom co-created by the students and inaugural instructor functioned as a microcosm of a democratic society where learners effectively balanced their personal opinions, judgments, and beliefs with the fundamentally interpersonal aspects of intellectual inquiry.

During some synchronous sessions, the instructor invited special guest speakers to address the class for a portion of the period. When extending these invitations, the instructor was mindful to showcase a range of voices and ideas (just as she had done assembling the course materials), which fed the group's shared desire to promote a sense of belonging throughout the community. Typically, however, ninety minutes of virtual learning time was fully dedicated to the students and exercises they could tailor to their personal interests by connecting the course content to their professional experiences and pursuing individual and collective learning goals during the session.

Sometimes, students were invited to take a few minutes at the beginning of the live session to respond in writing to prompts from the instructor. This practice helped to quiet the group, center their thinking, and put them in a reflective head space. Metacognition provided an essential bridge between instruction and student growth.

Following this type of exercise, students might be placed in breakout rooms that were used to facilitate small group discussions. In some cases, students were given agency to choose their small group partners. Other times, the instructor assigned students to the breakout rooms, paying close attention to the groupings each week to try to ensure that each student had an opportunity to be in a small group session with every other student in the cohort at least once during the semester.

The smaller number of participants in breakout groups (2-4 students per group) promoted trust, fluid conversation, and the ability for learners to engage with their cohort mates on a more direct and personal level. The instructor usually provided students with thought-sparking questions and exercises to stimulate the conversation, which gave the groups common ground to cover together. Typically, students would type out the salient points that emerged from their conversations in a shared Google document that all cohort members had access to in real-time. This collaborative document served as a tool the students relied upon to learn more about what was being discussed in other groups. This practice made the cohort feel cohesive even when students were working in separate groups, and also provided them with opportunities to bear witness to collective learning. While students engaged in their small groups, the instructor circulated among them—listening to the conversations, prompting with additional questions, or offering additional thoughts for their consideration, as the moments warranted. Still, the small group sessions remained student-led, with students retaining the autonomy to drive the conversation based on their learning interests.

Following small group breakout sessions, the class would come back together to report on what ideas came up in their small groups. Learners tended to build and expand on what others said, validating the experiences shared by their peers and showing their support and mutual regard for one another. This practice led to more conversation among the cohort, which could meander through different topics based on their preferences. Even when there was disagreement, the students were thoughtful, kind, and respectful. Regardless of the activity, large group discussions (and weekly live sessions, more broadly speaking) functioned as collaborative forums for the thoughtful and respectful exchange of ideas.

During these virtual classes, students were encouraged to use the chat function to comment more informally on class discussions. The chat provided a space for parallel discourse in which students could react to what was being said without interrupting the speaker. As people got to know each other better, they would use the chat function to make jokes, offer encouragement, and share resources relevant to the topics being discussed. These more intimate exchanges started to occur relatively early in the semester.

Although the instructor created a lesson plan for each live session online, she adopted a flexible, student-centered approach, which enabled her to adapt to the perceived needs and interests of the students at the time. In these sessions, the instructor assumed the role and identity of a navigational guide—someone who would moderate the discussions to help students integrate the learning with their daily practices. While there were always topics the instructor was interested in covering during live sessions, she tended to defer to the students to chart their own course, providing them with suggested points of discussion that they were free to take up or move in a different direction.

Whereas the instructor assumed a more traditional role of lecturer during the asynchronous time, she functioned in the live sessions as more of a peer—equally engaged in the learning alongside the students. By trusting the students to make these choices, the instructor was attempting to enhance their learning experience, strengthen their commitment to the community, and create discourse centered on a collaborative and iterative exchange of knowledge. Empowering learners to exercise increased ownership of their studies and priorities seemed to drive their motivation, participation, and engagement in the course. This facilitation approach was complemented by the instructor's willingness to share personal tidbits about her own life. By peppering the discourse with stories that allowed students to perceive her as a real person, she contributed to a sense of trust and community.

Another way the instructor aimed to build trust and engagement in the learning community was by regularly soliciting feedback from the cohort and being responsive to student ideas and concerns. The value that the instructor and program director placed on feedback communicated to students a high level of care and concern for their learning experience, as well as a commitment to iteration and continuous improvement. The instructor also showed her investment in the students' educational journeys by providing individualized feedback on all assignments. It was essential to her (and the program director) that all students feel known, heard, and valued.

Opportunities for Social and Interpersonal Connection

Students in the program had various opportunities for social and interpersonal connections that helped build community in this virtual learning environment. Some were formally facilitated through the program, and others were ones that the students created on their own. For example, the inaugural professor often stayed in the Zoom room after class, inviting anyone interested to remain and personally connect in a more casual setting. At the university level, students were invited to participate virtually in various university-sponsored events. On the more informal side, many students in the cohort participated in social hours they hosted via Zoom. Students also formed their own discussion groups related to the coursework and collaborated with thought partners on the assigned materials each week. The fact that the students independently created these communities of practice on their own illuminates the sense of community that was building within the cohort.

THE ANALYTIC CASE: WHAT THE DATA REVEALED ABOUT COMMUNITY BUILDING EFFORTS

In addition to investigating the lived experiences, observations, and field notes of the program director and the inaugural online course instructor, this case study examines survey data collected from students in the first online cohort to inform our inquiry into the factors contributing to the development of a sense of community within a virtual learning environment. Surveys were administered to all eighteen students at two critical junctures. The first was a course evaluation survey conducted in August 2022 upon the students' completion of the inaugural online class. The second was a survey more specifically oriented toward building community online, which was administered in June 2023, as the students were nearing completion of their degree program in SLP.

Below, we examine the findings from the survey data through the Community of Inquiry (CoI) framework. This analysis reveals the elements of the course content, environment, and instructional strategies and design, which positively contributed to the students' sense of belonging and satisfaction with the program as a whole.

End-of-Semester Course Evaluation Survey (August 2022)

At the end of the inaugural online course, students in the cohort were asked to voluntarily complete the university's course evaluation survey, which was designed as an opportunity for students to provide feedback on their learning and ideas on ways to improve the course in the future. The evaluation survey contained a combination of Likert scale questions and prompts for short answers regarding the instructor; the course content, objectives, and design; the elements of the course most contributing to learning; and any recommended improvements. Half of the students in the cohort (nine of the eighteen) completed and returned the survey.

In terms of the cognitive and teaching presence established in the community, one hundred percent (100%) of respondents either agreed (11.11%) or strongly agreed (88.89%) that: (i) the inaugural online instructor encouraged critical, original, or creative thinking; and (ii) the inaugural online course helped students consider connections between course material and other areas of their personal, academic, or professional lives. Similar results were reported concerning whether the instructor helped students understand the core ideas related to the course, with over three-quarters of students (77.78%) strongly agreeing and approximately one-quarter (22.22%) agreeing she did.

Expanding on the elements of the course that most contributed to learning in these cognitive aspects, one student commented, "The study of different leadership styles provides concrete information for personal and professional reflection and growth. The structure of the course enabled collaboration and fluid discussions." Another student responded similarly, highlighting as essential elements for learning the "great care" the instructor took "to craft readings and learning materials to expose the class to a variety of ideas that provoked meaningful class discussion." Other students specifically identified the interviews the instructor conducted and presented to the class, as well as the live Q&A sessions with interviewees that the instructor moderated during synchronous sessions, as instructional methods that "really made the learning come alive."

Another significant finding emerging from this evaluative survey is the extent to which students perceived the asynchronous content to be engaging and conducive to their overall learning experience. One learner described the material as "relevant and engaging," noting that appreciation for the instructor's use of "multiple modes to deliver information." The positive feedback on the online asynchronous learning modules was echoed by others who cited the asynchronous content that the instructor curated as "masterfully done and something to look forward to each week" and "the most helpful in learning material related to the course."

With respect to the social and teaching presences related to climate setting and engagement, one hundred percent (100%) of respondents strongly agreed that the instructor: (i) demonstrated interest in students' learning; and (ii) created a welcoming and inclusive classroom environment. The entire group (100%) also strongly agreed that they felt comfortable asking questions. All students also agreed or strongly agreed that the instructor clearly communicated course expectations.

Among the factors contributing most to their learning experiences, students cited the "engaging, communal environment that [the instructor] created," "[the instructor's] ability to build strong relationships virtually," the instructor's "ability to build community and bring together a bunch of different personalities," and the "psychologically safe space [established] for our class that allowed us to fully engage with the material and [learn] from each other." The synchronous class discussions were specifically identified as "helpful to connect with classmates and occasionally refine what was learned in the readings and asynchronous learning." One student summed up the experience in the first online class and its impact on the program as a whole by saying, "[The professor] laid the groundwork for us to be able to build strong relationships virtually ... I can't think of a better way for us to have begun our coursework for [SLP] study."

Various suggestions for course improvement were provided at the same time. For example, one student recommended more timely feedback. Another stated that the large whole group discussions "take too long," suggesting increased use of smaller breakout groups as "a way more productive [space] ... [where] we could actually learn about each other and our schools." The same student remarked that "the asynchronous work was way too long" and recommended the instructor assign portions of recorded lectures or podcasts rather than the entire pieces. This student also indicated that "[s]ome colleagues really struggled with the length of readings." Other recommendations made in the survey were to re-consider the type of required deliverables and further differentiate topics for the assigned papers. (Our case study did not explore how these critiques may have impacted the cohort's sense of community.)

Community Building Survey (June 2023)

In June 2023 (just weeks before their completion of the SLP), the cohort was asked to voluntarily participate in a survey aimed to explore whether, in what ways, to what extent, and how quickly the students in the inaugural cohort felt part of an online community in the beginning stages of SLP. The survey also explored the role (if any) that the inaugural online instructor played in building this virtual community.

The results discussed below are promising because they demonstrate that an instructor can help facilitate a powerful sense of community for adult learners in an online professional degree program. Beyond that, the data suggests that with the right strategies in place, students may perceive the online environment as highly additive to their ability to build a sense of belonging—one which, in their estimation, may rival the community formed in person by students participating in a brick-and-mortar version of the same program.

Demographics of Survey Participants

The second survey had almost unanimous participation, with seventeen out of eighteen students in the cohort responding (a 94.4% participation rate). This level of participation contributes to the reliability of the results outlined below.

The respondents included individuals ranging in age from their twenties to fifties, with the bulk of the respondents in their twenties and forties (Figure 2). Respondents reside in several different locations around the United States (mostly in the South and/or on the East Coast), and one student resides internationally in China.

Figure 2. Ages of cohort community members surveyed

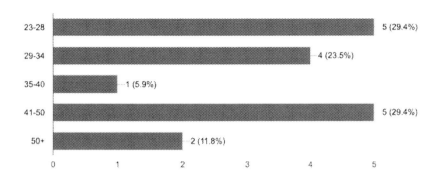

Attributes of the First Course Contributing to Students' Sense of Community

In the survey, students were asked to identify the top three attributes that contributed to their ability to build a sense of community within the cohort during the first online class. Students placed the highest value on the instructor's facilitation techniques (58.8%), the ability to bring their "true self" into the learning environment (58.8%), and the instructor's disposition (52.9%). Opportunities to engage in small group settings with cohort members and peer-to-peer collaboration were valued slightly lower, at 47.1% and 41.2%, respectively. Interestingly, students placed significantly less importance on onboarding activities/content (17.6%) and cognitive engagement (17.6%). Curricular content was rated the least influential, with only one student identifying it as one of the top three methods of community building (Figure 3). These findings suggest that the community-building strategies engaged in this case study may be generalizable to other contexts, regardless of curricular content.

Figure 3. Top three attributes contributing to sense of community
Note: Data collected from 17 of 18 cohort members in June 2023

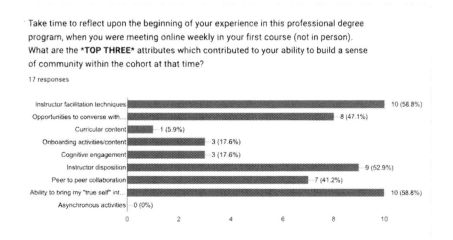

The survey provided students with the opportunity to expand upon why they selected these factors. Regarding the instructor's facilitation techniques, students called out the extended two-word check-ins, open reflections, personal anecdotes, small group discussions facilitated by the instructor, and the ability to "evaluate ourselves as people and leaders while building relationships with each other." The two-word check in was especially prominent in responses, with students highlighting the strengths of this instructional technique as a method of increasing their sense of belonging in the community as follows:

- "Allowing us time to 'check in' at the beginning of the class was instrumental in our connection. Whether it was super intentional or not, it created the opportunity for us to trust each other and get to know each other beyond the curriculum."
- "The extended check-ins were actually very powerful in allowing us to connect. I looked forward to hearing about what each of my classmates was up to at work or at home that particular week. It also led us into interesting discussions about what was happening at our schools during the springtime."
- "[The instructor] had us do a 'two word' check-in at the beginning of each class, which quickly turned into more than two words per person, but that time was perhaps the most meaningful."
- "Class check-ins were key early on. We probably took 30 minutes each of those early classes. We needed that time early on to create connections online. [The professor] created a totally safe space and so it felt easy to share and connect."
- "Particularly in the earliest classes, opening with a cohort check-in. Sometimes these were long but they helped us to learn about one another and build connections so that we would feel comfortable joining the discussions."

Students also valued the time they spent together in small breakout groups, along with the intentionality that the instructor engaged in "shuffling people through different groups … [so that they] knew a bit about everyone …" in the cohort.

Another strategy that students consistently identified as facilitating community was the opportunity "to help shape class with uninterrupted discussion." They described this approach as effective in helping them get to know one another and appreciate the unique personal and professional experiences of their cohort mates. In this regard, students emphasized the flexibility and nimbleness of the professor's approach to delivering instruction, stressing her willingness to "let [students] connect and drive the boat, while she pointed out key findings/recaps along the way." One student observed:

The content was interesting, and the course was facilitated in a way that took cues from the class. Discussions continued and shifted as needed—it felt as though the instructor was flexible and along on the journey with the class. There were clearly stated goals, but the methods for achieving them met the needs and developing personality of the group.

Along the same lines, another student remarked:

She invited and modeled deep conversations about content at hand with authenticity and honesty. Instructor had a plan but was quick to adapt to the needs of the group. She was respectful of everyone and yet confident to express herself fully. This made everyone comfortable doing the same.

Yet another learner pointed to how the instructor "provided fascinating reflections/content, but wasn't married to where the conversation would/should lead."

Students explained that this facilitation style allowed for "richer discussion and engagement" with course materials and one another and helped them to "grow and thrive" in the program. While the overwhelming majority of students spoke in general terms about how this approach affected community formation, one student was careful to qualify their perception of the broader impact of this facilitation style, commenting:

The instructor was very patient and willing to let discussions go in certain directions organically without being overly tied to the course lab for the evening. This worked well for leadership reflection topics but might not for other classes.

Thus, at best, these data validate an instructor's adoption of a facilitator or navigator identity in all online adult learning environments as a means of establishing a positive social and teaching presence in the community to accompany the cognitive work. At worst, the data demonstrate that this instructional style may be impactful only in certain settings. This uncertainty presents an opportunity for future research to clarify the context(s) most susceptible to the use of these instructional methods to build online community.

In terms of how the instructor's disposition operated in conjunction with instructional techniques to contribute to the sense of community in this cohort, a student explained:

I think there had to be a willingness from the group to be our most, or at least largely, authentic self. I went back and forth between the instructor's facilitation vs. instructor disposition, and while both contributed, the instructor's disposition invited us into the space of authenticity and cognitive inquiry and discussion.

Along similar lines, another shared, "Our professor played a gigantic role in our cohort community. Her flexibility, open mindset, and willingness to let discussion flow was the foundation of our community." These sentiments were echoed by others, who cited the instructor's candor and the way she provided non-judgmental space for vulnerability as being instrumental in enabling students to bring their true selves to the learning environment. This instructor's disposition also helped learners "engage openly and deeply in the topic and with one another" and "connect as humans, colleagues, and peers."

A student who seemed to capture all of these sentiments described the instructor as "[c]asual, open, with no pretense. She created a safe and trusting environment. There was no judgment ever." Other comments touched on how the instructor used acceptance, adaptability, openness, and respect for the students and their learning to facilitate community in the cohort:

- "I think our first instructor radiated an acceptance. She shared her own experiences and reflections which made it easier for us to share as well. It seemed like she was just as invested in the material as we were."
- "We were provided great space to explore our feelings and reflect on things. [The instructor] … always made us feel that the work we were doing was as important as she made us (personally) feel. It really set the stage for a culture of vulnerability and growth."

- "The nature of the course along with [the instructor] being so open about her own experiences as well really led to a sense of belonging to the wide group. It really felt like she was trying to coach us throughout the process and it was easy to then push others in the group as well."

How Quickly Students Experienced a Sense of Community

Students were asked to estimate how many synchronous sessions it took before they experienced a sense of community. Almost half of the students (47.1%) indicated that they felt a sense of community within five or six virtual sessions in the first online class. An equal percentage (47.1%) indicated that the community began to develop for them in four or fewer synchronous sessions, while one student (5.9% of the cohort) reported that it took between six and seven sessions. Notably, no students reported it taking more than seven synchronous sessions to build a sense of community during the first 14-week online course. This data indicates that all students in the cohort experienced a feeling of community no later than halfway through the first course in a 15-month program (Figure 4).

Figure 4. Number of sessions before students felt a sense of community
Note: Data collected from 17 of 18 cohort members in June 2023

In the early online class meetings of your professional degree program, how many synchronous sessions do you estimate occurred before you experienced a sense of community?

17 responses

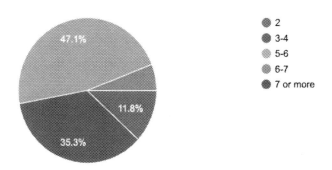

Perceived Importance of Experiencing a Sense of Community

Reflecting on their overall experience in SLP, over seventy percent (70.1%) of students categorized experiencing a sense of community as "extremely important" (a 10 out of 10) to the overall experience in their professional degree program. The remaining 30% rated community as a 7 or 8 out of 10.

The overall sense of community established in this cohort was categorized as "very strong" by 70.6% of students; as "strong" by 23.5%; and as "modest" by 5.9%. Notably, no students rated the sense of community as "weak." Students viewed the cohort model as instrumental in achieving these results, with one student remarking, "The cohort structure has been critical in my commitment to the program

Building an Adult Learning Community

and the learning environment that has been created." In the very same proportions (70.6%, 23.5%, and 5.9%), students indicated that on a scale of 1 to 5 (with 1 being "no impact" and 5 being a "very strong impact"), the impact that their sense of belonging had on their willingness to recommend the program to others was valued at 5, 4, or 3.

Interestingly, students reported that their status as online learners *helped* (rather than hindered) their ability to promote a sense of community in the SLP. More than half of students answered that the ability to form community was "significantly" (35.5%) or "modestly" aided by the virtual learning environment, while 11.8% indicated that community formation was not affected by their online learning status in either direction (positively or negatively). Only 23.5% of students indicated that being an online learner had a modest negative impact on their ability to form community (Figure 5).

Figure 5. Effect of online learning modality on ability to experience a sense of community
Note: Data collected from 17 of 18 cohort members in June 2023

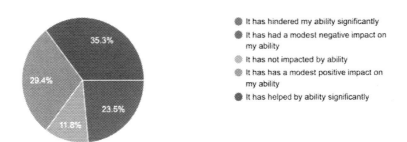

Expanding on this feedback, one student commented,

Community is EVERYTHING with the [SLP]. From the detailed application/selection process, to the first class ... it has blown me away. I would be the biggest cheerleader for this model because it has everything [ ] practitioners need. Community, connection, flexibility, reasonability, and high standards. How lucky I have been to have found a cohort and program like this one... it is truly life changing. Not many people get to feel that from their graduate program.

Other students expressed a certain level of surprise at how this level of community was established in a virtual environment, with one commenting, "I do not think about it that much anymore, but when I do, it surprises me how much we do (and how well-connected we are) even though most of our interactions are online." Another student reported feeling "more connected than I thought I'd be in a primarily online program," attributing this result to "intentional planning and execution by program leadership and excellent professors who helped pay extra attention on community building in those early months."

Although there was an overwhelming sense of community experienced by all members of the inaugural online cohort, some difficulties in building community online were still experienced. One student observed that "[c]reating a sense of vulnerability with people you've never met in person is a challenge," and claimed that all students felt "ready to be together in person" at some point during the first course. Another student noted that even though the consistent nature of the classes "made a big difference in building momentum for meaningful comments," some of the connections formed in the initial class "did not continue to grow" over time. Expanding further on why some connections may have faded after the first course, a student explained:

I think early on our first class allowed us to really bond and get to know each other. Overtime [sic], group dynamics have shifted...classes during the school year prioritize content (and to a lesser extent skills) leaving very little time to just talk. We don't do check-ins in any of our [other] classes. Some of our cohort does this separately, but with two courses a week and other commitments it has been hard to carve out time to talk. We generally only speak to each other when we have a problem of practice. I think it would be useful to find ways to integrate community and safe spaces into all of our classes. I think an easy way to do this is to allow us to reflect on our own practices more frequently in all classes.

On balance, however, the positives revealed in this survey certainly outweighed any negatives. In fact, 94.1% of students reported that they perceived their (online) cohort's sense of community as equal to or greater than that of the past residential (in-person) cohorts in the same professional degree program (Figure 6).

Figure 6. Perceptions of sense of community relative to past residential cohorts
Note: Data collected from 17 of 18 cohort members in June 2023

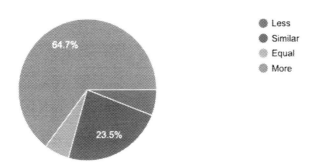

EVIDENCE-BASED RECOMMENDATIONS TO CULTIVATE ADULT LEARNING COMMUNITIES

When considering relevant applications of theory to practice, the following recommendations for the facilitation of effective online learning experiences for adult learners are suggested based on the findings of this case study. Although this case study examines data from only one specific online adult learning community, these general recommendations are also supported by the earlier synthesis of the literature pertaining to adult learners, high-quality online instruction, and drivers of a sense of community in learning environments.

Utilize a Dependable, User-Friendly LMS

The research has connected the use of an intuitive, user-friendly, consistently formatted LMS with a variety of positive outcomes, including a reduction of the cognitive load for online learners and an enhancement of the overall learning experience (Sweller et al., 2011). Because of how integral technology is to a successful online experience, we recommend leveraging the expertise of instructional designers to build a dependable learning management system (LMS) capable of offering easy access to educational materials and delivering opportunities for learner interaction and collaboration (Dabbagh & Kitsantas, 2012). By integrating multimedia and interactive elements in online instruction, the potential to enhance comprehension and retention of information among adult learners is also optimized (Mayer, 2014). The effective use of an LMS can provide a cognitive and teaching presence in a community of inquiry by facilitating students' engagement with course content and improving their overall learning experience.

Start with the End in Mind During the Curricular and Instructional Planning Stages

As with face-to-face instruction, it is imperative to begin with the end in mind by developing learning goals first (Froyd, 2008). This key strategy for effective online teaching presence within a community of inquiry framework encourages instructors to include a presentation of clear guidelines for the objective(s) of each class gathering at the onset. Instructors are encouraged to balance this structure with flexibility to allow discourse to unfold in accordance with the learners' expressions of engagement (Palloff & Pratt, 2013). Start by asking, "What are the key concepts and/or skills participants need to better understand by the end of this synchronous session?" The answer to this question will help the instructor select the appropriate technology and develop synchronous content and activities aligned with the learning goals of the lesson and the needs of adult learners engaging with the content (Caulfield, 2011).

Amplify Metacognitive Awareness

Since learners in an online setting have more autonomy and responsibility for carrying out the learning process, it is critical for instructors to proactively apply strategies that encourage student reflection on their learning. As the scholarship demonstrates, metacognition may be promoted in an online learning environment by incorporating instructional tools such as facilitated reflective practice, small group discussions, and the use of the multiple technical features of the virtual classroom (including digital polls, mind maps, and collaborative shared documents) (Berry, 2019; Khudhair et al., 2023). Data from this case study confirms that these tools serve as key learning methods for promoting awareness of one's personal learning process, which, in turn, drives up both individual and collective engagement in the learning community.

Create a Positive Learning Climate

The learning climate refers to the characteristics of a particular learning space that facilitate interpersonal interactions among the participants and help to build a supportive online community. Climate setting includes the expression and enactment of shared norms, goals, and values, which were effectively utilized in this case study to contribute to the social and teaching presences of this community of inquiry. Setting a positive learning climate requires attention to be paid to the specific context and ways the learning experiences are organized, facilitated, and developed to support desired student outcomes (such as academic achievement, a sense of belonging, and student well-being). Climate considerations must also integrate a respect for student identities and cultural backgrounds through instructional practices that acknowledge "that various groups have different experiences in relation to social power and privilege" (Jones & Wijeyesinghe, 2011, p.15). Climate-building also encompasses the need to embed opportunities for informal engagement among faculty and students in a virtual environment to take the place of the face-to-face meetings and impromptu gatherings that an in-person program can accommodate. This case study demonstrates that it is possible to develop caring and meaningful connections virtually when intentional steps are taken to contribute to a positive learning culture.

Promote Learner Empowerment

The research suggests that when facilitated effectively, online adult education can not only match—but even surpass—traditional face-to-face learning (Means et al., 2010). In an online adult learning community, consistently framing the modality of online learning as additive (rather than a "less than" version of in-person instruction) is key to cultivating a positive learning community in which adult learners feel empowered by the unique affordances of virtual learning (Ramos-Morcillo et al., 2020; Watson, 2008). Pairing this sensibility with high competence in the use of the technical features of an online classroom is essential to facilitating learner empowerment and autonomy, which lie at the intersection of social, cognitive, and teaching presence within a community of inquiry model (Ramos-Morcillo et al., 2020; Reeve, 2016).

Provide Opportunities for Reflective Practice

Structured time for engagement with pre- and post-reflection prompts in synchronous adult learning environments has been proven to contribute to a sense of community—promoting a climate in which participants are invited to directly engage with course material and facilitating the transition from the "real world" into the virtual learning setting (Hokanson et al., 2019). For adult learners (who are more likely to be transitioning into the learning space from professional and/or family environments), opening opportunities for quiet text-based reflection in online synchronous settings has been shown to facilitate smooth transitions, while promoting thinking about complex issues and contributing to deep, meaningful learning (Garrison et al., 2001). Adult learners who engaged in reflective practice during online learning experiences also reported an increased sense of trust, collaboration, and shared ownership over the learning process, which enhances both social and cognitive presences (Gunawardena & Zittle, 1997; Wei & Chen, 2012).

Facilitate Community Touchpoints

A sense of community has academic and social benefits for students in both online and in-person programs (Lai, 2015; Lovitts, 2001; Rovai, 2004). Rovai (2007) found that when online instructors created conditions where students could express themselves openly and present alternative viewpoints, students were more likely to feel a sense of community. In the facilitation of online instruction, strategies include limiting lecture time and dedicating class time to sharing personal and professional updates through the use of an interpersonal warm-up prompt, a chat waterfall, or an invitation to describe how they are feeling at the onset of each class (Berry, 2019; Brackett, 2020). Online instructors who invite social presence with adult learners in these ways have also reported an increase in emotional expression and socio-emotional support across the learning community. Humor and self-disclosure are common forms of emotional expression facilitated by community touchpoints, both of which are proven to contribute to group cohesion, task motivation, and learning outcomes for adult learners (Brookfield, 1987; Garrison, 2009). This study confirms that the strategic use of these touchpoints to increase social presence contributes favorably to students' ability to build community in an online environment.

Engage the Use of Multiple Technical Features for Collaboration

As previously mentioned, instructors who utilize many of the features afforded by the virtual classroom promote metacognition and community building (Berry, 2019). Common effective tools for adult learners include the utilization of the chat space, breakout rooms, digital mind maps, and collaborative documents and/or digital walls (Abutiheen et al., 2022). To facilitate robust, interactive synchronous discussions, instructors are encouraged to break students into groups of varying sizes, provide students with occasional opportunities to self-select their groups, and equip students with a digital repository (such as a collaborative document) for the sharing of ideas, emergent questions, and resources both during and after the synchronous class (Lin & Gao, 2020). A facility with the use of technical features is essential to establishing and maintaining an effective online teaching presence. Instructors are encouraged to seek support to advance their mastery of technical skills in order to optimize the educational experience for learners (Abutiheen et al., 2022; Ramos-Morcillo et al., 2020).

Solicit Feedback to Inform Continuous Improvement

Soliciting feedback from students is a useful technique to give instructors and students information on how the course is going and what might be done to enhance the learning environment (Lewis, 2002). To improve teaching and learning, instructors are encouraged to seek feedback across course elements, and evaluation processes should be ongoing, descriptive, diagnostic, and broad-based (Fuhrmann & Grasha, 1983). Wlodkowski and Ginsberg (2017) and Lyn and Broderick (2023) specifically examined the impact of iterative course feedback on adult online learners and found that the opportunity to offer feedback on instruction has a direct impact on adults' motivation to learn. This case study confirms these findings and emphasizes the importance of this type of communication for both learners and instructors.

CONCLUSION

As the domain of online professional degree programs for adult learners continues to expand, institutions have a responsibility to integrate evidence-based practices into their programmatic design and execution. The benefits of doing so are not only experienced by program participants, but also in the aggregate through key institutional indicators such as program referrals, enrollment growth, and revenue generation. This case study reveals the outsized impact that effective instructional techniques have on cultivating a sense of community within a cohort-based, online professional degree program in the brief space of 4-6 weekly synchronous sessions, as well as the residual impacts of that impact over the span of the degree experience. In addition, the orbiting variables of a high-quality, low-friction LMS interface and the animation of andragogically-minded instructional techniques are noted as key contributors to an overall experience of community for adult learners.

The implications for this case study are clear: institutions should invest in providing instructors with guidance and training on how to most effectively facilitate instruction for online learners and should also invest in skilled instructional designers to enable the implementation of high-quality digital platforms for online adult learners. The case study also illuminates the unique needs of the adult online learner: a busy professional with an appetite for learning experiences that are practically oriented, tethered to a greater sense of personal and professional purpose, and opportunistic in relationship building and reflection.

Implications for future study include the evaluation of the pace of establishing future cohorts' sense of community as instructional practices are refined and iterated; the role of brief, intermittent in-person gatherings on the overall sense of community for a mostly-online professional degree cohort; the durability of a sense of community for online learners following degree conferral; and the ways in which innovations related to artificial intelligence may contribute to future prospects for building community within these kinds of learning settings.

REFERENCES

Abutiheen, Z. A., Abdulmunem, A. A., & Harjan, Z. A. (2022). Assessment Online Platforms During COVID-19 Pandemic. In Advances in Intelligent Computing and Communication *Proceedings of ICAC, 2021,* 519–527.

Allen, I. E., & Seaman, J. (2017). *Digital Compass Learning: Distance Education Enrollment Report 2017.* Babson Survey Research Group.

Analytics, B. (2021). *Digital Learning Pulse Survey: Pandemic-Era Report Card Students, Faculty and Administrators Reflect Upon the Academic Year.* https://cengage.widen.net/view/pdf/ilw9jvg8hs/pandemic-era-report-card-digital-learning-pulse-survey-infographic-1649584.pdf?t.download=true&u=lpaabn

Ashar, H., & Skenes, R. (1993). Can Tinto's student departure model be applied to nontraditional students? *Adult Education Quarterly, 43*(2), 90–100. doi:10.1177/0741713693043002003

Ashforth, B. E., & Mael, F. (2004). Social identity theory and the organization. *Organizational identity. REAd (Porto Alegre),* 134–160.

Aslanian, C., & Fischer, S. (2021). *Online College Students 2021 Meeting Online Student Demands and Preferences in a Reshaped World.* EducationDynamics.

Bada, S. O., & Olusegun, S. (2015). Constructivism learning theory: A paradigm for teaching and learning. *Journal of Research & Method in Education, 5*(6), 66–70.

Barber, W., King, S., & Buchanan, S. (2015). Problem Based Learning and Authentic Assessment in Digital Pedagogy: Embracing the Role of Collaborative Communities. *Electronic Journal of e-Learning, 13*(2), 59–64.

Barnett, B. G., Basom, M. R., Yerkes, D. M., & Norris, C. J. (2000). Cohorts in educational leadership programs: Benefits, difficulties, and the potential for developing school leaders. *Educational Administration Quarterly, 36*(2), 255–282. doi:10.1177/0013161X00362005

Barnett, B. G., & Muse, I. D. (1993). Cohort groups in educational administration: Promises and challenges. *Journal of School Leadership, 3*(4), 400–415. doi:10.1177/105268469300300405

Bates, A. T., & Sangra, A. (2011). *Managing technology in higher education: Strategies for transforming teaching and learning.* John Wiley & Sons.

Bean, J., & Eaton, S. (2000). A psychological model of college student retention. In J. Braxton (Ed.), *Rethinking the departure puzzle: New theory and research Tinto 265 on college student retention* (pp. 48–62). Vanderbilt University Press.

Berry, S. (2019). Teaching to connect: Community-building strategies for the virtual classroom. *Online Learning : the Official Journal of the Online Learning Consortium, 23*(1), 164–183. doi:10.24059/olj.v23i1.1425

Bonk, C. J., & Khoo, E. (2014). Adding some TEC-VARIETY: 100+ activities for motivating and retaining learners online. OpenWorldBooks. com and Amazon CreateSpace.

Borup, J., Graham, C. R., West, R. E., Archambault, L., & Spring, K. J. (2020). Academic communities of engagement: An expansive lens for examining support structures in blended and online learning. *Educational Technology Research and Development, 68*(2), 807–832. doi:10.100711423-020-09744-x

Bouchrika, I. (2023, May 22). *50 online education statistics: 2023 data on Higher Learning & Corporate training.* https://research.com/education/online-education-statistics#:~:text=Moreover%2C%20findings%20from%20a%20survey,female%20(Duffin%2C%202019)

Brackett, M. (2019). *Permission to feel: Unlocking the power of emotions to help our kids, ourselves, and our society thrive.* Celadon Books.

Bransford, J. D., Brown, A. L., & Cocking, R. R. (2000). *How people learn* (Vol. 11). National academy press.

Bratlien, M. J., Genzer, S. M., Hoyle, J. R., & Oates, A. D. (1992). The professional studies doctorate: Leaders for learning. *Journal of School Leadership, 2*(1), 75–89. doi:10.1177/105268469200200107

Brookfield, S. D. (1987). *Developing Critical Thinkers.* Jossey-Bass.

Caffarella, R. S., & Merriam, S. B. (1999). *Perspectives on adult learning: Framing our research.* Academic Press.

Caulfield, J. (2011). *How to Design and Teach a Hybrid Course. Sterling.* Stylus Publishing.

Cercone, K. (2008). Characteristics of adult learners with implications for online learning design. AACE review (formerly. *AACE Journal, 16*(2), 137–159.

Conrad, D. (2005). Building and maintaining community in cohort-based online learning. *Journal of Distance Education, 20*(1), 1–20.

Dabbagh, N., & Kitsantas, A. (2012). Personal Learning Environments, social media, and self-regulated learning: A natural formula for connecting formal and informal learning. *The Internet and Higher Education, 15*(1), 3–8. doi:10.1016/j.iheduc.2011.06.002

Diep, N. A., Cocquyt, C., Zhu, C., & Vanwing, T. (2017). Online Interaction Quality among Adult Learners: The Role of Sense of Belonging and Perceived Learning Benefits. *Turkish Online Journal of Educational Technology-TOJET, 16*(2), 71–78.

Drezner, N. D., & Pizmony-Levy, O. (2021). I Belong, Therefore, I Give? The Impact of Sense of Belonging on Graduate Student Alumni Engagement. *Nonprofit and Voluntary Sector Quarterly*, *50*(4), 753–777. doi:10.1177/0899764020977687

Froyd, J. (2008, June). *White paper on promising practices in undergraduate STEM education*. Academic Press.

Fuhrmann, B. S., & Grasha, A. F. (1983). *A practical handbook for college teachers*. Little Brown.

Garrison, D. R. (2009). Communities of inquiry in online learning. In *Encyclopedia of distance learning* (2nd ed., pp. 352–355). IGI Global. doi:10.4018/978-1-60566-198-8.ch052

Garrison, D. R., Anderson, T., & Archer, W. (2001). Critical thinking, cognitive presence, and computer conferencing in distance education. *American Journal of Distance Education*, *15*(1), 7–23. doi:10.1080/08923640109527071

Garrison, R., Anderson, T., & Archer, W. (2021). *The Community of Inquiry model. The Community of Inquiry.* Athabasca University, Mount Royal University, KTH Royal Institute of Technology, Canadian Journal of Learning and Technology. Retrieved June 26, 2023, from https://creativecommons.org/licenses/by-sa/4.0/

Gunawardena, C. N., & Zittle, F. J. (1997). Social presence as a predictor of satisfaction within a computer-mediated conferencing environment. *American Journal of Distance Education*, *11*(3), 8–26. doi:10.1080/08923649709526970

Hewitt, J. (2003). How habitual online practices affect the development of asynchronous discussion threads. *Journal of Educational Computing Research*, *28*(1), 31–45. doi:10.2190/PMG8-A05J-CUH1-DK14

Hill, M. S. (1995). Educational leadership cohort models: Changing the talk to change the walk. *Planning and Changing*, *26*(3/4), 179–189.

Hokanson, S. C., Grannan, S., Greenler, R., Gillian-Daniel, D. L., Campa, H. III, & Goldberg, B. B. (2019). A study of synchronous, online professional development workshops for graduate students and postdocs reveals the value of reflection and community building. *Innovative Higher Education*, *44*(5), 385–398. doi:10.100710755-019-9470-6

Horn, R. A. (2000). Providing leadership for the new millennium. *Journal of the Intermountain Center for Education Effectiveness*, *1*(1), 1–6.

Horn, R. A. Jr. (2001). Promoting social justice and caring in schools and communities: The unrealized potential of the cohort model. *Journal of School Leadership*, *11*(4), 313–334. doi:10.1177/105268460101100404

Jaggars, S. S., & Xu, D. (2016). How do online course design features influence student performance? *Computers & Education*, *95*, 270–284. doi:10.1016/j.compedu.2016.01.014

Jiang, M., & Koo, K. (2020). Emotional presence in building an online learning community among nontraditional graduate students. *Online Learning : the Official Journal of the Online Learning Consortium*, *24*(4), 93–111. doi:10.24059/olj.v24i4.2307

Johnson, E., Morwane, R., Dada, S., Pretorius, G., & Lotriet, M. (2018). Adult Learners' Perspectives on Their Engagement in a Hybrid Learning Postgraduate Programme. *The Journal of Continuing Higher Education, 66*(2), 88–105. doi:10.1080/07377363.2018.1469071

Joksimovic, S., Gaševic, D., Kovanovic, V., Riecke, B. E., & Hatala, M. (2015). Social presence in online discussions as a process predictor of academic performance. *Journal of Computer Assisted Learning, 31*(6), 638–654. doi:10.1111/jcal.12107

Jones, S. R., & Wijeyesinghe, C. L. (2011). The promises and challenges of teaching from an intersectional perspective: Core components and applied strategies. *New Directions for Teaching and Learning, 2011*(125), 11–20. doi:10.1002/tl.429

Joyner, D. A., & Isbell, C. (2019, June). Master's at scale: Five years in a scalable online graduate degree. In *Proceedings of the Sixth ACM Conference on Learning@ Scale* (pp. 1-10). Academic Press.

Junco, R., & Mastrodicasa, J. (2007). *Connecting to the Net.Generation: What higher education professionals need to know about today's students* (1st ed.). National Association of Student Personnel Administrators.

Kara, M., Erdogdu, F., Kokoc, M., & Cagiltay, K. (2019). Challenges faced by adult learners in online distance education: A literature review. *Open Praxis, 11*(1), 5–22. https://search.informit.org/doi/10.3316/informit.234110355704611

Kauffman, H. (2015). A review of predictive factors of student success in and satisfaction with online learning. *Research in Learning Technology, 23*, 23. doi:10.3402/rlt.v23.26507

Kelly, K., & Zakrajsek, T. D. (2023). *Advancing online teaching: Creating equity-based digital learning environments*. Taylor & Francis.

Khudhair, A., Khudhair, M., Jaber, M., Awreed, Y., Ali, M., AL-Hameed, M., Jassim, M., Malik, R., Alkhayyat, A., & Hameed, A. (2023). Impact on Higher Education and College Students in Dijlah University after COVID through E-learning. *Computer-Aided Design and Applications*, 104–115. doi:10.14733/cadaps.2023.S12.104-115

Knowles, M. S. (1984). *Andragogy in action*. Academic Press.

Kolb, D. (1984). *Experiential Learning: Experience as the Source of Learning and Development*. Prentice Hall.

Lai, K. W. (2015). Knowledge construction in online learning communities: A case study of a doctoral course. *Studies in Higher Education, 40*(4), 561–579. doi:10.1080/03075079.2013.831402

LaPointe, L., & Reisetter, M. (2008). Belonging online: Students' perceptions of the value and efficacy of an online learning community. *International Journal on E-Learning, 7*(4), 641–665.

Leithwood, K., Jantzi, D., & Coffin, G. (1995). *Preparing school leaders: What works*. Ontario Institute for Studies in Education.

Lewis, K. G. (2001). Using midsemester student feedback and responding to it. *New Directions for Teaching and Learning, 2001*(87), 33–44. doi:10.1002/tl.26

Li, X., & Pei, Z. (2023). Improving effectiveness of online learning for higher education students during the COVID-19 pandemic. *Frontiers in Psychology*, *13*, 1111028. doi:10.3389/fpsyg.2022.1111028 PMID:36726501

Lim, H. L. (2007). Community of inquiry in an online undergraduate information technology course. *Journal of Information Technology Education*, *6*(1), 153–168. doi:10.28945/207

Lin, X., & Gao, L. (2020). Students' sense of community and perspectives of taking synchronous and asynchronous online courses. *Asian Journal of Distance Education*, *15*(1), 169–179.

Liu, X., Bonk, C. J., Magjuka, R. J., Lee, S. H., & Su, B. (2005). Exploring four dimensions of online instructor roles: A program level case study. *Journal of Asynchronous Learning Networks*, *9*(4), 29–48.

Loeng, S. (2020). Self-directed learning: A core concept in adult education. *Education Research International*, *2020*, 1–12. doi:10.1155/2020/3816132

Lovitts, B. E. (2001). *Leaving the Ivory Tower: The causes and consequences of departure from doctoral study*. Rowman & Littlefield.

Lyn, A. E., Broderick, M., & Spranger, E. (2023). Student well-being and empowerment: SEL in online graduate education. In *Exploring Social Emotional Learning in Diverse Academic Settings* (pp. 312–336). IGI Global. doi:10.4018/978-1-6684-7227-9.ch016

Mael, F., & Ashforth, B. E. (1992). Alumni and their alma mater: A partial test of the reformulated model of organizational identification. *Journal of Organizational Behavior*, *13*(2), 103–123. doi:10.1002/job.4030130202

Maulana, A. E., Patterson, P. G., Satria, A., & Pradipta, I. A. (2023). Alumni connectedness and its role in intention to contribute to higher education institutions. *Journal of Marketing for Higher Education*, 1–22. doi:10.1080/08841241.2023.2186560

Maunder, R. E. (2018). Students' peer relationships and their contribution to university adjustment: The need to belong in the university community. *Journal of Further and Higher Education*, *42*(6), 756–768. doi:10.1080/0309877X.2017.1311996

Mayer, R. E. (2014). Incorporating motivation into multimedia learning. *Learning and Instruction*, *29*, 171–173. doi:10.1016/j.learninstruc.2013.04.003

McFarland, J., Hussar, B., De Brey, C., Snyder, T., Wang, X., Wilkinson-Flicker, S., ... & Hinz, S. (2017). *The Condition of Education 2017*. NCES 2017-144. National Center for Education Statistics.

McInnerney, J. M., & Roberts, T. S. (2004). Online learning: Social interaction and the creation of a sense of community. *Journal of Educational Technology & Society*, *7*(3), 73–81.

McMillan, D. W., & Chavis, D. M. (1986). Sense of Community: A definition and theory. *Journal of Community Psychology*, *14*(1), 6–23. doi:10.1002/1520-6629(198601)14:1<6::AID-JCOP2290140103>3.0.CO;2-I

McPhail, C. J. (2000). *Transforming Community College Leadership Preparation: A Cohort Leadership Learning Model*. Academic Press.

Means, Toyama, Murphy, Bakia, & Jones. (2010). Department of Education, Office of Planning, Evaluation, and Policy Development. *Evaluation of evidence-based practices in online learning.*

Merriam, S. B., & Caffarella, R. S. (1999). *Learning in Adulthood* (2nd ed.). Jossey-Bass.

Mezirow, J. (1997). Transformative learning. *New Directions for Adult and Continuing Education, 74*(74), 5–12. doi:10.1002/ace.7401

Organisation for Economic Co-operation and Development. (2020). *The potential of online learning for adults: Early lessons from the COVID-19 crisis.* OECD Publishing.

Palloff, R. M., & Pratt, K. (2007). *Building online learning communities: Effective strategies for the virtual classroom.* John Wiley & Sons.

Palloff, R. M., & Pratt, K. (2013). *Lessons from the virtual classroom: The realities of online teaching.* John Wiley & Sons.

Pemberton, C. L. A., & Akkary, R. K. (2010). A cohort, is a cohort, is a cohort… or is it? *Journal of Research on Leadership Education, 5*(5), 179–208. doi:10.1177/194277511000500501

Price, E., Lau, A. C., Goldberg, F., Turpen, C., Smith, P. S., Dancy, M., & Robinson, S. (2021). Analyzing a faculty online learning community as a mechanism for supporting faculty implementation of a guided-inquiry curriculum. *International Journal of STEM Education, 8*(1), 1–26. doi:10.118640594-020-00268-7 PMID:33643775

Ramos-Morcillo, A. J., Leal-Costa, C., Moral-García, J. E., & Ruzafa-Martínez, M. (2020). Experiences of nursing students during the abrupt change from face-to-face to e-learning education during the first month of confinement due to COVID-19 in Spain. *International Journal of Environmental Research and Public Health, 17*(15), 5519. doi:10.3390/ijerph17155519 PMID:32751660

Reeve, J. (2016). Autonomy-supportive teaching: What is is, how to do it. In *Building autonomous learners: Perspectives from research and practice using self-determination theory* (pp. 129–152). Springer Singapore. doi:10.1007/978-981-287-630-0_7

Rovai, A. (2002). Building Sense of Community at a Distance. *International Review of Research in Open and Distance Learning, 3*(1), 1–16. doi:10.19173/irrodl.v3i1.79

Rovai, A. (2007). Facilitating online discussions effectively. *The Internet and Higher Education, 1*(1), 77–88. doi:10.1016/j.iheduc.2006.10.001

Rovai, A., & Jordan, H. (2004). Blended Learning and Sense of Community: A comparative analysis with traditional and fully online graduate courses. *International Review of Research in Open and Distance Learning, 5*(2), 1–13. doi:10.19173/irrodl.v5i2.192

Rovai, A. P. (2002). Development of an instrument to measure classroom community. *The Internet and Higher Education, 5*(3), 197–211. doi:10.1016/S1096-7516(02)00102-1

Rovai, A. P., & Downey, J. R. (2010). Why some distance education programs fail while others succeed in a global environment. *The Internet and Higher Education, 13*(3), 141–147. doi:10.1016/j.iheduc.2009.07.001

Ruey, S. (2010). A case study of constructivist instructional strategies for adult online learning. *British Journal of Educational Technology, 41*(5), 706720. doi:10.1111/j.1467-8535.2009.00965.x

Sadera, W. A., Robertson, J., Song, L., & Midon, M. N. (2009). The role of community in online learning success. *Journal of Online Learning and Teaching, 5*(2), 277–284.

Seaman, J. E., Allen, I. E., & Seaman, J. (2018). *Grade increase: Tracking distance education in the United States*. Babson Survey Research Group.

Shea, P., Li, C. S., Swan, K., & Pickett, A. (2005). Developing learning community in online asynchronous college courses: The role of teaching presence. *Journal of Asynchronous Learning Networks, 9*(4), 59–82.

Stebleton, M., Soria, K., Huesman, R. Jr, & Torres, V. (2014). Recent immigrant students at research universities: The relationship between campus climate and sense of belonging. *Journal of College Student Development, 55*(2), 196–202. doi:10.1353/csd.2014.0019

Strayhorn, T. (2008). Fittin' in: Do diverse interactions with peers affect sense of belonging for black men at predominantly white institutions? *Journal of Student Affairs Research and Practice, 45*(4), 953–979.

Strayhorn, T. (2012). *College students' sense of belonging*. Routledge. doi:10.4324/9780203118924

Swan, K. (2002). Building learning communities in online courses: The importance of interaction. *Education Communication and Information, 2*(1), 23–49. doi:10.1080/1463631022000005016

Sweller, J., Ayres, P., & Kalyuga, S. (2011). *Cognitive load theory*. Springer. doi:10.1007/978-1-4419-8126-4

Tajfel, H. (1974). Social identity and intergroup behaviour. *Social Sciences Information. Information Sur les Sciences Sociales, 13*(2), 65–93. doi:10.1177/053901847401300204

Tajfel, H., & Turner, J. C. (2004). The social identity theory of intergroup behavior. In *Political psychology* (pp. 276–293). Psychology Press. doi:10.4324/9780203505984-16

Tam, M. (2000). Constructivism, Instructional Design, and Technology: Implications for Transforming Distance Learning. *Journal of Educational Technology & Society, 3*(2).

Teitel, L. (1997). Understanding and harnessing the power of the cohort model in preparing educational leaders. *Peabody Journal of Education, 72*(2), 66–85. doi:10.120715327930pje7202_4

Thompson, J. J., & Porto, S. C. (2014). Supporting wellness in adult online education. *Open Praxis, 6*(1), 17–28. doi:10.5944/openpraxis.6.1.100

Tinto, V. (1987). *Leaving college: Rethinking the causes and cures of student attrition*. The University of Chicago Press.

Tinto, V. (1993). Building community. *Liberal Education, 79*(4), 16–21.

Tinto, V. (2017). Through the eyes of students. *Journal of College Student Retention, 19*(3), 254–269. doi:10.1177/1521025115621917

Watson, J. (2008). *Blended Learning: The Convergence of online and face-to-face education. Promising practices in online learning*. North American Council for Online Learning.

Wei, C. W., Chen, N. S., & Kinshuk. (2012). A model for social presence in online classrooms. *Educational Technology Research and Development, 60*(3), 529–545. doi:10.100711423-012-9234-9

Wlodkowski, R. J., & Ginsberg, M. B. (2017). *Enhancing adult motivation to learn: A comprehensive guide for teaching all adults.* John Wiley & Sons.

Wood, J. (2022, January 27). *These 3 charts show the global growth in online learning.* World Economic Forum. https://www.weforum.org/agenda/2022/01/online-learning-courses-reskill-skills-gap

Woods, R., & Ebersole, S. (2003). Using non-subject-matter discussion boards to build connectedness in online learning. *American Journal of Distance Education, 17*(2), 99–118. doi:10.1207/S15389286AJDE1702_3

Yamauchi, L. A., Taira, K., & Trevorrow, T. (2016). Effective instruction for engaging culturally diverse students in higher education. *International Journal on Teaching and Learning in Higher Education, 28*(3), 460–470.

Zigelman, I. (2018). Constructivism and the Community of Inquiry. *Technology and the Curriculum: Summer 2018.*

Chapter 3
Building Relationship Through Discussion:
Innovative Ideas to Connect and Empower

Crystal Ann Brashear
https://orcid.org/0000-0003-0577-1114
Colorado Christian University, USA

ABSTRACT

Distance education programs have proliferated, sometimes growing faster than instructors can innovate. A problem plaguing educators for decades is how to translate the synergism flowing naturally through in-seat discussion into an online environment. This chapter begins with an overview of the various purposes for class discussion and an exploration of best practices for facilitating transformative conversation. It examines the benefits and challenges of synchronous and asynchronous online discussion, offering practical, creative solutions for each approach. The ultimate goals are fostering generative conversation and genuine connection. Strategies to accomplish this include setting clear expectation, adopting a consistent, probing co-participant stance, and teaching students self-facilitation. Out-of-the-box ideas include social annotation and simulation activities.

Online higher education programs offer many benefits. They can be more accessible from fiscal, geographical, and temporal standpoints (Barrio Minton et al., 2018; Benshoff & Gibbons, 2011). For the instructor, online programs provide the opportunity to innovate, to generate creative solutions for forming genuine connection with students (Benshoff & Gibbons, 2011).

PURPOSES OF CLASS DISCUSSION

Class discussion is one component of the online educational experience. Meaningful discussion draws on the unique social, cultural, and environmental perspectives of each student and the instructor, exposing participants to new ways of thinking and fostering a whole that is larger than the sum of its parts. This

DOI: 10.4018/978-1-6684-8908-6.ch003

richer perspective can then transfer into other learning contexts, empowering more advanced critical thinking and problem solving (Murphy et al., 2009). With class discussion, learners process, analyze, synthesize, and reflect aloud, which can help reveal both what students know and (perhaps more importantly) what they don't yet know (Boettcher, 2018). Class discussion can take different stances, depending on the goal the professor hopes to help students accomplish. A *critical analytic* stance (e.g., Collaborative Reasoning and Paideia Seminar) prompts students to bring a critical eye toward a particular text or collection of texts (Murphy et al., 2009). An *efferent* stance (e.g., Shared Inquiry, Instructional Conversations, and Questioning the Author) prioritizes knowledge acquisition and retrieval, reinforcing a specific set of ideas or skills that must be mastered (Murphy et al., 2009). An *expressive* stance (e.g., Grand Conversations, Book Club, and Literature Circles) explores student's emotional response and connection to a text or collection of texts (Murphy et al., 2009).

One major purpose of class discussion is to enhance critical literacy, which involves higher order thinking reflection on course content. The goal is for students to achieve a higher level of textual comprehension, moving deeper than surface understanding (Murphy et al., 2009). Does classroom discussion help to meet these goals effectively? A meta-analysis focused on class discussion was conducted by Murphy et al. (2009). Quantitative synthesis of 42 studies found that a variety of discussion stances were highly effective in enhancing students' inferential and literal comprehension, especially *efferent* ones. However, only a few stances were effective at enhancing students' reasoning, critical thinking, and textual argumentation abilities. Additionally, most discussion stances effectively increased student talk time while decreasing instructor talk time. Unfortunately, increases in student talk did not seem to cause improvement in student comprehension. It is important to note that this meta-analysis synthesized studies on school-aged children, not higher education learners. However, this poses an important question: Is online classroom discussion in higher ed spaces working to accomplish the goals it purports to accomplish?

Another major purpose of class discussion is to transform the learner. Eschenbacher (2020) differentiates between discussion that informs and trains, versus conversation that transforms. The former assumes a deficit within the learner, while the latter expects the student to take an active role by leveraging personal experience and challenging previously accepted paradigms (Eschenbacher, 2020). Transformative conversations are best conducted within an environment of mutual respect and appreciation for others' unique ways of seeing things (Eschenbacher, 2020). These discussions open up choice for participants, who are invited to consider how they might want to live their lives (Eschenbacher, 2020). Discussants engage in *non-teleological* dialogue requiring them to risk critical self-reflection. This type of discussion, though challenging, offers potential for profound personal change. Authors Shohet and Shohet (2020, p. 18) kick off their book on transformative conversations in supervision by sharing the following story, from Anderson (2023):

Once upon a time, a very strong woodcutter asked for a job with a timber merchant. The pay was really good and so were the working conditions. For those reasons, the woodcutter was determined to do his best. His boss gave him an axe and showed him where he would work. The first day, the woodcutter felled 18 trees. 'Congratulations,' the boss said. 'Go on that way!' Motivated by the boss's words, the woodcutter tried harder the next day, but he could only bring down 15 trees. The third day he tried even harder, but he could only manage 10 trees. Day after day, he finished with fewer trees. 'I must be losing my strength,' the woodcutter thought. He went to the boss and apologised, saying that he could not understand what was going on. 'When was the last time you sharpened your axe?' the boss asked. 'Sharpen?' said the woodcutter. 'I've had no time to sharpen my axe. I've been so busy trying to cut trees.'

Transformative conversation provides the stone on which learners sharpen their axes. A typical online course is thick with trees, knowledge to be gained and skills to be mastered. Collaboratively pausing for self-reflection can solidify what has been gained and refresh for what is to come.

Businesses are calling for their leaders to engage in, and be able to facilitate, honest, transformative conversation (Beer, 2022). These types of conversations can identify "silent killers" of the organization, elicit truthful feedback by giving a voice to various stakeholders, identify strengths and growth areas, and point the way to an effective action plan for needed change (Beer, 2022). Professors can model this type of vulnerable, impactful discussion with their students. This in turn prepares them for future leadership in their chosen fields.

Effectiveness of Class Discussion

How important is classroom discussion, in the big picture of education? Professor John Hattie (2009) and his team at Visible Learning have synthesized over 2,100 metaanalyses on what works in education, including more than 132,000 studies involving over 300 million students worldwide (Corwin Visible Learning Plus, 2023). One such metaanalysis (examined in detail later in this chapter) explored the effectiveness of classroom discussion, and found a weighted mean effect size of 0.82 (Corwin Visible Learning Plus, 2023), which means it has the potential to considerably influence student achievement. Knowing that quality discussion has a transformational positive influence on student process and product raises questions. How can the dynamic, synergistic conversation that takes place in a physical classroom be translated into an online learning environment? With all that stands to be gained from online education, is deep, rich discussion a necessary sacrifice? And must transformative relationship be sacrificed as well?

ONLINE DISCUSSION: AN OVERVIEW

Educators have been pondering how to conduct quality discussion in an online platform for two and a half decades. In the mid 1990's, Harasim et al. (1996) gave us *Learning Networks*, and three years later Palloff and Pratt (1999) gave us *Building Learning Communities in Cyberspace*. At the same time, an andragogical shift was already underway, led by Malcolm Knowles (Knowles, 1980). Adult learners, previously assumed to be passive sponges soaking up knowledge via professor lecture, were increasingly being recognized as a *neglected species* (Knowles, 1990) desirous of opportunities to actively engage with the material and with one another. Educators recognized early that learners did not automatically understand how to successfully interact online (Conrad & Donaldson, 2011). What worked seamlessly in a traditional classroom did not easily translate to online learning.

The Purposes for Online Discussion

However, successfully translating classroom discussion to an online platform is worth the effort because this discussion meets crucial needs. Boettcher's (2011) lists several purposes for online discussion (derived from Goodyear, 2002; Painter et al., 2003). Online discussion carves out space for an open question and answer forum. It can help reinforce procedural and domain processes. It provides a chance for students to validate one another's experiences. It encourages innovative and critical thinking. It supports students as they reflect and curiously inquire. And of course, as this chapter highlights, it helps to build community and facilitate social interaction among students.

The most effective online instructors spend time casting a vision for the type of online community they would like to build. Here are some questions they might ponder as a jumping-off place:

· Is there language specific to the content area I am teaching?
· Are there certain processing styles, certain personality types of students that tend to work in this field?
· What have past iterations of this course taught me about what students ultimately need?
· What is the most appropriate ultimate goal for this virtual community? Is it a product, a client, a process, a standard?

Vision-casting can be accomplished collaboratively by asking students open-ended questions at the outset (e.g., "What do we want here?" and, "What do you predict you will most need to know by the end of this course?"). The type of online community the professor hopes to build will impact the stance that class discussion will take. This stance will then be reflected in the discussion prompts and the thrust of facilitative questions used throughout the course.

Best Practices in Online Discussion

The most effective online instructors behave with intentionality where discussion is concerned. They balance challenge with affirmation, rigor with support (Imad, 2020). They seek to positively influence their students (Edwards & Perry, 2005). They establish a clear presence by logging into their online courses several times throughout the week to post reminders, answer email, monitor discussion, and host virtual office hours (Boettcher, 2011). They are not afraid to present themselves as relatable people, operating in a connective manner (Imad, 2020). They speak with optimistic, hopeful language (Imad, 2020).

The most effective online instructors facilitate discussion that invites further question, reflection, and thoughtful response (Boettcher, 2011). They use Socratic probing and follow-up questioning that invites learners to explore and apply (Boettcher, 2011):

· What causes you to think that? What is your reasoning here?
· Might there be an alternative strategy or way of viewing this?
· What do you already know, and what would you like to know?

On the flip side, they avoid asking questions that solicit basic facts and closed-ended questions for which there is an obvious yes/no response. They reserve such fact-based questions for objective assignments like practice quizzes (Boettcher, 2011). Recognizing the demands students in higher education face, they stagger due dates of discussion responses and sprinkle encouraging comments throughout (Boettcher, 2011). They seek to connect discussion prompts to students' previous experiences and real world examples.

The most effective online instructors build a classroom community with a variety of activities and experiences (Boettcher, 2011) When possible, they provide choices for students, inviting personalized, customized learning (Boettcher, 2011). This includes allowing students to choose whether they would prefer to work in a group or on their own (Boettcher, 2011). When students must work in teams to address complex case studies or scenarios for the first time, the best online instructors allow students to pick their teams (Boettcher, 2011).

Last but not least, the most effective online instructors support growth-fostering relationships among students and between students and themselves; this sets the stage for quality learning (Lertora et al., 2020). This concept is derived relational-cultural theory and has recently been applied to higher education. Growth-fostering relationships in the online environment are characterized by mutuality, empathy, genuineness, repair when disconnection has occurred, and empowerment (Lertora et al., 2020). Growth-fostering relationships help make it safe to take risks when collaboratively processing experiential activities like role plays and real plays (Lertora et al., 2020).

Hosting Courageous Conversations

Growth-fostering relationships can set the stage for brave spaces in which students feel supported enough to take risks. Educators Arao and Clemens (2023) have observed that when it comes to dialogue about diversity and social justice, students often conflate safety with comfort. This confusion can motivate students to protest and/or avoid discussion that would be better faced with courage and vulnerability. Arao and Clemens (2023) concluded that students are more solidly prepared when educators stop promising safety and instead emphasize the role of bravery in potentially charged classroom discussion. In this manner, students can grow by allowing themselves to stretch outside their proverbial comfort zones (Arao & Clemens, 2023). Power, privilege, identity, oppression…these are challenging subjects to discuss. If safety is defined as freedom from risk and harm, how can such discussion be safe (Arao & Clemens, 2023)? In fact, expectation of safety in such conversations (if safety is taken to mean the absence of discomfort, conflict, and risk) may even represent a form of subordination of minority groups by the dominant group (Arao & Clemens, 2023).

In his book, Singleton (2015) provides a template for conducting courageous conversations in classroom discussions about race. This framework begins with Four Agreements: "stay engaged, experience discomfort, speak your truth, expect and accept non-closure" (Singleton, 2015, p. 70). The Courageous Conversations framework uses the Compass to graphically depict how people process and engage with information about race. It is broken into four quadrants: Emotional (feeling, heart), Intellectual (thinking, head), Moral (believing, soul), and Social (doing, hands and feet) (Singleton, 2015, p. 29). Last but not least, the Courageous Conversations method outlines Six Conditions of Courageous Conversation (Singleton, 2015, p. 27):

1. Establish a racial context that is personal, local, and immediate.
2. Isolate race while acknowledging the broader scope of diversity and the variety of factors and conditions that contribute to a racialized problem.
3. Develop understanding of race as a social/political construction of knowledge, and engage multiple racial perspectives to surface critical understanding.
4. Monitor the parameters of the conversation by being explicit and intentional about the number of participants, prompts for discussion, and time allotted for listening, speaking, and reflecting. Use the Courageous Conversation Compass to determine how each participant is displaying emotion—mind, body, and soul—to access a given racial topic.
5. Establish agreement around a contemporary working definition of race, one that is clearly differentiated from ethnicity and nationality.

6. Examine the presence and role of Whiteness and its impact on the conversation and the problem being addressed.

Instructors who wish to create brave discussion spaces and lead students in courageous conversations about race are encouraged to explore the abovementioned resources more deeply.

SYNCHRONOUS ONLINE DISCUSSION

Synchronous online discussion takes place in real time using various digital platforms (e.g., chat rooms, video conferencing, or instant messaging). The key characteristic of synchronous online discussion is the immediate interaction and response between participants. This enables a dynamic and interactive conversation that approximates face-to-face discussions.

Benefits of Synchronous Online Discussion

The obvious benefit of synchronous discussion is that it more closely mimics the organic synergy that emerges thorough in-seat discussion. This means that all the benefits of classroom discussion listed above apply. However, in one way online synchronous discussion may prove superior to in-seat discussion. During discussion there is always the potential for a few students to dominate the conversation, while the more reticent students are less involved. A savvy leader finds ways to draw these students out without publicly pressuring them, which requires ingenuity in a physical classroom space. This can easily be accomplished during synchronous online discussion sans pressure by using the chat feature. The professor poses an open-ended question to the entire group, meant to be answered via written chat. As answers populate, the professor verbally observes patterns of similar responses, as well as unique ideas and perspectives. The professor can also use quieter students' answers as a jumping off place to move the discussion in a new direction. In this way, students who might hesitate to speak out (because of cultural norms, shyer personalities, or other factors) are included, facilitating richer, more diverse conversation and creating a more connected online community.

Challenges of Synchronous Online Discussion

Synchronous online discussion, while advantageous, brings a set of unique challenges. One such challenge is video chat exhaustion (i.e., Zoom fatigue), caused by a combination of factors. The first factor is sensory deprivation (i.e., the lack of a dynamic physical classroom space). Participants cannot use the full range of non-verbal cues that are typically observed during in-person meetings; they must more heavily rely on the limited signals from facial expressions (Maheu, 2020). A second factor is the potential distraction of seeing one's own image (Dodgen-Magee, 2020). A third factor is physical strain. This includes the need to maintain a fixed posture to keep oneself within the camera's limited view. It can be exacerbated by using equipment (e.g., mobile phone) that is too small, which can lead to eye strain from squinting at a tiny screen (Maheu, 2020). Another factor is mental strain from being on camera nonstop, which requires great concentration and focus (Maheu, 2020).

Solutions for video chat exhaustion include (first and foremost) empowering your students to consistently evaluate what they want and need throughout the discussion and take action to get those needs met

Building Relationship Through Discussion

in healthy ways. Setting up the online workspace in a healthy manner helps, too. Encourage students to use adjustable chairs that support their lower backs and promote good posture. Instruct them to position their chairs at a height that allows their feet to rest flat on the floor or on a footrest and adjust their desk heights so that their arms are parallel to the floor when typing, with their wrists relaxed. Next, have them position their monitors directly in front of the, at eye level, about an arm's length away. They should be able to adjust the tilt and height of the monitor so they can view their screen comfortably without straining their necks or eyes. Inform students about ergonomic keyboards and mice that allow their hands and wrists to remain in a neutral position. Help them to ensure that their workspaces are well-lit to reduce eye strain and avoid glare on their screens. Occasionally, remind students to take their eyes off the screen and look up, focusing on an object further away. One fun game to play is the Triple-Twenty (Maheu, 2020): every twenty minutes, have students spend twenty seconds looking at something around twenty feet away. Periodically, remind students to maintain proper posture, sitting upright with their shoulders relaxed, backs supported, and heads aligned with their spines. As the discussion leader, initiate short breaks every 30 minutes to an hour. You can also facilitate a brief stretching exercise, which helps to promote blood circulation. If the synchronous discussion time is too short to allow a break, remind students to shift. They might not be able to walk away, but they can certainly make small adjustments to how they are seated, without becoming a distraction to their classmates (Maheu, 2020).

Another obvious challenge with synchronous online discussion is distraction. After all, students are not in a protected classroom setting. As an educator, you can help your students minimize distraction by offering the following suggestions. If they know that others will be nearby, students should ensure those around them realize they will be focused on class discussion. Beforehand, students can teach those with whom they share a space to respect their need for quiet and privacy (Maheu, 2020). Students can even post a *Do Not Disturb* sign to visually cue those in their immediate vicinity (Maheu, 2020). If students have pets, they should contain them where they won't disturb. This includes sound distractions (Maheu, 2020). Students should resist the urge to multitask. It can help to put one's phone on silent, close one's email browser, and turn off all social media apps prior to the discussion start time (Maheu, 2020). Invite students to hide self-view if it distracts them, and employ creativity to increase the authenticity and spontaneity of digital encounters (Dodgen-Magee, 2020).

ASYNCHRONOUS ONLINE DISCUSSION

Asynchronous online discussion occurs with a time delay, enabling participants to engage at their own convenience. Instead of real-time interaction, participants post messages or comments on digital platforms (e.g., forums, discussion boards, or email threads). The defining characteristic of asynchronous online discussion is that participants can participate at different times, providing greater flexibility and accommodating students in different time zones or with varied schedules.

Benefits of Asynchronous Online Discussion

There are many benefits of asynchronous online discussion. Students have the freedom to respond flexibly, without being confined by time and space (Thompson, 2006). Further, they may enjoy fuller participation, since multiple discussion threads occur simultaneously, sans chaos (Benshoff & Gibbons, 2011). Students may also benefit culturally from asynchronous online discussion because they can engage with classmates from various geographical locations, potentially providing richer cultural diversity (Chadha, 2017). Additionally, in asynchronous discussion it is the participant's message that takes prominence, not their cultural identity (Chadha, 2017).

Challenges of Asynchronous Online Discussion

One prevalent criticism of asynchronous discussion is that written threaded discussions can lack depth and quality. For example, Webb et al. (2004) found little thoughtful, reflective discussion in a class of over 500 students, though students did try to help one another master course content. Webb et al. (2004) further noted that in a smaller 30-student class, contributions primarily served a perfunctory purpose. Potential solutions to this problem include designing a prompt based on the Four Fields model (Scharmer, 2015), adopting a probing collaborative stance (Dennen & Wieland, 2007), and teaching students the process of self-facilitation (Scharmer, 2015). Students can be taught to self-reflect about the quality of their discussion contribution using Kantor's (2012) Four Player Model: move, follow, oppose, or bystand. Collectively, these strategies can help to foster generative conversation in online counseling education classrooms (Champion & Gunnlaugson, 2017).

Another criticism of asynchronous discussion boards is that they cannot approximate spontaneous, synergistic synchronous discussion. Asynchronous discussion threads can sometimes feel more like formalized message-posting or mini-papers, rather than real, responsive dialogue (Dennen & Wieland, 2007). Asynchronous discussion prompts do not organically emerge; they are planned in advance in the course process (Boettcher, 2018). The upside of this is that crafting prompts in advance helps the instructor focus on questions related to the specific desired knowledge and/or skillset to be discussed (Boettcher, 2018). A quality approach to creating prompts is to focus on addressing two to three core concepts, applied in different scenarios (Boettcher, 2018). This requires students to construct knowledge frameworks around these core concepts, and helps connect novel information with existing knowledge.

Online instructors are encouraged to set clear expectations around asynchronous discussion, to maximize student success (Champion & Gunnlaugson, 2017). Boettcher (2018) suggests explicitly sharing the following expectations with students:

- Post your initial response early in the week (e.g., by Wednesday night), so your classmates have ample time to respond to you. Revisit the thread often, rather than only at the end of the week right before the due date.
- Stick to an effective length for a discussion post, which is between one to two paragraphs.
- Move beyond generalized comments (e.g., 'I agree/disagree' or 'Great idea there') by elaborating on why you agree or disagree.
    - Support your comments with ideas and/or quotes from assigned readings, and don't forget to include appropriate citations and references, to avoid plagiarism.
    - Weave in personal knowledge you have gained from your own experiences, when you can.
- Stay on topic as much as possible; don't let your discussion stray too far from the original prompt.
- When responding to your classmates, demonstrate how different ideas are related and connected.
- Always employ professional etiquette when posting. This includes using proper tone, language, spelling, and grammar, etc.

Building Relationship Through Discussion

Mixing Synchronous and Asynchronous Discussion

Experts have advocated for mixing synchronous and asynchronous formats when conducting experiential learning and building community online (Boettcher, 2018; Christian et al., 2020). This type of mixed format provides space for social interaction during the synchronous parts, while also facilitating growth on a personal level (Raskin, 2008) during the asynchronous parts (Christian et al., 2020).

INNOVATING TO CONNECT AND EMPOWER

Online educators have a responsibility to innovate, to ameliorate the potential disconnection that an online environment can bring and to keep learning fresh and exciting. The best instructors challenge themselves to infuse creativity into learning opportunities (Benshoff & Gibbons, 2011). This section provides a whole host of ideas to inventively boost online discussion.

Innovative Ideas in Synchronous Discussion

Creative opportunities abound for synchronous online discussion. The innovative instructor leverages the virtual environment to enrich discussion. Here are some ideas.

Begin the discussion session with an icebreaker activity. Entire lists of virtual icebreaker activities are available. Here are some examples from (Mrvova, 2022):

- Use a mood barometer to assess how students are feeling. Alternatively, have students post the emoji that best represents their current mood, or have them depict their mood by drawing on a collaborative virtual whiteboard.
- Spark conversation with a "Would you rather…?" poll or a silly trivia question.
- Collaboratively create a virtual word cloud by having students contribute single words in response to a simple question.
- Elicit nostalgia by asking a question about a positive memory (e.g., What was your favorite candy when you were a child?).
- Have students rank their favorite…whatever, using a virtual ranking poll tool.
- Play *Guess Whose Desk?*. Have students send photos of their workspaces to you prior to the synchronous meeting, and then share one of them.
- Host an impromptu scavenger hunt. Give students one minute to find something in their environment that meets a specific criterion (e.g., something red, something odd). When time is up, invite students to show-and-tell what they found.

Icebreakers can shatter uncomfortable silences and facilitate lighthearted community building.

Craft a virtual gallery walk in a shared digital space (e.g., collaborative whiteboard or Google Slides) in which students can showcase their original ideas or creations. Assign each student or group of students a different topic or project. Have them present their final products visually, rather than in written format. During the synchronous session, students can explore the virtual gallery and discuss by leaving comments and asking questions.

Facilitate a fishbowl discussion. Divide students into two groups. Group A acts as the fish in a fishbowl, engaging in the discussion while Group B observes. After a set time, switch the roles. The fishbowl format works well when discussion groups are larger. It encourages active participation for more students. It also facilitates deep listening and reflection.

Host a speed debate. Provide students with a controversial statement or topic, then divide them into pairs. Assign each student a stance, favor or against the statement. Students in breakout rooms engage in timed mini debates (e.g., 1-2 minutes per round) with their partners. Encourage students to present their arguments and counterarguments with professionalism and respect. At the end of each round, students will rejoin the large group. They then rotate partners, and discussion continues. This fast-paced activity promotes c concise argumentation and critical thinking.

Conduct an interactive poll. Use an online polling tool (e.g., Mentimeter or Kahoot) to create a live poll or quiz that is related to the discussion topic. Pose a questions to the class, and have students submit their responses via the link you provide. These tools display the results in real-time. Use findings as a basis for further discussion. This interactive format encourages active engagement and provides immediate feedback.

Design a role play. Assign different roles or characters to students based on a scenario or historical event you as the instructor provided beforehand. Invite them to embody their assigned character and participate in a discussion or debate from that perspective. This immersive approach can help students develop empathy. Through role play, students can reach deeper understanding of differing perspectives.

Invite a guest speaker. Through the magic of virtual meeting rooms, students can interact with experts from around the globe. These virtual guests can bring a wealth of knowledge and experience to share. To prepare, students can craft questions for the guest speaker before the discussion begins.

Innovative Ideas in Asynchronous Discussion

Creative opportunities can also be found for asynchronous online discussion. Instructors need not settle for yet another traditional discussion thread. Here are a few ideas.

For more three-dimensional community connection, consider a video discussion thread. Invite students to record short video responses to discussion prompts using a tool designed for that purpose (e.g., Flipgrid or Loom). Each student can naturally share their thoughts, and then respond to other students' videos. This approach adds a personal touch and encourages students to express their ideas visually and verbally.

Have students engage in collaborative document editing. Use an online editing platform (e.g., Google Docs or Microsoft OneNote) to create shared documents in which students can contribute their own ideas, reflection, or respond to a specific prompt. Students can insert comments, provide feedback, or engage in threaded discussions within the document itself. This format promotes collaboration and enables students to build upon each other's ideas.

Organize an online debate. Assign students to different sides of a topic or issue. Invite them post their arguments, counterarguments, and rebuttals asynchronously in a platform like Padlet. Encourage students to engage with their peers' posts by providing constructive feedback and asking thought-provoking open-ended questions.

Host a multimedia discussion. Expand the traditional discussion format beyond text-based interactions by incorporating multimedia elements. Assign students to create and share their multimedia presentation, infographic, or original video related to the discussion topic. Students can then engage in asynchronous discussion by posting comments and feedback on their classmates' multimedia contributions.

Require students to maintain a reflective journals or blogs. Invite students to share their thoughts, insights, and reflections on the course material along the way. Encourage them to comment on each other's entries by providing constructive feedback and engaging in asynchronous conversations about their reflections.

Facilitate peer feedback exchange. Implement a structured feedback exchange system in which students provide feedback about each other's assignments or projects asynchronously. Assign students to specific peer groups, and provide clear guidelines and specific rubrics to ensure constructive and meaningful feedback. This fosters a sense of community and collaborative learning.

As the instructor, provide video-based feedback on major assignment submissions. This can help build connection between student and professor. Researchers Bahula and Kay (2021) conducted a systematic literature review of 58 scholarly articles and found that students overall preferred to receive video-based feedback, rather than text-based feedback. Benefits of video-based feedback on major assignments were numerous. Students found the feedback to be more clear, rich, and detailed when it was offered in video format. They expressed that this type of feedback increased their understanding. Most pertinent to this chapter, students felt more supported in this type of communication from their professors, and they felt the video feedback was more interactive. One noted drawback, however, was the linear nature of video feedback. To alleviate this drawback, students can respond to the professor via video, creating a back-and-forth conversation.

INNOVATIVE IDEAS THAT WORK FOR BOTH SYNCHRONOUS AND ASYNCHRONOUS DISCUSSION

Many innovative ideas can be adapted for either synchronous or asynchronous class discussion. The following section focuses on infusing experiential learning into discussion.

Experiential Learning in Online Discussion

Experiential learning is not just an activity for changing things up occasionally. It is actually an entire philosophy of education based on Dewey's theory of experience (Kolb & Kolb, 2017). This type of learner-centered education has grown in acceptance in the twenty-first century, and educators are increasingly experimenting with experiential learning approaches (Kolb & Kolb, 2017). Educators can employ the Experiential Learning Cycle (ELC; Kolb, 1984) when translating experiential learning in an online environment. The ELC has four steps: doing, reflecting, generalizing, and transferring (Kolb, 1984).

Problem-Based Learning

An experiential learning strategy that may be especially suited to creating rich discussion in online higher education is problem-based learning (PBL). PBL is an educational approach that focuses on solving real-world problems to promote active learning and critical thinking. In PBL, students are presented with a complex, open-ended problem or scenario that requires ongoing investigation and analysis. Students then work in small groups to identify what they already know, what they need to learn, and how to approach the problem. This collaboration can take place synchronously or asynchronously. Students engage in self-directed learning. Together, they conduct research, gather information, and apply their knowledge to develop possible solutions or recommendations. They are encouraged to integrate knowledge and skills from various disciplines, allowing for a more holistic understanding of the problem.

Throughout the PBL process, instructors serve as facilitators. They guide students' learning, provide resources, and offer support when needed. Students take ownership over their own learning, developing problem-solving strategies, critical thinking abilities, and effective communication skills for a true community experience. PBL encourages metacognition, as students reflect on their learning process and assess their problem-solving strategies. This metacognition can serve as the discussion component of the class. At the end of the PBL experience, students present their findings, solutions, or recommendations to the class or a wider audience, promoting communication and presentation skills. This presentation can also serve as a prompt for further discussion, as classmates respond to the group's work. Overall, Problem-Based Learning shifts the focus from passive knowledge absorption to active engagement, inquiry, and problem-solving, preparing students to tackle complex, real-world challenges.

Boetchetter (2011) suggests that instructors identify core concepts they want students to learn, transform these into performance goals, and mentor students through a collection of increasingly complex, customized projects (e.g., case studies, real-world professional problems, and analyses) that require them to apply the original core concepts. One study found that PBL in an undergraduate physical education course was associated student confidence about their own ability to think critically, to comprehend a current issue in the field, to present and discuss with their classmates, and to engage positively with their learning (Bethell & Morgan, 2011). Overall, PBL was found to be highly beneficial to students' educational experiences (Bethell & Morgan, 2011).

Service Learning

Service learning combines academic learning with community service to address real-world problems. It invites students to actively participate in organized service activities that meet identified community needs while also integrating their experiences into the academic curriculum. Service learning aims to enhance students' understanding of course content, develop civic responsibility, and promote social engagement and awareness. Through service learning, students can apply their knowledge and skillset to make a positive impact on their communities. They work closely with community partners or organizations to identify, plan, and carry out service projects that address specific needs or social issues. Service activities can range from environmental conservation to healthcare initiatives to advocacy work.

Reflection is integral to service learning is reflection, which is where classroom discussion enters the picture. Through reflection, students critically analyze their experiences, evaluate their impact, and connect their service work with the academic concepts and theories they are learning. Reflective discussion allows students to gain a deeper understanding of the community's challenges, develop empathy, and consider the broader social implications of their actions. Service learning benefits students by fostering personal growth, enhancing problem-solving and communication skills, promoting cultural sensitivity, and instilling a sense of civic responsibility. It also benefits the community by providing much-needed support, raising awareness about social issues, and facilitating sustainable change. Overall, service learning integrates meaningful community service with academic learning. In that way, students build online community by making a positive difference in their own communities.

Bielefeldt et al. (2011) explored how service learning has been integrated into undergraduate engineering capstone courses. They described a variety of structured and semi- structured reflection exercises that were used throughout the process and found service learning to be effective in helping students improve depth and breadth of both technical and non-technical skills (Bielefeldt et al., 2011). Brower (2011) described the use of service learning in a business elective, focusing on developing sustainable community in a third world country. There seems to be no end to the contexts in which students can develop interpersonally and professionally through serving their communities, enjoying rich reflective discussion.

Simulation Activities and Gaming

Simulation activities and gaming are increasingly popular approaches in higher education, designed to enhance student learning and engagement. Simulation activities replicate real-world scenarios or processes in a controlled and immersive environment. Students actively participate in simulated experiences that mimic the challenges they may encounter in their chosen field. Simulations can be computer-based in the online classroom. They provide students with opportunities to apply theoretical knowledge, develop problem-solving skills, and practice decision-making in a safe and supportive virtual community. Simulations can be used in various disciplines (e.g., business, healthcare, engineering, and social sciences) to enhance experiential learning and bridge the gap between theory and practice.

Gaming refers to the use of educational games or gamified elements in higher education. It incorporates game mechanics (e.g., point systems, levels, challenges, and rewards) into the learning process. Games can be digital, designed specifically for a specific educational purpose or adapted from an existing game. By introducing game elements, educators aim to increase student motivation, engagement, and active participation. Games can promote critical thinking, problem-solving, collaboration, and decision-making skills. They often provide immediate feedback, allow for experimentation and exploration, and create a dynamic and interactive learning environment.

Simulation activities and gaming offer unique benefits in higher education. They provide students with practical experiences, promote active learning, and offer opportunities for reflection and feedback. They can enhance student motivation, foster collaborative teamwork within community, and help develop skills that are valuable in real-world contexts. Furthermore, these approaches can accommodate different learning preferences and allow for personalized learning experiences. When incorporating simulation activities and gaming, online educators should align the activities with specific learning outcomes, provide clear instructions and guidelines, and offer adequate support. Debriefing sessions provide the perfect opportunity for synchronous or asynchronous discussion.

Social Annotation

Social annotation is a collaborative learning strategy in which the instructor assigns digital course readings on a web-based tool or platform. Students actively engage through critical discourse by annotating and discussing course materials, scholarly articles, or other relevant texts in an online environment. These annotations can be shared with the instructor and other students, fostering a sense of community and facilitating interactive discussions.

Here is how social annotation works. First, students read the assigned text individually and annotate it using the digital annotation tool. They can highlight key passages, insert comments, pose questions, and provide explanations. These annotations are typically text-based, but some tools also support multimedia annotations (e.g., images and videos). Next, the annotated text becomes a shared space for collaboration and online discussion. Students can view and respond to each other's annotations, sparking conversations, debates, and knowledge sharing. They can reply to comments, ask for clarification, provide alternative perspectives, and build upon one other's ideas. This collaborative dialogue deepens understanding, encourages critical thinking, and promotes active engagement with the text.

The online instructor plays a vital role in facilitating the social annotation process. They can provide prompts or discussion questions to focus the annotations, offer information, and participate in the discussions. The instructor may also moderate the conversation, steering it towards learning objectives, and highlight exemplary annotations to encourage meaningful engagement.

Social annotation offers several benefits. It promotes active reading and engagement with the course materials. Students are encouraged to think critically, analyze the text, and construct meaning through their annotations and discussions. It allows students to reflect on their reading processes, articulate their thoughts, and engage in metacognitive thinking. They gain insights into their own learning strategies and can refine their approach to reading and analyzing texts. Online social annotation tools also provide flexibility, enabling students to access and participate in discussions at their convenience. Students can contribute from anywhere, and asynchronous discussions accommodate diverse schedules and time zones. Most closely aligned with the purposes of this chapter, social annotation helps students to build a sense of community by sharing annotations and engaging in discussions. They learn from each other, exchange perspectives, and develop a deeper understanding of the subject matter.

When implementing social annotation in online higher education, instructors should familiarize students with the annotation tool, provide clear guidelines for its use, and set clear expectations for participation. The instructor's active presence and guidance foster meaningful interactions, ensuring that the social annotation activity aligns with the course objectives and enhances student learning outcomes. Lazzara and Clinton-Lisell (2022) have recently used social annotation in psychology courses. They found that students tended to submit high quality annotations above and beyond the minimum requirement and overall reported favorable perceptions of this innovative type of online discussion (Lazzara & Clinton-Lisell, 2022).

Virtual Makerspaces

A virtual makerspace is an environment in which students can use digital tools to think creatively, design and experiment, and construct innovative products (Duenyas & Perkins, 2021). Recently, makerspace enthusiasm has spread throughout academic institutions, nonprofit organizations, and community programs (Duenyas & Perkins, 2021). This excitement may be attributable to a contemporary movement to bolster STEM (i.e., Science, Technology, Engineering, and Math) disciplines in education (Fontichiaro, 2019) because STEM disciplines tend to emphasize problem-solving, reconciliation of diverse ideas, and creative inquiry (Karaahmetoglu & Korkmaz, 2019). Additionally, educators have proposed that creativity be included in STEM, expanding the acronym to STEAM (i.e., Science, Technology, Engineering, Arts and Mathematics) because all fields require the learner to find innovative solutions to problems (Bequette & Bequette, 2012).

Makerspaces have been used to help communities heal from grief and loss (Seymour, 2016). These environments are intentionally designed to promote safety in creative exploration (Duenyas & Perkins, 2021). They can be used to encourage students to open themselves up to novel experiences, to nurture innovation, to think critically, to problem-solve, and to deepen self-awareness (Duenyas & Perkins, 2021). All of this is undertaken within an environment of kinship, resource sharing, and mutual encouragement.

Conversation that flows from such spaces will likely be less structured, more organic and connective, than traditional online discussion.

CONCLUSION

Discussion is an important educational strategy for online learning. This chapter explored the purposes and processes of class discussion. Best practices were offered for facilitating transformative (Boettcher, 2011, 2018), generative (Champion & Gunnlaugson, 2017), and courageous (Singleton, 2015) conversation. Benefits of both synchronous and asynchronous online discussion were highlighted, and solutions for barriers were provided. Multiple innovative ideas for online discussion were broached. Here is one final suggestion to add to the online instructor's toolbelt. Plan a special experience to bring the course to a close, one that celebrates the online community discussion has helped to create. A celebratory activity carves out space for connective reflection about positive social and cognitive experiences (Boettcher, 2011). A wrap up experience can also help students solidify the knowledge they have acquired along the way (Boettcher, 2011). Endings can prove difficult when authentic connection has occurred. Honoring that connection models healthy social interaction, which benefits all students and the academic milieu at large.

REFERENCES

Anderson, B. (2023). *Sharpen your axe: A leadership lesson*. NetGain Technologies. https://www.netgainit.com/blogs/sharpen-your-axe/

Arao, B., & Clemens, K. (2023). From safe spaces to brave spaces: A new way to frame dialogue around diversity and social justice. In L. M. Landreman (Ed.), The Art of Effective Facilitation: Reflections from Social Justice Educators. Stylus Publishing LLC.

Bahula, T., & Kay, R. (2021). Exploring student perceptions of video-based feedback in higher education: A systematic review of the literature. *Journal of Higher Education Theory and Practice*, *21*(4), 248–258. doi:10.33423/jhetp.v21i4.4224

Barrio Minton, C. A., Morris, C. W., & Bruner, S. L. (2018). Pedagogy in counselor education: 2011-2015 update. *Counselor Education and Supervision*, *57*(3), 227–236. doi:10.1002/ceas.12112

Beer, M. (2022, December 2). *Honest transformative conversations: The key to successful change*. Udemy Blog. https://blog.udemy.com/keys-to-honest-transformative-conversations-workplace/

Benshoff, J. M., & Gibbons, M. M. (2011). Bringing life to e-learning: Incorporating a synchronous approach to online teaching in counselor education. *The Professional Counselor, 1*(1), 21–28.

Bequette, J. W., & Bequette, M. B. (2012). A place for ART and DESIGN education in the STEM conversation. *Art Education*, *65*(2), 40–47. doi:10.1080/00043125.2012.11519167

Bethell, S., & Morgan, K. (2011). Problem-based and experiential learning: Engaging students in an undergraduate physical education module. *Journal of Hospitality, Leisure, Sport and Tourism Education*, *10*(1), 128–134. doi:10.3794/johlste.101.365

Bielefeldt, A. R., Dewoolkar, M. M., Caves, K. M., Berdanier, B. W., & Paterson, K. G. (2011). Diverse models for incorporating service projects into engineering capstone design courses. *International Journal of Engineering Education*, *27*(6), 1206–1220.

Boettcher, J. V. (2011). *Ten best practices for teaching online*. Designing for Learning. http://www.designingforlearning.info/services/writing/ecoach/tenbest.html

Boettcher, J. V. (2018). ECoaching tip 2 online discussions – Why and how of using discussion forums. *Designing for Learning*. http://designingforlearning.info/ecoachingtips/e-coaching-tip-2/

Brower, H. H. (2011). Sustainable development through service learning: A pedagogical framework and case example in a third world context. *Academy of Management Learning & Education*, *10*(1), 58–76. doi:10.5465/amle.10.1.zqr58

Chadha, A. (2017). Comparing student reflectiveness in online discussion forums across modes of instruction and levels of courses. *The Journal of Educators Online*, *14*(2). Advance online publication. doi:10.9743/jeo.2017.14.2.8

Champion, K., & Gunnlaugson, O. (2017). Fostering generative conversation in higher education course discussion boards. *Innovations in Education and Teaching International*, 1–9. doi:10.1080/14703297.2017.1279069

Christian, D. D., McCarty, D. L., & Brown, C. L. (2020). Experiential education during the COVID-19 pandemic: A reflective process. *Journal of Constructivist Psychology*, 1–14. doi:10.1080/10720537.2020.1813666

Conrad, R.-M., & Donaldson, J. A. (2011). Engaging the online learner: Activities and resources for creative instruction. Jossey-Bass.

Corwin Visible Learning Plus. (2023, June). *Visible learning metax*. Visible Learning. https://www.visiblelearningmetax.com/

Dennen, V. P., & Wieland, K. (2007). From interaction to intersubjectivity: Facilitating online group discourse processes. *Distance Education*, *28*(3), 281–297. doi:10.1080/01587910701611328

Dodgen-Magee, D. (2020, April 17). *Why video chats are so exhausting*. Psychology Today. https://www.psychologytoday.com/blog/deviced/202004/why-video-chats-are-so-exhausting

Duenyas, D. L., & Perkins, R. (2021). Making space for a makerspace in counselor education: The creative experiences of counseling graduate students. *Journal of Creativity in Mental Health*, *16*(4), 537–547. doi:10.1080/15401383.2020.1790456

Edwards, M., & Perry, B. (2005). Exemplary online educators: Creating a community of inquiry. *Turkish Online Journal of Distance Education*, *6*(2), 45–54.

Eschenbacher, S. (2020). Transformative learning theory and migration: Having transformative and edifying conversations. *European Journal for Research on the Education and Learning of Adults, 11*(3), 367–381. doi:10.3384/2000-7426.ojs1678

Fontichiaro, K. (2019). What I've learned from 7 years of the maker movement in schools and libraries. *Teacher Librarian, 46*(4), 51.

Goodyear, P. (2002). Psychological foundations for networked learning. In C. Steeples & C. Jones (Eds.), *Networked Learning: Perspectives and Issues* (pp. 49–75). Springer London. doi:10.1007/978-1-4471-0181-9_4

Harasim, L. H., Hiltz, R., Teles, L., & Turoff, M. (1996). *Learning networks: A field guide to teaching and learning online*. MIT Press.

Hattie, J. A. C. (2009). *Visible learning: A synthesis of over 800 meta-analyses relating to achievement*. Routledge.

Imad, M. (2020, April 25). *10 strategies to support students and help them learn during the coronavirus crisis*. Google Docs. https://drive.google.com/file/d/1X63HVRzxHd41ZmlOZPxZ_UCC9QtgNMmf/view?usp=sharing&usp=embed_facebook

Kantor, D. (2012). *Reading the room: Group dynamics for coaches and leaders*. Jossey-Bass.

Karaahmetoglu, K., & Korkmaz, Ö. (2019). The Effect of project-based Arduino educational robot applications on students' computational thinking skills and their perception of basic STEM skill levels. *Online Submission, 6*(2), 1–14. doi:10.17275/per.19.8.6.2

Knowles, M. S. (1980). *The modern practice of adult education: From pedagogy to andragogy* (2nd ed.). Association Press.

Knowles, M. S. (1990). *The adult learner: A neglected species* (4th ed.). Gulf Publishing Company.

Kolb, A. Y., & Kolb, D. A. (2017). *The experiential educator: Principles and practices of experiential learning*. EBLS Press.

Kolb, D. A. (1984). *Experiential learning: Experience as the source of learning and development*. Prentice Hall.

Lazzara, J., & Clinton-Lisell, V. (2022). Using social annotation to enhance student engagement in psychology courses. *Scholarship of Teaching and Learning in Psychology*, 1–7. Advance online publication. doi:10.1037tl0000335

Lertora, I. M., Croffie, A., Dorn-Medeiros, C., & Christensen, J. (2020). Using relational cultural theory as a pedagogical approach for counselor education. *Journal of Creativity in Mental Health, 15*(2), 265–276. doi:10.1080/15401383.2019.1687059

Maheu, M. (2020, June 11). Zoom fatigue: What can you do about it. *TBH Institute Blog*. https://telehealth.org/blog/zoom-fatigue-what-it-is-what-you-can-do/

Mrvova, K. (2022, July 28). *35 icebreakers perfect for virtual and hybrid meetings*. Slido Blog. https://blog.slido.com/virtual-icebreakers/

Murphy, P. K., Wilkinson, I. A. G., Soter, A. O., Hennessey, M. N., & Alexander, J. F. (2009). Examining the effects of classroom discussion on students' comprehension of text: A meta-analysis. *Journal of Educational Psychology, 101*(3), 740–764. doi:10.1037/a0015576

Painter, C., Coffin, C., & Hewings, A. (2003). Impacts of directed tutorial activities in computer conferencing: A case study. *Distance Education, 24*(2), 159–173. doi:10.1080/0158791032000127455

Palloff, R. M., & Pratt, K. (1999). *Building learning communitities in cyberspace: Effective strategies for the online classroom.* Jossey-Bass.

Raskin, J. D. (2008). The evolution of constructivism. *Journal of Constructivist Psychology, 21*(1), 1–24. doi:10.1080/10720530701734331

Ratcliff, J. J., Minster, K. I., & Monheim, C. (2021). Engaging students in an online format during the COVID-19 pandemic: A jury voir dire activity. *Scholarship of Teaching and Learning in Psychology.* Advance online publication. doi:10.1037tl0000246

Scharmer, O. (2015, February 17). U.Lab: Seven principles for revolutionizing higher ed. *HuffPost.* https://www.huffpost.com/entry/ulab-seven-principles-for_b_6697584

Seymour, G. (2016). The compassionate makerspace: Grief and healing in a high school library makerspace. *Teacher Librarian, 43*(5), 28.

Shoet, R., & Shoet, J. (2020). *In love with supervision: Creating transformative conversations.* PCCS Books Ltd.

Singleton, G. E. (2015). Courageous conversations about race: A field guide for achieving equity in schools. SAGE Publications Ltd.

Thompson, J. T. (2006). Best practices in asynchronous online course discussions. *Journal of College Teaching and Learning, 3*(7), 7. Advance online publication. doi:10.19030/tlc.v3i7.1698

Webb, E., Jones, A., Barker, P., & van Schaik, P. (2004). Using e-learning dialogues in higher education. *Innovations in Education and Teaching International, 41*(1), 93–103. doi:10.1080/1470329032000172748

KEY TERMS AND DEFINITIONS

Asynchronous Online Discussion: Participants engage in discussion at different times by posting messages or comments on digital platforms (e.g., forums, discussion boards, or email threads).

Courageous Conversations: A framework created by Singleton (2015) for structuring transformative classroom discussions about race.

Gaming: An educational approach employing educational games or gamified elements and incorporating game mechanics (e.g., point systems, levels, challenges, and rewards).

Problem-Based Learning: An educational approach that focuses on solving real-world problems to promote active learning and critical thinking.

Service Learning: An educational approach that combines academic learning with community service to address real-world problems.

Simulation Activities: An educational approach that replicates real-world scenarios or processes in a controlled and immersive environment, mimicking challenges students may encounter in their chosen field.

Social Annotation: An educational approach in which students collaboratively annotate digital course readings, scholarly articles, or other relevant texts on a web-based tool or platform.

Synchronous Online Discussion: Participants engage in discussion in real time using various digital platforms (e.g., chat rooms, video conferencing, or instant messaging) to approximate face-to-face classroom interaction.

Transformative Conversation: Discussion in which participants actively leverage personal experience and challenge previously accepted paradigms.

Video Chat Exhaustion (i.e., Zoom Fatigue): Synchronous discussion depletion caused by a combination of sensory deprivation, distraction, and physical and mental strain.

Virtual Makerspace: An online educational environment in which students use digital tools to think creatively, design and experiment, and construct innovative products.

Chapter 4
Challenges With Sensitivity and Boundaries in an Imperfect, Ever-Changing World:
Online Counselor Education

Rosina E. Mete
https://orcid.org/0000-0001-7292-9079
Yorkville University, Canada

Alyssa Weiss
Yorkville University, Canada

ABSTRACT

This chapter provides an overview of the online educational environment and its context and outlines two realistic examples with suggested responses for counselor educators. The reflect, prepare, and respond approach was explained in detail for both examples. The historical context of societal changes was briefly explained within the chapter to further highlight how quickly the world may change as opposed to written resources for students. Schlossberg's research on coping with transitions enhances the chapter to provide counselor educators with an evidence-based framework to better address the challenges and inquiries that arise within an imperfect, ever-changing world in online education.

INTRODUCTION

Teaching graduate students can present overwhelming challenges for educators. Counselor educators employ knowledge, skills, and strategies to ensure that student learning is evidence-based and relevant (Malott et al., 2014). They engage with diverse student groups who bring their own complex backgrounds, lived experiences and perspectives which can lead to moments of disagreement within the classroom. Consequently, how can counselor educators ensure sensitivity and awareness regarding controversial topics in the online classroom in an ever-changing society? The dynamic societal and global transformations can create stress for educators. Counselor educators grapple with maintaining currency with theoretical concepts and practice strategies. Additionally, counselor educators struggle to increase connections within the classroom to empower and build online learning communities (Tackie, 2022). How should counselor educators respond when students are challenged by the course material and concepts?

The concept for this chapter evolved from current research examining the challenges within the online learning environment for counselor educators as well as the authors' own experiences, including mentoring other faculty. It presents the potential challenges educators face within an online graduate educational environment promoting a realistic application of current skills using two examples developed by the authors. The chapter covers evidence-based practices to address student inquiries regarding foundational literature which may not reflect changes in knowledge and awareness of issues in current society. The following chapter provides a thorough analysis of two examples of students' reactions to their learning process within the online setting. Consequently, counselor educators will learn how to ensure they are aware and informed in an imperfect world. They will also understand how to acknowledge and address their own reactions when challenged by students.

To assist with these questions, this chapter offers guidance and the initial integration of social justice related to counselor education. The authors outline and explain two examples of case scenarios to assist counselor educators who teach in an online environment adapt to the academic world that is continuously in flux while textbooks are unable to maintain currency as quickly. To conclude readers will learn strategies that promote professionalism, sensitivity, and awareness – all key skills of a counselor educator.

HISTORICAL CONTEXT OF SOCIAL JUSTICE AND CULTURAL SENSITIVITY

The history of social justice within higher education, and education in general, is complex (Francis et al., 2017). Davis et al. (2021) noted that "we are living in the most culturally diverse but perhaps least interculturally civil time in modern history, and the field of psychology is not immune. Over recent decades, our field has often engaged in divisive and uncivil dialogue..." (p. 79). Our world continues to shift. Research shows that social work education rapidly changed from the 1990s and forward (Payne, 2020). Similarly, counselor educators and students are currently in a different place than the original scholars within the field (Singh et al., 2020). The initial theories of Eurocentric perspectives and standards within counselor education programs have changed (Williams et al., 2021). This present place is constantly evolving and is a place where what is developed today may not be the same tomorrow (McAuliffe, 2019).

Counselor educators may also consider their understanding of social justice, how their conceptualizations do or do not include the social determinants of health, and how such beliefs affect their work. This is highlighted as a best practice approach for integrating and teaching multicultural and social justice topics in counselor education (Ratts et al., 2016; Waters et al., 2022, p.19).

Changes within society related to education and awareness regarding historical events, as well as social justice implications such as understanding injustice, privilege, and systemic issues are generally implicitly or explicitly discussed within the online classroom (Waters et al., 2022). For future counselors, these concepts are key to understanding a client's context, and the counselor's own positioning within the session, as well as understanding the role of advocacy which may be applicable in certain situations (Davis et al., 2021; Pace, 2022).

The concept of social justice may be analyzed via different lenses and focus on different elements. However, for the purposes of this chapter and the related analysis, the following definition developed by Goodman et al. (2004), specifically, "social justice work encompasses scholarship and professional action designed to change societal values, structures, policies, and practices, such that disadvantaged or marginalized groups gain increased access to these tools of self-determination" will be used (p.795). The definition encompasses the approach utilized within this chapter. Goodman et al. (2004) further utilized the ecological model of social analysis to identify social justice work on the following levels: "the micro level, including individuals and families; the meso level, including communities and organizations; and the macro level, including social structures, ideologies, and policies" (p.795). Additionally, Goodman et al. (2004) outlined the importance of understanding the context of the individual to specify that an individual does not act alone. A variety of factors may impact one's well-being such as social and financial. As counselors in training, it is important for students to recognize the impact of social justice.

Consequently, prior to addressing the ever-changing world, it is important to understand its historical roots and context in the research. Within counseling education, individuals such as Clifford Beers and Frank Parsons were historical advocates for social justice for those with mental illness and immigrants, respectively (Motulsky et al., 2014). Additionally, counseling theories from feminist theorists and culture-centered researchers began to emerge over time. Within different countries, such as Canada and Australia, specific diverse practices related to Indigenous healing for mental health have emerged (McKenna & Woods, 2012; Reeves & Stewart, 2015). However, different theories also developed within the counseling field, emphasizing the individual's journey and integrating the scientist-practitioner perspective. There are a variety of evidence-based practices that incorporate this type of lens however it may shift from a social justice lens within counseling care.

Additional challenges may occur when integrating a social justice lens within the counseling field. Many of the historical and original counselor educational texts were written with a North American or European Western lens linked to colonialist histories (Tatman, 2004). These authors were in the majority population and often had greater access to resources and fewer barriers or challenges. Unfortunately, this early knowledge may not encompass concepts related to social justice such as equity and equality or feminism and multiculturalism. However, professional organizations such as the American Counseling Association (ACA) have developed and continue to create evidence-based resources to incorporate a socially just perspective with multicultural and diverse considerations. The ACA also has a Code of Ethics which "emphasizes that counselors are ethically obligated to work at understanding the diverse cultural backgrounds of the clients they serve" (Barnett & Johnson, 2015, p.173). Further chapters within ACA, such as the Association for Multicultural Counseling and Development (AMCD), advocated for the creation of multicultural and social justice counseling competencies (Ratts et al., 2016; Singh et al., 2020).

The AMCD (2023) provides an updated framework for the Multicultural and Social Justice Competencies which consists of the following constructs:
"1. Counselor self-awareness,
2. Client worldview,
3. Counseling relationship, and
4. Counseling and advocacy interventions" (para 1).

It is divided into four parts which outline "intersection of identities and the dynamics of power, privilege, and oppression which influence the counseling relationship" (AMCD, 2023, para 1). Additionally, the first domain of the framework compasses "aspirational competencies of attitudes and beliefs, knowledge, skills, and action (AKSA)" (AMCD, 2023, para. 1).

Challenges With Sensitivity and Boundaries

The framework, competencies, and dynamics of the AMCD model provide a great map for counselors to integrate self-reflection, skills, and knowledge to ensure they are culturally aware and sensitive (Ratts et al., 2016). Additionally, the idea of cultural humility is interwoven within the framework. Cultural humility is defined as the ability to

(a) reflect on oneself as an embedded cultural being and (b) hear about and strive to understand others' cultural backgrounds and identities (Foronda et al., 2016; Hook et al., 2017; Hook & Watkins, 2015). It foremost is a form of humility that is specific to all matters of culture (e.g., race/ethnicity, gender, sexual orientation, ability status) and, most fundamentally, involves being curious about and respectful of others and their cultural identities, not making automatic, foreordained assumptions about them (Foronda et al., 2016; Hook et al., 2013) (Zhang et al., 2022, p.249).

The concept of cultural humility is related to social justice within the field of counseling and school psychology. It is important for counselors-in-training to recognize that the client is the expert regarding their own culture. Cultural knowledge and awareness can provide a foundation for the counselor but ultimately, listening, being open-minded, and allowing for safe space facilitates an environment that is culturally informed.

Within today's society, there is a wealth of information at our fingertips. One trend is the increase in technology which means the world is more connected and further informed about one another. Social justice along with globalization has highlighted the importance of cultural awareness and education, specifically within the field of counselor education. As the world becomes more connected, awareness, cultural sensitivity and cultural understanding are key concepts for connection and comprehension (Kennedy & Arthur, 2014). However, within an educational institution, the updates to curriculum may not occur as swiftly as changes within social justice. This may cause some issues with integrating cultural awareness and sensitivity (Chen et al., 2020; Snow & Coker, 2020).

An example may be related to gender binary. Individuals who identify as transgender and individuals who identify as gender-neutral have been present throughout our world for centuries (Beemyn, 2013). One could list famous scholars, writers, and artists to note who discussed concepts related to transgender or did not adhere to gender binaries (Kemp, 2019). If we examine the Western world, however, some of these topics were less understood by society as a whole and stigma and prejudice were rampant – for example in the 70s, 80s, and 90s (Hash & Rogers, 2013). Today, there is movement towards a gender-neutral/gender-fluid and accepting society although stigma and ignorance still occur worldwide. Similar patterns are found within awareness and understanding of sexuality as a spectrum. Heteronormativity was often at the forefront of societal expectations within the Western world. This was also evident as homosexuality was originally a mental health diagnosis within the *Diagnostic and Statistical Manual* system until 1974. However, distress related to sexuality replaced the original diagnosis until 2013 (Drescher, 2015).

Unfortunately, within the counseling field, seminal textbooks and even updated textbooks may not reflect societal understandings or awareness as quickly as they come to light. As a result, professors and students discuss the concept of cultural humility but some concepts –such as the gender binary – may still be prevalent within relevant readings for the course. Therefore, the ever-changing world moves so quickly that materials might be out of date and consequently, course updates need to occur regularly.

Professors can integrate evidence-based concepts such as the competencies outlined by the ACA and link information to the basics related to counseling such as treating others with respect and compassion.

However, students may express frustration with some outdated concepts and express concerns about marginalization or feeling unsafe. Within the chapter, an examination of a related example is explained. Other methods to address outdated materials are to bring in newer concepts via peer-reviewed data or multicultural sources.

STUDENT STRESS AND ADAPTABILITY

People's ability to cope with stress has been tested by the pandemic. In counseling programs, students are learning skills to help clients handle the uncertainty of loss, build resilience, adjust their coping strategies and self-care routines, and identify their individual and community strengths (Gallagher et al., 2020). Since the COVID-19 pandemic, expectations and outcomes within higher education environments shifted and consequently, university staff, counselor educators and students have had to adapt.

Schlossberg's Transition Theory is engrained in psychology and acts as a tool for comprehending adult development. Schlossberg (1981) wrote that her model offers a mechanism for "analyzing human adaptation to transition" (p.2). According to Evans (2010), Schlossberg defines these transitions as "any event or non-event that results in changed relationships, routines, assumptions, and roles" (p. 111). Transitions occur in various settings within an individual's life. Schlossberg refers to these as individual, relationship and work transitions. The question arises, as counselors how might we add Schlossberg's theory to our toolbox and apply it when working with clients during this health crisis transition? Researchers note that prior significant events such as 9/11, or events linked to climate change (such as hurricanes, earthquakes) impacted students and disrupted learning. However, there was an understanding that the changes would be temporary (Rapanta et al., 2021).

With the pandemic, there are arguments that its influence continues despite vaccines, managed care, and reduction of restrictions. Studies show that generally university students rated their emotional wellbeing as low or poor during COVID and many noted challenges with stress management (Lancaster & Arango, 2021). This may have impacted their current stress response and led to reactive responses within an online environment. Research shows that students may struggle with learning online due to a lack of self-regulation and stress management strategies (Araka et al., 2020; Wong et al., 2015).

DEFINITION OF ONLINE ENVIRONMENT

Distance learning, distance education online education or online environment depending on what one wants to call the term has been with us longer than one would remember. There was the teacher who traveled to provide students with knowledge and wisdom to Socrates and Apostle Paul conveying their expertise (Johnston, 2020). History has shown that the dispersion of knowledge and ideas is crucial to considering different perspectives. Online education has surfaced as another form of education in the last few decades (Lee, 2017; Xia, 2018). There are different eras that have evolved with distance education. According to Kentor (2015), he classified distance education into four groups based on their delivery system: (a) Parcel post; (b) radio; (c) television and (4) Internet. According to Keegan (1980) distance education is defined as: "separation of teacher and student; influence of educational organization; use of technical media; two-way communication; possibility of occasional seminars and participation in the most industrial education" (p. 33).

However, within an online environment, much of the dynamics between counselor educators and their students is asynchronous and incorporating controversial topics promotes challenging the student's status quo or ingrained beliefs (Haskins & Singh, 2015). Consequently, some students may become reactive or position their personal beliefs prior to examining the entire situation. Chein and Cui (2022) state that, "The online learning modalities have increased the possibilities of course content being shared and abused outside of the classroom boundary" (p.2). Professors may become concerned regarding potential backlash from students which results in one of the following outcomes: "skipping controversial issues, teaching with no change, advising students against sharing course content" (Chein & Cui, 2022, p.1). This may result in a detrimental impact on their student learning and understanding of issues. Further research has shown that teacher engagement in the online classroom, such as increased online engagement and increased posting, assists in student learning. When compared to peer-facilitated learning, instructor-facilitated learning increases student interest and fosters a sense of community (Phirangee et al., 2016). Additionally, the research identifies that students appreciate teacher self-disclosure as this phenomenon increases student satisfaction with learning, improved their level of knowledge obtained, and consequently led to improvement in teacher-student social interactions online (Song et al., 2019). Research identifies that, "not only do students benefit from supportive emotional connections to teachers but positive teacher–student relationships also increase teachers' feelings of self-efficacy and well-being" (Tackie, 2022, p.2). To effectively engage with students, communication, respect and compassion should be present. Tackie (2022) identifies the concept of intimacy as key:

Building intimacy and permitting vulnerability is a dynamic process that evolves, and shifts based on the interpersonal interactions of relationship participants (Reis & Shaver, 1988). The establishment of intimacy relies on a perception of the other as trustworthy, receptive, and accessible, which can be facilitated or hindered by differences in the social positioning—race, class, and or other status-holding identifications—of the participants. (p. 1)

McAuliffe (2019) noted that engaging students online is different from building relationships in the classroom—"it is undeniably harder, but it can be done if the educator is committed, interested, and prepared to put in the time and experiment with the various digital tools available" (p.111). There is less social interaction with online learning which impacts connection and attention within the classroom. Additionally, the professor's and students' technological knowledge and abilities can hinder rapport-building and professional educational relationships.

Counselor educators who manage to teach a variety of topics in today's imperfect world enhance their student relationships, increase student trust, and facilitate a learning environment that is inquisitive and good promotes growth and development. A variety of technological tools exist to assist counselor educators may use to bridge the gap between the online environment and the student learning from home (Martin, 2019).

BOUNDARIES WITHIN THE ONLINE ENVIRONMENT

How does one manage one's time when working online? How does one develop expectations when working online? How important are boundaries when working online? When working online these are questions to ask oneself. There are few clear boundaries when teaching within the online environment.

Explicit boundaries generally depend on the educational institution and may include being present in the course room four to five days a week and responding to emails within 24 hours. However, once instructors have completed those tasks, they spend most of the day and night checking emails and responding in the course room (Hansen & Gray, 2018).

Moving from textbook/theory-to-practice is essential but often challenging for new counselors. Finding unique ways to break down complex concepts into manageable pieces and implementing creative instructional strategies to teach these concepts can be challenging and cumbersome for counselor educators. Building educational rapport with students while ensuring they understand and can apply concepts can be a struggle when connecting virtually rather than in real-time and face-to-face with students. Within the online environment, "the opportunities for spontaneous, formative feedback between a teacher and student are lost" (Martin, 2019, p.1). Additionally, educational material may encompass a variety of topics which include controversial issues or those which challenge the students' beliefs or values.

Two examples are outlined to further develop skills and knowledge when interacting online with students and facilitating a culturally sensitive and informed perspective. They highlight concerns that may arise within the online asynchronous classroom related to boundaries as well as outdated information, as discussed earlier. The authors have developed the acronym RPR for Reflect, Prepare, and Respond which will be integrated into the example.

REFLECT, PREPARE AND RESPOND

Example 1: Online Discussion Forum Scenario

You are a faculty member in a graduate higher education program which is fully online and asynchronous. Consequently, students respond to scenarios via discussion forums each week within the course. One of your scenarios discussed a situation where an individual reflects on how they would approach a challenge within the counselling room. However, the individual is described as in "his/her opinion" and you receive complaints from other students that it is non-inclusive language and insensitive. The students are concerned that the gender binary is highlighted and that a non-binary option like "they" should be included. You receive an email from the student:

I am concerned with the scenario within our Week 3 discussion. The description of "his/her opinion" reflects gender bias and does not correlate with the APA 7 standards.

I believe when I read the scenario, I experienced invalidation and marginalization as a gender minority. I can provide research that shows the negative consequences on social and emotional health.

I hope this was helpful and informative for you, to help you be gender inclusive in the future. I would hope that our program embraces all genders instead of only the binary of he/her.

Response: As the Professor, How Do You Respond?

1). **Reflect** on the situation. Acknowledge that there is always growth and development in learning – our society continues to change and grow in its perspectives. Some materials may not immediately

Challenges With Sensitivity and Boundaries

reflect that and it's OK – changes can be made. Be gentle with yourself. Ask yourself, are you taking this personally?
2). **Prepare**. Review the course in its entirety. You may notice that this gender binary notation was a mix up and the rest of the course embraces inclusivity and diversity. Professors are humans and sometimes mistakes are made – but this can be a learning experience for you and the student. Incorporate self-compassion, awareness, and education within your perspective. This is a great reminder to review your course between sections (terms, semesters) and look at the vocabulary used, the scenarios described and update accordingly. Stay informed about our ever-changing society.
3). **Respond**. Consider your response to the student and try to balance the awareness of the client and counselor. Your response may include: *Thank you for bringing this to my attention. I will be reviewing the course to ensure that it aligns with an inclusive lens. Our graduate program embraces inclusivity and diversity as evidenced by (example: our mission, vision, goals...our department of...). However, I would like to return back to the original goal of the assignment: for the couple experiencing a disconnect, how do you suggest addressing this as the counselor?*

Your institution may have an Equity, Diversity, and Inclusion (EDI) department which may review your response prior to sending it to your student. They may also have relevant resources and training available.

Example 2: Online Interactions Throughout the Weekend

One of the benefits of asynchronous online learning is the accessibility of materials and the classroom. However, a challenge is the potential for inflated expectations from students for professor and their availability. An asynchronous course allows professors and students to access the course at convenient times for their own schedules. This ability may lead to issues with boundaries as students may expect professors to be consistently connected online. Hansen and Gray (2018) note, "the term ubiquitous can be used to describe the online environment because there are unclear boundaries and great flexibility when teaching online" (p.1).

Imagine you are teaching in a graduate-level online program and your students have an assignment due on Monday. It is the weekend before the due date and on Saturday morning you receive an email from a stressed-out student who is asking you to review all instructions and confirm that "they are on the right track" with a copy of the assignment to review. You respond by providing some clarity for the instructions and directing the student to the syllabus for further information. You also remind the student that your institution's policies prohibit reviewing assignments ahead of time or giving a preliminary grade before the due date. By 5pm Saturday evening, you had received three additional emails from this student. On Sunday morning, when you are at your laptop to write a response, you see an updated email from the student to your Dean, cc'ing you. The student wrote a lengthy complaint that you have not responded since Saturday morning and that they are concerned they will fail due to your lack of engagement. The student demands your response ASAP and now asks for an extension on their paper.

Response: As the Professor, How Do You Respond?

1). **Reflect** on the situation. Acknowledge the challenges that you face as a professor online. Respect your boundaries and your peace by responding on Monday as per the university policies.
2). **Prepare**. Review your response, syllabus, university policies and student's demands.

3). **Respond**. Please refer to a sample response below that you could edit. Reactivity within these situations generally leads to further frustration, however setting the boundaries and tone from the beginning is very important within these discussions. How you write and react electronically will go a long way.

Email to student Monday morning: attach first response – explain that your follow-up questions could be answered by my original email and information was in the syllabus.

I appreciate the challenges and stresses of completing assignments. I encourage you to connect with Student Services/Library resources for additional support in the future with your assignments. Furthermore, I provided a response to your first email within an hour of receipt. As per the syllabus, I respond to emails within 24 hours including on weekends. I cannot pre-grade assignments as you requested due to university policies. I also offer a weekly office hour or you can email me ahead of time if you are not available during those office hours. Additionally, as per university policy, I cannot grant an extension without further information – see the syllabus for next steps.

NEXT STEPS FOR COUNSELOR EDUCATORS

After reviewing the chapter, the question remains: How can the counselor educator prepare for the future? A variety of scenarios may occur in the future, especially given the continued societal changes, societal awareness, and technological advancements. How can the counselor educator ensure that they are prepared?

Schlossberg's 4S System for Coping With Transitions

To further expand upon the concepts of stress management, self-care, adaptability and resilience, the authors will provide information from Schlossberg's (1981) and Schlossberg et al. (1995) research that explains the 4S System for Coping with Transitions. Schlossberg (1981) explains transitions as any event or non-event that affects a change in relationships, routines, assumptions, and roles. Schlossberg's Transition Theory is engrained in psychology and acts as a tool for comprehending adult development. Transitions occur in various settings within an individual's life. Schlossberg refers to these as individual, relationship and work transitions. How might counselors add Schlossberg's theory to the theoretical toolbox and apply it when working with clients during this health crisis transition? How does one handle this journey, live through it, and learn from it adjusting or adapting to his/her new transition? Schlossberg's (1981) hallmark to the theory includes four major factors referred to as the 4Ss: situation, self, support and strategies.

Situation

This signifies the person's situation at the time of transition.

What kind of transition is it? Does the individual see the transition as positive, negative, expected, unexpected, desired or unwanted? Did the transition come at the worst or best possible time? Is it on time or off schedule? Is it voluntary or obligatory? Is the person at the beginning, middle or end of the transition? (Sargent & Schlossberg, 1988, p. 60)

Consider today's situation: a global pandemic occurs. This was an unpredicted event resulting in an unexpected transition. The transition came for most people at the worst time. Children were currently in school; people were engaged in their careers and/or jobs and had other commitments. COVID-19 imposed on and affected everyone. Some of the consequences of COVID-19 included children confined to home participating in digital learning, parents needing to home-school, and spouses or partners also working from home. Federal and state governments-imposed quarantines forcing all to remain home, and multiple businesses and recreation areas needed to close. This unforeseen event resulted in an unexpected situational transition. This S (situation) begs the following question: "How long will this transition last?" The length of the quarantine remained unknown which triggered stress. This situation also impacted self as in this case the multiple role changes from working parent to teacher, teaching children academics and physical education; entertainer, providing entertainment to children; and chef, as now the individual has assumed the role of full-time cook. At this point, individuals started to look at their resources to see if they had a previous experience of this type of situation.

Self

This signifies the person's inner strengths for coping with the situation. In self, one looks at the personal and demographic characteristics of how the individual views their life. Personal characteristics include socioeconomic status, gender age, stage of life and ethnicity which influence worldview. These characteristics affect how a person perceives his or her life (Pendleton, 2007).

What psychological resources does the individual have in terms of coping? What kinds of strengths and weaknesses does the individual bring to the situation? What is the person's previous experience in making a similar transition? Does he or she believe there are options? Is the person optimistic, resilient and able to deal with ambiguity? (Sargent & Schlossberg, 1988, p. 60)

Now the individual needs to find his/her inner strength in order to be able to move through this unexpected event. Individuals try to find coping skills to attain or maintain a balance during this unexpected event. The needed psychological resources to promote adaptation are ego development, outlook in optimism and self-efficacy, commitment and values, spirituality and resiliency. From the therapeutic and/or counseling standpoint some questions to ask in this phase include: What kind of strengths and weaknesses does the individual bring to the situation? Do they believe there are options? Is the individual optimistic?

Support

The support an individual gains during a transitional period can be a key element to success. Support comes in different forms and Schlossberg et al. (1995) discuss the types of support as: institutions or communities, family units, and intimate relationships. Brooks et al. (2020) offer a framework through which an onlooker can clearly see the different aspects of existential factors. When one utilizes this research lens, there is a further delineation of the loci of control that illuminate external and internal facets of pandemic living. External characteristics are strongly linked to social support which can influence an individual's internal facet (i.e. the ability to cope). Additional existential aspects of life that are examined include the psychological, physical and career related to sociability.

Strategies

The last "S" focuses on actionable goals that allow for progress. The literature demonstrates plans that allow for proactive and reactive measures during pandemics or cases of forced isolation. Most of the pandemic-related factors that are detrimental, as well as happiness and resilience attributes that aid in mitigating the influence of the health and psychological detractors that impact relationships (Achor, 2010; Brooks, et al., 2020; Choi, et al. 2019). The psychological aspects of an individual encompass functions of the mind and how the mind impacts behavior. Understanding the impact of isolative and disruptive events on relational networks brought forth by a pandemic can better aid individuals in creating resilience, while also reducing potential adverse psychological sequela.

Further Suggestions for Counselor Educators

In response to next steps and aligned with Schlossberg's (1981) and Schlossberg et al.'s (1995) research, a variety of tangible suggestions are provided to assist and empower counselor educators.

The strategies are provided in a list form below:

1). First and foremost, this is a gentle reminder to remember to grow, develop, and continue to learn. Counselor educators often place additional pressure on themselves to be "perfect," however, they are human. As counselors, learning and developing are two key components to ensure cultural awareness and relevant clinical skills.
2). When you encounter challenged students, consider a cognitive reframe. Rather than question, "what have I done wrong? Why are they so upset?" take a breath and ask the question, "how can I empower these students? Have these students been given space? How can I clarify the situation?"
3). The concept of self-reflection is highlighted throughout this chapter. As a counselor educator, recognize your own influences, prior development, and status. How do these concepts impact your teaching? How can you move away from assumptions and move towards equity within the classroom?
4). As stated within the chapter, the world continues to change. Consequently, adaptability and resilience are two concepts which allow for preparation. Adaptability is the "ability to adjust to different situations" (Oxford Concise English Dictionary, 2003, p.16). Counselor educators must adjust their perspective and recognize that continual changes will happen.
5). To enhance your learning, continue to stay informed about changes within the field. The authors encourage you to join your professional association or organizations that reflect diversity and inclusivity. Join your faculty curriculum committee and propose changes to the curriculum which are reflective of different voices and literature.
6). Schlossberg et al. (1995) highlight the importance of support during stressful times and times of transition. Remember your social network at the educational institution – faculty members, chair, department head and other colleagues. Or reach out to friends or relatives with whom you have positive relationships. Social support is key in managing stress and helping retain perspective.

Challenges With Sensitivity and Boundaries

7). Lastly, self-care is an important concept to highlight and integrate in your daily life. Incorporating resilience and adaptability will be challenging if you feel stressed most of the time or have intense reactions to emails or situations. Review your routine and what helps to "refill your cup."

CONCLUSION

In conclusion, counselor educators face challenges with sensitivity in today's ever-changing world. Societal changes and awareness continue to develop and grow, which is positive, however, counselor educators need to constantly adapt to these changes. This becomes overwhelming within the navigation of an online educational environment and its demands.

The chapter provided a brief overview of the historical context of social justice within counselor education as well as its impact on learning. To further the topic, the chapter integrated two evidence-based practices demonstrating how to address two possible examples within the online classroom. The readers were introduced to the strategy of Reflect, Prepare, and Respond to use in the future.

For future preparation, the authors incorporated Schlossberg's (1981) research and the 4S System for Coping with Transitions. Counselor educators now have a better understanding of the impact of Situation, Self, Support, and Strategies to better manage stress and adapting to student situations within the online educational environment. The chapter provides a detailed list for counselor educators to utilize in the future for a comprehensive approach to addressing student concerns within the online milieu of the imperfect, ever-changing world.

The authors encourage counselor educators to continue to reflect, learn, and grow throughout their professional career and integrate these strategies for further professional development.

REFERENCES

Achor, S. (2010). *The happiness advantage: the seven principles that fuel success and performance at work*. Virgin.

Araka, E., Maina, E., Gitonga, R., & Oboko, R. (2020). Research trends in measurement and intervention tools for self-regulated learning for e-learning environments—Systematic review (2008–2018). *Research and Practice in Technology Enhanced Learning, 15*(1), 1–21. doi:10.118641039-020-00129-5

Association for Multicultural Counseling and Development (AMCD). (2023). *Multicultural and social justice counseling competencies.* https://www.multiculturalcounselingdevelopment.org/competencies

Barnett, J. E., & Johnson, W. B. (2015). *EthicsDesk reference for counselors* (2nd ed.). American Counseling Association. doi:10.1002/9781119221555

Beemyn, G. (2013). A presence in the past: A transgender historiography. *Journal of Women's History, 25*(4), 113–121. doi:10.1353/jowh.2013.0062

Brooks, S. K., Webster, R. K., Smith, L. E., Woodland, L., Wessely, S., Greenberg, N., & Rubin, G. J. (2020). The psychological impact of quarantine and how to reduce it: Rapid review of the evidence. SSRN *Electronic Journal*. doi:10.2139/ssrn.3532534

Chen, F., & Cui, X. (2022). Teaching controversial issues online: Exploring college professors' risk appraisals and coping strategies in the US. *Teaching and Teacher Education, 115*, 1–9. doi:10.1016/j.tate.2022.103728

Chen, S. Y., Basma, D., Ju, J., & Ng, K. M. (2020). Opportunities and challenges of multicultural and international online education. *The Professional Counselor, 10*(1), 120–132. doi:10.15241yc.10.1.120

Choi, K. W., Chen, C. Y., Ursano, R. J., Sun, X., Jain, S., Kessler, R. C., Koenen, K. C., Wang, M. J., Wynn, G. H., Campbell-Sills, L., Stein, M. B., & Smoller, J. W. (2019). Prospective study of polygenic risk, protective factors, and incident depression following combat deployment in US Army soldiers. *Psychological Medicine, 50*(5), 737–745. doi:10.1017/S0033291719000527 PMID:30982473

Davis, E. B., Plante, T. G., Grey, M. J., Kim, C. L., Freeman-Coppadge, D., Lefevor, G. T., Paulez, J. A., Giwa, S., Lasser, J., Stratton, S. P., Deneke, E., & Glowiak, K. J. (2021). The role of civility and cultural humility in navigating controversial areas in psychology. *Spirituality in Clinical Practice, 8*(2), 79–97. doi:10.1037cp0000236

Drescher, J. (2015). Out of DSM: Depathologizing homosexuality. *Behavioral Sciences (Basel, Switzerland), 5*(4), 565–575. doi:10.3390/bs5040565 PMID:26690228

Evans, N. J., Forney, D. S., Guido, F. M., Patton, L. D., & Renn, K. A. (2010). *Student development in college. Theory, research, and practice* (2nd ed.). Jossey-Bass.

Francis, B., Mills, M., & Lupton, R. (2017). Towards social justice in education: Contradictions and dilemmas. *Journal of Education Policy, 32*(4), 414–431. doi:10.1080/02680939.2016.1276218

Gallagher, M. W., Zvolensky, M. J., Long, L. J., Rogers, A. H., & Garey, L. (2020). The impact of Covid-19 experiences and associated stress on anxiety, depression, and functional impairment in American adults. *Cognitive Therapy and Research, 44*(6), 1043–1051. doi:10.100710608-020-10143-y PMID:32904454

Goodman, L. A., Liang, B., Helms, J. E., Latta, R. E., Sparks, E., & Weintraub, S. R. (2004). Training counseling psychologists as social justice agents: Feminist and multicultural principles in action. *The Counseling Psychologist, 32*(6), 793–836. doi:10.1177/0011000004268802

Hansen, B., & Gray, E. (2018). Creating boundaries within the ubiquitous online classroom. *The Journal of Educators Online, 15*(3), 1–21. doi:10.9743/jeo.2018.15.3.2

Hash, K. M., & Rogers, A. (2013). Clinical practice with older LGBT clients: Overcoming lifelong stigma through strength and resilience. *Clinical Social Work Journal, 41*(3), 249–257. doi:10.100710615-013-0437-2

Haskins, N. H., & Singh, A. (2015). Critical race theory and counselor education pedagogy: Creating equitable training. *Counselor Education and Supervision, 54*(4), 288–301. doi:10.1002/ceas.12027

Johnston, J. P. (2020). Creating better definitions of distance education. *Online Journal of Distance Learning Administration, 23*(2).

Keegan, D. (1980). On defining distance education. *Distance Education*, *1*(1), 13–36. doi:10.1080/0158791800010102

Kemp, S. K. (2019). In that dimension grossly clad": Transgender rhetoric, representation, and Shakespeare. *Shakespeare Studies*, *47*, 120–13.

Kennedy, B. A., & Arthur, N. (2014). Social justice and counselling psychology: Recommitment through action. *Canadian Journal of Counselling and Psychotherapy*, *48*(3).

Kentnor, H. E. (2015). Distance education and the evolution of online learning in the United States. *Curriculum and Teaching Dialogue*, *17*(1), 21–34.

Lancaster, M., & Arango, E. (2021). Health and emotional well-being of urban university students in the era of COVID-19. *Traumatology*, *27*(1), 107–117. doi:10.1037/trm0000308

Lee, K. (2017). Rethinking the accessibility of online higher education: A historical review. *The Internet and Higher Education*, *33*, 15–23. doi:10.1016/j.iheduc.2017.01.001

Malott, K. M., Hall, K. H., Sheely-Moore, A., Krell, M. M., & Cardaciotto, L. (2014). Evidence based teaching in higher education: Application to counselor education. *Counselor Education and Supervision*, *53*(4), 294–305. doi:10.1002/j.1556-6978.2014.00064.x

Martin, J. (2019). Building relationships and increasing engagement in the virtual classroom: Practical tools for the online instructor. *The Journal of Educators Online*, *16*(1), n1–n8. doi:10.9743/jeo.2019.16.1.9

McAuliffe, D. (2019). Challenges for best practice in online social work education. *Australian Social Work*, *72*(1), 110–112. doi:10.1080/0312407X.2018.1534982

McKenna, T., & Woods, D. B. (2012). Using psychotherapeutic arts to decolonise counselling for Indigenous peoples. *Asia Pacific Journal of Counselling and Psychotherapy*, *3*(1), 29–40. doi:10.1080/21507686.2011.631145

Motulsky, S. L., Gere, S. H., Saleem, R., & Trantham, S. M. (2014). Teaching social justice in counseling psychology. *The Counseling Psychologist*, *42*(8), 1058–1083. doi:10.1177/0011000014553855

Oxford Concise English Dictionary. (2011). Adaptability. In Oxford Concise English Dictionary (12th ed., p.16). Academic Press.

Pace, J. L. (2022). Learning to teach controversial issues in a divided society: Adaptive appropriation of pedagogical tools. *Democracy & Education*, *30*(1), 1–11.

Payne, M. (2020). *The origins of social work: Continuity and change*. Bloomsbury Publishing.

Phirangee, K., Epp, C. D., & Hewitt, J. (2016). Exploring the relationships between facilitation methods, students' sense of community, and their online behaviors. *Online Learning : the Official Journal of the Online Learning Consortium*, *20*(2), 134–154. doi:10.24059/olj.v20i2.775

Rapanta, C., Botturi, L., Goodyear, P., Guàrdia, L., & Koole, M. (2021). Balancing technology, pedagogy and the new normal: Post-pandemic challenges for higher education. *Postdigital Science and Education*, *3*(3), 715–742. doi:10.100742438-021-00249-1

Ratts, M. J., Singh, A. A., Nassar-McMillan, S., Butler, S. K., & McCullough, J. R. (2016). Multicultural and social justice counseling competencies: Guidelines for the counseling profession. *Journal of Multicultural Counseling and Development, 44*(1), 28–48. doi:10.1002/jmcd.12035

Reeves, A., & Stewart, S. L. (2015). Exploring the integration of Indigenous healing and western psychotherapy for sexual trauma survivors who use mental health services at Anishnawbe Health Toronto. *Canadian Journal of Counselling and Psychotherapy, 49*(1).

Sargent, A. G., & Schlossberg, N. K. (1988). Managing Adult Transitions. *Training and Development Journal, 42*(12), 58–60.

Schlossberg, N. K. (1981). Adult Transitions. *The Counseling Psychologist, 9*(2), 2–18. doi:10.1177/001100008100900202

Schlossberg, N. K., Waters, E. B., & Goodman, J. (1995). *Counseling adults in transition* (2nd ed.). Springer.

Singh, A. A., Appling, B., & Trepal, H. (2020). Using the multicultural and social justice counseling competencies to decolonize counseling practice: The important roles of theory, power, and action. *Journal of Counseling and Development, 98*(3), 261–271. doi:10.1002/jcad.12321

Singh, A. A., Nassar, S. C., Arredondo, P., & Toporek, R. (2020). The past guides the future: Implementing the multicultural and social justice counseling competencies. *Journal of Counseling and Development, 98*(3), 238–252. doi:10.1002/jcad.12319

Snow, W. H., & Coker, J. K. (2020). Distance counselor education: Past, present, future. *The Professional Counselor, 10*(1), 40–56. doi:10.15241/whs.10.1.40

Song, H., Kim, J., & Park, N. (2019). I know my professor: Teacher self-disclosure in online education and a mediating role of social presence. *International Journal of Human-Computer Interaction, 35*(6), 448–455. doi:10.1080/10447318.2018.1455126

Tackie, H. N. (2022). (Dis) Connected: Establishing social presence and intimacy in teacher–student relationships during emergency remote learning. *AERA Open, 8*, 1–14. doi:10.1177/23328584211069525

Tatman, A. W. (2004). Hmong history, culture, and acculturation: Implications for counseling the Hmong. *Journal of Multicultural Counseling and Development, 32*(4), 222–233. doi:10.1002/j.2161-1912.2004.tb00629.x

Vagos, P., & Carvalhais, L. (2022). Online versus classroom teaching: Impact on teacher and student relationship quality and quality of life. *Frontiers in Psychology, 13*, 13. doi:10.3389/fpsyg.2022.828774 PMID:35250769

Waters, J. M., Gantt, A. C., Worth, A., Duyile, B., Johnson, K., & Mariotti, D. (2022). Motivated but challenged: Counselor educators' experiences teaching about social determinants of health. *The Journal of Counselor Preparation and Supervisor, 15*(2), 1–32.

Williams, J. M., Byrd, J. A., & Washington, A. R. (2021). Challenges in implementing antiracist pedagogy into counselor education programs: A collective self-study. *Counselor Education and Supervision, 60*(4), 254–273. doi:10.1002/ceas.12215

Wong, J., Baars, M., Davis, D., Van Der Zee, T., Houben, G. J., & Paas, F. (2019). Supporting self-regulated learning in online learning environments and MOOCs: A systematic review. *International Journal of Human-Computer Interaction*, *35*(4-5), 356–373. doi:10.1080/10447318.2018.1543084

Xiao, J. (2018). On the margins or at the center? Distance education in higher education. *Distance Education*, *39*(2), 259–274. doi:10.1080/01587919.2018.1429213

Zhang, H., Watkins, C. E. Jr, Hook, J. N., Hodge, A. S., Davis, C. W., Norton, J., Wilcox, M., Davis, D., DeBlaere, C., & Owen, J. (2022). Cultural humility in psychotherapy and clinical supervision: A research review. *Counselling & Psychotherapy Research*, *22*(3), 548–557. doi:10.1002/capr.12481

Chapter 5
Creating Care in the Online Classroom

Kim Cowan
https://orcid.org/0009-0003-7282-9221
The University of Arizona Global Campus, USA

William G. Davis
The University of Arizona Global Campus, USA

Stephanie Stubbs
The University of Arizona Global Campus, USA

ABSTRACT

This chapter explores care with respect to theoretical concepts including belonging and mattering. The authors utilize feedback from the academic resolution process and draw from faculty experiences to illustrate the unique challenges of the adult online learner and those who work with them. They highlight data from a study that aimed to give voice to the student as well, identifying elements of perceived care that may be particularly impactful in the online environment. Warm, inviting communication and recognition of individuality were particularly valued, suggesting a desire for connection. Finally, the authors identify clear strategies for practical actions to develop meaningful online relationships which may enhance student persistence.

CREATING CARING CONNECTIONS IN THE ONLINE CLASSROOM

Student persistence is one of the hottest topics in higher education. At the University of Arizona Global Campus (UAGC), one unique strategy to increase student persistence involves creating a *Culture of Care*. This culture urges faculty to provide flexibility and a more individualized approach to enhance student engagement. The initial phases of this shift emphasized flexibility, encouraging faculty to provide additional time and allow for resubmissions in the classroom to help students reach the learning outcomes in the course. Three members of the university community with a strong belief in this shift came together to focus on how they can reinforce and help this culture of care evolve. As we determined how we could

DOI: 10.4018/978-1-6684-8908-6.ch005

impact care and what that might look like in the classroom, we discussed the student experience from a Student Affairs perspective compared to the faculty experiences from the College of Arts and Sciences and the Forbes School of Business and Technology. We then sought to broaden our understanding of care in the online classroom, considering the characteristics of an adult online learner in light of research about student persistence.

Our research about student persistence leans on the work of Vincent Tinto and focuses on belonging, self-efficacy, and meaningful curriculum. (Tinto, 2017). We hoped to enhance and amplify the student perspective by reviewing Tinto's work and other theories for student mattering, connecting, caring, and supporting students. We focused on the student perspective as the best way to determine how and why the culture at our online university should continue to change. According to Tinto (2017), "Universities have to see the issue of persistence through the eyes of their students, hear their voices, engage with their students as partners, learn from their experiences" (p. 6) to understand how they can positively impact student persistence. Given the online modality of our institution, it was essential to understand our learners, what challenges they face, and how that fits within the broader concept of building trust and ensuring faculty engage with students in a way that is meaningful to them.

As staff and faculty of an online institution with a large nontraditional population, we wanted to better understand the experience of the adult learner. We therefore sought to find answers to questions such as how do we, as faculty and staff, impact an adult learner's sense of belonging and know how to support them without seeing them face to face? What are the challenges that students and faculty face in an online environment? How can we show care for our unique student population, thus increasing their connection to the university? How do we build trust in an online accelerated format? What does a meaningful online relationship look like? How can an online institution demonstrate care in a positively impactful way for students?

CONSIDERING CONTEXT: WHAT DO ONLINE LEARNERS WANT OR NEED?

The adult online learner faces unique challenges, especially in an open-access institution, which brings a set of impacts that may not be visible through the computer screen. Adult online learners may come from varying backgrounds and skill levels. Though academic preparedness does play a role in failure to thrive at the college level, non-academic or affective factors (i.e., personal variables such as self-confidence or motivation) present additional challenges (Fowler & Boylan, 2010). With an accelerated online course format and little time to build lasting relationships, students pursuing online education may feel disconnected or unsupported, especially given adult learners' additional obligations (e.g., work and family life). To successfully navigate these challenges, students need adequate support. Though faculty members may be willing to support students, they may not be fully aware of existing resources or opportunities to demonstrate care or identify students who could benefit from additional support services. Students may drop, fail, or even leave the institution because they do not perceive or receive support and flexibility from instructors and staff.

Hierarchy of Needs as Applied to Students

Student persistence is a crucial focus of higher education institutions. As the world changes, so do the needs of our students. Each year may bring about a different challenge for our student body, including increases in mental health concerns, housing, and rising costs. With these changes in mind, we considered Abraham Maslow's (1943) hierarchy of needs and how that might align with our understanding of student behavior. As student's needs change, institutions need to change; utilizing Maslow's hierarchy can help align support with student needs, resulting in academic and personal growth (Miller, 2023.) As we learned more about the levels of Maslow's hierarchy and considered its uses for higher education, we wondered how the online aspect of education might cause challenges in putting the tool into practice.

The assessment and encouragement associated with Maslow's model can positively impact students; however, having limited visibility of the needs and experiences of online students can make this a challenge. How do online institutions show empathy for students if they are not aware of the situation a student is experiencing or have ever experienced a particular situation for themselves? If an institution struggles to assess and provide appropriate resources to support student's physiological and safety needs, this could negatively impact their "sense of social connection and the desire to feel accepted and loved by others" (Miller, W., 2023, p. 2). When students are connected and feel accepted and loved by others, mainly faculty and staff with whom they interact consistently, their ability to build trust and relationships may support them in finding success. Given the limitations or challenges of assessing students who do not interact with faculty and staff face to face, how do institutions determine appropriate support and care?

Maximizing Student Success Retention Through Purposeful Strategies

Research suggests the most effective student retention strategies include practices that consider the expertise of all stakeholders (students, faculty, and staff), with a strong faculty presence (Carey-Butler & Myrick-Harris, 2008). Though much emphasis has been given to the value of innovative technologies and services available to assist students in their educational journey, faculty are the consistent face with whom students interact and therefore central to the student experience (Rhoades, 2012). In a recent focus group conducted among underrepresented first-year students, an evident concern emerged: "In short, students did not believe most college instructors were accessible, clear about their expectations of students, or supportive of their learning (Carrell & Kurlaender, 2020, p. 5). Student success and retention may suffer if instructors and staff fail to engage and support their students adequately. For example, during the pandemic, the need to accommodate online students' needs increased as the number of online learners grew globally. This included relaxing policies on how work was produced and submitted. Some students returned to on-campus courses while online adult learners continued their journey with little change. However, whether online or on campus, students may still feel the impact of lingering and unknown stressors. Therefore, caring instructors and staff should be familiar with academic policies and engage with student services to effectively guide students to the appropriate and necessary resources for success.

Student success and retention are critical concerns for all involved in higher education. The staggering financial costs of failure to graduate impact individual students and their families; the workforce is deprived of an educated pool of candidates; taxpayers bear an added economic burden, and the state and federal governments lose potential income tax gains (Schneider & Yin, 2011). Understanding factors that impact success and retention for adult online learners is therefore paramount.

THE STUDENT VOICE

Throughout our research, we found something was missing, and it was what Tinto (2017) alluded to: the student voice. Increasingly, authors have recognized this perspective's value in improving the educational system (Robinson & Taylor, 2007). While reading theories about belonging, student mattering, and caring in the classroom, we wondered whether anyone had asked students what they felt would be caring, how to build trust, or how to connect them to the university community. With these questions in mind, we created a survey for faculty, staff, and students to understand and bridge the gaps of what care in the online classroom means to each group. By asking what care looked or felt like to them, we hoped to find ways to better connect students to their course, materials, instructor, and institution.

We also focused on better understanding the challenges that faculty face, especially adjunct faculty who may be less connected to the institution than full-time staff and faculty, and finding ways to create meaningful relationships within an online realm. As we analyzed the demographics and the data, we considered the traditional theories that have positively impacted the higher education landscape and conducted our analysis through the lens of our unique student population. With a foundation of traditional educational theories and a perspective of what makes an adult online learner unique, we sought to help refine a caring culture within the classroom that boosts a sense of care and connection to positively impact the UAGC culture by increasing student persistence. This started with analyzing the student voice and the qualities they perceived as caring in the classroom and beyond.

CARE IN THE ONLINE CLASSROOM

While it can be challenging to juggle priorities and responsibilities like work and family, it can help to acknowledge those challenges and receive support from someone who cares. One might hope that staff and faculty recognize the positions of power they hold when teaching or supporting students within the classroom. Adult learners experience unique external impacts and would therefore need a type of care different from what traditional students require.

The adult online learner has external stressors and impacts that, as educators, we may not be privy to and over which they have no control. Situations in which we can identify the need for a student, even when they are not clearly or compellingly advocating for themselves, become key. According to Kathleen Sitzman (2016), a professor from East Carolina University, in her study about student cues that prompt online instructors to offer caring interventions, she found that when a student is struggling academically, reaching out for help, and communicating in a concerning way, these are the cues that should instigate caring interventions (p. 65). Students may not always advocate for themselves clearly and compellingly, so faculty may struggle with understanding the impacts they are experiencing. Instead of responding negatively or judging students who may find themselves failing, shouting, or demanding things in ways that may not feel normal, Sitzman (2016) suggests that these situations be treated as cues for care. These interventions deserve actionable responses from instructors, including offering different communication modalities, quick responses, assurances, and additional clarification for questions (Sitzman, 2016).

Students are more than just a picture or name on a screen. However, each experiences something unique that sets them apart from others and highlights a need for faculty to humanize them, personalize their approach, and attempt to demonstrate empathy. Although flexibility and these types of personalization can be time-consuming and challenging when faculty also face unique obstacles, this is what the student is seeking; this is what can positively impact a student's ability to thrive, engage, and connect with the university community. Moreover, although we may not have experienced these things on our academic journeys, we need to understand that the landscape of higher education is changing and better understand and accept that students' needs are changing too. According to the Student Voice survey by Coleen Flaherty (2023), 3004 students at 128 institutions indicated that the teaching style and action from faculty are the most impactful to success in their programs. Most students outlined concerns about the challenges they face with balancing their schoolwork with their personal and professional lives, challenges that come from keeping positive mental health. Though these students are of more traditional age with fewer external stressors than the adult learners may face, if traditional students are facing challenges with connecting with instructors, they see face-to-face, this trend can be magnified in the online modality simply because student impacts may be unknown as students may not clearly, or compellingly advocate for themselves. This also demonstrates the need to find ways to ask pertinent questions and engage with students to help them move through Maslow's (1943) hierarchical levels. Overall, this trend of students needing more individualized support and care both in on-ground and online institutions shows the importance of understanding the student perspective as we continue to evolve and build on theories associated with student persistence.

Research remains consistent with the survey we conducted and the College Pulse survey. Lynne Zajac (2020) from Northern Kentucky University focused research on student perceptions of faculty presence and care in an accelerated online format. Admitting that the online classroom poses challenges not always experienced in the traditional classroom, they found four themes emerge: students wanted authentic and empathetic communication, timely and respectful feedback, faculty interactions, and investment in student success (Zajac, 2020). Each of these themes highlights some action or feeling that a student would get based on the communication they received, how quickly they received it, and the need for faculty to be "visible to the other student in a fast-paced online environment" (Zajac, 2020, p. 74). This visibility humanizes the faculty member, and the timely responses and availability provided to the student can lead to the assumption that the student would feel more connected and engaged in progressing through the course. These perceptions from students are instrumental in helping to determine ways to consider innovative approaches to curriculum and how to facilitate care in an anonymous environment. Without understanding the student's perspective, lack of care or care applied carelessly can negatively impact the student experience, which may lead to a drop in student persistence.

DEFINITION OF CARE

Meaningful, caring connections between students, instructors, and staff may mitigate academic and non-academic challenges, improving student success and retention. In our view, the vast body of literature exploring the concept of care in the classroom can be distilled to four essential qualities: instructors and staff who CARE lead with *compassion*, taking the time to *acknowledge* the individual student's situation (including challenges and obstacles specific to adult learners pursuing online education), *respect* the unique contributions and strengths of each learner, and *encourage* development and growth toward meeting personal and career-related educational goals.

In recognition of the necessity of crafting intentional, meaningful student-faculty interactions and relationships (Correia & Strehlow, 2018), an efficacious approach will include caring relationships (Buskirk-Cohen & Plants, 2019; Miller, 2007; Olson & Carter, 2014; Walker-Gleaves, 2019). The present research will help identify the exact specifications of how the qualities reflected in CARE (compassion, acknowledgment, respect, and encouragement) can be most meaningfully modeled in instructor and staff behavior to best match student perceptions of care and support, fostering student success and retention.

METHOD

We focused our study on exploring perceptions and realities of CARE (compassion, acknowledgment, respect, and encouragement) in the classroom, from the perspective of both students and faculty, to determine awareness and utilization of support systems for student success and retention that are already in place and identify potential opportunities to expand services, understand the needs of adult online learners, and ways we could further develop the skills of faculty and staff to align with those needs.

This project utilized a convergent parallel mixed-methods design, collecting qualitative and quantitative data from interviews and surveys. This method is appropriate for gathering information from an identified group regarding their thoughts and experiences on a specific topic. The population of interest in this case was the entire UAGC student body. Survey data were collected by inviting students to respond to an anonymous online survey that consisted of closed-ended and open-ended questions regarding perceptions and experiences of CARE in the classroom.

Participants

Participants included 125 students (93 women, 28 men, 1 non-binary, and 1 preferred not to say) at UAGC. On average, they had been attending UAGC for 2.5 years, but they had been attending higher education in general for 7.5 years total. Of these students, 70% were first-generation college students, 74% were parents, and 78% were employed (15 part-time, 83 full-time).

Procedure

A purposeful convenience sample was drawn from students in the Forbes School of Business and Technology, the College of Arts and Sciences, and faculty and staff across UAGC. In the Fall of 2022, faculty received an announcement to share in their classrooms inviting students to participate in an anonymous survey. Participation was voluntary, and students were not compensated for their participation.

Instrument

Participants were asked to consider their current or most recent experience with 1) an instructor and 2) a staff member, indicating on a 7-point Likert-type scale whether that individual demonstrated compassion, acknowledgment, respect, and encouragement. In addition to the overall ratings of CARE, participants answered twelve items designed to identify specific features of care as we had conceptualized it. Rather than rating, participants indicated whether these actions were reflected in their interactions with their current or most recent instructor and staff member. In addition to the quantitative data, students responded to an open-ended question asking, "How else can instructors (staff) show that they care for you?"

Results

Overall, students indicated agreement (on a scale of 1 = *strongly disagree* to 7 = *strongly agree*) with items asking whether the instructor ($M = 5.76$) and staff member ($M = 5.84$) with whom they had most recently interacted demonstrated compassion, acknowledgment, respect, and encouragement (see Table 1).

Table 1. Demonstration of CARE (compassion, acknowledgement, respect, and encouragement) to students by current or most recent instructor and staff

	Instructor $M =$	Staff $M =$
Compassion	**5.64**	**5.81**
Acknowledgment	5.47	5.74
Respect	6.02	5.96
Encouragement	5.92	5.85

Instructors

Regarding instructors, students reported positive experiences (see Table 2). They especially appreciated warm, inviting communication, including knowing their names. Students were least likely to indicate that their instructor thought about them as an individual.

Table 2. How does my instructor care for me?

Communicates in a warm and inviting manner	75%
Knows my name	69%
Identifies support for my academic success	65%
Considers my point of view fairly	64%
Expresses genuine concern regarding my life circumstances	58%
Motivates me	58%
Offers support based on my individual needs	54%
Treats me in a way that helps me feel seen and heard	53%
Values my experience and skills	53%
Inspires me	53%
Recognizes my unique strengths and/or opportunities for growth	49%
Thinks about me as an individual	46%

The emphasis on individuality re-emerged in the qualitative data, in which we asked students to indicate, "How else can instructors show that they care for you?" (see Figure 1). Students shared that individuality and current life circumstances needed to be recognized. For example, one student mentioned, "We are all adults but just knowing that a teacher may understand your current situation helps." Another indicated appreciation for teachers "showing respect for your age and experience." Another student provided the following recommendation: "Make sure the [sic] speak to us as adult [sic] and though we do not have degrees yet know we are intelligent and aware of how they respond to us. As well as understand that we do not have as much free time as they think we do to complete tasks."

Figure 1. Students: How do instructors show they care?

Staff

Regarding staff, students also reported positive experiences (see Table 3). They especially appreciated warm, inviting communication and support based on individual needs. Students were least likely to indicate that their staff member valued their experience and skills or recognized their unique strengths and/or opportunities for growth.

Table 3. How does my staff member care for me?

Communicates in a warm and inviting manner	67%
Offers support based on my individual needs	62%
Knows my name	60%
Identifies support for my academic success	60%
Expresses genuine concern regarding my life circumstances	56%
Considers my point of view fairly	51%
Treats me in a way that helps me feel seen and heard	47%
Thinks about me as an individual	44%
Motivates me	43%
Inspires me	41%
Recognizes my unique strengths and/or opportunities for growth	39%
Values my experience and skills	38%

Understanding the whole person was a theme that emerged in the qualitative data, particularly concerning the openness of staff members to be present and real (see Figure 2). For example, one student mentioned, "Interaction/engagement is important in virtual settings. Just by showing they are virtually active and giving students easier ways to approach them." One student provided the following recommendation: "Be willing to have genuine conversations;" another stated the same sentiment differently: "Show some type of realness when interacting."

Figure 2. Students: How do staff show they care?

Summary

Overall, the data suggest that the Culture of Care we have implemented positively impacts the student experience. What does CARE look and feel like to a student (refer to Figure 1 and Figure 2)? It seems

Creating Care in the Online Classroom

understanding—and support—is vital! For some adult learners, this may look like a phone call, questions about who they are and what they are experiencing. For others, it might be an email that uses their name and even an acknowledgment of something posted in the classroom. For some learners, flexibility may look like an extra day or two to submit work for credit due to a situation at work. To others, there might be an external event or hardship impacting their ability to engage in the course at that time, and they may need the option to extend the course an additional thirty days beyond the original five weeks to find success. CARE is action-oriented, and the challenge becomes a race to actively identify needs, engage promptly, and determine the best way forward for everyone. These results help us consider how we can implement impactful actions that indicate their needs on Malow's (1943) hierarchy are being met and consider our learners as individuals with unique circumstances who need those actions to succeed.

THE UNIQUE CASE OF THE ONLINE LEARNER

As we sought to gather additional student perspectives from our unique population, we wanted to understand the diversity, challenges, and obstacles our learners might face. As a baseline for this understanding, we compared the demographics of The University of Arizona Global Campus (UAGC) versus the traditional on-ground learner admitted to The University of Arizona (UArizona) in 2022 (see Table 4). UArizona had approximately fifty-thousand students enrolled at the institution in 2022; 66% self-identified as White, and 6.7% as Black or African-American; 26.5% were above the age of twenty-five; and 50.6% were Arizona residents. Twenty-five percent of students were Pell Grant recipients, which indicates their economic status (The University of Arizona, 2023). In contrast, The University of Arizona Global Campus, which is strictly online, had approximately twenty-three thousand students enrolled in 2022; 41% identified as White and 30% as Black or African-American; 87% were above the age of 25; and 5.6% of students were Arizona residents. Fifty percent of students were Pell Grant Recipients at UAGC (The University of Arizona Global Campus, 2023). Based on the demographic information alone, we can see differences in age, ethnicity, geographical location, and financial status. We can then differentiate the challenges adult learners might face compared to traditional students.

Table 4. UA vs. UAGC student demographics, 2022

	University of Arizona	University of Arizona Global Campus
	%	%
Ethnicity		
White	66	30
Black or African-American	6.7	41
Age		
Under 25	73.5	13
25+	26.5	87
Arizona Resident	50.6	5.6
Pell Grant Recipient	25.1	50

Non-College Life Events

We can recognize that adult learners may face additional stressors or impacts that typical traditional students do not. Cox and colleagues (2016) focused their research on what they considered to be non-college life events, which they defined as "events occurring outside the control of the institution that are likely to cause a change in a student's relationships, routines, assumptions, or roles" (p.7). These events include external stressors that college students face, but do adult online learners face the same challenges? The biggest difference they found for traditional-aged college students was that they tend to have more familial, cultural, and financial support. Their work pointed to the most significant external stressors stemming from students whose parents separated or experienced financial trouble. However, based on the UAGC student demographics, we can assume that online adult learners navigate more pressures and stressors from their own familial and financial situations and not necessarily from their parent's situation.

Feedback From the Academic Resolution Process

To help us better understand whether our assumptions were on track, we reviewed student feedback shared with us through the academic resolution process at UAGC. The academic resolution process "provides students with an opportunity to seek redress of academic concerns to ensure their instructional experience represents a fair and consistent evaluation of student performance" (University of Arizona Global Campus, 2023, para. 1). In this process, students engage with staff members to better understand the situation and determine the best support and resources and resolution outcomes that best serve the needs of the institution and the individual. The outcomes from these areas help UAGC determine those factors or non-college life events that adult online learners tend to experience, which negatively impact their ability to find success in the classroom.

Through the academic resolution process, students can challenge a final letter grade in a course or report a concern about an instructor or course (The University of Arizona Global Campus, 2023, para. 6). The process helps Student Affairs staff better understand the student experience as each resolution request includes a comprehensive review of the concerns along with a consultation which is a learning opportunity for all parties. For staff, the goals are to understand the request better, facilitate connections to appropriate support services and resources, and determine potential resolution options, if applicable. For students, the goals are to identify appropriate resources and resolution pathways, gain a deeper understanding of policies and expectations at UAGC, and help them feel heard and valued, which can help them better connect with the university community.

Generally, the feedback we reviewed consisted of obstacles from every imaginable perspective. The online adult learner enrolled at UAGC may face homelessness, medical impacts (personal or family), multiple jobs, deaths, and everything else. With most UAGC students over the age of 25 using the Pell Grant, we can understand that their experience and external stressors differ from a typical traditional student focused solely on their academic journey. Although these are only snapshots of the situations and experiences adult learners at our institution face, we can safely assume that consistent events happening outside of the classroom directly impact an adult online learner's ability to find success in the classroom. When these non-college life events occur, students may not be able to successfully submit an assignment, meet deadlines, engage in online discussions, or complete their coursework in a way that demonstrates their true abilities. When a student experiences external stressors, they may engage in the academic resolution process to seek additional support if they believe they did not receive the support necessary to meet the course's learning outcomes.

Through the academic resolution process, we have seen many successes. We define success as providing the student in need the ability or opportunity to engage with (or re-engage with) the classroom materials to reach the course learning outcomes. This could be through an opportunity to revise and resubmit an assignment or a chance to submit an assignment that the student missed, all for a potential revised letter grade at the end of the course. It also might be an opportunity for the student to receive additional feedback that meets them where they are so they can utilize that moving forward to find success. In each of these situations, students may have initially requested support from their instructor and failed.

What the Students Tell Us

When reviewing the student feedback in the academic resolution process from 2022, we found that out of 420 requests received, 66% of students reported concerns about the grading or feedback received in the course. Fifty-nine percent related to alleged policy violations or support not provided within the expectations for faculty and courses. Moreover, 27% of students reported hardships, which we equate to non-college life events, in which the student reported that extenuating circumstances prevented them from having an opportunity to operate within the classroom expectations and University policy. Similar to what we assumed based on the demographics alone, students experience impacts outside of the classroom for many reasons. The academic resolution data shows that students may need more support during the course to meet the learning outcomes. At the same time, students may be experiencing an external stressor, not sharing that with the instructor, and are not able to engage in the accelerated classroom in a way that demonstrates their abilities. After in-depth conversations with students, we found that students reaching out via email are both hesitant to share their stories and unable to articulate or advocate for themselves clearly and compellingly, and faculty struggle to find ways to support student success or identify an individualized approach that shows that individual that they care.

Overall, the data we have reviewed has supported the idea that the adult learner is a unique student population, and they experience numerous non-college life events. They are navigating and balancing different priorities daily, unlike a traditional-age learner whose sole focus may be only on their academics. Flexibility has become one way UAGC has aimed to focus its cultural shift, providing students with additional time or chances to overcome their external obstacles and find ways to meet those learning outcomes. Although it is not always easy to determine how much time would support student success depending on the individual impact they might be experiencing, even the smallest amount of flexibility in an accelerated format could lessen the stress adult learners experience.

The debate on whether providing flexibility impacts academic rigor in classrooms has caused challenges with embracing this cultural shift. This idea of flexibility stemmed from the pandemic in which "many professors sought to decrease the logistical demands they put on students, relaxing their policies about how work was produced and when it was handed in" (Supiano, 2023, para 16). Many institutions sought ways to lessen the physical and mental impacts on students during the pandemic. Although the external impacts and stressors students felt during the pandemic were unprecedented, it is not too far-fetched to understand that adult online learners, including those who struggle economically, may continue to feel those stressors and experience unknown impacts that limit their ability to engage with their courses successfully. Although the height of the pandemic is over, the long-lasting effects are still unknown, and flexibility is still needed for students. However, the idea of providing flexibility is not always embraced. Academic rigor is defined as the grade a student receives or how much time is spent on a given assignment (Supiano, 2023). In that case, flexibility can change how we consider student outcomes in a course. Moreover, with the concerns higher education staff and faculty have raised regarding rigor and flexibility, we were determined to find additional ways to define our culture of care through actions beyond flexible timelines. However, though we understand that the online adult learner may experience non-college life events that impact their ability to succeed, we can also safely assume that online faculty, especially adjunct faculty, face unique challenges that limit or hinder their ability to give time and space (and thought) to individual student circumstances and find ways to show they care.

FACULTY PERSPECTIVES AND CHALLENGES

All faculty at UAGC have been onboarded and introduced to the online classroom, policies, and procedures, and the unique characteristics of the adult online learner. Most faculty have also been introduced to the idea of this culture of care and have embraced attempts to build relationships and support specific student situations. With this training, we ask faculty to navigate technical challenges and policies they may need help understanding and be the front line for student situations. The question we began to ask is what challenges faculty face that could impact their ability to engage and support students in the way that most benefit the student. Often, we consider the student's needs and create resources and support pathways for them. However, what do faculty need, how can they get support when they do not know how to guide and direct students, and how do they bring their best self to each interaction?

Catherine Adams from the University of Alberta and Ellen Rose from the University of New Brunswick joined to explore connecting with students. Their phenomenological research explored care through the stories of instructors in an online institution (2014). Their work focused on areas like availability, student demands, work/life balance, and the solitude of online work. The story from the instructors highlights that teaching online involves "constant tinkering and attention" (Adams, 2014, p. 13), and this "demanding quality sometimes imparts itself through messages from students, which may be experienced as a relentless bombardment from faceless entities, rather than a means of connecting with other individuals" (Adams, 2014, p. 13). If faculty struggle to humanize students due to the anonymity and ability to hide behind a screen, how would they impart a caring tone or support? Can we humanize students through the online modality, or does the modality itself cause the issues?

For adjunct faculty who may work a full-time job outside of the classroom and conduct their teaching responsibilities late at night after a long day of balancing work and family, how they approach their mental well-being and connection to the institution can have a direct impact on their communication and engagement with their classrooms. One of the instructor's stories from Adams and Rose's (2014) research focuses on "the duties of reading and responding to discussion posts may be experienced as a continuation of an already busy day into the evening and the night" (p. 11). We all know how it feels to come home after a long day of work, family, or anything else and devote ourselves entirely to another responsibility. In this case, adjunct faculty must have the luxury of turning off for the evening. Although students may be experiencing the same thing, the screen tends to amplify that disconnect and lack of empathy for others. Faculty may feel bombarded by written text in the form of emails and discussion posts by students "without faces" (Adams, 2014, p. 11). Our survey results indicate that this is different from the care students seek. They want to be recognized for their individuality and for there to be an understanding and support for their unique situations.

Creating Care in the Online Classroom

The reality of anonymity can cause a disconnect, leading to terse, direct communication, and lacking a component of caring for the human on the other side of the screen. The more students struggle with the technology or the concept of their paper, the more they may reach out for support. The more faculty must manage all aspects of the classroom, including their unique challenges, situations, and demands for their attention, the more we can assume that it is likely that faculty will not always take the additional steps and time needed to show care in a way that meets a student where they are.

Faculty may also encounter students needing technical or writing skills to succeed. With the world amplifying and focusing on informal written communication, we may experience more formal writing in classes, specifically in discussion forums. In these cases, faculty become more focused on helping students navigate basic-level skills and take time away from the content meant to move the course forward. The more students' needs take away from the classroom experience, the more likely faculty will forget their own needs, possibly leading to potential burnout (Adams, 2014). With this burnout, care for themselves, and students becomes strained and limited. As higher education continues to change due to student needs, we must remember the effect that may have on our faculty pool. If faculty do not feel cared for, how can they inspire care and trust, demonstrate empathy, and effectively support students?

Although this chapter has focused on the non-college life events that our adult learners may face, faculty, especially adjunct faculty working multiple roles across multiple institutions, might face their own events and impacts outside the classroom. The challenges faculty face tend to stem from their need to be a faculty, mentor, coach, counselor, technical support, and available anytime. Although the needs of students will continue to evolve, the need for supporting faculty should, too. Keeping these challenges for faculty in mind can help to find ways to take a breath, find a positive workspace and routine, and even lean on colleagues to ensure that the challenges faculty face do not negatively impact the classroom experience for the student.

ONLINE COMMUNICATION

With the challenges that online learning and teaching can bring, we found it essential to focus on ways communication can undermine the student and instructor relationship. Online communication already comes with complications, so adding the human component can make or break the engagement and focus of an adult online learner. For example, a faculty member at Texas A & M University at Commerce informed the students in his course via email that they could fail the course due to the use of ChatGPT. Although there are broad concerns about the ability to concretely identify the use of AI in assignments, students were told they would not complete the course should any AI be found (Verma, 2023). A student spoke with the Washington Post, stating that the "accusation sent her into a frenzy," and "the thought of [her] hard work not being acknowledged, and [her] character being questioned" caused frustrations (Verma, 2023, para. 5-7). This is just one example of the negative impact online communication can have if students are treated as anonymous names behind a screen. In this case, the fear that faculty felt for this modern technology and the challenges they faced in grading assignments manifested in accusations and lack of empathy and opportunity for understanding. The student did not feel valued or respected, and according to Maslow's hierarchy of needs, if a student does not feel accepted or connected to others within the institution, this can limit their ability to feel a "sense of self-worth, recognition, and respect from others" (Miller, W. 2023, p. 3). This lack of reaching the fourth level of Maslow's hierarchy could impact students' engagement and desire to continue their education.

It is common to see conflicts arise when navigating concerns around plagiarism; however, the instructor's alarming response and reaction led to less substantive feedback and more accusatory communication toward students. Without an opportunity to engage in understanding or treat the student as someone who could have made a mistake or needed a teachable moment, more punitive action caused confusion and panic in students. We then see a rise in defensiveness and students reacting to the accusations and lack of feedback by calling the instructor names and shutting down all future opportunities to engage in a meaningful way to learn and find success. These students do not feel cared for, do not feel valued, and are not given a chance to identify needs or opportunities for understanding, which could negatively impact their engagement and desire to persist in their programs.

STUDENT MATTERING AND TRUST

Our service and the learning environment we create for our students positively impact their learning and future success. It is vital to understand how our students perceive situations, like our communication and feedback, how they view relationships we have established with them, the learning environments we create, and how we teach to reach them. These are just some reasons we conducted our research on this topic. As we lead in our academic and personal lives, it is important to pause, evaluate, and consider what we can do better, whether that be our communication, mental health, work/life balance, and/or understanding of student impacts and experiences. Leading with care, empathy, and acting with compassion can help meet students where they are which can help build trust and self-efficacy, and it shapes an environment that furthers learning. According to Schlossberg's research (1989) on mattering theory, he concludes that people's beliefs are important to them and that they are objects of their attention and deserve care and appreciation. In a collegiate environment, it is important that our students feel they matter and that their instructor and their university community care about them as a person. Suppose students feel cared for through communication, interactions, feedback, and support. In that case, they will trust that they are in a space that works for them, which can positively affect their engagement and motivation.

If establishing trust in the online classroom positively impacts student engagement and motivation, it can positively impact student progression, persistence, and success. Building positive connections with them helps faculty help students transcend negative beliefs and creates a positive experience of belonging by reducing unacceptable feelings (Schlossberg, 1989). Schlossberg (1989) believes that everyone feels marginal sometimes, and focusing on the four dimensions of mattering theory can help instructors connect with their students and develop meaningful relationships. The four dimensions include attention, importance, ego-extension, and dependence. If students are given attention and instructors are sensitive to their needs, they will feel more connected and supported. By showing interest in student success, providing supportive and honest feedback, and following through with what faculty say they will do, students will feel those actionable care responses, which will help them feel more connected and more driven to find success. Just as the survey results and feedback we received from students in the academic resolution process, these are action-oriented and can be felt by students. Mattering theory aligns well with the student voices we heard and the research we have conducted and should be used as a guide to help faculty find ways to put their active listening into action so that they can build meaningful relationships.

Building and sustaining trust in the online classroom is essential to student success. Displaying a positive instructor presence and making a positive impression is significant and lasting. According to Janelle Cox (n.d), "Trust is the foundation of any relationship, and it is one of the most important things for a teacher to develop with their students" (p. 1). Our research shows that when students trust their teachers and their peers, they are more likely to engage in the learning process, take risks, and share their ideas and thoughts openly. By showing students we lead with care by example and treating them as humans who can make mistakes, we are showing students we are committed and dedicated to their success. If we work to earn the students' respect and trust, and they know that what they perceive and experience matters, the more they will engage in the classroom meaningfully.

MEANINGFUL ONLINE RELATIONSHIPS

It is not only essential to build trust in our online classrooms, but we also need to build relationships with students and across departments throughout the university. Similar to the relationships built across Student Affairs and Faculty in this group of researchers, these positive working relationships strengthen our system and further student success. The University of Arizona Global Campus is one team, and we all collaborate to find ways to further student success. The vision of UAGC is to empower, enrich, support, and graduate our students; this is always at the core of what we do (The University of Arizona Global Campus, 2023). Harvard Business School and author of renowned leadership and strategy books, Dr. Rosabeth Moss Kanter (2007), stated that it is crucial to understand that principles are fundamental and moral. She provided three principles for changing times that are still relevant today: "1) Have a higher sense of purpose, 2) Be open to experience, and 3) Find common ground" (11:31). We believe that Dr. Kanter's framework and principles fit in an online environment. It is important to understand our purpose as educators and to commit and remain dedicated to what we do for our students. As faculty and staff, they see their university's vision, and they should align, embrace, and serve. They support and work to achieve their vision, mission, and purpose, and contribute to their own culture of care. They should be committed and dedicated to serving and supporting their students and committed to providing them with a meaningful and gratifying learning experience. They should want to be there to support them even after their education ends.

Some ways to focus on and form meaningful relationships through actions include being authentic, engaging in conversations, and leading with and showing empathy. Faculty and staff should not use the anonymity of the computer screen to empower them to react negatively and carelessly to communication from a student that may be harsh or demanding. Instead, they should act in the way they would in person. Showing their personalities and being mindful of others can speak volumes about who they are, which can limit assumptions. Participating in online communities and dialogues allows them to show interest in what others say, ask questions, and lessen their own bias and assumptions about their students (Davis & Korpi, 2022). Although empathy might look different online than in person, it is important to be mindful and seek to understand others' perspectives and feelings, especially when in an online university community that can lead itself to make judgments based on avatars, images, and written text.

As meaningful participants in a university community, members are responsible for being open to diverse cultures, perspectives, and ideologies, as that can help us grow as individuals. It is also important to be respectful, supportive, and forgiving. Respect can be subjective, so it is better to be curious, respect others' beliefs, opinions, and values, and attempt to avoid instigating arguments, attacking, or judging others. It is also important to offer support and encouragement to others who may be going through something. As an online institution, knowing what is happening outside of the classroom is impossible. Considering the information about our student population we shared earlier and other impacts the world has experienced, like the pandemic, we can safely assume that something is constantly occurring outside the classroom. Our survey results support that students want action and encouragement, including sending them a message and letting them know someone is there for them (Davis & Korpi, 2022). Although the unknown can bring about anxiety or fear and even trigger biases due to a lack of face-to-face interactions, it can be helpful to remember that relationships may encounter misunderstandings, and mistakes will happen. Intentionally practicing forgiveness and empathy, remaining curious, and moving past the issues to find favorable resolutions can support a caring relationship, even in the most challenging times.

Bringing together so many anonymous people from varying backgrounds and cultures, especially at a Global Campus, it is essential to be open-minded, share individual experiences, invest time in oneself and students, and find ways to make a more human connection. As we all work with people who may not have the same experiences, background, or culture, it is important to be open to different ideas, perspectives, and beliefs and not be too quick to dismiss or judge others. Sharing experiences helps create opportunities to connect and find similarities. This can also help create a deeper connection to build trust and understanding (Schlossberg, 1989). Furthermore, getting out from behind the screen and connecting over the phone, in person, or even via a Zoom call can help humanize each person and strengthen bonds.

Each suggestion above takes time, and as we discussed, students and faculty face challenges within the online realm. Do faculty have time to invest in each student as an individual while trying to also care for themselves? Do students have the time to invest in themselves and with each faculty member within an accelerated classroom? Although time may not be on the side of the faculty or the student, we have some compelling information that focuses on action. How do we take what we have learned from theories like a hierarchy of needs, student mattering, and student persistence supporting the positive effects of belonging and self-efficacy and move beyond that to focus on what students say they need to succeed?

CONCLUSION AND RECOMMENDATIONS

Student persistence is important, and universities need to continue to find ways to help students feel a sense of connection, engagement, and support that is meaningful to them. Higher Education Institutions that are solely online may have additional challenges beyond what more traditional institutions might face. Recognizing and understanding the adult online learner experience and perspective is only the first step in identifying ways to help students reach their goal of graduation. Throughout our research, we identified the unique challenges adult online learners face and the expectation that non-college life events are a reality for these students. We also identified that faculty and staff can support an adult learner's sense of belonging without seeing them face to face by asking questions, being action-oriented, treating them as individuals, and listening to students about their experiences and what might be most meaningful to them. Overall, students at online institutions want to be something other than faceless names; they want faculty and staff to be aware and open to their unique situations, provide flexible deadlines, connect them with resources, acknowledge their challenges, and treat them as human beings.

Building trust in an online accelerated format is a challenge, but it includes providing substantive, individualized, and empathetic communication. Helping students feel that they matter can help connect them to the institution and motivate them to engage with the materials and course. Trust and student mattering are a starting point for building meaningful online relationships. An institution can demonstrate care by building an internal community that works together with students as the focus. Being authentic and engaging in conversations with students can help lessen judgments and allow students to feel safe and appreciated, even when mistakes or life events occur. Online institutions can help adult learners develop skills, reach their educational goals, and support them in achieving their career aspirations. Moving past the images and words on a computer screen can humanize the experience for students and instructors and create a positively impactful university community.

Online faculty, especially adjunct faculty, face challenges in connecting to their institution, ensuring they practice self-care, and navigating the ever-growing role of what it means to teach today's students. The following steps include creating resources and training to support faculty and staff's ability to provide a more individualized approach to engaging with students. The Culture of Care at UAGC identified the need for flexibility for students as it is the first step. However, to move forward we need to listen to the student voice and find more ways to humanize them yet support their busy lives. We also need to find ways to humanize faculty and staff and determine ways to move the needle away from transactional efficiencies and focus on supporting and understanding the individual. Is this shift difficult and does it take more time? Yes, but it can be done.

As each faculty and staff member connects to the institutional purpose, they need to lean on their community to find ways to create trusting and meaningful relationships. The better we understand the ins and outs of the university, the better we can serve any unique student need. The more we are patient and remain curious rather than judgmental, the more we can understand something we may not have experienced ourselves. The more we seek a positive resolution and communicate with empathy the more the students will feel valued. The power of anonymity can be diminished when we take the time to understand and recognize our student population and the uniqueness of the online modality. As we continue to unmask the students we serve, the more we are likely to lessen our reactions and personalize our solutions.

REFERENCES

Adams, C., & Rose, E. (2014). Will I ever connect with the students?" Online teaching and the pedagogy of care. *Phenomenology & Practice*, 8(1), 5–16. doi:10.29173/pandpr20637

Buskirk-Cohen, A. A., & Plants, A. (2019). Caring about success: Students' perceptions of professors' caring matters more than grit. *International Journal on Teaching and Learning in Higher Education*, 31(1), 108–114. https://files.eric.ed.gov/fulltext/EJ1206948.pdf

Carey-Butler, S., & Myrick-Harris, C. (2008, November 21-22). *Faculty's role in student success: Engagement in and outside of the classroom* [Conference presentation]. Defining and Promoting Student Success: A National Symposium, San Francisco, CA.

Carrell, S. E., & Kurlaender, M. (2020). *My professor cares: Experimental evidence on the role of faculty engagement* (Working Paper Series No. w27312). National Bureau of Economic Research. https://www.nber.org/system/files/working_papers/w27312/w27312.pdf

Correia, H. M., & Strehlow, K. (2018). Mindful care and compassion in higher education: Cultivating communities of practice. In N. Lemon & S. McDonough (Eds.), *Mindfulness in the academy: Practices and perspectives from scholars* (pp. 189–202). Springer. doi:10.1007/978-981-13-2143-6_12

Cox, B. E., Reason, R. D., Nix, S., & Gillman, M. (2016). Life happens (outside of college): Non-college life-events and students' likelihood of graduation. *Research in Higher Education, 57*(7), 823–844. doi:10.100711162-016-9409-z

Cox, J. (n.d.). *How to build trust with students.* Western Governors University. https://www.wgu.edu/heyteach/article/how-build-trust-students1808.html

Davis, B., & Korpi, S. (2022). Authentic human connection: Coaching with care to promote student perceptions of belonging. *UAGC Chronicle*, (Winter Issue), 2022.

Flaherty, C. (2023, March 23) What students want (and don't) from their professors. *Inside Higher Ed College Pulse.* https://www.insidehighered.com/news/2023/03/24/survey-faculty-teaching-style-impedes-academic-success-students-say

Fowler, P. R., & Boylan, H. R. (2010). Increasing student success and retention: A multidimensional approach. *Journal of Developmental Education, 34*(2), 2. https://files.eric.ed.gov/fulltext/EJ986268.pdf

Kanter, R. (2007). *Enduring principles for changing times.* Long Now Foundation. https://www.youtube.com/watch?v=ga0VXYlbK7M

Maslow, A. H. (1943). A theory of human motivation. *Psychological Review, 50*(4), 370–396. doi:10.1037/h0054346

Miller, A. S. (2007). *Students that persist: Caring relationships that make a difference in higher education.* https://files.eric.ed.gov/fulltext/ED497500.pdf

Miller, W. (2023, May 25). Maslow's hierarchy in action: How student affairs can use the framework for better assessment of well-being. *Student Affairs Assessment Leaders.* http://studentaffairsassessment.org/entries/announcements/maslow-s-hierarchy-in-action-how-student-affairs-can-use-the-framework-for-better-assessment-of-wellbeing

Olson, J. N., & Carter, J. A. (2014). Caring and the college professor. *National Forum Journals: Focus on Colleges, Universities, and Schools, 8*(1), 1-9. http://www.nationalforum.com/Electronic%20Journal%20Volumes/Olson,%20James%20Caring%20and%20the%20College%20Professor%20FOCUS%20V8%20N1%202014.pdf

Rhoades, G. (2012). *Faculty engagement to enhance student attainment* [White paper]. National Commission on Higher Education Attainment. https://www.acenet.edu/news-room/Documents/Faculty-Engagement-to-EnhanceStudent-Attainment--Rhoades.pdf

Robinson, C., & Taylor, C. (2007). Theorizing student voice: Values and perspectives. *Improving Schools, 10*(1), 5–17. doi:10.1177/1365480207073702

Schlossberg, N. K. (1989). Marginality and mattering: Key issues in building community. *New Directions for Student Services, 48*(1), 5–15. doi:10.1002s.37119894803

Schneider, M., & Yin, L. (2011). *The high cost of low graduation rates: How much does dropping out of college really cost?* American Institutes for Research. https://files.eric.ed.gov/fulltext/ED523102.pdf

Sitzman, K. L. (2016). What student cues prompt online instructors to offer caring interventions? *Nursing Education Perspectives*, *37*(2), 61–71. doi:10.5480/14-1542 PMID:27209863

Supiano, B. (2022, March 29). The redefinition of rigor. *The Chronicle of Higher Education*. https://www.chronicle.com/article/the-redefinition-of-rigor

The University of Arizona. (2023a) *Interactive Factbook: Enrollment*. https://uair.arizona.edu/content/enrollment

The University of Arizona. (2023b). *Interactive Factbook: Academic College Diversity*. https://uair.arizona.edu/content/academic-college-diversity

The University of Arizona Global Campus. (2023a). *About UAGC*. https://www.uagc.edu/about

The University of Arizona Global Campus. (2023b). *Academic Resolution*. https://www.uagc.edu/catalog/student-rights-responsibilities/academic-resolution

The University of Arizona Global Campus. (2023c). *Student Rights and Responsibilities*. https://www.uagc.edu/student-experience/rights-responsibilities

The University of Arizona Global Campus. (2023d). *Institutional Data at UAGC*. https://www.uagc.edu/institutional-data

Tinto, V. (2017). Reflections on student persistence. *Student Success.*, *8*(2), 1–8. doi:10.5204sj.v8i2.376

Verma, P. (2023, May 18). A professor accused his class of using ChatGPT, putting diplomas in jeopardy. *The Washington Post*. https://www.washingtonpost.com/technology/2023/05/18/texas-professor-threatened-fail-class-chatgpt-cheating/

Walker-Gleaves, C. (2019). Is caring pedagogy really so progressive? Exploring the conceptual and practical impediments to operationalizing care in higher education. In P. Gibbs & A. Peterson (Eds.), *Higher Education and Hope* (pp. 93–112). Palgrave Macmillan. doi:10.1007/978-3-030-13566-9_5

Zajac, C. (2020). *Outstanding first year teacher perceptions*. Northeastern University Library. doi:10.17760/D20350267

KEY TERMS AND DEFINITIONS

Academic Resolution: A process at The University of Arizona that provides students an opportunity to seek redress of academic concerns to ensure their instructional experience represents a fair and consistent evaluation of student performance.

Adjunct Faculty: A part-time faculty member hired on a contractual basis.

Adult Online Learner: Adults (typically age 25 and over) with a wide range of educational and professional experiences who choose to return to school and take online classes for the flexibility to maintain work and family responsibilities; also known as "non-traditional students."

Culture of Care: A culture promoting greater flexibility and a more individualized approach to faculty engagement with students.

Hardship(s): Extenuating circumstance(s) that prevented a student from having an opportunity to operate within classroom expectations and University policy.

Non-College Life Events: Events that occur outside of the collegiate classroom that impacts a student's ability to engage positively.

Pell Grant Recipients: Awarded to students who display exceptional financial need.

Self-Efficacy: An individual's belief in their capacity to complete actions necessary to achieve goals.

Chapter 6
Cultivating Cultural Competence and Meaningful Bonds in the Virtual Classroom Using a Narrative Approach

Selin Philip
Colorado Christian University, USA

Shalini Mathew
https://orcid.org/0000-0001-7640-8449
Northern State University, USA

ABSTRACT

The narrative theoretical approach to content delivery is a powerful tool for educators and students to cultivate their cultural competencies and meaningful connections in the virtual classroom. By utilizing this approach, students can gain a deeper understanding and appreciation for their peers' diverse perspectives and experiences while nurturing community and belonging among themselves. Drawing upon current research, the chapter focuses on exploring the significance of cultural competence and fluency in establishing meaningful connections in online education. It introduces a novel approach to cultivating cultural competence and meaningful connections in the virtual classroom by providing practical examples of narratives and cultural content. It also includes a range of assignments and a case study that highlight different cultural perspectives and experiences, further reinforcing the importance of cultural understanding and empathy in virtual educational settings.

"Welcome to the online classroom!" has become the mantra of modern-day academia. The traditional face-to-face teaching method has given way to the integration of virtual or online teaching and learning. Online education differs greatly from typical in-person classroom instruction. We have seen how the internet has changed educational delivery methods by enabling universal access to education regardless of one's location. Educators and students now have new ways to communicate due to the use of

DOI: 10.4018/978-1-6684-8908-6.ch006

technology in the classroom. However, in this virtual realm, where physical proximity is not required, intentional efforts to establish and cultivate meaningful connections are essential for an effective educational experience. In the absence of committed efforts to establish instructor-student and student-student relationships, decreased student retention and a decline in the overall quality of online education loom large. Due to the impersonal nature of online interactions, strengthening a sense of community, belonging, and involvement among students and instructors is necessary. As educators, we cannot underestimate the significance of collaboration and the pedagogical approach of collective learning in online education.

STORYTELLING TO CLASSROOM CONNECTIONS

Vygotsky (1962) asserts that interaction is fundamental to shaping meaningful learning experiences. This applies to both traditional face-to-face and virtual learning environments. According to constructivist theory, engaging in social learning within a group setting holds considerable significance as it enables students to actively collaborate and acquire the essential skills of co-constructing knowledge (Brindley et al., 2009). This approach rises above cultural differences and promotes an inclusive learning environment. *Storytelling* is a constructivist pedagogical technique that is culturally inclusive and has a powerful influence on creating meaningful connections (Gunawardena, 2021). The impact of stories on humans is significant, affecting them at intellectual, emotional, and relational levels. In education, stories are essential for aiding in the transfer and retention of knowledge and fostering deep bonds between students and teachers. Why do stories hold such power? The answer points to their ability to align seamlessly with the human thought process, information processing and absorption, self-perception, and the ability to influence others. Scholars have reported that when information is presented in a narrative form, it is stored in memory as fragments that can be easily retrieved as a whole (Baldwin & Ching, 2017; Black & Bower, 1979). By weaving new information into the fabric of a story, students can connect it with their existing knowledge, and it helps with comprehension and retention (Baldwin & Ching, 2017; Liston, 1994).

Storytelling has a remarkable capability to help students navigate and make sense of unfamiliar concepts by relating them to their past experiences and understanding. Through the reflective process of engaging with a story, students actively construct meaning by synthesizing the information presented (Baldwin & Ching, 2017). The story's narrative structure serves a cognitive function, and it allows students to store and comprehend the information effectively while also developing a coherent understanding of the world around them (Baldwin & Ching, 2017; Bers & Cassell, 1998).

THE PURPOSE OF THE CHAPTER

Stories remain a dynamic force even in this digital age, as human brains have not evolved as rapidly as technology. As a result, storytelling continues to be one of the most successful ways to engage students, and the key is to identify the narratives that resonate deeply with each individual student. The narrative theoretical approach to content delivery is a powerful tool for educators and students to cultivate their cultural competencies and explore how stories align with the natural processes of human thinking, information processing, self-perception, and social influence. Narrative theory is a valuable framework for understanding cultural competence in online education. According to narrative theory, people construct their reality through the stories they tell themselves and others (Morris, 2006). The stories, or narratives, represent their reality, which is unique, personal, subjective, and open to change (Prochaska & Norcross, 2018). From a constructivist viewpoint and recognizing the value of diverse narratives, the narrative approach can promote understanding and empathy among students and educators from diverse cultural backgrounds. Utilizing personal narratives can enhance cultural competence online by providing opportunities for students to learn about various cultural perspectives and experiences.

The narrative approach can also help students understand and appreciate their peers' diverse perspectives and experiences while nurturing community and belonging among students from various cultural backgrounds. Researchers (Gopalan & Brady, 2019; Gopalan et al., 2022; Murphy, 2002) have indicated that students' sense of belonging is a significant factor in their retention in and completion of the program and better mental health outcomes. This matter carries particular importance for first-generation college students and students from racial minority backgrounds (Gopalan & Brady, 2019; Gopalan et al., 2022; Murphy, 2022). Additionally, online courses can incorporate narratives and cultural content that promote cultural competence. These online courses can include case studies, videos, and other multimedia materials highlighting cultural perspectives and experiences. By exposing students to various cultural narratives, they can better understand and appreciate different cultural perspectives, values, and beliefs (Landrum et al, 2019).

Drawing upon current research, in this chapter we focus on exploring the significance of cultural competence and fluency in establishing meaningful connections in online education. To provide a structured and well-defined approach to content delivery, we introduce storytelling from a narrative theoretical perspective to cultivate cultural competence and meaningful connections. The crucial aspect is considering the communication factors that are most advantageous for promoting interaction and facilitating students' learning.

BACKGROUND AND LITERATURE REVIEW

The Strengths and Challenges of Virtual Classroom

Online education, usually referred to as virtual education, has become a common way to provide instruction in higher education. It offers more flexibility than the in-person classroom; however, some studies have found that online students' dropout rate is higher than in traditional classroom settings (Allen & Seaman, 2011; Angelino et al., 2007; Herbert, 2006). Recent studies suggest that even with the surge in online learners, the success of students in online learning environment has been diminishing (Hamann, 2021), and undergraduate students generally performed better in and preferred traditional face-to-face classes than online learning (Spencer & Temple, 2021). Consequently, there is a growing consensus among researchers urging universities to implement strategies aimed at enhancing the online student community's success (Hamann et al., 2021; Seery et al., 2021).

Additionally, current literature highlights social, technological, and motivational challenges for students and instructors in online education (Seery et al., 2021). Instructors face challenges establishing meaningful relationships with online students, leading to decreased engagement, lower quality work, and lower overall student satisfaction (Martin, 2019). The lack of direct interaction between a teacher and a student reduces opportunities for impromptu, informative feedback (Cela et al., 2016). In certain programs, rather than receiving verbal instructions from the instructor, students are expected to read written instructions. This disconnect can cause frustration for many students. Thus, relationship-building is crucial in the virtual classroom, as its absence can impact the educational experience significantly.

Furthermore, higher education has the potential to diversify and broaden the workforce (Gordon & Whitchurch, 2009); however, traditional in-person programs present hurdles for individuals facing social, physical, geographical, or economic challenges. Online education, on the other hand, offers more versatility regarding the method and location of learning, allowing students to integrate their studies with work, family responsibilities, and other personal obligations (Moessenlechner et al., 2015). Considering this scenario, how might virtual learning platforms attract and support a more diverse student population, potentially leading to a more diverse workforce?

According to Palloff and Pratt (2013), the online learning environment has the potential to be a highly effective platform for teaching and learning. They suggest innovative approaches and interpersonal connections within this arena that can significantly enhance the learning experience. To fully utilize the educational potential of online platforms, instructors should receive training in technology usage and adapt their instructional methods and delivery approaches to empower the student learning process and nurture a sense of community and collaboration among them.

Culturally Competent Connections in the Classroom

Cultural competence is crucial to forming meaningful relationships in in-person and online educational environments. It refers to a person's ability to interact effectively, be sensitive to cultural differences, work well in a team, and establish trusting relationships with people from different cultural backgrounds. Cultural competence involves an empathetic understanding of various cultural groups and their distinct beliefs, traditions, and practices (Deardorff & Jones, 2009). Cultural competency is skill-based (Sue, 1998), and acquiring cultural competence is a continuous journey that involves enhancing self-awareness, refining social awareness and skills related to diversity, and supporting others.

Developing cultural competence is a prerequisite for meaningful connections in a group environment (de Hei et.al., 2020). In the virtual classroom, it can lead to more accepting and respectful online interactions, improved communication, and less or no misunderstandings and conflicts. Through cultural empathy and responsiveness, students and instructors can build stronger connections and more productive and collaborative learning experiences in online settings.

Developing Cultural Competence Through Digital Communications

Researchers have posited that individuals can cultivate cultural competence through various educational methods, including digital learning platforms (Hutchins & Goldstein, 2021). Two examples of digital learning platforms are learning management systems (LMS) and learning content management systems (LCMS). All digital learning platforms, regardless of type, serve the same purpose: to provide students with a seamless and efficient learning experience (Bouchrika, 2022).

Similar to traditional face-to-face learning environments, students' cultural competence can be cultivated by intentionally integrating cultural aspects into online courses. One aspect of online courses that is effective in this regard is online discussion. Researchers have found that students in online courses who participated in these discussions experienced growth in their cultural competence as they provided the students with opportunities to study challenging topics in depth, express their opinions, and ask questions on sensitive issues with a sense of security (Lee et al., 2010; Van Soest et al., 2000).

THEORETICAL FRAMEWORK

Narrative Theory: Key Concepts and Definitions

The word *narrative* refers to a representation of an event or series of events (Abbott, 2020). Narrative theory examines and describes the nature, structure, and function of narratives, which are the stories we tell or encounter in different forms of media and communication (Moen, 2006). As Fisher (1984, p. 2) puts it, a story sees the world as a "sequence with meaning." Therefore, a *narrative* in narrative theory refers to a sequence of events or experiences that are presented in a coherent and meaningful way. It typically involves characters, settings, plot, and a specific point of view or perspective (Abbott, 2020). The narrator, or the one who shares the story, has a vital role in narrative theory. The narrator is the entity or voice that tells the story (Bal & Van Boheemen, 2009). The narrator may be a character within the story (a first-person narrator) or an external observer (a third-person narrator) (Abbott, 2020). This implies that the position of narrator influences the perspective and interpretation of the events.

Another concept in narrative theory is focalization, coined by Gerard Genette in 1972, which refers to the perspective through which a narrative is presented or experienced (Edmiston, 1989). It determines what information is revealed to the audience and how it is filtered or interpreted. Focalization can be internal (limited to the thoughts and experiences of a character) or external (providing an objective view) (Toolan, 1994).

In narrative theory, there is the *protagonist*, the main character, or the central figure, who is the character with whom the audience empathizes or follows closely throughout the story. On the other hand, an *antagonist* is a character or force that opposes or creates conflict for the protagonist (Herman et al., 2012). They serve as an obstacle or source of tension within the narrative. Some other concepts worth mentioning in narrative theory are setting and theme. The term *setting* denotes the time, place, and social context in which the events of a narrative transpire. It includes the physical environment, cultural background, and historical period (Krizek, 2017). The theme is the central idea, message, or morale that underlies a narrative. It is a broader concept or universal truth inferred from the events and characters' experiences. In summary, narrative learning refers to "learning through stories—stories heard, stories told, and stories recognized" (Clark & Rossiter, 2008, p. 2).

Narrative Theory for Infusing Cultural Competence in Virtual Classrooms

Narrative theory and its practical applications can serve as a valuable tool for infusing cultural competence into virtual classrooms within higher education. Additionally, educators must encourage sharing of stories that encourage cultural awareness, empathy, and cross-cultural communication in light of the expanding globalization and diversity of student populations. Research suggests that humans prefer storytelling over theoretical information. It is often attributed to the belief that narratives are ingrained in both our cultural and biological nature and explains the innate tendency of humans to communicate through stories (Boyd, 2009). Cultivating cultural competence among students is essential to navigate and appreciate diverse cultural perspectives in the classroom. Narrative theory offers a promising approach to infusing cultural competence into virtual classrooms. Educators may build a rich and culturally responsive learning environment that fosters the growth of empathy, understanding, and respect by including stories that reflect varied cultural experiences.

Incorporating Diverse Narratives Into the Curriculum

By including a variety of narratives in the curriculum, educators can create a learning environment that is more diverse and sensitive to cultural differences there by prepare students to navigate a diverse and interconnected world (Parsazadeh et al., 2021).

An example of this approach is a project that school counselors-in-training can implement for middle school students. The goal of the project is to honor students' diverse cultural backgrounds and empower them to develop cultural responsiveness and empathy. Educators may allow students to convey their own narratives and cultural experiences through a variety of mediums, including written storytelling, digital presentations, and visual artwork, in order to accomplish this purpose. This is supported by researchers, who defined narrative as the expression of stories through words or images (Bal & Van Boheemen, 2009). The curriculum can include activities to explore and reflect on students' own cultural heritage, traditions, and family histories. Before starting the project, instructors may introduce students to the definition of cultural diversity and the importance of sharing and understanding different cultural narratives. The importance of varied viewpoints in creating a culturally sensitive community may be highlighted in class discussions and activities.

Students can interview their family, friends, or people of the community as part of the project's practical application. Additionally, they may gather tales, customs, and artifacts from the various cultures represented in their communities. The interviews and gathered materials serve as the foundation for their projects. Instructors may offer students the opportunity to choose personal stories or created fictional narratives incorporating cultural heritage elements, digital presentations using multimedia tools, combining images, videos, and audio recordings to present their cultural backgrounds. It can also include visual artwork that represents their cultural traditions and identities. Once they complete the project, students may share it with the school community through an exhibition or a digital platform, to highlight their narratives and share their cultural experiences with their peers. It provides students from different backgrounds with an opportunity to learn from one another and appreciate the richness of their diverse cultural heritage. This example demonstrates how school counselors-in-training can use narrative theory in a classroom curriculum. A rubric for this activity is given in Table 1 in the Appendix.

Using Narratives to Challenge Stereotypes and Biases

According to Lewis and Shah (2021), educators use narratives to explore stereotypes and biases, empower college students to think critically, question assumptions, and enhance empathy and knowledge towards each other. Through these efforts, students actively promote inclusivity, justice, and equality within their groups. An instance of how educators can use this in an online classroom is through an activity that can be named, "Voices of Diversity." The objectives of this activity are to explore and address stereotypes and biases through sharing narratives and cultivating curiosity and empathy among college students. This course can be used for both undergraduate and graduate students and it introduces them to stories and how they could utilize digital resources, guest speakers, and interactive discussions to enhance their knowledge on diverse values, beliefs, and cultural systems.

The narratives constitute distinctive cultural, racial, ethnic, religious, and social backgrounds and help challenge commonly held stereotypes and biases. At the onset of the course, instructors can introduce the concept of stereotypes and biases and their effects on individuals and society as a whole. Throughout their learning, students would engage in online dialog, discussing narratives that explore and address stereotypes and biases. Instructors may offer students with readings, videos, and case studies that portray people who challenge stereotypes and are successful in their respective fields.

If allowed by the university and the program, instructors may invite guest speakers from diverse backgrounds to share their personal stories and experiences. They offer unique perspectives that break down stereotypes and demonstrate the complexities of diverse identities. Instructors may require students to research and present narratives that challenge specific stereotypes or biases as part of their assignments. Additionally, the requirements can also include evidence and examples to support students' arguments and engage in respectful dialogue with their peers. The instructor may facilitate meaningful student interactions and discussions, and create a conducive learning environment. In this activity, instructors must be actively engaging on the virtual learning platforms and consistently encouraging students to share their narratives, experiences, and perspectives. They may also gently challenge students to examine their biases, think critically about stereotypes, and develop empathy toward others. Through engaging with diverse stories and participating in reflective discussions, students may gain a deeper understanding of the complexities of human identities. A rubric for this activity is given in Table 2 in the Appendix.

Cultivating Empathy and Cross-Cultural Communication Through Narratives

By utilizing narratives as a tool, educators can effectively cultivate empathy and cross-cultural communication among students (Seay et al., 2022). Educators may encourage students to choose narratives thoughtfully, and engage in reflective discussions, to develop a deeper appreciation for diverse cultures. Educators may deliver lecture or seminar on the effectiveness of these activities in enhancing their ability to connect with others and navigate the increasingly interconnected world. One real-life example of how educators can cultivate empathy and cross-cultural communication through narratives in online higher education is a project that can be named the *Global Stories Exchange* project. In this project, instructors may pair up students from diverse cultural backgrounds as storytelling partners. The assignment for each student is to present personal narratives that are representative of their cultural identity, experiences, and values. By sharing personal experiences with one another, the intention is to foster intercultural understanding, empathy, and communication.

As students begin the project, instructors may provide them with guidelines on storytelling techniques and the importance of active listening. In order to select stories that reflect their distinct histories and viewpoints, students are required to reflect on their cultural heritage. The students then participate in online discussion forums and share with their partners about their experiences. Instructors must be present on the virtual learning platform and hold a space for students to engage in reflective discussions, which would allow them to share their thoughts, reactions, and insights prompted by their partner's story.

The *Global Stories Exchange* project can provide students with opportunities to communicate cross-culturally and develop empathy by enabling them to connect personally and find meaning through storytelling. Students may gain a greater knowledge of various cultural viewpoints and the human experiences that shape them through active listening and reflecting on each other's narratives. A rubric to measure the objectives of this project is given in Table 3 in the Appendix.

Narrative Theory for Building Meaningful Connections in Virtual Classrooms

Due to the challenge of creating educator-student relationships in virtual classroom environment, it is essential for educators to be intentional in implementing narrative pedagogical strategies. The goal must be to cultivate engagement and critical thinking, and to provide their students with meaningful cultural learning experiences. Some strategies for applying narrative pedagogy in a virtual classroom can include sharing personal narratives, story-based assignments, collaborative storytelling, and narrative assessments.

Personal Narratives and Story-Based Assignments

Research has shown that students belonging to different backgrounds find storytelling particularly valuable, as it captivates and pleases them while also acknowledging its relevance to their educational journey (Keehn, 2015). The findings have emphasized the importance of incorporating personal narratives as an authentic, transformative, and essential educational strategy in diversity-oriented courses (Keehn, 2015). An example of personal narratives can begin with instructors sharing their personal narratives related to the topic. This will open an avenue for students to have a sense of community and belonging as they may be able to resonate with the instructors' stories. Another way of using personal narratives is by giving story-based assignments. Here, educators can assign projects or assignments that require students to create narratives or stories related to the subject. This could involve writing a fictional story, producing a video, or designing a visual narrative. This approach may allow students to explore the content creatively and apply their understanding meaningfully.

For example, in an online literature course, if the instructor plans to engage students in a discussion about the impact of storytelling on individuals and communities, they can incorporate personal narratives into the lesson to provide a real-life perspective. The instructor may assign a task for each student to prepare a short video or audio recording and share a personal story about the power of literature or storytelling in their lives. The students have the freedom to choose a specific book, author, or literary experience that has influenced them significantly. Once the students submit their recordings, the instructor can create a discussion forum within the online learning platform. Educators may share an announcement to the students to watch or listen to their peers' narratives and reminding them to engage in a respectful conversation about shared experiences. In the discussion forum, students may reflect on the emotions, lessons, and connections they draw from personal narratives. They can discuss how literature and storytelling have impacted their lives, broadened their perspectives, or helped them navigate challenges.

Collaborative Storytelling

Educators can advance collaboration among students by engaging them in collaborative storytelling activities. They may use online discussion boards where students can collectively build a story or narrative, contributing their ideas and perspectives. This activity can be instrumental in the students' ability to work as a team, developing critical thinking, and the co-construction of knowledge (Vygotsky, 1962). According to Dooly and Tudini (2022), by integrating personal experiences into the social action of completing a university assignment, students and teachers establish connections that demonstrate mutual affiliation during their collaborative efforts in the online environment. An example would be introducing fictional or historical characters in the virtual classroom experience. This experience may allow students to explore the characters' backgrounds, motivations, and challenges and engage with the content through narrative lenses, promoting empathy, analysis, and deeper understanding.

Narrative Assessments

Narrative theory can also be used to design assessments. Instead of traditional tests, instructors who teach in virtual environments can consider projects or assignments that require students to create narratives to demonstrate their understanding of the content. This could include writing reflective essays, recording podcasts, or creating multimedia presentations. By incorporating reflective activities, instructors can provide narrative-based feedback to students. Instructors can encourage students to reflect on their learning experiences and growth throughout the virtual classroom sessions and provide constructive feedback highlighting specific examples and narratives from their work, facilitating self-reflection and improvement. These projects diminish the potential for artificial intelligence (AI) emulation and promote the original application of classroom-learned concepts. This approach not only stimulates critical thinking but also elevates students' cognitive processes from mere passive observation or rote memorization to evaluation, creativity, and innovation. It enhances student engagement and nurtures a sense of connection and relevance in the virtual learning environment.

CULTURAL COMPETENCE AND MEANINGFUL CONNECTIONS IN THE VIRTUAL CLASSROOM USING NARRATIVE THEORY: A CASE STUDY

The following case study focuses on the use of strategies from narrative theory in a virtual classroom. The specific example selected is narrative storytelling. It highlights the importance of how narrative theory can be used to infuse cultural competence and meaningful connections in a virtual classroom.

Dr. Sam is an online instructor in the school of education at central college. Dr. Sam was excited to find that her students hailed from diverse cultural traditions. Part of the course curriculum was developing cultural competence as educators. Being an educator of educators-in-training, Dr. Sam was excited about the ice-breaker activity she planned for the class. One day, as the class began, Dr. Sam introduced herself, emphasizing her own cultural traditions and her experiences of growing up in a household that respected other cultures. She shared her experiences that influenced her understanding of cultural diversity. She hoped that her vulnerability in sharing her own cultural story would lead to her students sharing their stories without fear of judgment. Just as she hoped, students began to share their stories. One student, Mariam, shared her story of her family's journey through immigration and what it meant for her to be a person from Hispanic background in the U.S. She shared about her challenges of adapting to a new culture. Her vulnerability and genuineness touched the hearts of her classmates, and it was the turn of Praveen to share about his story of growing up in the U.S as a person of Indian origin. He shared about living between two worlds, the U.S. culture outside the home and the Indian culture inside the home. This reminded Mika how sharing of stories is an inherent part of his American Indian culture. He began to share about how stories are passed down through generations in his family. Dr. Sam observed that students were curious about learning each other's cultural stories. She took this opportunity to gently remind students of their need to be sensitive in their curiosity and while asking their peers questions about their cultural heritage. Dr. Sam facilitated the discussion and invited others to join the conversation. It was heartwarming to hear the story of John, who was an international student from Ghana and how his journey through the immigration process of obtaining student visa helped him see the opportunities granted to him in the U.S. This led to Jasmine, a Muslim student, whose family is from Egypt, sharing her story of practicing her religious and cultural beliefs in a foreign land.

Dr. Sam skillfully incorporated narrative theory techniques into their discussion with the goal of students learning about each other and creating meaningful relationships with one another. As the session drew close, Dr. Sam provided the students with opportunities to reflect on their own sharing and listening to stories. The discussion that ensued was eye opening as each student shared how respectful and appreciative, they have grown after hearing the stories and sharing them. They shared that they felt belonged to the group and were looking forward to their next class together.

Ethical Considerations in Narrative Approach to Virtual Learning

A narrative approach to content delivery may benefit student-to-student and instructor-to-student connections and develop cultural competence. However, what ethical considerations exist at the intersection of narrative influence and cultivating cultural competence and meaningful connections in the virtual classroom? Primarily, the constructivist nature of narrative theory can raise validity issues in the context of virtual learning. The narrative theory depends on students' or instructors' personal stories. It can lead to potential validity issues, such as the chance of presenting a false story or the distortion of a story. They may also be unable or unwilling to give the complete story due to trauma or limitations in their memory. Instructors should be aware of these issues and may mitigate the risk of validity by emphasizing the importance of honesty and integrity in the classroom. Instructors may also provide prompts and clear guidelines to help students structure their stories to meet specific requirements within the course. This can include focusing on critical aspects such as the context, emotions, and cultural influences within their stories. Instructors may also create a comfortable environment for sharing students' stories without fear or intimidation.

In addition to establishing a culture of empathy and respect, instructors may open opportunities for alternative expressions. This might include encouraging artistic or verbal modes of communication for students who find it challenging to convey their narratives in written form or those who wish to explore more creative ways of expressing their ideas. Storytelling is a universally common human activity that is passed down through generations, but certain cultures have been particularly well-known for their rich storytelling traditions. Some of them are, American Indian/Native American (AI/NA) (Shiri et al., 2022), and some Asian cultures, African cultures, and some European cultures, that have a strong tradition of storytelling (Cvorovic & Coe, 2022). It is important for educators to be aware of these diverse cultural traditions and preference of expression in the online classroom.

Another ethical consideration is the potential for countertransference in the virtual classroom. Within virtual learning, countertransference can be defined as emotional and psychological reactions that instructors or students may experience in response to the narratives shared by others in the classroom. There may be intense emotional reactions that can affect their perceptions, behaviors, and interactions with one another when instructors or students share personal accounts of sensitive or painful experiences. In an online learning environment, countertransference might manifest when educators unconsciously projects their own unresolved issues, biases, or emotions onto a student. For example, if a student's experiences or comments trigger strong emotional reactions in the educator, such as frustration, anger, stress, sympathy, or discomfort, this could be a sign of countertransference. Instructors' mindfulness of the possible power dynamics when delivering narrative-based information is warranted. They must be aware that how they understand and react to students' narratives may be influenced by their experiences, prejudices, and personal histories. This awareness is essential for maintaining an ethical and supportive learning environment.

In addition, instructors should engage in self-reflection and cultivate self-awareness. They may practice 'bracketing' to avoid judgment and separate their experiences from students' stories (Moustakas, 1994). Bracketing is a qualitative research method developed by Moustakas (1994) and is commonly used in cross-cultural counseling settings. It refers to an individual's ability to be aware of and acknowledge their own biases, preconceptions, and personal experiences that may influence the effectiveness of interactions with others. By modeling this practice, instructors can highlight its usefulness to students. This process involves ongoing self-examination to enhance self-awareness, professional development for ongoing learning of different cultures, identities, and experiences, and seeking support from colleagues or supervisors when needed. Additionally, embracing a mindset of cultural humility (Abbott, 2019; Foronda et al., 2022), which goes beyond cultural competency, helps educators to acknowledge that they do not fully understand or know about every culture and be open to learning from students of their cultural traditions and belief systems.

CONCLUSION

It is our belief based on our conceptualization of narrative theory in creating meaningful connections in the online classroom, and our personal experiences of teaching students from diverse backgrounds, that the integration of narrative theory and its applications in virtual classroom can improve student participation and lead to student persistence in the program. Through allowing each student to bring their authentic self into the classroom as well as creating a climate of safe student to student and instructor to student interactions, online learning becomes a culturally responsive experience that potentially empowers everyone involved. In this era of technology, educators are especially positioned to set an example of exercising cultural competence and humility and lead the next generation of students to cultivate meaningful connections. They have the opportunity to empower each student to be agents of their own learning through the sharing of their own stories and to create long lasting relationships in the virtual classroom. We believe that this would ultimately lead to student persistence and higher retention and success in the virtual learning environment.

REFERENCES

Abbott, D. M., Pelc, N., & Mercier, C. (2019). Cultural humility and the teaching of psychology. *Scholarship of Teaching and Learning in Psychology*, 5(2), 169–181. doi:10.1037tl0000144

Abbott, H. P. (2020). *The Cambridge introduction to narrative*. Cambridge University Press. doi:10.1017/9781108913928

Allen, I. E., & Seaman, J. (2011). *Going the distance: Online education in the United States*. Sloan Consortium.

Angelino, L. M., Williams, F. K., & Natvig, D. (2007). Strategies to engage online students and reduce attrition rates. *The Journal of Educators Online*, 4(2). doi:10.9743/JEO.2007.2.1

Bal, M., & Van Boheemen, C. (2009). *Narratology: Introduction to the theory of narrative*. University of Toronto Press.

Baldwin, S., & Ching, Y. H. (2017). Interactive storytelling: Opportunities for online course design. *TechTrends*, *61*(2), 179–186. doi:10.100711528-016-0136-2

Black, J. B., & Bower, G. H. (1979). Episodes as chunks in narrative memory. *Journal of Verbal Learning and Verbal Behavior*, *18*(3), 309–318. doi:10.1016/S0022-5371(79)90173-7

Bouchrika, I. (2022, August 23). *Best Digital Learning Platforms for 2023*. Research.Com. https://research.com/software/best-digital-learning-platforms

Boyd, B. (2009). *On the Origin of Stories: Evolution, Cognition, and Fiction*. Harvard University Press. doi:10.4159/9780674053595

Brindley, J., Walti, C., & Blaschke, L. (2009). Creating effective collaborative learning groups in an online environment. *International Review of Research in Open and Distance Learning*, *10*(3), •••. doi:10.19173/irrodl.v10i3.675

Cela, K., Silcilia, M., & Sanches-Alonso, S. (2016). Influence of learning styles on social structures in online learning environments. *British Journal of Educational Technology*, *47*(6), 1065–1082. doi:10.1111/bjet.12267

Clark, M. C., & Rossiter, M. (2008). *Narrative learning in the adult classroom*. https://newprairiepress.org/cgi/viewcontent.cgi?article=2897&context=aerc

Cvorovic, J., & Coe, K. (2022). *Storytelling around the World: Folktales, Narrative Rituals, and Oral Traditions*. Bloomsbury Publishing USA. doi:10.5040/9798216019398

de Hei, M., Tabacaru, C., Sjoer, E., Rippe, R., & Walenkamp, J. (2020). Developing Intercultural Competence Through Collaborative Learning in International Higher Education. *Journal of Studies in International Education*, *24*(2), 190–211. doi:10.1177/1028315319826226

Deardorff, D. K. (2019). *Manual for developing intercultural competencies: Story circles*. Routledge. doi:10.4324/9780429244612

Deardorff, D. K., & Jones, E. (2009). Intercultural Competence. In V. Savicki (Ed.), *Developing Intercultural Competence and Transformation* (pp. 32–52). Stylus Pub. doi:10.4135/9781071872987.n28

Dooly, M., & Tudini, V. (2022). 'I Remember When I Was in Spain': Student-Teacher Storytelling in Online Collaborative Task Accomplishment. In A. Filipi, B. T. Ta, & M. Theobald (Eds.), *Storytelling Practices in Home and Educational Contexts*. Springer. doi:10.1007/978-981-16-9955-9_15

Edmiston, W. F. (1989). Focalization and the first-person narrator: A revision of the theory. *Poetics Today*, *10*(4), 729–744. doi:10.2307/1772808

Fisher, W. R. (1985). The narrative paradigm: In the beginning. *Journal of Communication*, *35*(4), 74–89. doi:10.1111/j.1460-2466.1985.tb02974.x

Foronda, C., Prather, S., Baptiste, D. L., & Luctkar-Flude, M. (2022). Cultural humility toolkit. *Nurse Educator*, *47*(5), 267–271. doi:10.1097/NNE.0000000000001182 PMID:35324491

Gait, S., & Halewood, A. (2019). Developing countertransference awareness as a therapist in training: The role of containing contexts. *Psychodynamic Practice*, *25*(3), 256–272. doi:10.1080/14753634.2019.1643961

Gopalan, M., & Brady, S. T. (2020). College Students' Sense of Belonging: A National Perspective. *Educational Researcher*, *49*(2), 134–137. doi:10.3102/0013189X19897622

Gopalan, M., Linden-Carmichael, A., & Lanza, S. (2022). College Students' Sense of Belonging and Mental Health Amidst the COVID-19 Pandemic. *The Journal of Adolescent Health*, *70*(2), 228–233. doi:10.1016/j.jadohealth.2021.10.010 PMID:34893423

Gordon, G., & Whitchurch, C. (2010). *Academic and professional identities in higher education*. Routledge.

Gunawardena, M., & Brown, B. (2021). Fostering Values Through Authentic Storytelling. *The Australian Journal of Teacher Education*, *46*(6), 36–53. Advance online publication. doi:10.14221/ajte.2021v46n6.3

Hamann, K., Glazier, R. A., Wilson, B. M., & Pollock, P. H. (2021). Online teaching, student success, and retention in political science courses. *European Political Science*, *20*(3), 427–439. doi:10.105741304-020-00282-x

Herbert, M. (2006). Staying the course: A study in online student satisfaction and retention. *Online Journal of Distance Learning Administration*, *9*.

Herman, D., Phelan, J., Rabinowitz, P. J., Richardson, B., & Warhol, R. (2012). *Narrative theory: Core concepts and critical debates*. The Ohio State University Press.

Hutchins, D., & Goldstein Hode, M. (2021). Exploring faculty and staff development of cultural competence through communicative learning in an online diversity course. *Journal of Diversity in Higher Education*, *14*(4), 468–479. doi:10.1037/dhe0000162

Keehn, M. G. (2015). "When You Tell a Personal Story, I Kind of Perk up a Little Bit More": An Examination of Student Learning From Listening to Personal Stories in Two Social Diversity Courses. *Equity & Excellence in Education*, *48*(3), 373–391. doi:10.1080/10665684.2015.1056712

Krizek, R. L. (2017). Narrative and storytelling. The International Encyclopedia of Organizational Communication, 1-17. doi:10.1002/9781118955567.wbieoc146

Landrum, R. E., Brakke, K., & McCarthy, M. A. (2019). The pedagogical power of storytelling. *Scholarship of Teaching and Learning in Psychology*, *5*(3), 247–253. doi:10.1037tl0000152

Lawrence, A. (2020). Teaching as Dialogue: Toward Culturally Responsive Online Pedagogy. *Journal of Online Learning Research*, *6*, 5–33. https://www.learntechlib.org/primary/p/210657/

Lee, E., & Bertera, E. (2007). Teaching diversity by using instructional technology: Application of self-efficacy and cultural competence. *Multicultural Education & Technology Journal*, *1*(2), 112–125. doi:10.1108/17504970710759602

Lee, E.-K. O., Brown, M., & Bertera, E. M. (2010). The use of an online diversity forum to facilitate social work students' dialogue on sensitive issues: A quasi-experimental design. *Journal of Teaching in Social Work*, *30*(3), 272–287. doi:10.1080/08841233.2010.499066

Lewis, K. R., & Shah, P. P. (2021). Black students' narratives of diversity and inclusion initiatives and the campus racial climate: An interest-convergence analysis. *Journal of Diversity in Higher Education*, *14*(2), 189–202. doi:10.1037/dhe0000147

Liston, D. D. (1994). *Storytelling and narrative: A neurophilosophical perspective*. Retrieved from https://files.eric.ed.gov/fulltext/ED372092.pdf

Littlefield, M. B., & Bertera, E. M. (2004). A discourse analysis of online dialogs in social work diversity courses: Topical themes, depth, and tone. *Journal of Teaching in Social Work*, *24*(3-4), 131–146. doi:10.1300/J067v24n03_09

Martin, J. (2019). Building relationships and increasing engagement in the virtual classroom: Practical tools for the online instructor. *The Journal of Educators Online*, *16*(1). doi:10.9743/jeo.2019.16.1.9

Moen, T. (2006). Reflections on the narrative research approach. *International Journal of Qualitative Methods*, *5*(4), 56–69. doi:10.1177/160940690600500405

Moessenlechner, C., Obexer, R., Sixl-Daniell, K., & Seeler, J. M. (2015). E-learning degree programs: A better way to balance work and education? *Studies*, *23*(24), 25. http://learningideasconf.s3.amazonaws.com/Docs/Past/2015/Papers/Moessenlechner_Obexer_et_al.pdf

Morris, C. C. (2006). *Narrative theory: A culturally sensitive counseling and research framework*. http://www.counselingoutfitters.com/Morris.htm

Moustakas, C. (1994). *Phenomenological research methods*. Sage Publications. doi:10.4135/9781412995658

Murphy, M. C. (2022). How Social Belonging Impacts Retention at Broad-Access Colleges. *Academic Upshot*. https://www.thirdway.org/report/how-social-belonging-impacts-retention-at-broad-access-colleges

Palloff, R. M., & Pratt, K. (2013). *Lessons from the Virtual Classroom* (2nd ed.). Jossey-Bass.

Parsazadeh, N., Cheng, P.-Y., Wu, T.-T., & Huang, Y.-M. (2021). Integrating Computational Thinking Concept Into Digital Storytelling to Improve Learners' Motivation and Performance. *Journal of Educational Computing Research*, *59*(3), 470–495. doi:10.1177/0735633120967315

Prochaska, J. O., & Norcross, J. C. (2018). *Systems of psychotherapy: A transtheoretical analysis*. Oxford University Press.

Seay, A. K. M., Benavides, M. T., Eddington, S. M., & Coleman, J. A. (2022). Beyond perspective taking: Fostering equity through critical empathy and intercultural listening. In A. M. Seay, M. T. Benavides, S. M. Eddington, & J. A. Coleman (Eds.), *Achieving equity in higher education using empathy as a guiding principle* (pp. 141–171). IGI Global. doi:10.4018/978-1-7998-9746-0.ch007

Sherry, J., Warner, L., & Kitchenham, A. (2021). What's Bred in the Bone: Transference and Countertransference in Teachers. *Brock Journal of Education*, *30*(1), 136–154. doi:10.26522/brocked.v30i1.859

Shiri, A., Howard, D., & Farnel, S. (2022). Indigenous digital storytelling: Digital interfaces supporting cultural heritage preservation and access. *The International Information & Library Review*, *54*(2), 93–114. doi:10.1080/10572317.2021.1946748

Sue, S. (1998). In search of cultural competence in psychotherapy and counseling. *The American Psychologist*, *53*(4), 440–448. doi:10.1037/0003-066X.53.4.440 PMID:9572007

Toolan, M. J. (1994). Narrative: Linguistic and structural theories. In R. E. Asher & J. M. Y. Simpson (Eds.), *The Encyclopedia of Language and Linguistics* (Vol. 6, pp. 2679–2696). Pergamont Press.

Van Soest, D., Canon, R., & Grant, D. (2000). Using an interactive website to educate about cultural diversity and societal oppression. *Journal of Social Work Education*, *36*(3), 463–479. doi:10.1080/10437797.2000.10779022

Vygotsky, L. (1962). *Thought and language*. MIT Press. doi:10.1037/11193-000

KEY TERMS AND DEFINITIONS

Bracketing: This is a qualitative research method that is commonly used in cross-cultural counseling settings. It refers to an individual's ability to be aware of and acknowledge own biases, preconceptions, and personal experiences that may influence the effectiveness of interactions with others.

Countertransference: It refers to the emotional or psychological reactions and responses that an educator may experience in response to a student's verbal or written expressions, behaviors, comments, or circumstances. It is a concept that originates from psychotherapy and counseling (Gait & Hailwood, 2019) but can also apply to the teaching and learning environment (Sherry et al., 2021). In an online learning environment, countertransference might manifest when educators unconsciously projects their own unresolved issues, biases, or emotions onto a student. For example, if a student's experiences or comments trigger strong emotional reactions in the educator, such as frustration, anger, stress, sympathy, or discomfort, this could be a sign of countertransference.

Cultural Competency: It refers to the ability of individuals to be aware of their own cultural values, beliefs, and behaviors and respond to individuals of other cultural values, beliefs, and behaviors with sensitivity and respect.

Culture: Culture is a holistic, learned, and relative system that shapes behavior, identity, and group cohesion. It is acquired from one generation to the next and affects individuals' perception and organization of their lives while adapting to change. Similar to an iceberg, culture has visible and hidden aspects, including core values and beliefs that are less prone to change (Department of Education, University of Oxford, n.d.).

Meaningful Bonds or Connections: It refers to student-instructor and student-student interactions to cultivate collaboration, peer support, and a sense of belonging and community in online learning.

Narrative Approach: It refers to using narrative techniques, such as storytelling to engage students in online learning environments.

Virtual Classroom and Online Classroom: It replicates the traditional brick and mortar classroom dynamics in a digital environment. These terms are used interchangeably in this chapter and signify the same meaning.

APPENDIX

Table 1. Rubric for an activity for infusing narrative theory into curriculum

Criteria	Excellent	Proficient	Developing	Unsatisfactory
Introduction to Cultural Diversity	Student demonstrates a strong understanding of cultural diversity, and the importance of sharing and understanding different narratives.	Student demonstrates a clear understanding of cultural diversity but lacks depth or fail to understand its importance effectively.	Students demonstrates some understanding of cultural diversity, with limited depth of understanding of its importance.	Student does not demonstrate an understanding of cultural diversity.
Creative Expression	Student demonstrates creativity and skill in presenting their cultural backgrounds through written stories, digital presentations, and visual artwork.	Student effectively use various creative methods but exhibits minor deficiencies in creativity or skill.	Student attempts creative expression, but there are significant deficiencies in creativity or skill.	Student makes no effort to demonstrate creative expression.
Cultural Learning and Appreciation	Students from different backgrounds effectively learn from one another and appreciate the richness of their diverse cultural heritage.	Students learn from one another and appreciate cultural diversity to some extent, but there is room for improvement.	Students show limited evidence of learning from one another or appreciating cultural diversity.	There is no evidence of learning or appreciation of cultural diversity among students.

Table 2. Rubric for the "voices of diversity" project

Performance Level	Description
Exemplary (4)	Student demonstrates an exceptional understanding of human identities through engagement with diverse narratives. - Actively engages in reflective discussions and consistently contribute profound insights.
Proficient (3)	Student shows a solid understanding of human identities through engagement with diverse narratives. - Actively participates in reflective discussions through meaningful contributions.
Developing (2)	Student displays a basic understanding of human identities through some engagement with diverse narratives. - Participates in reflective discussions with occasional meaningful contributions.
Limited (1)	Student exhibits limited understanding of human identities through minimal engagement with diverse narratives. - Participates passively in reflective discussions with minimal or no meaningful contributions.

Table 3. A rubric for the global stories exchange project

Criteria	Excellent (4)	Proficient (3)	Developing (2)	Limited (1)
Cross-Cultural Communication	Student effectively and consistently engages in cross-cultural communication, demonstrating a deep understanding of different cultural perspectives and the human experiences that shape them.	Student generally engages in cross-cultural communication, showing some understanding of different cultural perspectives and human experiences.	Student struggles to engage in cross-cultural communication, with limited understanding of different cultural perspectives and human experiences.	Student does not engage in cross-cultural communication.
Empathy Development	Student consistently demonstrates empathy and find meaning through storytelling, actively listening to, and reflecting on each other's narratives. They connect personally with the stories shared.	Student demonstrates empathy and find meaning through storytelling, but their engagement in active listening and reflection is inconsistent. They somewhat connect personally with the stories shared.	Student struggles to demonstrate empathy and find meaning through storytelling. Their active listening and reflection are limited, and they have difficulty connecting personally with the stories shared.	Student does not demonstrate empathy, find meaning, or engage in active listening and reflection during storytelling.

Chapter 7
Cultural Competency and Meaningful Online Relationships:
Creating Safe Spaces for BIPOC Students

Ariel Harrison
https://orcid.org/0009-0007-3444-0249
Walden University, USA

ABSTRACT

Since their creation, online and distance-learning programs have afforded traditional and non-traditional students access to learning. Black, Indigenous, and People of Color (BIPOC) students represent many enrollments each year in online and distance-learning undergraduate, master's, and doctoral programs. While the absence of in-person and synchronous learning can impact the connections made by all students, this learning modality has also amplified some existing challenges for BIPOC students in these higher educational settings. This chapter will describe themes of isolation, a sense of belonging, and the quest for safe spaces amongst BIPOC students. This chapter will also discuss the role and responsibilities of mentorship; the importance of fostering meaningful relationships that combat isolation linked to BIPOC students' perception of support, safety, and belonging; and the position of culturally specific virtual affinity spaces in uncovering links to connectedness in online programs.

The growth of online post-secondary education and educational programs with online components in North America has encouraged the discussion of inclusiveness and connection for students. Attending classes, receiving training, and attaining degrees while dwelling in places that provide internet access provide an opportunity and flexibility for many individuals to grow in their lives and careers. Access to this style of learning has supported working adults, frequent travelers, parents, caretakers, and individuals in rural areas with receiving education and training remotely.

While an advantage of online education includes the ability to provide access to learning for students all over the world, literature has disclosed an isolating component to online education, as different pro-

DOI: 10.4018/978-1-6684-8908-6.ch007

grams may not consistently provide optimal opportunities for student connection (Ajmal & Ahmad, 2019; Sadeghi, 2019). Students attend online colleges and universities for many reasons, including program type, accreditation, reputation, and lifestyle alignment. However, for many students, their selections also depend on their abilities to succeed and their capabilities to form professional relationships with faculty and other students. Online education provides access to learning, but programs can lack the component of social connection that also contributes to student success characteristics (Sadeghi, 2019). Factors such as isolation, lack of social interaction, loneliness, and disconnection can significantly influence students' academic success and retention in online programs (Ajmal & Ahmad, 2019; Sadeghi, 2019). Despite the efforts of many online schools and programs to provide social opportunities, Phirangee and Malec (2017) explained that students still reported negative feelings, resulting in a disconnection from course content and instructors and a lack of community within peer groups and possibly dropping out of their programs.

The goals of fostering cultural competency and strategies to develop meaningful relationships have become increasingly significant for academic leaders in online institutions. Instructors and programs must understand how to provide opportunities for connection and inclusion for all students in educational environments. However, explicitly focusing on the needs of historically isolated cultural groups, such as Black, Indigenous, and People of Color (BIPOC) individuals, can become a starting point in helping to bridge educational and opportunity gaps. Identifying and understanding challenges and successful strategies that impact these students can support academic leaders in establishing systemic changes and supporting the retention of students (Hradilová & Chovancová, 2023). By understanding the challenges that BIPOC students may experience, academic leaders may find ways to evaluate their current resources and develop new support strategies to foster a positive educational experience and transition into the workforce.

This chapter will address specific challenges BIPOC students may experience that influence their perception of support, safety, and belonging in online degree programs. This chapter will also include the role and responsibilities of mentorship and the development of culturally specific virtual affinity spaces in uncovering links to connectedness and fostering meaningful relationships.

EXAMINING THE ACADEMIC EXPERIENCES OF BIPOC STUDENTS IN NORTH AMERICA

The description of Black, Indigenous, and People of Color (BIPOC) involves person-first language that shifts away from the traditional labels such as "marginalized" and "minority" used to describe the cultural groups of Black, American Indians, or Native Americans, First Nations, Native Alaskans or Alaska Natives, Hispanic, East Asian, South Asian, and Hawaiian and Pacific Islander racial and ethnic individuals (Silverstein et al., 2022). These populations should not be viewed as monoliths but recognized as individuals with distinctive and shared life experiences based on historical occurrences, cultural traditions, physical attributes, and societal practices and treatments. As with all scholars, BIPOC students enter the field of higher education bringing life experiences and perceptions into their academic journeys (Silverstein et al., 2023). On the one hand, these understandings can shape how BIPOC students contribute to the practice of their future careers. On the other hand, these understandings can also impact how BIPOC students view their learning institutions, the educational process, their future career fields of choice, and the people responsible for preparing them for their future careers (Scott et al., 2022).

While the United States Census Bureau (2022) reported an increase in BIPOC individuals with bachelor's degrees from 2011 to 2021, Clarke and Davison (2020) and the National Center for Education Statistics (2022) denoted the existence of underrepresented BIPOC populations in graduate and post-graduate institutions. The BIPOC student population has increasingly received access to academic opportunities and success; however, Preston (2017) shared that BIPOC students have historically faced additional obstacles to educational success from grade school to post-graduate work. These struggles represent an ongoing systemic issue involving a deficiency in resources and support for these students, which can result in inequalities in retention rates, underrepresented populations in higher education, and disparities in degree completion rates (Preston, 2017).

Isolation of BIPOC Students

As the literature has established an isolating component to online learning for all students (Almazova et al., 2020; Hradilová & Chovancová, 2023), BIPOC students may experience an amplified negative perception of support, safety, and belonging in the online environment associated with racial and ethnic identity and culture. In the college environment, Keels (2020) described the existence of additional and inequitable stressors for BIPOC students compared to White college students. These stressors included pressure to adapt to stereotypes, navigating racial conflict, and disparities in treatment by staff and other students.

Williams (2020) and Nadal et al. (2014) thoroughly acknowledged the presence of experienced racial microaggressions (verbal, nonverbal, or visual offensive exchanges that emphasize the power differentials amongst racial groups) that can shape how students connect with their universities and, over time, can impact the mental health and self-esteem of BIPOC students. These microaggressions can develop in response to interactions with others and the entrenchment of institutional racism in systems such as media, education, politics, and the economy (Solórzano & Perez Huber, 2020). Additionally, Bonilla-Silva (2014) described the presence of color-blind racism, which includes a belief that suggests racism no longer exists and rationalizes racial events as nonracial, exhibited in many academic environments. Individuals who exercise the beliefs of color-blind racism negate the understandings and opinions of those who recognize and address racist experiences. This lens of color-blind racism can create socialized and internalized comprehensions that impact the accuracy and interpretation of information regarding racial experiences and inequalities for BIPOC students (Ayala & Chalupa Young, 2022). In addition to the pressures associated with educational requirements and progress, BIPOC students can experience racial battle fatigue, involving psychological, physiological, and behavioral stressors throughout their educational journeys (Solórzano & Perez Huber, 2020; Williams, 2020). Given these additional difficulties and a lack of resources or individuals to mitigate these circumstances, BIPOC students might view their college and university environments as unwelcoming or hostile, which can significantly impact their social and academic functioning and achievement (Banks & Landau, 2022).

Specifically, regarding the experiences of BIPOC students online, Phirangee and Malec (2017) described the environment of higher education as exposing a struggle between societal beliefs and students' individual and cultural beliefs. Black, Indigenous, and People of Color students reported feeling as though they were outsiders or othered through differences in educational expectations and employment obligations while attaining degrees and cultural identities that did not align with those of peers, instructors, or course curricula (Phirangee & Malec, 2017). Shavers and Moore (2014) explained an extension of perceptions of discrimination, racism, or sexism leading to further feelings of othering or isolation as non-BIPOC faculty or administrators were more likely to minimize, ignore, or even reject BIPOC student complaints. Students experienced discomfort in asking for help from faculty and students or bore the task of directly searching for their academic resources and support (Shavers & Moore, 2014). This additional work placed a burden of responsibility on BIPOC students to create avenues that non-White students did not have to explore. As Kumi-Yeboah et al. (2017) examined the perceptions of BIPOC graduate students regarding online collaborative learning activities, they found that BIPOC students valued being in culturally diverse settings that permitted them to have social interactions with others. However, BIPOC students experienced multicultural exclusion in the curriculum, online reading content, and often felt marginalized in online discussions due to lack of acknowledgment.

An additional aspect of the isolation of BIPOC students consists of the absence of opportunities to see and connect with others who look like them in the online environment (Harrison PhD, 2022; Kumi-Yeboah et al., 2017; Phirangee & Malec, 2017). Taylor (2019) explained:

Perception acts as a lens through which we view reality. Our perceptions influence how we focus on, process, remember, interpret, understand, synthesize, decide about, and act on reality. In doing so, our tendency is to assume that how we perceive reality is an accurate representation of what reality truly is. But it's not. The problem is that the lens through which we perceive is often warped in the first place by our genetic predispositions, past experiences, prior knowledge, emotions, preconceived notions, self-interest, and cognitive distortions. (para. 5)

Even in culturally diverse online programs or institutions that may include large numbers of BIPOC students and faculty, students may be limited to interacting only with the other students in their courses or cohorts and their specific course instructors (Kumi-Yeboah et al., 2017). Given the social experiences and marginalization of BIPOC students, the lens through which students experience their academic journey can become shaped by their perceptions of the environment (Taylor, 2019). In these cases, the lack of visibility, cultural representation, and perception of the shortage of diversity at online institutions may lead BIPOC students to feel disengaged or excluded, which may impact their academic success.

Cultural and Ethnic Representation

The paradigm of culture includes a set of shared beliefs or practices that connect individuals. Culture can incorporate race, gender, ethnicity, religion, geographic location, age, and many other social or physical constructs that can characterize a group of people (Hall, 1997). These commonalities contribute to social traditions that create meaning. Cultural and ethnic representation, focusing on race and ethnicity, can include the visibility and recognition of individuals who share physical and social connections with others (Hall, 1997). In academic institutions, cultural or ethnic representation can involve the physical presence of BIPOC individuals and the acknowledgment and existence of racial and ethnic diversity in policies and practices, curricula, activities, celebrations, and course content (Keels, 2020; Williams, 2020). For BIPOC students, finding areas of connection can be significant in counteracting stressors associated with being in the academic setting; however, a substantial factor in the journey of BIPOC students can also include identifying how the institution or program embraces cultural and ethnic representation.

Representation in Faculty and Students

One aspect of cultural or ethnic representation in academic institutions includes the presence of BIPOC individuals. Seeing others who mirror students' physical images can become very effective when educating students of all ages (Kumi-Yeboah et al., 2017; Phirangee & Malec, 2017). While many individuals might interpret the term "affirmative action" with negative sentiments, people often misinterpret its purpose as placing selection on specific demographic groups rather than shaping policies and practices to address cultural inequalities (Petts, 2022). Okechukwu (2019) defined affirmative action as "policies and programs that provide special consideration to historically excluded groups, such as racial and ethnic minorities and women in the spheres of education and employment" (p. 4). Affirmative action goals included using special considerations and intentionality in hiring practices and student admissions procedures to foster a diverse and inclusive educational setting. While used and interpreted in various ways in higher education, this practice ensured the physical presence (employment and enrollment) of underrepresented population groups in faculty and student bodies (Okechukwu, 2019).

In 2023, colleges and universities evolved the language and practices of affirmative action to address the need for cultural representation through Diversity, Equity, and Inclusion (DEI) (Paul & Maranto, 2023). Many areas of employment and college and university policies advertised these DEI statements to convey the acknowledgment of cultural acceptance and applicable practices. This term, which describes policies and procedures that promote the representation and involvement of diverse groups of individuals, incorporates people of different ages, races, ethnicities, abilities, disabilities, genders, religions, cultures, and sexual orientations (Barnett, 2020; Brissett, 2020). By using the language of DEI in college and university marketing, public perception assumes the existence of policies and programs that allow colleges and universities to admit, hire, and retain BIPOC faculty, staff, and students. The evolution of affirmative action practices, while intended to increase access for historically excluded groups, transformed into loosely interpreted definitions that did not always include the constructs of race, ethnicity, or gender (Paul & Maranto, 2023). Meeting an intentional method of increasing diversity changed to broader characteristics, which still provided opportunities for many people but, at face value, impacted the perception of a heterogeneous population of faculty and students. This evolution in strategies led consumers to question many colleges and universities that may advertise support of social justice, equality, diversity, equity, and inclusion, yet neglect to definitively state or show how they act on this support and the effectiveness of these practices with faculty and students (Rinke et al., 2021).

In 2020, the National Center for Education Statistics (2022) reported approximately 1.5 million faculty members at degree-granting post-secondary institutions in the United States, with 840,000 categorized as full-time faculty. Out of this number, approximately 25% of full-time faculty identified as BIPOC. In 2020, Educationdata.org (2022) reported that 40.9% of college graduates identified as BIPOC, with 93% of BIPOC graduates earning 43.8% of associate degrees, 49% of BIPOC graduates earning 37.7% of bachelor's degrees, 93% of BIPOC graduates earning 45% of master's degrees, and 94% of BIPOC graduates earning 39.8% of doctorate or professional degrees. These statistics revealed that while approximately 25% of full-time faculty fell into the racial category of BIPOC, this compared to roughly 40% of college graduates meeting the BIPOC racial classification. Regarding cultural and ethnic representation in physical presence (employment and enrollment), faculty-student disparities and underrepresentation seem to exist (National Center for Education Statistics, 2022). Despite fostering these DEI statements, many advocates address the concern that university faculty do not represent the student body based on race, ethnicity, and gender (Paul & Maranto, 2023). Coincidentally, recent statistics may support this claim and create the need for academic leaders to examine the cultural statistics regarding the empirical relationship of BIPOC faculty-to-student ratios (Educationdata.org, 2022; National Center for Education Statistics, 2022).

Representation in Policies and Practices

Another aspect of cultural or ethnic representation in academic institutions includes the authenticity of policies and initiatives directed at inclusiveness for BIPOC individuals. These policies and practices can include distinct resources or programs provided for BIPOC faculty and students, targeted efforts to recruit and retain BIPOC faculty and students, and procedures that address racial, discrimination, or inequity concerns raised by BIPOC faculty and students. Scott et al. (2022) explained that despite institutional efforts on behalf of colleges and universities to support BIPOC students, these efforts frequently possess foundations that yield poor results in transformational change, regardless of the appearance of success. Sangaramoorthy and Richardson (2020) described the term *performative whiteness*, which characterizes the tendency for colleges and universities to issue statements or use strategies that present the idea of valuing racial justice, diversity, equity, and inclusion, but do not execute practical policy initiatives or programs that result in systemic change. Lack of cultural representation in policies and practices might include excluding BIPOC individuals on decision-making panels, programs that consider the impact of and input of BIPOC individuals and causes, and comprehensive procedures that permit BIPOC individuals to voice their concerns (Sangaramoorthy & Richardson, 2020). Normalized practices or traditions deemed culturally insensitive over time can also pose challenges when colleges, universities, or programs choose to continue or not acknowledge any offenses (McCavanagh & Cadaret, 2022). This deficit can lead to a lack of consideration or the perceived lack of consideration of processes that significantly impact BIPOC students who enroll in various colleges and programs.

Representation in Curriculum and Teaching

Black, Indigenous, and People of Color students may identify cultural or ethnic representation through the course curricula, syllabi, and subject matter of what educators teach. Representation in this area includes the selection of content that educational institutions provide and the method by which teachers disseminate information. Overall, courses retain great value in proper curriculum and text selections. Morgan and Houghton (2011) stated, "An inclusive curriculum design approach is one that takes into account students' educational, cultural, and social background and experience as well as the presence of any physical or sensory impairment and their mental well-being" (p. 5). Inclusive curricula involve discussions, assignments, projects, case studies, assessments, and resources that incorporate theories, topics, input, and ideas created by or associated with BIPOC individuals in addition to their White counterparts. When instructors incorporate diverse resources and assignments, all students can find and value their cultures, histories, experiences, and voices (Morgan & Houghton, 2011). Rinke et al. (2021) expressed a considerable need for higher education to prepare graduates better to live and work in a global and pluralistic society. Lack of cultural representation in the curriculum negates intersectionality in culture and uniqueness in cultural groups and provides students with limited information beyond that of White or dominant cultural groups.

Developing an inclusive curriculum becomes the first step in supporting cultural representation; however, the necessity also exists for nurturing a safe environment for discourse regarding cultural information and topics. Virtual activities that include small group collaboration can support students with participation in course discussions, collaboration with others, sharing ideas with other classmates and instructors, and developing their cultural identities (Kumi-Yeboah et al., 2017). Barnett (2020) explained that diverse and inclusive curricula must extend beyond course topics, and faculty and staff should adopt it as a fundamental and authentic aspect of the institution's culture. The National Education Association describes cultural competence as "the ability to successfully teach students who come from a culture or cultures other than our own" through developing "personal and interpersonal awareness and sensitivities, understanding certain bodies of cultural knowledge, and mastering a set of skills that taken together, underlie effective cross-cultural teaching and culturally responsive teaching" (Van Roekel, 2008, p. 6). As faculty of all cultures are responsible for disseminating curriculum, a lack of cultural representation in teaching involves faculty dismissing the responsibilities of being open to new and unique ideas, addressing biases and stereotypes, and welcoming more profound, respectful, and safe discourse on culturally related principles and topics (Morgan & Houghton, 2011). This practice includes promoting positive interactions between students of different cultures, understanding, respecting, and integrating diverse cultural perspectives into their lessons (Puhy et al., 2021). Lack of cultural representation also includes educators who must examine and address their personal cultural competence and cultural biases that may impact their relationships with students and the content they teach.

Impact on Students and Implications

Kornbluh et al. (2022) explained that when BIPOC students observed the recognition of their backgrounds, culture, and voices in their academic institutions, they were more likely to feel a sense of connection with their environment and perceive themselves as acknowledged as individuals. Kornbluh et al. (2022) continued by describing gaps in racial and ethnic representation as influencing feelings of hypervisibility, marginalization, and tokenization, which impacted BIPOC students' perceptions of emotional belonging and engagement at their academic institutions. Blatant differences in race and ethnicity also impacted the likelihood of students requesting educational support from faculty, impacting retention and academic success.

Many academic institutions may adapt or promote diversity in official statements, but the assessment of the inclusion practices implemented by these settings rests on the perceptions of their students (Barnett, 2020). Black, Indigenous, and People of Color individuals hold multiple lived experiences, realities, voices, and perspectives; however, the physical component of cultural representation begins with having the attendance of BIPOC individuals in multiple areas of the college or university experience. Black, Indigenous, and People of Color students benefit from diverse instructors who look like them (Nadal et al., 2014). Nadal (2021) explained that BIPOC individuals might experience challenges with racial and ethnic identity development in which a lack of representation can impact their overall self-esteem. Additionally, many BIPOC students may not pursue careers or academic paths when a lack of exposure to others in those roles or positions exists (Nadal, 2021). Purposeful and measurable practices that provide special consideration to historically excluded groups can help to provide cultural and ethnic representation in the classroom, but representation requires much more than numbers. Barnett (2020) encourages academic leaders to include diverse representatives across college and university stakeholder groups with the understanding that there is value and respect for multiple perspectives in decision-making processes. Academic leaders must accurately assess the level of cultural representation in their institutions and programs to help support the experiences of BIPOC students. Intentionality in developing diverse cultural representation might support creating a more welcoming academic environment for students, staff, and scholars (Paul & Maranto, 2023).

RECOGNIZING THE FUNCTIONALITY OF SUPPORT

At this point, the chapter has addressed isolation and the challenges that BIPOC students can undergo without cultural competency, consideration, and intentionality. However, the literature provides many examples of elements within the academic journeys of BIPOC students that can also promote endurance and matriculation when well executed by and with suitable individuals. Formally and informally, safe spaces and mentorship can help to further the discussion on cultural competency and strategies to develop meaningful relationships for BIPOC students.

The Role of Safe Spaces

A substantial component of the functionality of support for BIPOC students involves the presence of safe spaces. In-person and virtual safe spaces include settings where individuals experience safety and security in expressing opinions, taking risks, and exploring their actions, feelings, and familiarities (Hernandez Rivera, 2020; Yosso et al., 2009). While safe spaces may include the safeguarded physical environment of an individual, this term typically consists of circumstances that provide emotional and psychological protection (Nadal et al., 2014; Williams, 2020). Many literature reviews of the concept of safe spaces address its use in establishing a sense of belonging for Lesbian, Gay, Bisexual, Trans, and gender diverse, Intersex, Queer, and questioning (LGBTIQ+) groups (Mann, 2022; McCavanagh & Cadaret, 2022). However, in response to experiences of ostracism, loneliness, discrimination, or lack of understanding, BIPOC students may also desire and create safe or counter spaces to forge a sense of belonging in response to being marginalized (Hernandez Rivera, 2020). These safe or counter spaces involve physical and virtual meeting spaces for individuals who share cultural commonalities and experiences.

Black, Indigenous, and People of Color individuals can form many safe spaces that serve several purposes for students in different settings. Yosso et al. (2009) described the existence of *academic counter spaces* or environments where students can feel safe discussing culturally based content in various courses, and *social counter spaces*, or spaces to share frustrations and connect based on shared experiences. Sief (2009) expanded on this definition of safe spaces by adding *politicized spaces* where the connection goes beyond academic and social connection and serves a role in organizing civic engagement and advocacy. The existence of safe cultural spaces can foster authentic dialogue and support and foster relationship building when individuals may not feel as though their opinions or cultural experiences possess value inside and outside of their academic setting (Sief, 2009; Yosso et al., 2009).

The goal of an intentional effort to create a space of belonging includes the opportunity to connect with other professionals, students, or culturally based groups and to support the ongoing retention of students and future professionals (McCavanagh & Cadaret, 2022). Many colleges and universities promote the value of DEI yet might not be aware of or acknowledge the experiences of BIPOC students who may experience an adverse racial climate of situations that span from institutional neglect to racial micro and macroaggressions (Nájera, 2020). Black, Indigenous, and People of Color students and faculty may become reluctant to share culturally based experiences, opinions, and needs due to fear of retaliation, the concern of impact on academic or professional success, and threats to the confidentiality of communicated information (Cisneros et al., 2022; Nájera, 2020; Shavers & Moore, 2014; Tuitt, 2012). However, as Butnaru et al. (2021) explained:

High aspirations, care, positive attitude toward learning, motivation, and encouragement of group members (teacher-student or student-student) can all contribute to obtaining good academic results. Students who do not receive significant support from their families compensate with the moral and social support provided by teachers and their peers and can still attain good school results and be successful in general. (p. 16)

Brick-and-mortar institutions have housed organizations such as Black Student Unions, Hispanic Student Union/Latinos Unidos, and Asian Student Alliances to provide a sense of cultural connection for self-identified cultural groups on college campuses (Graham, 2023; TBS Staff, 2022), yet little research verifies the existence of similar groups in online colleges either categorized by university, school, or program. Harrison, PhD (2022) encouraged students in online programs to find or create networks based on their needs and cultural identities as people and students. This strategy included encouraging online students to explore their comfort levels, availability, and best methods of communication in a distance-learning environment (Harrison PhD, 2022). Virtual or online safe spaces can facilitate meetings or communication using video applications, group text messages or phone calls, or plans to meet in person in various locations. As online education can establish a physical disconnect for students regarding in-person or synchronous interactions and communication, safe spaces become especially important when addressing ways to retain, influence, guide, and connect students in ways that align with their needs.

The Role of Mentorship

Mentorship includes influence or direction from one more experienced person to another, and support networks include individuals who provide social, financial, emotional, and spiritual guidance (Cisneros et al., 2022; Hebert et al., 2023; Pollard & Kumar, 2021). The literature has noted several benefits to mentorship for all online college and university students. Some advantages include fewer restrictions due to distance and time, abilities to document or record interactions that students and faculty can use for clarification, reflection, or research, and the choice to work synchronously or asynchronously based on the schedules of the mentee and mentor (Pollard & Kumar, 2021). For students, best practices in online mentoring included responsiveness, concern for the well-being of students as individuals, and consistent communication (Hebert et al., 2023).

The challenge in online environments, specifically for BIPOC students, includes creating constructive and successful opportunities for personal relationships, mentorship, and practical support networks (Hradilová & Chovancová, 2023; Payne et al., 2023; Phirangee & Malec, 2017). Two components of practical retention efforts for BIPOC students in higher education include mentoring and establishing an intensified support network (Chapman, 2018; Cisneros et al., 2022; Kornbluh et al., 2022; Kramarczuk et al., 2021; Liu, 2021). Scott and Sharp (2019) found that Black males who achieved advanced degrees mentioned cultural identity, supportive social networks, and self-beliefs contributing to their academic success. Black, Indigenous, and People of Color students reported experiencing connection and comfort when mentored by individuals with similar cultural beliefs (Barker, 2011; Cisneros et al., 2022; Esposito et al., 2017; Tuitt, 2012). Additionally, Gooden et al. (2020) found that when it pertained to culturally specific mentor-mentee relationships, a shared mindset of the value of educational attainment for family and community existed, which included pride, hope, and investment that reinforced the drive to be academically successful and impactful in their cultural community. Chapman (2018) explained, "Effective mentoring, advocacy, and scholar development relationships rely on open, race-aware engagement, value and respect for the scholar's personhood and scholarship, to realize a strong foundation for scholar success" (p. 600). Though non-BIPOC professors can foster meaningful mentorship relationships with BIPOC students, several authors note the significance of student connection with faculty members from their own racial or ethnic group, leading to an increase in matriculation and retention rates for BIPOC students (Barker, 2016; Brooms & Davis, 2017; Esposito et al., 2017; Tillman, 1998; 2001). These conclusions coincide with the benefits and ramifications of creating academic environments focusing on cultural and ethnic representation.

Complexities Associated With Mentorship

Although mentorship can positively impact BIPOC students, it is also essential to possess awareness of potential challenges when creating this professional relationship. Complexities can exist when crafting mentor-mentee relationships that may impact students' quality of the experience. Reddick (2015) and Santa-Ramirez (2022) explained the term *troll models*, a recreation of the concept of role models, referring to faculty tasked with mentoring and modeling ways for students to progress despite having unrelated values in comparison to students. This arrangement can include forced or disingenuous relationships between students where an absence exists in focusing on the needs of students, creating a supportive bond, or supporting the student holistically during their academic journey. Just as positive mentorship relationships can help students succeed, adverse mentorship relationships can damage students' academic path, goals, and retention (Reddick, 2015; Santa-Ramirez, 2022). Garrett et al. (2022) described negative mentor behaviors, such as setting unrealistic goals, not delivering adequate or clear direction, or communicating poorly, as diminishing the efficacy of the mentoring connection. These negative characteristics and behaviors can impact students' mental health, their motivation to succeed, and the potential for having students reach out for support when experiencing academic challenges (Nadal et al., 2014). Understanding the complexities of mentorship and the quality, dedication, and qualifications of the designated mentor or mentors become key when creating a support system for BIPOC students. Capriciously pairing students and faculty of similar races and ethnicities without understanding the needs, experiences, goals, values, and dedication of the individuals involved can potentially become more damaging for students than not providing any support.

The Weight of Service for BIPOC Faculty. The literature has addressed the effectiveness and preference for mentorship, support networks, and creating safe spaces for BIPOC students to include the support of BIPOC faculty (Cisneros et al., 2022; Nájera, 2020; Tuitt, 2012). Equally, the literature has also addressed the challenges and lack of compensation that BIPOC faculty receive for their directed support of BIPOC students. An aspect of these challenges includes an unwarranted assumption that BIPOC faculty will instinctively or routinely assume the role of mentor due to cultural similarities, in addition to their educational duties (Shavers & Moore, 2014).

The term *cultural taxation* incorporates the expectation that BIPOC faculty maintain requirements to excel in instruction, research, and professional service while also undertaking cultural tasks that other faculty do not possess, such as advocate or therapist for BIPOC students or consultant for BIPOC concerns (Padilla, 1994; Santa-Ramirez, 2022). While many BIPOC faculty possess a pride, professional proclivity, and personal inclination to support the academic growth of BIPOC students, academic leaders should not view this social responsibility as a professional obligation (Brissett, 2020; Scott et al., 2022). Brissett (2020) and Santa-Ramirez (2022) explain that BIPOC faculty can spend a disproportionately large amount of time mentoring BIPOC students during their tenure. The disproportional expectation placed upon BIPOC faculty includes the presence of *invisible labor* that generally remains unrecognized in performance, tenure, and promotion reviews. Brissett (2020) shared:

Rewards systems in colleges and universities are meant to create incentive structures that determine how faculty prioritize their work. Based on this logic, the mentorship ethos that guides faculty of color in their work with students of color is comparatively less valued by the academy based on how it is ranked in the rewards system. (p. 571)

Santa-Ramirez (2022) explains that as the culture of white dominance in academia can impact the professional careers and aspirations of BIPOC faculty, academic leaders must understand that many BIPOC faculty may also need levels of support, mentorship, and safe spaces that can mirror the needs of BIPOC students. In essence, BIPOC faculty may face the challenges of providing the guidance, encouragement, and resources to students that they require (Brissett, 2020). Additionally, expanding on the concept of *troll models*, arbitrarily pairing BIPOC faculty with BIPOC students in a mentorship capacity does not guarantee mutual interests or values (Reddick, 2015; Santa-Ramirez, 2022). A disingenuous or forced mentoring relationship or obligation between BIPOC faculty and BIPOC students based on mutual cultural identity can become detrimental to creating an environment of inclusion, awareness, and belonging.

As educational institutions strive to promote initiatives in DEI through the creation and development of formal or informal mentorship and safe spaces, Garrett et al. (2022) communicated the need for colleges and universities to provide comprehensive support resources and adjust evaluation methods to reward BIPOC faculty who mentor students throughout their tenure. Establishing formal or informal safe spaces to promote student belonging and retention requires academic leaders to consider what support and safe spaces they provide for BIPOC faculty, as well (Garrett et al., 2022). Furthermore, in understanding the risks and benefits that BIPOC mentorship can have on students, academic leaders must exercise diligence in informally and formally pairing students and faculty. An assessment should appraise the interest, training, compensation, and recognition of BIPOC faculty in creating and fostering these DEI efforts for BIPOC students (Brissett, 2020; Santa-Ramirez, 2022).

The Role of Non-BIPOC Faculty and Cross-Cultural Support. Multicultural knowledge, skills, and abilities through experience and professional development become essential for all mentors (Suriel et al., 2018). As statistics reveal a disproportionate balance between the number of BIPOC faculty in high education and BIPOC students (Educationdata.org, 2022; National Center for Education Statistics, 2022), complexities may exist for institutions and programs when addressing the need for culturally conscious mentorship opportunities. Merriweather et al. (2022) found that some cross-cultural mentorships fell into the categories of pragmatic, focusing on the universal language of the subject area and culture minimization. Mentors directed their support to the objective completion of academic tasks or milestones, solely enforced the expectations of the field rather than acknowledging mitigating factors for students, and did not address any culturally based concerns or needs outside of the student meeting curricula requirements. Merriweather et al. (2022) also explained that these types of relationships could perpetuate social and epistemological barriers and maintain borders of marginalization. In addressing cross-cultural support barriers for non-BIPOC faculty in mentorship roles, Harris and Lee (2019) recommended adopting the role of an advocate-mentor. Advocate-mentors work to reinforce the intellectual abilities of BIPOC mentees, acknowledge their value to the program, validate their academic interests, and support academic opportunities that will develop career advancement in BIPOC mentees. Using compassion and respect, Harris and Lee (2019) suggest integrating racial, professional, and intellectual privilege to advocate for their BIPOC mentees. This advocacy involves a commitment to encouraging accountability for the needs of BIPOC students and faculty, as well as challenging the department and institution to promote diversity, equity, inclusion, and systemic change (Harris & Lee, 2019). Some scholars also recommended providing connections or referrals to BIPOC colleagues at other institutions or culturally based organizations within the academic field to help support students who may seek a cultural connection with a faculty mentor (Harrison PhD, 2022; Suriel et al., 2018).

ESTABLISHING SAFE SPACES FOR BIPOC STUDENTS

For BIPOC students to communicate their needs and understandings to academic leaders, opportunities for dialogue must exist. Colleges and universities, academic programs, and students retain responsibility for creating and maintaining protected settings and opportunities for students and faculty to connect culturally (Cisneros et al., 2022; Clarke & Davison, 2020; Kramarczuk et al., 2021). Although BIPOC students can experience a lack of safety in many social and academic settings, when promoting the value of DEI in their colleges and programs, academic leaders must strive to identify ways to develop safe spaces that promote belonging and support. This identification includes knowledge of the people, processes, and trust necessary to establish safe spaces.

Understanding Virtual Cultural Affinity Spaces

Cultural affinity groups involve spaces for connection created to support individuals who share common demographic and cultural profiles (Young & Hockfield, 2019). In addition to fostering dialogue amongst participants, these groups can promote professional development, establish social events, and create awareness about cultural celebration months meant to educate and appreciate the contributions of their respective cultures. Like the conception of safe or counter spaces, cultural affinity groups can provide emotional and psychological protection for individuals looking for safety and security in expressing opinions, taking risks, and exploring their actions, feelings, and familiarities (Sief, 2009; Yosso et al., 2009). Virtual cultural affinity spaces utilize the technological capabilities of online programs, telephone, or electronic communication to bond with other individuals without being in person. Whether connected synchronously or asynchronously, the benefits of belonging to a virtual cultural affinity space parallel the appeal of online education (Payne et al., 2023). Members or participants can exist in various physical or geographic locations, communicate during times that align with their schedules, and choose when and how to connect with others.

Given the information regarding the academic experiences of BIPOC students concerning inequalities, stressors, additional responsibilities, and perceptions of cultural and ethnic representation, creating a designated online environment may provide an opportunity for connection, mentorship, and support. Virtual cultural affinity spaces may provide a setting for students to share their life and academic experiences while sharing their success needs with each other and trusted faculty (Payne et al., 2023). For BIPOC students in online education, developing a virtual cultural affinity space may include presenting a safe space for students, establishing a setting to share or garner resources for academic success, and cultivating a way to exhibit cultural and ethnic representation (Silverstein et al., 2022). Virtual cultural affinity spaces may also provide an opportunity to embrace the elements of DEI, assess the effectiveness of inclusivity, and provide opportunities to learn about ways to improve the online educational experience for BIPOC students.

Implications for Development

While the number of BIPOC students entering higher education spaces and matriculating has increased over the years (United States Census Bureau, 2022), there is a growing need to create cultural affinity spaces that provide mentorship, a safe space, and a sense of belonging for students desiring a culturally based connection to others in online educational environments (Cisneros et al., 2022; Clarke, 2020; Kramarczuk et al., 2021; Yosso et al., 2009). Creating virtual cultural affinity groups requires planning and possession of relevant resources to implement. Online educational institutions must consider the interest and availability of BIPOC faculty, staff, and student leaders; the presence of methods to effectively communicate with BIPOC students; an idea to develop institution-wide, program-specific, or school-specific groups; access to a virtual meeting technology program, and the validity of opportunities to communicate with administrators to evoke change when necessary (Butnaru et al., 2021; Cisneros et al., 2022; Kramarczuk et al., 2021).

As previously mentioned in the chapter, creating virtual cultural affinity spaces requires more than just the existence of BIPOC faculty, staff, or students. Proper development of culturally specific virtual affinity spaces necessitates individuals with a genuine interest and passion for providing influence, social, financial, emotional, and spiritual guidance, and direction to students (Cisneros et al., 2022; Clarke, 2020; Kramarczuk et al., 2021). Faculty leaders must possess the power and desire to evoke or enact change, when necessary, involving issues from institutional and cultural neglect to racial micro and macroaggressions. Hiring processes should include proactive individuals and resources provided to maintain virtual cultural affinity spaces, such as video applications to hold meetings and marketing or communication to promote the presence of these spaces for new and current BIPOC students (Kramarczuk et al., 2021). Academic leaders should offer sufficient compensation and recognition of these faculty leadership roles and the time commitment required to mentor students, as well (Brissett, 2020). These spaces also necessitate the requirement of BIPOC students who desire leadership roles in facilitating the times when students have a place to speak freely amongst themselves.

Academic leaders must be aware that BIPOC individuals do not exist in a monolith despite similarities in racial or ethnic identity. Although some students might benefit from joining a virtual cultural affinity space, other students may feel unsafe in these groups with other students or faculty leaders despite possessing a cultural connection (McCavanagh & Cadaret, 2022). Each student should be able to experiment with membership in these virtual cultural affinity spaces to gain reassurance of its safety and alignment with the needs of their cultural and educational encounters. Academic leaders should also understand that the mere existence of these spaces may not correlate with success in addressing DEI or the effectiveness of BIPOC student mentorship and support. Academic leaders must be diligent in assessing the interest in these groups and consistently evaluate the effectiveness of these spaces for students (Payne et al. 2020, 2021, 2023).

Modeling an Existing Virtual Cultural Affinity Space Structure

Payne et al. (2020, 2021, 2023) described successfully creating Tapestry, a structured virtual cultural affinity space for Black women Counselor Education and Supervision doctoral students and a group that provided connection and visibility for students, faculty, and professionals. This cultural affinity group began by explicitly sharing emailed and posted communication with students in the classroom regarding the availability of an online space for Black women to connect, noting the personal and professional challenges Black women faced while pursuing a doctoral degree. The group met monthly using an online video application and intentionally was formatted to provide connection and a safe space for Black women.

According to Payne et al. (2020, 2021), the faculty member(s) and students reserved the first portion of the meeting for connection and dialogue with an established mentor or mentors with similar cultural self-identity. This setting provided a casual space for students to ask questions and communicate about the program, career paths, challenges, and successes through the lens of race and gender. An additional aspect of the first portion of this meeting provided an opportunity for Black women guest speakers (professional and other faculty) to casually speak to students about directed topics or lessons learned during their academic and professional journeys through the lens of race and gender.

Payne et al. (2020, 2021) described the second portion of the meeting as sister circle time. Allen (2019) defined a sister circle as a "welcoming physical and emotional coping space that allows Black women to unpack and manage the oppressive societal situations they encounter" (p. 6). In sister circle time, the faculty leader(s) and guest speaker(s) exited the meeting to allow the students a safe space to connect. In this space, facilitated by a student leader or student leaders, students were free to discuss directed topics in academics, current events, work/life/school balance, accomplishments, or recent experiences or need for support. While the faculty leaders did not participate in sister circle time, the student leader or student leaders regularly met with faculty leaders to discuss needs that required extra support from faculty, the program, and content or people of interest in which students requested to enhance their learning and experience (Payne et al., 2020, 2021). This monthly virtual cultural affinity group meeting was optional for students to relieve the pressure of adding obligations to their schedules. It also provided a consistent connection as leaders scheduled monthly meetings for specific times and dates. Students also received professional and academic resources and opportunities through email communication and a student-created newsletter throughout the year.

Similarly, Silverstein et al. (2022) described the virtual implementation of Scholars Committed to Opportunities in Psychological Education (SCOPE), an antiracist and culturally informed program that provided workshops and mentorship for BIPOC undergraduates interested in pursuing graduate education in psychology. Initially conducted as an in-person weekend program, the virtual adaptation of SCOPE involved large group sessions and smaller breakout group sessions covering research, clinical, and advocacy interests (Silverstein et al., 2022). SCOPE organizers emphasized recruiting BIPOC faculty members or graduate students to lead the breakout groups; however, a requirement existed for all team members (BIPOC and non-BIPOC) to complete multicultural competency and advocacy training to understand the issues faced by racial/ethnic minority individuals (Silverstein et al., 2023). Workshops provided academic and career support, such as finding financial resources, searching for graduate programs, creating curriculum vitae (CVs), and interviewing skills. Workshops also covered healthcare and educational disparities, self-care when experiencing microaggressions and racism, racial and ethnic identity development, and relationships with mentors. Participants of SCOPE reported an increase in self-efficacy, increased knowledge of the graduate application process, a decrease in stress, and no experienced microaggressions throughout the program (Silverstein et al., 2022).

The purpose of creating a virtual cultural affinity space for BIPOC students includes the opportunity to incorporate safety, mentorship, advocacy, academic, professional, and personal support, connection, and visibility for students who may feel culturally isolated in their online environments. Although enrollment numbers may determine the membership criteria, Payne et al. (2020, 2021) and Silverstein et al. (2022, 2023) provide designs for other online organizations and approaches to developing virtual cultural affinity spaces for connection. Faculty and student leaders can use these blueprints, along with knowledge of their BIPOC students, as a basis and structure to meet the needs and capabilities of their colleges, universities, and students. Many students may require various meeting times or management of smaller groups separated by college, programs, student levels, gender, geographic location, or other cultural intersectionality characteristics. However, as the cultural membership of these virtual spaces might vary, the plan and structure of virtual cultural affinity can begin by using Tapestry and SCOPE as model formats (Payne et al., 2020, 2021; Silverstein et al., 2022, 2023).

CONCLUSION

The goals of fostering cultural competency and strategies to develop meaningful relationships have become increasingly significant for academic leaders in online institutions. Instructors and programs must understand how to provide opportunities for connection and inclusion for all students in educational environments by identifying and understanding challenges and successful strategies that impact students, as well as establishing systemic changes that support the retention of students in historically excluded groups, such as BIPOC individuals or racial and ethnic minorities.

This chapter described common themes of isolation, a sense of belonging, and the quest for safe spaces amongst BIPOC students in online educational environments. This chapter also discussed the role of mentorship and culturally specific virtual affinity spaces in uncovering links to connectedness and the importance of fostering meaningful relationships that combat isolation linked to BIPOC students' perception of support, safety, and belonging in online degree programs. A goal of higher education institutions includes educating future professionals, which includes retaining them and supporting their matriculation. In the mission to address cultural competency and meaningful online relationships for BIPOC students, academic leaders must intentionally understand these students' unique experiences. Effective planning and implementation require the presence of BIPOC faculty, staff, and student leaders, adequate compensation, effective communication with students, increased visibility, institution-wide or division by program or school, access to a virtual meeting technology program, and space and opportunity to communicate with administrators to evoke change when necessary.

REFERENCES

Ajmal, M., & Ahmad, S. (2019). Exploration of anxiety factors among students of distance learning: A case study of Allama Iqbal Open University. *Bulletin of Education and Research August, 41*(2), 67–78.

Allen, C. (2019). Calling all the sisters: The Impact of sister circles on the retention and experiences of Black womyn collegians at predominantly White institutions. *All Dissertations*, 2374. https://tigerprints.clemson.edu/all_dissertations/2374

Almazova, N., Krylova, E., Rubtsova, A., & Odinokaya, M. (2020). Challenges and opportunities for Russian higher education amid COVID-19. *Education Sciences*, *10*(12), 368. doi:10.3390/educsci10120368

Ayala, M. I., & Chalupa Young, D. (2022). Racial microaggressions and coping mechanisms among Latina/o college students. *Sociological Forum*, *37*(1), 200–221. doi:10.1111ocf.12785

Banks, B. M., & Landau, S. (2022). Take a deep breath: Coping and the cognitive consequences of racial microaggression among Black college women. *Journal of College Student Psychotherapy*, 1–20. doi:10.1080/87568225.2022.2100855

Barker, M. J. (2016). The Doctorate in Black and White: Exploring the engagement of black doctoral students in cross-race advising relationships with White faculty. *The Western Journal of Black Studies*, *40*(2), 126–140.

Barnett, R. M. (2020). Leading with meaning: Why diversity, equity, and inclusion matters in US higher education. *Perspectives in Education*, *38*(2), 20–35. doi:10.18820/2519593X/pie.v38.i2.02

Bonilla-Silva, E. (2014). *Racism without racists: Color-blind racism and the persistence of racial inequality in the United States*. Rowman & Littlefield Publishers.

Brissett, N. (2020). Inequitable rewards: Experiences of faculty of color mentoring students of color. *Mentoring & Tutoring*, *28*(5), 556–577. doi:10.1080/13611267.2020.1859327

Brooms, D. R., & Davis, A. R. (2017). Staying focused on the goal: Peer bonding and faculty mentors supporting Black males' persistence in college. *Journal of Black Studies*, *48*(3), 305–326. doi:10.1177/0021934717692520

Butnaru, G. I., Haller, A.-P., Dragolea, L.-L., Anichiti, A., & Tacu Hârşan, G.-D. (2021). Students' well-being during the transition from onsite to online education: Are there risks arising from social isolation? *International Journal of Environmental Research and Public Health*, *18*(18), 9665. doi:10.3390/ijerph18189665 PMID:34574589

Chapman, R. N. (2018). The Thrive Mosaic developmental framework: A systems activist approach to marginalized STEM Scholar success. *The American Behavioral Scientist*, *62*(5), 600–611. doi:10.1177/0002764218768859

Cisneros, D., Anandavalli, S., Brown, E. M., Whitman, J. S., & Chaney, M. P. (2022). Anti-racist mentorship: A multicultural and social justice approach to mentoring students identifying as Black, Indigenous, and persons of color in counselor education. *Journal of Counselor Leadership & Advocacy*, 1–13. doi:10.1080/2326716X.2022.2162462

Clarke, R., & Davison, R. M. (2020). Through whose eyes? The critical concept of researcher perspective. *Journal of the Association for Information Systems*, *21*(2), 483–501. doi:10.17705/1jais.00609

Educationdata.org. (2022). *College graduation statistics*. https://educationdata.org/number-of-college-graduates

Esposito, J., Lee, T., Limes-Taylor, H. K., Mason, A., Outler, A., Rodriguez Jackson, J., ... Whitaker-Lea, L. (2017). Doctoral students' experiences with pedagogies of the home, pedagogies of love, and mentoring in the academy. *Educational Studies (Ames)*, *53*(2), 155–177. doi:10.1080/00131946.2017.1286589

Garrett, S. D., Williams, M. S., & Carr, A. M. (2022). Finding their way: Exploring the experiences of tenured Black women faculty. *Journal of Diversity in Higher Education*, *16*(5), 527–538. doi:10.1037/dhe0000213

Gooden, M. A., Devereaux, C. A., & Hulse, N. E. (2020). #BlackintheIvory: Culturally responsive mentoring with Black women doctoral students and a Black male mentor. *Mentoring & Tutoring*, *28*(4), 392–415. doi:10.1080/13611267.2020.1793083

Graham, C. (2023). *The History of the Black Student Union*. https://www.bestcolleges.com/blog/history-of-black-student-union/

Hall, S. (Ed.). (1997). Representation: Cultural representations and signifying practices. Sage Publications, Inc.

Harris, T. M., & Lee, C. N. (2019). Advocate-mentoring: A communicative response to diversity in higher education. *Communication Education*, *68*(1), 103–113. doi:10.1080/03634523.2018.1536272

Harrison, A. (2022). 10 tips for navigating online graduate school: A Guide for single parents & primary caretakers. Author.

Hebert, H. S., Dye, C. K., Lauber, D. E., Roy, D. P., Harden, V., Wrye, B. A., Harris, A., Hendrix, S. P., Sheehan-Smith, L., & Zhang, H. (2023). Connecting online graduate students to the university community. *Journal of Higher Education Theory and Practice*, *23*(2), 190–201. doi:10.33423/jhetp.v23i2.5815

Hernandez Rivera, S. (2020). A space of our own: Examining a womxn of color retreat as a counterspace. *Journal of Women and Gender in Higher Education*, *13*(3), 327–347. doi:10.1080/26379112.2020.1844220

Hradilová, A., & Chovancová, B. (2023). *Visual representations as a means to motivate students and curb feelings of isolation in distance learning*. https://www.hltmag.co.uk/feb23/visual-representations

Keels, M. (2020). *Campus counter spaces: Black and Latinx Students' search for the community at historically White Universities*. Cornell University Press. doi:10.7591/cornell/9781501746888.001.0001

Kornbluh, M., Bell, S., Vierra, K., & Herrnstadt, Z. (2022). Resistance capital: Cultural activism as a gateway to college persistence for minority and first-generation students. *Journal of Adolescent Research*, *37*(4), 501–540. doi:10.1177/07435584211006920

Kramarczuk, K., Atchison, K., Plane, J., & Narayanasamy, M. (2021). The Power of mentoring programs in retaining women and Black, Indigenous, and students of color in undergraduate computing majors. *2021 International Conference on Computational Science and Computational Intelligence (CSCI), Computational Science and Computational Intelligence (CSCI), 2021 International Conference on CSCI*, 1125–1128. 10.1109/CSCI54926.2021.00237

Kumi-Yeboah, A., Yuan, G., & Dogbey, J. (2017). Online collaborative learning activities: The perceptions of culturally diverse graduate students. *Online Learning : the Official Journal of the Online Learning Consortium, 21*(4), 5–28. doi:10.24059/olj.v21i4.1277

Liu, T. (2021). *Relationships among mentoring support and student success in a Chinese first-year experience program* [Doctoral dissertation, Chapman University]. Chapman University Digital Commons. doi:10.36837/chapman.000329

Mann, G. (2022). Allies as guides in the borderlands: The development of an online ally program to foster belonging for LGBTIQ+ students and staff at a regional university. *Journal of University Teaching & Learning Practice, 19*(4), 1–18.

McCavanagh, T. M., & Cadaret, M. C. (2022). Creating safe spaces for lesbian, gay, bisexual, transgender, and queer (LGBTQ+) student–athletes. In Affirming LGBTQ+ students in higher education. (pp. 141–159). American Psychological Association. doi:10.1037/0000281-009

Merriweather, L. R., Howell, C. D., & Gnanadass, E. (2022). Cross-cultural mentorships with Black and Brown US STEM Doctoral Students: Unpacking the perceptions of International faculty. *2022 IEEE Frontiers in Education Conference (FIE), Frontiers in Education Conference (FIE), 2022 IEEE*, 1–9. 10.1109/FIE56618.2022.9962715

Morgan, H., & Houghton, A. (2011). *Inclusive curriculum design in higher education: Considerations for effective practice across and within subject areas.* The Higher Education Academy.

Nadal, K. L. (2021). *Why representation matters and why it's still not enough: Reflections on growing up brown, queer, and Asian American.* https://www.psychologytoday.com/us/blog/psychology-the-people/202112/why-representation-matters-and-why-it-s-still-not-enough

Nadal, K. L., Wong, Y., Griffin, K. E., Davidoff, K., & Sriken, J. (2014). The adverse impact of racial microaggressions on college students' self-esteem. *Journal of College Student Development, 55*(5), 461–474. doi:10.1353/csd.2014.0051

Nájera, J. R. (2020). Creating safe space for undocumented students: Building on politically unstable ground. *Anthropology & Education Quarterly, 51*(3), 341–358. doi:10.1111/aeq.12339

National Center for Education Statistics. (2022). *Race/ethnicity of college faculty.* https://nces.ed.gov/fastfacts/display.asp?id=61

Okechukwu, A. (2019). *To fulfill these rights: Political struggle over affirmative action and open admissions.* Columbia University Press. doi:10.7312/okec18308

Padilla, A. M. (1994). Research news and comment: Ethnic minority scholars; research, and mentoring: Current and future issues. *Educational Researcher, 23*(4), 24–27. doi:10.3102/0013189X023004024

Paul, J. D., & Maranto, R. (2023). Elite schools lead an empirical examination of diversity requirements in higher education job markets. *Studies in Higher Education, 48*(2), 314–328. doi:10.1080/03075079.2022.2134334

Payne, R., Harrison, A., & Griffin, M. (2020, September). *Mentorship and African American women: Exploring topics that arise in safe spaces* [Presentation]. Walden University National Faculty Meeting, Virtual.

Payne, R., Harrison, A., & Griffin, M. (2021, August 19). *Confronting integration, belonging and isolation of graduate students of color* [Presentation]. Walden University Real-World Solutions to Real-World Problems: Expanding the Women-in-Leadership Advantage, Virtual.

Payne, R., Harrison, A., & Griffin, M. (2023). *"Safe spaces are built": How African American women discuss personal and professional connectedness in online doctoral program* [Manuscript submitted for publication].

Petts, A. L. (2022). Attitudes about affirmative action in higher education admissions. *The Sociological Quarterly*, *63*(4), 711–732. doi:10.1080/00380253.2021.1951627

Phirangee, K., & Malec, A. (2017). Othering in online learning: An examination of social presence, identity, and sense of community. *Distance Education*, *38*(2), 160–172. doi:10.1080/01587919.2017.1322457

Pollard, R., & Kumar, S. (2021). Mentoring graduate students online: Strategies and challenges. *International Review of Research in Open and Distance Learning*, *22*(2), 267–284. doi:10.19173/irrodl.v22i2.5093

Preston, D. (2017). *Untold barriers for Black students in higher education: Placing race at the center of developmental education*. https://southerneducation.org/wp-content/uploads/untold-barriers-for-black-students-in-higher-ed.pdf

Puhy, C., Prakash, N., Lacson, C., & Bradt, J. (2021). Multicultural teaching competence among undergraduate faculty: A convergent mixed methods study. *Journal for Multicultural Education*, *15*(4), 459–473. doi:10.1108/JME-05-2021-0059

Reddick, R. J. (2015). Of feral faculty and magisterial Mowgli: The domestication of junior faculty. In C. Turner (Ed.), *New directions for higher education* (pp. 43–51). Jossey-Bass., doi:10.1002/he.20141

Rinke, C. R., Williams, S. A. S., Conlin, V., & Coshal, S. (2021). Shaping an inclusive higher education curriculum: Building capacity for transformational change. *School Psychology Training & Pedagogy*, *38*(1), 24–36.

Sadeghi, M. (2019). A shift from classroom to distance learning: Advantages and limitations. *International Journal of Research in English Education*, *4*(1), 80–88. doi:10.29252/ijree.4.1.80

Sangaramoorthy, T., & Richardson, B. J. (2020). *Black lives matter without Black people?* https://www.insidehighered.com/advice/2020/10/16/many-people-deny-how-pervasive-racism-higher-ed-and-how-its-often-reproduced

Santa-Ramirez, S. (2022). Sink or swim: The mentoring experiences of Latinx PhD students with faculty of color. *Journal of Diversity in Higher Education*, *15*(1), 124–134. doi:10.1037/dhe0000335

Scott, B. L., Muñoz, S. M., & Scott, S. B. (2022). How whiteness operates at a Hispanic serving institution: A qualitative case study of faculty, staff, and administrators. *Journal of Diversity in Higher Education*. Advance online publication. doi:10.1037/dhe0000438

Scott, L., & Sharp, L. A. (2019). Black males who hold advanced degrees: Critical factors that preclude and promote success. *The Journal of Negro Education*, *88*(1), 44–61. doi:10.7709/jnegroeducation.88.1.0044

Seif, H. (2009). *The Civic education and engagement of Latina/o immigrant youth: Challenging boundaries and creating safe spaces*. Research Paper Series on Latino Immigrant Civic and Political Participation, no 5. University of Illinois.

Shavers, M. C., & Moore, J. L. III. (2014). Black female voices: Self-presentation strategies in doctoral programs at predominately White institutions. *Journal of College Student Development*, *55*(4), 391–407. doi:10.1353/csd.2014.0040

Silverstein, M. W., Fix, R. L., Nuhu, N., & Kaslow, N. J. (2023). Disseminating a mentoring program for undergraduates of color: Lessons learned. *Scholarship of Teaching and Learning in Psychology*, *9*(1), 38–49. doi:10.1037tl0000224

Silverstein, M. W., Miller, M., Rivet, J., & Nuhu, N. (2022). Program evaluation of a virtual mentoring program for BIPOC undergraduates in psychology. *Scholarship of Teaching and Learning in Psychology*. Advance online publication. doi:10.1037tl0000322

Solórzano, D. G., & Pérez Huber, L. (2020). *Racial microaggressions: Using critical race theory to respond to everyday racism*. Teachers College Press.

Staff, T. B. S. (2022, August 30). *The ultimate guide to campus clubs and organizations.* https://thebestschools.org/magazine/popular-college-clubs/

Suriel, R. L., Martinez, J., & Evans-Winters, V. (2018). A Critical co-constructed autoethnography of a gendered cross-cultural mentoring between two early career Latin@ scholars working in the deep South. *Educational Studies (Ames)*, *54*(2), 165–182. doi:10.1080/00131946.2017.1356308

Taylor, J. (2019). *Perception is not reality.* https://www.psychologytoday.com/us/blog/the-power-prime/201908/perception-is-not-reality

Tillman, L. C. (1998). The mentoring of African American faculty: Scaling the promotion and tenure mountain. In H. T. Frierson (Ed.), *Diversity in Higher Education* (pp. 141–155). JAI Press.

Tillman, L. C. (2001). Mentoring African-American faculty in predominantly White institutions. *Research in Higher Education*, *42*(3), 295–325. doi:10.1023/A:1018822006485

Tuitt, F. (2012). Black like me: Graduate students' perceptions of their pedagogical experiences in classes taught by Black faculty in a predominantly White institution. *Journal of Black Studies*, *43*(2), 186–206. doi:10.1177/0021934711413271

United States Census Bureau. (2022). *Educational attainment in the United States: 2021*. Author.

Van Roekel, N. P. D. (2008). *Promoting educators' cultural competence to better serve culturally diverse students*. National Education Agency.

Williams, M. T. (2020). Microaggressions: Clarification, evidence, and impact. *Perspectives on Psychological Science*, *15*(1), 3–26. doi:10.1177/1745691619827499 PMID:31418642

Yosso, T., Smith, W., Ceja, M., & Solarzano, D. (2009). Critical race theory, microaggressions, and campus racial climate for Latina/o undergraduates. *Harvard Educational Review, 79*(4), 659–690.

Young, S., & Hockfield, B. (2019). Bringing the curtain down on affinity groups: Cultural equity teams wait in the wings. *Profiles in Diversity Journal*, 66–69.

KEY TERMS AND DEFINITIONS

Black, Indigenous, and People of Color (BIPOC): Person-first language that shifts away from the traditional labels such as "marginalized" and "minority" used to describe the cultural groups of Black, American Indians or Native Americans, First Nations, Native Alaskans or Alaska Natives, Hispanic, East Asian, South Asian, and Hawaiian and Pacific Islander racial and ethnic individuals.

Cultural and Ethnic Representation: The visibility and recognition of individuals who share physical and social connections with others in physical presence, curricula, and policies.

Diversity, Equity, and Inclusion: Policies and procedures that promote the representation and involvement of diverse groups of individuals incorporate people of different ages, races, ethnicities, abilities, disabilities, genders, religions, cultures, and sexual orientations.

Mentorship: Influence, guidance, and direction from one more experienced person to another, and support networks include individuals who provide social, financial, emotional, and spiritual guidance.

Online Educational Programs: Training or academic courses that include remote or virtual access to connect with course materials or teachers.

Racial Microaggressions: Verbal, nonverbal, or visual offensive exchanges that emphasize the power differentials amongst racial groups.

Safe Spaces: Settings where individuals experience safety and security in expressing opinions, taking risks, and exploring their actions, feelings, and familiarities.

Virtual Cultural Affinity Groups: Spaces for connection utilizing the technological capabilities of online programs, telephone, or electronic communication to support individuals who share common demographic and cultural profiles.

Chapter 8
Cultural Sensitivity in the Distance Learning Sphere

Nancy Thomas
https://orcid.org/0000-0001-6759-8287
Colorado Christian University, USA

Crystal A. Brashear
Colorado Christian University, USA

Rebecca Mathews
https://orcid.org/0000-0002-3322-6351
University of North Carolina at Greensboro, USA

Donna Hickman
University of North Texas, USA

ABSTRACT

As the old adage states, "With great power comes great responsibility." Distance education is a double-edged sword – one with great power and also great responsibility. It can impact millions more than the average brick-and-mortar program, which increases the need for sensitivity to those receiving the learning. The need for competence related to multicultural factors in distance education is greater now with the sharp rise in popularity. In 2016, there were over 6 million students in the United States utilizing distance education, half of whom were fully remote. This begets the need for awareness and training at an institutional level to combat the lack of sensitivity and effectively equip students of all backgrounds to adjust to the virtual world. Students, instructors, and institutions will be best equipped to carry the load with careful attention to the three core components of professional training, professional development, and professional identity. This is an ethical and professional responsibility.

DOI: 10.4018/978-1-6684-8908-6.ch008

Distance learning has been an educational format for millions of students and has increased in popularity over time. In 2012, 25.9% of all students were enrolled in at least one distance course (Seaman et al., 2018). By 2016, this number had increased to 31.6%, representing 6,359,121 students enrolled in distance learning. The COVID-19 pandemic adjusted how education was delivered (UNESCO, 2020) and in 2020, approximately three-fourths of undergraduate and graduate students had at least one class that was completed online (National Center for Education Statistics, 2022).

Distance education has its roots in making education more accessible (Kentnor, 2015). Removing the requirement that a teacher and student must reside in the same space at the same time opened educational doors for those in rural areas. It reduced the financial barriers associated with attending a brick-and-mortar institution. Additionally, its flexibility supported students who needed to fit education around their schedules (Turan et al., 2022). These factors increased educational access to students and faculty from diverse backgrounds, cultures, races, and identities (Snow & Coker, 2020) and removed geographic barriers.

How do educators meet the needs of an ever-changing student population? It begins with providing education in a culturally responsive manner, meeting the needs of students with diverse backgrounds and identities. Each student has individualized needs and culturally responsive distance learning will allow instructors to cater to these unique needs. In a study of student success, Becker et al. (2009) found that "feelings of safety and security" (p. 147) were correlated with student performance. Understanding what helps to create that connection and sense of safety for students, particularly minoritized students, will benefit educators as they craft courses to meet students' needs.

In this chapter, we will discuss competencies for culturally responsive educators in the distance learning sphere. We will establish the need for training and professional development. We will explore the connection between cultural competency and an educator's professional identity. Finally, we will describe some practical tools educators can utilize in this ever-expanding space and present case studies to apply theory to practice.

LITERATURE REVIEW

Multicultural Competence

With the rapid growth of immigrants in the United States, it is easy to see the need for sensitivity to the diverse needs and expectations of the various cultures represented. Often, we are trapped in a Western worldview that blinds us to the needs of other populations that might look different than our own. Unlike the helping professions where multicultural competence training is provided and assessed, many other schools of thought may not emphasize this in the same way (Attilee, 2019). According to the Pew Research Center (Budman, 2020), the number of foreign-born individuals in the United States in 2018 was 44.8 million, or about 13.7% of the entire population. By 2065, 88% of the population is projected to be immigrants or descendants of immigrants in the United States (Budman, 2020). With the growing diversity comes the responsibility to appropriately honor the needs that arise.

Distance Education

The mainstream classroom has shifted significantly over the last several decades as distance education continues to rise in popularity (Seaman et al., 2018). There has been a similar strength in the decline of residential students, a reduction of over a million students between 2012 and 2016 (Seaman et al., 2018). For many students, the shift to distance education may have been the only way they could secure higher education training along with full-time jobs and other responsibilities (Ragusa & Crampton, 2018). In the Fall of 2021, 9.4 million students, or 61% of undergraduate students, were enrolled in at least one online class, according to the National Center for Education Statistics (2022). What was once housed in a brick-and-mortar institution is now largely housed in a digital world where the potential impact is far greater. Students from around the globe can have immediate access in moments. Distance education may eliminate the need for international students to relocate, secure visas, and leave their homes to be able to secure a prolific educational experience (Kung, 2017). Distance education also provides institutions access to a larger collection of instructors and faculty members (Snow & Coker, 2020). The benefits are many, but the challenges are too.

Multicultural Considerations in Distance Education

Growth in the online classroom and the reach of online education all point towards a need for continued assessment and improvement of the online classroom. Since making the shift during the pandemic, in many institutions, the virtual classroom has found a permanent home. One of many motivations for its continued use is its ability to reach historically underserved populations in remote areas within the United States (Bennett-Levy et al., 2012). The growth of distance education has reduced barriers and improved access for many cultural groups around the world without the limitation of proximity (Sells et al., 2012). Particularly in minoritized populations, reducing barriers has increased access for people groups that have never had the privilege of experiencing higher education. Despite the convenience, the domestic and international reach poses far greater challenges for educators.

Researchers recommend that instructors of all disciplines make extra efforts to improve their knowledge of cultural diversity as they determine resources for their classroom (Kung, 2017, Kumi-Yeboah et al. 2020). Fifty full-time educators across three universities in the United States participated in a qualitative study in which researchers found that the perception of diversity differed based on the discipline taught. Despite the instructional strategies available, significant challenges exist related to incorporating diversity in the online classroom, including time limitations, risk of stereotyping, and language barriers (Kumi-Yeboah et al., 2020). Students in online settings were surveyed and they reported limited knowledge acquisition and heightened perceptions of isolation (Chen & Bennett, 2012). Barbera and Linder-VanBerschot (2011) found that students from different cultures have, though satisfactory, dissimilar perceptions of the online learning environment, highlighting the variety of needs and experiences.

The power that distance education wields is to be handled with care – care for the person first. Barbera and Linder-VanBerschot (2011) assessed the constructs of "social presence" – the understanding that the person on the other side of the screen genuinely cares about you as a person – and "instructor interaction" – the active engagement in the online classroom. Ragusa and Crampton (2018) explored the sense of connection as it relates to student experiences in distance education and the rising attrition rates. These are valuable constructs that will both bridge cultural gaps and support learning outcomes for students despite their backgrounds. The consideration of cultural factors will improve the disparity many students face when engaging in distance education, especially outside of their home country.

CORE COMPONENTS

The need for multicultural competence is heightened in a distance learning environment where there is far more room for misinterpretation and misunderstanding of cues. Since the online classroom is growing more and more popular, it is important to consider the ways we must expand our knowledge base to adjust to change. Verbal and nonverbal communication are often inhibited and lost in translation over the World Wide Web (Westbrook, 2014). Therefore, the need for competence and sensitivity to cross-cultural needs from a distance is greater.

Ideally, all segments of the educational system would work in unison to support one another toward the endeavor of long-term societal change. At the individual level, learners from multicultural backgrounds can advocate for their educational needs by maintaining timely communication with instructors, requesting accommodations as necessary, and taking time to immerse and educate themselves in the educational culture of their institution while also engaging in vulnerable sharing of their own culture with peers. Educators can broach one-on-one and group conversations of needs within the classroom, maintain honest and timely communication around course expectations, seek to build authentic relationships and connections and strengthen their cognitive flexibility to adapt to the needs at a given moment. Finally, at the organizational level, institutions and accrediting bodies can have policies and procedures surrounding connection in the classroom, educate and train staff and faculty on the need for awareness and competence, and enact review systems to assess and evaluate over time. Barbera and Linder-VenBerschot (2011) similarly discussed a systemic approach that includes learner factors, institutional factors, and outcome factors to impact success. These joint efforts will support the ongoing growth and development of distance education and thereby its potential far-reaching impact.

Despite the ideal, educators must work towards enhancing their self and other awareness throughout their professional journey to best support the needs of their learners, particularly awareness of the importance of cultural sensitivity (Kumi-Yeboah et al., 2020). The following core components provide a framework for consistent ethical practice around multicultural competence in distance learning: professional training, professional development, and professional identity. These will support, not only present-day knowledge and practice but more importantly long-term growth in an ever-evolving world.

Professional Training

The core component of professional training highlights the need for a solid foundation of education about the needs of various populations in an online setting. The awareness of the need for multicultural sensitivity in the classroom begins with the instructor's commitment to consistent growth within their training. It also depends on the institutional commitment to model the pedagogical framework that will foster continued growth beyond the training experience. There are various levels of protection against unethical practice – accrediting bodies that ensure a level of institutional compliance beyond what is visible to the naked eye, licensing boards that ensure a level of ethical compliance before entrusting individuals with a certificate to practice professionally, and many more. Professional training may begin in the classroom but far surpasses the bounds of a classroom into the potential lifelong impact of a full career.

Once formal training is complete, the onus of continued education, awareness, and growth shifts to the practicing professional. There will no longer be a hand to hold once learners graduate from the educational institution. It will be imperative to their continued development in the profession to pursue training and specialization based on their desired goals. Seeking a mentor or participating in an apprenticeship experience can help individuals evade stagnancy. This pursuit of learning beyond the formal training experience is a mark of commitment to lifelong learning. As times change and people evolve, it will be necessary to continuously reexamine our perspectives and learn new ways of connecting with people in your circles of influence. Many professions require a certain number of continuing education units (CEUs), which can have either a significant or insignificant effect on the professional practice postgraduation. There are several opportunities to grow our awareness and knowledge of cultural diversity in this digital age, but the intentionality with which instructors engage in them makes the difference in the classroom. Faculty and staff can greatly impact students' learning experiences by growing their awareness and modeling as recipients of cultural competence training. Furthermore, support in the form of consultation from colleagues and mentors can be a source of strength when feeling stuck in a dilemma. Certain professions require a level of supervised practice post-graduation, but even otherwise, mentorship from people who have gone before you can ameliorate the classroom learning experience. Therefore, the training ground is a seed that is planted that requires continuous watering to see the fruit on the other side.

Professional Development

The core component of professional development highlights the need for consistent reassessment and refinement of previously normed practices. The world is ever-changing and transforming and educators need to understand the movement of the times to serve their students well. As long as we are educating dynamic human beings, we will need to be lifelong learners committed to consistent professional and personal development. This starts from the inside, with a growth mindset rather than a fixed mindset. Online educators need to approach the technologically driven world of distance education with a tremendous level of flexibility. Technological issues emerge without warning and the willingness to pivot and provide alternatives will influence the success of the classroom environment. The growth mindset also lends well to your personal growth journey as instructors bring biases into the classroom. It is important to arrive with a level of openness to understand and digest other perspectives than your own in the world of academia.

There are several professional organizations that help support individuals in their lifelong career journey. Engagement within professional organizations will help educators remain abreast of current events and stressors in students' worlds. This can include seeking additional training, attending conferences, engaging in mentor groups in the profession, and more to help ensure accountability for continuous growth. Research is often normed for the general Caucasian population in the United States and minorities are often underrepresented (Bussing & Gary, 2012), so as the body of research grows and we learn more about the needs of other ethnicities and multiethnic communities, instructors would benefit tremendously from continued research development.

Involvement in consistent development ideally translates to action or advocacy. Educators carry a significant influence over future generations. Their support of students in the classroom may extend well past the learning experience into the future. Therefore, instructor comprehension of students' various needs and cultural complexities goes a long way inside and outside of the classroom. Often, in positions of power, instructors have an opportunity to give voice to the voiceless and act on behalf of the powerless within and outside of the classroom to impact systemic change. Part of an educator's continued professional development is the leadership they exercise in meeting a need outside of their scope. Educators have a beautiful opportunity to pave the way for many who may otherwise not have believed there was a way. Researchers found that mentorship particularly for minority individuals can prove useful for their continued motivation in the field (Cannon et al., 2020). As educators, our training plants a seed within us that has potential, but since the classroom is continuously changing, as evidenced by the growth in distance learning, we must continue to nurture our development to fit the ever-growing demands of the classroom. Our responsibility to professional development can be likened to the needed soil, water, and sunlight for every fruit-bearing seed. Even the harshest conditions can be withstood with the right nutrients, but it often depends on the impact of your training and development on your professional identity.

Professional Identity

The core component of professional identity highlights the need for our behavior and practices to align with the values that undergird our identity in the profession. Garber (2007) discusses the importance of your "being" aligning with your "doing," particularly as educators model this for students in their formative years in college. Similarly, the Multicultural and Social Justice Counseling Competencies highlight the importance of attitudes and beliefs in the shaping of a counselor's knowledge, skills, and actions related to multicultural or social justice issues (Ratts et al., 2015). One's professional identity is impacted by a wide variety of nature and nurture factors. It is supported by the training and ongoing development, but can also largely influence the absorption of said training and development. Therefore, though listed last, professional identity has the most potential to motivate long-term change. At the core, if an educator can maintain a level of cognitive flexibility (Brashear & Thomas, 2020) and self-awareness, any number of adverse circumstances within the classroom can be effectively handled. The pivot to distance learning as a result of the COVID-19 pandemic caused many struggles for educators with no experience online at all. However, if your professional identity encapsulates the value of flexibly meeting student needs, this will drive your continued production of fruit in the classroom.

An instructor's professional identity speaks to who they are rather than just what they might do for a living. We can respond with action when our knowledge and awareness can penetrate through our lens and worldview. Creating a safe space and broaching difficult conversations (King & Summers, 2020) feel less taxing when there is a greater purpose beyond the transmission of book knowledge from one individual to another. It has been said that you may not remember what a person said to you, but you'll remember how they made you feel. Your professional identity, supported by both your training and continuous development, can have a significant impact on each student in your classroom. The results of this can be exponential. Therefore, the seed that has now been well-watered and nourished can now produce fruit and provide life and sustenance for many others.

The interweaving of these three core components will strengthen the educator's resolve to provide the best learning experience possible for all the unique personalities and cultures represented in their classroom. They honor the work of the training in the past and present, continued development in the present and future, and an identity that is timeless and will carry you through an impactful career. Perera-Diltz and Greenidge (2018) describe multicultural competence as a journey and one that calls for ownership of the concept rather than a surface-level application of the idea. Educators, particularly in the distance learning sphere, have a responsibility to honor the unspoken voices in their classroom by sensing and responding to needs expressed both verbally and nonverbally.

PRACTICAL SOLUTIONS

The rapid acceleration of online learning presents both opportunities and challenges for educators. Facilitating an online course requires innovation, creativity, and flexibility, and instructors must intentionally create an impactful online presence (Benshoff & Gibbons, 2011; Sharoff, 2019). Educators teaching online are charged with striking a thoughtful balance between delivering course content and keeping students motivated and engaged. With careful planning, instructors can design an active, student-centered learning environment that provides a meaningful experience for every student in their class. In this section, practical strategies for facilitating a dynamic online classroom environment will be discussed.

Setting the Stage

Educators can begin to create a meaningful learning experience for students before the semester starts. Students will start forming an impression of the instructor and the learning environment very quickly, and instructors can lay the groundwork for a successful start by introducing themselves before class begins. The goal of this first interaction is for students to know that there is a human being behind the instructor's name on the syllabus. This introduction can be delivered via email, as an announcement posted to the class learning management system, or, preferably, in a video link sent to students. A video enables students to experience the instructor as a three-dimensional being. Instructors can introduce themselves by sharing:

· Any identifying information you would like to share, what you would like to be called, and where you are located in the United States.
· Contact information (*Email address, office hours, how to schedule a meeting*)
· Their education, credentials, and background experience (*What makes you the perfect person to teach this class?*)
· Any personal information they feel comfortable sharing: career journey, experience in the field, family information, cultural background, pets, favorite books/movies/music/restaurants, etc. (*What pieces of your personality could you share with students to demonstrate your personality?*)
· The overall goal and purpose of the class (*Why should students be excited to be taking this class? What will they take away from this semester?*)

Another strategy for setting the stage for a successful semester is to send out a check-in survey to students before the semester begins. A link to this survey can be included in the above introduction or sent separately during the first week of class. The goals of this interaction are to (1) assess student needs, (2) gather information about the knowledge and skills that students already have, and (3) provide students with an opportunity to communicate informally with the instructor as the class begins. Instructors can use the information from this survey to design inclusive learning activities that support the needs of diverse learners (Woodley et al., 2017). Some prompts to include in a student check-in survey can include:

- Any identifying information you would like to share, what you would like to be called, and where you are located in the United States.
- What is your degree track? Where are you in the program? What are your career plans after you graduate?
- What are your expectations for the course? What are you hoping to learn about the subject matter?
- Is there anything you would like me to know about you as a student? How can I best support you this semester?
- What is your comfort level with online learning? Tell me about your experience using our learning management system.
- Is there anything else you would like to share with me?

First Week of Class

After laying the groundwork for a successful start, instructors can create an inclusive and welcoming environment by asking students to introduce themselves during the first week of class. These introductions can take place via an online discussion board or during a synchronous class meeting. The goals of this initial introduction are to (1) build rapport and create classroom connections, (2) foster a sense of belonging and inclusivity, and (3) gauge students' communication abilities, an essential component of online classes (Woodley et al., 2017). Instructors can provide a variety of prompts for students to stimulate this discussion. This will foster a healthy and connective classroom. The use of icebreaker activities during the first few days of class encourages student interaction and builds the foundation of a supportive community. Furthermore, taking the time to build meaningful relationships helps students understand that there is more to each person than what meets the virtual eye (Woodley, 2007).

Throughout the Semester

As the semester progresses, educators should continue to maintain an active and connected learning community. Snow and Coker (2020) suggest that instructors should focus on regular and substantive interactions in their online classrooms. These interactions reduce the amount of apparent distance, culturally or physically, between students and faculty and help encourage quality student engagement. This also improves the sense of ongoing presence in the course. Some practical strategies that instructors can use to promote and maintain engagement include:

- *Broach difficult conversations.* Instructors have a responsibility in the classroom to initiate conversations that their students may be resistant to broaching. They can initiate a conversation about cultural identity, needs within the classroom, expectations of the instructor and assignment feedback, and the meaning of verbal and nonverbal communication in a respectful and nonjudgmental manner. Sharing examples of successes, educating about ways to respectfully communicate, and modeling open and flexible listening will all be important supports for this process.
- *Use a variety of instructional methods.* Instructors should utilize diverse teaching methods to support different learning styles and keep students engaged. Combine live and pre-recorded lectures, interactive discussions, multimedia content, and experiential learning activities to create a dynamic and interactive learning environment. The flexibility of this approach lends well to learners of all different needs and backgrounds.

- *Encourage collaborative learning.* Instructors can support interaction and engagement by incorporating interactive activities such as online discussions, group work, role plays, hands-on activities, and breakout rooms during synchronous class meetings. These collaborative experiences might lend to improved self-awareness and growth in personal and professional identity. Instructors' willingness to be flexible with assignment instructions may open the door for far more self-reflection on cultural identity intersections within small groups or as a big classroom experience.
- *Provide quality feedback.* Instructors should strive to provide students with regular and substantive feedback on assignments and assessments. The tone of written feedback can often be misunderstood, and providing students with different types of feedback can help ensure that students feel encouraged and supported throughout the semester. It can be helpful for some learners to hear and see the instructor's feedback rather than read it in two-dimensional form. Feedback and grading can be personalized to support diverse student needs by providing students with audio or video feedback or by meeting individually with students to discuss their progress. This three-dimensional engagement can support student success and avoid mistranslations over the World Wide Web.
- *Be present and accessible.* Instructors can maintain a strong online presence throughout the semester by holding regular office hours where students can informally ask questions. It may be helpful to utilize discussion forums to answer questions publicly so all students can benefit from the responses. Educators can also provide students with an online forum to submit and ask questions anonymously. Timely responses to emails and discussion threads will ensure your presence is tangible in the online classroom. Finally, heeding student feedback about expectations will also help them feel seen and heard for their unique needs.
- *Utilize self-disclosure as a tool for connection.* Culturally responsive instructors will model the vulnerability and honor the courage it takes for some people groups to engage in direct conversation and broach difficult conversations. Instructors might share their own negative experiences or disclose their desire to learn from the individual in humility and openness. This willingness to be human in the educator-student relationship will improve students' sense of connectedness and feelings of safety and trust.
- *Provide multidimensional learning opportunities.* Culturally responsive teaching creates a learning environment that acknowledges and validates the differences that exist among students. When instructors actively engage students in the learning process, students move from being passive participants in their learning to navigating their educational paths (Gay, 2010; Woodley et al., 2017). For example, when assigning a reflection activity, instructors can provide students with options for completing the assignment. Students can be encouraged to submit their reflections in one of the following ways: a traditional written response, a video response, an expressive arts activity, or by meeting one-on-one with the instructor (Woodley, 2017). Experiential activities or assignments allow flexibility in expression, whereby students can decide how best to interpret and respond to the prompts to attain the same learning outcome, but do it in ways that are unique to their individual identity.

Finishing Strong

After the semester has ended, instructors should engage in a reflective process to evaluate successes and growing edges. Educators can encourage students to provide feedback via university course evaluations or ask students to reflect on their experiences in class during end-of-term class meetings. Providing students with an opportunity to share their thoughts encourages students to actively participate in a self- and course-assessment process and provides instructors with opportunities for continued development. It is helpful to consistently encourage students to meet with instructors for support. This way, the request to provide feedback at the end can be genuine and honest feedback founded on a firm relationship that has been built over the term. This is an additional opportunity to utilize self-disclosure and share instructors' growth that has happened in the course, gratitude to the students for their engagement and courage in the learning process, and invite ongoing feedback and connection even post-course completion.

CASE STUDIES

Mei Zhang

Mei is a Chinese-American undergraduate student who has been grappling with the challenge of balancing her dual cultural identity while pursuing higher education. Mei grew up in a traditional Chinese household in the United States. Through the years, she has frequently found herself caught between her Chinese heritage and the American society in which she is immersed. Lately, at college, the pressure to conform to both cultures' expectations, maintain strong ties with her family's customs, and excel academically has become an overwhelming burden. During an asynchronous discussion in her Anthropology class, Mei's struggle to reconcile her Chinese roots with her American experiences becomes apparent.

Her professor, Dr. Sharma, believes that Mei's struggle poses a significant hurdle to her personal growth and self-acceptance. Dr. Sharma has observed a search for an authentic sense of identity amidst the convergence of her two worlds in Mei's written assignments. Reflecting upon the discussion thread, Dr. Sharma realizes that even in an online environment, she has managed to cultivate a safe and inclusive classroom environment. This set the stage for Mei to feel comfortable enough to reveal her struggle. Perhaps, thinks Dr. Sharma, this was accomplished by open and non-judgmental interactions in previous discussion threads. Early in the semester, Dr. Sharma broached issues of cultural diversity in the context of Anthropology. Dr. Sharma has worked hard to celebrate many cultures in this introductory class.

Ultimately, Dr. Sharma concludes that it is not her job to resolve Mei's struggle *for* her. Rather, it is Dr. Sharma's job to continue cultivating safety in her online classroom and to expose all students to a wide range of experiences. By honoring the richness that culture brings, perhaps Mei will begin to discover what harmony between these two cultures looks like in her unique life. Dr. Sharma decided to create several self-reflective assignments that help students explore their cultural intersectionality and what this means to them. Dr. Sharma knows that Mei is not alone in this quest, but she also recognizes that an online environment can pose a barrier to connecting with peers. Dr. Sharma resolves to highlight the various student organizations on campus that promote intercultural appreciation in an upcoming video announcement. Finally, Dr. Sharma decides to reemphasize to the class as a whole that she is available as a listening ear if any students ever want a place to connect during office hours or to set up a Zoom to talk individually.

Alejandro Ramirez

Alejandro is a Peruvian graduate student facing the complex task of assimilating into a new culture while pursuing his Master of Science in Education from an online American program. Alejandro feels passionately about pursuing his academic dreams, especially because he desires to help students from impoverished neighborhoods. However, even from the comfort of his own home in Lima, Alejandro finds himself grappling with the tension between preserving his cultural heritage and integrating into the American way of conceptualizing education. The pressure to adapt to unfamiliar social norms, language barriers, and cultural expectations has created a sense of displacement and isolation. Alejandro suspects that being in an online program has made this feeling worse. Balancing the pursuit of academic success with the desire to stay connected to his South American roots increasingly becomes a struggle for Alejandro as he seeks to find a harmonious balance between his past and present, ultimately shaping his journey of self-discovery in a new cultural context.

Dr. Shepard, Alejandro's professor for Early Childhood Education, notices that Alejandro is gradually disappearing from the class. Once a vibrant voice during synchronous Zoom discussions, Alejandro's participation has dwindled to meeting minimum expectations. Dr. Shepard misses Alejandro's contribution to the class. After all, Alejandro has brought an alternative perspective to the class. He has challenged his classmates' worldviews on education and increased their curiosity and innovation. But maybe, Dr. Shepard reflects, Alejandro has borne that burden mostly by himself.

Dr. Shepard explores ways to incorporate more culturally inclusive perspectives into the curriculum. This becomes a fun game, as Dr. Shepart brainstorms ways to highlight the importance of multicultural education in the existing curriculum. For example, he tasks students with beginning the next synchronous discussion with a greeting in another language they would like to learn. Dr. Shepard also designs a final project in which students create a virtual classroom space celebrating the cultures of their young students. Additionally, Dr. Shepard reworks discussion prompts so they explicitly invite students to explore and share their cultural backgrounds. This allows Alejandro to express his experiences and perspectives in a context of mutual exploration. Dr. Shepard believes that the new assignments he is developing will help Alejandro feel validated and supported to maintain a connection with his South American roots. However, he does not stop there. During the next synchronous discussion, Dr. Shepard sends a private message to Alejandro to let him know how much he values what Alejandro has brought to the class. Alejandro feels as if Dr. Shepard truly cares about his well-being, and asks if he can make an appointment for virtual office hours next week.

Emily Foster

Emily is an undergraduate Biology student who moved from London to the United States last fall. Emily is surprised to discover that cultural differences are profoundly affecting her educational experience. She is finding herself challenged to adjust, even though she and her professors and classmates tend to share European heritage. While Emily initially embraced the opportunity to study in a new country, she finds herself struggling with the American academic system's distinct approach to education. Specifically, the emphasis her online classes place on participation during virtual class discussions directly contrasts with the more reserved and formalized educational environment Emily was accustomed to in London. She feels as if her voice does not matter in her group projects and partnered virtual lab assignments because other students are more assertive in expressing themselves. Her struggle to adapt to these cultural nuances is now affecting her confidence and impeding her ability to fully engage with her coursework. This in turn has been leading to feelings of frustration and being misunderstood.

Dr. Baird, Emily's professor for Principles of Biochemistry, has always prided himself on facilitating lively discussions and crafting interactive learning opportunities in his online classes. For a few years, though, he has noticed that some students seem to engage more readily and vocally than others. Dr. Baird recognizes the disparity between some students' low social interactiveness, versus their stellar work in individual assignments. He decides to increase student autonomy by offering students choices in how they approach assignments. Rather than requiring students to work in groups, Dr. Baird begins encouraging them to decide for themselves how they will accomplish required assignment tasks. Further, Dr. Baird hypothesizes that perhaps all students, regardless of their majors, can benefit from more structure. He decides that next discussion, he will keep track of who has yet to speak. If, near the end of the discussion, some have yet to contribute, he will intentionally invite them into the conversation.

Alem Tadesse

Alem is an Ethiopian graduate student studying counseling in a hybrid program in the United States. Since the beginning of her program, Alem has been grappling with the complex task of reconciling her Ethiopian cultural values with the cultural norms of the profession of counseling. Raised in a society deeply rooted in traditions, collectivism, and respect for elders, Alem has been thrust into a contrasting individualistic society that prizes independence and assertiveness. The clash between these cultural values leaves Alem feeling torn between honoring her Ethiopian heritage and adapting to the expectations and pressures of her American academic environment. She finds that her online classes are posing the most challenge because she feels disconnected from her professor and her peers. Where, she wonders, is there a place to process all of this? And how can her professional identity develop in a vacuum?

Early in the semester, Alem's professor for the online Counseling Theories, Dr. Willis, began watching for signs of struggle. Primed with the knowledge that some international students find navigating the intricate dynamics of cultural integration and self-acceptance stressful, Dr. Willis initiated a meeting with Alem. In this virtual meeting, Dr. Willis inquired specifically about how Alem has been adjusting to life in America and to the Western view of mental health. When Alem courageously revealed her struggles, Dr. Willis offered to mentor her. Together, the two of them envisioned what a supportive mentoring relationship would look like and set clear expectations about meeting frequency and duration. Dr. Willis specifically broached discussion about what Alem believed would prove most helpful for her, and Alem shared that she would value spiritual practices like prayer to be a part of their times together. Even before their first mentoring meeting, Alem found that she felt seen and understood. She witnessed firsthand the difference that a caring relationship can make for a person who feels isolated and confused. She vowed to take that experiential learning into her work with her future clients.

CONCLUSION

Distance learning has played an important role in increasing access to education, and breaking through geographic barriers. Currently, millions of adults have engaged in distance learning, and due to the flexibility, cost-savings, and increased flexibility of this learning format, it is anticipated that the number will only increase. As education continues to be a global experience, the need for multicultural competence in teaching in this medium will only grow. Educators have the responsibility to anticipate how to create a supportive environment and navigate how individual differences may impact the learning environment.

Professional training and ongoing development for educators are part of the equation. Our professional identity requires flexibly meeting the needs of students and maintaining core competencies for training.

This approach necessitates professional and individual attributes such as cultural humility, sensitivity to the intersectionality of identities, curiosity, and flexibility in working with diverse student populations. Additionally, the intentional use of strategies, such as establishing clear expectations, broaching difficult conversations, engaging in consistent and clear communication, providing students with detailed feedback, encouraging collaborative learning, and promoting multidimensional learning opportunities, can create environments conducive to learning. While strategic pedagogy benefits students, multicultural competence is a journey that requires in-depth exploration and construct adjustment (Perera-Diltz & Greenidge, 2018).

Additional research can inform teaching and learning strategies. While the body of research is growing, it will continue to be important to evaluate distance learning formats (online versus offline, degree of synchronicity) and pedagogical interventions. We encourage an evaluation of methods that support learning with minoritized populations. Finally, research that demonstrates the impact of applied teaching competencies can further strengthen the field of education.

Culturally competent educators are a big part of the equation. The world needs scholarship surrounding the role and responsibility of institutions in the construction of programs and student experiences. Additionally, it would be beneficial for institutions, faculty, and students to analyze the educator's role in identifying systemic barriers that may be negatively affecting their responsibility in the widening educational system. Individuals and institutions can join forces in the meaningful work of creating a safe and secure learning environment for every student.

REFERENCES

Attilee, S. (2019). Multicultural competency in online counseling courses: Before and after a multicultural counseling course. *Walden Dissertations and Doctoral Studies.* https://scholarworks.waldenu.edu/dissertations/6302

Barbera, E., & Linder-VanBerschot, J. A. (2011). Systemic multicultural model for online education: Tracing connections among learner inputs, instructional processes, and outcomes. *Quarterly Review of Distance Education, 12*(3), 167–180.

Becker, C., Cooper, N., Atkins, K., & Martin, S. (2009). What helps students thrive? An investigation of student engagement and performance. *Recreational Sports Journal, 33*(2), 139–149. doi:10.1123/rsj.33.2.139

Bennett-Levy, J., Hawkins, R., Perry, H., Cromarty, P., & Mills, J. (2012). Online cognitive behavioural therapy training for therapists: Outcomes, acceptability, and impact of support. *Australian Psychologist, 47*(3), 174–182. doi:10.1111/j.1742-9544.2012.00089.x

Benshoff, J. M., & Gibbons, M. M. (2011). Bringing life to e-learning: Incorporating a synchronous approach to online teaching in counselor education. *The Professional Counselor, 1*(1), 21–28. doi:10.15241/jmb.1.1.21

Brashear, C. A., & Thomas, N. (2020). Core competencies for combatting crisis: Fusing ethics, cultural competence, and cognitive flexibility in counseling. *Counselling Psychology Quarterly, 35*(1), 1–15. doi:10.1080/09515070.2020.1768362

Budiman, A. (2020). *Key findings about U.S. immigrants.* Pew Research Center. Retrieved May 26, 2023, from https://www.pewresearch.org/short-reads/2020/08/20/key-findings-about-u-s-immigrants/

Bussing, R., & Gary, F. A. (2012). Eliminating mental health disparities by 2020: Everyone's actions matter. *Journal of the American Academy of Child and Adolescent Psychiatry, 51*(7), 663–666. doi:10.1016/j.jaac.2012.04.005 PMID:22721587

Cannon, Y., Haiyasoso, M., & Tello, A. (2020). Relational aspects in research mentoring of women doctoral counseling students. *Journal of Creativity in Mental Health, 15*(3), 278–291. doi:10.1080/15401383.2019.1689213

Chen, R., & Bennett, S. (2012). When Chinese learners meet constructivist pedagogy online. *Higher Education, 64*(5), 677–691. 10.100710734-012-9520-9

Garber, S. (2007). *The fabric of faithfulness: Weaving together belief and behavior* (Expanded edition). IVP.

Gay, G. (2010). Culturally responsive teaching: Theory, research, and practice (2nd ed.) (Multicultural education series). Teachers College.

Kentnor, H. E. (2015). Distance education and the evolution of online learning in the United States. *Curriculum and Teaching Dialogue, 17*(1/2), 21.

King, K. M., & Summers, L. (2020). Predictors of broaching: Multicultural competence, racial color blindness, and interpersonal communication. *Counselor Education and Supervision, 59*(3), 216–230. doi:10.1002/ceas.12185

Kumi-Yeboah, A., Dogbey, J., Yuan, G., & Smith, P. (2020). Cultural diversity in online education: An exploration of instructors' perceptions and challenges. *Teachers College Record, 122*(7), 1–46. doi:10.1177/016146812012200708

Kung, M. (2017). Methods and strategies for working with international students learning online in the U.S. *TechTrends, 61*(5), 479–485. doi:10.100711528-017-0209-x

National Center for Education Statistics. (2023). Undergraduate Enrollment. In *Condition of Education.* U.S. Department of Education, Institute of Education Sciences. https://nces.ed.gov/programs/coe/indicator/cha

Perera-Diltz, D. M., & Greenidge, W. L. (2018). Mindfulness techniques to promote culturally appropriate engagement. *Journal of Creativity in Mental Health, 13*(4), 490–504. doi:10.1080/15401383.2018.1459215

Ragusa, A. T., & Crampton, A. (2018). Sense of connection, identity and academic success in distance education: Sociologically exploring online learning environments. *Rural Society, 27*(2), 125–142. doi:10.1080/10371656.2018.1472914

Ratts, M. J., Singh, A. A., Nassar-McMillan, S., Butler, S. K., & McCullough, J. R. (2017). Multicultural and Social Justice Counseling Competencies: A leadership framework for professional school counselors. *Professional School Counseling, 21*(1b). doi:10.1177/2156759X18773582

Seaman, J. E., Allen, I. E., & Seaman, J. (2018). *Grade increase: Tracking distance education in the United States*. https://www.bayviewanalytics.com/reports/gradeincrease.pdf

Sells, J., Tan, A., Brogan, J., Dahlen, U., & Stupart, Y. (2012). Preparing international counselor educators through online distance learning. *International Journal for the Advancement of Counseling, 34*(1), 39–54. doi:10.100710447-011-9126-4

Sharoff, L. (2019). Creative and innovative online teaching strategies: Facilitation for active participation. *The Journal of Educators Online, 16*(2). Advance online publication. doi:10.9743/JEO.2019.16.2.9

Snow, W. H., & Coker, J. K. (2020). Distance counselor education: Past, present, future. *The Professional Counselor, 10*(1), 40–56. doi:10.15241/whs.10.1.40

Turan, Z., Kucuk, S., & Cilligol Karabey, S. (2022). The university students' self-regulated effort, flexibility and satisfaction in distance education. *International Journal of Educational Technology in Higher Education, 19*(1), 35. Advance online publication. doi:10.118641239-022-00342-w PMID:35891707

Undergraduate enrollment. (2022). National Center for Education Statistics. https://nces.ed.gov/programs/coe/indicator/cha

UNESCO. (2020). *Policy brief: Education during COVID-19 and beyond*. United Nations. https://www.un.org/development/desa/dspd/wp-content/uploads/sites/22/2020/08/sg_policy_brief_covid-19_and_education_august_2020.pdf

Westbrook, T. P. (2014). Global contexts for learning: Exploring the relationship between low-context online learning and high-context learners. *Christian Higher Education, 13*(4), 281–294. doi:10.1080/15363759.2014.924888

Woodley, X., Hernandez, C., Parra, J., & Negash, B. (2017). Celebrating difference: Best practices in culturally responsive teaching online. *TechTrends, 61*(5), 470–478. doi:10.100711528-017-0207-z

Chapter 9
Enhancing Online Adult Learning Communities Through the Lens of Social Climate Theory

Carrie M. Grimes
https://orcid.org/0009-0007-5937-0048
Vanderbilt University, USA

ABSTRACT

The dramatic expansion of online learning programs for adult degree-seeking professionals has opened significant access and opportunity for institutions of higher education, as well as for the adult learners they serve. However, this recent dramatic increase in online graduate degree offerings has posed challenges to educators and students. One of the most significant challenges is building and maintaining strong connections, and a sense of community, among the participants within the online setting. Social climate theory provides a useful lens for a reconsideration of the social climate of an online learning environment (synchronous and asynchronous) as embodying a "personality" that iteratively shapes the learning community and the experience of participants, and is shaped in return. This chapter presents an in-depth analysis of how educators can strategically enhance online classroom communities for adult degree-seeking professionals through the application of social climate theory principles and a proposed conceptual framework.

INTRODUCTION

In the recent literature regarding online learning for adults, the critical role of community for successful achievement of learning outcomes is more widely recognized than one to two decades ago when a more technical and self-directed conceptualization of online learning predominated (Hartley Bendixen, 2001; Land Greene, 2000; Rovai, 2002; Song, 2005). In the early days of online learning, numerous studies explored its key attributes including flexibility (Chizmar Walbert, 1999) and convenience (Poole, 2000),

DOI: 10.4018/978-1-6684-8908-6.ch009

while a lack of community in online learning environments was specifically identified as a key challenge and cause for learner dissatisfaction (Song, et al., 2004; Rovai, 2002; Shea, et al., 2001). The ways in which adult learners and their instructors adapt, perceive, and co-create community within the virtual classroom is influenced by the extent to which social connections are engendered by all participants, contributing to an overall social climate (Oren, et al., 2002; 2015; Ni, 2013). F Moreover, studies have consistently signaled that virtual classroom social climate elements, such as having more opportunities for human interaction with instructors and classmates, directly impact student satisfaction with their online learning experience (Ghaderizefreh Hoover, 2018; Shea, et al., 2002). Although research suggests that the virtual classroom climate with regard to community is affected—positively and negatively—by instructor behaviors, course design and structure, course clarity, and student connectedness (Kaufmann, et al., 2015), the strategic cultivation of a positive climate remains elusive to some faculty who are responsible for the facilitation of high quality online learning experiences for adults in professional degree programs (Dewaele, et al., 2022; Sithole, et al., 2019). The increased enrollment in online education for adult learners in the wake of COVID-19 has put significant additional pressure on instructors to demonstrate a facility with employing different strategies to create a positive climate in online classes (Qui, 2022; Shahnama et al., 2021; Dewaele et al., 2022).

Given that the role of classroom climate is central to adult learners' assessment of their educational experience (Reid, et al., 2003; Ghaderizefreh Hoover, 2018), and online professional degree programs are growing exponentially, understanding how to facilitate a positive social climate for adults learning in an online community is an essential skill for instructors (Sriharan, 2020; Sithole, et al., 2019). Larger institutional implications for high quality online instruction in professional degree program contexts also exist, as colleges and universities seek to expand online offerings to enhance revenue and promote organizational sustainability (Elliot, et al., 2015; Gamage, et al., 2020). Therefore, a consideration of social climate in online learning environments, and the affiliated theoretical framework (Moos,1979,1984,1987) should provide deeper insight into the way social climate is constructed within an online adult professional degree learning community, and effective means for leveraging it for the benefit of students, instructors, and the institution.

WHAT IS COMMUNITY?

The notion of community has long been the subject of diverse definitions and interpretations within academic discourse. The seminal contribution of McMillian and Chavis (1986) provides a useful theory for understanding the meaning of a sense of community as a social force. Their framework highlights four fundamental attributes of a sense of community: membership, influence, integration and fulfillment of needs, and shared emotional connection (McMillian Chavis, 1986). The notion of membership describes an individual's perception of belonging or interconnectedness within a specific group, distinguished by a sense of personal identification and investment. The term "influence" is conceptualized by McMillan and Chavis as the perception of members' abilities to exercise an impact on the group, coupled with the notion of the group being valued by its members. Integration and fulfillment of needs describes the ways in which resources which are furnished to the members of a group through their membership will satisfy certain needs. When individual needs are met within a community, this reinforces loyalty to the group which inspires ongoing engagement. Elements which drive need fulfillment within the community include shared values, competence of fellow members, and the success and status of the community. A sense of community is made more salient by a shared emotional bond that is manifested through ongoing social contact and community spirit, along with shared history, environments, and beliefs in the value of the investment of time spent together among members (McMillan and Chavis, 1986).

The construct of community within adult learning spaces builds upon the work of McMillan and Chavis, and is a multidimensional concept that encompasses both cognitive and emotional dimensions, shaping the holistic experiences of adult learners. A student's experience of community bears significance in adult online learning environments, and directly influences outcomes such as retention, perceptions of curricular/program quality, feelings of affiliation with the university, and a sense of belonging within the learning environment and larger university community (Kauffman, 2015; Ruey, 2010; Tinto, 1993; Yamauchi et al., 2016). Cognitive experiences which contribute to a sense of community within learning environments include intellectual engagement, knowledge sharing, and collaborative learning. Adult learners in online environments who participate in critical discussions, knowledge co-construction, and problem-solving activities facilitated by interactions with peers and instructors express a more salient sense of community through social presence (Palloff Pratt, 2013; Thoms, et al., 2008). These social and cognitive experiences contribute to deeper learning and interpersonal connection, as learners collectively participate in meaningful discourse, witness diverse perspectives, and participate in acts of metacognition and reflection (Rovai Jordan, 2004). Research about online learning community building by Conrad (2005) further emphasizes that a sense of community in online learning spaces is correlated with higher levels of cognitive engagement and the development of critical thinking skills among adult learners. Regardless of an in-person or online learning modality, scholars concur that a sense of community is a major contributor to an adult learner's overall academic success; when adult learners feel connected to their peers and instructors, they are more likely to actively engage in the learning process, participate meaningfully in the activities of the learning community, and experience positive learning outcomes (Rovai, 2002; Swan, 2002).

The socio-emotional characteristics of a learning environment, whether online or in-person, are closely linked to the emotional experiences individuals have within a learning community. According to Rovai (2002), adult learners seek feelings of affiliation, partnership, and engagement with their peers and instructors. Garrison, Anderson, and Archer (2001) claim that an atmosphere of emotional support within a learning community has the potential to enhance the overall perceptions of the learning environment, boost students' motivation and minimize disengagement. Woods and Ebersole (2002) highlight the broader institutional value of community, contending that the establishment of a sense of community is a significant factor in enhancing learner satisfaction and emotional well-being, and consequently contributing to increased retention rates among adult learners in professional degree programs. Interestingly, adult learners may sometimes conflate their perceptions of a strong communal atmosphere within their learning environment with their assessment of a graduate program's curricular quality (Conrad, 2005). Hewitt's (2003) scholarship echoes Conrad, affirming that adult learners are motivated to persist and invest in their educational journey due to the conviction that a supportive and engaging community is equivalent to high-quality learning experiences (Hewitt, 2003). It follows that a robust sense of community is a crucial factor in determining the effectiveness of a learning experience, and is also considered to be a reliable predictor of students' assessments of individual courses and the overall degree program quality (Rovai, 2002).

Shea, Li, Swan, and Pickett (2005) emphasize that a strong sense of community significantly influences adult learners' feelings of affiliation with the university or the professional graduate program. When adult learners perceive a supportive and engaging community, they develop a sense of connection and social identification with the educational institution, which strengthens their loyalty and commitment (Tafjel, 1974; Tafjel Turner, 2004; Ashforth Mael, 2004). This sense of affiliation enhances the overall learning experience and fosters a positive relationship between the adult learner and the university. Junco and Mastrodicasa (2007) suggest that adult learners who feel a strong sense of community are more likely to engage in campus activities, seek out campus resources, and develop meaningful relationships with faculty and staff. This integration into the broader university community contributes to a more holistic educational experience and enhances the adult learner's overall satisfaction with their graduate program. It also benefits the institution, as feelings of loyalty toward one's alma mater are correlated with positive alumni relations behaviors such as financial contributions, a willingness to advise others to attend the institution, and volunteer engagement (Mael and Ashforth, 1992).

A student's sense of community is also tightly coupled with their feelings of belonging within the learning environment and the larger university community. Numerous scholars (Bean Eaton, 2000; Stebleton, Soria, Huesman, Torres, 2014; Strayhorn, 2008, 2012) underscore the importance of students' capacity to develop a sense of belonging and membership within their academic community. Feelings of belongingness and membership are directly facilitated by a student's ability to recognize the value of their contributions to the community in conjunction with possessing an understanding of their role and place amongst faculty and fellow students (Maunder, 2018; Tinto, 2017). Tinto articulates the outcome of this kind of membership as a cohesive force that unites the learner with the community, despite obstacles that may emerge (Tinto, 1987). Through his theory of student persistence, Tinto (1993) further claims that a sense of belonging and social connection is essential for student retention and academic success. Ashar and Skenes (1993) advance Tinto's theory by specifically investigating the experiences and persistence outcomes of adult learners, finding that both the social environment and one's sense of social integration have a significant and positive effect on persistence. Those who feel a strong sense of community and belonging are more likely to persist in their studies, actively engage in the learning process, and seek out opportunities for involvement and collaboration. These positive behaviors have cascade effects across the learning community and broader institution during a student's enrollment and into their alumni experience (Drezner, 2021).

THEORETICAL FRAMEWORK: SOCIAL CLIMATE THEORY

Foundational to understanding social climate theory is the overarching field of environmental assessment, which is a domain of applied psychology that seeks to understand and measure the ways in which the characteristics of an environment shape human behavior (Moos Holahan, 2004). By investigating the intertwinement of the spaces we inhabit and our behaviors within them, researchers have an opportunity to contribute to a body of evidence which can influence individuals' experiences, and in turn, their quality of life (Moos Holahan, 2004). Environmental assessment may be conceptualized as an umbrella term which encompasses four primary domains: physical features, institutional structures, suprapersonal factors, and social climate (Moos Holahan, 2004).

The study of one of these domains, social climate, represents a highly productive research initiative at the intersection of environmental assessment, community, and psychology. This social-ecological methodology developed by Moos and colleagues has been used to assess the social environments of a wide array of organizational settings from hospitals to schools to prisons (Moos, 1974, 1976, 1984). Emergent from this scholarship is Moos' (1987) social climate theory, which is concerned with the social environment and its impact on individuals within various settings, particularly educational and organizational contexts. Moos defines social climate as "the social characteristics and expectations of setting, such as its level of support, goal orientation, and structure" (Moos Holahan, 2004, p. 787). Moos' research (1987) contributes to a collective understanding of how social climates influence individuals' attitudes, behaviors, and well-being through its consideration of the ways in which "human contexts and coping resources promote human adaptation and growth" (p.231). Social climate theory emphasizes the importance of understanding the social environment as a critical determinant of individuals' experiences and outcomes; in learning communities this is integrative of the cognitive processes that underlie an individual's perception of their environment and their ability to effectively cope within it (Moos, 1979).

The early scholarship of Moos was significantly shaped by the works of several eminent scholars, most notably Murray (1938), whose primary focus was on the impact of environmental perceptions on human behavior. Lewin's (1935) seminal research on field theory also had important implications for the later development of Moos' social climate theory. Advancing the work of Murray and Lewin, Moos' perspective is grounded in a fundamental tenet that an individual's perception of their surroundings has a significant impact on their behavior within those surroundings; this is known as individual adaptation. Moos posits that environments, much like individuals, possess distinctive personalities; therefore it is imperative to be able to describe the environment in a manner similar to that of describing an individual's personality. To better investigate these ideas, Moos (1987) developed an integrative person-environment framework, proposing that people and environments influence one another in a reciprocal manner. The person-environment framework postulates that the relationship between the environmental system and individual adaptation is bidirectional and characterized by ongoing, iterative, transactional processes. The person-environment framework is useful in that it asserts that an individual's capacity to thrive within a particular context is a result of experiencing congruence between the individual and their environment (Moos, 1987).

According to social climate theory, social climate is characterized by the interactions, norms, and expectations within a particular setting, and is grounded in three key dimensions: relationships, personal development, and the upkeep of organizational systems and change responsiveness within those systems. The relationship dimension considers individuals' levels of involvement and support towards each other, and includes behaviors which foster peer cohesion (Moos, 1987). The dimension of personal growth considers the fundamental goals of a given setting; in an educational setting an example would be clear learning objectives which are aligned with particular tasks and activities, and designed to promote cognitive development. Moos (1984) defines the system maintenance and change dimension as the level of structure, organization, and clarity within a setting which coexists with the relative openness to change that characterizes that setting. When attempting to grasp how individual and group personal characteristics interact with the environment to influence outcomes in the educational settings, researchers must take these dimensions into account (Finney Moos, 1986).

With regards to educational experiences, Moos asserts that the social-ecological and physical environments of learners must be considered concurrently. "The socio-ecological setting in which students function can affect their attitudes and moods, their behavior and performance, and their self-concept and general sense of well-being" (Moos, 1979, p. 3). Moos and other scholars (Allodi, 2010; Darkenwald, 1989; Fraser, 2002; Kauffman, 2015; Rovai, 2002) coalesce around the following key components of social climate within learning settings: interpersonal relationships (student-instructor and peer-to-peer); instructor behaviors and beliefs; classroom facilitation and group activities; and instructor communication style. Swirling within and around these facets are an array of affiliated forces, which ebb and flow in the classroom environment. Some of these include cooperation and competition, trust, shared values, self-efficacy, participation and exclusion, and systems of democracy and hierarchy (Allodi, 2010; Givens Rolland, 2012; Hong, et al., 2021; Kurt, et al., 2022; Platz Platz, 2021).

When students in higher education settings draw upon coping resources in order to exercise adaptation within their learning environments, this positively impacts their personal interests and values, and motivation and achievement levels (Graham Gisi, 2000; Myers Rocca, 2001). A classroom social climate which is perceived as beneficial has also been proven to generate positive course evaluations from both students and instructors (Dwyer et al., 2004). Accordingly, the application of social climate theory principles should be a top priority for higher education instructors and leaders, given its capacity to foster key outcomes such as academic accomplishment, student retention, and student well-being (Alonso-Tapia Nieto, 2019; Mustika, 2021; Rutter, 2000; Thomas, et al., 2014, Tinto, 1993; Yamauchi, et al., 2016).

SOCIAL CLIMATE SCALES IN LEARNING SETTINGS

Moos (1984) devised a series of reliable, validated scales to evaluate social climate and further his development of social climate theory. Among these scales, the Classroom Environment Scale (Trickett Moos, 1973) is noteworthy, as it specifically measures social climate in school settings, and demonstrates that in order to foster academic growth and comprehension, classrooms must possess an intellectually stimulating atmosphere. The CES, which is focused on the psychosocial environments of students in junior and senior high school settings, also confirms that student engagement and motivation are byproducts of maintaining a classroom environment which is cohesive and gratifying for participants (Trickett Moos, 1973; Trickett, et al., 1993). Darkenwald Gavin (1987) advanced the work of Trickett and Moos with their design of the Adult Classroom Climate Scale (ACCS), a multidimensional scale to assess the social climate of adult learning environments. Like the CES, the ACCS conceptualizes the classroom environment "as a dynamic social system that includes not only teacher behavior and teacher-student interaction but also student-student interaction" (Moos, 1979, p. 138). The ACCS is comprised of five subscales to measure the social climate of adult learning settings: organization and support, student centeredness, student affiliation, student influence, and task orientation (Brandes, 1998). These subscales represent significant iteration from the original nine subscales of the Moos' CES. Darkenwald's work (1989) distinguishes the ways in which adults' diverse life experiences and individual characteristics uniquely inform a classroom's environment, effectively adding a whole other dimension to the social climate.

Dwyer et al. (2004) and Gokcora (1989) each also offer validated classroom climate scales designed for traditional in-person undergraduate classroom environments. While Dwyer's unidimensional Connected Classroom Climate Inventory (CCCI) measures the ways in which student and instructor perceptions of peer-to-peer communication contribute to a positive perception of classroom climate, Gokcora's Class Climate Scale (CCS) is focused upon examining undergraduates' perceptions of their instructor's communication behaviors as predictive of their perceptions of classroom climate. In their quest to address the need for a standardized, valid and reliable tool to assess classroom climate within online learning environments, Kaufmann, et al. (2016) leveraged the CCCI and the CCS through the conceptual application of an instructional beliefs model. They proposed the design of the online learning climate scale (OLCS) to be used within higher education. This multidimensional scale is predicated upon student self-efficacy as a derivative of instructor behaviors, student characteristics/ behaviors, and course-specific structural issues. While the OLCS may be able to contribute to the enterprise of assessing climate in online classroom settings in the future, it remains a draft inventory which requires further analysis.

REVIEW OF RELATED LITERATURE

In order to best conceptualize the complexity and breadth of the landscape of the issues encompassing classroom social climate and its impact on community for adult learners in online professional degree programs, an examination of the relevant scholarship is essential. Source materials of this literature review include peer reviewed journal articles and chapters, along with research study reports generated by think tanks and government agencies. Constructs of classroom climate, adult learning, online learning, a sense of community in learning environments, and the proven benefits of positive social climate for individuals and institutions are examined. This synthesis of the literature empowers us to better understand the relevant applications of social climate theory to the phenomenon of improving a sense of community for adults enrolled in online professional degree programs.

CLASSROOM CLIMATE AND RAPPORT

Anderson's (1982) landmark synthesis of school climate literature underscores the importance of cultivating a positive classroom climate, which is distinguished by nurturing relationships, transparent communication, and a sense of inclusivity. Her analysis reveals that favorable teacher-student interactions and amicable teacher-student relationships are significant elements in cultivating an environment that is conducive to learning. The empirical evidence further indicates that a positive climate within the classroom promotes student engagement, motivation, and academic accomplishment. Anderson also emphasizes the bidirectional nature of the classroom climate, recognizing that the conduct and exchanges amongst students also play a significant role in shaping the broader climate. A well-rounded instructional approach that encompasses both the affective and cognitive dimensions of the classroom environment, and exercises intentionality in fostering an inclusive, democratic atmosphere contributes to a positive classroom climate (Anderson, 1982). Scholars such as Fraser (1986, 1998, 2002) and Wang Eccles (2012) enhance the scholarship, reinforcing key benefits of a positive classroom climate such as increased student engagement, increased feelings of belongingness, greater student persistence in the face of challenges, and increased achievement outcomes.

Classroom climate has also been described by some scholars as the learning environment created in the classroom by teachers (Hirschy Wilson, 2002). Current research, focused on students in secondary school settings, has sought to distill the complex and multifaceted construct of classroom climate into three primary dimensions emanating from instructor actions (Evans, et al., 2009). These include actions which organize the instructional climate with the intent of motivating specific learning behaviors and outcomes (Alonso-Tapia, et al., 2020; Wang, et al., 2020); actions aimed at resolving classroom disruptions and discipline problems (Simon Alonso-Tapia, 2016; Lee Gage, 2020); and actions involved in the emotional exchange between members of the classroom community (Wang, et al., 2020, Alonso-Tapia Nieto, 2019).

Alternatively, Dwyer et al. (2004), Frisby Martin (2010), and Myers (1995) define classroom climate as the perceived connection and rapport that exists between instructor and students. This view is influenced by both the instructor-student interactions, the student-student interactions, and the course structure or organization (Moos, 1979). This scholarly perspective has more fitting applications to the landscape of adult learners, including those who participate in virtual classroom environments. When classroom climate is conceptualized as being based upon perception, it may illuminate how welcomed, supported, and comfortable students feel in the classroom with each particular instructor. Every student has an individual perception of the environment of the classroom; however, a collective perception and feeling can also be generated and shared by the students and their instructor (Alonso-Tapia Ruiz-Díaz, 2022). The classroom climate primarily consists of these perceptions that evolve amidst exposure to several learning contexts over time, and the existing opportunities and resources within the learning environment which help participants to develop impressions and make judgments accordingly regarding the climate (Fraser and Treagust, 1986).

Classroom rapport, a prosocial bond which is defined as harmonious interactions between teachers and students (Bernieri, 1988), is believed to be based in interpersonal relationships characterized by connection and mutual trust (Murphy Rodriguez, 2012). Rapport-building communication behaviors include confirming behaviors, which are "the transactional processes by which teachers communicate to students that they are endorsed, recognized, and acknowledged as valuable, significant individuals" (Ellis, 2000. P. 266). Rapport is co-constructed (Sidelinger Booth-Butterfield, 2010) by students and faculty when active participation is encouraged and made manifest; however instructors play the lead role in cultivating rapport. Notably, an atmosphere in which rapport is resonant fosters higher levels of participation, satisfaction, motivation, and enhanced classroom participation (Frisby Myers, 2008); consequently, positive social climate conditions are reinforced (Coupland, 2003; Frisby Myers, 2008; Jorgenson, 1992).

Parker Herrington (2015) specifically consider classroom climate in adult online courses through a blend of theoretical frames, including authentic learning principles (Herrington, et al., 2010), community of inquiry elements (Garrison, et al., 2001) and technologies as cognitive tools (Jonassen Reeves, 2001). They assert that setting climate in online learning communities is less about encouraging students to share personally at the onset of the course, and more about attending to four main elements throughout the duration of the course: "designing a friendly learning environment, building rapport, engendering a sense of belonging, and developing a sense of purpose to assist student learning" (Parker Herrington, 2015).

CLASSROOM CLIMATE'S INFLUENCE ON STUDENT WELL-BEING

According to well-being theory (Seligman, 2011), several elements contribute to students' well-being, including positive emotions, engagement, relationships, meaning and accomplishments. Research pertaining to the social climate of learning communities demonstrates that school climate parameters influence factors such as students' optimistic acceptance of life, their psychological and physiological well-being, and academic success (Ruus, et al., 2007). Research by Rania, et al. (2013) reinforces the existence of a strong correlation between well-being and climate in their study of how classroom climates impact undergraduate nursing students' well-being. While these studies focused on in-person learning communities, the work of Mustika, et al. (2021) specifically investigated how the atmosphere of an online learning environment is connected to graduate students' well-being, and found that almost all aspects of the online learning climate were significantly predictive of students' well-being. Climate inputs in the online setting such as peer-to-peer communication, the quality of instructors' communication, the personal relevance of content, and the opportunity to receive feedback were all important predictors of students' well-being (Mustika, et al., 2021). This evidence affirms Moos' (1979) seminal postulate of social climate theory: that "the social-ecological setting in which students function can affect their attitudes and moods, their behavior and performance, their self-concept and general sense of well-being" (p. 3).

ADULT LEARNERS ONLINE

Recent studies indicate that adult online learners identify the top benefits of online education as access to a more diverse community of learners, access to more institutions and degree programs, an increased sense of agency/independence, the ability to work at one's own pace, and flexibility and convenience (Castro Tumibay, 2021; Paudel, 2021; Tareen Haand, 2020). When considering how to best serve adult learners in professional graduate degree online programs, it is important to recognize that they are a distinctive category of learners with unique needs and motivations, which have important implications for the design and facilitation of online learning environments. Cercone (2008) asserts that adult learners have significant personal and professional responsibilities (childcare, work) that interfere with and/or influence their learning experiences. Typically, adults electively enroll in graduate educational programs and juggle their classes and coursework around these responsibilities. Due in part to the fact that they are self-selecting into professional degree studies, adult learners are also more likely to be highly motivated and focused (Merriam Caffarella, 1999). For adults, the learning process involves self-discovery, and transforming not just what one learns, but also the way in which one learns (Cercone, 2008). Understanding these distinctive features is essential for designing effective learning experiences for adults. Key conceptual frameworks, including transformative learning theory, self-directed learning, and Knowles' theory of andragogy (1984), shed light on the specific needs and motivations of adult learners in context.

Andragogy provides a useful window into better understanding the specific characteristics and learning preferences of adult learners (Knowles, 1984). A fundamental aspect of andragogy is the concept of self-directed learning. Adult learners are typically intrinsically motivated, and have a strong desire to take ownership of their learning journey, engaging in learning that is relevant and applicable to their personal and professional lives (Merriam Caffarella, 1999). Providing clear learning objectives and guidance, while still allowing flexibility for learners to pursue their specific interests and goals, promotes a self-directed learning process for adults. Transformative learning theory complements andragogy by emphasizing the transformative process that adult learners undergo as they engage in the learning process (Mezirow, 1997). Adult learners in professional graduate programs are often seeking opportunities for critical reflection, in order to challenge their existing assumptions and beliefs. Adult learners are more likely to feel as if their needs are being effectively met if learning experiences incorporate reflection, dialogue, and the exploration of diverse points of view which contribute to a sense of transformation for the learner.

Another key principle of andragogy is the emphasis on the learners' prior experiences. Adult learners bring their life experiences and pre-existing knowledge into the learning process, which shapes their perspectives and contributes to their understanding of the course material. Andragogy also emphasizes the importance of practical application; adult learners are motivated by the immediate relevance and applicability of what they learn (Cercone, 2008; Knowles, 1984). By integrating practical, job-related applications into the learning experience such as case studies, simulations, and authentic assessments that bridge the gap between theory and practice, educators can enhance the motivation and engagement of adult learners. In the specific context of professional graduate degree programs, adult learners have a strong appetite for the application of newly acquired knowledge and skills directly to their professional contexts, fostering deeper learning and skills transfer to the work environment.

Merriam (2001) asserts that self-directed learning theory is tightly coupled with andragogy in its aim to enable adults to achieve autonomy and develop a lifelong learning mindset by establishing learner-centered environments that foster opportunities for individual discovery. Candy's (1991) research identifies four key elements of self-directed learning: preparedness for learning, existence of learning initiatives, efficient learning techniques, and a conducive learning atmosphere. Self-directed learning interventions such as goal setting, self-monitoring, and reflective practice have beneficial effects on adult learners, including favorable impacts on their knowledge, skills, and attitudes (Loeng, 2020). Du Toit-Brits' (2019) study on self directed learning underscored the significant role that educators play in transforming their learning environments into spaces that fostered individuals' empowerment and provided them with opportunities to learn actively and cooperatively. Additional strategies for enhancing self-directed learning for adults include allowing classroom discourse to unfold in flexible accordance with learners' expressed needs and interests, granting options for assessments, and providing ongoing feedback (Merriam, et al., 2007; Cho Heron, 2015).

Online learning contexts are particularly promising as complementary environments for principles of self-directed learning and andragogy. Recent studies indicate that adult online learners identify an increased sense of agency/independence and the ability to work at one's own pace as top benefits of online education (Castro Tumibay, 2021; Paudel, 2021; Tareen Haand, 2020). Online students need to proficiently navigate digital environments, efficiently manage their time, and proactively seek out resources and assistance. Online learning provides adults with opportunities to customize their learning experiences, study asynchronously at their own pace, and explore personal interests (Cho Heron, 2015). Online environments also offer various digital resources, interactive tools, and collaborative platforms that support self-directed learning. Studies indicate a positive correlation between these kinds of self-directed learning activities and learner autonomy, motivation, and satisfaction (Candy, 1991). When empowered with self-direction, adult learners are more likely to actively engage and persist in their online studies. Self-regulatory skills, perceived control, self-efficacy, a sense of comfort online, and course design are crucial factors affecting self-directed learning in online settings (du Toit-Brits, C., 2019; Futch, et al., 2016; Song, 2005). Instructors can facilitate the success of adult learners in online education by promoting self-directed learning, which enables learners to take an active and independent approach to their learning process.

EFFECTIVE ONLINE INSTRUCTION FOR ADULT LEARNING COMMUNITIES

Research demonstrates that effective online instruction for adult learning communities necessitates particular attributes and methodologies to cater to the distinct needs and preferences of adult learners (Johnson, 2018; Thompson and Porto, 2014). Proficient online instructors can best meet adult learners' needs by demonstrating an aptitude for communication and facilitation, both of which foster a sense of connection and ensure that instructions, expectations, and feedback are effectively conveyed to students (Palloff Pratt, 2007). Evidence-based ingredients for instructional success include creating a welcoming and supportive climate for learners that fosters active engagement, encourages ongoing participation in discussions, invites the sharing of perspectives, and capitalizes on peer-to-peer learning.

Palloff and Pratt (2013) posit that an effective online instructor is someone "who is open to giving up control of the learning process" by making students active participants in their learning process. A learner-centered approach acknowledges what students bring to the online classroom—their backgrounds, needs, professional roles, and interests—and what they take away as relevant and meaningful outcomes. With the instructor serving as facilitator rather than lecturer, students are given more control and responsibility around how they learn, including the opportunity to actively engage in inquiry, and to teach one another through collaboration and personal interactions (Palloff Pratt, 2013). Effective online instruction for adults also provides chances for students to reflect upon their learning experiences and practice metacognition (Bransford, Brown Cocking, 2000). In synchronous learning environments, metacognition may be supported through facilitated reflective practice, small group discussions, and the utilization of multiple technical features of the virtual classroom during instruction such as digital polls, chat waterfalls, mind maps, and collaborative shared documents (Khudhair et al., 2023; Berry, 2019).

The integration of authentic and experiential learning methodologies in online educational settings also affords adult learners the chance to apply new knowledge and competencies to practical settings (Bonk Khoo, 2014). Establishing connections between theoretical concepts and real-world contexts is a highly effective instructional practice to deploy with adult online learners, as it enhances the utility of course material. Rovai and Downey (2010) advance the construct of learning-by-doing with their emphasis on the efficacy of collaborative activities for adults learning in virtual environments. Simulations, peer-to-peer role plays, and small group case examinations are all proven means of promoting both engagement and academic success for adult learners online.

The smooth integration of technology plays an important role in the delivery of effective online instruction for adult learners, who seek a low-friction virtual learning experience. Leveraging the expertise of instructional designers to build a learning management system (LMS) that is both user-friendly and intuitive has been shown to significantly reduce the cognitive load for online learners, and enhance the overall learning experience (Sweller, Ayres, Kalyuga, 2011). Offering easy access to educational materials, and delivering opportunities for learner interaction and collaboration have been emphasized by Dabbagh and Kitsantas (2012) as elemental to the learner's positive perceptions of the online learning both asynchronously and synchronously. By integrating multimedia and interactive elements in online instruction, such as videos, graphics, and interactive simulations, the potential to enhance comprehension and retention of information among adult learners is also optimized (Mayer, 2014).

APPLICATION OF SOCIAL CLIMATE THEORY TO INSTRUCTIONAL PRACTICES IN ADULT ONLINE PROFESSIONAL DEGREE PROGRAMS: CONCEPTUAL FRAMING

As previously mentioned, social climate theory (Moos, 1979) suggests that people's behavior and attitudes are influenced by the environments they inhabit. The ways in which an individual perceives the environment tends to influence the way they will behave in that environment. This theory provides space for a consideration of the social climate of online learning spaces as embodying a "personality" which iteratively shapes the learning community and the experiences of participants, and is shaped in return. Social climate theory is particularly relevant in online learning environments, where the absence of a physical in-person presence makes it all the more critical to intentionally animate strategies which have the capacity to nourish a positive social climate that contributes to the development of the aforementioned "personality". Given the scholarship's strongly established positive correlations between learners' sense of community and a wide array of beneficial outcomes for individuals and institutions, equipping instructors with evidence-based tools to facilitate the formation of a positive classroom climate which enables a sense of community is paramount.

Moos' definition of social climate as "the social characteristics and expectations of setting, such as its level of support, goal orientation, and structure" (Moos Holahan, 2004, p. 787), and the affiliated key dimensions of relationships, personal development, and system maintenance and change serve as an appropriate scaffolding for a consideration of effective instructional strategy. An overlapping framing construct, distilled from multiple scholars who advanced Moos' theory within learning environments, emphasizes interpersonal relationships (student-instructor and peer-to-peer); instructor behaviors and beliefs; classroom facilitation and group activities; and instructor communication style (Allodi, 2010; Alonso-Tapia Nieto, 2019; Darkenwald, 1989; Fraser, 2002; Kauffman, 2015; Rovai, 2002). Finally, an integration of what is understood about the needs of adult learners (Knowles, 1984) and the affordances and constraints of online learning environments provides additional essential context to inform a strategy for manifesting a positive social climate for adult online learners. The following representation (Figure 1) of a social climate framework for online adult learners which synthesizes key research is proposed to inform evidence-based instructional practices.

Figure 1. Conceptual frame of social climate for online adult learners
Source: Grimes (2023)

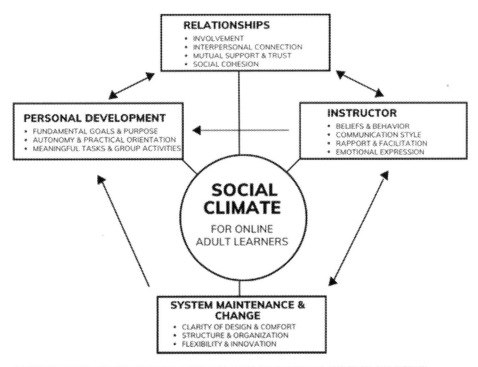

This conceptual framework illustrates the unidirectional and bidirectional iterative forces which contribute to the formation of a social climate within an online adult learning community. Relationships are the predominant dimension, with the other three dimensions serving as both antecedents of and reinforcements to relationships. A consideration of each factor follows, along with recommended instructional practices. Instructional practices are integrative of efforts put forward by the faculty member tasked with teaching the course as well as contributions from institutional colleagues in roles related to overall degree program administration and instructional design. An optimization of the social climate for online adult learning communities is realized when these individuals work in concert, with a shared understanding of the driving forces.

Relationships

The relationship dimension of social climate for online adult learners encompasses both peer-to-peer and student-to-instructor interpersonal connections and is elemental to the existence of a social climate. Relationships within a social climate for adult learners online are bidirectional in nature, demonstrating reciprocity with the domains of personal development and the instructor. That is to say, the instructor has an impact on relationships, and relationships, in turn, shape the instructor. Similarly, relationships influence personal development, and vice versa. This dynamic is illustrative of the conceptualization of the social climate as the outcome of a kind of alchemy of interactive forces between people, systems, tools and environments. Once relationships are initiated, specific activities and behaviors within the learning environment enable their development, including involvement. Involvement describes a learner's participation in the environment, both behaviorally, emotionally and cognitively, as well as the provision of such an environment by the instructor and the system. Interest in peers and subject matter facilitates involvement and inspires a sense of motivation, morale, and self-efficacy amongst learners that contributes to the building of relationships.

While the absence of in-person engagement in online programs is observed by some as a social climate deficiency, virtual learning environments offer pathways for involvement that are distinct from in-person instruction and additive in nature, including private and public chat features and discussion tools, synchronous and asynchronous locations for interaction, access to recordings of learning sessions, and the improvisational implementation of randomized and coordinated small groups. For adult learners, involvement opportunities which allow students to go "deeper and further" into the material through their interactions with others (Palloff Pratt, 2007, p.111) enhance both the level of participation and the capacity for interpersonal connection. Given that students in online programs express a desire to avoid isolation and feel a sense of connection with fellow students and instructors (Thomas Teras, 2014; Song, et al., 2016) it follows that they will take up synchronous and asynchronous involvement opportunities which have the capacity to fulfill that need.

As involvement occurs over time, students may experience a sense of increased investment in the learning experience, which further motivates ongoing behaviors that serve to reinforce both interpersonal and suprapersonal relationships. Interpersonal connections which are fostered through student involvement generate other benefits which are foundational to the social climate dimension of relationships. These include mutual support and trust, and social cohesion. The ability for students to develop prosocial bonds (student-to-student and student-to-instructor) which are characterized by mutual trust and support is fundamental to a positive social climate for adult learners online, and to bridging the divide that may be felt by them in the absence of physical in-person presence and proximity. When amalgamated, the ingredients of involvement, interpersonal and suprapersonal connection, mutual support, and trust advance the establishment of social cohesion in the learning climate. Social cohesion, a suprapersonal phenomenon that reflects students' and instructor's knowledge of one another, and their interest in getting to know each other more, is further characterized by supportive and friendly intra-group behaviors which promote harmony and belonging (Dwyer, et al., 2004; Fraser Treagust, 1996; Thomas, et al., 2014). The sense of community which is animated through social cohesion and its antecedents helps to define the "personality" of an online learning environment (Moos, 1979).

Relationships are the cornerstone for generating a positive social climate in online learning environments for adults. With the above in mind, the following key recommendations are offered to optimize the relationship dimension of social climate to promote community in adult online learning environments, keeping in mind that these efforts significantly overlap with the instructor dimension and may vary in accordance with the kind of online learning model (cohort-based, self-paced). The elements of the relationship dimension which are present in each recommendation are noted.

Orient adult online learners to their new degree program community in advance of the onset of their studies. Materials such as a shared collection of student biographies (provided by students and assembled and disseminated by administration) which highlight both personal *and professional identities, are recommended. (interpersonal connection, social cohesion)*

Orient adult online learners to their new degree program community by hosting a welcoming online orientation. This should occur outside of class time, where students meet and learn about one another as individuals prior to onset of studies, and a shared group identity is introduced. (interpersonal connection, social cohesion)

At the onset of the degree program, lead the learning community in co-creating a set of agreed upon core values and/or norms of engagement. Co-creating and periodically referencing core values and/or norms of engagement across learning environments and experiences, as appropriate, reifies and promotes suprapersonal connection and a collective sense of identity. (involvement, interpersonal connection, trust, social cohesion)

Promote learner involvement and social presence through the provision of a variety of spaces and activities for learners to engage in peer-to-peer discourse, knowledge sharing, problem solving, teaming, and collaborative work. This includes both synchronous and asynchronous spaces and activities such as breakout groups, team projects, video-based (VoiceThread©, Flip©) and written discussions, and collaborative documents (Google Docs©), mind maps (LucidChart©, Miro©, MindMeister©), and white/post-it boards (Padlet©, Mural©, Jamboard©,). (involvement, interpersonal connection, mutual support, trust, social cohesion)

Exercise intentionality with use of breakout rooms including purposeful selection and rearrangement of groupings of students as well as providing students with opportunities to self-select groups. (interpersonal connection, social cohesion, involvement)

Provide invitations and opportunities for adult online learners to engage with the broader institution through ongoing communication, programming, and resources such as career services offerings, digital newsletters, student engagement and wellness online events, university-sponsored webinars and colloquiums, and regional in-person gatherings. (involvement)

Instructor

Like the captain of a ship, the instructor has an outsized influence on successfully developing an online learning environment "personality" (Moos, 1987) and its conjoined collective sense of community. This is displayed through the trilogy of impacts the instructor has on the other social climate domains of relationships, personal development, and system maintenance and change. When teaching adult professionals online, an instructor's comprehension of their needs and preferences is critical to the genesis of a positive social climate, as are instructional behaviors which signal high competence with relevant technology tools. In addition to these competencies, each instructor brings a unique set of beliefs and values into the learning community with them; the ways in which these are communicated to students through an instructor's persona, behavior and dialogue in asynchronous and synchronous settings serves to establish an overall tone and atmosphere of social climate, particularly in the early weeks of community building when students are more impressionable to an instructor's style. An instructional communication style that incorporates affirming messages which encourage student effort and commitment, clearly articulates course expectations, and portrays a genuine enthusiasm for the content drives a positive social climate. (Barr, 2016).

An instructional facilitation style which is characterized by centering the learner is most effective in adult online learning communities. By focusing on the learners' experiences, interests, perspectives, and needs, as opposed to primarily lecturing about course material, the instructor is modeling a posture of care for students which fosters mutual respect and promotes class participation (Dallimore, et al., 2004). This facilitation approach aligns with andragogical principles (Knowles, 1984) and is proven to foster positive student-instructor relationships, positive student perceptions of the class, and a positive environmental "personality" (McCombs, 1997; Moos, 1987). Intentional facilitation of a dynamic learner-centered environment is essential in online spaces, which are two dimensional and therefore inherently predisposed to feeling more flat in nature. Optimal facilitation calls for activities which are interactive, inviting, and affirming, where adult learners feel seen and have chances to assert their identities and perspectives with one another. Andragogically informed facilitation also reminds instructors that their interactions with students serve two ends: interpersonal connection and content delivery. Consequently instructors are responsible not only for providing useful content and promoting impactful cognitive experiences for students, but also for playing the lead role in developing classroom rapport (Frymier Houser, 2000) which paves the way for a positive social climate.

With the above in mind, the following key recommendations are offered to optimize the instructor dimension of social climate to promote community in adult online learning environments, noting the high overlap with the relationship and personal development dimensions.

Conceptualize and convey that high quality online education offers unique benefits and is not deficient vis à vis in-person learning for adult professionals. An instructor's awareness of, belief in, and positive communication about the benefits of online learning for adult degree seeking professionals will have a cascade effect across the learning community, promoting shared buy-in regarding the learning modality. To uphold their endorsement, online instructors should possess technical competency with tools and platforms, along with some fluency regarding current evidence which supports the key benefits of online learning for adults. (beliefs, behavior, communication style)

Model and clarify expectations for social presence at the onset. This includes clearly articulating an expectation for students to leave their cameras on; promoting active utilization of the chat space for parallel discourse, inquiry, and expressions of support; articulating preferred means of signaling a desire to participate (virtual or manual hand raising); modeling active and appropriate participation through instructor eye contact, nodding, listening and other forms of verbal and non-verbal communication; and eliciting participation from members of the community who are less vocal in the learning environment to promote inclusion and illumination of a variety of perspectives. (facilitation, behavior, rapport)

Regularly use socio-emotional rituals and rapport-building techniques. Self-disclosure, expressions of warmth, openness, and concern, an encouragement for students to share personal life stories and identities, and the playful incorporation of humor and levity are recommended instructional strategies. Exhibiting a friendly tone, performing confirming behaviors (such as demonstrating interest, calling students by name, nodding, answering questions) and welcoming social conversation in the online environment should also be priorities for online instructors of adult learners. One clear technique for demonstrating interest is visiting breakout rooms while they are in session. Listening to student discussions, observing their interactions, chiming in when appropriate, and engaging with nods and facial expressions are instructor behaviors which signal that breakout rooms are meaningful, valuable learning spaces. In addition, a democratic instructional style which eschews favoritism and incorporates behaviors such as personal instructor-student emails or other forms of one-to-one outreach enhance the capacity for a positive social climate. One ritual that promotes interpersonal connection and rapport is opening each class with a "two word check-in" during which each student has the opportunity to share how they are feeling, or share something personal about themselves with the larger group. This valuable socio-emotional technique not only promotes rapport and interpersonal connection, but softens the sometimes abrupt transitions adults make from their personal and professional lives into the synchronous environment. (emotional expression, rapport, behavior, facilitation, communication style)

Exercise intentional limitations on instructional lecturing in synchronous settings. When lecturing, limit it to spans of under five minutes, strategically using the instructor voice as a means of clarifying agenda and objectives, providing meaningful feedback and affirmation to students, facilitating discussion amongst students, and synthesizing collective learnings. (facilitation, behavior, rapport)

Use chunking of time and a variety of activities to maintain a sense of energy, momentum, agency, and variety for learners. While overly rigid lesson planning is not in alignment with principles of self-directed learning and andragogy, instructors are still encouraged to be mindful of the resource of time, and the phenomenon of "zoom fatigue" in planning their teaching online methods (Toney, et al., 2021). In synchronous meetings this includes bookending focal small group activities with time-bounded large group discourse: a large group introduction of the activity and clarifications of objectives at the onset, and a large group share out and synthesis of small group learnings at the conclusion. In asynchronous meetings this includes the thoughtful integration of a variety of learner inputs such as recorded lectures, reflection prompts, collaboration boards, readings, and external media. (facilitation)

Personal Development

The dimension of personal development (also known as "personal growth") emphasizes the fundamental goals of a given setting (Moos, 1987); in an educational setting an example would be the provision of clear learning objectives which are aligned with particular tasks and activities, and designed to promote cognitive development. In the case of the formation of social climate within adult online learning communities, the dimension of personal development demonstrates interdependence with relationships, and is directly impacted by both the instructor and by system maintenance and change. Given that adult learners who self-select into online professional degree programs are much more likely to share an interest in the subject matter, there is fertile ground for personal development. A collective affinity for course content inspires productive engagement within a community of adult learners, who are more likely to be intrinsically motivated and eager to excavate meaning and relevant applications of content to practice (Merriam, 2001; Knowles, 1984). When considering the constraints of a lack of physical proximity for adult online professional degree learners, the ongoing pursuit and articulation of a shared purpose and collective values is beneficial to upholding the dimension of personal development in relation to social climate. While traditional face-to-face environments possess more universally agreed upon expectations and norms that signal a high quality learning environment, the benchmarks of excellence within the virtual landscape of adult learning are still relatively novel, ambiguous, and uncodified. Therefore, any and all adaptive activities which promote the illumination of shared goals and purposes, and empower program participants with a sense of self-direction and practical orientation are beneficial to the enterprise of supporting a positive social climate.

The instructor's impact on the domain of personal development cannot be understated, as established by the conceptual frame (Figure 1). In particular, the instructor serves as an ongoing navigational beacon of purpose throughout the online adult learning experience and is tasked with repeatedly reminding adult learners of the essential "why" of their participation in their studies in order to promote a positive social climate and sense of social cohesion (Mezirow, 1993; Sinek, 2011). This reification of purpose is particularly significant in the landscape of higher education online professional graduate degree programs, where the investment of resources is typically substantial and the geographic location distal. With the above in mind, the following key recommendations are offered to optimize the personal development dimension of social climate to promote community in adult online learning environments:

Consistently and clearly communicate learning objectives, desired learning outcomes, programmatic goals, and aims of synchronous and asynchronous activities. In order to fulfill the need for a sense of purpose, autonomy and self-direction that adult learners typically crave, clarity regarding the fundamental goals of learning and the rationale for selected course materials and activities is essential. This need may be amplified by the feeling of distance and inaccessibility adult online learners may experience as a result of their geographic dislocation from the physical campus. Therefore, programmatic communications, digital interfaces (LMS), syllabi, and learning activities and assignments should reflect a cohesive quality of purpose and shared mission that serves to motivate learners' appetite for ongoing learning and accrual of knowledge, even amidst setbacks. Tools like agendas, branded and consistent LMS content for a program, and readily sharable instructor slides and resources promote clarity for adult online learners. The repetition of course learning objectives and program mission, clearly stated expectations regarding tasks and activities, and habitually asking learners if clarification is needed regarding assessments, activities, or course content are highly recommended practices. (fundamental goals and purpose, autonomy, meaningful tasks)

Demonstrate responsiveness through efficient, ongoing, high-quality feedback which optimizes technology interfaces (LMS). (fundamental goals purpose, autonomy)

Regularly invite learners to bring their life experiences and pre-existing knowledge into class, and to practically apply their learning to their professional lives. Adult learners are motivated by the immediate relevance and applicability of what they learn (Cercone, 2008; Knowles, 1984) which shapes their perspectives and contributes to their understanding of the course material. Practical application can be achieved through the use of simulations, role plays, case studies (provided and self-generated), participatory action research, and authentic assessments that bridge the gap between theory and practice. Given that enhanced diversity of participants is a benefit of online learning communities (Paudel,

2021; Tareen Haand, 2020), engagement in practical application with others provides adult learners with important chances to participate in dialogue which allows for the exploration of diverse points of view. Therefore, particular attention should be paid to practical application enterprises that enable group work or teaming. (meaningful tasks and group activities, autonomy and practical orientation)

Promote agency for the learner. Adult learners are eager to experience a sense of self-determination, particularly in the context of online learning. This can be animated through practices such as allowing students to self-select into virtual breakout groups, providing choice with assessments, readings, and activities, and using tools like polling and surveys to empower learners. (autonomy)

Make time for individual and collective reflective practice. Adult learners in professional graduate programs are often seeking opportunities for critical reflection, in order to challenge their existing assumptions and beliefs. Opening synchronous or asynchronous learning sessions with a reflective prompt (a question about their lives, a quote from the readings, a video clip, a piece of music or poetry) and an invitation to engage in introspection about the prompt can be both meaningful and inspire valuable metacognition about one's identity and greater purpose. A subsequent sharing of individual reflections in the larger group escalates collective meaning making. (fundamental goals and purpose, meaningful tasks and group activities)

In synchronous meetings, leverage small group breakout rooms as a predominant involvement method. Small group work for sensemaking and sharing findings back out to the larger group is an effective way for adult learners to build a sense of reliance upon and support for one another in the acquisition of knowledge. (involvement, interpersonal connection, mutual support, trust)

System Maintenance and Change

Moos (1984) defines the system maintenance and change dimension of social climate theory as the level of structure, organization, and clarity within a setting which coexists with the relative openness to change that characterizes that setting. This dimension has clear implications for the enterprise of building social climate in adult online learning settings given that the scholarly panorama and best practices of the field are still evolving. The massive growth in online professional degree program offerings post COVID-19 has outpaced the available population of instructors who are equipped with a repertoire of effective skills and training. While many scholars have identified specific inputs which contribute to a sense of structure, organization, and clarity for consumers of online education, an aptitude for innovation is somewhat lagging. Therefore, system maintenance and change is a dimension which should actively and strategically incorporate the expertise of instructors' university partners such as instructional designers and programmatic leaders, in order to promote systems for students which depict a sense of organization, clarity, agility, and continuous improvement.

The LMS (learning management system) of an online course serves as the primary systemic interface for online adult learners, and is where courses are typically introduced, organized, engaged with and delivered. Common current learning management platforms such as Blackboard, Brightspace, and Canvas offer particular integrations and student-facing structures which may or may not contribute to a learner's sense of clarity and comfort, depending upon how they are structured. In many ways, the LMS functions as the opening act for a course or degree program, overtly signaling the the brand of the institution, the "personality" (Moos, 1987) of a course environment, the overall level of organization, and the quality of the design of the learning experience for current and future courses. With the above in mind, the following key recommendations are offered to optimize the system maintenance and change dimension of social climate to promote community in adult online learning environments:

Utilize a flipped curriculum, in which asynchronous content is taken up by learners in advance of synchronous gatherings, and synchronous gatherings minimize lecture/direct instruction. In this model learners encounter information before class, and synchronous class time is dedicated to interactive activities that involve higher order thinking and investigation of relevant themes, knowledge, and practical applications. (Brame, 2013).(structure and organization)

Have instructors, program leaders, and instructional designers engage in conversation and strategy regarding the scaffolding, branding, and overall interface experience of the LMS for online adult learners, to promote clarity and comfort.

For adult online learners, who are often busy with competing personal and professional obligations and paying a premium for a degree, an LMS interface which is aesthetic, low-friction, and institutionally branded offers a more welcoming, comfortable, and predictable online learning experience that contributes to overall perceptions of social climate and reduces cognitive load. Easy to access online course materials, nimble interactive asynchronous content, and seamless integration of external engagement platforms contribute to clarity and comfort. Student comfort-level is defined as a reduction of students' vulnerabilities, brought about by high quality instructional design and teaching strategies, so that students are more likely to succeed in their online courses (Futch, et al., 2016).

(clarity of design and comfort, structure and organization)

Instructors should demonstrate flexibility and openness to their instructional plans, content, and assessments--in real time--to fit the needs of the adult online learners they are serving. Instructors who make room for iteration, innovation, and deviation from rigid structures and lesson plans contribute to a more positive social climate for adult online learners, who prefer a more self-directed learning experience which is rooted in autonomy, practicality, and collective needs. The facility of LMS content, which can be updated in real time throughout the course experience, liberates both instructor and student from static structures. Other ways to demonstrate flexibility that appeals to adult learners is by offering choices when it comes to assessments, readings, and self-selected project teams and breakout groups. (flexibility and innovation, structure and organization)

CONCLUSION

Social climate theory (Moos, 1987) provides a useful theoretical framework for considering the dynamics of adult online learning communities; when synthesized with the broader scholarship pertaining to online learning, community, climate, adult learning, and socio-emotional constructs such as belonging and well-being, the conceptual lens for investigating these phenomena is sharpened. As previously mentioned, the benefits of a perceived favorable social climate and a sense of community for adult online learners are irrefutable and include increased academic achievement and motivation; lasting positive perceptions of academic experience; increased sense of belonging, well-being, and self-efficacy; and enhanced affiliation with and loyalty towards the institution (Hong, et al., 2021; Rania, et al., 2014; Shea, et al., 2005; Tafjel Turner, 2004; Thomas Teras, 2014; Wang, et al., 2020). Therefore, as online professional degree programs for adults continue to advance in their ubiquity, it behooves institutions of higher education to be equipped to compete in the marketplace by offering high quality online learning experiences for adults. It follows that the instructors and university personnel responsible for these programs must be provided with the necessary training, resources, evidence-based tools, and practices to effectively build online learning communities which radiate a positive social climate.

One productive avenue for further scholarly investigation is to more strategically lean into Moos' (1987) construct of person-environment congruence to design mechanisms for more accurately predicting congruence within these particular settings. This would likely have positive ramifications for institutions and for learners. As more and more programs become available, savvy consumers of online education will proactively seek out programs which provide not only a high profile brand name, academic reputation, and affordability, but are also well-known for possessing a positive social climate characterized by student-centeredness, relationships, and a sense of community.

REFERENCES

Allodi, M. W. (2010). The meaning of social climate of learning environments: Some reasons why we do not care enough about it. *Learning Environments Research*, *13*(2), 89–104. doi:10.100710984-010-9072-9

Alonso-Tapia, J., & Nieto, C. (2019). Classroom emotional climate: Nature, measurement, effects and implications for education. Revista de Psicodidáctica (English ed.), 24(2), 79-87.

Alonso-Tapia, J., Ruiz, M. Á., Huertas, J. A. (2020). Differences in classroom motivational climate: Causes, effects and implications for teacher education. A multilevel study. *Anales De Psicología/Annals of Psychology, 36*(1), 122-133.

Alonso-Tapia, J., & Ruiz-Díaz, M. (2022). Student, teacher, and school factors predicting differences in classroom climate: A multilevel analysis. *Learning and Individual Differences*, *94*, 102115. doi:10.1016/j.lindif.2022.102115

Anderson, C. S. (1982). The Search for School Climate: A Review of the Research. *Review of Educational Research*, *52*(3), 368–420. doi:10.3102/00346543052003368

Ashar, H., & Skenes, R. (1993). Can Tinto's student departure model be applied to nontraditional students? *Adult Education Quarterly*, *43*(2), 90–100. doi:10.1177/0741713693043002003

Ashforth, B. E., & Mael, F. (2004). Social identity theory and the organization. *Organizational identity. REAd (Porto Alegre)*, 134–160.

Barr, J. J. (2016). *Developing a Positive Classroom Climate. IDEA Paper# 61*. IDEA Center, Inc.

Bean, J., & Eaton, S. (2000). A psychological model of college student retention. In J. Braxton (Ed.), *Rethinking the departure puzzle: New theory and research Tinto 265 on college student retention* (pp. 48–62). Vanderbilt University Press.

Bernieri, F. J. (1988). Coordinated movement and rapport in teacher-student interactions. *Journal of Nonverbal Behavior*, *12*(2), 120–138. doi:10.1007/BF00986930

Berry, S. (2019). Teaching to connect: Community-building strategies for the virtual classroom. *Online Learning : the Official Journal of the Online Learning Consortium*, *23*(1), 164–183. doi:10.24059/olj.v23i1.1425

Bonk, C. J., & Khoo, E. (2014). Adding some TEC-VARIETY: 100+ activities for motivating and retaining learners online. OpenWorldBooks. com and Amazon CreateSpace.

Brame, C. (2013). *Flipping the classroom*. Vanderbilt University Center for Teaching. Retrieved 06/1/23 from http://cft.vanderbilt.edu/guides-sub-pages/flipping-the-classroom/

Brandes, A. H. (1998). *Assessment of the validity of the Adult Classroom Environment Scale*. Rutgers The State University of New Jersey, School of Graduate Studies.

Bransford, J. D., Brown, A. L., & Cocking, R. R. (2000). *How people learn* (Vol. 11). National academy press.

Brooks, D. (1997). *Web-Teaching: A guide to interactive teaching for the World Wide Web*. Plenum Press.

Candy, P. C. (1991). *Self-Direction for Lifelong Learning*. Jossey-Bass.

Casañ-Núñez, J. C. (2021). Creating a Positive Learning Environment in the Online Classroom with Flipgrid. *The EuroCALL Review*, *29*(2), 22–32. doi:10.4995/eurocall.2021.15347

Castro, M. D. B., & Tumibay, G. M. (2021). A literature review: Efficacy of online learning courses for higher education institutions using meta-analysis. *Education and Information Technologies*, *26*(2), 1367–1385. doi:10.100710639-019-10027-z

Cercone, K. (2008). Characteristics of adult learners with implications for online learning design. AACE review (formerly. *AACE Journal*, *16*(2), 137–159.

Chizmar, J. F., & Walbert, M. S. (1999). Web-based learning environments guided by principles of good teaching practice. *The Journal of Economic Education*, *30*(3), 248–264. doi:10.1080/00220489909595985

Cho, M. H., & Heron, M. L. (2015). Self-regulated learning: The role of motivation, emotion, and use of learning strategies in students' learning experiences in a self-paced online mathematics course. *Distance Education*, *36*(1), 80–99. doi:10.1080/01587919.2015.1019963

Conrad, D. (2005). Building and maintaining community in cohort-based online learning. *Journal of Distance Education*, *20*(1), 1–20.

Coupland, J. (2003). Small talk: Social functions. *Research on Language and Social Interaction*, *36*(1), 16. doi:10.1207/S15327973RLSI3601_1

Dabbagh, N., & Kitsantas, A. (2012). Personal Learning Environments, social media, and self-regulated learning: A natural formula for connecting formal and informal learning. *The Internet and Higher Education*, *15*(1), 3–8. doi:10.1016/j.iheduc.2011.06.002

Dallimore, E. J., Hertenstein, J. H., & Platt, M. B. (2004). Classroom participation and discussion effectiveness: Student-generated strategies. *Communication Education*, *53*(1), 103–115. doi:10.1080/0363452032000135805

Darkenwald, G. G. (1987). Assessing the Social Environment of Adult Classes. *Studies in the Education of Adults*, *19*(2), 127–136. doi:10.1080/02660830.1987.11730484

Darkenwald, G. G. (1989). Enhancing the adult classroom environment. *New Directions for Adult and Continuing Education*, *1989*(43), 67–75. doi:10.1002/ace.36719894308

Dewaele, J. M., Albakistani, A., & Ahmed, I. K. (2022a). Levels of foreign language enjoyment, anxiety and boredom in emergency remote teaching and in-person classes. *Language Learning Journal*, •••, 1–14. doi:10.1080/09571736.2022.2110607

Drezner, N. D., & Pizmony-Levy, O. (2021). I Belong, Therefore, I Give? The Impact of Sense of Belonging on Graduate Student Alumni Engagement. *Nonprofit and Voluntary Sector Quarterly*, *50*(4), 753–777. doi:10.1177/0899764020977687

du Toit-Brits, C. (2019). A focus on self-directed learning: The role that educators' expectations play in the enhancement of students' self-directedness. *South African Journal of Education*, *39*(2), 1–11. doi:10.15700aje.v39n2a1645

Dwyer, K. K., Bingham, S. G., Carlson, R. E., Prisbell, M., Cruz, A. M., & Fus, D. A. (2004). Communication and connectedness in the classroom: Development of the connected classroom climate inventory. *Communication Research Reports*, *21*(3), 264–272. doi:10.1080/08824090409359988

Elliott, M., Rhoades, N., Jackson, C. M., & Mandernach, B. J. (2015). Professional development: Designing initiatives to meet the needs of online faculty. *The Journal of Educators Online*, *12*(1), n1. doi:10.9743/JEO.2015.1.2

Ellis, K. (2000). Perceived teacher confirmation: The development and validation of an instrument and two studies of the relationship to cognitive and affective learning. *Human Communication Research*, *26*(2), 264291. doi:10.1111/j.1468-2958.2000.tb00758.x

Evans, I. M., Harvey, S. T., Buckley, L., & Yan, E. (2009). Differentiating classroom climate concepts: Academic, management, and emotional environments. *Kotuitui*, *4*(2), 131–146. doi:10.1080/1177083X.2009.9522449

Finney, J., & Moos, R. (1986). Matching patients with treatments: Conceptual and methodological issues. *Journal of Studies on Alcohol*, *47*(2), 122–134. doi:10.15288/jsa.1986.47.122 PMID:3713174

Fraser, B. (2002). Research involving classroom environmental instruments. Learning Environments Research: Yesterday, Today and Tomorrow. In *Studies In Educational Learning Environments: An International Perspective*. World Scientific Publishing Company. doi:10.1142/9789812777133_0001

Fraser, B. J. (1986). *Classroom environment* (Vol. 234). Routledge.

Fraser, B. J. (1998). Classroom environment instruments: Development, validity and applications. *Learning Environments Research*, *1*(1), 7–34. doi:10.1023/A:1009932514731

Fraser, B. J. (2002). Learning environments research: Yesterday, today and tomorrow. In Studies in educational learning environments: An international perspective (pp. 1-25). Academic Press.

Fraser, B. J., & Treagust, D. F. (1986). Validity and use of an instrument for assessing classroom psychological environment in higher education. *Higher Education*, *15*(1-2), 37–57. doi:10.1007/BF00138091

Frisby, B. N., & Martin, M. M. (2010). Instructor–student and student–student rapport in the classroom. *Communication Education*, *59*(2), 146–164. doi:10.1080/03634520903564362

Frisby, B. N., & Myers, S. A. (2008). The relationships among perceived instructor rapport, student participation, and student learning outcomes. *Texas Speech Communication Journal*, *33*, 2734.

Frymier, A. B., & Houser, M. L. (2000). The teacher-student relationship as an interpersonal relationship. *Communication Education*, *49*(3), 207–219. doi:10.1080/03634520009379209

Gamage, K. A., Wijesuriya, D. I., Ekanayake, S. Y., Rennie, A. E., Lambert, C. G., Futch, L. S., DeNoyelles, A., Thompson, K., & Howard, W. (2016). Comfort" as a Critical Success Factor in Blended Learning Courses. *Online Learning : the Official Journal of the Online Learning Consortium*, *20*(3), 140–158.

Garrison, D. R., Anderson, T., & Archer, W. (2001). Critical thinking, cognitive presence, and computer conferencing in distance education. *American Journal of Distance Education*, *15*(1), 7–23. doi:10.1080/08923640109527071

Ghaderizefreh, S., & Hoover, M. L. (2018). Student satisfaction with online learning in a blended course. *Int. J. Digit. Soc*, *9*(3), 1393–1398. doi:10.20533/ijds.2040.2570.2018.0172

Gigone, D., & Hastie, R. (1997). The impact of information on small group choice. *Journal of Personality and Social Psychology*, *72*(1), 132–140. doi:10.1037/0022-3514.72.1.132

Givens Rolland, R. (2012). Synthesizing the evidence on classroom goal structures in middle and secondary schools: A meta-analysis and narrative review. *Review of Educational Research*, *82*(4), 396–435. doi:10.3102/0034654312464909

Gokcora, D. (1989, November). *A descriptive study of communication and teaching strategies used by two types of international teaching assistants at the University of Minnesota, and their cultural perceptions of teaching and teachers.* Paper presented at the meeting of the National Conference on Training and Employment of Teaching Assistants, Seattle, WA. (ERIC Document Reproduction Service No. ED351730)

Graham, S. W., & Gisi, S. L. (2000). The effects of instructional climate and student affairs services on college outcomes and satisfaction. *Journal of College Student Development*, *41*, 279–291.

Granitz, N. A., Koernig, S. K., & Harich, K. R. (2009). Now it's personal: Antecedents and outcomes of rapport between business faculty and their students. *Journal of Marketing Education*, *31*(1), 52–65. doi:10.1177/0273475308326408

Gunawardhana, N. (2020). Online delivery of teaching and laboratory practices: Continuity of university programmes during COVID-19 pandemic. *Education Sciences*, *10*(10), 291. doi:10.3390/educsci10100291

Hartley, K., & Bendixen, L. D. (2001). Educational research in the Internet age: Examining the role of individual characteristics. *Educational Researcher*, *30*(9), 22–26. doi:10.3102/0013189X030009022

Herrington, J., Reeves, T. C., & Oliver, R. (2010). *A guide to authentic e-learning*. Routledge.

Hewitt, J. (2003). How habitual online practices affect the development of asynchronous discussion threads. *Journal of Educational Computing Research*, *28*(1), 31–45. doi:10.2190/PMG8-A05J-CUH1-DK14

Hirschy, A. S., & Wilson, M. E. (2002). The sociology of the classroom and its influence on student learning. *Peabody Journal of Education*, *77*(3), 85–100. doi:10.1207/S15327930PJE7703_5

Hong, F.-Y., Shao-I., C., Huang, D.-H., & Chiu, S.-L. (2021). Correlations among classroom emotional climate, social self-efficacy, and psychological health of university students in Taiwan. *Education and Urban Society*, *53*(4), 446–468. doi:10.1177/0013124520931458

Jack, B. M., Lin, H. S., & Yore, L. D. (2014). The synergistic effect of affective factors on student learning outcomes. *Journal of Research in Science Teaching*, *51*(8), 1084–1101. doi:10.1002/tea.21153

Johnson, E., Morwane, R., Dada, S., Pretorius, G., & Lotriet, M. (2018). Adult Learners' Perspectives on Their Engagement in a Hybrid Learning Postgraduate Programme. *The Journal of Continuing Higher Education*, *66*(2), 88–105. doi:10.1080/07377363.2018.1469071

Jonassen, D., & Reeves, T. C. (2001). Learning with technology: Using computers as cognitive tools. In D. H. Jonassen (Ed.), *The handbook of research for educational communications and technology*. Lawrence Earlbaum.

Jorgenson, J. (1992). Social approaches: Communication, rapport, and the interview: A social perspective. *Communication Theory*, *2*(2), 148156. doi:10.1111/j.1468-2885.1992.tb00034.x

Junco, R., & Mastrodicasa, J. (2007). *Connecting to the Net.Generation: What higher education professionals need to know about today's students* (1st ed.). National Association of Student Personnel Administrators.

Kauffman, H. (2015). A review of predictive factors of student success in and satisfaction with online learning. *Research in Learning Technology*, *23*, 23. doi:10.3402/rlt.v23.26507

Kaufmann, R., Sellnow, D. D., & Frisby, B. N. (2016). The development and validation of the online learning climate scale (OLCS). *Communication Education*, *65*(3), 307–321. doi:10.1080/03634523.2015.1101778

Khudhair, A. K., Jaber, M., Awreed, M., & Ali, Y. (2023). Impact on Higher Education and College Students in Dijlah University after COVID through E-learning. *Computer-Aided Design and Applications*, 104–115. doi:10.14733/cadaps.2023.S12.104-115

Knowles, M. S. (1984). *Andragogy in action*. Academic Press.

Kurt, Y., Özkan, Ç. G., & Öztürk, H. (2022). Nursing students' classroom climate perceptions: A longitudinal study. *Nurse Education Today*, *111*, 105311. doi:10.1016/j.nedt.2022.105311 PMID:35240399

Land, S. M., & Greene, B. A. (2000). Projectbased learning with the World Wide Web: A qualitative study of resource integration. *Educational Technology Research and Development*, *48*(1), 45–68. doi:10.1007/BF02313485

Lee, A., & Gage, N. A. (2020). Updating and expanding systematic reviews and meta-analyses on the effects of school-wide positive behavior interventions and supports. *Psychology in the Schools*, *57*(5), 783–804. doi:10.1002/pits.22336

Lewin, K. (1935). *A dynamic theory of personality: Selected papers*. McGraw-Hill.

Loeng, S. (2020). Self-Directed Learning: A Core Concept in Adult Education. *Education Research International*. doi:10.1155/2020/3816132

Mael, F., & Ashforth, B. E. (1992). Alumni and their alma mater: A partial test of the reformulated model of organizational identification. *Journal of Organizational Behavior, 13*(2), 103–123. doi:10.1002/job.4030130202

Maor, D. (2008). Changing relationship: Who is the learner and who is the teacher in the online educational landscape? *Australasian Journal of Educational Technology, 24*(5), 627–638. doi:10.14742/ajet.1195

Mayer, R. E. (2014). Incorporating motivation into multimedia learning. *Learning and Instruction, 29*, 171–173. doi:10.1016/j.learninstruc.2013.04.003

Mazer, J. P., Murphy, R. E., & Simonds, C. J. (2007). I'll see you on "Facebook": The effects of computer-mediated teacher self-disclosure on student motivation, affective learning, and classroom climate. *Communication Education, 56*(1), 1–17. doi:10.1080/03634520601009710

McCombs, B. L. (1997). Self-assessment and reflection: Tools for promoting teacher changes toward learner-centered practices. *NASSP Bulletin, 81*(587), 1–14. doi:10.1177/019263659708158702

McMillan, D. W., & Chavis, D. M. (1986). Sense of Community: A definition and theory. *Journal of Community Psychology, 14*(1), 6–23. doi:10.1002/1520-6629(198601)14:1<6::AID-JCOP2290140103>3.0.CO;2-I

Merriam, S. B. (2001). Andragogy and self-directed learning: Pillars of adult learning theory. *New Directions for Adult and Continuing Education, 2001*(89), 3–14. doi:10.1002/ace.3

Merriam, S. B., & Caffarella, R. S. (1999). *Learning in Adulthood* (2nd ed.). Jossey-Bass.

Merriam, S. B., Cafferella, R. C., & Baumgartner, L. M. (2007). *Learning in adulthood* (3rd ed.). Jossey-Bass.

Mezirow, J. (1981). A critical theory of adult learning and education. *Adult Education, 32*(1), 3–24. doi:10.1177/074171368103200101

Moos, R. H. (1979). *Evaluating educational environments*. Jossey-Bass.

Moos, R. H. (1984). Context and coping: Toward a unifying conceptual framework. *American Journal of Community Psychology, 12*(1), 5–36. doi:10.1007/BF00896933 PMID:6711492

Moos, R. H. (1987). Person-environment congruence in work, school, and health care settings. *Journal of Vocational Behavior, 31*(3), 231–247. doi:10.1016/0001-8791(87)90041-8

Moos, R. H., & Holahan, C. J. (2017). Environmental Assessment. In *Reference Module in Neuroscience and Biobehavioral Psychology*. Elsevier Inc. doi:10.1016/B978-0-12-809324-5.05552-8

Moos, R. H., Trickett, E. (1974). *Classroom environment scale*. Academic Press.

Murphy, E., & Rodriguez, A. M. (2012). Rapport in distance education. *International Review of Research in Open and Distance Learning, 13*(1), 167–190. doi:10.19173/irrodl.v13i1.1057

Murray, H. A. (1938). *Explorations in personality*. Oxford University Press.

Mustika, R., Yo, E. C., Faruqi, M., & Zhuhra, R. T. (2021, October). Evaluating the Relationship Between Online Learning Environment and Medical Students' Wellbeing During COVID-19 Pandemic. *The Malaysian Journal of Medical Sciences : MJMS*, *28*(5), 108–117. doi:10.21315/mjms2021.28.5.11 PMID:35115893

Mustika, Yo, Faruqi, & Zhuhra. (n.d.). *Evaluating the Relationship Between Online Learning Environment and Medical Students' Wellbeing During COVID-19 Pandemic*. Academic Press.

Myers, S. A. (1995). Student perceptions of teacher affinity-seeking and classroom climate. *Communication Research Reports*, *12*(2), 192–199. doi:10.1080/08824099509362056

Myers, S. A., & Rocca, K. A. (2001). Perceived instructor argumentativeness and verbal aggressiveness in the college classroom: Effects on student perceptions of climate, apprehension, and state motivation. *Western Journal of Communication*, *65*(2), 113–137. doi:10.1080/10570310109374696

Ni, A. Y. (2013). Comparing the effectiveness of classroom and online learning: Teaching research methods. *Journal of Public Affairs Education*, *19*(2), 199–215. doi:10.1080/15236803.2013.12001730

Oren, A., Mioduser, D., & Nachmias, R. (2002). The development of social climate in virtual learning discussion groups. *International Review of Research in Open and Distance Learning*, *3*(1), 1–19. doi:10.19173/irrodl.v3i1.80

Palloff, R. M., & Pratt, K. (2007). *Building online learning communities: Effective strategies for the virtual classroom*. John Wiley Sons.

Palloff, R. M., & Pratt, K. (2013). *Lessons from the virtual classroom: The realities of online teaching*. John Wiley Sons.

Parker, J., & Herrington, J. (2015). *Setting the Climate in an Authentic Online Community of Learning*. Australian Association for Research in Education.

Paudel, P. (2021). Online education: Benefits, challenges and strategies during and after COVID-19 in higher education. *International Journal on Studies in Education*, *3*(2), 70–85. doi:10.46328/ijonse.32

Pawlak, M., Derakhshan, A., Mehdizadeh, M., & Kruk, M. (2022). Boredom in online English language classes: Mediating variables and coping strategies. *Language Teaching Research*. Advance online publication. doi:10.1177/13621688211064944

Platz, M., Platz, M. (2021). Trust in the Teacher-Student Relationship. *Good Relationships in Schools: Teachers, Students, and the Epistemic Aims of Education*, 65-81.

Poole, D. M. (2000). Student participation in a discussion-oriented online course: A case study. *Journal of Research on Computing in Education*, *33*(2), 162–177. doi:10.1080/08886504.2000.10782307

Qiu, F. (2022, October 21). Reviewing the role of positive classroom climate in improving English as a foreign language students' social interactions in the online classroom. *Frontiers in Psychology*, *13*, 1012524. doi:10.3389/fpsyg.2022.1012524 PMID:36337469

Rania, N., Siri, A., Bagnasco, A., Aleo, G., & Sasso, L. (2014). Academic climate, well-being and academic performance in a university degree course. *Journal of Nursing Management, 22*(6), 751–760. doi:10.1111/j.1365-2834.2012.01471.x PMID:23617787

Reid, L. D., & Radhakrishnan, P. (2003). Race matters: The relation between race and general campus climate. *Cultural Diversity & Ethnic Minority Psychology, 9*(3), 263–275. doi:10.1037/1099-9809.9.3.263 PMID:12971093

Rovai, A. (2002). Building Sense of Community at a Distance. *International Review of Research in Open and Distance Learning, 3*(1), 1–16. doi:10.19173/irrodl.v3i1.79

Rovai, A., & Jordan, H. (2004). Blended Learning and Sense of Community: A comparative analysis with traditional and fully online graduate courses. *International Review of Research in Open and Distance Learning, 5*(2), 1–13. doi:10.19173/irrodl.v5i2.192

Rovai, A. P., & Downey, J. R. (2010). Why some distance education programs fail while others succeed in a global environment. *The Internet and Higher Education, 13*(3), 141–147. doi:10.1016/j.iheduc.2009.07.001

Ruey, S. (2010). A case study of constructivist instructional strategies for adult online learning. *British Journal of Educational Technology, 41*(5), 706720. doi:10.1111/j.1467-8535.2009.00965.x

Rutter, M. (2000). School effects on pupil progress: Research findings and policy implications. In Psychology of education: Major themes (Vol. 1, pp. 3–50). London: Falmer Press.

Ruus, V. R., Veisson, M., Leino, M., Ots, L., Pallas, L., Sarv, E. S., & Veisson, A. (2007). Students wellbeing, coping, academic success, and school climate. *Social Behavior and Personality, 35*(7), 919–936. doi:10.2224bp.2007.35.7.919

Seligman, M. E. (2011). *Flourish: A visionary new understanding of happiness and well-being.* Simon and Schuster.

Shahnama, M., Yazdanmehr, E., & Elahi Shirvan, M. (2021). Challenges of online language teaching during the COVID-19 pandemic: A process tracing approach. *Teaching English as a Second Language, 40*(3), 159–195.

Shea, P., Li, C. S., Swan, K., & Pickett, A. (2005). Developing learning community in online asynchronous college courses: The role of teaching presence. *Journal of Asynchronous Learning Networks, 9*(4), 59–82.

Shea, P., Swan, K., Fredericksen, E., & Pickett, A. (2002). Student satisfaction and reported learning in the SUNY learning network. *Elements of Quality Online Education, 3*, 145–156.

Sidelinger, R. J., & Booth-Butterfield, M. (2010). Co-constructing student involvement: An examination of teacher confirmation and student-to-student connectedness in the college classroom. *Communication Education, 59*(2), 165–184. doi:10.1080/03634520903390867

Simón, C., & Alonso-Tapia, J. (2016). Positive Classroom Management: Effects of Disruption Management Climate on Behaviour and Satisfaction with Teacher//Clima positivo de gestión del aula: efectos del clima de gestión de la disrupción en el comportamiento y en la satisfacción con el pro. *Revista de Psicodidáctica, 21*(1), 65–86. doi:10.1387/RevPsicodidact.13202

Sinek, S. (2011). *Start with why: How great leaders inspire everyone to take action*. Penguin.

Sithole, A., Mupinga, D. M., Kibirige, J., Manyanga, F., & Bucklein, B. K. (2019). Expectations, challenges and suggestions for faculty teaching online courses in higher education. *International Journal of Online Pedagogy and Course Design*, 9(1), 62–77. doi:10.4018/IJOPCD.2019010105

Sloan Consortium. (2004). *Entering the mainstream: The quality and extent of online education in the United States, 2003 and 2004*. Retrieved March 10, 2005, from http://www.sloan-c.org/resources/

Song, L. (2005). *Adult learners' self-directed learning in online environments: Process, personal attribute, and context* [Unpublished Dissertation]. The University of Georgia, Athens, GA.

Song, L., & Hill, J. R. (2007). A conceptual model for understanding self-directed learning in online environments. *Journal of Interactive Online Learning*, 6(1), 27–42.

Song, L., Singleton, E. S., Hill, J. R., & Koh, M. H. (2004). Improving online learning: Student perceptions of useful and challenging characteristics. *The Internet and Higher Education*, 7(1), 59–70. doi:10.1016/j.iheduc.2003.11.003

Sriharan, A. (2020, October 14). Teaching Online: Tips for Engaging Students in Virtual Classrooms. *Medical Science Educator*, 30(4), 1673–1675. doi:10.100740670-020-01116-7 PMID:33078083

Sriharan, A. (2020). Teaching online: Tips for engaging students in virtual classrooms. *Medical Science Educator*, 30(4), 1673–1675. doi:10.100740670-020-01116-7 PMID:33078083

Stebleton, M., Soria, K., Huesman, R. Jr, & Torres, V. (2014). Recent immigrant students at research universities: The relationship between campus climate and sense of belonging. *Journal of College Student Development*, 55(2), 196–202. doi:10.1353/csd.2014.0019

Strayhorn, T. (2008). Fittin' in: Do diverse interactions with peers affect sense of belonging for black men at predominantly white institutions? *Journal of Student Affairs Research and Practice*, 45(4), 953–979.

Strayhorn, T. (2012). *College students' sense of belonging*. Routledge. doi:10.4324/9780203118924

Swan, K. (2002). Building learning communities in online courses: The importance of interaction. *Education Communication and Information*, 2(1), 23–49. doi:10.1080/1463631022000005016

Sweller, J., Ayres, P., & Kalyuga, S. (2011). *Cognitive load theory*. Springer., doi:10.1007/978-1-4419-8126-4

Tajfel, H. (1974). Social identity and intergroup behaviour. *Social Sciences Information. Information Sur les Sciences Sociales*, 13(2), 65–93. doi:10.1177/053901847401300204

Tajfel, H., & Turner, J. C. (2004). The social identity theory of intergroup behavior. In *Political psychology* (pp. 276–293). Psychology Press. doi:10.4324/9780203505984-16

Tareen, H., & Haand, M. T. (2020). A case study of UiTM post-graduate students' perceptions on online learning: Benefits challenges. *International Journal of Advanced Research and Publications*, 4(6), 86–94.

Thomas, L., Herbert, J., & Teras, M. (2014). A sense of belonging to enhance participation, success and retention in online programs. *The International Journal of the First Year in Higher Education*, *5*(2), 69–80. doi:10.5204/intjfyhe.v5i2.233

Thompson, J., Porto, S. (2014). *Supporting wellness in adult online education*. Academic Press.

Thoms, B., Garrett, N., Herrera, J. C., & Ryan, T. (2008). Understanding the Roles of Knowledge Sharing and Trust in Online Learning Communities. *Proceedings of the 41st Annual Hawaii International Conference on System Sciences (HICSS 2008)*. 10.1109/HICSS.2008.481

Tinto, V. (1987). *Leaving college: Rethinking the causes and cures of student attrition*. The University of Chicago Press.

Tinto, V. (1993). Building community. *Liberal Education*, *79*(4), 16–21.

Tinto, V. (2017). Through the eyes of students. *Journal of College Student Retention*, *19*(3), 254–269. doi:10.1177/1521025115621917

Toney, S., Light, J., & Urbaczewski, A. (2021). Fighting Zoom fatigue: Keeping the zoombies at bay. *Communications of the Association for Information Systems*, *48*(1), 10. doi:10.17705/1CAIS.04806

Trickett, E. J., Leone, P. E., Fink, C. M., & Braaten, S. L. (1993). The perceived environment of special education classrooms for adolescents: A revision of the classroom environment scale. *Exceptional Children*, *59*(5), 411–420. doi:10.1177/001440299305900504 PMID:8440299

Trickett, E. J., & Moos, R. H. (1973). Assessment of the psychosocial environment of the high school classroom. *Journal of Educational Psychology*, *65*, 93–102. doi:10.1037/h0034823

Tu, C. H. (2002). The measurement of social presence in an online learning environment. International *Journal of eLearning, Corporate, Government, Healthcare*, *2*, 34–45.

Wang, M. T., Degol, J. L., Amemiya, J., Parr, A., & Guo, J. (2020). Classroom climate and children's academic and psychological well being: A systematic review and meta-analysis. *Developmental Review*, *57*, 100912. doi:10.1016/j.dr.2020.100912

Wang, M. T., & Eccles, J. S. (2012). Social support matters: Longitudinal effects of social support on three dimensions of school engagement from middle to high school. *Child Development*, *83*(3), 877–895. doi:10.1111/j.1467-8624.2012.01745.x PMID:22506836

Woods, R., & Ebersole, S. (2003). Using non-subject-matter discussion boards to build connectedness in online learning. *American Journal of Distance Education*, *17*(2), 99–118. doi:10.1207/S15389286AJDE1702_3

Yamauchi, L. A., Taira, K., & Trevorrow, T. (2016). Effective instruction for engaging culturally diverse students in higher education. *International Journal on Teaching and Learning in Higher Education*, *28*(3), 460–470.

Chapter 10
Fostering Connections in the Online Learning Environment:
Using Intentionality, Empathy, Creativity, and Accessibility as Tools for Connection

Fatma Ouled Salem
Walden University, USA

Corinne W. Bridges
Walden University, USA

ABSTRACT

Student retention and success in online programs seems to be closely related to their perceived sense of connection with their faculty, peers, and institution. Using activities that create opportunities for interactions and communal learning reduces attrition rates and enhances the learner's experience. In fact, Ouled Salem identified four critical strategies that distance educators can use to foster meaningful connections in the online learning environment: intentionality, creativity, empathy, and accessibility. This chapter will go into detail about each of the four skills and outline evidence-based activities that can be used in the online classroom to create and maintain meaningful relationships.

Forming meaningful connections is essential in online education (Harrison, 2021). In fact, an extensive body of research supports that student success in online classrooms relies heavily on the confluence of pedagogy, faculty-student interactions, student engagement, and connections between students (Harrison, 2021; Ouled Salem, 2023). Moore's (1997) theory of transactional distance, which discussed the important facets of distance education, highlighted the importance of adopting a comprehensive approach that uses creativity to engage students in activities that foster connections and create a sense of belonging. Using activities that create opportunities for interactions and communal learning reduces attrition rates and enhances the learner's experience (Haddock et al., 2020; Christian et al., 2021). Further, Moore (1997) put great emphasis on effective, consistent, and ongoing communication between teachers and students and highlighted dialogue as a predictor of student satisfaction and success. Similarly, Ouled

DOI: 10.4018/978-1-6684-8908-6.ch010

Salem (2023) identified four critical strategies that distance educators can use to foster meaningful connections in the online learning environment: intentionality, creativity, empathy, and accessibility. In this chapter, we will go into detail about each of the four skills and outline the benefits of fostering meaningful relationships and connections among students and between students and their faculty. Further, we will suggest evidence-based activities that can be used in the online classroom to create and maintain meaningful relationships.

Learning Objectives

After reading this chapter you will be able to:

- Identify how intentionality, creativity, empathy, and accessibility facilitate students' perception of positive connections in the online classroom.
- Apply strategies to increase intentionality, creativity, empathy, and accessibility in the online classroom.
- Apply strategies that infuse multicultural awareness in creating online classrooms that facilitate connections.

INTENTIONALITY

While the world has largely resumed its pre-COVID-19 state, new strains of the virus, most recently Arcturus, continue to emerge and cause unprecedented challenges. As a result, the present and future of face-to-face education remain precarious, despite the availability and accessibility of vaccinations (Weintraub, 2021). When COVID-19 unexpectedly forced an expedited shift to fully online instruction in 2019, many institutions were not equipped to ensure a smooth transition. Martin et al. (2022) therefore highlighted the importance of continuing to elicit research on effective online education and transcend the initial response to the COVID-19 pandemic by putting in place clear guidelines on intentional transitions from face-to-face to online instruction.

Martin et al. (2022) discussed the importance of intentionality in online education within the context of COVID-19. They highlighted the importance of using a trauma-informed lens and creating a variety of opportunities to interact with students on affective, cognitive, and behavioral levels. Intentional online instruction must transcend traditional pedagogy to create effective and comprehensive syllabi that meet online students' learning and contextual needs (Raza & Reddy, 2021; Martin et al. 2022; Tse et al. 2018). By implementing a trauma-informed lens, online educators are better equipped to provide students with the necessary support and resources (Martin et al. 2022). Martin et al. (2022) further argued the importance of intentionality in creating opportunities for social engagement as it is critical for students' wellbeing.

There exists substantial potential for online learning environments (Martin et al., 2022; Tse et al., 2018). In fact, student reports indicate higher satisfaction rates when instructors are intentional and thoughtful about their pedagogical approach (Tse et al., 2018). Moreover, instructors who have a long-term commitment to the course, meaning that they teach the course more than once, take a hands-on instructional approach using different technologies and resources, and use a collaborative approach to curriculum design elicit student engagement and success (Tse et al., 2018). Further, instructors must design e-portfolios that use a variety of modalities that intentionally meet learning outcomes and students' needs as spending sufficient time designing and implementing e-portfolios is a way to increase intentionality (Tse et al., 2018).

The use of a variety of interactive and engaging modalities in the online learning environment can serve as a precursor to student engagement and satisfaction (Raza & Reddy, 2021). Due to the importance of instructor sensitivity to students' needs, it is important for online instructors to use intentionality to create safe spaces where students from various geographic, cultural, and socioeconomic backgrounds can thrive. In fact, in terms of pedagogy, a student-centered approach while developing and teaching courses as well as discussing challenges specific to the online learning environment could enhance instructors' ability to identify issues like "cybersecurity, cheating, and plagiarism" (Raza & Ready, p. 2, 2021). With the recent rise in the use of artificial intelligence (AI) content generation tools such as Chat-GPT, instructors have yet another complex issue to navigate (Pophal, 2023). There are no clear liability guidelines surrounding the use of AI content-generation tools. While tools like Chat-GPT are designed to generate original content, it is possible for the tool to produce the same response if several people use the same prompts (Pophal, 2023). Instructors are gaining awareness that some students use AI content generation tools to write papers that they pass as their own original work. However, there exist tools such as GPTZero the creators of which claim can immediately detect AI generated content (Pophal, 2023). Due to the complex challenges of online instruction, some educators resort to implementing face-to-face instructional pedagogies; while face-to-face instructional strategies may be beneficial in an online environment, they should not be used excessively or exclusively (Raza & Reddy, 2021). Further, trying to force a "one-size-fits-all" approach by implementing a face-to-face pedagogy in an online environment can be detrimental and counterproductive because traditional paradigms do not translate seamlessly into online programs (Raza & Reddy, 2021).

There is a considerable amount of published research showing the connection between intentionality in online teaching pedagogy and students' motivation, engagement, and retention (Bridges & Frazier, 2018; Dixon-Saxon & Buckley, date; Raza & Reddy, 2021). In addition, there is a positive correlation between the instructor's teaching style and students' motivation and success (Raza & Reddy, 2021). The onus is on the educator to intentionally design and implement curricula that are meaningful, effective, and practical.

Strategies to Increase Intentionality

In a 2023 qualitative study conducted to explore the experiences of online counselor educators in creating and enhancing connections with students during the COVID-19 pandemic, Ouled Salem (2023) outlined intentionality as an integral aspect of faculty-student connections. The results of this research highlight strategies to foster student motivation and engagement while experiencing a global pandemic. These strategies include the optimal use of technology, building individual connections with students, providing supportive feedback, intentional pairing for group activities, and regular assessment strategies.

Optimal Use of Technology

Online faculty can leverage technology to create learning environments that are engaging and meet different students' needs. It is critical that online faculty use intentionality in selecting technologies that can help learners meet the course's learning outcomes. For example, faculty can post an announcement using Powtoons to help clarify difficult concepts, while also hosting an optional mid-week live event via Zoom. While not all students will attend, offering the space and time can help faculty and students build individual connections.

There are several categories of technologies that meet different online classroom needs. First, faculty must become efficient in using a variety of learning management systems (LMS). The LMS is the foundation of the online classroom and will serve as the home base for the course. The LMS typically houses the course materials and assignments and can serve as a point of connection between the students and their faculty. Popular options include Moodle, Canvas, Blackboard, and Google Classroom. Once the online teacher acquires a good grasp of the working terrain that is the LMS, other technologies can be incorporated to enhance the learning experience. The following table provides a non-exhaustive list of possible technologies.

Table 1. Technology toolbox

Engaging Course Materials	o Prezi o Thinglink o PowerPoint o EdPuzzle o Flip (Formerly Flipgrid) o Flippity o Powtoons
Synchronous Communication	o Zoom o Microsoft Teams o Google Meet
Collaboration and Discussion	o Google Docs o Google Jamboard o Google Sheets o Linoit o Mindmeister o Mindomo o Padlet
Assessments	o Kahoot o Quizlet o Google Forms o Gimkit o Socrative
Individualized Feedback	o Bongo o Kaltura o Kaizena through Google Docs o Vocaroo o Audacity
Virtual Simulations	o Labster o PhET o Concord Consortium o EduMedia o PBS NOVA o APA Online Psychology Laboratory
Collaboration Tools	o Popplet o Nearpod o Wakelet o Whiteboard.chat o Whiteboard.fi
Engaging Multimedia	o Response Cards o Book Creator o VoiceThread

Through mastery of the appropriate LMS followed by the intentional preparation of engaging course materials, facilitating real-time communication, encouraging collaboration and discussion, using the proper assessment tools, providing personalized feedback, incorporating virtual simulations, using online collaboration tools, and creating opportunities for students to engage with multimedia, online educators optimize their use of the virtual classroom. Further, faculty must continue to explore and incorporate emerging technologies that can enhance the online learning experience and enrich the learning environment. Faculty must stay connected with online communities, attend webinars, and participate in professional development events to stay up to date with recent trends and effective tools.

Building Individual Connections With Students

Ouled Salem (2023) discussed the importance of connecting with students individually, when possible, to better understand unique student needs. The online learning environment attracts learners from diverse backgrounds and walks of life, which requires intentional attention to their diverse needs. One strategy is to periodically send non-assignment-related emails to students to encourage open communication. Another strategy is to use discussion boards to make students feel seen and encourage them to elaborate on their original thoughts (Ouled Salem, 2023). While this may seem time intensive, it demonstrates that students are at the center of the learning environment. In fact, Dingel and Punti (2023) noted that when faculty intentionally express their openness by initiating, maintaining, and actively creating spaces for communication, they create an iterative cycle that facilitates mutual and ongoing responsiveness. They explained that initiatives like checking on students, asking open-ended questions, and showing interest in students' learning build positive relationships with students. They highlighted the importance of consistency in welcoming questions by students and explained that this technique can be particularly important for minority and first-generation students. Snijders et al. (2020) added that faculty must make intentional efforts to build individual connections with students. These efforts foster trust and create immense opportunities for individual assessments and attending to unique student needs. Individual connections help students feel heard and seen in the classroom which gives them a sense of belonging, enhances their academic performance, and decreases attrition rates (Snijders et al., 2020). By building individual, intentional, and consistent connections with students, faculty increase students' affective commitment, which in turn enhances students' engagement and satisfaction (Dingel & Punti, 2023; Snijders et al., 2020).

Providing Supportive Feedback

Tse et al. (2018) noted the importance of using feedback intentionally to increase student engagement. Faculty providing constructive feedback and creating activities where students engage in providing peer feedback can provide students with opportunities to reflect on their work and increase their critical thinking skills (Tse et al., 2018). Moreover, providing constructive feedback allows students to apply course concepts at a higher level (Ockerman & Adams, 2019). Bridges & Frazier (2019) highlighted the need for individualized qualitative feedback in addition to numerical with specific attention to language and tone, as well as creativity in that faculty can use various tech tools to increase student understanding of the feedback. For example, many online learning platforms now offer voice or video feedback, which could reduce confusion and negative interpretation of tone.

Similarly, creating space to learn and ask questions about the individual interests of students is important (Salem, 2023). For example, blogs or discussion boards can be created for students to interact with one another, request to engage about specific shared interests, or even share resources relative to course concepts. This kind of engagement can allow for an increase in student autonomy and understanding on a higher level (Bridges & Frazier, 2019). This engagement allows online students from diverse backgrounds to apply what they are learning to their lived experiences and share real-world examples that further learning for all.

Intentional Pairing for Group Activities

Technologies like Zoom and Google Meet have increased in popularity since the COVID-19 pandemic (Cai & King, 2020). Such tools offer opportunities for small group activities by creating rooms where a few students can engage in a live discussion. Ouled Salem (2023) discussed the importance of intentional pairing when conducting small group activities. By purposely pairing students who demonstrate a better understanding of the topic with those who do not, students can engage with one another in sharing and constructing new knowledge (Ouled Salem, 2023). In addition, purposeful pairing can increase student-student relationships when faculty identify commonalities. For example, in research courses, faculty can pair students interested in similar content areas or research designs. This will help students support one another in various ways including using shared materials and experiences.

Regular Assessment Strategies

Raza and Reddy (2021) noted that frequent, intentional, and consistent assessment of students' learning is a best practice in online education. Weekly assessment strategies such as discussion boards, reflection papers, and quizzes not only increase interactive and engaging learning but also provide the instructor with the necessary data to track students' progress and attend to emerging needs (Raza & Reddy, 2021). Further, various strategies to engage students consistently can help meet the needs of a diverse student body with myriad learning styles. For example, using skills simulations in certain courses allows students to engage in experiential learning. Hwang and Nurtantyana (2022) conducted an experimental study where they assessed English as a foreign language (EFL) students' writing skills using an AI generated Q&A tool and found that the use of AI enhanced the students' experiences and learning. Students were able to use the tool to interact with and enhance the knowledge base of the AI tool, thus enhancing their own learning (Hwang & Nurtrantyana, 2022).

Multicultural Considerations

Nacu et al. (2016) acknowledged the importance of intentionality in increasing multicultural awareness and competence in online education. The online environment provides educators with an unequivocal opportunity to get to know students on an individual and personal level (Nacu et al. 2016). In doing so, educators foster an equitable learning environment that attends to the diverse needs of learners. In fact, Ouled Salem (2023) noted that the accessibility of online education creates learning environments with a wide range of student capacities; some of which come from cultural backgrounds that foster open communication and requesting support when needed, while others may come from environments where autonomy in problem-solving is heavily enforced. It is, therefore, the educator's responsibility to identify these idiosyncrasies and engage with reserved students (Salem, 2023). Educators must practice intentionality in creating inclusive learning environments that embrace the diverse backgrounds, perspectives, and cultural identities of students.

Online educators, therefore, adopt strategies that promote meaningful engagement of all students. This can be demonstrated through the intentional selection of course materials and resources that reflect various cultural perspectives (Bista, 2015; Tatum & McBride, 2021). Further, educators must implement inclusive instructional practices such as flexible assessment methods and collaborative learning opportunities to accommodate various learning styles and needs, as well as facilitate cross-cultural interactions among students to foster cultural humility and empathy (Tatum & McBride, 2021). According to Bista (2015), counselor educators are responsible for self-awareness which includes multicultural limitations, biases, and social identities. This highlights the need for faculty to undergo a continuous reflexive journey of assessing their own biases and blinders to create truly inclusive and equitable learning environments (Bista, 2015).

Creativity

Raymundo (2020) posited that creativity is typically defined as the ability to generate new and practical ideas. Educational institutions across a variety of disciplines consider creativity as an integral competency that is essential to educational and vocational success (Raymundo, 2020). For example, LinkedIn lists creativity at the top of the skills most sought after by a variety of companies worldwide (Raymundo, 2020). In the context of online higher education, creativity is not only necessary as an effective curriculum implementation tool but is also a powerful catalyst for fostering connections. Creative online education recognizes the capacity of the educator and the learner to engage experientially with the materials; thus, expanding learning opportunities beyond didactic structures (Dennen & Burner, 2020). Technological tools used creatively in the classroom can provide a more meaningful learning experience (Bridges & Frazier, 2019). By incorporating interactive strategies that immerse learners in multisensory experiences, educators create inclusive and stimulating online learning experiences that inspire collaboration and active participation among students (Dennen & Burner, 2020).

Kinesthetic learning for example, which involves physically engaging the learner in examining and interacting with the course materials is shown to enhance problem-solving and critical thinking skills in students (Pacansky-Brock, 2013). By incorporating physical movement, hands-on activities, and interactive exercises, kinesthetic learning allows students to apply their acquired knowledge to real-world scenarios, thus moving the student from a theoretical understanding to a practical application of the materials (Davies & Forsery, 2019). In fact, Bloom's taxonomy (2001) displayed application as the next educational objective, following understanding. Creating opportunities for students to engage with and apply the materials promote students' sense of self-efficacy, autonomy, and motivation as they become active generators of knowledge rather than passive consumers (Franklin & Peat, 2018). With the ongoing advancements in technology and online educational tools, kinesthetic learning is becoming more and more accessible and applicable. Educators can use both synchronous and asynchronous activities, simulations, and exercises to allow students to actively participate in the learning process (Pacansky-Brock, 2013). Students can manipulate objects, perform experiments, engage with other students, or practice virtual simulations that mimic real-world situations.

Creativity in online higher education can also facilitate peer-to-peer connections. Students in online educational programs crave peer connections and are eager to engage with one another (Ouled Salem,

2023). When students are encouraged to think creatively and express themselves through various activities such as class presentations, discussions, and group projects, it provides them with opportunities to connect with their peers and co-create meaning. Using dyadic, triadic, and group projects involving brainstorming, problem-solving, and co-creation of content opens avenues for students to learn from one another, share ideas, and build connections (Shapiro, 2020). Such opportunities for collaboration enhance the learners' experiences by promoting deeper learning and cultivating a sense of community (Shapiro, 2020). Similarly, Berry (2019) encouraged shortening lecture time and increasing discussion time in the classroom and identified frequent dialogue as integral to online education. By providing students with the space to discuss topics, negotiate ideological differences, interact with course content, and collaborate to answer questions, the educator promotes a sense of community which is intrinsically lacking in online education (Berry, 2019).

Creativity is also important for the online educator as it allows for the incorporation of hobbies, interests, and ingenious expression (Ouled Salem, 2023). It enables instructors to use their talents and existing tools to engage students in fun and interactive ways that foster positive and exciting connections between the instructor and the students and amongst students (Ouled Salem, 2023). Further, creativity allows instructors to personalize the learning experience and connect with students on an individual level. By using creative assessments such as multimedia projects, artistic expression, and digital portfolios, instructors can stimulate students' unique styles of expression and engage them in a multisensory learning experience (Johnson et al., 2015). This encourages students to tap into their creative self-expression and demonstrates the instructor's appreciation of students' diverse skills, abilities, and autonomy.

Strategies to Increase Creativity in Online Education

Richardson et al. (2021) identified creativity as essential in online education as it allows the educator to engage students in a meaningful experience of course content. The continuous search for creative outlets that produce impactful results also helps the educator stay relevant and avoid stagnation (Richardson et al., 2021). Further, Richards and Schubert-Irastorza (2013) highlighted the importance of creativity in increasing life satisfaction and facilitating self-actualization. Moreover, creativity is at the epicenter of successful individuals and organizations in a variety of fields. In fact, Richards and Schubert-Irastorza (2013) shared that success in any field generally depends on three key skills: analytical abilities, practical abilities, and creative abilities. Similarly, through his theory of Multiple Intelligences, Gardner (2011) explained that while creativity was not rewarded in the past, it is essential to thriving in our quickly evolving and demanding society. The following are examples of creative methods to engage students in online learning; however, there is no finite list to present as creativity is limitless.

Use of Technology

Educators are seldom aware of all the technological options that are available to them, especially with the rapid evolution and expansion of the internet and available applications and software (Ouled Salem, 2023). It has become extremely important for educators to familiarize themselves with the available technologies and use them in ways that stimulate enthusiasm and creativity in students (Bridges & Frazier, 2019; Ouled Salem, 2023; Richards & Schubert-Irastorza, 2013). The use of open-option activities where students can choose the format in which they present their work is important along with the use of multi-media resources which give students the opportunity to interact with one another using the available technologies (Richards & Schubert-Irastorza, 2013). The use of recorded videos that educators and students share within the classroom is a useful tool to make the online environment more personable and engaging (Bridges & Frazier, 2019; Ouled Salem, 2023). Additionally, online educators can incorporate gamification elements like interactive quizzes and virtual simulations to enhance student motivation and participation (Barbetta, 2023). Educators must encourage project-based learning and use assignments that require students to apply acquired knowledge to real-world scenarios. These activities stimulate critical thinking and problem-solving and give students the opportunity to creatively apply their knowledge. Further, collaborative tools such as Google Docs and online discussion forums can also be used to create opportunities for students to creatively interact with course content and one another (Barbetta, 2023).

Exercise 1.1

Creative Technology Integration in the Online Classroom: Flippity Quiz Show
This is an interactive activity that can be used during live classes to help students practice their knowledge. Students will be divided into teams and will work together to answer the questions and earn points.
Instructions:
    1- Identify specific course concepts or lessons (up to six categories) that you want your students to master.
    2- Visit the Flippity site https://flippity.net and hover over Flippity Quiz Show.
    3- Select the option "Instructions"
    4- Follow the instructions to create your own Quiz Show relating to your course topics.
    5- Save your Quiz Show and share it with your students during your live class.

Engaging Students in Their Interests

One way to foster creativity and intrinsic motivation in students is to engage them using their hobbies and interests (Richards & Schubert-Irastorza, 2013). Online educators must maintain awareness of the inherent lack of non-content related student interactions and make intentional efforts to create opportunities for students to have a space for casual banter which occurs naturally in land-based institutions (Ouled Salem, 2023). In fact, Richards and Schubert-Irastorza (2013) and Ouled Salem (2023) suggested faculty create spaces in the online environment where students can talk about their interests and have open and ongoing discussions. For example, during the first week of class, faculty can use discussion boards or chatrooms to engage students in introducing themselves to the class by sharing three pictures that represent their interests (Richards & Schubert-Irastorza, 2013). Activities like these can facilitate connections with students and transmit a message that the educator cares about the students. Richardson et al. (2021) also talked about engaging students through interests and hobbies and discussed the efficacy of storytelling in creatively engaging the students in the course content. Storytelling allows educators to use analogies, metaphors, hyperboles, allegories, and more to engage students in an immersive experience of the course content (Richardson et al. 2021). Further, art is another way of engaging students' creativity to process course content. Ouled Salem (2023) outlined the case of an online educator who creates music videos and raps to help students process and memorize important information. Similarly, pictures, interactive videos, graphics, and movement can be used to appeal to students who favor visual and kinesthetic learning (Pacansky-Brock, 2013).

Exercise 1.2

Engaging Students in Their Interests: Sand Tray Activity
This activity can serve as an icebreaker or a regular check-in and can be tailored to a variety of topics and contexts. The instructor can alter the directive/prompt provided to students to meet the desired outcome of the activity. This activity can be used in synchronous or asynchronous class discussions. It can also serve as a class introduction activity.
　1- Identify a prompt that can serve as an icebreaker, check-in, or a way to help students engage with a course topic. List of possible prompts provided below.
　2- Visit the online sand tray tool at https://onlinesandtray.com/
　3- Share the link with students and allow them some time to explore the website. There are seven pages of possible images that students can select from.
　4- Provide students with a prompt and allow adequate time to complete the activity.
　5- Follow up prompts can be used if needed.
　6- Allow students to share what they created if they choose to.
　7- Allow time for reflection and processing.
Possible Prompts:
　o Build a tray representing your ideal world.
　o Build a tray about your hopes for this course/semester.
　o Build a tray about your concerns about this course/semester.
　o Build a tray representing your strengths.
　o Build a tray representing your goals.
　o Build a tray representing your current challenges.

Humor

Implementing humor in the classroom is another creative outlet that allows students to feel an increase in connection with peers and faculty on a more personal level (Bridges & Frazier, 2019). Humor can make the educator seem more accessible to students, thus fostering educator-student connection. It helps students feel safe and comfortable in the online classroom (Ouled Salem, 2023). Educators can combine student and faculty interests with humor and technology using videos, pictures, graphics, or emojis to communicate with students. An instructor can use a quote or an image from a popular video game or a movie to motivate students or elucidate content. For example, an educator uses an image from the video game Zelda with the quote, "it's dangerous out there, take this" to highlight the importance of the American Psychological Association (APA) manual to students (Ouled Salem, 2023).

Case Studies, Labs, and Simulations

When possible, case studies can be a great way to connect theory to reality and provide students with real life situations to problem solve. Case studies engage students in critical thinking and reflection (Richards & Schiert-Irastoza, 2013), which can increase multicultural understanding and encourages constructivist thought (Ockerman & Adams, 2019). While case studies are typically generated by educators, it can be beneficial to engage students in identifying case studies that represent difficult concepts (Richards & Shciert-Irastoza, 2013). Ockerman and Adams (2019) highlighted the multidimensional use of case studies in the medical and mental health fields. Similarly, virtual labs and simulations can be used to provide students in myriad of disciplines with the opportunity to apply their knowledge to real-world examples. These digital resources provide realistic and interactive experiences through which students can explore and experiment in a low-risk environment (Hoxha et al., 2020). Virtual labs and simulations allow students to practice skills and techniques in an accessible and controlled environment and receive immediate feedback. Some labs and simulations allow students to practice in an open-ended fashion, which allows them to deepen their understanding of the underlying concepts without fearing the repercussions of experimenting with real materials or living subjects (Hoxha et al., 2020).

Multicultural Considerations

Creativity allows instructors to stretch out of the typical didactic model of teaching to incorporate modalities that speak to all types of students. Ouled Salem (2023) noted that the nature of online education makes it accessible to all learners of all backgrounds, which makes it increasingly important to use creativity in the online environment to facilitate learning for all types of learners. Educators must maintain awareness of the different types of learning styles and the variety of instruments that students respond to. Gardner (2011) identified eight types of intelligence, which further highlights the diversity of skills that students possess. Further, Kolb (1984) identified four learning styles and encouraged catering to individual students' needs and abilities in higher education. Similarly, Pacansky-Brock (2013) discussed the flexibility inherent to the online environment that allows the educator to creatively engage students by integrating visual, auditory, and kinesthetic elements. Skilled educators recognize the cross-cultural realities of students that expand beyond the geographical location of the university (Khamis et al, 2021).

It is important for educators to use an intersectional lens to maintain mindfulness of the interaction between the systems of oppression and privilege that the students experience and how those intersections affect their learning (Case, 2017). Educators must be aware of the environmental resources available to their students while incorporating creative activities and catering to the student's level of ability. For example, some students may be artistically or technologically inclined and can thrive in assignments that require artistic creativity, while other students may struggle to use technology or use art to display their understanding of course content. It is also critical to be mindful of students with visible and invisible disabilities and create a safe learning environment for them that caters to their individual needs. Using intersectionality as a pedagogy empowers students and educators and fosters equity and social justice (Thompson & Bridges, 2019; Ouled Salem, 2023).

EMPATHY

Empathy is an innate and essential human characteristic that has been proven to be a driving force in online education (Kuhfeld et al., 2020; Trifu, 2021). Empathy is an essential educator trait that facilitates the creation of a supportive learning environment where students can feel heard, seen, and understood (Kuhfeld et al., 2020). By demonstrating empathy, educators can create authentic connections with students based on the understanding and consideration of unique needs and challenges in the online learning environment. Online education inherently lacks interactive factors that help students connect with their educators and feel a sense of belonging and trust (Ouled Salem, 2023). This makes it extremely important for online educators to actively and intentionally incorporate empathy as an educational tool. Empathy can enhance student engagement, motivation, and achievement by reducing the physical and psychological distance between the student and the educator (Kuhfeld et al., 2020).

Trifu (2021) noted that empathy helps the educator learn about the student's motivations and find strategies to foster positive behavior. Further, online educators can use empathy to assess the emotional well-being of their students and provide appropriate guidance. This became more imminent and critical during the COVID-19 pandemic, where students were experiencing a whirlwind of emotional and psychological challenges (Ouled Salem, 2023). Online learning is inherently isolating which leaves students vulnerable to feelings of stress, anxiety, and loneliness (Reyes, 2020). With the added complications of the COVID-19 pandemic and social distancing mandates, online students were facing increasingly challenging times (Ouled Salem 2023). By regularly checking in with students and expressing genuine empathy and care, educators can decrease students' feelings of isolation and ease their anxiety (Reyes, 2020). Additionally, educators should be knowledgeable about the available resources that students can benefit from when experiencing emotional or psychological turmoil. Online educators play an integral role in directing students toward the proper resources and creating a positive and supportive online community that encourages peer interactions.

Ultimately, empathy is integral to online education as it increases the educator's ability to anticipate students' needs which enhances the quality of instruction. Becker and Schad (2022) explained that researchers commonly define empathy as an honorable emotion that increases the individual's awareness of others' needs and encourages prosocial and altruistic engagement. An empathetic educator is therefore a mindful facilitator of learning who acts in ways that benefit students and foster positive and supportive relationships. Educator empathy is directly related to student success (Becker & Schad, 2022).

Becker and Schad (2022) emphasized the use of empathetic skills as a precursor to effective higher education. Educators must tap into their empathetic abilities to put themselves in the students' shoes and assess students' emotional, psychological, and educational needs. This will not only help educators design effective curricula, but also create trusting connections where students can provide honest feedback (Trifu, 2021). In fact, Trifu (2021) conducted a study to assess the level of understanding of course material by online students versus face-to-face students. The results showed that while online students can have good knowledge of the subject, it appears that the face-to-face interaction increased students' understanding of the materials at a higher rate than those who did not interact with their instructor. Interactions with instructors not only increase course performance but are also beneficial to students' emotional and behavioral wellbeing (Trifu, 2021). Further, frequent and intentional interactions between the instructor and students increase instructor empathy and understanding of students' needs.

Strategies to Increase and Demonstrate Empathy

Research suggests that educators can learn to be more empathetic, especially in online education (Becker & Schad, 2022). In fact, Becker and Schad (2022) encouraged more phenomenological research on students' experiences in online education to increase educators' insight and empathy toward students. By searching the literature for existing phenomenological research on distance education as well as conducting original research, educators can gain a level of understanding of students' experiences which can increase effective pedagogy. Trifu (2021) explained that empathy is a skill that can be innate or acquired and identified three strategies to increase empathy in educators. We will outline these strategies along with others.

Perspective Taking

Trifu (2021) explained the importance of putting oneself in the students' shoes. This means trying to understand students' scope of the course as well as their learning objectives. Students' understanding of the learning outcomes will vary and depend on individual goals; it is therefore important for the educator to be attuned to each student's learning needs and goals. By actively engaging in perspective taking, educators can gain insight into their students' individual needs, goals, learning styles, and cultural backgrounds, which facilitates inclusive and effective instruction (Colby et al., 2018).

Considering Student's Feelings

While perspective taking allows the educator to understand the practical circumstances and needs of the student, it is equally important for the former to be attuned to the latter's feelings, character, and traits(Trifu, 2021). Understanding the student's feelings can help the instructor provide adequate and effective support that is sensitive to the individual student's needs. When the educator creates a safe space where the student's feelings are explored and understood, the student will feel supported and motivated to adopt positive behaviors (Ouled Salem, 2023).

Communicate Understanding

As much as it is important to empathize with and understand the student, it is equally important to convey that understanding. Educators must use effective communication skills such as reflection of content and reflection of feeling to display their understanding of the student (Trifu, 2021). Trifu (2021) noted that when students feel understood and cared for by their instructors, they are more likely to feel positively about the learning environment. Thus, educators must communicate with their students in clear and culturally sensitive ways that display their understanding and consideration of the student's individuality (Trifu, 2021).

Active Listening

Educators must set the tone for healthy interpersonal connections in the online learning environment through leading by example and displaying adequate and effective communication. Active listening is an essential skill that demonstrate empathy and care (Stinson & Liu, 2019). By actively listening, educators show genuine interest and engagement in the thoughts and concerns of their students. This helps reduce the social distance between the educator and the student and creates a safe space where the latter feels heard. Active listening involves not only listening to what is being verbally communicated, but also paying close attention to nonverbal cues, reflecting content to clarify understanding, and empathetically responding to what the student is sharing (Stinson & Liu, 2019).

Create Opportunities for Student Feedback

One way to communicate empathy toward students is to provide them with opportunities to provide feedback about course content and their learning experiences. By giving students the space to share their perspectives and provide input, educators demonstrate that they value and respect their students' opinions (Freeman et al., 2014). This fosters a collaborative approach that encourages open communication and promotes a sense of belonging. Educators can therefore create a space where students feel valued and can be actively engaged in creating a positive learning community. This increases students' motivation as they feel responsible for their learning experience (Freeman et al., 2014).

Multicultural Considerations

Educators must consider their students' cultural backgrounds when using empathy-based practices. It is important to recognize that students' diversity can dictate the level to which they feel comfortable to engage with their instructor (Ouled Salem, 2023). Educators must engage in ongoing self-reflection and learning about their students' backgrounds. This involves examining one's own cultural biases, blinders, and assumptions while actively seeking knowledge about students' preferences and experiences (Hurtado, 2019). Educators must engage in ongoing professional development and consult with peers to expand their understanding of diverse cultures and improve cultural competence. Educators can cultivate an environment that celebrates diversity by demonstrating a willingness to learn and inviting students to share their perspectives. Educators must create opportunities for students to share their unique experiences and validate one another; therefore, fostering collective empathy within the classroom. Further, educators must empathetically accommodate diverse students through providing flexible deadlines or accommodating different learning styles to help students feel valued and supported (Cavanagh, 2020). By embracing cultural diversity, educators can create a supportive space where students feel seen, heard, and understood, leading to enhanced learning outcomes (Cavanagh, 2020).

Case Illustration 1.1

Struggling Student
You are an online faculty teaching a sociology course in a graduate program. During the winter semester, one of your students, Sam, reaches out to you asking for support and guidance. Sam
is missing several assignments and participates sporadically in discussion boards. Sam expressed feeling overwhelmed with the number of assignments as this is his first graduate course. Sam also disclosed struggling with seasonal depression.

    1- Consider the challenges Sam is facing and the way they impact his academic performance. How would you demonstrate empathy in your response?
       2- What specific language or words would you use to express empathy and show Sam that his concerns are heard?
       3- What questions would you use to encourage Sam to provide further information on specific areas that he needs support with?
       4- How would you convey your willingness to provide support and guidance and demonstrate your commitment to Sam's success and wellbeing?
       5- What accommodations and/or resources could you provide Sam with to support his learning journey?
       6- How can you demonstrate multicultural considerations in your response to Sam?

ACCESSIBILITY

Accessibility relates to the level of instructor visibility, availability, and engagement within the online environment (Ouled Salem, 2023). One of the main struggles in online education is ensuring student engagement, which can be mitigated by creating and maintaining channels of communication between faculty and students (Elshami et al., 2022; Kordrostami & Seitz, 2022). Elshami et al. (2022) noted that faculty must improve their techno-pedagogical skills to foster a learning environment that is engaging and beneficial to all types of students. They highlighted the importance of faculty availability and accessibility to students as an essential element to student retention and success. In fact, Elshami et al. (2022) conducted a quantitative study compiling responses from 370 online students in health professions about engagement strategies that they find most beneficial. The results showed that strategies that increase instructor accessibility such as regular posts, announcements, and email reminders as well as having a forum where students can interact with their instructor are most favored by students.

Similarly, Kordrostami and Seitz (2022) established that instructor techno-pedagogical skills can positively impact students' perceptions of the online learning experience. Instructor online competence can increase student engagement by using different online resources to create opportunities for students to interact with their faculty and peers. Further, Kordrostami and Seitz (2022) highlighted the importance of instructor affective engagement skills as they increase positive perceptions of the learning environment. They explained that instructors must create a learning environment where students feel safe to engage in discussion, understand that their contributions are an important part of the learning community, and feel a sense of belonging and collaboration with their peers and instructors. Affective engagement makes students feel seen, heard, and safe to express themselves within the classroom.

Online instructor competencies fall within three general categories: basic instructor competence, student engagement skills, and evaluation skills (Kodrostami & Seitz, 2022). Basic instructor competence refers to the instructor's knowledge of the course content, mastery of the online environment, and motivation to adapt to the demands of the learning environment. Student engagement skills refer to the instructor's ability to create an inclusive and equitable environment where students feel like their contributions matter. Finally, evaluation skills relate to the instructor's ability to reflect on the effectiveness of the implemented processes.

Similarly, and using the community of inquiry COI framework, Robb et al. (2022) identified course design and facilitation, and direct instruction as factors of which instructors must be mindful. Further, students greatly value course reminders and consistent communication from instructors. Environments that foster student engagement and success rely on instructor availability, responsiveness, and support (Robb et al., 2022; Zheng et al., 2021). The COI framework defines direct instruction as the consistent presence of the educator within the online classroom. This can be demonstrated by providing timely and consistent feedback and creating opportunities to interact with students individually and as a group (Bridges & Frazier, 2019; Robb et al., 2022). Students feel connected and are motivated to succeed in the program when instructors show direct involvement through frequent check-ins and consistent feedback (Ouled Salem, 2023; Elshami et al., 2022; Robb et al., 2022).

Strategies to Increase Accessibility

Zheng et al., (2021) identified a positive relationship between faculty availability and accessibility and students' perceived effectiveness in the online classroom. By being accessible, faculty reduce the intimidating effects of the power differential that exists between faculty and students and create an inviting space where students feel comfortable to seek support when needed (Elshami et al., 2022: Ouled Salem, 2023). Kordrostami and Seitz (2022) talked about faculty motivation as perceived by students and explained that students gauge faculty motivation by their presence in the online environment. They further explained that students experience better course satisfaction when they perceive that their instructor is actively present in the classroom. The following are strategies to increase accessibility in the online learning environment.

Regular Check-ins

Robb et al. (2022) talked about regular check-ins as fuel to the students and likened an instructor who consistently checks in on students to a cheerleader. They noted that checking in with students can be useful for many reasons: to ensure their appropriate understanding of course content, to assess their level of need and offer support, and to request constructive feedback on the course and instruction. Regular check-ins in the form of emails or announcements can increase student motivation and reduce the transactional distance between them and the instructor. This further creates an inviting space where students can openly share their needs and express their concerns (Robb et al., 2022).

Consistent and Timely Feedback

Kordrostami and Seitz (2022) noted that because of the nature of the online environment which reduces the face-to-face interaction between faculty and students, instructors must be intentional and consistent in providing feedback to students. Feedback must be individualized and timely as it creates opportunities for direct interaction with students as well as increases the student's understanding of course content (Bridges & Frazier, 2019). Because of the lack of face-to-face interactions, students perceive that they are responsible for most of their learning in the online classroom. Timely and consistent feedback can therefore be a powerful tool that the instructor can use to move the student to a higher level of understanding of course materials (Kordrostami & Seitz, 2022). Further, students value instructor feedback and perceive that some faculty do not review all assignments which can negatively impact student performance. Therefore, educators should only assign work that the instructor will have time to thoroughly review and provide individual feedback (Kordrostami & Seitz, 2022).

Presence in the Classroom

Elshami et al. (2022) talked about the importance of instructor presence in the classroom through different modalities. The online instructor must use available resources to engage creatively in the online environment and have a consistent presence that allows students to feel cared for and comfortable (Elshami et al., 2022). Timely feedback communicates that the instructor is present, invested, and serious about the learning environment (Tanis, 2020). Therefore, Tanis (2020) recommended grading assignments within a week of submission. Further, Elshami et al. (2022) suggested recording short videos and sharing them consistently within the classroom to create a sense of ongoing connection with the students. For example, the instructor can create an orientation video at the beginning of the semester to communicate course expectations and learning outcomes. Elshami et al. (2022) encouraged using diverse modalities when providing feedback (e.g., text, video, graphics, emoticons, and audio). Moreover, faculty can use various modalities during synchronous meetings to engage with students, such as creating polls, using the whiteboard function, and sharing videos. In fact, student engagement in online classrooms peaked when faculty used visuals, audio, emoticons, and videos (Elshami et al., 2022).

Facilitate Contact

Instructor accessibility relies largely on the student's ability to contact the instructor. Instructors may have different preferences for how students can contact them, however, regardless of the modality of contact, instructors must be responsive and available (Ouled Salem, 2023). Some faculty may feel comfortable providing students with their personal phone numbers while others may create forums within the classroom for students to contact them (Elshami et al., 2022). The mode of contact must be available and easy to use by students as well as easily accessed by instructors. It is important to clearly communicate the preferred method of communication at the beginning of the course and ensure its availability throughout the semester (Kordrostami & Seitz, 2022).

Multicultural Considerations

Accessibility is a critical element of effective and equitable online education (Ouled Salem, 2023). It is important for the instructor to be mindful of the diverse learning environment and to intentionally implement strategies that increase accessibility for minority students. For example, Tanis (2020) explained that using various modalities to communicate with students fosters an inclusive environment. Implementing video introductions for faculty and students as well as using written, visual, and auditory ways to communicate within the classroom improve diverse students' perceptions of the online classroom as this variety transcends language, culture, and geographic locations (Tanis, 2020). Further, Elshami et al., (2022) encouraged the use of collaborative learning activities within the online environment as it increases cross-cultural communication and learning. This fosters empathy within the classroom, increases knowledge integration, and creates a sense of community. By supporting the creation of a collaborative learning environment, instructors can increase the visibility of minority students. Therefore, instructors must intentionally make themselves available and accessible and create individual connections with students to encourage minority students to share their concerns and feel safe in the classroom. Further, by creating a collaborative space where students feel connected, privileged students may engage in advocacy efforts to vocalize the needs of their minority peers (Ouled Salem, 2023).

SUMMARY

In this chapter, we discussed evidence-based strategies to facilitate and increase connections in the online classroom. Online students must perceive a positive sense of connection to their peers, faculty, and university to engage in their learning effectively and successfully. Online faculty must be mindful of the challenges that online students face such as isolation and disconnection and must facilitate connections as a mitigating agent. By practicing intentionality, empathy, creativity, and accessibility, online faculty can enhance the overall learning experience, promote students' engagement, and ensure inclusivity. Intentionality increases deliberate planning and execution of strategies that are intended to meet students' learning needs. Empathy allows instructors to create a learning environment where students feel seen, heard, and understood. Creativity fosters an innovative learning environment where both the instructor and the students can engage in fun and playful interactions that enhance motivation and critical thinking. Accessibility ensures inclusivity and multicultural competence by creating a space that is welcoming and equitable to diverse learners. By embracing these tools, online faculty can create meaningful learning experiences that are engaging, exciting, and motivating, leading to improved student outcomes.

REFERENCES

Barbetta, P. M. (2023). Technologies as tools to increase active learning during online higher-education instruction. *Journal of Educational Technology Systems*, *51*(3), 317–339. doi:10.1177/00472395221143969

Becker, J. D., & Schad, M. (2022). Understanding the lived experience of online learners: Towards a framework for phenomenological research on distance education. *Online Learning : the Official Journal of the Online Learning Consortium, 26*(2), 296–322. doi:10.24059/olj.v26i2.2642

Berry, S. (2019). Teaching to connect: Community-building strategies for the virtual classroom. *Online Learning : the Official Journal of the Online Learning Consortium, 23*(1), 164–183. doi:10.24059/olj.v23i1.1425

Bista, K. (2015). Examining the role of multicultural competence in online teaching. *International Journal of Online Pedagogy and Course Design, 5*(2), 17–30. doi:10.4018/IJOPCD.2015040102

Bridges, C. W., & Frazier, W. (2019). Teaching across settings. In L. Haddock & J. Whitman (Eds.), *Preparing the educator in counselor education: A comprehensive guide to building knowledge and developing skills* (pp. 190-212). Routledge.

Cai, H., & King, I. (2020). Education technology for online learning in times of crisis. *2020 IEEE International Conference on Teaching, Assessment, and Learning for Engineering (TALE), Teaching, Assessment, and Learning for Engineering (TALE), 2020 IEEE International Conference*, 758–763. 10.1109/TALE48869.2020.9368387

Case, K. A. (2017). Toward an intersectional pedagogy model: Engaged learning for social justice. In K. A. Case (Ed.), *Intersectional pedagogy: Complicating identity and social justice* (pp. 1–24). Routledge.

Cavanagh, S. R. (2020). *The online class: Empathy, equity, and the future of education*. Harvard University Press.

Christian, D. D., McCarty, D. L., & Brown, C. L. (2021). Experiential education during the COVID-19 pandemic: A reflective process. *Journal of Constructivist Psychology, 34*(3), 264–277. doi:10.1080/10720537.2020.1813666

Colby, S. A., Ort, S. W., Pearson, C. S., & Conway, M. (2018). Seeing possibility through a new lens: An exploratory study of teachers' perspective taking. *Teaching and Teacher Education, 73*, 87–97.

Davies, D. J., & Forsey, M. (2019). *Making sense of the modern world: An anthropological perspective*. Oxford University Press.

Dennen, V. P., & Burner, K. J. (2020). Creative engagement in online learning environments. In *Learning Online: The Student Experience* (2nd ed., pp. 193–211). Routledge.

Dingel, M., & Punti, G. (2023). Building faculty-student relationships in higher education. *Mentoring & Tutoring, 31*(1), 61–82. Advance online publication. doi:10.1080/13611267.2023.2164976

Dixon-Saxon, S., & Buckley, M. R. (2020). Student selection, development, and retention: A commentary on supporting student success in distance counselor education. *The Professional Counselor, 10*(1), 57–77. doi:10.15241ds.10.1.57

Elshami, W., Taha, M. H., Abdalla, M. E., Abuzaid, M., Saravanan, C., & Al Kawas, S. (2022). Factors that affect student engagement in online learning in health professions education. *Nurse Education Today, 110*, 105261. doi:10.1016/j.nedt.2021.105261 PMID:35152148

Franklin, T., & Peat, M. (2018). Beyond passive consumption: Encouraging active participation in online learning. *EDUCAUSE Review*. Retrieved from https://er.educause.edu/articles/2018/10/beyond-passive-consumption-encouraging-active-participation-in-online-learning

Freeman, S., Eddy, S. L., McDonough, M., Smith, M. K., Okoroafor, N., Jordt, H., & Wenderoth, M. P. (2014). Active learning increases student performance in science, engineering, and mathematics. *Proceedings of the National Academy of Sciences of the United States of America*, *111*(23), 8410–8415. doi:10.1073/pnas.1319030111 PMID:24821756

Gardner, H. (2011). Frames of mind: The theory of multiple intelligences. Hachette. In R. J. Sternberg & W. M. Williams (Eds.), *Theory Instruction, and Assessment: Theory Into Practice* (pp. 17–42). Lawrence Erlbaum Associates.

Haddock, L., Cannon, K., & Grey, E. (2020). A comparative analysis of traditional and online counselor training program delivery and instruction. *The Professional Counselor*, *10*(1), 92–105. doi:10.15241/lh.10.1.92

Harrison, K. L. (2021). A call to action: Online learning and distance education in the training of couple and family therapists. *Journal of Marital and Family Therapy*, *47*(2), 408–423. doi:10.1111/jmft.12512 PMID:33755219

Hoxha, E., Sahiti, N., Fetaji, M., & Berisha-Shaqiri, A. (2020). Virtual laboratories in engineering education: A systematic literature review. *IEEE Access : Practical Innovations, Open Solutions*, *8*, 176000–176014.

Hurtado, S. (2019). Making higher education more inclusive. *Journal of Diversity in Higher Education*, *12*(3), 147–155.

Hwang, W. Y., & Nurtantyana, R. (2022). X-Education: Education of all things with AI and edge computing—one case study for EFL learning. *Sustainability (Basel)*, *14*(12533), 12533. doi:10.3390u141912533

Johnson, L., Adams Becker, S., Estrada, V., & Freeman, A. (2015a). *NMC/CoSN Horizon Report: 2015 K-12 Edition*. The New Media Consortium. Retrieved from https://www.learntechlib.org/p/152103/

Johnson, R. D., Adams Becker, S., Estrada, V., & Freeman, A. (2015b). *NMC/CoSN Horizon Report: 2015 Higher Education Edition*. The New Media Consortium. Retrieved from https://www.learntechlib.org/p/152102/

Khamis, T., Naseem, A., Khamis, A., & Petrucka, P. (2021). The COVID-19 pandemic: A catalyst for creativity and collaboration for online learning and work-based higher education systems and processes. *Journal of Work-Applied Management*, *13*(2), 184–196. doi:10.1108/JWAM-01-2021-0010

Kolb, D. A. (1984). *Experiential learning: Experience as the source of learning and development*. Prentice-Hall.

Kordrostami, M., & Seitz, V. (2022). Faculty online competence and student affective engagement in online learning. *Marketing Education Review*, *32*(3), 240–254. doi:10.1080/10528008.2021.1965891

Kuhfeld, M., Soland, J., Tarasawa, B., Johnson, A., Ruzek, E., & Liu, J. (2020). Projecting the potential impact of COVID-19 school closures on academic achievement. *Educational Researcher*, *49*(8), 549–565. doi:10.3102/0013189X20965918

Martin, F., Xie, K., & Bolliger, D. U. (2022). Engaging learners in the emergency transition to online learning during the COVID-19 pandemic. *Journal of Research on Technology in Education*, *54*(sup1), S1–S13. doi:10.1080/15391523.2021.1991703

Moore, M. G. (1997). Theory of transactional distance. In D. Keegan (Ed.), *Theoretical principles of distance education* (pp. 22–38). Routledge.

Nacu, D. C., Martin, C. K., Pinkard, N., & Gray, T. (2016). Analyzing educators' online interactions: A framework of online learning support roles. *Learning, Media and Technology*, *41*(2), 283–305. doi:10.1080/17439884.2015.975722

Ockerman, M., & Adams, B. (2019). Teaching across settings. In L. Haddock & J. Whitman (Eds.), Preparing the educator in counselor education: A comprehensive guide to building knowledge and developing skills (pp. 190-212). Routledge.

Ouled Salem, F. (2023). *Faculty-student and student-student connections amidst the COVID-19 pandemic* (Order No. 30527974). Available from Dissertations & Theses @ Walden University. (2827837803). https://www.proquest.com/dissertations-theses/faculty-student-connections-amidst-covid-19/docview/2827837803/se-2

Pacansky-Brock, M. (2013). *Best practices for teaching with emerging technologies*. Routledge.

Pophal, L. (2023). ChatGPT: Opportunities and Risks Related to AI-Generated Content. *Information Today*, *40*(2), 36–38.

Raymundo, M. R. D. R. (2020). Fostering creativity through online creative collaborative group projects. *Asian Association of Open Universities Journal*, *15*(1), 97–113. doi:10.1108/AAOUJ-10-2019-0048

Raza, S. H., & Reddy, E. (2021). Intentionality and players of effective online courses in mathematics. *Frontiers in Applied Mathematics and Statistics*, *7*, 612327. Advance online publication. doi:10.3389/fams.2021.612327

Reyes, M. R. (2020). The role of empathy in creating a sense of belonging in online learning environments. *The Journal of Scholarship of Teaching and Learning*, *20*(3), 1–12.

Richards, J., & Schubert-Irastorza, C. (2013). Valuing creativity in online teaching. *Journal of Research in Innovative Teaching*, *6*(1), 68–79.

Richardson, C., Mishra, P., & Henriksen, D. (2021). Creativity in online learning and teacher education: An interview with Leanna Archambault. *TechTrends*, *65*(6), 914–918. doi:10.100711528-021-00669-7

Robb, M., & Spadaro, K. (2022). Exploration of online doctor of nursing practice students' perceptions of effective teaching methods using the critical incident technique. *Nurse Educator*, *47*(6), 328–331. doi:10.1097/NNE.0000000000001217 PMID:35503108

Scarpena, K., Riley, M., & Keathley, M. (2018). Creating successful professional development activities for online faculty: A reorganized framework. *Online Journal of Distance Learning Administration*, *21*(1), 1–8.

Shapiro, S. (2020). Fostering online learning communities: Strategies to support collaboration and interaction in virtual classrooms. *EDUCAUSE Review*. Retrieved from https://er.educause.edu/articles/2020/10/fostering-online-learning-communities-strategies-to-support-collaboration-and-interaction-in-virtual-classrooms

Snijders, I., Wijnia, L., Rikers, R. M. J. P., & Loyens, S. M. M. (2020). Building bridges in higher education: Student-faculty relationship quality, student engagement, and student loyalty. *International Journal of Educational Research*, *100*, 101538. Advance online publication. doi:10.1016/j.ijer.2020.101538

Stinson, D. W., & Liu, Y. (2019). The influence of teacher empathy on collective teacher efficacy: Examining the mediating role of teacher-student relationships. *Teaching and Teacher Education*, *85*, 215–225.

Tanis, C. J. (2020). The seven principles of online learning: Feedback from faculty and alumni on its importance for teaching and learning. *Research in Learning Technology*, *28*(0). Advance online publication. doi:10.25304/rlt.v28.2319

Tatum, A. L., & McBride, R. (2021). Creating inclusive online classrooms through intentional course design. *Online Learning Journal*, *25*(2), 74–90. doi:10.24059/olj.v25i2.2467Thompson, J., & Bridges, C. W. (2019). Intersectionality pedagogy in the classroom: Experiences of counselor educators. *Teaching and Supervision in Counseling*, *1*(2), 98–112. doi:10.7290/tsc010207

Trifu, A. (2021). Can we talk of empathy in online communication in education and business? *Anuarul Universitatii "Petre Andrei" Din Iasi - Fascicula: Drept, Stiinte Economice. Stiinte Politice*, *28*, 300–305. doi:10.18662/upalaw/83

Tse, C. T., Scholz, K. W., & Lithgow, K. (2018). Beliefs or intentionality? Instructor approaches to ePortfolio pedagogy. *The Canadian Journal for the Scholarship of Teaching and Learning*, *9*(3). Advance online publication. doi:10.5206/cjsotl-rcacea.2018.3.10

Weintraub, K. (2021). New coronavirus variants aren't cause for alarm yet, but mutations could make COVID-19 harder to fght, experts say. *USA Today*. Retrieved January 22, 2021, from https://www.usatoday.com/story/news/health/2021/01/09/new-coronavirus-strains-variants-not-yet-cause-formore-covid-vaccine-concerns-experts-say/6575267002/

Zheng, M., Bender, D., & Lyon, C. (2021). Online learning during COVID-19 produced equivalent or better student course performance as compared with pre-pandemic: Empirical evidence from a school-wide comparative study. *BMC Medical Education*, *21*(1), 495. doi:10.118612909-021-02909-z PMID:34530828

Chapter 11
Going Viral:
Using Social Media to Build Relationships in Online Courses

Marla J. Lohmann
https://orcid.org/0000-0002-2236-7140
Colorado Christian University, USA

Kathleen A. Boothe
https://orcid.org/0000-0002-7667-4832
Southeastern Oklahoma State University, USA

ABSTRACT

The number of students wanting an online education is on the rise, thus the need for higher education faculty to ensure they are meeting the needs of their students in a way that is familiar to them. One way to do this is through the use of social media. Research is limited on the impact of social media in the remote classroom. However, the use of social media may support and enhance relationship-building in the online classroom, as well as students' perceptions of social presence in learning. This chapter provides faculty with an overview of the current research on relationship building in learning and social media for educational purposes, as well as offers practical examples of how faculty might use social media in their online coursework.

INTRODUCTION

Online learning is becoming increasingly more popular with 75% of undergraduate students (National Center for Education Statistics, 2022) and 71% of graduate students (Best Colleges, 2022) taking at least one course online. With the rise of online instruction, faculty must ensure that student needs are met in the virtual classroom. Previous research indicates that students have a higher likelihood of staying enrolled in the course and the university (Jacobs & Archie, 2008), increased engagement in their own learning (Pike et al., 2011) and a reduction in their self-reported levels of stress related to the coursework

DOI: 10.4018/978-1-6684-8908-6.ch011

(Benson & Whitson, 2022) when they build relationships in their classes. Additionally, some learners are intentionally seeking out these relationships with classmates and professors (Berry, 2019).

One emerging solution for supporting relationship building in the virtual classroom is the use of social media. Due to the interactive nature of social media platforms, they are often an ideal tool for supporting the sharing of knowledge and collaboration between online learners (Arnold & Paulus, 2010). Almost three-fourths of Americans use social media on a regular basis, with the 18-29 demographic using it the most frequently (Pew Research Center, 2021). According to the Pew Research Center (2021), the ten most popular social media platforms are: (a) Facebook, (b) Pinterest, (c) Instagram, (d) Linkedin, (e) X, (f) Snapchat, (g) YouTube, (h) WhatsApp, (i) Reddit, and (j) TikTok. Not all of these platforms are ideal for instructional purposes, but several of them offer unique opportunities for university faculty to support student learning.

As noted previously, young adults use social media more frequently than do other adults. In fact, about 60% of college students report checking their social media accounts multiple times per day (Sponcil & Gitimu, 2013). College students use social media for a variety of reasons, including building relationships and engaging socially (Kim & Kim, 2017; Liu, 2010). In addition, students taking online courses spend more time using social media to support their learning than do their peers taking traditional face-to-face courses (Abrahim et al., 2019).

Research is limited on the impact of social media in the remote classroom, but both university faculty and students report that its use increases learning (Alalwan, 2022; Rigamonti et al, 2020; Stathopoulou et al., 2019), engagement in the course (Alalwan, 2022; Stathopoulou et al., 2019), and collaboration between students (Stathopoulou et al., 2019). In addition, the use of social media may support and enhance relationship-building in the online classroom (Ha & Shin, 2014), as well as students' perceptions of social presence in learning (Akcaoglu & Lee, 2018).

This book chapter will provide university faculty with an overview of the current research on relationship building in learning and social media for educational purposes. In addition, the authors will offer practical suggestions for how faculty might use social media in their coursework, with a specific focus on how its use can increase relationships between students, relationships between students and faculty, and relationships between students and the broader community in their field.

BACKGROUND

Humans were created with a desire for connection (Cacioppo & Patrick, 2009). Not surprisingly, online learners are more successful when they feel a sense of connection to the course, the university, and their classmates and instructor. Previous research (Canty et al., 2020; Wang et al., 2019) indicates that student attrition rates are decreased by a sense of community. In addition, student stress levels are reduced (Benson & Whitson, 2022) and students are more engaged in their own learning (Pike et al., 2011) when they feel a sense of community in the online classroom.

The term "social media" refers to a variety of online tools that include (a) networking platforms, (b) blogs, (c) virtual communities, (d) websites for sharing photographs, (e) online product review websites, and (f) countless other online platforms (Aichner et al., 2021). The Merriam-Webster Dictionary (2023, paragraph 1) defines the term "social media" as "forms of electronic communication…through which users create online communities" based on this definition, we posit that social media is specifically designed to support the development and maintenance of relationships. In fact, the use of social media has been shown to support young adults in learning social and relationship skills (Wang & Edwards, 2016) and aids people in meeting their need for social connection (Kim et al., 2023). Because it can be used to share information quickly and widely, social media is an ideal avenue for dissemination of knowledge and for use within coursework (Abbas et al., 2019). In fact, social media is being widely used as an instructional tool in high school (Mulenga & Marban, 2020; Otchie & Pedaste, 2020) and university (Dutta, 2020; Greenhow & Galvin, 2020) classrooms around the world.

CULTIVATING STUDENT-STUDENT RELATIONSHIPS

As noted earlier, online learners are seeking opportunities to connect with their classmates (Berry, 2019). These learning communities are sometimes referred to as communities of practice (COP), which is a term that indicates a group of people with a common goal of supporting one another in learning and exploring new ideas (Heinnen et al., 2022). These online learning communities can mitigate the impacts of geographic restrictions by allowing learners to connect with other students from around the world (Kimmel et al., 2019). Jiang and Koo (2020) note that the use of COPs within online coursework can increase students' self-reported levels of emotional presence, which has a positive impact on their satisfaction with learning. The use of online COPs can also support learners as they navigate personal and professional challenges (Yi, 2022). It is clear that there are both learning and social-emotional benefits to intentional community-building online coursework. In addition to the use of tools within the course LMS, we recommend using social media tools, such as Facebook, Pinterest, and TikTok, to build community and relationships between students.

Facebook

The first social media tool that we recommend is Facebook. Facebook is a virtual space where people can connect with one another in a digital environment (Chayka, 2021). Facebook users can connect with others through their personal profiles, but also through pages and groups that are specific to certain groups of people (Facebook, 2023). On a monthly basis, almost three billion people worldwide use Facebook to connect with others (Campbell, 2023). The popularity of this social media tool, as well as the flexibility inherent in its design, makes it ideal for online learning communities. According to Roblyer et al. (2010), college students report liking using Facebook as a learning tool. The use of Facebook increases online learners' sense of social presence and learning interactions with peers and instructors (Akcaoglu & Lee, 2018). Social presence is a term often used to describe the extent to which students feel they are able to connect with others in an online setting in a way that reflects themselves as unique and authentic individuals (Aldosari et al., 2022).

University faculty can use private Facebook groups in lieu of traditional LMS course discussion boards. Whittaker et al. (2014) used a course Facebook group in an animal science course; the use of this social media tool led to students self-reporting high levels of group cohesion and an increased level of group problem solving as compared to previous sections of the same course that did not use this tool. In order to establish this, instructors must provide students with guidelines to follow when participating. Figure 1 below provides example guidelines that can be presented to students as they embark in participating in Facebook groups, or can even be tweaked for other social media platforms.

Figure 1. Guidelines for Facebook group participation

> **Be Kind** - Treat everyone in the group the way you want to be treated. It is ok to disagree with one another, but do so while being respectful of each other's viewpoints. Remember, we all come from different places and have different experiences.
>
> **Be Proactive** - Check-in often. Respond often. Do not wait until the last minute.
>
> **Be Professional** - Remember you are a professional, act like one; someday you may be looking for a job and this person might be in a hiring position!
>
> **Be Truthful** - Ensure the comments you are posting are truthful and accurate. If they are ideas say so, if the ideas are not your own, give proper credit.
>
> **Be Respectful of Others' Privacy** - Not everyone enjoys their business being blessed all over social media, be respectful of this and do not share information learned about others outside of this group.

Pinterest

Pinterest is a social media tool in which users can share ideas by saving (known as "pinning") websites or images; these pins can be organized by topic area on "boards" designed by the user (Pinterest, 2023a). Pinterest is a visual tool and the pins are images linked to specific websites, such as blogs (Popolo, 2013). Over 400 million people use Pinterest and the majority of users are women (Pinterest, 2023b). While Pinterest users may select to create boards and not interact with others, they can also follow other users or follow specific trends and boards, thus making it a social media tool (Popolo, 2013). Users can also interact with others by liking and sharing the pins of others (Pearce & Learmonth, 2013).

Pinterest has proven to be a successful teaching tool for college instruction and has been used in a variety of ways. Holt (2012) reports that Pinterest boards can be used as inspiration portfolios in a media graphics course. It could be used in a similar manner in other art courses and students can be encouraged to share their inspiration boards with one another. Another idea for sharing ideas in Pinterest is to create weekly Pinterest boards and have all students add pins to the weekly theme. This has been done successfully in an anthropology course; a board was created for the weekly learning topic and all students added pins related to that topic, including academic journal articles, news stories, and information from museum websites (Pearce & Learmonth, 2013). This concept of a class-wide Pinterest board for each topic in the course could be used in any academic subject.

Holmes and Rusmussen (2018) had students create Pinterest boards in an accounting course and students were required to comment on one another's pins. This intentional required engagement with classmates can increase their level of connection to one another, thus building relationships between students. It is clear that Pinterest is a valuable social media tool for supporting student-student relationships. Figure 2 offers a sample Pinterest assignment that a college instructor might assign.

Figure 2. Vocabulary word board via Pinterest

> Welcome to French 101! Your first activity will to familiarize yourself with common French words. To do this follow the directions below:
>
> - Create a Pinterest Account.
>
> - Choose a theme that interests you - food, travel, electronics, greetings, etc.
>
> - Add a new board and title it Vocabulary Words_ThemeNameHere for example "Vocabulary Words_Food"
>
> - Find images/pictures to add to your board. Create images that include a picture of the item (photos or from internet) as well as the English and French word. For example - take a picture of an apple and write Apple/Pomme. Add each newly created image to your Pinterest Board.
>
> - Obtain a direct link to your vocabulary board and share the link in this week's discussion board.
>
> - Review several student's boards and make sure to bookmark them so you have them throughout the semester. In your peer responses share words that you would like to know so that the original poster can work on adding those additional words to the board.
>
> - Continue updating your Pinterest Board throughout the next few weeks.

Tik Tok

Tik Tok is a social media platform in which users share content via short-form videos, all less than ten minutes in length (Tik Tok, 2023). Over 500 million people had TikTok accounts before COVID (Herrman, 2019) and that number had grown to more than one billion just two years later (Shepherd, 2023). Almost half of TikTok users are under the age of 30 (Shepherd, 2023) and the younger demographic uses the platform more often than do older TikTok users (Montag et al., 2019). Females use this social media tool more frequently than do males (Wang, 2020).

The use of TikTok for sharing information has been the focus of recent research. During the COVID-19 pandemic, health information was shared from agencies such as the US Centers for Disease Control (Basch et al., 2020). TikTok videos have also been used to share information about other topics including (a) chemistry (Hayes et al., 2020), (b) sports science (Escamilla-Fajardo et al., 2021), (c) radiology (Lovett et al., 2021), and (d) sociology (Lampe, 2023).

The use of TikTok supports student-student relationships by offering an opportunity to connect with one another (Escamilla-Fajardo et al., 2021). One way to incorporate TikTok in online teaching is to have students create a getting to know you video and then asking students to view and comment on one another's videos. A second way to use TikTok is to have a jigsaw assignment, in which each student learns a different concept and the students teach the content they are learning to one another.

One benefit about TikTok is that students can create these videos from anywhere and those students who are inclined to edit and "bling" out their videos can, whereas other students can do a simple video and post. It is also a great way for students to talk to one another through the comment section function. If you would prefer to not use actual social media but still reap some of the benefits, you can have students do short video clips that are similar to the TikTok format and post to the discussion board in your LMS. Figure 3 offers a sample TikTok assignment.

Figure 3. Sample TikTok assignment with participation guidelines

> Social media has become a vital aspect of our society and an ideal way to share information. In your future careers, you will likely need to use social media. With this in mind, this week's discussion will occur through TikTok. Our discussion topic this week is The American Revolution.
>
> 1. First things first, create a TikTok account.
> 2. Choose an article from the list provided in Canvas.
> 3. Create a 1-3-minute TikTok in which you summarize your article. Be sure to include the APA reference for your chosen article.
> 4. In the Discussion board found in Canvas, share your TikTok link.
> 5. When responding to your peers, do so in the TikTok app.
> 6. You are expected to respond to a minimum of three peers by asking questions to further the discussion, responding to questions they asked you, or providing information to further the discussion.

CULTIVATING STUDENT-FACULTY RELATIONSHIPS

While relationships between students are important in the online classroom, relationships between faculty and students are also a vital aspect of the virtual learning experience for both students and faculty. Sabin and Olive (2018) report that the connections they are able to build in online courses are stronger than those in traditional face-to-face courses, likely due to the opportunities for daily interactions with students in online coursework. A variety of benefits occur when students feel connected to the faculty teaching their courses. First, these relationships lead to student academic success within the university coursework as evidenced by student course grades (Kim & Lundberg, 2015; Raposa et al., 2021). Secondly, student-faculty interactions and relationships lead to increased cognitive learning and development of critical thinking skills among students (Kim & Lundberg, 2015). Additionally, student engagement within the course is increased when strong faculty-student relationships are present (Gares et al., 2020). A fourth benefit is that student persistence and completion of their degrees is increased when they report feeling connected to university faculty (Guzzardo et al., 2021; Seery et al., 2021; Tygret et al., 2022). Finally, students' overall sense of connection and belonging in the university setting is increased through quality relationships with faculty members (Tygret et al., 2022).

It is important to note that interactions are not the same as relationships, but the building of relationships between students and faculty occurs through frequent positive interactions (Hagenauer et al., 2023). Guzzardo et al. (2021) note that students report feeling more connected to university faculty members when those faculty members do more than simply teach; connections are established when faculty demonstrate care for students and support student needs beyond academics. Caring behaviors, which includes actions such as showing empathy when students are struggling and encouraging students, are a critical component of these interactions that lead to positive faculty-student relationships (Hagenauer et al., 2023). Raposa and colleagues (2021) note that students report feeling more supported and more connected to faculty members when they have shared interests. With this in mind, we recommend that faculty utilize social media tools, such as Zoom and Slack, to connect with one another on topics in addition to coursework.

Synchronous Sessions via Online Video Conferencing Platforms

While over a third of university students prefer fully asynchronous courses (Bentrim et al., 2022), faculty-student relationships may be formed or enhanced through the use of synchronous video conferencing platforms such as Zoom, InSpace, and Google Meet. Celuch et al. (2021) suggest that live sessions may increase faculty-student relationships due to the ability to view one another and have questions answered in real-time. For asynchronous courses, we recommend offering optional synchronous sessions to support the development of faculty-student relationships.

Zoom is an online platform in which people can connect online via video, audio, or written chat; users can access Zoom through a phone, computer, or other internet-enabled device (Zoom, 2022). Similarly, Google Meet offers video conferencing services for up to 100 participants at no cost and up to 500 people for a fee (Google, 2023). The ability to see the instructor and hear them speak can help students feel more connected to the instructor and to the learning.

There are a few considerations when using video conferencing software; we would like to specifically address two of these. First, when using video conferencing for courses, almost half of students keep their cameras off (Meletiou-Mavrotheris et al., 2022). There are a variety of reasons that students make this choice. Some students feel self-conscious about their own image on the screen (Fauville et al., 2021), which distracts them from focusing on the instruction. A second reason is that students may feel uncomfortable about others seeing their home or the surroundings in which they are attending the online meeting (Trust & Goodman, 2023). Other students may have unreliable internet that makes connecting to online sessions and using video challenging (Boerngen & Rickard, 2021). In addition, students may select to remain off camera so they can engage in other tasks, such as eating or moving around while listening to the professor speak (Trust & Goodman, 2023). There are numerous other reasons that students make the choice to keep their video off. In order to accommodate individual student needs, we suggest not making the use of video a requirement in online learning. One solution may be to allow students to create avatars if they would prefer to remain off-screen (Shockley et al., 2021)

Secondly, when designing instruction in a synchronous format, we do recommend being cautious about the amount of time students are required to be online. A phenomenon known as "zoom fatigue" can occur from too much time spent on a screen; this can lead to decreased sleep quality and higher levels of student stress and anxiety (Salim et al., 2022). It can also reduce student engagement when required to engage in live Zoom sessions (Shockley et al., 2021). Research indicates that women have a greater likelihood of experiencing "zoom fatigue" than do men (Fauville et al., 2021).

In order to address these two concerns and use video conferencing software effectively, we suggest that university faculty intentionally plan all sessions conducted via video conferencing platforms. This can ensure that high quality synchronous learning is occurring and increase the likelihood of positive faculty-study relationships. Figure 4 offers a plan that a faculty member might use for a one-hour synchronous online class session.

In addition to whole-class sessions via video conferencing, Kordrostami and Seitz (2022) suggest offering one-on-one individualized meetings between instructors and students. In our experiences, these sessions can provide an opportunity for faculty and students to discuss unique student needs and for faculty to address any challenges that students might be facing in the course. In addition, these sessions allow faculty and students to discuss shared areas of interest and for faculty to offer advice and guidance to students as they prepare for their future careers. These individual video conference meetings can be optional or may be a required component of the course. We have found that in some courses, required meetings ensure that students are prepared to meet the requirements for large projects.

Figure 4. Teaching plan for synchronous class session

Catching up - Take time to create a poll or have informal conversations with students to see how they are doing, what is going on in their lives, etc.

Review Last Week - Take this as opportunity to review what was covered last week, especially if they need to remember the information to help them with the current week's assignment

Provide an Overview/Agenda - Tell the students what to expect during today's class meeting

Lecture - Provide content instruction

Break-Outs - Allow time for students to interact with each other. This can be done as think-pair-shares, or small group discussion and share with whole group afterwards

Assignment Overview - Take time to go over the course requirements for the week. This is a good time to clarify assignment expectations.

Preview Next Week - Tell students what they should expect next week and include any connection to this week's content/assignments.

Closing - Bid your students goodbye with a positive quote or something to think about this coming week. Make sure to let them know you are available throughout the remainder of the week if they need anything.

Slack

Another social media tool that can support faculty-student relationships is Slack. Slack is an online messaging tool that teams can use for asynchronous communication (Slack Technologies, 2023). Within the tool, different conversations occur within "channels" and the professor and students may be in several channels, holding different conversations in each one (Lien, 2020). Slack may be used for either synchronous (Lu, 2023) or asynchronous (Muller, 2023) text-based discussions in lieu of using the discussion board within the course Learning Management System (LMS). Slack conversations may involve a large number of people or may be limited to just a few people.

Sabin & Olive (2018) used Slack channels to communicate announcements and information to students. In addition to information sharing, one specific channel can be a question and answer discussion, where students ask questions about course content and get answers about course content and assignments. We suggest that instructors create specific Slack channels for each course topic and direct students to engage with one another and the professor within each of those channels. These channels could function similar to a traditional LMS discussion board, but with Slack, students can access the information via the app. In these discussions, it is vital that faculty engage with students, which helps to build student-faculty relationships.

Müller (2023) notes that the use of Slack can ensure communication and responses to student questions and needs in a timely manner. Instructor responsiveness in a timely manner is one way that faculty can build relationships with their students (Martin et al., 2019). Students report that Slack is a good tool for learning and that it emulates real-world communication needs they may encounter in their jobs (Ross, 2019); this indicates that the use of this social media tool supports student learning in addition to building relationships. In addition, students report preferring direct messages in the Slack tool (Alvarez Vazquez et al., 2020), which is ideal for relationship-developing.

Figure 5 offers an example of how an instructor might use a Slack channel to start building a relationship with each individual student. This figure offers the beginning of a conversation between the professor and a student, with the expectation that the discussion would be ongoing throughout the semester.

Figure 5. Sample Slack channel for 1:1 connection between faculty and students

> Professor: Hello, Rafael, and welcome to this course on World History. I am so glad that you are here. This channel is a designated space for you and I to communicate privately. Over the next several days, I want to get to know you better and will be asking you questions in this channel. As the course progresses, please feel free to use this space to ask me questions or gain any support you need to be successful in this class. First, I am interested in learning why you chose to take this course. As an undergraduate student, I know that you are required to take a history course, but I am curious why you chose this specific history course.
>
> Rafael: Hello, Dr. Churchill. Thank you for taking the time to chat with me. I am very excited about this class! I am taking this course for two reasons. First, I want to better understand the history of the world. I know that we can only improve for the future when we fully understand the past. I am hoping to better understand the mistakes (and successes) from the past so that I can help ensure we make better decisions in the future. Second, I am taking this course because it is an asynchronous online class. I am the father of three and I work two jobs, so getting to classes on campus is very hard for me. And, it is even hard for me to attend online class sessions between my work schedules and being there for my kids.

CULTIVATING STUDENT-PROFESSIONAL COMMUNITY RELATIONSHIPS

In addition to building relationships with classmates and university faculty, online learners should build connections with others in their professional community. The building of relationships for professional gain is referred to as networking (Gibson et al., 2014). Blickle and colleagues (2009) state that networking aids employees in a variety of fields to build social capital within their organizations and the broader professional field. In addition, engaging in networking allows professionals to share career-related resources, such as information, support, and influence, with one another (Porter et al., 2016). For university students, professional networking activities are an important part of the job searching process and university faculty can assist students to build professional relationships.

Part of the networking process involves professionals discovering their own professional identity. A student's professional identity within their field of study helps as they transition from being college students to working professionals in their field (Tomlinson & Jackson, 2021). University students build their professional identities in a variety of ways, including active engagement with communities of professionals in their field (Jackson, 2016). The use of social media tools such as X and LinkedIn can support students in locating and connecting with these professional communities.

X

X is a social media app that allows for communication with others through the use of text-based, video-based, or image-based messages referred to as Tweets; other X members can reply to these Tweets (X, 2023). Tweets often include hashtags, which are words or short phrases starting with the pound symbol; hashtags help X users to categorize Tweets on the same topic and locate Tweets they may be interested in viewing (Macready, 2022).

X is popular for professional networking and learning. Current and future teachers use X to grow their professional network and increase their knowledge of their professional field by sharing professional ideas with one another (Carpenter & Krutka, 2014; Staudt Willit, 2019). Similarly, nursing students used X during the COVID-19 pandemic to share their experiences with others and make connections with others in the medical field (DeGagne et al., 2021). Scientists and those engaged in scientific research use X to debate ideas, share theories, and disseminate knowledge to one another and the broader community (Walter et al., 2019). Due to its popularity with professionals in a variety of fields, X is an ideal platform for university students to use when seeking to build relationships with professionals in their fields. Junco and colleagues (2011) indicate that the use of X in university courses increases student engagement in learning. It also can support learners in connecting their course learning to authentic contexts in their daily personal and professional lives (Hsu & Ching, 2012).

Due to its international appeal and its interactive nature, it is a popular tool for educational communities of practice, in which learners share ideas with one another, as well as for connecting with professionals in your field around the world (Zheng & Beck Dallaghan, 2022). In addition, the use of X may lead to discussions with people outside the course who share differing or opposing views on course-related topics, thus leading to critical debate on topics and enhancing student learning (Rohr et al., 2022). These interactions with individuals outside of the course, but still interested in course content, can support online learners in building relationships with others in the field. Zheng and Beck Dallaghan (2022) found that about half of college students who follow a X hashtag do so to learn from others, but do not engage in conversation on these topics. With this in mind, we recommend that university faculty set clear guidelines and expectations for participation in X and model for students what this looks like.

A common interaction method on X is the use of X chats, which are real-time discussions on a topic in which any X user can participate in the discussion. They serve as an open forum and people from all over the world can participate in a discussion on a specific topic (Admon et al., 2020; Zimmerle, 2020). X chats are held at pre-arranged times and include a planned discussion topic facilitated by chat moderators (Admon et al., 2020). The chat moderators ask a series of numbered questions on the topic and anyone involved can respond to the questions and should use the dedicated chat hashtag to ensure the responses are part of the ongoing conversation (Alton, 2023). The use of X chats can aid online learners in gaining access to resources from professionals outside of their own community and tailor their learning to their own professional development goals and needs (Zimmerle, 2020).

When hosting a X chat, you need to have a specific topic. Many X chats occur on a regular basis and each chat session is focused on one specific aspect of the broader chat topic. Your X chat should include a dedicated hashtag that will be used to post each question and that participants will include in their responses to the questions. It can be helpful to post the list of questions prior to the chat to allow participants the opportunity to prepare their responses. During the chat itself, only one question will be asked at a time and chat participants will be given time to respond before the next question is asked. Participants should be directed to respond to each question, as well as respond to other chat participants.

For an example of information that may be developed to prepare participants for a X chat, see Figure 6. In order to support students in using X chats to build professional relationships, we suggest having your students participate in a popular chat in your field or co-hosting a X chat with colleagues at other universities who are teaching a course similar to yours.

Figure 6. Sample X chat

Online Learning Chat

This week's topic: Building Relationships in Online Learning

Tuesday, July 11 from 8:00-9:00 pm eastern time

Question 1: Introduce yourself by stating your name, place of employment, and your experience with online learning. In addition, share your favorite meme about online teaching and learning

Question 2: In your experience (and based on the research), why do you feel relationships are vital to learning?

Question 3: What strategies have you used to support students in building relationships with one another in the online classroom?

Linked In Profile and Following Others on LinkedIn

A second social media tool for connecting with professionals in the broader field of study is LinkedIn. LinkedIn is an online professional network that assists professionals in a variety of fields with job hunting or gaining professional networks that will support their career advancement (LinkedIn, 2023). In addition to the ability for members to post their resumes, LinkedIn also allows users to endorse one another for job-related knowledge and skills, which indicates that a user has a professional expertise in the endorsed area (Urdaneta-Ponte et al., 2022).

Currently, more than 875 million people from 200 countries use LinkedIn (Macready, 2023). Despite its popularity among professionals worldwide, the majority of university students do not use LinkedIn or use it infrequently (Carmack & Heiss, 2018). Because LinkedIn is a popular social media tool for building professional networks among already-working professionals, it is an ideal medium for supporting university students in building their own professional networks and we argue that university students should learn the skills to use it effectively to advance their own careers.

Davis et al. (2020) found that the frequency of engagement on LinkedIn, not the number of LinkedIn connections one has, had the largest impact on career advancement and other career benefits. Previous research has noted that students are more likely to use LinkedIn and use it more frequently after its use has been taught in a university course (Laird-Magee, 2013). With this in mind, university faculty can support students in using LinkedIn effectively by teaching them how to use it and offering opportunities within coursework to engage with others via LinkedIn.

Within the university classroom, there are a variety of ways that LinkedIn can be used.

Students can be given an assignment that requires them to create a LinkedIn profile that includes the key components of their professional resume (McCorkle & McCorkle, 2012; Slone & Gaffney, 2016). To build on this, students may also be asked to evaluate the LinkedIn profiles of others and identify the characteristics of a good profile and how various aspects of a profile may reflect on a job candidate (Slone & Gaffney, 2016). Finally, students may be required to join professional groups on LinkedIn and engage with others in those groups ((McCorkle & McCorkle, 2012). Figure 7 provides a sample assignment prompt that a university faculty member might use to support students in learning to use LinkedIn; please note that this prompt is not specific to any field of study and could be used for professionals of virtually any university major.

Figure 7. Sample LinkedIn assignment

Many of you will be entering the profession within the next few semesters. There is no better time to begin networking and see what job are available. One way to do this is through LinkedIn. Your assignment is as follows.

1. Download the LinkedIn App and create an account. If you do not have a smartphone then you can access Linkedin through a web browser. Complete the following sections of the profile
    a. Add picture
    b. About Me
    c. Current Position
    d. Education
    e. Work Experience
    f. Any other areas that are applicable to you.

2. Once you have completed your profile, take time to start networking. Click on the My Network icon and begin reviewing other profiles. Add people as you begin finding people who have similar career interests as you.

3. Now, go to the Jobs icon and begin reviewing the job postings. Identify at least one job that you may want to apply for and save it so you can turn it in.

4. Create with a cover letter in Microsoft Word

5. Turn in the following:
    a. A link to your LinkedIn account
    b. A copy of the job posting you found
    c. A cover letter that you would use to apply for the job you found

FURTHER RESEARCH

Due to the relatively recent use of social media within learning contexts, there are significant opportunities for continued research on the topic. We recommend two specific areas for focused research on social media in online learning. First, there is minimal data on the impacts of social media on student learning. We recommend studies that examine how the use of social media affects students' understanding of the course content as compared to comparable peers who were taught the same content using other methods. The other area that requires additional research is on the topic of accessibility. Not all social media tools are accessible for college students with disabilities. We recommend future research that examines the barriers that prevent students with disabilities from fully utilizing social media tools for learning, as well as accommodations that may remove those barriers.

CONCLUSION

Social media is a vital tool for supporting both student learning and relationship building in the online classrooms. Through social media-based course assignments and discussions, as well as optional activities that utilize social media, faculty can support online learners in increasing their sense of connection to others. While this chapter covers many different types of social media that can be used to help build relationships in online courses, we know that there are many more that can be used. We challenge readers to explore the ideas we have shared and create their own activities for using social media to support online learners in building relationships with one another, with faculty, and with the broader community in their field.

REFERENCES

Abbas, J., Aman, J., Nurunnabi, M., & Bano, S. (2019). The impact of social media on learning behavior for sustainable education: Evidence of students from selected universities in Pakistan. *Sustainability (Basel)*, *11*(6), 1683. Advance online publication. doi:10.3390u11061683

Abedini, A., Abedin, B., & Zowgi, D. (2021). Adult learning in online communities of practice: A systematic review. *British Journal of Educational Technology*, *52*(4), 1663–1694. doi:10.1111/bjet.13120

Abrahim, M., & Suhara, M. (2019). Structural equation modeling and confirmatory factor analysis of social media use and education. *International Journal of Educational Technology in Higher Education*, *16*(1), 32. doi:10.118641239-019-0157-y

Admon, A. J., Kaul, V., Cribbs, S. K., Guzman, E., Jiminez, O., & Richards, J. B. (2020). Twelve tips for developing and implementing a medical education X chat. *Medical Teacher*, *42*(5), 500–506. doi:10.1080/0142159X.2019.1598553 PMID:30999789

Aichner, T., Grunfelder, M., Maurer, O., & Jegeni, D. (2021). Twenty-five years of social media: A review of social media applications and definitions from 1994 to 2019. *Cyberpsychology, Behavior, and Social Networking*, *24*(4), 215–222. doi:10.1089/cyber.2020.0134 PMID:33847527

Akcaoglu, M., & Lee, E. (2018). Using facebook groups to support social presence in online learning. *Distance Education*, *39*(3), 334–352. doi:10.1080/01587919.2018.1476842

Alalwan, N. (2022). Actual use of social media for engagement to enhance students' learning. *Education and Information Technologies*, *27*(7), 9767–9789. doi:10.100710639-022-11014-7 PMID:35399784

Aldosari, A. M., Alramthi, S. M., & Eid, H. F. (2022). Improving social presence in online higher education: Using live virtual classroom to confront learning challenges during COVID-19 pandemic. *Frontiers in Psychology*, *13*, 994403. Advance online publication. doi:10.3389/fpsyg.2022.994403 PMID:36467142

Alton, L. (2023). *How X chats can improve your audience engagement strategy*. https://business.X.com/en/blog/how-to-promote-your-X-chat.html

Alvarez VazquezE.Cortes-MendezM.StrikerR.SingelmannL.PearsonM.SwartzE.

Arnold & Paulus. (2010). Using a social networking site for experiential learning: Appropriating, lurking, modeling and community building. *The Internet and Higher Education, 13*(4), 188-196.

Basch, C. H., Hillyer, G. C., & Jaime, C. (2020). COVID-19 on TikTok: Harnessing an emerging social media platform to convey important public health messages. *International Journal of Adolescent Medicine and Health*, *34*(5), 367–369. doi:10.1515/ijamh-2020-0111 PMID:32776899

Benson, O. M., & Whitson, M. L. (2022). The protective role of sense of community and access to resources on college student stress and COVID-19-related daily life disruptions. *Journal of Community Psychology*, *50*(6), 2746–2764. doi:10.1002/jcop.22817 PMID:35142379

Bentrim, E. M., Grygier, J., Ralicki, J., Schiller, J., & Widenhorn, M. (2022). *Nationwide student survey: Opportunities to grow student success and career preparation.* https://thestacks.anthology.com/wp-content/uploads/2022/05/White-Paper_Student-Success-and-Career-Preparation.pdf?_ga=2.15546033.643518578.1652197075-1075087224.1652197075

Berry, S. (2019). Faculty perspectives on online learning: The instructor's role in creating community. *Online Learning : the Official Journal of the Online Learning Consortium*, *23*(4), 181–191. doi:10.24059/olj.v23i4.2038

Best Colleges. (2022). *Online Education Trends Report*. https://www.bestcolleges.com/research/annual-trends-in-online-education/

Blickle, G., Witzki, A. H., & Schneider, P. B. (2009). Mentoring support and power: A three year predictive field study on protege networking and career success. *Journal of Vocational Behavior*, *74*(2), 181–189. doi:10.1016/j.jvb.2008.12.008

Boerngen, M. A., & Rickard, J. W. (2021). To zoom or not to zoom: The impact of rural broadband on online learning. *Natural Sciences Education*, *50*(1), e20044. Advance online publication. doi:10.1002/nse2.20044

Cacioppo, J. T., & Patrick, W. (2009). *Loneliness: Human nature and the need for social connection.* W. W. Norton & Company.

Campbell, S. (2023). *How many people use Facebook in 2023?* https://thesmallbusinessblog.net/facebook-statistics/

Canty, A. J., Chase, J., Hingston, M., Greenwood, M., Mainsbridge, C. P., & Skalicky, J. (2020). Addressing student attrition within higher education online programs through a collaborative community of practice. *Journal of Applied Learning and Teaching, 3*(Special Issue), 1–12. doi:10.37074/jalt.2020.3.s1.3

Carmack, H. J., & Heiss, S. N. (2018). Using the theory of planned behavior to predict college students' intent to use LinkedIn for job searches and professional networking. *Communication Studies, 69*(2), 145–160. doi:10.1080/10510974.2018.1424003

Carpenter, J. P., & Krutka, D. G. (2014). How and why educators use X: A survey of the field. *Journal of Research on Technology in Education, 46*(4), 414–434. doi:10.1080/15391523.2014.925701

Celuch, K., Milewicz, C., & Saxby, C. (2021). Student and faculty interaction in motivated learning for face-to-face and online marketing classes. *Journal of Education for Business, 96*(6), 366–372. doi:10.1080/08832323.2020.1848767

Chayka, K. (2021). *Facebook wants us to live in the metaverse.* https://www.newyorker.com/culture/infinite-scroll/facebook-wants-us-to-live-in-the-metaverse

Davis, J., Wolff, H. G., Forret, M. L., & Sullivan, S. E. (2020). Networking via LinkedIn: An examination of usage and career benefits. *Journal of Vocational Behavior, 118*, 103396. doi:10.1016/j.jvb.2020.103396

De Gagne, A. C., Cho, E., Park, H. K., Nam, J. D., & Jung, D. (2021). A qualitative analysis of nursing students' tweets during the COVID-19 pandemic. *Nursing & Health Sciences, 23*(1), 273–278. doi:10.1111/nhs.12809 PMID:33404157

Dutta, A. (2020). Impact of digital social media on Indian higher education: Alternative approaches of online learning during COVID-19 pandemic crisis. *International Journal of Scientific and Research Publications, 10*(5), 604–611. doi:10.29322/IJSRP.10.05.2020.p10169

Escamilla-Fajardo, P., Alguacil, M., & Lopez-Carril, S. (2021). Incorporating TikTok in higher education: Pedagogical perspectives from a corporal expression sport sciences course. *Journal of Hospitality, Leisure, Sport and Tourism Education, 28*, 100302. Advance online publication. doi:10.1016/j.jhlste.2021.100302

Facebook. (2023). *Differences between profiles, groups, and pages on Facebook.* https://www.facebook.com/help/337881706729661

FauvilleG.LuoM.Muller QueirozA. C.BailensonJ. N.HancockJ. (2021). Nonverbal mechanisms predict zoom fatigue and explain why women experience higher levels than men. SSRN, 1–18. https://doi.org/doi:10.2139/ssrn.3820035

Gares, S. L., Kariuki, J. K., & Rempel, R. P. (2020). Community matters: Student-instructor relationships foster student motivation and engagement in an emergency remote teaching environment. *Journal of Chemical Education, 97*(9), 3332–3335. doi:10.1021/acs.jchemed.0c00635

Gibson, C., Hardy, J. H., & Buckley, M. R. (2014). Understanding the role of networking in organizations. *Career Development International, 19*(2), 146–161. doi:10.1108/CDI-09-2013-0111

Google. (2023). *Google Meet.* https://apps.google.com/meet/

Greenhow, C., & Galvin, S. (2020). Teaching with social media: Evidence-based strategies for making remote higher education less remote. *Information and Learning Science, 121*(7-8), 513–524. doi:10.1108/ILS-04-2020-0138

Guzzardo, M. T., Khosla, N., Adams, A. L., Bussman, J. D., Engelman, A., Ingraham, N., Gamba, R., Jones-Bey, A., Moore, M. D., Toosi, N. R., & Taylor, S. (2021). "The ones that care make all the difference:" Perspectives on student-faculty relationships. *Innovative Higher Education, 46*(1), 41–58. doi:10.100710755-020-09522-w PMID:33012971

Ha, J., & Shin, D. H. (2013). Facebook in a standard college class: An alternative conduit for promoting teacher-student interaction. *American Communication Journal, 16*(1), 36–52.

Hagenauer, G., Muehlbacher, F., & Ivanova, M. (2023). "It's where learning and teaching begins- is this relationship" - insights on the teacher-student relationship at university from the teachers' perspective. *Higher Education, 85*(4), 819–835. doi:10.100710734-022-00867-z PMID:37128236

Hayes, C., Stott, K., Lamb, K. J., & Hurst, G. A. (2020). "Making every second count:" Utilizing TikTok and systems thinking to facilitate scientific public engagement and contextualization of chemistry at home. *Journal of Chemical Education, 97*(10), 3858–3866. doi:10.1021/acs.jchemed.0c00511

Hennein, R., Ggita, J. M., Turimumahoro, P., Ochom, E., Gupta, A. J., Katamba, A., Armstrong-Hough, M., & Davis, J. L. (2022). Core components of a community of practice to improve community health worker performance: A qualitative study. *Implementation Science Communications, 3*(1), 27. Advance online publication. doi:10.118643058-022-00279-1 PMID:35272705

Herrman, J. (2019). *How TikTok is rewriting the world.* https://www.nytimes.com/2019/03/10/style/what-is-tik-tok.html

Holmes, A. F., & Rasmussen, S. J. (2018). Using Pinterest to stimulate student engagement, interest, and learning in managerial accounting courses. *Journal of Accounting Education, 43*, 43–56. doi:10.1016/j.jaccedu.2018.03.001

Holt, K. (2012). *Teachers Pin With Their Students.* https://mashable.com/2012/03/22/teachers-using-pinterest/

Hsu, Y. C., & Ching, Y. H. (2012). Mobile micoblogging: Using X and mobile devices in an online course to promote learning in authentic contexts. *International Review of Research in Open and Distance Learning, 13*(4), 211–227. doi:10.19173/irrodl.v13i4.1222

Jackson, D. (2016). Re-conceptualising graduate employability: The importance of pre-professional identity. *Higher Education Research & Development, 35*(5), 925–939. doi:10.1080/07294360.2016.1139551

Jacobs, J., & Archie, T. (2008). Investigating sense of community in first-year college students. *Journal of Experiential Education, 30*(3), 282–285. doi:10.1177/105382590703000312

Jiang, M., & Koo, K. (2020). Emotional presence in building an online learning community among non-traditional graduate students. *Online Learning : the Official Journal of the Online Learning Consortium, 24*(4), 93–111. doi:10.24059/olj.v24i4.2307

Junco, R., Heibergert, G., & Loken, E. (2011). The effect of X on college student engagement and grades. *Journal of Computer Assisted Learning, 27*(2), 119–132. doi:10.1111/j.1365-2729.2010.00387.x

Kim, B., & Kim, Y. (2017). College students' social media use and communication network heterogeneity: Implications for social capital and subjective well-being. *Computers in Human Behavior, 73*, 620–628. doi:10.1016/j.chb.2017.03.033

Kim, M., Jun, M., & Han, J. (2023). The relationship between needs, motivation, and information sharing behaviors on social media: Focus on the self-connection and social connection. *Asia Pacific Journal of Marketing and Logistics, 35*(1), 1–16. doi:10.1108/APJML-01-2021-0066

Kim, Y. K., & Lundberg, C. A. (2015). A structural model of the relationship between student-faculty interaction and cognitive skills development among college students. *Research in Higher Education, 57*(3), 288–309. doi:10.100711162-015-9387-6

Kimmel, S. C., Burns, E., & DiScala, J. (2019). Community at a distance: Employing a community of practice framework in online learning for rural students. *Journal of Education for Library and Information Science, 60*(4), 265–284. doi:10.3138/jelis.2018-0056

Kordrostami, M., & Seitz, V. (2022). Faculty online competence and student affective engagement in online learning. *Marketing Education Review, 32*(3), 240–254. doi:10.1080/10528008.2021.1965891

Laird-Magee, T. (2013). Teams build a wiki to teach each other four social media platforms. *Journal of Advertising Education, 17*(1), 46–54. doi:10.1177/109804821301700107

Lampe, N. M. (2023, October). (online first 2023). Teaching with TikTok in online sociology of sex and gender courses. *Teaching Sociology, 51*(4), 323–335. Advance online publication. doi:10.1177/0092055X231159091

Lien, B. (2020). *Why understanding channel types makes using Slack more awesome.* https://uit.stanford.edu/blog/why-understanding-channel-types-makes-using-slack-more-awesome

LinkedIn. (2023). *What is LinkedIn and how can I use it?* https://www.linkedin.com/help/linkedin/answer/a548441/what-is-linkedin-and-how-can-i-use-it-?lang=en

Liu, Y. (2010). Social media tools as a learning resource. *Journal of Educational Technology Development and Exchange, 3*(1), 8. Advance online publication. doi:10.18785/jetde.0301.08

Lovett, J. T., Munawar, K., Mohammed, S., & Prabhu, V. (2021). Radiology content on TikTok: Current use of a novel video-based social media platform and opportunities for radiology. *Current Problems in Diagnostic Radiology, 50*(2), 125–131. doi:10.1067/j.cpradiol.2020.10.004 PMID:33250298

Lu, W. (2023). Socrates on Slack: Text-based persistent-chat platforms as an alternative to "Zoom classes" in synchronous online learning. *Communication Teacher, 37*(2), 141–150. doi:10.1080/17404622.2022.2117395

M. (2020). *Lessons learned using Slack in engineering education: An innovation-based learning approach.* Paper presented at 2020 ASEE Virtual Annual Conference. https://peer.asee.org/34916

Macready, H. (2022). *How to use hashtags in 2023: A guide for every network.* https://blog.hootsuite.com/how-to-use-hashtags/

Macready, H. (2023). *47 LinkedIn Statistics you need to know in 2023.* https://blog.hootsuite.com/linkedin-statistics-business/

Martin, F., Ritzhaupt, A., Kumar, S., & Budhrani, K. (2019). Award-winning faculty online teaching practices: Course design, assessment and evaluation, and facilitation. *The Internet and Higher Education, 42,* 34–43. doi:10.1016/j.iheduc.2019.04.001

McCorkle, D. E., & McCorkle, Y. L. (2012). Using LinkedIn in the marketing classroom: Exploratory insights and recommendations for teaching social media/networking. *Marketing Education Review, 22*(2), 157–166. doi:10.2753/MER1052-8008220205

Meletiou-Mavrotheris, M., Eteokleoius, N., & Stylianou-Georgiou, A. (2022). Emergency remote learning in higher education in Cyprus during COVID-19 lockdown: A zoom-out view of challenges and opportunities for quality online learning. *Education Sciences, 12*(477), 477. Advance online publication. doi:10.3390/educsci12070477

Merriam-Webster Dictionary. (2023). *Social media.* https://www.merriam-webster.com/dictionary/social%20media

Montag, C., Yang, H., & Elhai, J. D. (2021). On the psychology of TikTok use: A first glimpse from empirical findings. *Frontiers in Public Health, 9,* 641673. Advance online publication. doi:10.3389/fpubh.2021.641673 PMID:33816425

Mulenga, E. M., & Marban, J. M. (2020). Is COVID-19 the gateway for digital learning in mathematics education? *Contemporary Educational Technology, 12*(2), 269. Advance online publication. doi:10.30935/cedtech/7949

Müller, S. (2023). How Slack Facilitates Communication and Collaboration in Seminars and Project-Based Courses. *Journal of Educational Technology Systems, 51*(3), 303–316. doi:10.1177/00472395231151910

Muller, S. (2023). How "Slack" facilitates communication and collaboration in seminars and project-based courses. *Journal of Educational Technology Systems, 51*(3), 303–316. doi:10.1177/00472395231151910

National Center for Education Statistics. (2022). *Undergraduate Enrollment. Condition of Education.* https://nces.ed.gov/programs/coe/indicator/cha

Otchie, W. O., & Pedaste, M. (2020). Using social media for learning in high schools: A systematic literature review. *European Journal of Educational Research, 9*(2), 889–903. doi:10.12973/eu-jer.9.2.889

Pearce, N., & Learmonth, S. (2013). Learning beyond the classroom: Evaluating the use of Pinterest in learning and teaching in an introductory anthropology class. *Journal of Interactive Media in Education, 2*(2), 12. Advance online publication. doi:10.5334/2013-12

Pew Research Center. (2021). *Social Media Fact Sheet.* https://www.pewresearch.org/internet/fact-sheet/social-media/

Pike, G. R., Kuh, G. D., & McCormick, A. C. (2011). An investigation of the contingent relationships between learning community participation and student engagement. *Research in Higher Education*, *52*(3), 300–322. doi:10.100711162-010-9192-1

Pinterest. (2023a). *All about Pinterest.* https://help.pinterest.com/en/guide/all-about-pinterest

Pinterest. (2023b). *Why Pinterest.* https://business.pinterest.com/

PopoloM. (2013). *How to use Pinterest for beginners.* https://www.pcmag.com/news/how-to-use-pinterest-for-beginners

Porter, C. M., Woo, S. E., & Campion, M. A. (2016). Internal and external networking differentially predict turnover through job embeddedness and job offers. *Personnel Psychology*, *69*(3), 635–672. doi:10.1111/peps.12121

Raposa, E. B., Hagler, M., Liu, D., & Rhodes, J. E. (2021). Predictors of close faculty-student relationships and mentorship in higher education: Findings from the Gallup-Purdue Index. *Annals of the New York Academy of Sciences*, *1483*(1), 36–49. doi:10.1111/nyas.14342 PMID:32242962

Rigamonti, L., Dolci, A., Galetta, F., Stefanelli, C., Hughes, M., Bartsch, M., Seidelmeier, I., Bonaventura, K., & Back, D. A. (2020). Social media and e-learning use among European exercise science students. *Health Promotion International*, *35*(3), 470–477. doi:10.1093/heapro/daz046 PMID:31071200

Roblyer, M. D., McDaniel, M., Webb, M., Herman, J., & Witty, J. V. (2010). Findings on Facebook in higher education: A comparison of college faculty and student uses and perceptions of social networking sites. *The Internet and Higher Education*, *13*(3), 134–140. doi:10.1016/j.iheduc.2010.03.002

Rohr, L., Squires, L., & Peters, A. (2022). Examining the use of X in online classes: Can X improve interaction and engagement? *The Canadian Journal for the Scholarship of Teaching and Learning*, *13*(1), 9. Advance online publication. doi:10.5206/cjsotlrcacea.2022.1.10892

Ross, S. M. (2019). Slack it to me: Complementing LMS with student-centric communications for the millenial/post-millenial student. *Journal of Marketing Education*, *41*(2), 91–108. doi:10.1177/0273475319833113

Sabin, J., & Olive, A. (2018). Slack: Adopting social-networking platforms for active learning. *PS, Political Science & Politics*, *51*(1), 183–189. doi:10.1017/S1049096517001913

Salim, J., Tandy, S., Arnindita, J. N., Wibisono, J. J., Haryanto, M. R., & Wibisono, M. G. (2022). Zoom fatigue and its risk factors in online during the COVID-19 pandemic. *Medical Journal of Indonesia*, *31*(1), 13–19. doi:10.13181/mji.oa.225703

Seery, K., Barreda, A. A., Hein, S. G., & Hiller, J. K. (2021). Retention strategies for online students: A systematic literature review. *Journal of Global Education and Research*, *5*(1), 72–84. doi:10.5038/2577-509X.5.1.1105

Shepherd, J. (2023). *21 Essential TikTok statistics you need to know in 2023.* https://thesocialshepherd.com/blog/tiktok-statistics#:~:text=Most%20of%20the%20Platform's%20Users,600%20million%20daily%20active%20users.

Shockley, K. M., Gabriel, A. S., Robertson, D., Rosen, C. C., Chawla, N., Ganster, M. L., & Ezerins, M. E. (2021). The fatiguing effects of camera use in virtual meetings: A within-person field experiment. *The Journal of Applied Psychology*, *106*(8), 1137–1155. doi:10.1037/apl0000948 PMID:34423999

Slack Technologies. (2023). *What is Slack?* https://slack.com/help/articles/115004071768-What-is-Slack-

Slone, A. R., & Gaffney, A. L. H. (2016). Assessing students' use of LinkedIn in a business and professional communication course. *Communication Teacher*, *30*(4), 206–214. doi:10.1080/17404622.2016.1219043

Sponcil, M., & Gitimu, P. (2013). Use of social media by college students: Relationship to communication and self-concept. *Journal of Technology Research*, *4*, 1–13.

Staudt Willet, K. B. (2019). Revisiting how and why educators use X: Tweet types and purposes in #Edchat. *Journal of Research on Technology in Education*, *51*(3), 273–289. doi:10.1080/15391523.2019.1611507

Tik Tok. (2023). *About Tik Tok*. https://www.tiktok.com/about?lang=en

Tomlinson, M., & Jackson, D. (2021). Professional identity formation in contemporary higher education students. *Studies in Higher Education*, *46*(4), 885–900. doi:10.1080/03075079.2019.1659763

Trust, T., & Goodman, L. (2023, May 03). (online first 2023). Cameras optional?: Examining student camera use from a learner-centered perspective. *TechTrends*. Advance online publication. doi:10.100711528-023-00855-9 PMID:37362589

X. (2023). *New user FAQ*. https://help.X.com/en/resources/new-user-faq

Tygret, J., Green, P., & Mendez, S. (2022). Promoting faculty-student relationships. *Journal of College Orientation, Transition, and Retention*, *29*(1), 6. https://pubs.lib.umn.edu/index.php/jcotr/article/view/4873

Urdaneta-Ponte, M. C., Oleagoria-Ruiz, I., & Mendez-Zorrilla, A. (2022). Using LinkedIn endorsements to reinforce an ontology and machine learning-based recommender system to improve professional skills. *Electronics (Basel)*, *11*(8), 1190. doi:10.3390/electronics11081190

Walter, S., Lorcher, I., & Bruggemann, M. (2019). Scientific networks on X: Analyzing scientists' interactions in the climate change debate. *Public Understanding of Science (Bristol, England)*, *28*(6), 696–712. doi:10.1177/0963662519844131 PMID:31027461

Wang, V., & Edwards, S. (2016). Strangers are friends I haven't met yet: A positive approach to young people's use of social media. *Journal of Youth Studies*, *19*(9), 1204–1219. doi:10.1080/13676261.2016.1154933

Wang, W., Guo, L., He, L., & Wu, Y. J. (2019). Effects of social-interactive engagement on the dropout ratio in online learning: Insights from MOOC. *Behaviour & Information Technology*, *38*(6), 621–636. doi:10.1080/0144929X.2018.1549595

Wang, Y. (2020). Humor and camera view on mobile short-form video apps influence user experience and technology-adoption intent, an example of TikTok. *Computers in Human Behavior*, *110*, 106373. Advance online publication. doi:10.1016/j.chb.2020.106373

Whittaker, A. L., Haworth, G. S., & Lymn, K. A. (2014). Evaluation of Facebook to create an online learning community in an undergraduate animal science course. *Educational Media International*, *51*(2), 135–145. doi:10.1080/09523987.2014.924664

Yi, P. (2022). Teachers' communities of practice in response to the COVID-19 pandemic: Will innovation in teaching practices persist and prosper? *Journal of Curriculum and Teaching*, *11*(5), 241–251. doi:10.5430/jct.v11n5p241

Zheng, B., & Beck Dallaghan, G. (2022). A X-facilitated professional learning community: Online participation, connectedness, and satisfaction. *BMC Medical Education*, *22*(1), 577. Advance online publication. doi:10.118612909-022-03639-6 PMID:35897094

Zimmerle, J. (2020). Nice to Tweet you: Supporting rural preservice teachers through X chats. *SRATE Journal*, *29*(2), Article 10. https://www.srate.org/z_journal_archive_29_2.html

Zoom. (2022). *What is Zoom video conferencing?* https://support.zoom.us/hc/en-us/articles/4420426401037-What-is-Zoom-Video-Conferencing-

ADDITIONAL READING

Allen, K. A., Jimerson, S. R., Qiuntana, D. S., & McKinley, L. (2022). *An academic's guide to social media*. Routledge. doi:10.4324/9781003198369

Carrigan, M. (2019). *Social media for academics* (2nd ed.). Sage Publications.

Chugh, R. (2023). *The role and use of social media in higher education*. https://www.thehighereducationreview.com/opinion/in-my-view/the-role-and-use-of-social-media-in-higher-education-fid-38.html

Davis, M. (2015). *Social media for teachers: Guides, resources, and ideas*. https://www.edutopia.org/blog/social-media-resources-educators-matt-davis

Greenhow, C., Sonnevend, J., & Agur, C. (2016). *Education and social media: Toward a digital future*. The MIT Press. doi:10.7551/mitpress/9780262034470.001.0001

Joosten, T. (2012). *Social media for educators: Strategies and best practices*. Wiley.

Rowell, C. (2020). *Social media in higher education: Case studies, reflections, and analysis*. Saint Philip Street Press.

West, C. (2021). *12 ways to use social media for education*. https://sproutsocial.com/insights/social-media-for-education/

KEY TERMS AND DEFINITIONS

Asynchronous Learning: Learning that occurs when convenient for students with no required live meetings.

Learning Communities: Learning communities is a type of collaboration where groups of students or other like-minded professionals share a common goal or vision.

Learning Management System (LMS): Platform that houses course content. Students can submit assignments, complete discussion boards, etc. Examples of LMS's are Canvas, D2L, and Blackboard.

Professional Networks: A group of individuals working in the same field who share ideas.

Relationships: A connection between one or more people. In online learning, this connection can be between students or between students and instructors, or even students and the larger professional community.

Social Media: Interactive ways to share ideas, information, and/or interests using an online or technology platform.

Synchronous Learning: Learning that occurs in real-time and may include live meetings in which students and teachers meet at the same time to review course content.

Chapter 12
Hello, Is Anyone There?
Strategies for Building Relationships in the Online Classroom

Heather Pederson
The University of Arizona Global Campus, USA

Stephanie Stubbs
The University of Arizona Global Campus, USA

ABSTRACT

It is well known that the online classroom structure can cause students to feel isolated and unsupported. Asynchronous discussion boards and digitally submitted assignments as well as not seeing the instructor or classmates face to face make for an impersonal learning experience. Knowing how to effectively connect with all students and working to build caring, authentic relationships can improve the online education experience for both the faculty member and the student. This chapter includes a review of evidence-based existing literature on building faculty-student relationships and making caring connections in the online environment. In this chapter, two online doctoral faculty members who have a combined 34 years of experience teaching in online classrooms provide practical strategies for building faculty-student relationships with the hope that current and future online educators can implement these strategies to better support student well-being and success while simultaneously promoting faculty satisfaction.

INTRODUCTION

In 1985, the first online degree program was made available by the National Technological University, according to *Forbes.com*, and since then, the growth of online training and education has nearly mirrored the success of the Internet (Learn.org, n.d.). Online learning has grown exponentially with each year's enrollments exceeding the previous year. According to the National Center for Education Statistics (2023), among postbaccalaureate students in Fall 2020, 2.2 million (or 71 percent) enrolled in at least one distance education course. 1.6 million students (or 52 percent) of total postbaccalaureate enrollment, took online courses exclusively. With the enormous number of enrollments in online undergraduate and

DOI: 10.4018/978-1-6684-8908-6.ch012

graduate degree programs, it is critical that faculty go beyond sharing content knowledge and know how to build relationships with students to create caring connections in the online classroom. Online instructors oftentimes struggle to engage with and build meaningful relationships with students in the virtual environment, and without this critical component in place, online students report a lack of interest, in turn, they produce a lower quality of work and report less overall satisfaction. There are a host of tools and strategies that may be used by the online instructor to build meaningful relationships with students and increase these satisfaction levels (Jeffrey, 2019). It is well known that the online classroom structure can cause students to feel isolated and unsupported. Asynchronous discussion boards and digitally submitted assignments, as well as not seeing the instructor or classmates face to face make for an impersonal learning experience. Knowing how to effectively connect with all students and working to build caring, authentic relationships can improve the online education experience for both the faculty member and the student.

The Community of Inquiry (CoI) framework is threaded through the content of this chapter. In particular, Garrison's CoI framework is known for three elements – social presence, teaching presence, and cognitive presence – that are deemed critical for fostering a community of actively engaged participants (Garrison et al., 2010). The three elements combined contribute to student engagement, performance, and building community. Social presence (participants' ability to establish themselves as real/authentic selves in their academic community), cognitive presence (participants' ability to construct meaning and confirm understanding), and teaching presence (instructor's ability to design, facilitate, and provide direct instruction) as a trifecta cultivate a community that provides optimal support for student learning. Purposeful community building using the CoI is a critical component of fostering successful student engagement and performance in class.

Existing research about online teaching and learning includes mostly factors related to student success, persistence to degree completion, and student satisfaction (Alison et al., 2020). It is widely understood by stakeholders that online learners need support beyond academic instruction. In addition, instructors who teach online doctoral courses play a vital role in students' experiences as these students are engaged in the highest level of academic study and require specific types of connection, communication, and support. When students feel connected in the classroom, stronger classroom interactions and discussions often occur and that feeling of connectedness helps retain learners and create classroom community investment. The connections that can occur in a community of practice are incredibly important when considering the implementation of online courses (Blevins et al., 2021). Cultivating trusting relationships by providing students with numerous opportunities for authentic, spontaneous, supportive discussion with people they know well emerged as central to fostering a sense of community among online learners (Cornell et al., 2019). This highlights the importance of building faculty-student relationships.

In a survey of 344 faculty at land-grant and research-intensive institutions, Bolliger et al. (2019) discovered that faculty found students' sense of community to be key to engagement and satisfaction in online programs. Eighty-eight percent strongly agreed that community was important. Sixty-six percent said community extends beyond classes. However, only 37% said that there was a system in place at their institution to help online students build community. Given that faculty are the primary point of contact for online students, learning more about their perceptions of the online community is critical for supporting online students' success.

There are numerous strategies that faculty members can use to connect with students, including one-on-one video meetings, group video meetings, recorded announcements and messages in the classroom, phone calls, text messages, and other technological tools. While the use of technology is a critical component, the way in which a faculty member engages and communicates with students is equally, if not more so, critical. Demonstrating empathy, caring, understanding, and flexibility are just some of the ways a faculty member can build strong relationships with online doctoral students. According to Jeffrey (2019), students want to know that a real, caring person is collaborating with them to complete the course, and this support and personal guidance can be the difference between success and failure for some students.

What does a successful partnership between online students and the instructor really look like? What qualities define this relationship, and how can faculty implement these strategies into their courses as well as one-on-one conversations and digital communications with students? How are genuine connections made in the virtual environment? This chapter includes a review of evidence-based existing literature on building faculty-student relationships and making caring connections in the online environment. In this chapter, two online doctoral faculty members who have a combined 34 years of experience teaching in online classrooms provide practical strategies for building faculty-student and student-to-student relationships with the hope that current and future online educators can implement these strategies to better support student well-being and success while simultaneously promoting faculty satisfaction.

COMMUNITY OF INQUIRY

Much of the literature surrounding the idea of the classroom as a community has emerged from the Community of Inquiry framework developed by Garrison and colleagues (2010). The goal of their research was to delineate the elements of a collaborative, worthwhile pursuit. The framework that emerged, which was developed precisely for the context of online learning, identifies three key elements that contribute to a student's educational experience: social presence, cognitive presence, and teaching presence (Garrison & Arbaugh, 2007). These three facets are fundamentally interconnected and rely upon each other for fulfillment.

Social presence refers to the ability to project and perceive personhood (Garrison & Arbaugh, 2007). The online setting, as previously mentioned, creates many challenges, not least of which includes the presentation of an authentic self. Social presence includes interaction, discourse, and a sense of camaraderie, all of which evolve, as the development of trust necessary for an individual to engage with others in the online setting takes time. Indicators of social presence in the online classroom may include encouragement to collaborate and the expression of emotion via the use of emoticons. Instructors can facilitate social presence by modeling genuine care and open communication, creating an environment in which students feel safe and empowered to allow their true selves opportunities to shine.

Cognitive presence refers to the ability to construct meaning through sustained reflection (Garrison & Arbaugh, 2007). More specifically, a triggering event may prompt a student to explore; the student may then integrate the new insight and apply their learning. Indicators of cognitive presence in the online classroom may include connection and application of new knowledge, as well as exchange of knowledge. Instructors can facilitate cognitive presence by providing material or examples that pique curiosity, inspiring students to go beyond superficial consideration of the material. They can ask questions that prompt students to engage in critical thinking or apply their new knowledge.

Teaching presence refers to the traditional elements of instruction that best support meaningful learning, including the design and organization of information, facilitation of discourse, and direct instruction (Garrison & Arbaugh, 2007). Indicators of teaching presence in the online classroom may include clear instructional materials and focused discussion. Instructors can facilitate teaching presence by providing additional tips for the completion of assignments or examples to clarify misconceptions.

Though each of these elements is distinct, they function together to support the development of a community of learners, one in which students and instructors work together to draw meaning out of the experience. The overlap of social presence and cognitive presence supports healthy discourse in the classroom; the overlap of social presence and teaching presence set the climate; and, the overlap of cognitive presence and teaching presence provides guidance for selecting content (Flock, 2020).

Building a community can prove challenging in the online setting. The instructor plays a key role in the development of a sense of connection and belonging (Berry, 2017). The instructor can promote community by fostering elements of the CoI through communication practices as well as curriculum choices. Communication practices that encourage all students to participate in open and honest dialogue build a foundation for continued interaction. Though instructors may not always have the liberty of choosing the curriculum, one common method of interaction in the online classroom is the discussion board, which necessitates peer contributions. Instructors can prompt students to make the most of this opportunity, including cross-peer references or questions that pertain to multiple students in the class. Assignments that require collaboration offer additional opportunities for students to engage and build relationships that may further support a sense of community.

Strategy 1- Support Social Presence: Promote authenticity: As mentioned earlier, genuine concern for individual students can foster trust and build caring connections. But, social presence is a two-way street. Instructors can model appropriate self-disclosure, sharing information about themselves that will help students see them as a real person, thus making them more likely to reciprocate. Students want to know their instructor as an individual, and they want to be known individually too. Though students are interested in the professional biographies of their instructors, they also find their personal stories more relatable. Share a picture, mention a hobby, or identify likes and dislikes. Sharing personal characteristics helps establish relationships by encouraging interaction and a feeling of emotional connection, prompting students to share more about themselves. Students might be especially relieved to hear that their instructors also experienced doubt, embarrassment, or even failure, especially if the example is framed humorously. Students will be more willing to take chances when they feel as though they can relate to their instructors as imperfect humans, with emotions and desires, and interests that extend beyond the classroom. In terms of course design, integrating multiple and varied opportunities for collaboration and expression will be most beneficial in establishing a sense of community from a social perspective (Flock, 2020).

Strategy 2- Support Cognitive Presence: Pique curiosity: In reality, most students in most courses are not intrinsically interested in every individual topic, or even in the discipline as a whole. It is the responsibility of the instructor to help every student see the relevance of the subject matter on a personal or professional level. Identifying outside materials that relate the topic to current issues or sharing examples that make clear the relevance of the topic for a given personal or professional setting might prompt a student to reconsider the value of an assignment. Because students prefer different types of learning, a best practice might include the use of multimedia (e.g., videos, websites, blogs, audio, images, etc.) or multiple forms of communication (e.g., written, spoken, illustrated, etc.). Thought-provoking questions are particularly useful in prompting dialogue and a quest for further information. In terms of course design, assignments that allow students to self-select topics and discussions that encourage different perspectives support student engagement and foster further exploration, thus enhancing a sense of community from a cognitive perspective (Flock, 2020).

Strategy 3- Support Teaching Presence: Provide clarity: If students are confused or frustrated, they are unlikely to engage with materials or others in the course (instructor or peers). The use of varied avenues in the course to convey helpful information may be welcomed by the new student. Instructors should be mindful, however, of overwhelming students. Goals and instructions should be explicit, and redundant, with concrete guidelines for grading. Announcements can be used to provide an overview or identify points that students are likely to miss in the instructions or rubrics, such as detailed course expectations or policies; discussions can be used to scaffold information from previous and into future weeks; and feedback in the grade book provides a space to identify opportunities for individual growth along with explanation and helpful resources. Timely feedback with specific steps for improvement is also important. In terms of course design, creating a narrative that guides students through the course using multiple avenues of instruction, supporting a sense of community from a teaching perspective (Flock, 2020).

Recognizing that a classroom does not automatically equate to a community is essential. Instructors must be proactive in seeking to make their presence (teaching, cognitive, and social) seen, heard, and felt through purposeful words and actions across the many means available to them, making use of technology and resources.

BUILDING RELATIONSHIPS AND CARING CONNECTIONS

Arguably, building strong faculty-student and student-student relationships and "rapport" in an online classroom may be the number one, most integral piece of the "student success and satisfaction" puzzle. Online relationships, where there are zero in-person meetings or conversations, require consistent intentional effort, a high degree of flexibility, and thoughtful communication strategies. Findings from Flanigan et al. (2022) indicated that online instructors rely upon different rapport-related strategies and contextual factors to initiate and maintain rapport, for example, during the first weeks of the semester. These instructors rely upon connecting, information sharing, and common grounding behaviors to initiate a sense of rapport among the class. We have found success in making strong, positive, initial connections with online students in similar ways. The faculty introduction posting, a warm welcome announcement and email, and faculty responses to student introductions should take place as soon as possible once the course begins, ideally on days one, two, and three. Note: It is critical to ensure that all communication between faculty and students inside and outside of the classroom platform is inclusive and that faculty follow the diversity, equity, and inclusive best-practices and policies set forth by their institutions. In addition, it is important to set the stage for relationship-building between students. There are activities to help students get to know each other on a personal level. Asking students to share personal interests, hobbies, and experiences can help create a sense of connection and provide the foundation for a relationship.

Strategy 1- Connect: When instructors are making initial connections with students, it is important to initiate communication and make introductions as soon as the course begins. A friendly and warm welcome announcement and email can set a positive tone on the very first day of class. During the first week, and on the very first days of the course, incorporating a discussion prompt or activity that encourages students to meet the faculty member and communicate with each other as students can relieve tension and offer an opportunity to make initial friendly contact in the online classroom. Based on student feedback, we have found that students enjoy and appreciate a pre-recorded instructor welcome video.

On the introductory or week one discussion board, an instructor prompt may include specific requirements, phrased in a friendly, warm manner, as well as an opportunity for optional information sharing:

Prompt: *Welcome to (course name), which begins on Monday, (insert date)! My name is Dr. Jane Doe and I look forward to meeting all of you. I hope that you have already watched my recorded video in the announcements and have read my introductory post on the week one introduction discussion board. As you can see from my photos, my dog loves to swim and my partner and I love to travel to the mountains 12. For this "getting to know each other" discussion, please feel free to share any or all of the following (plus more!): interesting or informative personal or professional details, hobbies, special interests, goals, place of residence or travel destinations, a "fun fact" about you, favorite food or recipes, special traditions, and family, pets, or other photos. You are welcome to post anything that may help us get to know you better! I hope this initial discussion will allow all of us to connect and jump-start our relationship-building. Your well-being and success are important to me. I will be with you every step of the way over the next nine weeks of the course. Warmly, Dr. Doe*

It is ideal for the faculty member to post first as it demonstrates a willingness to be vulnerable. We have found that posting a family photo, vacation photo, pet photo, interesting, amazing, or funny story, a brief biography, or sharing anything authentic publicly with the group offers a strong invite to connect and can serve as the foundation for building relationships. Photos can be great conversation starters and allow students to see the instructor as a real person instead of just a name. Sharing stories of travel or pets oftentimes sparks an initial connection and students find that they have something in common with the instructor and each other or realize they share the same interest or hobby, or even dog breed! These types of informal, and oftentimes fun, initial contacts can be the very first building blocks of the faculty-student relationship and connection. Instructors can also put out an open invite for one-on-one or group virtual meetings on day one of the course, and then send meeting invites as students provide mutually agreed-upon dates and times.

Strategy 2- Personalize: Creating a respectful and inclusive online environment takes special care and consideration. In all classroom announcements, on discussion boards, in emails, during virtual meetings, and on phone calls, the faculty tone should be positive, respectful, and safe. Students and faculty alike deserve an inclusive and equitable online environment. Meeting with or speaking with students individually can help faculty demonstrate an interest in students' lives and personalize the learning experience. One-to-one virtual meetings allow for the faculty member and student to see each other and hear each other's voices. This is a critical component for online students to feel recognized and understood and can motivate them as well (Singh et al., 2022). In our experience, one-to-one virtual meetings are the single best way for the faculty member to learn about student interests, goals, learning preferences, and challenges. These types of meetings are an ideal way to truly connect and build an authentic relationship. Students almost always express gratitude for being willing to connect in a personal manner. We have found that when a student can see our smiles, and eyes, and hear the tone of our voices, it alleviates their apprehension and allows them to engage with us on a deeper and more personal level.

Prompt or Email: *Hi, (student name): I hope you are well! I would enjoy learning more about how to best support you during this course so I would like to meet virtually sometime, at your convenience, within the next 5-7 days. The meeting will be casual in nature- an informal chat where you can ask questions, get clarification, and let me know what you need as a student. Can you please email me with your available days/times when you have 15-20 minutes to connect? I'm looking forward to it! Warmly, Dr. Doe*

Personalized, consistent, and proactive communication, using a variety of tools, is vital for building relationships. Faculty can use email, text, virtual meeting platforms, discussion boards, and phone calls to connect with students. Not only do students benefit from supportive emotional connections to teachers, but positive faculty–student relationships also increase faculty feelings of self-efficacy and well-being (Tackie, 2022). Faculty can establish and then maintain initial relationships and connections with students when they show empathy, and flexibility, and acknowledge a job well done. Even in the online asynchronous classroom, there are numerous strategies and tools for effective communication. Once relationships are established, continuing to build and connect is an ongoing process. It takes faculty commitment and effort that goes beyond a certain percentage of discussion board postings or returning graded papers on time. Creating and fostering caring connections with online students can result in a positive and nurturing educational environment that fosters meaningful learning experiences and personal, authentic connections with students.

Strategy 3: Foster peer-to-peer community: Faculty may use one or more activities to build and support peer-to-peer relationships and community. Icebreaker activities can be used during week one to help learners get to know each other on a personal level. Students should be encouraged to share personal interests, hobbies, or experiences as these can create a sense of connection with others who are simply interested in the same things or wish to learn something new. Meaningful and authentic group projects or discussions can foster empathy as learners collaborate and understand different perspectives. The instructor, to the extent possible, should ensure that groups are diverse in terms of backgrounds and abilities, and incorporate activities that help students put themselves in others' shoes. Socratic method can also be incorporated by asking students to share personal stories or experiences related to the course material. Hosting virtual office hours or Q&A sessions where students can interact with both the instructor and their peers is another informal way to foster peer-to-peer relationships. Some courses provide an opportunity to include gamification elements in the course, such as leaderboards, badges, or collaborative challenges, which motivate students to engage with their peers. To make even more peer-to-peer connections, when appropriate, the instructor can rotate group members throughout the course to help students interact with different peers.

TOOLS AND STRATEGIES IN THE ONLINE CLASSROOM

As online education continues to evolve, faculty and students have access to a wide variety of digital tools, both synchronous and asynchronous. A quick search online will provide dozens of free tools along with tutorials and best-practice ideas for using them. These tools, when used appropriately and effectively, can be used to build relationships both privately and publicly while fostering a sense of connection between faculty and students and among the student group. Asynchronous tools, like discussion boards, support online students by allowing them to participate at their own pace and on their own schedule and allows for the instructor to monitor communications among the group and check for understanding (University of Michigan, 2021). In nearly all online classrooms, there are discussion boards, chat rooms, or forums where faculty and students can interact with each other asynchronously. Asynchronous tools provide convenience and flexibility for both the instructor and the student. In addition, these types of tools allow for easily accessible reviews of previously posted notes, chats, responses to prompts, questions, answers, or anything that is published within the classroom platform. In addition to asynchronous tools, the use of synchronous "real-time" tools can also be beneficial when building relationships and making connections. Video conferencing platforms like Zoom, Facetime, Microsoft Teams, or Google Meet allow for face-to-face interactions. These face-to-face interactions allow the instructor and student to hear each other's voices and see each other's faces, fostering a more authentic and personal connection. Using asynchronous and synchronous tools effectively and consistently can help instructors and students stay in close, frequent, and varied communication with each other, which helps build strong relationships and allows for connections to be made using a variety of modalities.

Strategy 1- Use of Asynchronous Tools (not an exhaustive list): *Email, discussion boards, annotation tools, audio and video recordings, blogs, wikis, podcasts, chat forums, games, recorded presentations or webinars, interactives, texts, social media, virtual reality, simulations*

Strategy 2- Use of Synchronous Tools (not an exhaustive list): *One-on-one video conferences, group video conferences, live presentations, virtual office hours, phone calls, instant messaging, collaborative "real-time" tools such as Google Docs or other project management platforms, polls, breakout rooms*

Because asynchronous and synchronous tools have different benefits, challenges, and overall characteristics, students benefit most when the faculty member uses a combination of modalities. Faculty should use a variety of tools as well as learn students' communication preferences to provide individual attention and support to students. Connecting with faculty and classmates in a variety of ways allows students to choose their preferred way to discuss their concerns, seek clarifications, engage with classmates, or receive guidance on assignments. According to Barbetta (2023), students learn more with instruction that includes active learning opportunities rather than simply passively attending, and this is true for both face-to-face and online classrooms. When both asynchronous and synchronous tools are used, the instructor can promote a sense of community, which may lead to more meaningful relationships among students.

CULTIVATING TRUST

Building trust with online students requires creating an atmosphere and environment where students can take risks, express themselves, and be authentic without fear of shame, reprimand, ridicule, or dismissal. When students trust the instructor and each other, it boosts their confidence and improves their overall relationships. Online students can sometimes feel isolated and insecure since they spend much of their time reading and writing, and at no time are they physically present with the instructor or other classmates. Creating and then cultivating an authentic, trusting relationship requires a personalized approach and intentional, consistent effort. Many of the asynchronous and synchronous tools previously mentioned can provide multiple communication channels, and some students will feel more comfortable with one or another so individualized preferences should be met. It is important for instructors to clearly communicate availability and response times, and then ensure that those are adhered to. To build trust, students must feel supported and heard, even though they are unable to physically meet the instructor by walking into a building to attend office hours. When students do not understand something or have a misconception about something, they sometimes panic and send off multiple emails or leave multiple voicemails. Faculty can quickly de-escalate those feelings by being responsive and approachable. In our experience, an immediate five-minute phone call or video meeting clears up nearly all of those insecure, panicked, high-stress moments that students experience. Communications from the instructor should demonstrate a genuine interest in response to student questions, concerns, and contributions. Keeping personal matters private and not reprimanding or harshly correcting students publicly helps build trust. Constructive criticism, done in a way to teach, not scold, using a warm tone can build confidence and trust in the relationship. Written communications should be personalized by addressing students by their preferred names. Remembering important details about a student and then circling back to those later shows a personal touch and can help demonstrate that the instructor values and recognizes their individuality. The factors found to be important to student achievement and overall satisfaction in online coursework include the quality of faculty-student interaction, academic support, and the establishment of trust and a sense of community in the online course (Lockman & Schirmer, 2020). Some students have a difficult time trusting due to past trauma or negative experiences with instructors. We have found that sometimes our students lack trust due to misunderstandings, using incorrect emails that do not get delivered, or improper inferences of faculty communications or assignment feedback. Tone is difficult to assess in written form; this is why phone calls and video meetings are crucial to building trust.

Strategy 1- Within the online classroom platform: *Create a consistent presence, if you will be out of the office be sure to communicate that as an announcement and email, adhere to established timelines for answering questions and providing feedback or answering emails, and provide specific office hours, share your phone number and email address, when appropriate, use emojis to demonstrate tone, share personal and professional experiences, be empathetic and understanding, offer flexibility, be fair, point out the good, be relatable, create a safe, inclusive and equitable environment*

Strategy 2- Outside of the online classroom platform: *meet virtually using audio and video, ask how the student is doing and how you can help, offer to text, provide supplemental resources or interesting articles based on what you know about the student, provide clear expectations, ask what they need from you for them to be successful, ask about learning and communication preferences, have a sense of humor, be kind*

Showing a genuine interest in each student and telling them that their success is important to you are two main building blocks of establishing trust. It is easy to get into the habit of only providing constructive criticism in assignment feedback, but also pointing out areas that were done well or uniquely provides positive reinforcement. Active listening and acknowledging their triumphs and tribulations are also keys to building trusting relationships. To establish and then maintain trust between the instructor and student, consistency and feeling safe are imperative. The efforts that go into building a trusting relationship should not be taken lightly as they will likely enhance both student and faculty success and satisfaction in online classes.

DEMONSTRATING EMPATHY AND CARE

Time and again, students and faculty alike cite empathy and care as key factors in the development of relationships in the online learning environment. The responsibility for building rapport in the online classroom rests largely on the instructor, who must engage in a continuous, concerted, deep effort to be productive; the results benefit the student, who may earn better grades and demonstrate greater retention (Glazer, 2016). This may be especially critical for students who are at risk, facing challenges in their pursuit of a degree. Thus, gaining a better understanding of the actual behaviors that promote perceptions of each of these will allow faculty to more fully support students as they pursue their educational objectives.

Empathy refers to the ability to understand another person's thoughts and feelings from their perspective (i.e., to step into another's shoes). Instructors and students may struggle to connect on this level in the online setting since they do not have the same opportunities to interact. This may be especially true if they come from different backgrounds. Though online education offers access to low-income individuals, students from minoritized groups may experience less success in this setting (Pacansky-Brock et al., 2020). One pedagogical strategy identified by Pacansky-Brock and colleagues (2020) that seeks to address this equity gap is known as "humanizing". Humanizing strives to shift the burden of engagement and achievement barriers some students may experience to educators, who then support practices that encourage greater success among all students, starting with recognizing each name should be recognized as a real human on the other side of the screen. Their approach suggests several concrete strategies:

- First, if instructors imagine the physical situation of the online student, they can consider sharing information in a variety of ways so that students can access it without having to log into the learning management system, via a mobile device. Friendly emails prior to the course, highlighting need-to-know information can assist them as they prepare for the first day. Attachments that are easily downloadable and printable may be appreciated by students.
- Instructors can also ask questions to provide students the opportunity to share information that may be relevant to their satisfaction or success but perhaps is not requested or required as part of a course introduction (e.g., Identify any concerns you have regarding your success in this class). This opens the door for a student to share and provides an opportunity for the instructor to follow up later in the course, demonstrating empathy.
- Instructors can strive to development a visually appealing course, as this may lend itself to more positive first impressions and entice students to spend more time engaging with the course.
- Instructors can incorporate video throughout the course (e.g., announcements, discussions, grading feedback). Though many avoid this avenue for fear of looking unprofessional or unprepared, the use of video, even and perhaps especially unpolished and informal clips that portray the instructor as a real person (at home, with a pet or child in the background, or on the go) can help a student see them as more approachable and relatable.
- Instructors can also offer multiple means for students to communicate in the context of the course. Writing (and reading) paper after paper becomes monotonous and both students and instructor are quickly disengaged. If opportunities and technology allow, incorporate multiple options for expression in discussions or assignments. However, instructors should be vigilant to recognize this may make some students uncomfortable or place them at risk, and care should be taken to prevent bias.
- Instructors can provide an opportunity for students to reflect on their learning, throughout or at the end of the course, providing advice for future students. Various tools allow for this.

Efforts by instructors to demonstrate recognition and appreciation for the humanness each and every student need not be elaborate actions, but rather intentional and individualized with the goal of building relationships and ultimately community.

Similar to empathy, caring for students provides another avenue for fostering relationships in the online classroom. This is particularly important for students who may be facing academic, personal, financial, or professional challenges impacting their ability to succeed (Guzzardo et al., 2020). Instructors are in a prime position to support students by engaging them in learning, thus enhancing motivation to persist, and pointing them toward the myriad of resources and services provided within the university community. To truly care, instructors must be willing to suspend preconceived notions or expectations and truly listen to the needs of their students. Guzzardo and colleagues (2020) identified four specific strategies instructors may apply to foster supportive, responsive relationships:

- Instructors can create pedagogical space, demonstrating a willingness to support accommodations. This may also include flexibility of deadlines or sharing of additional support, especially during times of distress or crisis. When instructors adjust policies or practices to support student success, students feel respected and valued, rather than frustrated or disappointed, and this may translate to greater success.
- Instructors can be inclusive and aware. Instructors should create a welcoming environment for all students, and one in which all students are encouraged to broaden their perspectives. Students who feel excluded or whose concerns are dismissed prematurely may not perform as well as they could if they felt greater efficacy.
- Instructors can be engaged and engaging. Though very few students would refute an "easy A", nearly all appreciate a challenge when presented by a passionate instructor with high expectations who motivates students to engage with the content. Similarly, instructors may feel energized by students who get excited about a topic and put forth extra effort. One might reinforce the other, resulting in positive growth for both. Instructors should strive to be present, frequently and substantively throughout the various modalities present in the online classroom.
- Instructors can do more than teach. Students notice when instructors go above and beyond, offering academic or career advice or pointing students in the direction of campus support services when needed. Instructors who are available and approachable increase students' feelings of value and may motivate them toward future achievement.

For students, a high-quality online learning experience consists of an instructor who is interactive, responsive, and available (Cashion & Palmieri, 2002). When instructors demonstrate that they truly care for their students through supportive relationships, students may experience better learning, higher achievement, and improved well-being. Instructors may find their interactions more rewarding as well. Happy students are more successful, with well-being corresponding to better learning—more focused attention as well as more creative and holistic thinking (Seligman et al, 2009). Researchers have demonstrated that people with positive relationships are most likely to be happy (Diener & Seligman, 2002). Students with caring and supportive relationships report more positive attitudes and greater satisfaction, and they are more academically engaged (2004). Positive relationships build motivation, create safe spaces for taking chances, build new pathways for learning, and promote better behavior (Kaufman, n.d.). Moreover, well-being in the classroom context is socially contagious (King & Datu, 2017). Therefore, creating a context that fosters a supportive, genuine connection between instructor and students is imperative.

ADDITIONAL CONSIDERATIONS FOR PROMOTING SUCCESS

While instructors may be unable to control student differences, they do have the ability to account for some qualities that students may possess that have an impact on online learning. In particular, students may differ in their self-efficacy concerning technology as well as their personality. Instructors can take purposeful action to minimize detrimental effects and maximize positive outcomes in both regards.

Students who lack efficacy in their ability to navigate technology may experience less satisfaction and success in the learning environment (Rios et al., 2018). Instructors may need to be especially cognizant of students who are new to the experience or platform and provide supportive materials or offer to assist. They can also strive to create a course experience free from the hassle of unnecessary clicking and scrolling. Information overload may prevent students from progressing. The use of tools such as simple videos or tipsheets may guide students through new and unfamiliar or more complex processes necessary to navigate the course or complete assignments. Because many online instructors have spent years in their world, they may take for granted that students understand commonplace practices such as the use of track changes in Microsoft Word; then, when students fail to take into account comments, instructors assume they disregarded the feedback, but in reality, the student did not even know it was available. Instructor strategies include encouraging peer support and mentoring among learners and pairing more experienced online learners with newcomers, which can help build empathy and care. Instructors can gauge student preparation with a few simple questions and careful observation, followed by the provision of appropriate support to enhance the student experience.

Another student difference that can impact the interactions in the classroom is personality. Extraversion, conscientiousness, and openness all play a prominent role in the engagement of students and instructors (Rios et al., 2018). Extraverted students may thrive in the discussion setting, enjoying the opportunity to share and interact, while introverted students may need additional prompting to engage, and may prefer more private means of communication more generally. Conscientious students may be especially motivated to achieve and adhere to course requirements, whereas less conscientious students may be less apt to persevere or perform as meticulously. Instructors can provide feedback for both, recognizing that they may not share the same goals in terms of achievement of particular grades or other metrics of success. Students who are open to experience may enjoy new and challenging assignment opportunities, while less open students may find them somewhat unpleasant or threatening. Instructors can be sensitive to each, encouraging and motivating them to pursue intellectual curiosity. Instructors can also design assignments that require students to work in small groups, fostering teamwork and communication.

Respecting individual differences can contribute to more positive relationships, thus fostering successful outcomes in the online classroom. Finally, instructors must be mindful of their preparation and preconceived notions, as well as the personality and situational characteristics that drew or forced them into online education. Though many may feel that traditional face-to-face teaching can easily be adapted to the online setting, or that teaching online is easier or less time-consuming, in reality, there are advantages and challenges unique to each. Recognizing individual strengths and employing them to achieve maximum benefit for both self and others is ideal; admitting to weaknesses and seeking opportunities for professional development is essential. Even experienced instructors muse that they are still refining their methods (Schmidt et al., 2013). The development of rewarding relationships is not just a benefit for students; it can also foster greater satisfaction and enjoyment in the online setting for instructors. Hence, putting forth the time and effort necessary to improve skills as well as fostering individual relationships within a community of learners is worth the investment. Though the student must demonstrate an interest in, a positive attitude about, and effort toward learning, the well-prepared instructor can foster an environment in which students are actively engaged and excited to learn, particularly when engaged in a mutually supportive relationship (Mandernach, 2009).

SUMMARY

Teaching online requires a diverse skill set and the ability of the instructor to build relationships and create connections with students. High-quality programs in which learning communities develop require the input of creative and innovative educators (Aitken et al., 2021). Online education will continue to evolve, and scholars must continue to explore strategies for creating connections in the virtual environment. We have been teaching online since 2005 and 2007, respectively, and have experienced the evolution of online higher education, which has become highly sophisticated, well-accepted, and a readily available means of delivering high-quality education. One thing remains consistent; the student experience is dependent on the instructor and it is clear that authentic faculty-student relationships and student-student relationships improve faculty and student success and satisfaction.

REFERENCES

Adams, B., & Wilson, N. S. (2020). Building Community in Asynchronous Online Higher Education Courses Through Collaborative Annotation. *Journal of Educational Technology Systems*, *49*(2), 250–261. doi:10.1177/0047239520946422

Aitken, G., & Hayes, S. (2021). Online Postgraduate Teaching: Re-Discovering Human Agency. In T. Fawns, G. Aitken, & D. Jones (Eds.), *Online Postgraduate Education in a Postdigital World. Postdigital Science and Education*. Springer. doi:10.1007/978-3-030-77673-2_8

Barbetta, P. M. (2023). Technologies as Tools to Increase Active Learning During Online Higher-Education Instruction. *Journal of Educational Technology Systems*, *51*(3), 317–339. doi:10.1177/00472395221143969

Berry, S. (2017). Building community in online doctoral classrooms: Instructor practices that support community. *Online Learning : the Official Journal of the Online Learning Consortium*, *21*(2), n2. doi:10.24059/olj.v21i2.875

Bolliger, D. U., Shepherd, C. E., & Bryant, H. V. (2019, October 31). Faculty members' perceptions of the online program community and their efforts to sustain it. *British Journal of Educational Technology*. https://eric.ed.gov/?id=EJ1232104

Cashion, J., & Palmieri, P. (2002). *'The secret is the teacher': the learner's view of online learning*. NCVER.

Cornell, H. R., Sayman, D., & Herron, J. (2019). Sense of community in an online graduate program. *Journal of Effective Teaching in Higher Education*, *2*(2), 117–132. doi:10.36021/jethe.v2i2.52

Diener, E., & Seligman, M. E. P. (2002). Very happy people. *Psychological Science*, *13*(1), 81–84. doi:10.1111/1467-9280.00415 PMID:11894851

Flanigan, A. E., Akcaoglu, M., & Ray, E. (2022). Initiating and maintaining student-instructor rapport in online classes. *The Internet and Higher Education*, *53*, 100844. doi:10.1016/j.iheduc.2021.100844

Flock, H. (2020). Designing a community of inquiry in online courses. *International Review of Research in Open and Distance Learning*, *21*(1), 135–153. doi:10.19173/irrodl.v20i5.3985

Garrison, D. R., Anderson, T., & Archer, W. (2010). The first decade of the community of inquiry framework: A retrospective. *The Internet and Higher Education*, *13*(1), 5–9. doi:10.1016/j.iheduc.2009.10.003

Garrison, D. R., & Arbaugh, J. B. (2007). Researching the community of inquiry framework: Review, issues, and future directions. *The Internet and Higher Education, 10*(3), 157–172. doi:10.1016/j.iheduc.2007.04.001

Glazier, R. A. (2016). Building rapport to improve retention and success in online classes. *Journal of Political Science Education, 12*(4), 437–456. doi:10.1080/15512169.2016.1155994

Guzzardo, M. T., Khosla, N., Adams, A. L., Bussmann, J. D., Engelman, A., Ingraham, N., Gamba, R., Jones-Bey, A., Moore, M. D., Toosi, N. R., & Taylor, S. (2020). "The ones that care make all the difference": Perspectives on student-faculty relationships. *Innovative Higher Education, 46*(1), 41–58. doi:10.100710755-020-09522-w PMID:33012971

How Has Online Education Evolved. (n.d.). https://learn.org/articles/How_Has_Online_Education_Evolved.html

Kaufman, T. (n.d.). Building positive relationships with students: What brain science says. *Understood.* https://www.understood.org/en/articles/brain-science-says-4-reasons-to-build-positive-relationships-with-students

King, R. B., & Datu, J. A. (2017). Happy classes make happy students: Classmates' well-being predicts individual student well-being. *Journal of School Psychology, 65*, 116–128. doi:10.1016/j.jsp.2017.07.004 PMID:29145940

Klem, A. M., & Connell, J. P. (2004). Relationships matter: Linking teacher support to student engagement and achievement. *The Journal of School Health, 74*(7), 262–273. doi:10.1111/j.1746-1561.2004.tb08283.x PMID:15493703

Lively, C. L., Blevins, B., Talbert, S., & Cooper, S. (2021). Building community in online professional practice doctoral programs. *Impacting Education: Journal on Transforming Professional Practice, 6*(3), 21–29. doi:10.5195/ie.2021.187

Lockman, A., & Schirmer, B. (2020). Online instruction in Higher Education: Promising, research-based, and evidence-based practices. *Journal of Education and e-learning Research, 7*(2), 130–152. doi:10.20448/journal.509.2020.72.130.152

Mandernach, B. J. (March 2009). Three ways to improve student engagement in the online classroom. *Online Cl@ssroom: Ideas for Effective Online Instruction.* 1-2.

Martin, J. (2019). Building relationships and increasing engagement in the virtual classroom. *The Journal of Educators Online, 16*(1). Advance online publication. doi:10.9743/jeo.2019.16.1.9

National Center for Education Statistics | U.S. Department of Education. (2023). https://www.ed.gov/category/keyword/national-center-education-statistics

Pacansky-Brock, M., Smedshammer, M., & Vincent-Layton, K. (2020). Humanizing online teaching to equitize higher education. *Current Issues in Education (Tempe, Ariz.), 21*(2).

Rios, T., Elliot, M., & Mandernach, B. J. (2008). Efficient instructional strategies for maximizing online student satisfaction. *The Journal of Educators Online, 15*(3). Advance online publication. doi:10.9743/jeo.2018.15.3.7

Schmidt, S. W., Hodge, E. M., & Tschida, C. M. (2013). How university faculty members developed their online teaching skills. *Quarterly Review of Distance Education, 14*(3), 131–140.

Seligman, M. E., Ernst, R. M., Gillham, J., Reivich, K., & Linkins, M. (2009). Positive education: Positive psychology and classroom interventions. *Oxford Review of Education, 35*(3), 293–311. doi:10.1080/03054980902934563

Singh, J., Singh, L., & Matthees, B. (2022). Establishing social, cognitive, and teaching presence in online learning—A panacea in covid-19 pandemic, post vaccine and Post Pandemic Times. *Journal of Educational Technology Systems, 51*(1), 28–45. doi:10.1177/00472395221095169

Tackie, H. N. (2022). (Dis)Connected: Establishing Social Presence and Intimacy in Teacher–Student Relationships During Emergency Remote Learning. *AERA Open, 8*. Advance online publication. doi:10.1177/23328584211069525

University of Michigan Center for Academic Innovation. (2020). *Asynchronous tools and how to use them.* https://onlineteaching.umich.edu/asynchronous-tools-and-how-to-use-them/

Chapter 13
Keeping It Compliant:
ADA in the Online Classroom

Cara L. Metz
https://orcid.org/0000-0002-2447-2665
The University of Arizona Global Campus, USA

Sarah H. Jarvie
https://orcid.org/0000-0001-9401-4275
Colorado Christian University, USA

ABSTRACT

This chapter will discuss what disabilities are, how they can impact students in an online classroom, and what it means to be ADA compliant. In addition, this chapter will provide some examples of practical applications for designing ADA compliant online classrooms with the purpose of creating relationships. Higher education faculty are at the frontline, making online classrooms accessible and setting the tone for the learning environment. They can engage in relationships with all students and work actively to come alongside those who may need additional support in the classroom. It is in creating relationships with students that barriers are broken and more opportunities for access arise.

INTRODUCTION

When it comes to building relationships, it is important that a student feel seen and understood. Instructors who design their classroom to meet the needs of students at all ability levels can begin to build trust and empathy with students, especially those with disabilities that affect how they learn. Instead of waiting until a student discloses a need that might cause them to get behind in their courses (Huss & Eastep, 2016), instructors can proactively build a classroom that is usable for all students (Edwards et al., 2022; Guilbaud et al., 2021; Terras et al., 2015). This approach demonstrates empathy and a culturally inclusive environment, possibly opens up higher education to those who might not have had access to it before (Barnard-Brak & Sulak, 2012), and creates from the start an environment of inclusion and equity (Huss & Eastep, 2016). Even when instructors are unaware of their attitude toward disability accommodations, if they approach their classrooms with an ableist attitude, students are less likely to reach out for the support they need (Evans et al., 2017). Viewing disability as an element of diversity to be celebrated in the student body can foster access for all students (Cory, 2011).

People who have a disability are less likely than those without to complete a higher education degree and be employed (Bureau of Labor Statistics, 2019). A student with a disability is defined as someone who has different physical, cognitive, sensory, or emotional characteristics from a normative population to the extent that they require services or accommodations to be fully active in a classroom (Heward et al., 2017, as cited by Kurea et al., 2021). Online education provides an opportunity to remove barriers that exist in other educational settings (Moorefield-Lang et al., 2016).

Disabilities will be both disclosed and undisclosed in the classroom. The National Center for Education Statistics (NCES) (2022) reports that only one-third of students who had a disability reported it to their college. Even with only one-third reporting, 19 percent of non-veteran undergraduates reported having a disability, and 26 percent of all veteran undergraduates reported having a disability (NCES, 2018). It is essential that instructors create a classroom that is welcoming to all students, regardless of disability. Additionally, they must advocate for students who need more services. Building relationships with students is a great way to have conversations about what might help them best. Disabilities might be undiagnosed, the student may not be used to advocating for themselves, especially if they are younger and their parents or guardians were able to advocate for them before (Barnard-Brak et al., 2010; Hong, 2015). Perhaps students who transition into college are eager to not be identified as a disabled student with their new start in higher education (Hong, 2015). Students who have a disability are less likely to complete their education compared to those who are non-disabled (NCES, n.d.).

This chapter will also provide some examples of practical applications for designing ADA compliant online classrooms with the purpose of creating relationships. Higher education faculty are at the frontline, making online classrooms accessible and setting the tone for the learning environment. They can engage in relationships with all students and work actively to come alongside those who may need additional support in the classroom. It is in creating relationships with students that barriers are broken and more opportunities for access arise.

HISTORY OF ADA

First implemented in 1990, the Americans with Disabilities Act (commonly referred to as ADA) was a way to establish guidelines and standards to provide accessibility and equal access for all (Betts, 2013). It covers physical disabilities and mental health challenges and provides an equal opportunity for employment and education by prohibiting discrimination against such individuals. Section 504 of the Rehabilitation Act of 1973 as amended (Section 504) (King & Piotroski, 2021) is the other federal statute that governs accessibility of online education. Section 504 is a national law that provides protection from discrimination based on disability for those who qualify (U.S. Department of Health and Human Services, 2006). All educational institutions that receive federal financial assistance are subject to Section 504 (King & Piotroski, 2021). In 1998, the Section 508 Amendment to the Rehabilitation Act of 1973 was added requiring federal agencies to make their electronic and information technology accessible. Together these statutes require materials like websites, videos, PDF files, and other information technology be made available to all individuals, including those with disabilities.

As technology and culture have evolved, so have the needs and challenges of Americans with disabilities (Betts, 2013). The Americans with Disabilities Act Amendments Act (ADAAA) of 2008 provided further clarification of the term disability. This amendment expanded the definition of disability and added such disabilities as depression, anxiety, and asthma with symptoms that are episodic or in remission. For the higher education setting, this amendment plays a significant role by clarifying that students are provided more protection under the law and do not need severe disabilities to qualify. "Mitigating measures" like an individual's using medication or assistive technology to lessen the impact of their disability are also considered under this amendment (ADA Amendments Act, 2008).

Accessibility requirements have moved to the forefront of higher education legal responsibilities as Section 504 and ADA are increasingly challenged in courts (King & Piotroski, 2021). King and Piotrowski (2021) present an overview of accessibility standards related to ADA laws and regulations in the context of online instruction. They highlight the importance of providing accessible content for students with disabilities to avoid the legal implications of failure to do so (King & Piotroski, 2021). Creating accessible classrooms is not merely a practicality; legal responsibilities have become increasingly scrutinized (King & Piotroski, 2021). For example, the National Association for the Deaf (NAD) cited violations of accessibility in lawsuits against Harvard University and Massachusetts Institute of Technology (MIT) (King & Piotroski, 2021). The lawsuits focused on the universities' alleged failure to provide appropriately accurate and comprehensive captioning for online course materials (King & Piotroski, 2021). Both Harvard and MIT offer free online educational lectures and programming through such platforms as YouTube and iTunes through edX, a nonprofit that offers dozens of MOOCs (massive open online courses) free to students around the world. The NAD claimed both institutions failed to give equal access to meet the needs of deaf and hard of hearing individuals.

These two universities are not the only ones struggling with lawsuits due to noncompliance with ADA regulations. According to King & Piotroski (2021) these lawsuits are notable and focus attention on three important things. First, they highlight the significance of publicly available online content falling under the purview of Section 504 and ADA. Secondly, providing accurate and quality captions is necessary for any publicly available audio and audio-visual content. Lastly, colleges and universities should follow Web Content Accessibility Guidelines (WCAG) 2.1 AA, which provides detailed guidelines for accessibility compliance. (WCAG 2.1 AA standards are discussed in a subsequent section in this chapter).

ADA COMPLIANT VIRTUAL CLASSROOMS

As the world of online education continues to grow, it is becoming even more important to provide students of all abilities access to quality online education. A recent systematic review of the literature from 2000 to 2021 revealed that students with disabilities are not being supported in the online learning environment (She & Martin, 2022). She & Martin (2022) found barriers in online education that focused on four themes including accessibility standards, assistive technology, Universal Design for Learning (UDL), and need for online accessibility training and development.

The Center for Universal Design was developed in 1989 at North Carolina State University with a grant from the National Institute on Disability and Rehabilitation Research (Center for Universal Design, 1997). The mission of the center is "to improve the built environment and related products for all users by impacting change in policies and procedures through research, information, training, and design assistance" (Center for Universal Design, 1997, para 3). Although Universal Design was used previously, this center researched its efficacy and interventions. There are seven principles for universal design. These include 1) the ability to be used by people with diverse abilities; 2) flexible design based on people's preferences and abilities; 3) ease of use without a lot of knowledge or experience; 4) providing users the necessary information regardless of their abilities; 5) few consequences to accidents; 6) use with little fatigue; and 7) usability for all, regardless of mobility, posture, or size (Center for Universal Design, 1997).

When applied to teaching, the concept of Universal Design means that the design of education should be fully accessible to those with and without disabilities (Helvacioglu & Karamanoglu, 2012). CAST (2018) states that UDL guidelines require instructors to provide multiple ways of engaging with the end goal so that students understand the purpose and stay motivated. This means finding ways to keep a person's interest, helping them persist, and encouraging them to self-regulate. The UDL guidelines also require numerous ways of representation to achieve the goal of learners who are knowledgeable. Instructors must consider the ways students can gain or perceive the information, use language and symbols that can be understood with all students, and provide various channels for students to comprehend the information. Finally, UDL guidelines include providing multiple modes of action and expression like various ways to access and manipulate tools, different avenues to communicate knowledge, and options for executive functions. The goal here is to develop learners who are goal-directed.

All resources that instructors put in their online classrooms must be ADA compliant. Even when they are not responsible for their design, instructors are responsible for ensuring materials are accessible to all students (Lowenthal et al., 2020). For example, if an instructor is sharing an online resource like a website or a video, they must ensure that the colors are readable and not the only cue about information, alternative text exists for images and pictures, accurate captions are on videos, forms can be read by a screen reader, and websites can be navigated beyond the use of a mouse (ADA.gov, 2022). Programs can caption videos, but may not be accurate; for example, they may not include punctuation. Faculty must update transcripts of their own videos to reflect accuracy and use videos created by others only if the closed captioning is accurate. As another example, if an instructor uses a PDF, the file must be readable by a screen reader. Scanning a document into a PDF will make the document inaccessible to some unless the instructor uses technology that can convert it into digital text. Lowenthal et al. (2020) suggest to test the readability of the document with text-to-speech software, instructors can highlight words or phrases on the page, copy them, and then paste them into another document. If this process works, the document can be read with text-to-speech software. If the resource does not meet these expectations, the materials should not be used in the online classroom. The stronger the accessibility, the stronger the potential learning (Betts, 2013).

Further, screen readers can be a great tool for those who are visually impaired, who have suffered a traumatic brain injury, or who have attention-deficit/hyperactivity disorder (Lowenthal et al., 2020). Huss and Eastetp (2016) explain that faculty must be informed about how a screen reader works. Users learn shortcuts and keys to operate a screen reader. A screen reader will read everything on a page and cannot read separate colors or bolded prints. Additionally, a screen reader will read everything on a screen. When instructors post a website, they should create a linked text description of the website instead of listing the entire URL because the screen reader will only read the linked text. Also, using phrases such as "click here" prohibits screen-reader users from understanding the context. Additionally, screen-readers might struggle with indents and asterisks, so if lists are included in PDFs and other documents, the use of numbers or bullet points are important. If tables are used, the top row should contain headers.

In addition to ADA compliance, faculty can design a classroom that is consistent and repetitive (Moorefield-Lang et al., 2016), not only within the classroom itself but also across courses in the program or university (Lowenthal et al., 2020). This offers students with disabilities a familiar and predictable environment. Each week the classroom schedule should follow a similar format, instructions on how to submit assignments should be the same, and information should be available to the students in multiple locations (Moorefield-Lang et al., 2016). Instructors can provide an orientation that reviews classroom setup before students start their first course to help them become acquainted and comfortable with the university's online environment.

ACCESSIBILITY GUIDELINES AND STANDARDS

Web Content Accessibility Guidelines (WCAG) (2018) 2.1 AA created by the World Wide Web Consortium (W3C) provides detailed instructions about how to make web content more accessible to people with disabilities. WCAG accessibility encompasses a wide range of disabilities "including visual, auditory, physical, speech, cognitive, language, learning, and neurological disabilities" ("Background on WCAG 2," paragraph 1). As of this writing, the guidelines for WCAG 2.2 are in the final draft stages (https://www.w3.org/TR/WCAG22/). The WCAG provides three conformance levels: A, AA, and AAA; these set success criteria that go beyond captioning to include requirements for perceivable content, operable interface, and a robust website that can work with a variety of user agents like assistive technologies, to name a few. Because the online classroom is like a website, faculty must ensure that everything within the classroom meets these standards.

The WCAG 2.1 AA provides four standards: 1) perceivable, 2) operable, 3) understandable, and 4) robust which relate to the web content and technology that house the content (King & Piotrowski, 2021; W3C, 2018). Each of these accessibility standards will be discussed below.

Perceivable describes how the information and user interface components must be presented in ways that are not invisible to the users' senses. King and Piotrowski (2019) cite this standard as most relevant to faculty creating online courses. Non-text material should have a text equivalent; the text equivalent can be accomplished via text transcripts or captions (King & Piotrowski, 2021; Moorefield-Lang et al., 2016). For example, audio-only content (like a podcast) should be accompanied by full-text transcripts of the content; if an individual is hearing impaired, they will not perceive the content in the same way as one who is not hearing impaired. Keep in mind that "structure and text elements should be used depending upon whether what is presented is an image, audio-only file, video-only file, pre-recorded video with audio file or a live streaming of video with audio" (King & Piotrowski, 2021, p. 131). Video communication platforms like Google Meet and Zoom have live captioning capabilities that make them useful educational tools (King & Piotrowski, 2021). Making the text distinguishable and utilizing proper headings (such as H1 to H6) to allow a screen reader to properly navigate the material (King & Piotrowski, 2021; W3C, 2018) are additional important perceivable elements.

W3C (2017) outlines that when using images, instructors must include descriptions that relay to users what the image portrays. If instructors include a picture that is more than decorative, does not include information that is important or has value, and does not contain links, they must use alternative, or alt, text. This provides a description of the image so that if a user cannot see the image, they can still gain the information from the alt text. Most images should be described in a sentence or short phrase, with the most important information presented first. If instructors use more complicated images like charts, diagrams, and maps, they must include a short description and a long description that fully represents the necessary information (W3C, 2022). To check if an image has an alt text that is accessible with a screen reader, instructors can right click on an image and choose "inspect." The alt text will appear in quotes. Whether they are using the image as a part of their classroom or including a website with images, it is important for faculty to ensure that alt text is available.

Operable is merely the ability to operate the interface (W3C, 2018). It considers if the individual can navigate the information. For example, if an individual lacks the mobility to utilize a mouse but can operate a keyboard, faculty must ensure there are keyboard accessibility shortcuts in place. Links should be easy to read and descriptive unlike the short phrases, "click here" or "next."

The understandable principle relates to ensuring the information on the website is structured in a manner that the user can understand and operate the interface. According to King and Piotrowski (2019), "the main focus of the understandable principle is on individuals with visual impairments, learning difficulties and cognitive disabilities" (p. 132). Thus, part of this standard is readability and making sure the text is well organized and uses proper <h1-h6> headings. Headings and subheadings provide an organization and structure to the information but also allow accessibility tools to move through the information and navigate the page.

Robust means that content must be developed enough so it can be interpreted by a variety of user agents including assistive technologies (W3C, 2018). Websites must be developed enough so individuals can use the best assistive technologies to meet their needs.

While these standards refer to websites, King and Piotrowski (2019) highlight practical tips that faculty can take from making sure any images such as photographs or tables are accompanied by alternate text describing the image to creating documents with programs that have built-in accessibility checks like Microsoft Word or Adobe Acrobat.

Finally, there must be a partnership across university disciplines and departments. Collaboration between instructors and the instructional technologists, librarian, and office for disability services administrators ensures the university achieves compliance (She & Martin, 2022) and enhances efforts to provide accommodations. "Access is an institution-wide responsibility" (Betts, 2013, p. 4).

ACCOMMODATIONS

The Accommodation Process

An individual faculty member does not decide on the accommodations that a student receives. Nearly all colleges and universities (including those online) offer services through a disability services (DS) department (Cory, 2011). DS exists to guide institutions through the process of ensuring reasonable accommodations are provided and met for students who need them (Cory, 2011). Cory (2011) frames DS as both a legal and ethical obligation in terms of providing access to education for all students. By law, the process starts with a student; this is a unique aspect of disability accommodations in higher education versus accommodations in primary or secondary school (Cory, 2011; Izzo & Horne, 2016). To receive accommodations, students are required to disclose their disability, and the institution is authorized to request third-party documentation of that disability from a medical doctor or psychologist (Cory, 2011; Simon, 2000). The documentation should provide a clear diagnosis and functional impact of the disability on classroom activities that may be impacted by the disability like test taking, completing homework assignments, or even reading (Cory, 2011). DS staff will use the provided documentation and have a conversation with the student to gain more information regarding the impact of disability on function as well as verify the third-party report (Cory, 2011). After these steps, the DS staff member will make accommodation recommendations. The accommodation recommendation is most often presented in the form of a letter that outlines the accommodations (for example, extra time to complete tests or the use of a screen reader). The letters do not disclose the disability but rather outline the accommodations that are allowed (Tamjeed et al., 2021). These letters are then given to the individual student, who is responsible for distributing them to their instructor. Due to this process, more responsibility is placed on the student to self-identity and self-advocate. Additionally, there is more pressure on the student to disclose their disability and provide the appropriate documentation(s) (Izzo & Horne, 2016).

Barriers of Accommodation

Toutain's (2019) literature review of barriers to accommodations for students reported three main themes: barriers of knowledge, function, or attitude. Barriers of knowledge refer to a lack of awareness related to the resources available. Student interviews by Lyman et al. (2016) further supported these findings; they found that students did not know about the resources available to them. Barriers of function refer to the function of the accommodation. Students were either unable to provide appropriate documentation of a disability or receive accommodations that they found useful (Toutain, 2019). Students are often unaware that a disability services department exists or how accommodations may help them in higher education (Izzo & Horn, 2016; Toutain, 2019). Barriers of attitude can include the student's negative attitude toward their disability or their desire not to disclose it because they have experienced related shame (Izzo & Horn, 2016; Toutain, 2019). Additionally, many students do not understand how accommodations may allow them to be more successful in higher education (Izzo & Horn, 2016; Toutain, 2019).

Faculty Perceptions

Faculty report being hesitant to provide accommodations based on feeling unprepared, not being compensated for the extra work, not having enough time (Guilbaud et al., 2021; Hsiao et al., 2019; Huss & Eastep, 2016), believing those who are receiving accommodations may have an unfair advantage (Hsiao et al., 2019; Stevens et al., 2018), not being supported by the university (Hsiao et al., 2019), and not receiving the necessary tools (Guilbaud et al., 2021; Huss & Eastep, 2016). These perceptions can lead faculty to approach students who have disabilities with a negative attitude (Sniatecki et al., 2015). Faculty may not be aware of all the compliance requirements (Huss & Eastep, 2016; Sniatecki et al., 2015) thinking they fall on "someone else." In many cases, faculty do not contact appropriate departments in the university to get help or think it is not their responsibility to ensure accessibility compliance (Huss & Eastep, 2016). These perceptions can hinder their willingness to make changes.

THE IMPORTANCE OF THE RELATIONSHIP IN BEING ADA COMPLIANT

Instructors want to support all students in the classroom and provide them opportunities to engage with the material and learn course content. Morina (2019) cites faculty as key inclusion enablers for students with disabilities. Positive interactions between faculty and students, concern for student well-being, and personal respect and connection were attributed to spurring student learning, thus supporting the importance of relationships (Morina, 2019). One of the barriers to accommodations (Ehlinger & Roper, 2020; Hong, 2015) is students' understanding of faculty perception. Students do not want to feel judged (Hong, 2015; Terras et al., 2015), embarrassed, and less capable. Students reported that they felt that no one believed in them (Hong, 2015). These are powerful findings that support the need for strong, empathetic, supportive relationships between faculty and students who have a disability. A classroom that is designed from the start to meet the needs of all students sends the message that faculty are thinking about and understanding their students' diverse abilities and are open to making the classroom more accommodating if needed. Faculty must understand the impact of disabilities on a student's ability to learn, access resources, and navigate requirements. By understanding how a student interacts with and absorbs information, faculty will gain a greater appreciation for accommodations and UDL.

Communication

Faculty should work on creating ways to personally communicate with students individually and in a group (Moorefield-Lang et al., 2016), not only through lectures but by building relationships with their students (Terras et al., 2015). A course can be designed to include all abilities, but without the presence of an empathetic, effective instructor, the course's efficacy can deteriorate (Lowenthal et al., 2020). Open communication and self-disclosure from instructors who convey care for the well-being and learning of students are key to helping students with disabilities learn in the classroom. Faculty should not hesitate to talk about their own struggles (Ehlinger & Ropers, 2020); it is important for faculty to introduce humanness into instruction.

Using multiple communication methods within and outside the classroom can help students with disabilities (Ehlinger & Roper, 2020). Instructors might consider how weekly video announcements give the students an overview of the course's content and provide a way for students to see and hear from them, thus building a virtual relationship. Providing non-text content like a prerecorded video with accurate closed captions and a transcript is an effective method for an announcement, lecture, or even message of encouragement during finals week. By utilizing the W3C standards, faculty can ensure they are creating content that is compliant and accessible. Additionally, establishing office hours and allowing students to schedule individual appointments is helpful, especially if students can communicate in multiple ways (Ehlinger & Roper, 2020).

It is also important to communicate information through multiple channels in the classroom. Students learn in different ways, especially when they have a disability. When students are given a variety of methods to gain information, they have a better chance for comprehension and success. For example, faculty can write assignment instructions and create an accompanying video that verbally explains the directions. They might consider creating a set of short videos for the student to consume, not allowing any video to exceed five minutes (Tobin, 2014). This not only helps with attention; it can also aid in breaking the material down into easy-to-find and consumable sections. In comparison, receiving a lot of information all at once or having to find where the information is located can prove frustrating when people do not have a diagnosed disability and becomes even more difficult with various disabilities.

Social Presence

Instructors should work on their social presence before day one in an online classroom. Syllabi should use language that is inclusive to all learners and backgrounds (Lowenthal et al., 2020). This creates an inviting environment where students feel safe and seen. Faculty can also contact each student individually through email or a short five-minute phone or video conference appointment (Ehlinger & Roper, 2020; Lowenthal et al., 2020). In this introductory meeting, faculty can get to know the student and ask about any special needs, accommodations, or learning styles the student prefers. Through this initial interaction, faculty can begin to validate the identity of students who might have disabilities and encourage them to bring their perspectives (Ehlinger & Roper, 2020), while also understanding a student might not want their disability to be a big part of their identity (Hong, 2015). The faculty can then tailor their further interactions with the student based on this information and include resources that represent the varied identities within the classroom (Ehlinger & Roper, 2020).

Collaboration

Faculty are not the only people who must work on their relationship with students. It is important that academic advisors also understand the student, their disability, and its impact. Academic advisors can be advocates for students and help them find resources and understand the processes. Students who do not seek out their advisors tend to have a harder time understanding the impact of their disability on their studies (Hong, 2015). Creating open communication between the student, advisor, and faculty develops an environment where the student's needs are met. Building a strong relationship from the start of the student's educational experience can help to reduce their stress load throughout their studies.

Being reluctant to change teaching methods and adapt can be a barrier to learning (Lipka et al., 2019). Faculty must be open to hearing from students and making adjustments (Moorefield-Lang et al., 2016). An inclusive classroom is one that is open to change and adaptive. Although faculty want to provide a perfect classroom that is completely inclusive, they might overlook something. Hong (2015) explains that when faculty build relationships with students and are open to hearing about their roadblocks, the classroom overall can improve. It is important that students do not feel they are a burden (Hong, 2015), but that faculty welcome feedback and communication. This process can be hard work and overwhelming; however, faculty must understand how an inaccessible classroom impacts their students and support their students with disabilities by ensuring they have access to the same education as their peers. Making all aspects of the online classroom including the course shell, time allowances, videos, reading materials, and websites available and usable to each student can help to remove barriers to those who might have a disability.

Faculty might consider asking students at the start (Ehlinger & Roper, 2020; Moorfield-Lang et al., 2016) or the end of the course what they need from the classroom and adjust accordingly (Moorefield-Lang et al., 2016). Sharing resources or helping students to find resources that are needed can reduce the struggle for students with disabilities (Ehlinger & Ropers, 2020). Being proactive at the beginning of class can help put people at ease. When faculty show they care, want feedback, and will make accommodations, students might feel comfortable speaking up about their needs. Providing a solid relationship can increase the likelihood that students will voice their needs, better ensuring their success in class.

FUTURE RESEARCH

As technology continues to develop and online learning becomes more popular and available, higher education faculty must continue to understand how they can improve their classroom to make it accessible to all. Future research should include program development and evaluation about how to train faculty beyond accessibility awareness. Research and training must focus on how faculty can create a universally accessible classroom with easy-to-use tools, develop relationships with students that enhance learning opportunities and accessibility, and understand the needs of the students that have yet to be addressed. This is especially important because many faculty state that what they know about ADA they learned from their own formal education for their degree (Stevens et al., 2018). Many programs do not teach ADA-compliant education, so it is important faculty learn about it elsewhere.

CONCLUSION

While it may seem overwhelming to consider all the aspects of ADA compliance and accessibility in an online classroom, awareness is the critical first step. By learning how to take these steps to implement changes, faculty can work toward creating online classrooms that are more compliant and meet the needs of all learners. This is not a one-time process and may require ongoing updating and testing to ensure the course continues to meet accessibility and compliance requirements. Implementing UDL guidelines can be a good starting point to create an accessible course. Other recommendations involve adding descriptive headers and titles for assistive technologies, including transcripts and closed captions for video and audio, writing alt-text for non-textual materials such as images and graphics, and paying attention to the color scheme of graphics and text (Betts, 2013; Betts et al., 2013; She & Martin, 2022). Finally, a supportive learning environment that fosters learning through relationship building between students and faculty will help students feel comfortable to reach out for help or with questions.

Points to remember:

- Accessibility standards: guidelines that apply to providing accommodations of access.
- Assistive technology: a term that relates to software, programming, or devices that help individuals with disabilities participate more independently (i.e., screen reader).
- Universal Design for Learning: use this model as a guide to create a more inclusive environment for all learners and consider the physical and sensory needs of all users in the design process.
- Need for training and development on online accessibility: collaborate with your disability services department to provide training.

REFERENCES

ADA Amendments Act of 2008, H.R.3195 - 110th Congress (2007-2008). (2008, June 27). https://www.congress.gov/bill/110th-congress/house-bill/3195/text

ADA.gov. (2022, March 18). *Guidance on web accessibility and the ADA.* https://www.ada.gov/resources/web-guidance/

Barnard-Brak, L., & Sulak, T. (2012). The relationship of institutional distance education goals and students requests for accommodations. *Journal of Postsecondary Education and Disability, 25*(1), 5–19.

Barnard-Brak, L., Sulak, T., Tate, A., & Lechtenberger, D. (2010). Measuring college students' attitudes toward requesting accommodations: A national multi-institutional study. *Assessment for Effective Intervention, 35*(3), 141–147. doi:10.1177/1534508409358900

Betts, K. (2013). National perspective: Q&A with national federation of the blind & association of Higher education and disability. *Online Learning : the Official Journal of the Online Learning Consortium, 17*(3). Advance online publication. doi:10.24059/olj.v17i3.379

Betts, K., Welsh, B., Pruitt, C., Hermann, K., Dietrich, G., Trevino, J. G., ... Coombs, N. (2013b). Understanding disabilities & online student success. *Online Learning : the Official Journal of the Online Learning Consortium, 17*(3), 15–48. doi:10.24059/olj.v17i3.388

Bureau of Labor Statistics. (2019, October 29). *Employment characteristics of people with a disability in 2018.* https://www.bls.gov/opub/ted/2019/employment-characteristics-of-people-with-a-disability-in-2018.htm

Burke, D. D., Clapper, D., & McRae, D. (2016). Accessible online instruction for students with disabilities: Federal imperatives and the challenge of compliance. *Journal of Law & Education, 45*(2), 135–180.

CAST. (2018). *Universal Design for Learning guidelines version 2.2.* http://udlguidelines.cast.org

CAST. (2023). *About Universal Design for Learning.* https://www.cast.org/impact/universal-design-for-learning-udl

Center for Universal Design. (1997). *Center for Universal Design.* North Carolina State University. https://design.ncsu.edu/research/center-for-universal-design/

Cory, R. C. (2011). Disability services offices for students with disabilities: A campus resource. *New Directions for Higher Education, 154*(154), 27–36. doi:10.1002/he.431

Edwards, M., Poed, S., Al-Nawab, H., & Penna, O. (2022). Academic accommodations for university students living with disability and the potential of universal design to address their needs. *Higher Education, 84*(4), 779–799. doi:10.100710734-021-00800-w PMID:35079174

Ehlinger, E., & Ropers, R. (2020). "It's all about learning as as community": Facilitating the learning of students with disabilities in higher education classrooms. *Journal of College Student Development, 61*(3), 333–349. doi:10.1353/csd.2020.0031

Evans, N. J., Broido, E. M., Brown, K. R., Wilke, A. K., & Herriott, T. K. (2017). *Disability in higher education: A social justice approach.* John Wiley & Sons, Incorporated.

Guilbaud, T. C., Marin, F., & Newton, X. (2021). Faculty perception on accessibility in online learning: Knowledge, practice and professional development. *Online Learning : the Official Journal of the Online Learning Consortium, 25*(12), 6–35. doi:10.24059/olj.v25i2.2233

Helvacioglu, E., & Karamanoglu, N. N. (2012). Awareness of the concept of universal design in design education. *Procedia: Social and Behavioral Sciences, 51*, 99–103. doi:10.1016/j.sbspro.2012.08.125

Hong, B. (2015). Qualitative analysis of barriers college students with disabilities experience in higher education. *Journal of College Student Development, 56*(3), 209–226. doi:10.1353/csd.2015.0032

Hsiao, F., Burgstahler, S., Johnson, T., Nuss, D., & Doherty, M. (2019). Promoting an accessible learning environment for students with disabilities via faculty development. *Journal of Postsecondary Education and Disability, 32*(1), 91–99.

Huss, J. A., & Eastep, S. (2016). Okay, our courses are online, but are they ADA compliant? An investigation of faculty awareness of accessibility at a Midwestern university. *Inquiry in Education, 8*(2). https://eric.ed.gov/?id=EJ1171774

Izzo, M. V., & Horne, L. R. (2016). *Empowering students with hidden disabilities: A path to pride and success*. Brookes Publishing.

King, C., & Piotrowski, C. (2021). Navigating the ADA accessibility requirements and legal pitfalls in online education. *College Student Journal, 55*(2), 127–134.

Kourea, L., Christodoulidou, P., & Fella, A. (2021). Voices of undergraduate students with disabilities during the COVID-19 pandemic: A pilot study. *European Journal of Psychology Open, 80*(3), 111–124. doi:10.1024/2673-8627/a000011

Lipka, O., Khouri, M., & Shecter-Lerner, M. (2019). University faculty attitudes and knowledge about learning disabilities. *Higher Education Research & Development*, 1–15. doi:10.1080/07294360.2019.1695750

Lowenthal, P. R., Humphrey, M., Conley, Q., Dunlap, J. C., Greear, K., Lowenthal, A., & Giacumo, L. A. (2020). Creating accessible and inclusive online learning: Moving beyond compliance and broadening the discussion. *Quarterly Review of Distance Education, 21*(2), 1–21.

Moorfield-Lang, H., Copeland, C. A., & Haynes, A. (2016). Accessing abilities: Creating innovative accessible online learning environments and putting quality into practice. *Education for Information, 32*(1), 27–33. doi:10.3233/EFI-150966

Moriña, A. (2019). The keys to learning for university students with disabilities: Motivation, emotion and faculty-student relationships. *PLoS One, 14*(5), e0215249. doi:10.1371/journal.pone.0215249 PMID:31116748

National Center for Education Statistics. (2018, May). *Digest of education statistics*. https://nces.ed.gov/programs/digest/d20/tables/dt20_311.10.asp

National Center for Education Statistics. (2022, April 26). *A majority of college students with disabilities do not inform school, new NCES data shows*. https://nces.ed.gov/whatsnew/press_releases/4_26_2022.asp

National Center for Education Statistics. (n.d.). *Beginning postsecondary students: 2012/2017 (BPS)*. https://nces.ed.gov/datalab/powerstats/71-beginning-postsecondary-students-2012-2017 /percentage-distribution

She, L., & Martin, F. (2022). Systematic review (2000 to 2021) of online accessibility research in higher education. *American Journal of Distance Education, 36*(4), 327–346. doi:10.1080/08923647.2022.2081438

Sniatecki, J. L., Perry, H. B., & Snell, L. H. (2015). Faculty attitudes and knowledge regarding college students with disabilities. *Journal of Postsecondary Education and Disability, 28*(3), 259–275.

Stevens, C. M., Schneider, E., & Bederman-Miller, P. (2018). Identifying faculty perceptions of awareness and preparedness relating to ADA compliance at a small, private college in NE PA. *American Journal of Business Education, 11*(2), 27–40. doi:10.19030/ajbe.v11i2.10142

Terras, K., Phillips, A., & Leggio, J. (2015). Disability accommodations in online courses: The graduate student experience. *Journal of Postsecondary Education and Disability, 28*(3), 329–340.

Tobin. (2014). Increase online student retention with universal design for learning. *The Quarterly Review of Distance Education, 15*(3), 13-24.

U.S. Department of Health and Human Services. (2006, June). *Your Rights Under Section 504 of the Rehabilitation Act (H-8/June 2000 – revised June 2006 - English)*. https://www.hhs.gov/sites/default/files/ocr/civilrights/resources/factsheets/504.pdf

U.S. Department of Health and Human Services. (n.d.). *Introduction to Section 508 Compliance and Accessibility*. https://www.hhs.gov/sites/default/files/Intro%20to%20Accessibility%20and%20508.pdf

W3C. (2017, April 12). *Tips and tricks*. https://www.w3.org/WAI/tutorials/images/tips/

W3C. (2018, June 5). *Web Content Accessibility Guidelines (WCAG) 2.1*. https://www.w3.org/TR/WCAG21/

W3C. (2022, January 17). *Complex images*. https://www.w3.org/WAI/tutorials/images/complex/

KEY TERMS AND DEFINITIONS

Accessibility: Being able to easily obtain or use.
ADA: Americans with Disabilities Act, which prohibits discrimination based on disability in school, work, and all other public areas.
Assistive Technology: Anything used to increase the accessibility of learning resources.
Compliance: Being in line with guidelines.
Disability: Impairment or lack of functioning related to a physical or mental ability.
Relationship: A state of being connected.
Universal Design for Learning: "A framework to improve and optimize teaching and learning for all people based on scientific insights into how humans learn" (CAST, 2023, para 1).

Websites and Resources

The following is a list of helpful websites and resources. This is not an exhaustive list but a starting point.

Accessibility Bookmarklets: Website that highlights accessibility features of webpages https://accessibility-bookmarklets.org/

Accessible Rich Internet Applications (ARIA): A W3C specification that provides a way to make dynamic web applications and advanced user interface controls more accessible to people with disabilities https://www.w3.org/WAI/standards-guidelines/aria/

Accessibility Requirements Tool (ART): Step-by-step guide to identify accessibility requirements from the 508 standards https://www.section508.gov/art/#/

Accessible Technology Resource List: A collection of accessible technology resources developed by the University of Washington https://www.washington.edu/doit/resources/popular-resource-collections/accessible-technology

Apple Accessibility Web Page: Guide to accessibility options on Apple products http://www.apple.com/accessibility/ios/#vision

Contrast Checker Resources: Resources to check the color contrast https://webaim.org/resources/contrastchecker/

https://www.tpgi.com/color-contrast-checker/

Disabled World: List of Invisible Disabilities: Comprehensive list of invisible disabilities https://www.disabled-world.com/disability/types/invisible/

Information Technology Industry Council: https://www.itic.org/public-policy/accessibility

Tech Republic's Accessibility Information on the Android 4.0: Guide to accessibility options on Android smartphones https://www.techrepublic.com/blog/smartphones/android-accessibility-options-for-vision-and-hearing- impaired

Types of Motor Disabilities: List of motor disabilities https://webaim.org/articles/motor/motordisabilities

Universal Design for Learning (UDL) Guidelines: Website which provides guidelines and recommendations for creating UDL https://udlguidelines.cast.org/

Working Together: Computers and People with Sensory Impairments: Information on sensory impairments https://www.washington.edu/doit/Brochures/Technology/wtsense.html

W3C website: World Wide Web Consortium (W3C) website which lists the Web Content Accessibility Guidelines (WCAG) 2.1 AA https://www.w3.org/

Chapter 14
Leveraging Online Communities for Building Social Capital in University Libraries:
A Case Study of Fudan University Medical Library

Yuanjun Ni
The University of Hong Kong, Hong Kong

Apple Hiu Ching Lam
https://orcid.org/0000-0002-2587-6979
The University of Hong Kong, Hong Kong

Dickson K. W. Chiu
https://orcid.org/0000-0002-7926-9568
The University of Hong Kong, Hong Kong

ABSTRACT

This study investigates the development of social capital in university libraries using the Fudan University Medical Library (FUML) as the case. The authors first use the SWOT matrix to analyze the FUML based on librarian interviews, official websites, and previous literature. Next, they construct a social capital evaluation framework for university libraries with four dimensions (degree of user demand, level of trust, visibility, and status in users' minds). Guided by the framework, our findings indicate that FUML's user demands in recent years are optimistic, though trust, visibility, and library status vary in users' minds. Thus, they suggest some strategies to help improve patron-library relations through online communities, such as using social media, multi-online channel user feedback, and improving related employee training. This study provides insights into how university libraries can build online relations from social capital concepts. Scant studies have applied social capital to investigate the relationship between university libraries and students, especially in East Asia.

DOI: 10.4018/978-1-6684-8908-6.ch014

INTRODUCTION

The concept of social capital can be traced back to the nineteenth century as some intangible capital that could potentially contribute to future development and effective resources available to the group through building relationships (Farr, 2004; Fong et al., 2020; Leung, Chiu, et al., 2022). Libraries, as public institutions, have long been seen as producers of social capital (Goulding, 2004; T. Jiang et al., 2019; Kee et al., 2023; Zheng et al., 2023). From the perspective of community development, university libraries should undoubtedly consider how to build social capital more effectively. At the same time, the building of social capital should be anticipated for future beneficial feedback to the institutions that produce it.

However, due to recent mobile technology advancements and the general availability of electronic resources, students can access learning materials anytime, anywhere (Lau et al., 2017; 2020), and thus fewer students visit the physical library (Leung, Chiu, et al., 2022; Lu et al., 2023). Worse still, the general lockdown due to the COVID-19 pandemic has further accelerated this change (Meng et al., 2023; P. Y. Yu et al., 2023) because their information habit has significantly changed (Dai & Chiu, 2023; Yi & Chiu, 2023). Thus, libraries should develop new online strategies to reinforce their patron community, which can be effectively and systematically guided by social capital concepts (Fong et al., 2021; Kee et al., 2023).

The Fudan University Medical Library (FUML), which was selected as the case of the study, has a unique cultural heritage that evolved from the Shanghai Medical University Library in the Republic of China, combining intelligence, high professionalism, and rich resources (Q. Liu et al., 2022). It has effectively utilized resources and reduced unnecessary capital loss by establishing a cross-institutional resource-sharing consortium (Fang et al., 2017). Yet amid COVID-19 and economic austerity, FUML still needs to consider how to increase its social capital in the long run through online communities to cope with technological and user habit changes.

Unfortunately, scant studies have addressed the social capital of university libraries, particularly the relationship with online communities, which is essential for their positioning and mission amid the health crisis, especially in East Asia. Thus, this study investigated how university libraries can build social capital for long-term development in the post-COVID era. Through a literature review, we first established a social capital evaluation framework with four dimensions. Next, we analyzed FUML using the SWOT matrix to classify the results into our 4-dimensional university library social capital assessment framework to diagnose FUML in building social capital. Based on the problems revealed, we suggested some online and other associated strategies to improve FUML's deficiencies in building social capital.

LITERATURE REVIEW

Social capital

The definition of social capital has been well-discussed continuously since the 1980s. Mark Granovetter (1985) suggests that social behavior, including economic behavior, is influenced by social relations, and James S. Coleman (1988) refers to the binding effect of social capital on responsibility and obligation in his theoretical system.

The period from 2000 to 2005 was a significant period in which many theories defining social capital were proposed. Robert D. Putnam's (1995) concept of social capital demonstrates a more understandable system of social capital theory based on social networks that include trust and mutual benefits. From the relationship between the measurement system and the theory, the question of how to measure social capital has become new.

In addition to social capital in a broad sense, organizational density (VO) in Putnam's theory has been analyzed as a more practical way to measure the system, which fits the perception of general trust derived from public opinion surveys. In this approach, social capital is the resources available to people in social networks or trust networks (Paldam, 2000). By this stage, the definition of social capital began to emerge. However, it is questionable whether social capital belongs to the category of physical capital. The transformative capacity, persistence, substitutability, decay, reliability, ability to invest and divest, and ability to create other forms of capital that physical capital cannot fully explain the state of social capital or its utility. Thus, empathy is proposed as a behavioral motivation and can be used to explain the difference between social capital and physical capital (Robison et al., 2002).

The collision of ideas among the various schools of thought during the five years (2000-2005) provided a comprehensive perspective for later studies. However, many new voices still emerged from 2005 to 2010. Although these voices proceeded based on the conclusions of their predecessors, they still innovated in critiquing the argumentative gaps referred to in classical theories. Social homogeneity (people's subconscious tendency to develop friendships with people like them) has influenced empirical research on the effects of social capital variables (Mouw, 2006). Mouw (2006) suggests that although individual factors (differences in individual interests) can cause biased results, findings can be enhanced by critically examining causality issues. Research methods in other disciplines that address social capital may provide a reference for subsequent researchers.

The social capital structure's composite and complex nature provides a venue for interdisciplinary research. Weather as a variable proposed in the study of Mexican immigrant employment (Munshi, 2003) is an innovative use of existing data to study social capital. Interdisciplinary research has likewise been applied to the intersection of mental health and social capital. The focus is on whether the evidence has undergone rigorous evaluation and analysis and whether the evidence applies to the mental health field (Almedom, 2005).

In the 2010s, the trend of interdisciplinary research became more prominent. The impact of media technology on social capital (Campante et al., 2022) highlights that the use of social capital is not necessarily benign. The cross-national ability of social capital and race relations has been proposed in studies on micro-multinational companies (Prashantham, 2010). Cross-agency programs for providing individualized practice for children can also develop networks of stakeholder trust from the perspective of social capital cohesion (McKean et al., 2016). When social capital was studied as an important measure of sustainable communities, results indicated the more sustainable the community, the higher the level of social capital (Rogers et al., 2012).

In summary, social capital is an available resource based on trust networks and social relationships generated by maintaining stakeholder relationships. It originates from and can benefit social activities and is a crucial topic for organizational, group, and community research.

Social Capital and Libraries

Even though the direction of causality is unclear, there is a strong association between public library use and higher levels of social capital (Johnson, 2010). Libraries can be seen as a tool for creating social capital for society (Kee et al., 2023; Vårheim, 2007). The way libraries build social capital is related to the ability to create shared public spaces that meet the requirements of various groups and enhance social interaction and trust (Hillenbrand, 2005; Leung, Chiu, et al., 2022). Although the share of different ways in which libraries generate social trust is difficult to measure (Vårheim et al., 2008), libraries can help change the quality of life in local communities from the perspective of serving as meeting places and providing universal services (Wojciechowska, 2021).

Research on the relationship between libraries and social capital has gradually shifted from the macro to the micro level. Individuals in libraries (people, organizations, functions) became the research subject. For example, for the level of personal social capital, social networks, social status, and trust in other staff in public libraries, a 2018 study was conducted for librarians in 20 different countries (Wojciechowska, 2019). The survey showed that public librarians tend to trust others more than other librarians, which can give insights to library administrators. For example, administrators can use the more approachable nature of public librarians to arrange more social activities to build links between librarians and people in the community, thus increasing social capital for the community and public librarians. The reason is that although public librarians are prone to trust others, they are mostly passive and closed-minded about socializing, which leads to lower personal social capital for public librarians (Wojciechowska & Topolska, 2021). On the contrary, Kee et al. (2023) found major US public libraries actively building social capital to enhance their services.

University libraries, libraries, and learning commons can serve as places to build social capital (M. K. Y. Chan et al., 2020; Deng et al., 2019; Leung, Chiu, et al., 2022; Zhou et al., 2022). Also, some studies have shown that the frequency of library visits is positively correlated with the perception of meetings to some extent (Leung, Chiu, et al., 2022). This suggests that although university libraries do not reach as broad an audience as public libraries, they also have the potential to serve as social asset generators (Leung, Chiu, et al., 2022).

Online Social Capital for Libraries

The recent COVID-19 outbreak has harmed libraries and many other cultural organizations (Chiu & Ho, 2022b, 2022c; Huang et al., 2021, 2022, 2023). Many organizations had to stop opening their venues (Meng et al., 2023; P.Y. Yu et al., 2023). Thus, people have changed their information and learning consumption habits to electronic and online resources, particularly led by the trend of the younger generation (Chan & Chiu, 2022; A. W. Y. Chan et al., 2022; Chiu & Wong, 2023; Dai & Chiu, 2023; Guo et al., 2022; Sung & Chiu, 2022; Wai et al., 2018; Yi et al., 2023; H. Y. Yu et al., 2022; X. Zhang et al., 2021). However, the outbreak has accelerated the rethinking of services and the transformation of online and intelligent information services (V. H. Y. Chan et al., 2022; W. Cheng et al., 2023; Chin & Chiu, 2023; Q. Li et al., 2023; S. M. Li et al., 2023; Lin et al., 2022; Lo, Allard, Anghelescu, et al., 2020; Tsang & Chiu, 2022; A. K.-k. Wong & Chiu, 2023; Wu et al., 2023; Xue et al., 2023), especially supported by ubiquitous mobile Internet services, apps, and devices (Dukic et al., 2015; Ezeamuzie et al., 2023; Fan et al., 2020; Fung et al., 2016; Gong et al., 2017; Hui et al., 2023; K. P. Lau et al., 2017; K. S. N. Lau et al., 2020; Law et al., 2019; Ni et al., 2022; Yip et al., 2021).

The richness and high quality of digital library services give them the potential to make a remarkable impact in the future (Ding et al., 2021; Lo & Chiu, 2015; Lo et al., 2015, 2017; Mehta & Wang, 2020; Suen et al., 2020; Sun et al., 2022; P. Wang et al., 2016; K. C. Wong & Chiu, 2023; Zuo et al., 2023). The closed environment and the unfolding of online work have increased the demands for online library services and learning (Y. Liu, Lei, et al., 2023; Tse et al., 2022; P.K. Yu et al., 2023). A study of the experiences of Australian public librarians working during the epidemic showed that a significant proportion of the demand for offline services came from the need to use document printing equipment to prepare materials for relief claims (Garner et al., 2022). The study also showed that librarians took on more responsibility and workload during the pandemic. Further, libraries should focus on balancing their staff's well-being and stress.

Libraries have gradually adopted social media to maintain a social presence for building online social capital, besides being widely adopted for promotion and learning aids (K.-y. Cheung et al., 2023, Chung et al., 2020; Fong et al., 2020; K. K. W. Ho et al., 2018; M. Jiang et al., 2023; A. H. C. Lam et al., 2023; E. T. H. Lam et al., 2019; Lei et al., 2021; Leung, Hui, et al., 2023; S. Li, Xie, et al., 2023; Y. Liu, Chiu, & Ho, 2023; Lo et al., 2013; Mak et al., 2022; Xie, Chiu, & Ho, 2023; Xie, Wong, et al., 2023; W. Wang et al., 2021; Yang et al., 2022), especially during the COVID-19 outbreak. A comparative study of two public libraries in Claudia (low digitization) and Singapore (digitization) (Sabolović-Krajina, 2021) also points out the importance of digitization and technology for the development of libraries.

Literature Gap and Methodology

Despite the increased related studies in the last two decades, social capital studies have not received enough attention in China. The results of the literary analysis of all articles titled "social capital" in the Chinese Social Sciences Citation Index (CSSCI) using Citespace indicate that the centrality of keywords and the linkage between keywords is low. Most studies on social capital in China occurred from 2000 to 2005, being a valuable research gap for this study to fill.

While libraries have been the subject of building online social capital, there has been little corresponding research on the impact of social resources on libraries, particularly for university libraries in East Asia. There is insufficient literature on how libraries obtain sufficient financial and social support to provide sound services meeting user requirements and preferences in East Asia. As public service institutions, libraries sometimes carry heavier expectations and responsibilities than commercial institutions. Neglecting may result in losing talent, atrophy, and the organization's demise.

University libraries are particularly limited in their social groups but need more professional librarians, more communication and learning, and more frequent information updates (W. W. H. Cheng et al., 2020 A. H. C. Lam et al., 2023; E. T. H. Lam et al., 2019), especially through online with the advent of the Internet. With many more expensive collections (e.g., academic databases and journal subscriptions) than public libraries, they may face a greater crisis due to financial constraints. Very few studies show how university libraries benefit from the network of online social capital, building and managing relationships with online communities at a lower cost. To study this case, we first collect information regarding FUML from librarian interviews (e.g., Q. Liu et al. (2022)), official websites, and previous literature (e.g., Fang et al. (2017)) and perform a SWOT analysis of FUML on the general level, followed by a 4-dimensional university social capital assessment, before providing our suggestions to enhance their online social capital building.

SWOT ANALYSIS OF FUML

Strengths

A rich community of resources. FUML has cooperated with several libraries. The inter-university lending platform of Shanghai University Library gives it more opportunities to communicate with quality universities. These are more relevant as an online community because resources are mainly shared electronically (Sun et al., 2022).

Professional staff and internal training system. Most librarians of FUML are multi-disciplinary talents with professional subjects and librarianship knowledge. Their strong academic backgrounds make them more trusted by patrons. The library provides regular training for the staff to consolidate the professional standard and enhance the communication of the internal network.

State-of-the-art equipment and scientific arrangement. Extensive organizational and operation experience has made the library's resources more available online and increased the library's audience. Collection management with artificial intelligence has reduced the onsite storage space required, and more interactive spaces, such as reading rooms and VR (Virtual Reality) spaces, can be used for developing social capital (Chiu & Wong, 2023).

Weaknesses

User limitations of university libraries. The user base of FUML is restricted to campus members and scholars and is not open to the large potential public user base. Thus, social visibility is much less than that of public libraries.

Staff shortage. Many FUML programs require specialized subject librarians for analytical services and information research. Staffing shortages may hinder reference services required by research projects and student learning. As these are crucial activities for the whole university, staffing shortages will likely affect FUML's social activities and community engagement.

Inadequate information literacy and promotion. Many library resources and functions are unknown to students and faculty, hindering them from efficiently and wisely using these services. Thus, many resources that can be used more efficiently and effectively are neglected and become a maintenance burden.

Opportunities

FUML's geographical advantages. Fudan University is located in Shanghai, a fast-growing, well-connected metropolis. The faster information flow and numerous channels mean the latest important information is available earlier. High-quality online information resources also help attract users to build the library's online social capital, even if they do not visit the library physically.

FUML's public reputation. Fudan University School of Medicine is one of the top medical schools in China and has a high reputation. The bonds of trust formed from respect for knowledge and prestige provide the foundation for building social capital. The school has provided numerous local hospitals in Shanghai with many talented medical professionals. The strong network of relationships between the hospital and the community can potentially become a source of social capital building. Thus, FUML serves as a platform for providing online information to these medical professionals in various medical institutions and can fully utilize these social relationships, especially when more online services are provided.

Threats

Epidemic policy and fear of COVID-19. China is now reopening from the COVID-19 pandemic, and local policies have been adjusted to better suit urban development and the normal movement of people (Yi & Chiu, 2023). However, the high infectiousness of the Omicron variation (Ledford, 2021) has caused widespread infection outbreaks. Users become more reluctant to leave their homes to visit the library, hindering social capacity building (Lu et al., 2023) and thus rendering online communities an opportunity.

Lack of professional acceptance. Library and other information professions generally lack social acceptance, especially in East Asia (Li & Chiu, 2022; Ng et al., 2022; Yew et al., 2022). As a result, the work of librarians is not sufficiently valued. Lack of understanding by users sometimes has an impact on staff motivation.

Pressure on information services demands from hospitals and medical schools. The library's opening strategy of limiting visitors during COVID-19 has increased the pressure on the library to serve accordingly, regardless of the increased demand reduction from users (as they are medical professionals and students). COVID-19 has increased the burden on hospitals and pushed various research institutions to conduct relevant medical research, thus increasing the demand for online information services. Yet, with the disrupted access, library staff are burdened with heavier responsibilities and more difficulties in work because remote and online reference services are often less effective than face-to-face ones (Guo et al., 2022; Tsang & Chiu, 2022).

4-DIMENSIONAL LIBRARY SOCIAL CAPITAL ASSESSMENT

The social capital created in the library's operation should circulate and flow to the library itself. In other words, in exploring the social capital assessment system, whether the criteria are appropriate per the developability of the library itself needs to be considered. From the review of the concept of social capital above, for libraries, the expansion of social capital can be proposed as these four main dimensions (Table 1): the volume of public equipment, services, and public spaces available for effective use (VP); the level of trust between individuals (LT); the number of visits by registered users (students and staffs for academic libraries) and visitors (NV); and the extent to which users are proactive in providing feedback on the service (PF). The types of social capital corresponding to the criteria of these four dimensions cater to the trend of developing smart libraries and socializing university libraries. We then analyze FUML using the SWOT matrix analysis method and compare the library's performance on VP, LT, NV, and PF to reveal FUML's problem in building social capital for some pragmatic solutions.

Table 1. Proposed 4-dimensional social capital assessment framework

Dimension	Content	Types of Social Capital
VP	Volume of effective public facilities	The degree of user demand
LT	Level of trust between individual users	Level of trust
NV	Number of visits by registered users and visitors	Visibility
PF	The extent to which users are proactive in providing feedback on the service	Status in people's minds

VP: The Degree of User Demand

To facilitate LT, NV, and PF, the equipment and services of a library should be in constant use. The amount of equipment and spaces available for effective use can provide an assessment dimension for evaluation. The usage status of the equipment and services can also indicate the level of knowledge of the library's visiting community about the basic functions and the tendency to use them to satisfy user needs.

The COVID-19 pandemic has catalyzed medical research in which the library was not actively involved. According to the CSSCI index, FUML's published articles have increased from zero before the pandemic to around 250 yearly in recent years. Thus, the demand for medical professional information services has also increased much during this period. Yet, undergraduate students' connections need improvement. Although FUML has been designed with "the library as place" concept with rich reading and study rooms providing space and facilities for exchange and discussions (Q. Liu et al., 2022; Zheng et al., 2023), lockdowns during COVID-19 have greatly affected the usage. With the reopening and recovery after COVID-19, the situation of FUML on VP is currently optimistic. Because user demand and preferences have changed during and after COVID-19, providing more online services should be the main strategy to facilitate the building of online academic communities (H. Y. Yu et al., 2023).

LT: Level of Trust

Users can establish a basic level of trust by receiving satisfactory services to build an impression of the library in their minds (V. H. Y. Chan et al., 2022; Chiu et al., 2009). Bonding social capital is social capital that occurs between individuals closely related (Ellison et al., 2007). Trusting relationships between library users are positively correlated with this social capital to some extent. Becoming a bond that deepens social relationships among users may be seen as another way for libraries to create social capital.

FUML has professional librarians who can provide quality academic information services. Most of their efforts target faculties and researchers and successfully build trust. Yet, the development of trust with students was much affected during the COVID-19 lockdowns. After COVID-19, with the full reopening of the facilities, more efforts can be spent on developing students' trust. On the other hand, online communities of learning and practice can facilitate building online social capital, satisfying next-generation students' changed demands after COVID-19.

NV: Visibility

The number of visits by registered users represents the extent to which professional information services are used. That is, when viewed as a tool for delivering information, whether the library itself is the most accessible and familiar option for the user. Meanwhile, the number of visits by non-registered users represents the visibility of a library outside the regular patron groups. That is, whether the circle of influence of a library can be further extended beyond the library's core community. Thus, online communities can extend visibility through service utilization and user interactions anytime, anywhere (Lei et al., 2021).

Fudan University School of Medicine has a high reputation locally (in Shanghai) and throughout China. The concept of *face* is a prominent feature of human relations in China (L. Li et al., 2023; Wu & Cheng, 2019), and people tend to chase after what is famous and looks gorgeous. FUML is attractive to scholars as a famous public institution providing medical information services. Yet, similar to many famous universities in East Asia, the inadequate publicity and the official website of FUML, including online, may not help attract more attention required for building social capital (W. W. H. Cheng et al., 2020; Fong et al., 2020; E. T. H. Lam et al., 2019), especially online social capital. The status of FUML on NV can be further enhanced with online communities, which can also overcome some of its barriers to non-medical and non-university visitors.

PF: Status in People's Minds

The extent to which users are proactive in providing feedback on the service is an essential measure of user attention to the organization (Guo et al., 2022; A. H. C. Lam et al., 2023; E. T. H. Lam et al., 2019). That is, whether users care enough about the organization and are willing to point out service shortcomings for improvement. PF can also serve as a reflection of user stickiness. As a place where a small group of people accesses information services, user stickiness in university libraries can represent the quality of FUML's services among the same type of institutions visited by that group (Lien et al., 2017) with the status of FUML in people's minds. Thus, online communities can enhance stickiness to facilitate user services and communication anytime, anywhere.

According to an interview with FUML's Director (Q. Liu et al., 2022), patrons generally have good impressions of FUML. Yet, continuous user research and feedback collection are essential for sustainability and long-term planning (C. Y. Ho et al., 2022; H. H. K. Yu et al., 2023).

SUGGESTIONS

Using Social Media

Library administrators are suggested to create more user-oriented forums by building real-name social platforms for research (Yang et al., 2022) or through existing social media sites, especially international ones (e.g., ResearchGate). People tend to develop trust in peers on reliable platforms that meet their needs (Chiu et al., 2019; Dunning et al., 2019). When recurring scientific themes, scholarship, or updates become the focus of communication, participants with common interests tend to increase intra-group cohesion in expressing their opinions (Hirvonen, 2022), which is essential for developing connections. Platforms oriented towards, but not limited to, fixed groups, constructed by voicing out, can increase intra-group trust, thus also increasing online social capital. However, librarians and administrators should lead in promoting services and communications and actively communicate with users to understand and respond to their needs (Guo et al., 2022; A. H. C. Lam et al., 2023).

Social media has been utilized by numerous research institutes, government agencies, and major universities as a successful medium for conveying influence (Au et al., 2021; Ho et al., 2022). The use of social media for academic communication is even becoming a trend (Dong et al., 2021; Sobaih et al., 2020; Yang et al., 2022).

As part of a university, FUML is an excellent knowledge provider. Regarding strategies for knowledge transfer, university libraries should also reflect the academic institution's broader goals and unique characteristics to the public through social media (Giuri et al., 2019) and lead its online communities through proactive participation (Fong et al., 2020; A. H. C. Lam et al., 2023). The content should consider a wider audience each time, using more non-specialist terms to convey their outstanding medical research results and give health advice to the (K. K. W. Ho et al., 2023; C. Y. Ho et al., 2022; Kwan, Chan, & Chiu, 2023), forming a community of practice (X. Jiang et al., 2023; Lei et al., 2021; Mak et al., 2023). If FUML wants to increase its visibility and reach people in non-academic circles, it needs to cater to the social media usage habits of a wide range of people and their knowledge preferences (S. Li, Chiu, et al., 2023; S. Li, Xie, et al., 2023; S. M. Li et al., 2023).

Stimulating Academic Knowledge Exchanges Through Online Communities

Much of the disconnect between faculties and students stems from social status and the restraints imposed by evaluative authority. To address this issue, university libraries may utilize their status as knowledge providers to bridge different stakeholders in the university through social media to connect and communicate, thus building social capital in the online community (Fong et al., 2020).

University libraries can analyze the hotness of topics and users' views on these topics based on data about the frequency of users' search terms and comment threads, together with relevant bibliometric studies collaborating with faculties and students (Chiu & Ho, 2022a, 2023). They can also develop an online community to discuss divergent topics and research trends (Yang et al., 2022) and encourage users to participate. The online community may also allow users to post anonymously to avoid the restrictions imposed by identity and social roles. Such an online community can provide further information for user sentiment and other social media analytics (Deng & Chiu, 2023; S. Li, Xie, et al., 2023; Y. Liu, Chiu, & Ho, 2023;).

Multi-Online-Channel User Feedback

When people use mobile devices (laptops, cell phones, etc.), they often do not have the patience to write detailed comments and complete questionnaires (Guo et al., 2022; A. H. C. Lam et al., 2023; Tsang & Chiu, 2022). Rating invitations may render annoying messages, especially when patrons come to the library to study and find answers in silence. Thus, FUML can get user feedback in various ways to improve its services and build trust, especially through online communities.

First, FUML should enhance its internal forums on social media to attract more patrons to participate and form online communities by providing more attractive and useful content and responding timely (V. H. Y. Chan et al., 2022; W. W. H. Cheng et al., 2020; Fong et al., 2020). In particular, the younger generation prefers videos and infographics to text content (W. Cheng et al., 2023; V. S. Y. Cheung et al.,

2023; Y. Liu, Chiu, & Ho, 2023; I. H. S. Wong et al., 2023). Thus, these forums can become gathering places for feedback discussion. The analysis of topic keywords can serve as a reference for libraries to improve their services (Deng & Chiu, 2023; He et al., 2022; J. Wang et al., 2022). Secondly, post-service feedback requests can be added to FUML's base service. For online services, especially virtual reference services (Guo et al., 2022; Tsang & Chiu, 2022), the users can be prompted with "service to be evaluated" to actively obtain feedback after the user has finished the manual consultation, information retrieval, literature checkout, room checkout, etc.

To expand the connection and offer the community's entry offline, QR codes and pressing devices can be placed at various convenient locations in the library, at the entrance of various rooms, and in corridors to collect brief feedback ratings, with links to relevant social media groups for further feedback and discussions. Besides, libraries can distribute such rating links in the online communities. Besides, this multi-channel approach can facilitate patrons to seek help and provide feedback more proactively, especially because the younger generation is more ready to share their opinions on social media (Au et al., 2022; W. Cheng et al., 2023; J. Wong et al., 2023).

User feedback is an asset to the service provider, as the user has accepted the institution's invitation. The institution can respond effectively to the user that their behavior is meaningful to create a sense of belonging (Smith et al., 2021), which can further sustain trust in the institution for building online social capital.

Employee Well-Being and Training

Librarians are valuable assets to university libraries. Libraries' service excellency requires librarians' professionalism, proficiency, and sociability due to its services' professionalism and richness and association with other institutions (Lo, Allard, Wang, & Chiu, 2020; Lo et al., 2018). Once a brain drain occurs, it may impact the library operations. Thus, FUML should provide regular incentives for staff to work diligently, such as time off, fruit and refreshments in the lounge, and staff dinners to help staff release their stress.

Besides, adequate training, especially regarding social media and other new technologies, such as the Internet of Things (Chang et al., 2018; T. Y. Cheung et al., 2021; Lin et al., 2022), VR (virtual reality) (Lo et al., 2019), and AR (augmented reality) (Suen et al., 2020), are essential to keep staff knowledgable and work effectively in the current digital age (A. W. Y. Chan et al., 2022; A. W. Y. Chan et al., 2019; Lin et al., 2022; Yip et al., 2019). Such training is also essential because librarians should provide advanced information and technology literacy to next-generation students (Hui et al., 2023; Y. Zhang et al., 2020), especially for developing online communities. Recruiting volunteers and interns from students and alums to help relief employees work and provide longer service hours (which is facilitated by the online communities for anytime, anywhere participation) can also help these community members develop a sense of belonging through their work (T. T. W. Chan et al., 2020; T. Y. Cheung et al., 2021; Guo et al., 2022; Li & Chiu, 2022; Yew et al., 2022).

CONCLUSION

This study attempted to address the lack of literature gap on university libraries and social capital, especially in Asia, by suggesting social media for sustainable social capital development. A 4-dimensional college library social capital assessment system is innovatively tailored through a literature review. In this case study, the social capital status of the four dimensions of FUML has undergone preliminary analysis. Results indicate some developmental suggestions to help FUML develop trust and social capital accordingly. The study results could give academic researchers, librarians, and policymakers of institutions, especially those with similar cases as FUML, some insights into how to build and manage connections and relationships through online communities, particularly social media.

However, this study has some limitations. Due to time and traffic control constraints during COVID-19, some conclusions requiring onsite observation and face-to-face interviews were infeasible. Besides, literature on user feedback on library services in mainland China, especially via social media, has been scarce in the last five years, implying this aspect of library research has much room for development. We are interested in exploring the previously mentioned options for building social capital: social media, academic knowledge exchange, multi-channel communication, and employee well-being and training.

REFERENCES

Almedom, A. M. (2005). Social capital and mental health: An interdisciplinary review of primary evidence. *Social Science & Medicine*, *61*(5), 943–964. doi:10.1016/j.socscimed.2004.12.025 PMID:15955397

Au, C. H., Ho, K. K. W., & Chiu, D. K. W. (2021). Does political extremity harm the ability to identify online information validity? Testing the impact of polarisation through online experiments. *Government Information Quarterly*, *38*(4), 101602. Advance online publication. doi:10.1016/j.giq.2021.101602

Au, C. H., Ho, K. K. W., & Chiu, D. K. W. (2022). Managing users' behaviors on open content crowd-sourcing platform. *Journal of Computer Information Systems*, *62*(2), 1125–1135. doi:10.1080/08874417.2021.1983487

Campante, F., Durante, R., & Tesei, A. (2022). Media and social capital. *Annual Review of Economics*, *14*(1), 69–91. doi:10.1146/annurev-economics-083121-050914

Chan, A. W. Y., Chiu, D. K. W., & Ho, K. K. W. (2022). Workforce information needs for vocational guidance system design. *International Journal of Systems and Service-Oriented Engineering*, *12*(1), 34. doi:10.4018/IJSSOE.297134

Chan, A. W. Y., Chiu, D. K. W., Ho, K. K. W., & Wang, M. (2019). Information needs of vocational training from training providers' perspectives. *International Journal of Systems and Service-Oriented Engineering*, *8*(4), 26–42. doi:10.4018/IJSSOE.2018100102

Chan, M. K. Y., Chiu, D. K. W., & Lam, E. T. H. (2020). Effectiveness of overnight learning commons: A comparative study. *Journal of Academic Librarianship*, *46*(6), 102253. Advance online publication. doi:10.1016/j.acalib.2020.102253 PMID:34173399

Chan, M. M. W., & Chiu, D. K. W. (2022). Alert driven customer relationship management in online travel agencies: Event-condition-actions rules and key performance indicators. In A. Naim & S. K. Kautish (Eds.), *Building a brand image through electronic customer relationship management* (pp. 286–303). IGI Global. doi:10.4018/978-1-6684-5386-5.ch012

Chan, T. T. W., Lam, A. H. C., & Chiu. D. K. W. (2020). From Facebook to Instagram: Exploring user engagement in an academic library. *Journal of Academic Librarianship*, *46*(6), 102229. Advance online publication. doi:10.1016/j.acalib.2020.102229 PMID:34173399

Chan, V. H. Y., Chiu, D. K. W., & Ho, K. K. W. (2022). Mediating effects on the relationship between perceived service quality and public library app loyalty during the COVID-19 era. *Journal of Retailing and Consumer Services*, *67*, 102960. Advance online publication. doi:10.1016/j.jretconser.2022.102960

Chang, V., Chiu, D. K. W., Ramachandran, M., & Li, C.-S. (2018). Internet of Things, Big Data and Complex Information Systems: Challenges, solutions and outputs from IoTBD 2016, COMPLEXIS 2016 and CLOSER 2016 selected papers and CLOSER 2015 keynote. *Future Generation Computer Systems*, *79*(3), 973–974. doi:10.1016/j.future.2017.09.013

Cheng, W., Tian, R., & Chiu, D. K. W. (2023). Travel vlogs influencing tourist decisions: Information preferences and gender differences. *Aslib Journal of Information Management*. Advance online publication. doi:10.1108/AJIM-05-2022-0261

Cheng, W. W. H., Lam, E. T. H., & Chiu, D. K. W. (2020). Social media as a platform in academic library marketing: A comparative study. *Journal of Academic Librarianship*, *46*(5), 102188. Advance online publication. doi:10.1016/j.acalib.2020.102188

Cheung, K.-y., Lam, A. H. C., & Chiu, D. K. W. (2023). Using YouTube and Facebook as German Language Learning Aids: A pilot study in Hong Kong. *German as a Foreign Language*, *2023*(1), 146–168.

Cheung, T. Y., Ye, Z., & Chiu, D. K. W. (2021). Value chain analysis of information services for the visually impaired: A case study of contemporary technological solutions. *Library Hi Tech*, *39*(2), 625–642. doi:10.1108/LHT-08-2020-0185

Cheung, V. S. Y., Lo, J. C. Y., Chiu, D. K. W., & Ho, K. K. W. (2023). Evaluating social media's communication effectiveness on travel product promotion: Facebook for college students in Hong Kong. *Information Discovery and Delivery*, *51*(1), 66–73. doi:10.1108/IDD-10-2021-0117

Chin, G. Y. L., & Chiu, D. K. W. (2023). RFID-based robotic process automation for smart museums with an alert-driven approach. In R. K. Tailor (Ed.), *Application and adoption of robotic process automation for smart cities*. IGI. Global. doi:10.4018/978-1-6684-7193-7.ch001

Chiu, D. K. W., & Ho, K. K. W. (2022a). Editorial: Special selection on bibliometrics and literature review. *Library Hi Tech*, *40*(3), 589–593. doi:10.1108/LHT-06-2022-510

Chiu, D. K. W., & Ho, K. K. W. (2022b). Editorial: Special selection on contemporary digital culture and reading. *Library Hi Tech*, *40*(5), 1204–1209. doi:10.1108/LHT-10-2022-516

Chiu, D. K. W., & Ho, K. K. W. (2022c). Editorial: 40th anniversary: Contemporary library research. *Library Hi Tech*, *40*(6), 1525–1531. doi:10.1108/LHT-12-2022-517

Chiu, D. K. W., & Ho, K. K. W. (2023). Editorial: Special selection on contemporary bibliometric analytics. *Library Hi Tech*, *41*(2), 277–286. doi:10.1108/LHT-04-2023-586

Chiu, D. K. W., Leung, H.-F., & Lam, K.-M. (2009). On the making of service recommendations: An action theory based on utility, reputation, and risk attitude. *Expert Systems with Applications*, *36*(2), 3293–3301. doi:10.1016/j.eswa.2008.01.055

Chiu, D. K. W., & Wong, S. W. S. (2023). Reevaluating remote library storage in the digital age: A comparative study. *portal*. *Portal (Baltimore, Md.)*, *23*(1), 89–109. doi:10.1353/pla.2023.0009

Chung, C., Chiu, D. K. W., Ho, K. K. W., & Au, C. H. (2020). Applying social media to environmental education: Is it more impactful than traditional media? *Information Discovery and Delivery*, *48*(4), 255–266. doi:10.1108/IDD-04-2020-0047

Coleman, J. S. (1988). Social capital in the creation of human capital. *American Journal of Sociology*, *94*, S95–S120. doi:10.1086/228943

Dai, C., & Chiu, D. K. W. (2023). Impact of COVID-19 on reading behaviors and preferences: Investigating high school students and parents with the 5E instructional model. *Library Hi Tech*, *41*(6), 1631–1657. Advance online publication. doi:10.1108/LHT-10-2022-0472

Deng, Q., Allard, B., Lo, P., Chiu, D. K. W., See-To, E. W. K., & Bao, A. Z. R. (2019). The role of the library café as a learning space: A comparative analysis of three universities. *Journal of Librarianship and Information Science*, *51*(3), 823–842. doi:10.1177/0961000617742469

Deng, S., & Chiu, D. K. W. (2023). Analyzing the Hong Kong Philharmonic Orchestra's Facebook community engagement with the Honeycomb Model. In M. Dennis & J. Halbert (Eds.), *Community engagement in the online space* (pp. 31–47). IGI. Global. doi:10.4018/978-1-6684-5190-8.ch003

Ding, S. J., Lam, E. T. H., Chiu, D. K. W., Lung, M. M., & Ho, K. K. W. (2021). Changes in reading behavior of periodicals on mobile devices: A comparative study. *Journal of Librarianship and Information Science*, *53*(2), 233–244. doi:10.1177/0961000620938119

Dong, G., Chiu, D. K. W., Huang, P.-S., Ho, K. K. W., Lung, M. M., & Geng, Y. (2021). Relationships between research supervisors and students from coursework-based Master's degrees: Information usage under social media. *Information Discovery and Delivery*, *49*(4), 319–327. doi:10.1108/IDD-08-2020-0100

Dukic, Z., Chiu, D. K. W., & Lo, P. (2015). How useful are smartphones for learning? Perceptions and practices of Library and Information Science students from Hong Kong and Japan. *Library Hi Tech*, *33*(4), 545–561. doi:10.1108/LHT-02-2015-0015

Dunning, D., Fetchenhauer, D., & Schlösser, T. (2019). Why people trust: Solved puzzles and open mysteries. *Current Directions in Psychological Science*, *28*(4), 366–371. doi:10.1177/0963721419838255

Ellison, N. B., Steinfield, C., & Lampe, C. (2007). The benefits of Facebook "Friends:" Social capital and college students' use of online social network sites. *Journal of Computer-Mediated Communication*, *12*(4), 1143–1168. doi:10.1111/j.1083-6101.2007.00367.x

Ezeamuzie, N. M., Rhim, A. H. R., Chiu, D. K. W., & Lung, M. M. (2022). (in press). Exploring gender differences in foreign domestic helpers' mobile information usage. *Library Hi Tech*. Advance online publication. doi:10.1108/LHT-07-2022-0350

Fan, K. Y. K., Lo, P., Ho, K. K. W., So, S., Chiu, D. K. W., & Ko, K. H. T. (2020). Exploring the mobile learning needs amongst performing arts students. *Information Discovery and Delivery*, *48*(2), 103–112. doi:10.1108/IDD-12-2019-0085

Fang, F., Ying, J., Chen, Y., Qiu, X., Hou, X., & Zhang, Y. (2017). Practical exploration of resource co-construction and sharing alliance of medical libraries in Fudan University. *Chinese Journal of Medical Library and Information*, *26*(6), 30–32.

Farr, J. (2004). Social capital. *Political Theory*, *32*(1), 6–33. doi:10.1177/0090591703254978

Fong, K. C. H., Au, C. H., Lam, E. T. H., & Chiu, D. K. W. (2020). Social network services for academic libraries: A study based on social capital and social proof. *Journal of Academic Librarianship*, *46*(1), 102091. Advance online publication. doi:10.1016/j.acalib.2019.102091

Fung, R. H. Y., Chiu, D. K. W., Ko, E. H. T., Ho, K. K. W., & Lo, P. (2016). Heuristic usability evaluation of University of Hong Kong Libraries' mobile website. *Journal of Academic Librarianship*, *42*(5), 581–594. doi:10.1016/j.acalib.2016.06.004

Garner, J., Wakeling, S., Hider, P., Jamali, H. R., Kennan, M. A., Mansourian, Y., & Randell-Moon, H. (2022). The lived experience of Australian public library staff during the COVID-19 library closures. *Library Management*, *43*(6/7), 427–438. doi:10.1108/LM-04-2022-0028

Giuri, P., Munari, F., Scandura, A., & Toschi, L. (2019). The strategic orientation of universities in knowledge transfer activities. *Technological Forecasting and Social Change*, *138*, 261–278. doi:10.1016/j.techfore.2018.09.030

Gong, J. Y., Schumann, F., Chiu, D. K. W., & Ho, K. K. W. (2017). Tourists' mobile information seeking behavior: An investigation on China's youth. *International Journal of Systems and Service-Oriented Engineering*, *7*(1), 58–76. doi:10.4018/IJSSOE.2017010104

Goulding, A. (2004). Libraries and social capital. *Journal of Librarianship and Information Science*, *36*(1), 3–6. doi:10.1177/0961000604042965

Granovetter, M. (1985). Economic action and social structure: The problem of Embeddedness. *American Journal of Sociology*, *91*(3), 481–510. doi:10.1086/228311

Guo, Y., Lam, A. H. C., Chiu, D. K. W., & Ho, K. K. W. (2022). Perceived quality of reference service with WhatsApp: A quantitative study from user perspectives. *Information Technology and Libraries*, *41*(3). Advance online publication. doi:10.6017/ital.v41i3.14325

He, Z., Chiu, D. K. W., & Ho, K. K. W. (2022). Weibo analysis on Chinese cultural knowledge for gaming. In Z. Sun & Z. Wu (Eds.), *Handbook of research on foundations and applications of intelligent business analytics* (pp. 320–349). IGI Global. doi:10.4018/978-1-7998-9016-4.ch015

Hillenbrand, C. (2005). A place for all: Social capital at the Mount Barker Community Library, South Australia. *Australasian Public Libraries and Information Services*, *18*(2), 41–58.

Hirvonen, N. (2022). Nameless strangers, similar others: The affordances of a young people's anonymous online forum for health information practices. *The Journal of Documentation*, *78*(7), 506–527. doi:10.1108/JD-09-2021-0192

Ho, C. Y., Chiu, D. K. W., & Ho, K. K. W. (2022). Green space development in academic libraries: A case study in Hong Kong. In V. Okojie & M. O. Igbinovia (Eds.), *Global perspectives on sustainable library practices* (pp. 142–156). IGI Global. doi:10.4018/978-1-6684-5964-5.ch010

Ho, K. K. W., Chan, J. Y., & Chiu, D. K. W. (2022). Fake news and misinformation during the pandemic: What we know, and what we don't know. *IT Professional, 24*(2), 19–24. doi:10.1109/MITP.2022.3142814

Ho, K. K. W., Chiu, D. K. W., & Sayama, K. L. C. (2023). When privacy, distrust, and misinformation cause worry about using COVID-19 contact-tracing apps. *IEEE Internet Computing, 27*(2), 7–12. doi:10.1109/MIC.2022.3225568

Ho, K. K. W., Takagi, T., Ye, S., Au, C. K., & Chiu, D. K. W. (2018). The use of social media for engaging people with environmentally friendly lifestyle – A conceptual model. *Pre-ICIS Workshop Proceedings 2018,* Article 2. https://aisel.aisnet.org/sprouts_proceedings_siggreen_2018/2/

Huang, P.-S., Paulino, Y. C., So, S., Chiu, D. K. W., & Ho, K. K. W. (2021). Editorial. *Library Hi Tech, 39*(3), 693–695. doi:10.1108/LHT-09-2021-324

Huang, P.-S., Paulino, Y. C., So, S., Chiu, D. K. W., & Ho, K. K. W. (2022). Guest editorial: COVID-19 pandemic and health informatics part 2. *Library Hi Tech, 40*(2), 281–285. doi:10.1108/LHT-04-2022-447

Huang, P.-S., Paulino, Y. C., So, S., Chiu, D. K. W., & Ho, K. K. W. (2023). Guest editorial: COVID-19 pandemic and health informatics part 3. *Library Hi Tech, 41*(1), 1–6. doi:10.1108/LHT-02-2023-585

Hui, S. C., Kwok, M. Y., Kong, E. W. S., & Chiu, D. K. W. (2023). (in press). Information security and technical issues of cloud storage services: A qualitative study on university students in Hong Kong. *Library Hi Tech.* Advance online publication. doi:10.1108/LHT-11-2022-0533

Jiang, M., Lam, A. H. C., Chiu, D. K. W., & Ho, K. K. W. (2023). Social media aids for business learning: A quantitative evaluation with the 5E instructional model. *Education and Information Technologies, 28*(9), 12269–12291. doi:10.100710639-023-11690-z PMID:37361768

Jiang, T., Lo, P., Cheuk, M. K., Chiu, D. K. W., Chu, M. Y., Zhang, X., Zhou, Q., Liu, Q., Tang, J., Zhang, X., Sun, X., Ye, Z., Yang, M., & Lam, S. K. (2019). 文化新語:兩岸四地傑出圖書館、檔案館及博物館傑出工作者訪談 [New cultural dialog: Interviews with outstanding librarians, archivists, and curators in Greater China]. Systech Publications.

Jiang, X., Chiu, D. K. W., & Chan, C. T. (2023). Application of the AIDA model in social media promotion and community engagement for small cultural organizations: A case study of the Choi Chang Sau Qin Society. In M. Dennis & J. Halbert (Eds.), *Community engagement in the online space* (pp. 48–70). IGI Global. doi:10.4018/978-1-6684-5190-8.ch004

Johnson, C. A. (2010). Do public libraries contribute to social capital? *Library & Information Science Research, 32*(2), 147–155. doi:10.1016/j.lisr.2009.12.006

Kee, H. C., Chan, M. M., & Chiu, D. K. W. (2023). Building social capital in contemporary major U.S. public libraries: Leading Information services and beyond. In D. K. W. Chiu & K. K. W. Ho (Eds.), *Emerging technology-based services and systems in libraries, educational institutions, and non-profit organizations* (pp. 239–269). IGI Global. doi:10.4018/978-1-6684-8671-9.ch010

Kwan, Y. K. C., Chan, M. W., & Chiu, D. K. W. (2023). (in press). Youth Marketing Development of Special Libraries in the Digital Era: Viewpoint from the Taste Library with 7Ps Marketing Mix. *Library Hi Tech*. Advance online publication. doi:10.1108/LHT-03-2023-0129

Lam, A. H. C., Ho, K. K. W., & Chiu, D. K. W. (2023). Instagram for student learning and library promotions? A quantitative study using the 5E Instructional Model. *Aslib Journal of Information Management*, *75*(1), 112–130. doi:10.1108/AJIM-12-2021-0389

Lam, E. T. H., Au, C. H., & Chiu, D. K. W. (2019). Analyzing the use of Facebook among university libraries in Hong Kong. *Journal of Academic Librarianship*, *45*(3), 175–183. doi:10.1016/j.acalib.2019.02.007

Lau, K. P., Chiu, D. K. W., Ho, K. K. W., Lo, P., & See-To, E. W. K. (2017). Educational usage of mobile devices: Differences between postgraduate and undergraduate students. *Journal of Academic Librarianship*, *43*(3), 201–208. doi:10.1016/j.acalib.2017.03.004

Lau, K. S. N., Lo, P., Chiu, D. K. W., Ho, K. K. W., Jiang, T., Zhou, Q., Percy, P., & Allard, B. (2020). Library and learning experiences turned mobile: A comparative study between LIS and non-LIS students. *Journal of Academic Librarianship*, *46*(2), 102103. Advance online publication. doi:10.1016/j.acalib.2019.102103

Law, T. Y., Leung, F. C. W., Chiu, D. K. W., Lo, P., Lung, M. M.-W., Zhou, Q., Xu, Y., Lu, Y., & Ho, K. K. W. (2019). Mobile learning usage of LIS students in Mainland China. *International Journal of Systems and Service-Oriented Engineering*, *9*(2), 12–34. doi:10.4018/IJSSOE.2019040102

Ledford, H. (2021). How severe are Omicron infections. *Nature*, *600*(7890), 577–578. doi:10.1038/d41586-021-03794-8 PMID:34934198

Lei, S. Y., Chiu, D. K. W., Lung, M. M., & Chan, C. T. (2021). Exploring the aids of social media for musical instrument education. *International Journal of Music Education*, *39*(2), 187–201. doi:10.1177/0255761420986217

Leung, T. N., Chiu, D. K. W., Ho, K. K. W., & Luk, C. K. L. (2022). User perceptions, academic library usage, and social capital: A correlation analysis under COVID-19 after library renovation. *Library Hi Tech*, *40*(2), 304–322. doi:10.1108/LHT-04-2021-0122

Leung, T. N., Hui, Y. M., Luk, C. K. L., Chiu, D. K. W., & Ho, K. K. W. (2022). (in press). Evaluating Facebook as aids for learning Japanese: Learners' perspectives. *Library Hi Tech*. Advance online publication. doi:10.1108/LHT-11-2021-0400

Li, K. K., & Chiu, D. K. W. (2022). A worldwide quantitative review of the iSchools' archival education. *Library Hi Tech*, *40*(5), 1497–1518. doi:10.1108/LHT-09-2021-0311

Li, L., Chiu, D. K. W., & Ho, K. K. W. (2023). How important is it to be beautiful?: The effect of beauty premium on wages. In Z. Sun (Ed.), *Handbook of Research on driving socioeconomic development with big data* (pp. 320–340). IGI Global. doi:10.4018/978-1-6684-5959-1.ch015

Li, Q., Wong, J., & Chiu, D. K. W. (2023). School library reading support for students with dyslexia: A qualitative study in the digital age. *Library Hi Tech*. Advance online publication. doi:10.1108/LHT-03-2023-0086

Li, S., Chiu, D. K. W., Kafeza, E., & Ho, K. K. W. (2023). Social media analytics for non-governmental organizations: A case study of Hong Kong Next Generation Arts. In Z. Sun (Ed.), *Handbook of research on driving socioeconomic development with big data* (pp. 277–295). IGI Global. doi:10.4018/978-1-6684-5959-1.ch013

Li, S., Xie, Z., Chiu, D. K. W., & Ho, K. K. W. (2023). Sentiment analysis and topic modeling regarding online classes on the Reddit Platform: Educators versus learners. *Applied Sciences (Basel, Switzerland)*, *13*(4), 2250. Advance online publication. doi:10.3390/app13042250

Li, S. M., Lam, A. H. C., & Chiu, D. K. W. (2023). Digital transformation of ticketing services: A value chain analysis of POPTICKET in Hong Kong. In J. Santos, I. Pereira, & P. Pires (Eds.), Management and marketing for improved retail competitiveness and performance (pp. 156-179). IGI Global. doi:10.4018/978-1-6684-8574-3.ch008

Lien, C., Cao, Y., & Zhou, X. (2017). Service quality, satisfaction, stickiness, and usage intentions: An exploratory evaluation in the context of WeChat services. *Computers in Human Behavior*, *68*, 403–410. doi:10.1016/j.chb.2016.11.061

Lin, C.-H., Chiu, D. K. W., & Lam, K. T. (2022). (in press). Hong Kong academic librarians' attitudes towards robotic process automation. *Library Hi Tech*. Advance online publication. doi:10.1108/LHT-03-2022-0141

Liu, Q., Lo, P., Zhou, Q., Chiu, D. K. W., & Cheuk, M. K. (2022). 走進大專院校圖書館: 圖書館員視角下的大中華區高等教育 [Why the Library? The Role of Librarians in the Higher Education Systems of Greater China]. City University Press.

Liu, Y., Chiu, D. K. W., & Ho, K. K. W. (2023). Short-form videos for public library marketing: Performance analytics of Douyin in China. *Applied Sciences (Basel, Switzerland)*, *13*(6), 3386. Advance online publication. doi:10.3390/app13063386

Liu, Y., Lei, J., Chiu, D. K. W., & Xie, Z. (2023). Adult learners' perception of online language English learning in China. In A. Garcés-Manzanera & M. E. C. García (Eds.), *New approaches to the investigation of language teaching and literature* (pp. 123–140). IGI Global. doi:10.4018/978-1-6684-6020-7.ch007

Lo, P., Allard, B., Anghelescu, H. G. B., Xin, Y., Chiu, D. K. W., & Stark, A. J. (2020). Transformational leadership practice in the world's leading academic libraries. *Journal of Librarianship and Information Science*, *52*(4), 972–999. doi:10.1177/0961000619897991

Lo, P., Allard, B., Wang, N., & Chiu, D. K. W. (2020). Servant leadership theory in practice: North America's leading public libraries. *Journal of Librarianship and Information Science*, *52*(1), 249–270. doi:10.1177/0961000618792387

Lo, P., Chan, H. H. Y., Tang, A. W. M., Chiu, D. K. W., Cho, A., See-To, E., Ho, K. K. W., He, M., Kenderdine, S., & Shaw, J. (2019). Visualising and revitalising traditional Chinese martial arts: Visitors' engagement and learning experience at the 300 years of Hakka KungFu. *Library Hi Tech, 37*(2), 269–288. doi:10.1108/LHT-05-2018-0071

Lo, P., & Chiu, D. K. W. (2015). Enhanced and changing roles of school librarians under the digital age. *New Library World, 116*(11/12), 696–710. doi:10.1108/NLW-05-2015-0037

Lo, P., Chiu, D. K. W., Cho, A., & Allard, B. (2018). *Conversations with leading academic and research library directors: International perspectives on library management.* Chandos Publishing.

Lo, P., Chiu, D. K. W., & Chu, W. (2013). Modeling your college library after a commercial bookstore? The Hong Kong Design Institute Library experience. *Community & Junior College Libraries, 19*(3-4), 59–76. doi:10.1080/02763915.2014.915186

Lo, P., Cho, A., Law, B. K.-K., Chiu, D. K. W., & Allard, B. (2017). Progressive trends in electronic resources management among academic libraries in Hong Kong. *Library Collections, Acquisitions & Technical Services, 40*(1-2), 28–37. doi:10.1080/14649055.2017.1291243

Lo, P., Yu, K., & Chiu, D. K. W. (2015). A research agenda for enhancing teacher librarians' roles and practice in Hong Kong's 21st century learning environments. *School Libraries Worldwide, 21*(1), 19–37. doi:10.29173lw6881

Lu, S. S., Tian, R., & Chiu, D. K. W. (2023). (in press). Why do people not attend public library programs in the current digital age? A mix method study in Hong Kong. *Library Hi Tech.* Advance online publication. doi:10.1108/LHT-04-2022-0217

Mak, M. Y. C., Poon, A. Y. M., & Chiu, D. K. W. (2022). Using social media as learning aids and preservation: Chinese martial arts in Hong Kong. In S. Papadakis & A. Kapaniaris (Eds.), *The digital folklore of cyberculture and digital humanities* (pp. 171–185). IGI Global. doi:10.4018/978-1-6684-4461-0.ch010

McKean, C., Law, J., Laing, K., Cockerill, M., Allon-Smith, J., McCartney, E., & Forbes, J. (2016). A qualitative case study in the social capital of Co-professional collaborative Co-practice for children with speech, language and communication needs. *International Journal of Language & Communication Disorders, 52*(4), 514–527. doi:10.1111/1460-6984.12296 PMID:27813256

Mehta, D., & Wang, X. (2020). COVID-19 and digital library services – A case study of a university library. *Digital Library Perspectives, 36*(4), 351–363. doi:10.1108/DLP-05-2020-0030

Meng, Y., Chu, M. Y., & Chiu, D. K. W. (2023). The impact of COVID-19 on museums in the digital era: Practices and challenges in Hong Kong. *Library Hi Tech, 41*(1), 130–151. doi:10.1108/LHT-05-2022-0273

Mouw, T. (2006). Estimating the causal effect of social capital: A review of recent research. *Annual Review of Sociology, 32*(1), 79–102. doi:10.1146/annurev.soc.32.061604.123150

Munshi, K. (2003). Networks in the modern economy: Mexican migrants in the U. S. labor market. *The Quarterly Journal of Economics, 118*(2), 549–599. doi:10.1162/003355303321675455

Ng, T. C. W., Chiu, D. K. W., & Li, K. K. (2022). Motivations of choosing archival studies as major in the i-Schools: Viewpoint between two universities across the Pacific Ocean. *Library Hi Tech*, *40*(5), 1483–1496. doi:10.1108/LHT-07-2021-0230

Ni, J., Rhim, A. H. R., Chiu, D. K. W., & Ho, K. K. W. (2022). Information search behavior among Chinese self-drive tourists in the smartphone era. *Information Discovery and Delivery*, *50*(3), 285–296. doi:10.1108/IDD-05-2020-0054

Paldam, M. (2000). Social capital: One or many? Definition and measurement. *Journal of Economic Surveys*, *14*(5), 629–653. doi:10.1111/1467-6419.00127

Prashantham, S. (2010). Social capital and Indian Micromultinationals. *British Journal of Management*, *22*(1), 4–20. doi:10.1111/j.1467-8551.2010.00720.x

Putnam, R. D. (1995). Bowling alone: America's declining social capital. *Journal of Democracy*, *6*(1), 65–78. doi:10.1353/jod.1995.0002

Robison, L. J., Schmid, A. A., & Siles, M. E. (2002). Is social capital really capital? *Review of Social Economy*, *60*(1), 1–21. doi:10.1080/00346760110127074

Rogers, S., Aytur, S., Gardner, K., & Carlson, C. (2012). Measuring community sustainability: Exploring the intersection of the built environment & social capital with a participatory case study. *Journal of Environmental Studies and Sciences*, *2*(2), 143–153. doi:10.100713412-012-0068-x

Sabolović-Krajina, D. (2021). Društveni utjecaj narodnih knjižnica tijekom pandemije COVID-19 u kontekstu koncepta pametnih gradova – komparacija Singapura I Hrvatske [The social impact of public libraries during the COVID-19 pandemic in the context of the concept of the smart cities – Comparison of Singapore and Croatia]. *Vjesnik bibliotekara Hrvatske*, *64*(1), 250-278. doi:10.30754/vbh.64.1.853

Smith, D., Leonis, T., & Anandavalli, S. (2021). Belonging and loneliness in cyberspace: Impacts of social media on adolescents' well-being. *Australian Journal of Psychology*, *73*(1), 12–23. doi:10.1080/00049530.2021.1898914

Sobaih, A. E., Hasanein, A. M., & Abu Elnasr, A. E. (2020). Responses to COVID-19 in higher education: Social media usage for sustaining formal academic communication in developing countries. *Sustainability (Basel)*, *12*(16), 6520. Advance online publication. doi:10.3390u12166520

Suen, R. L. T., Chiu, D. K. W., & Tang, J. K. T. (2020). Virtual reality services in academic libraries: Deployment experience in Hong Kong. *The Electronic Library*, *38*(4), 843–858. doi:10.1108/EL-05-2020-0116

Sun, X., Chiu, D. K. W., & Chan, C. T. (2022). Recent digitalization development of buddhist libraries: A comparative case study. In S. Papadakis & A. Kapaniaris (Eds.), *The digital folklore of cyberculture and digital humanities* (pp. 251–266). IGI Global. doi:10.4018/978-1-6684-4461-0.ch014

Sung, Y. Y. C., & Chiu, D. K. W. (2022). E-book or print book: Parents' current view in Hong Kong. *Library Hi Tech*, *40*(5), 1289–1304. doi:10.1108/LHT-09-2020-0230

Tsang, A. L. Y., & Chiu, D. K. W. (2022). Effectiveness of virtual reference services in academic libraries: A qualitative study based on the 5E Learning Model. *Journal of Academic Librarianship*, *48*(4), 102533. Advance online publication. doi:10.1016/j.acalib.2022.102533

Tse, H. L. T., Chiu, D. K. W., & Lam, A. H. C. (2022). From reading promotion to digital literacy: An analysis of digitalizing mobile library services with the 5E Instructional Model. In A. P. Almeida & S. Esteves (Eds.), *Modern reading practices and collaboration between schools, family, and community* (pp. 239–256). IGI Global. doi:10.4018/978-1-7998-9750-7.ch011

Vårheim, A. (2007). Social capital and public libraries: The need for research. *Library & Information Science Research*, *29*(3), 416–428. doi:10.1016/j.lisr.2007.04.009

Vårheim, A., Steinmo, S., & Ide, E. (2008). Do libraries matter? Public libraries and the creation of social capital. *The Journal of Documentation*, *64*(6), 877–892. doi:10.1108/00220410810912433

Wai, I. S. H., Ng, S. S. Y., Chiu, D. K. W., Ho, K. K. W., & Lo, P. (2018). Exploring undergraduate students' usage pattern of mobile apps for education. *Journal of Librarianship and Information Science*, *50*(1), 34–47. doi:10.1177/0961000616662699

Wang, J., Deng, S., Chiu, D. K. W., & Chan, C. T. (2022). Social network customer relationship management for orchestras: A case study on Hong Kong Philharmonic Orchestra. In N. B. Ammari (Ed.), *Social customer relationship management (Social-CRM) in the era of Web 4.0* (pp. 250–268). IGI Global. doi:10.4018/978-1-7998-9553-4.ch012

Wang, P., Chiu, D. K. W., Ho, K. K. W., & Lo, P. (2016). Why read it on your mobile device? Change in reading habit of electronic magazines for university students. *Journal of Academic Librarianship*, *42*(6), 664–669. doi:10.1016/j.acalib.2016.08.007

Wang, W., Lam, E. T. H., Chiu, D. K. W., Lung, M. M., & Ho, K. K. W. (2021). Supporting higher education with social networks: Trust and privacy vs perceived effectiveness. *Online Information Review*, *45*(1), 207–219. doi:10.1108/OIR-02-2020-0042

Wojciechowska, M. (2019). *Kształtowanie kapitału społecznego - ujęcie z perspektywy bibliotekoznawczej* [Shaping social capital. A view from the library science perspective]. Difin.

Wojciechowska, M., & Topolska, K. (2021). Social and cultural capital in public libraries and its impact on the organization of new forms of services and implementation of social projects. *Journal of Library Administration*, *61*(6), 627–643. doi:10.1080/01930826.2021.1947053

Wojciechowska, M. D. (2021). The role of public libraries in the development of social capital in local communities – A theoretical study. *Library Management*, *42*(3), 184–196. doi:10.1108/LM-10-2020-0139

Wong, A. K.-k., & Chiu, D. K. W. (2023). Digital transformation of museum conservation practices: A value chain analysis of public museums in Hong Kong. In R. Pettinger, B. B. Gupta, A. Roja, & D. Cozmiuc (Eds.), *Handbook of research on the digital transformation digitalization solutions for social and economic needs* (pp. 226–242). IGI. Global. doi:10.4018/978-1-6684-4102-2.ch010

Wong, I. H. S., Fan, C. H., Chiu, D. K. W., & Ho, K. K. W. (2023). (in press). Social media celebrities' influence on youths' diet behaviors: A gender study based on the AIDA marketing communication model. *Aslib Journal of Information Management*. Advance online publication. doi:10.1108/AJIM-11-2022-0495

Wong, J., Ho, K. K. W., Leung, T. N., & Chiu, D. K. W. (2023). Exploring the associations of youth Facebook addiction with social capital perceptions. *Online Information Review*, *47*(2), 283–298. doi:10.1108/OIR-06-2021-0300

Wong, K. C., & Chiu, D. K. W. (2023). Promoting the use of electronic resources of international schools: A case study of ESF King George V School in Hong Kong. In E. Meletiadou (Ed.), *Handbook of research on redesigning teaching, learning, and assessment in the digital era* (pp. 123–143). IGI Global. doi:10.4018/978-1-6684-8292-6.ch007

Wu, M., Lam, A. H. C., & Chiu, D. K. W. (2023). Transforming and promoting reference services with digital technologies: A case study on Hong Kong Baptist University Library. In B. Holland (Ed.), Handbook of research on advancements of contactless technology and service innovation in library and information science (pp. 128 – 145). IGI Global. doi:10.4018/978-1-6684-7693-2.ch007

Wu, Y., & Cheng, Z. (2019). Formation of user stickiness in an online knowledge community in China. *Social Behavior and Personality*, *47*(9), 1–14. doi:10.2224bp.8292

Xie, Z., Chiu, D. K. W., & Ho, K. K. W. (2023). (in press). The role of social media as aids for accounting education and knowledge sharing: Learning effectiveness and knowledge management perspectives in Mainland China. *Journal of the Knowledge Economy*. Advance online publication. doi:10.100713132-023-01262-4

Xie, Z., Wong, G. K. W., Chiu, D. K. W., & Lei, J. (2023). Bridging K-12 Mathematics and computational thinking in the Scratch community: Implications drawn from a creative learning context. *IT Professional*, *25*(2), 64–70. doi:10.1109/MITP.2023.3243393

Xue, B., Lam, A. H. C., & Chiu, D. K. W. (2023). Redesigning library information literacy education with the BOPPPS Model: A case study of the HKUST. In R. Taiwo, B. Idowu-Faith, & S. Ajiboye (Eds.), *Transformation of higher education through institutional online spaces*. IGI Global. doi:10.4018/978-1-6684-8122-6.ch017

Yang, Z., Zhou, Q., Chiu, D. K. W., & Wang, Y. (2022). Exploring the factors influencing continuance usage intention of academic social network sites. *Online Information Review*, *46*(7), 1225–1241. doi:10.1108/OIR-01-2021-0015

Yew, A., Chiu, D. K. W., Nakamura, Y., & Li, K. K. (2022). A quantitative review of LIS programs accredited by ALA and CILIP under contemporary technology advancement. *Library Hi Tech*, *40*(6), 1721–1745. doi:10.1108/LHT-12-2021-0442

Yi, Y., & Chiu, D. K. W. (2023). Public information needs during the COVID-19 outbreak: A qualitative study in mainland China. *Library Hi Tech*, *41*(1), 248–274. doi:10.1108/LHT-08-2022-0398

Yip, K. H. T., Lo, P., Ho, K. K. W., & Chiu, D. K. W. (2021). Adoption of mobile library apps as learning tools in higher education: A tale between Hong Kong and Japan. *Online Information Review*, *45*(2), 389–405. doi:10.1108/OIR-07-2020-0287

Yip, T., Chiu, D. K. W., Cho, A., & Lo, P. (2019). Behavior and informal learning at night in a 24-hour space: A case study of the Hong Kong Design Institute Library. *Journal of Librarianship and Information Science*, *51*(1), 171–179. doi:10.1177/0961000617726120

Yu, H. H. K., Chiu, D. K. W., & Chan, C. T. (2022). Resilience of symphony orchestras to challenges in the COVID-19 era: Analyzing the Hong Kong Philharmonic Orchestra with Porter's five force model. In W. J. Aloulou (Ed.), *Handbook of research on entrepreneurship and organizational resilience during unprecedented times* (pp. 586–601). IGI Global. doi:10.4018/978-1-6684-4605-8.ch026

Yu, H. Y., Tsoi, Y. Y., Rhim, A. H. R., Chiu, D. K. W., & Lung, M. M.-W. (2022). Changes in habits of electronic news usage on mobile devices in university students: A comparative survey. *Library Hi Tech*, *40*(5), 1322–1336. doi:10.1108/LHT-03-2021-0085

Yu, P. Y., Lam, E. T. H., & Chiu, D. K. W. (2023). Operation management of academic libraries in Hong Kong under COVID-19. *Library Hi Tech*, *41*(1), 108–129. doi:10.1108/LHT-10-2021-0342

Zhang, X., Lo, P., So, S., Chiu, D. K. W., Leung, T. N., Ho, K. K. W., & Stark, A. (2021). Medical students' attitudes and perceptions towards the effectiveness of mobile learning: A comparative information-need perspective. *Journal of Librarianship and Information Science*, *53*(1), 116–129. doi:10.1177/0961000620925547

Zhang, Y., Lo, P., So, S., & Chiu, D. K. W. (2020). Relating library user education to business students' information needs and learning practices: A comparative study. *RSR. Reference Services Review*, *48*(4), 537–558. doi:10.1108/RSR-12-2019-0084

Zheng, J., Lam, A. H. C., & Chiu, D. K. W. (2023). Evaluating the effectiveness of learning commons as third spaces with the 5Es usability model: The case of Hong Kong University of Science and Technology Library. In C. Kaye & J. Haynes Writer (Eds.), *Third-space exploration in education* (pp. 123–143). IGI Global. doi:10.4018/978-1-6684-8402-9.ch007

Zhou, J., Lam, E., Au, C. H., Lo, P., & Chiu, D. K. W. (2022). Library café or elsewhere: Usage of study space by different majors under contemporary technological environment. *Library Hi Tech*, *40*(6), 1567–1581. doi:10.1108/LHT-03-2021-0103

Zuo, Y., Lam, A. H. C., & Chiu, D. K. W. (2023). Digital protection of traditional villages for sustainable heritage tourism: A case study on Qiqiao Ancient Village, China. In A. Masouras, C. Papademetriou, D. Belias, & S. Anastasiadou (Eds.), *Sustainable growth strategies for entrepreneurial venture tourism and regional development* (pp. 129–151). IGI Global. doi:10.4018/978-1-6684-6055-9.ch009

KEY TERMS AND DEFINITIONS

4-Dimension Library Social Capital Assessment: A proposed framework, including the degree of user demand (VP), level of trust (LT), visibility (NV), and status in people's minds (PF), to evaluate a library's current situation regarding social capital and exploring future potentials of development of social capital.

FUML: Abbreviation of the Fudan University Medical Library, which is an associated library of the Fudan University located in Shanghai, Republic of China, especially for its School of Medicine. Developed from Shanghai Medical University Library, it comprises a unique cultural heritage, professional medical librarians, and a well-established cross-institutional recourse-sharing consortium.

Social Capital: It is a sort of capital consisting of shared values or recourses, both tangible and intangible, allowing people to harmoniously live or work together (or bond together), in other words, social relationships in a community or society.

Social Media: These technologies boost users' interactivity by expressing themselves to online communities through creation and sharing in various formats.

SWOT Analysis: Abbreviation of Strengths, Weaknesses, Opportunities, and Threats. It assists in identifying an organization's internal strengths and weaknesses and assessing any external opportunities and threats existing in the environment that may affect the organization's operation, uncovering possible potential future development.

University Libraries: A sort of libraries associated with its parent institution, i.e., a university. They aim to support teaching and learning and academic research conducted in the university community.

Chapter 15
Making the Connection:
Engaging and Impacting Student Outcomes by Building Self-Efficacy

Paula Louise McMahon
Montana State University, Billings, USA

ABSTRACT

Self-efficacy refers to a person's belief in their ability to execute behaviors necessary to produce specific performance outcomes. Bandura explained that there are four main sources of efficacy: performance accomplishments, vicarious experiences, social persuasion, and physiological reactions. Adapting a class structure and creating scaffolding that supports students does not mean that the content is less rigorous; it means how they meet these challenges is supported and developed with faculty guidance and input. Creating online learning environments that nurture students, motivate them, and engage them requires intentional practice and planning, using techniques to build student self-efficacy can assist in this process. This chapter will address how to identify tools and strategies to develop these skills.

The education landscape has undergone a profound transformation in recent years with the rapid proliferation of online learning platforms. This shift has created unprecedented opportunities for students to access education from virtually anywhere in the world. While online learning offers flexibility and convenience, it also presents unique challenges for educators and learners alike. One of the key challenges in online education for instructors is ensuring that students participate actively and thrive academically. Regarding online teaching, the concept of self-efficacy is particularly relevant because online instructors must navigate a diverse set of challenges compared to traditional classroom instructors. These challenges include technology proficiency, course design for online environments, and facilitating student engagement in virtual settings. "From a theoretical perspective, Self-Efficacy can be strengthened through the experience of mastery, observing someone succeed, and social persuasion such as direct encouragement" (Yokoyama, 2019, p.2).

One of the evident advantages of online learning is that "students can potentially download and stream media, whatever, wherever, and whenever they like, affording great flexibility in learning experiences, and potentially de-tethering learning from the bricks and mortar university classroom" (Thomson et al., 2014, p.67). This broad-reaching statement assumes that online access is readily available and that the ability to finance this does not present an obstacle. An article in Forbes found that "In 2021, about 60% of all postsecondary degree seekers in the U.S. took at least some online classes. Around 30% studied exclusively online" (Hamilton, 2023, para 6). We need to be able to accommodate this growing demand.

Undergraduate students can present retention concerns, which often occur when they struggle with adjusting to working online, "to address the lack of persistence of undergraduate online students, universities must create and implement interventions that prepare students for the online learning environment and help them develop as autonomous learners" (Stephen, Rockinson-Szapkiw, 2021).

Learning can be both formal and informal in nature. When online, there are adaptable formats that can be used, such as videos, texts, audio, and graphics. Faculty have a unique opportunity to communicate with students utilizing structures that are accessible and flexible. Online schooling created a mechanism for students with personal commitments, income limits, disabilities, work responsibilities, and a myriad of other concerns to access a quality education successfully. The education system serves an increasingly diverse demographic of students, which the traditional classroom environment needed to be designed to meet. Adapting a class structure and creating scaffolding to support students' success does not mean that the content is less rigorous; instead, it means these students meet the challenges in supportive environments through the tireless efforts of faculty guidance. Creating online learning environments that nurture, engage, and motivate students requires intentional practice and planning to identify the means for students to not connect with the content and develop a relationship with their instructors.

Through this chapter's exploration of self-efficacy in online learning, we aim to provide educators and institutions with the tools and insights needed to maximize the potential of their online learners and shape the future of education in the digital age and beyond.

WHAT IS SELF-EFFICACY?

Self-efficacy is important in instruction and student achievement. It refers to the person's belief in their ability to execute behaviors necessary to produce specific performance outcomes (Bandura, 1997). In the online environment, this is demonstrated when "the capability for learning vicariously allows individuals to acquire beliefs, cognitions, affects, skills, strategies, and behaviors from observations of others in their social environments and vicariously via media outlets" (Schunk & Mullen, 2012, p.221). Bandura explained that there are four primary sources of efficacy: performance accomplishments, vicarious experiences, social persuasion, and physiological reactions (1997). Self-efficacy is pivotal in instructional settings and significantly impacts student achievement, particularly in online environments.

Performance Accomplishments

Bandura's concept of "performance accomplishments" plays a pivotal role in understanding self-efficacy, which is the belief in one's ability to carry out specific actions to achieve desired outcomes. A performance accomplishment is when "students who have successfully completed similar experiences in the past will have stronger beliefs about their ability to complete future tasks" (Medaille et al., 2022, p.3). Successful task completion builds a sense of skill development in a student that is only reinforced by repeated positive experiences. "Performance accomplishments, the first source of information, are the most influential as it is based on learners' previous successful experience. Repeated successes develop strong efficacy expectation that leads to reducing the negative affect of failure" (Alqurashi, 2016, p.46). It is worth noting that in an online environment, there are factors that contribute to the sense of accomplishment. "Supportive feedback from a university instructor or professor about a student's performance in completing course assignments using online learning technology could be an important source of efficacy information" (Bates and Khasawneh, 2007 p. 179). Performance accomplishments, as one of the four primary sources of self-efficacy, refer to an individual's personal experiences and achievements, which can significantly impact their confidence and beliefs in their capabilities (Bandura, 1997).

In online learning environments, self-efficacy becomes particularly significant as it reflects the learner's confidence in their capability to acquire knowledge and skills effectively through digital means (Bandura, 1997). Academic Self-Efficacy always influences students' perceived capability in addressing class expectations and content. (Jan, 2015). Students' ability to navigate an online class format was determined to be equally valuable in determining their success. A possible solution is to have "first-time online students undertake a trial short course, similar to a real course so that students develop what Bandura called "performance accomplishment," which, if successful, would lead to a sense of self-efficacy for online learning" (Jan, 2015, p.38). This is just one approach to providing students the opportunity to achieve a performance accomplishment in the online environment.

Bates and Khasawneh's also noted that "Students who reported receiving some type of training in online learning system use at the beginning of their course also had higher outcome expectations, mastery perceptions, and reported higher efficacy beliefs than students who did not receive such training" (2007, p189). The pandemic familiarized students with online instruction, but each Learning Management System used for instruction has distinct differences. Each has a specific and sometimes unique method for accessing and submitting information. It is advisable:

Since task values are closely related to the relationship between Academic Self Efficacy and academic performance, students, teachers, and parents may need to choose the online learning software they believe will have the most valuable content and/or tasks for students. (Yokoyama 2019, p. 3)

Through a comprehensive examination of 122 students, Wang and Newlin's 2002 study, in addition to Aragon and Johnson's 2008 research, shed light on the critical role of self-efficacy and early course experiences in online learning, challenging conventional assumptions about factors affecting student performance and completion rates in web-based courses. In a study of 122 students, Wang and Newlin evaluated students' personal choices for taking web-based courses. They found that their research supported the idea that "age, gender, the number of hours employed per week, the number of children living at home, and distance traveled to campus do not correlate with final grades in an on-line class" (2002, p. 159). Instead, it was found that "self-efficacy beliefs regarding both course content and technology skills correlated with scores on the cumulative final exam." Similarly, Aragon and Johnson (2008, Para 1) did not find age as a factor but instead highlighted that "learners' early course experience were important factors affecting completion rates in online facilitated courses." These studies highlight the importance of students' confidence in their abilities and initial experiences in online learning environments as critical factors impacting their performance and course completion.

Vicarious Experience

We learn in some specific ways differently online than in the in-person classroom. Vicarious experiences come from observing others successfully manage challenging situations or completing complicated tasks. In a paper analyzing the effect of different types of vicarious experience with 136 participants of varying ages, Wilde and Hsu found that "participants with high general self-efficacy found many of the vicarious experience information presented to be beneficial to their self-efficacy to complete the set task as they were more likely to dismiss any information, they interpreted to be negative" (2019, p. 1). This method did not encourage those with low self-efficacy because they engaged in negative self-comparison. They suggest that those with low self-efficacy need help visualizing success. Therefore, your level of self-efficacy has a bearing on successfully navigating the learning process online, especially when the learning is vicarious.

The specific influence that self-efficacy has on vicarious learning in the online format may seem surprising. This may reflect that an online format needs to be more intuitive to create vicarious experiences. Hodges suggested that "in conveying cognitive skills, models should verbalize their thought processes. When cognitive skills are modeled, the competence of the model and whether the model displays coping strategies or mastery are important factors to consider" (Hodges 2008, P. 15). Brown and Inouye (1978) also found that students given tasks after seeing them modeled by others, judged their skills for solving a selected puzzle before and after watching someone else work on it. Those who watched someone persist at it while indicating verbally that they felt confident about their ability to solve the puzzle, had higher self-efficacy than those who made negative comments. So, messaging while providing vicarious experiences may be as important as observing the experiences themselves."

The importance of position messaging to subsequent self-efficacy also needs to be considered. It was suggested that messaging such as positive testimonials could impact perceived self-efficacy: "some participants felt reassured in their own abilities by reading information regarding other successes, this was especially the case for the successful testimonial information" (Wilde & Hsu, 2019, p. 17). Students are affected by the positive and negative messages around them, especially when considering the impact on their self-efficacy.

Social Persuasion

Messaging is directly related to the importance of the persuasion of others. Social persuasion can occur from the modeling behavior of others, and when affirmation occurs, this should "focus on cultivating positive self-assessments and substantive self-improvement" (Medaille et al., 2022, p. 4). Utilizing social persuasion in online learning may seem dissonant. However, it can be considered a form of social intimacy which "refers to a factor that is not directly related to learning contents, but which makes learners perceive their social change through the introduction, greetings and exchange of personal information in online learning environments" (Kang, and Im, 2013 p.293). In reviewing the literature on self-efficacy in online learning Alqurashi found that in determining the value of feedback from peers or faculty, students wanted to "see the persuader as someone who is qualified enough to provide authentic feedback" (2016 p. 46). The influence of the feedback provider is, not surprisingly, dependent on their perceived expertise around feedback.

Let us delve a little deeper into the method or mode of feedback. For a semester, eighty-three students were provided with audio and written feedback. The researchers found that "audio feedback was associated with increased retention of content" and "that students were three times more likely to apply content for which audio commenting was provided in class projects than was the case for content for which text-based commenting was provided" (Ice, Curtis, Philips, and Wells. 2007, p. 3). Ice et al. posited that "an enhanced ability to detect nuance impacts student perceptions of the instructor's use of humor, and openness toward and encouragement of student ideas and discussion" (2007, p. 18). The feedback method impacts the students' reactions and subsequent self-efficacy. There is a weight of responsibility on the instructor regarding tone, timeliness of feedback, and clarity. Bates and Khasawneh (2007, p. 179) found that:

The development of efficacy beliefs requires that individuals get clear information about their mastery and acquisition of knowledge or skills being pursued. Instructor feedback about performance supports this process by clarifying the outcomes and pattern of progress being made, and by providing data upon which efficacy judgments can be made.

Likewise, the personal quality of the method used to persuade students is essential. In a study of 690 students in a biology class over a semester, it was hypothesized that persuasive technology could engage students and positively motivate them. They found that positive personalized interaction amplifies the persuasive impact and reflects the use of similar technology in other contexts. (Adaji, Oyibo, and Vassileva, 2018) Utilizing strategies that provide positive encouragement can encourage and empower students. Although verbal persuasion has its limits, it is easier to distribute, and can help develop opportunities for performance practice. (Bandura, 1977; Hodges, 2008) Together, performance practice and verbal persuasion can have a significant impact.

Physiological Reactions

Next, let us consider physiological reactions. Physiological reactions can be an instinctive reaction to a stimulus. The emotions associated with that reaction can impact our ability to respond to and navigate tasks. These reactions can be experienced across a spectrum of positive and negative emotions. Even in an online learning environment: "people rely on physiological and emotional feedback when forming their self-efficacy beliefs. Stress, emotion, mood, pain, and fatigue are interpreted in making judgments of one's physiological and affective states" (Hodges, 2008 p. 16). Instructor affect needs to be monitored when providing instruction and feedback when considering students' reactions to perceived well-being. Recognizing physiological reactions as a key element in self-efficacy assessment highlights the profound influence of our instinctive responses and the associated emotions on our task performance.

Next, consider the importance of the method used for discussions, primarily online. When creating opportunities for in-person virtual discussion, online instructors impact "the physiological arousal of students engaged in online learning," which "can be enhanced via interactive teaching methods and pointed towards clear correlations between higher physiological responses and elementary criteria of learning experience such as engagement and attention" (Gellisch, et al., 2023 para. 1). Therefore, the instructor must consider interactive methods to grab the attention and engage the student.

The emotional state of the student is also essential to self-efficacy. Students can also be driven by anxiety when preparing for exams, which can negatively impact their sense of self-efficacy if fueled by negative test-taking experiences. Alkış and Temizel found that "providing students with sample exams and previous year's questions or organizing a mock-up exam can decrease their anxiety about the course." (2018 p.44) Considering the students' anxiety is being recognized as an essential consideration for promoting student success.

People tend to engage in assignments or activities in which they feel capable, and they will procrastinate about or avoid activities where they do not feel capable. The individuals' sense of their own self-efficacy will help them decide the level of effort they can devote to an assignment or task, the amount of time they will have to spend when faced with difficulties, and how much resilience they will have to demonstrate when confronted with a crisis. If they perceive themselves as capable, their effort, perseverance, and flexibility will increase. This is the path to increased productivity and effectiveness. (Bandura, 1986).

Getting a sense of students' comfort with online learning predicts success:

Students' who viewed online learning ability as an alterable and acquirable skill reported higher self-efficacy levels, more positive expectations about e-learning outcomes, less anxiety about using the technology, and a higher mastery level with respect to those systems. On the other hand, students who tended to believe that online learning ability was a relatively fixed skill reported higher anxiety levels, less previous success, and lower efficacy levels. (Bates & Khasawneh, 2007, p. 179)

Offering instructional resources that are universally accessible and offering guidance about maneuvering the online class format allows students with those reservations to learn how to manage the format.

As instruction increasingly shifts towards an on-screen format, "Understanding self-efficacy in online learning is critical to improving education, which can be a key component of academic success in distance education" (Peechapol et al., 2018, p. 65). For some students' "Self-efficacy belief may also diverge from action because of genuine faulty self-appraisal" (Bandura, 2012, p. 11). Faculty must navigate and manage student expectations for themselves and others and demystify the learning process so that they can start to feel confident in themselves. Self-efficacy in online learning is a fundamental concept that influences a student's perception of their ability to succeed in an online educational environment. It plays a crucial role in motivation, persistence, and effective use of resources and strategies, impacting online courses' overall learning experience and outcomes.

Instructor Presence

In literature evaluating the factors that impact student learning, instructor presence was consistently identified as a reinforcement to students and opportunities to interact with faculty in different capacities. It tended to build student confidence and a sense of their own capacity. (Bialowas & Steimel, 2019; Draus, Curran, and Trempus, 2014; Eom & Ashill, 2016; Glazier, 2016; Martin & Bolliger, 2018; Smith Jaggars & Xu, 2016) Learning that direct contact between students and faculty builds student confidence is heartening.

Draus, Curran, and Trempus (2014) determined that overall satisfaction with an online class and student engagement (measured by the amount and depth of discussion posts) in a course increased based on the provision of an instructor-generated video as an alternative to viewing a slide show. Faculty creating online content that provides context and insight into the reading materials provided students with a richer learning experience. Providing videos and other media to contextualize the learning increases student engagement and subsequent satisfaction with the course.

In a study at one university, students were asked through a survey to review instructor video announcements versus individual video feedback. The following was determined: When asked to compare videos directed at the entire class (e.g., general assignment videos) with videos directed at the individual student (e.g., individual-level assignment feedback videos), the videos directed at the entire class in a general way were rated more positively both in terms of instructor immediacy and student motivation (Bialowas & Steimel, 2019). They also found that while it can be helpful, individualized feedback for new students can be perceived as too critical. Sometimes, too much individualized feedback can be perceived as intimidating and makes the student anxious (Bialowas & Steimel, 2019).

Faculty can engage via class announcements and weekly class reviews and demonstrate enthusiasm and engagement with a topic, encouraging and stimulating student interest and avoiding making students feel anxious. Learning the common concerns of students over time for a given course allows an instructor to provide general guidance to the whole class; this avoids direct individual interactions from the instructor that tend to intimidate students. Faculty can also make announcements stemming from a single student's question to resolve possible shared concerns of other students.

On one Midwestern University campus, 372 responses were solicited from students who had completed at least one online course. These responses were used to examine student perception of online learning. It was found that "Instructor-student dialogue, student-student dialogue, instructor, and course design significantly affect students' satisfaction and learning outcomes" and that "the importance of student-student and instructor-student dialogue as predictors of perceived user satisfaction and learning outcomes" (Eom & Ashill, 2016, p. 185). The presence and opportunity for students to interact with faculty meant that students felt that they could get their concerns addressed and questions answered in a timely manner. It was found that faculty could "also intervene at any subprocess (forethought, performance, self-regulation) to enhance and improve student motivation, set appropriate course goals, or provide metacognitive feedback concerning student progress" (Eom & Ashill, 2016, p. 204).

In Australia, an undergraduate nursing program created online learning content using YouTube, which was positively received by the students, allowing them to engage in self-directed learning. The result was that "the cumulative total of accesses exceeded an average of ten views per video by each individual student" (Johnston et al., 2018, p. 7). The students could access the content at their convenience, and it took "a relatively small investment of staff time equated to large volume of student learning time" (Johnston et al., 2018, p. 7). Consequently, student engagement and outcomes improved with access to this content. This is an example of how minor revisions to a course, taking very little time, can tremendously impact student learning.

Glazier (2016) showed that a professor can build rapport with online students and increase their competency by establishing the means to communicate with students on a routine basis by using personalized reminders for deadlines and check-ins. Providing feedback on assignments to measure final course grades and retention also measurably increases student self-efficacy as they learn and develop skills based on this instruction (Wang & Wu, 2008; Glazier, 2016). Creating an online presence using interactive media resources so that students can learn about you and each other helps to build "rapport and collaboration between students and instructors in an interactive environment" (Martin & Bolliger, 2018, p. 208). These resources can include using "group work and instructive feedback, (which) are important for student engagement resulting in learning success" (Martin & Bolliger, 2018, p. 208). Students also identified icebreakers with professor involvement as an effective way to engage with the class and collaborate with each other using online communication tools. Banna, Lin, Stewart, and Fialkowski (2015) stress that faculty responsiveness and developed relationships are the critical solutions to addressing the issues of learner isolation, retention, and graduation rate in online learning. Working to build relationships in a course leads to greater engagement and increased learning.

Glazier (2016) found that regular engagement and periodic reminders positively impacted student grades as well as class involvement and reduced student withdrawals from class; by doing this, he was messaging his investment in the student's success in the class. Some Learning Management Systems (LMS) are designed to embed these types of reminders for students, although they tend to have a formatted impersonal style. Instructors should note that courses with "high interpersonal interaction ratings, (where) instructors tended to post frequently, invite student questions through a variety of modalities, respond to student queries quickly, and solicit and incorporate student feedback " (Smith Jaggars & Xu, 2016, p. 25) tended to be well received with better student outcomes. Smith Jaggars & Xu, explained that "effective teacher interaction and the sense that the teacher "cares" carried much weight in students' assessments (2016 p. 21). Efforts made by an instructor to increase feedback and interaction send a message to students that the instructor cares.

When changing from an in-person classroom to an online environment, gauging student interest and engagement in each topic area can be difficult. In their research, Vayre and Vonthro found that "Self-Efficacy fosters the engagement of online students regardless of the component considered" (2017, p. 213). When students begin to develop their sense of self-efficacy, they become more confident, especially in a setting where mutual exchange is encouraged, and students' sense of autonomy is developed. Self-efficacy is the foundation for students to advocate for themselves and provide the feedback needed to develop online content and learning opportunities. It also means that when they struggle with information, they can express their concerns without feeling that this reflects on their abilities, giving the instructor the insight to know when to adjust the content as needed. Developing student self-efficacy builds the resilience of students and assists in their academic success. Looking at the intrinsic factors that predict success, "locus of control, self-efficacy, and task value were significant predictors of learner satisfaction, while self-efficacy and task value predicted achievement" (Joo & Kim, 2013, p. 149). These are qualities that can be developed over time.

The need for instructor support and interaction was reiterated in a study at an online survey with 645 respondents, where it was determined that interaction with the instructor predicted learning achievement and that the "presence of instructor significantly predicted learners' perceived satisfaction." These findings underscore the enduring significance of instructor support and interaction in predicting learning achievement and learners' overall satisfaction with the educational experience. (Kang and Im, 2013 p. 299)

Peer-to-Peer Interaction

The traditional face-to-face model found that:

Students learn a great deal by explaining their ideas to their peers and by participating in activities in which they can learn from their peers. They develop skills in organizing and planning learning activities, working collaboratively with others, giving and receiving feedback, and evaluating their own learning. (Shekhar & Shailendra, 2021, p. 161)

Creating these opportunities in an online format creates a challenge for faculty, and they often default to discussion posts as a standard method of getting students to engage with each other. In reviewing the literature to determine the formats desirable to online learning for students, Smith et al. found that "many students viewed peer interactions in their online courses as an imposed requirement, rather than as a helpful and necessary component of learning" (2016, p. 280). For online discussions to be practical, faculty presence tended to generate increased participation, and some minor facilitation is a significant factor in successful discussions (Smith Jaggars & Xu, 2016). It is also interesting to note that the number of discussion boards could impact participation. Courses with more discussion forums appeared to result in less interaction among learners. Although incorporating discussion forums is a method to enhance student collaboration and communication, this study found that "assigning too many discussion forums in a course decreased interaction among online students" (Kuo & Belland, 2016, p. 675). Relying too much on any one method or modality for class instruction results in decreased impact. Although discussion boards are effective for student-to-student engagement, other methods are also needed to elicit this engagement.

Sometimes, faculty assign student moderators to maintain a group discussion and encourage participation. Evaluation of this format has shown that much hinges on the assigned moderator's responsiveness or lack thereof to determine the level of engagement from the rest of the class (Xie et al., 2014). Moderator observation was positively associated with active engagement and feedback. However, students often lack the skills to manage a group effectively the way a faculty member might, and training was recommended prior to allocating students the responsibility of managing their peers in a group environment. The advantage of these online discussion formats is that "Asynchronous online discussions enable knowledge to be constructed socially and cooperatively, give students time to think before contributing, and allow them to progress at their own pace" (Yilmaz & Yilmaz, 2019, p. 1304). With faculty engagement and affirmation, students can build a sense of competency around contributing to the online environment and feel less concerned about being vulnerable.

Interestingly, Yilmaz and Yilmaz's research showed that student engagement increased when students were assigned various roles, such as starter, moderator, and summarizer of a discussion topic. They found that "assigning different roles to group members helps discussions get started, enables their sustainability, affects social construction of knowledge positively" (Yilmaz & Yilmaz, 2019, p. 1307). When students had a mutually shared responsibility for the group's success and were able to encourage and incentivize one another, discussion boards were more effective.

Another approach to be considered is online group projects. These projects create not only an opportunity to demonstrate learning and mastery but also the opportunity for vicarious learning. When students develop a sense of connection with their classmates, they experience social persuasion, helping them to adopt ideas and develop their attitudes and insights into the work. However, students may be resistant, and scaffolding may be necessary. Over the duration of six semesters, with 204 students participating, researchers concluded that "Students' self-efficacy beliefs in groupwork are shaped by mastery experiences" where "mastery experience refers to personal interpretations of student performances on groupwork tasks" (Du et al., 2019, p. 781). If the students felt equipped to handle the group assignments' expectations, they became "more efficacious when they feel that they are able to handle problems or challenges in groupwork" (Du et al., 2019, p. 781). Providing guidance, outlining expectations, and giving students a foundation so that they are prepared ensures their willingness to engage in the challenges of collaborative online learning. A positive result related to this approach is that a "sense of community has a direct positive effect on enthusiasm and also plays an important role regarding self-efficacy in online education" (Vayre & Vonthron, 2017, p. 213). However, building a sense of community in the online setting requires thoughtful planning by the instructor.

Taking a creative approach to course projects could be helpful in online learning. Engaging students in service-learning projects and giving them the opportunity to engage in the community can have a positive effect. It is essential to work with students to identify industry-related or neighborhood-based issues for which they could identify solutions and the "use of structured reflections for promoting personal understanding and community self-efficacy" (Sanders et al., 2016, p.73). Many activities associated with such a project can be incorporated into an online format. Students can offer reflections online throughout the service-learning experience, including personal goal-writing, peer-to-peer interaction via online discussions, and a final reflection paper. These activities allow students to develop knowledge by engaging in assignments that offer a real-world context and allow them to utilize critical thinking skills in a scaffolded environment while exercising greater autonomy. This approach also provides opportunities to target desired outcomes carefully and allows students to demonstrate a skill or knowledge acquisition. Self-efficacy and service go together and build the students' connection to their community and the understanding that they, as individuals, can provide solutions and impact their community.

Being creative with online learning opportunities can develop "students who demonstrate generally higher perceptions of active learning practices online (and) may be more engaged in an online course" (Cole et al., 2021, p. 876). Once students feel comfortable navigating an online space, they can engage with their peers and faculty more effectively. An online survey of 151 postgraduate business students identified a positive relationship between self-efficacy and student relationships with peers (Prior et al., 2016). Developing student online competencies to enhance relationships and class involvement may sound counterintuitive. However, it impacts students' ability to navigate the platform comfortably. Prior identified that if a student had digital literacy, they would be able to locate information and manage the expectations of an online format if faculty gave them time and instruction to develop these skills (2016).

Developing a high level of computer self-efficacy reduces student anxiety and builds confidence in interacting with this medium (Wolverton et al., 2020). Although, as instructors, we are focused on the specific content of a course, effort needs to be made to consistently build the students' information technology capability in every course. In reviewing six studies evaluating the impact of self-efficacy and student outcomes, Yokoyama determined that mastery-approach goal approach and intrinsic motivation were qualities that predicted success in learning. Also, students with previous experience with online learning, a higher educational level, and help-seeking abilities, as well as self-regulated learning strategies and cognitive strategy use, are more likely to succeed. (2019) Where a faculty member must focus their energies initially is on the students who find this to be an unfamiliar format to help develop skills.

Representation

The student demographics of online higher education learning have been changing in recent years, reflecting a growing trend toward digital education and the evolving needs of students. Online education has made higher education more accessible to historically underrepresented minority groups. When working with underrepresented, nontraditional, and minority groups, faculty must consider using inclusive practices in their core content. Pumptow and Brahm posited, "Research suggests a link between students' diversity, in particular, their socio-economic background, academic self-efficacy expectations, study-related attitudes, and academic achievement" (2021, p. 555). When students feel that the core content or coursework is meaningful to them and reflects their goals and objectives for themselves, they are more likely to remain engaged in learning. The challenge for faculty is that "with such a potentially varied online audience, viewing teaching and learning as "student-centered," or "learner-centered," is perhaps even more important online" (Cole et al., 2021, p. 867). Online teaching is intimate, where faculty are given an opportunity to be the focus of the student facing the screen.

Educators should be sensitive to the diverse cultural backgrounds of their students. This includes understanding diverse cultural norms, values, and educational expectations. By acknowledging and respecting these differences, educators can help students feel more comfortable and valued in the online learning environment.

Gay offers a model of culturally responsive teaching (CRT) that is broken down into five principles. The first requires developing a cultural diversity knowledge the second requires that faculty develop a culturally relevant curriculum, and that they can display cultural caring and building a learning community, and utilize cross-cultural communications, while communicating cultural consistency in classroom instruction (Gay, 2002, Fitchett, Starker, & Salyers, 2012).

Designing an inclusive curriculum incorporating diverse perspectives, authors, and cultural references can help students from diverse backgrounds relate to the content. When students see themselves reflected in the materials, they may be more motivated and confident in their ability to succeed. Faculty should be aware that:

Integrating a culturally responsive framework within a ... class has the potential to not only inform students of multicultural dispositions but also increase their efficaciousness to interact with diverse learners, work in diverse environments, and instructionally engage learners in culturally diverse content. (Fitchett et al., 2012, p.603)

In a survey of 199 minority students, 167 responded that instructor presence and class content were highly rated factors in students' evaluation of their own success. Notably, it was found that:

Personalized or individualized online learning approaches that are adaptive to learning or cultural differences and needs of a diverse group of students may support minority students who usually show less confidence in taking online or web-based courses when compared with Caucasian students. (Kuo & Belland, 2016, p.671)

Essential in-person class practices still have efficacy in the online environment and must be considered and implemented.

Working with students in an online environment, particularly when navigating language challenges, institutes of education and faculty need to consider:

The challenges associated with ... online education such as the speed of Internet access, the type of learning device, online test anxiety, and lack of face-to-face interaction, as well as the challenges associated with the pandemic including, task overload, pandemic fears, social isolation, and confinement, those with higher self-efficacy would better accept challenging tasks, retain their interest in class discussions and tasks, and recover from disappointments sooner. (Abdolrezapour et al., 2023, p. 7)

These issues can impact first-generation students, transfer students, foreign language students, and older students, amongst a few. Identifying methods to ease the transition into higher education and online learning can help address these concerns. Building self-efficacy from the beginning of instruction is essential due to the many challenges students face in their transition to higher education.

Online education is no longer limited to traditional college-age students. It attracts learners of various age groups, including working professionals seeking to upskill or change careers, parents balancing family responsibilities, and retirees looking to continue learning. These nontraditional students are sometimes concerned that they are starting at a disadvantage because they are uncomfortable with the online learning format. Providing the opportunity to meet in person or virtually and then talking students through navigating the learning management system can go a long way to diminishing their concerns. Creating short five-minute videos guiding students through the class and explaining the online library system demystifies these systems and makes them more accessible. Students often assume campus resources are for in-person students, so it is essential to identify the relevant supports, provide points of contact, and encourage online students to use them. A study evaluating large-scale online classes found that students tend to be more responsive and engaged when video lectures are shorter, averaging a five-to-ten-minute duration, when offering conceptual information and covering curriculum (Hew et al., 2018). The ability to watch videos on their own time and repeatedly as needed assists with learning and concept development and helps familiarize them with the necessary content. In face-to-face classes, students can ask for clarification when colloquial terms or jargon are used. In online classes, faculty need to be mindful of this; students' can feel that "the complex and abstract vocabulary and technical terms used in academic courses was challenging…the academic language hindered their self-efficacy in academic learning in courses" (Shi, 2018, p.483). Nontraditional students may not expect to build relationships through online learning, but the relationship between self-efficacy and student success remains relevant for nontraditional students.

Students with disabilities utilize online learning platforms for their convenience, although accessibility is not always guaranteed, and it presents both opportunities and challenges. Ensuring that online courses are accessible and inclusive is essential to support these students in their pursuit of higher education. In a survey of 278 students with a wide variety of identified disabilities, including learning, physical, and neurodivergence, their online learning abilities and self-efficacy were evaluated. Technology competence proved to be a predictor of student success. "These learners with a high level of technology competency can enjoy the various benefits that a distance education modality provides e. g., saving commute time, audio transcripts, class recordings, etc." (EunKyoung et al., 2021, p. 300). As reflected in their research, "students with disabilities in this study appeared to benefit from direct communication with instructors via emails, highlighting the importance of effective communication in the virtual classroom and remote learning" (Lee et al., 2021, p. 300). Embedding accessible practices, such as documents that can be reviewed by read-out-loud software, was also highly rated by students with disabilities and minority status. Faculty getting their classes reviewed for accessibility is considered best practice, so students do not have to make a request whenever they are confronted with an access issue (because they are readily addressed), thereby slowing down their access to education and limiting their opportunity. Online institutions should consider that "as the number of online courses offered by higher education institutions is rocketing upward, cultivating a growth mindset to promote accessibility across all campus stakeholders is critical" (EunKyoung et al., 2021, p. 303).

Guest Speakers

Using guest speakers in online education can be a powerful strategy for building student self-efficacy. Guest speakers bring real-world expertise and diverse perspectives into the virtual classroom, providing students valuable insights and inspiration. They can provide a vicarious learning experience for students and identify possibilities that focus on the career aspirations of students. "Real-world application of projects that enhances subject mastery and critical thinking skills is one strategy related to fostering learner-to-content engagement" (Martin & Bolliger, 2018, p. 209). Utilizing speakers already in the fields students aspired to work in helped provide motivation as well as insight. Hebert et al. (2014, p. 47) noticed that "Role models who share their experiences completing research tasks successfully, and also share characteristics with class members, such as age, gender, and student status, have a greater potential to raise the student's sense of research self-efficacy."

Content experts working in the field could provide context to the theories being learned in class and allow students to learn through observing others. In a survey of 545 journalism students, certain practices were identified as being the most effective to engage students. Two of these were to "work with a speaker to emphasize personal examples and share professional tips linked to course objectives; and ensure speakers utilize an active presentation style, such as a question-and-answer format, rather than deliver a formal lecture" (Merle & Craig, 2017, p. 46). Guest speakers reduce student anxiety about their desired career path and shape their aspirations in an achievable and realistic manner.

Test Anxiety

Test anxiety can be a significant barrier to building self-efficacy in online learning, as it can undermine students' belief in their ability to perform well in assessments and coursework. Students' anxiety about tests can often undermine other identified strategies to build self-efficacy, as the looming deadlines concern and preoccupy them. For some, this can be severe: "Those affected by test anxiety typically report feelings of despair, hopelessness, and failure, but also panic-like physiological reactions such as accelerated heart rate, bladder and intestinal activation, sweating, and nausea" (Maier et al., 2021, p.3). In a study with nontraditional doctoral students, opportunities to retake tests were allowed. "From the course design perspective, students believed retaking quizzes and redoing assignments allowed them to correct misunderstanding as it took away the anxiety and reinforced fundamental concepts" (Jiang & Ballenger, 2023, p. 8). It reduced student test anxiety, allowed them to re-learn core themes, and allowed them to work on their problem-solving skills. Since the essential goal is to develop skills and knowledge, online learning is positioned to provide students with an opportunity to demonstrate their knowledge and skills in alternative methods that reduce student test anxiety and do not rely upon the time restraints of traditional instruction models.

Incorporate frequent formative assessments into the online learning process. These smaller, low-stakes assessments can help students build confidence by providing opportunities for practice and feedback without the high-pressure feeling of a major exam.

Power of Positive Self-Talk

Coaching students to use positive self-talk in online higher education instruction can be a valuable strategy to enhance their learning experience, motivation, and overall academic success. Positive self-talk can help students manage stress, build confidence, and focus on their goals. Galanis and Comoutos (2018) reiterate this indicating that positive self-talk can help task focus, even with external distractions occurring. And that those actively practicing while on task perform better that their silent peers.

Online, there are ways to support; instructors can model positive self-talk by using optimistic and motivating language when providing feedback, discussing challenges, or setting expectations. Demonstrating this behavior can inspire students to adopt it themselves. They can help students identify negative self-talk patterns by encouraging students to become aware of their negative self-talk patterns. This could involve asking them to reflect on their inner dialogue and identify any recurring negative thoughts or beliefs hindering their progress.

In a study of 146 undergraduate students completed by Markland & Hardy, they investigated whether the surveyed students' interpretation of self-talk used during a lecture by faculty was associated with their post-lecture affect. The results indicated a positive association between informational self-talk and positive affect. (2010)

When students persist, it can help challenge negative beliefs by teaching them how to challenge and reframe them. When they identify a negative thought, help them rephrase it into a more positive and constructive statement. For example, "I cannot do this" can become "I can overcome this challenge with effort and determination."

Format and Structure

Online platforms vary, and there can be a significant learning curve for students to adapt to each platform. A well-designed LMS can make it easier for students to navigate course materials, track their progress, and access resources, boosting their confidence and belief in their ability to succeed. There is an expectation in many classes that students should be prepared to engage the library websites databases, manage to look for things online, and be able to coordinate using e-mails and instant messaging with peers. (Knutsson et al., 2012). Embedding videos, providing written explanations, and providing guidance on navigating the LMS reduces student fears. Providing video guidance to students to explain the online library demystifies the system, making it more user-friendly.

For new faculty starting teaching online, the primary concerns are technical issues and organization. However, "previous studies show that the learning environment and interactions with online teachers and students can also influence student education" (Liu et al., 2020, p. 5). As mentioned previously, faculty responsiveness and engagement are highly valued by students. In reviewing different learning platforms, Liu and her colleagues found the value of these systems was the "control that it gives students over their academic performance" (2020). It indicates that their desire for autonomy and self-efficacy is often built in and that if fostered with the right tools, it will increase student knowledge, outcomes, and involvement in class.

The assumption is that students respond positively to in-person classes because of the opportunity to interact with faculty and the ability to ask questions. However, research has shown this to be an oversimplification. Students react to a course based on multiple factors, including the content, the instructor, the climate, and each other, with modality being less a predictor of success or withdrawal. They did not suggest student 'satisfaction' to be equivalent by modality (Dziuban & Moskal, 2011; Marzano & Allen, 2016). Faculty engagement, class format and instruction, and students' sense of themselves kept them involved in the class content. We need to consider the following: Understanding how students access different kinds of learning materials and how their behaviors in accessing these materials affect their learning performance may give teachers helpful information to improve their instructional design and provide insights for content and instructional designers to develop personalized learning supports (Li & Tsai, 2017).

One of the interesting shifts that online learning environments create for faculty is that instead of working with "human-human persuasion," we are shifting to "computer-human persuasion" (Orji et al., 2018, p. 1). Learning to utilize the tools where "computer software is used to motivate a target audience to achieve a specific goal" (Orji et al., 2018, p. 1). Utilizing group-based activities, discussions, and opportunities for peers to assess each other's work allows students to "evaluate themselves by comparing themselves to similar others" (Orji et al., 2018, p. 2). High-interaction instructors who post announcements regularly to remind students about requirements for assignments, coming deadlines, newly posted documents, examinations, and other logistic issues are well received. In contrast, in courses where the instructor minimizes engagement, students are more likely to express dissatisfaction with the course (Smith Jaggars & Xu, 2016).

Example-based learning has proven to be another effective strategy, particularly in math and engineering:

Studying examples plays an essential role in learning. Unlike conventional instruction that emphasizes problem-solving after initial presentation of a few examples in instruction, example-based learning underscores the importance of having learners study a much heavier number of examples to facilitate learning by reducing unnecessary cognitive load induced by problem solving. (Huang & Mayer, 2019, p. 1006)

Vicarious gains could occur through modeled performance (which can be provided online or via recording). Students are given the opportunity to practice and apply the theory, and feedback is encouraged to improve learning outcomes.

Researchers implementing similar practices found that "students' understanding of material increases on subsequent works and in all cases, student satisfaction with the course increases" (Schuessler, 2017, p. 119). Undergraduate students working on thesis projects expressed anxiety about managing expectations. They found that "Learning how to break down their projects into "manageable chunks" helped to ensure that they did not feel overwhelmed and made steady progress" (Medaille et al., 2022, p. 10).

Because there is increased demand for online learning, incorporating strategies that maximize learning outcomes and enhance academic achievement is essential. The developing research in this area points towards the need to ensure that students are provided with a baseline knowledge of the learning platforms and the tools necessary to be effective. When utilizing these:

Students with higher levels of technology, self-interventions and strategies to support students and build their confidence can provide the foundation for intrinsic motivation, a sense of well-being, and personal accomplishment. This can impact learning outcomes and exam competency, and "learners with higher Internet self-efficacy were more confident and found the course more relevant than those with lower Internet self-efficacy. (Chang et al., 2014, p. 373)

This means those who can seamlessly navigate the online learning system are more receptive to the content. Students can then begin to build on developed skill sets and mastery when working online.

A well-organized and user-friendly LMS can empower students to take ownership of their learning, stay engaged, and build confidence in their ability to succeed in online courses. It is important to continually assess and refine the LMS based on user feedback and evolving best practices in online education.

Utilizing a spectrum of activities to build self-efficacy can help students with goal setting for the class and help them develop skills and a sense of their abilities that will reinforce their ability to engage in study. A group of 95 students enrolled in an online course were invited to engage in a survey, and data from a convenience sample of 48 participants was analyzed. "The eight-week class was delivered synchronously and asynchronously using the university's learning management system (LMS) and video conference application" (Stephen & Rockinson-Szapkiw, 2021, p. 7). The instructors reviewed the expectations for the students in the class. They identified tools and skills that would help them, "time management, critical thinking, study habits, study skills, technology use, information literacy skills, knowledge of university academic policies and procedures, access to academic support services and resources, and knowledge of the university culture and history" (Stephen, Rockinson-Szapkiw, 2021 p. 7). It identified a variety of resources to assist students in developing their skills. Students used learning logs as a strategy, which proved useful in developing self-regulation and self-direction. "Students set goals, identified the resources and strategies they needed to achieve their goals, and evaluated their progress to attribute actions to results" (Stephen, Rockinson-Szapkiw, 2021, p. 13). Overall, the results illustrated that "online students need to incorporate reflection activities (i.e., learning logs, self-assessments, rubrics) to help them to develop an awareness of what they did before, during, and after a learning experience" (Stephen, Rockinson-Szapkiw, 2021, p. 14).

Practices Nurturing Self-Efficacy

Given the pivotal role of self-efficacy in online education, it becomes essential for educators and instructional designers to implement strategies that foster and enhance students' belief in their abilities.

1. **Instructor Support and Interaction:** Creating a supportive learning community where students can collaborate and seek assistance when needed can positively influence self-efficacy. Students felt supported by "high-interaction instructors (who) posted announcements on a regular basis to remind students about requirements for assignments, coming deadlines, newly posted documents, examinations, and other logistic issues" (Smith Jaggars & Xu, 2016, p. 278). Creating open forums for discussion, encouraging feedback, and identifying strategic opportunities for peer-to-peer interaction were also highly valued.
2. **Constructive Feedback:** Providing timely and constructive feedback can help students gauge their progress and build confidence in their abilities. When faculty provide students with "structure by means of support and encouragement, giving constructive, informational feedback, and thereby making students feel that they have more control over the outcome of their studies; and helping them to gain control over valued outcomes" (Ayllón & Colomer, 2019, p.2).
3. **Peer-to-Peer Interaction:** Peer-to-peer interaction promotes self-directed learning. When students engage in group discussions, peer review, or collaborative projects, they take on more responsibility for their education. When implemented strategically, discussion boards, peer reviews, and group projects can help students engage and develop genuine ideas (Aghaee & Keller, 2016).
4. **Setting Realistic Goals:** Guiding students to set attainable learning objectives that allow them to experience incremental successes can boost self-efficacy. Schunk and Mullen explain, "before embarking on a task, individuals determine their goals and what strategies to use, and they feel self-efficacious about performing well. As they engage in tasks, they monitor their performances, assess their progress toward goals, and decide whether their strategy needs adjusting. As tasks are completed, they reflect on their experiences, make modifications, and determine the next steps (2012, p. 222).
5. **Promoting Self-Regulated Learning:** Teaching students strategies for managing their learning processes, such as time management and study techniques, can empower them to take control of their education. For some students, this may be a new concept. Faculty should consider developing online materials, the class readings, videos, and other materials, that provide information about

the importance of self-regulation and how to manage and be successful when managing online schoolwork (Hu & Driscoll, 2013; Wandler & Imbriale, 2017). Training can offer guidance about test preparation, note-taking, and time management. Some students are accustomed to reminders and the defined structure of a K-12 environment; "prompting students to consider their actions in relation to their courses will provide reminders as to what is necessary to succeed in their class" (Wandler & Imbriale, 2017 p. 8).

Anecdotal Experience

When first teaching an online class, I added chapters and articles that I had identified to supplement content, created discussion prompts, and written assignments for each week. My classes, overwhelmingly, were loaded with content, and there was an abundance of reading and written work to do. Students were given so much information that it became difficult for them to identify the critical takeaway details, and I did not offer clarity. Students expressed to me that they were stressed trying to keep up with the materials and required reading and engaged less in class.

Even though students were provided some feedback on assignments, which I assumed was helpful, they felt as though they were teaching themselves and were overwhelmed by the amount of information they were expected to process. Later, I added video content from different sites. However, the same concerns persisted; the available downloaded lectures and materials (videos, podcasts) sometimes consisted of many hours of content. The graduate students I taught were largely self-directed, engaged in reading articles and chapters and managing multiple online tasks despite the unrealistic expectations that had been set. The undergraduates tended to be more vocal about their difficulty managing the class, and their work suffered. The adverse outcomes were clear for the undergraduate students, and the student concerns were universally felt in both groups.

In one of the undergraduate classes I taught, retention was impacted, and I lost over 30 percent of the students enrolled in the class. Enrollment was already low because students were reluctant to work with a new professor. Of the remaining students, two failed the class. My teaching evaluation scores were on a five-point Likert scale, where 5 is the most favorable evaluation, and 1 is the lowest. My overall mean evaluation score was 3.3 from the handful of students that responded to the survey. Students expressed that the class was not well organized, they had a difficult time searching for items online needed for the class, and they struggled with the due dates because of the amount of work due. The average of all student GPAs was 3.0, but this did not reflect the disparity in grades. As expressed by Kuo et al. (2014), "Student satisfaction is important in the evaluation of distance education courses as it is related to the quality of online programs and student performance.

The approach to all my classes needed to be changed. I began to restructure my assignments and identify ways to determine student progress and their understanding of the core content, so the needed adjustments were identified and made.

The first thing I needed to consider was the digital literacy of the students. I had assumed a standard understanding of online technology across student groups. Most people have internet access but need to gain more knowledge of the different Learning Management Systems typically utilized in higher education. In time, I learned that while most students had experience with technology in some capacity, they had a broad range of understanding and expertise of the system they were using.

I developed video content for undergraduate classes with a more qualitative focus, highlighted certain concepts or content embedded within the class materials, and talked them through how to access

Making the Connection

on-campus resources. For graduates, I encouraged those new to the format to reach out to me and meet with them online outside of class to talk through the different online modalities. Utilizing these methods, the students began to respond to me and each other more positively.

I share my digital story with students to illustrate my own developing self-efficacy in online work. Upon first arriving in America from England, making long-distance phone calls was expensive and completed via dial-up phones. My husband suggested using emails as a method to communicate with them, and I asked him, "What is an email?" Now, I teach almost exclusively online and can communicate using different platforms. It disarms students and makes them less embarrassed about asking questions. Working with students from varying backgrounds, I learned that it was important to promote the idea that abilities are not fixed, and that online efficacy can be developed through effort and learning.

In undergraduate classes, I incorporated short weekly quizzes, which could be taken as many times as needed, which gave students the opportunity to research and understand the questions they had gotten wrong. Then, some of these answers were incorporated into the mid and end-of-semester exams. Students had the opportunity to revisit concepts, review mistakes, and embed key concepts utilizing research and repetition.

While students' writing skills are developed in general education classes, their ability to research the content and organize the material to write a paper or a long-form assignment varied greatly. For larger tasks, I incorporated chunking, breaking a paper into four sections, each section to be submitted at different times during the semester. Students would then receive feedback on each section, to be incorporated into their work prior to submitting the final project.

The most significant change was creating a greater online presence, incorporating short videos into my weekly announcements, highlighting details for the week, and reviewing concepts discussed in the prior week's content in all classes. Also, scheduling online interactive discussions, which students could attend synchronously and observe asynchronously because each opportunity was recorded, and making a reflection on the discussion a required weekly assignment. This offered me insight into when content was poorly understood, what worked to highlight critical content, and a way to get to know students better. These discussions were also consistently well-received by students in all classes. I also started inviting guest speakers from around the state and country who either had work experience fitting the objectives of the students or expertise in the subject matter.

The following year, when I taught the same higher-level undergraduate class, I was able to evaluate the same metrics: 14 percent of the students dropped out, which I could attribute to natural attrition. Enrollment was higher, and only one student failed the class. My teaching evaluation scores were on a five-point Likert scale again; response rates were higher, and, in the survey, my overall mean evaluation score was 4.9, and the student's GPA averaged out at 3.5. I have now taught this class for five years, where the overall scores have remained consistent. An example of students' feedback from my most recent year of teaching this class: "This course was not like what I was expecting; it was very informative. I like the professor's teaching skills. The way she taught us to write a research paper was genius. I really got a lot of good skills from the class that I can use going forward." Another student "The speakers who we had come in were probably my favorite part of this class. It is nice seeing people in the real world being successful in doing what we are learning to do."

In an educational landscape characterized by increasing diversity and technological advancement, empowering students through self-efficacy enhancement is a crucial component of promoting student success and ensuring that online learning truly delivers on its promise of accessible and effective education.

Self-efficacy is a powerful catalyst for success in online learning environments:

Efficacy beliefs can influence individuals to become committed to achieve their desired outcomes successfully. People who have high confidence in their capabilities are considered to have a strong sense of efficacy. They don't take difficult tasks as obstacles to avoid, but instead they take it as a challenge to develop their skills. (Quraeshi, 2016, p. 45)

When students believe in their abilities to set goals, persevere through challenges, and master the material, they become more motivated and engaged learners. This sense of self-efficacy enhances their academic performance and fosters lifelong skills of self-discipline, problem-solving, and adaptability. As online education continues to grow in importance, nurturing and promoting self-efficacy among students will be vital to unlocking their full potential and ensuring their continued success in an increasingly digital and knowledge-driven world.

REFERENCES

Abdolrezapour, P., Jahanbakhsh Ganjeh, S., & Ghanbari, N. (2023). Self-efficacy and resilience as predictors of students' academic motivation in online education. *PLoS One*, *18*(5), e0285984–e0285984. doi:10.1371/journal.pone.0285984 PMID:37220147

Adaji, I., Oyibo, K., & Vassileva, J. (2018). Shopper types and the influence of persuasive strategies in E-commerce. *Proceedings of the Personalization in Persuasive Technology Workshop, Persuasive Technology*, *2089*, 58–67.

Aghaee & Keller, C. (2016). ICT-supported peer interaction among learners in Bachelor's and Master's thesis courses. *Computers and Education*, *94*, 276–297. doi:10.1016/j.compedu.2015.11.006

Alkış, N., & Temizel, T. T. (2018). The Impact of Motivation and Personality on Academic Performance in Online and Blended Learning Environments. *Journal of Educational Technology & Society*, *21*(3), 35–47. https://www.jstor.org/stable/26458505

Alqurashi. (2016). Self-Efficacy In Online Learning Environments: A Literature Review. *Contemporary Issues in Education Research*, *9*(1), 45–52. doi:10.19030/cier.v9i1.9549

Aragon, S. R., & Johnson, E. S. (2008). Factors influencing completion and noncompletion of community college online courses. *American Journal of Distance Education*, *22*(3), 146–158. doi:10.1080/08923640802239962

Ayllón, S., Alsina, Á., & Colomer, J. (2019). Teachers' involvement and students' self-efficacy: Keys to achievement in higher education. *PLoS One*, *14*(5), e0216865–e0216865. doi:10.1371/journal.pone.0216865 PMID:31125346

Bandura, A. (1986). *Social foundations of thought and action: A social cognitive theory*. Prentice Hall.

Bandura, A. (1997). *Self-efficacy: The exercise of control*. Freeman.

Bandura, A. (2012). On the Functional Properties of Perceived Self-Efficacy Revisited. *Journal of Management*, *38*(1), 9–44. doi:10.1177/0149206311410606

Banna, J., Grace Lin, M. F., Stewart, M., & Fialkowski, M. K. (2015). Interaction matters: Strategies to promote engaged learning in an online introductory nutrition course. *Journal of Online Learning and Teaching*, *11*(2), 249–261. PMID:27441032

Bates, R., & Khasawneh, S. (2004). Self-efficacy and college students' perceptions and use of online learning systems. *Computers in Human Behavior*, *23*(1). doi:10.1016/j.chb.2004.04.004

Bialowas, A., & Steimel, S. (2019). Less is more: Use of video to address the problem of teacher immediacy and presence in online courses. *International Journal on Teaching and Learning in Higher Education*, *31*(2), 354–364. https://eric.ed.gov/?id=EJ1224346

Brown, I., & Inouye, D. K. (1978). Learned helplessness through modeling: The role of perceived similarity in competence. *Journal of Personality and Social Psychology*, *36*(8), 900–908. doi:10.1037/0022-3514.36.8.900

Casey, G., & Wells, M. (2015). Remixing to design learning: Social media and peer-to-peer interaction. *Journal of Learning Design*, *8*(1). Advance online publication. doi:10.5204/jld.v8i1.225

Chandra, S., & Palvia, S. (2021). Online education next wave: Peer to peer learning. *Journal of Information Technology Case and Application Research*, *23*(3), 157–172. doi:10.1080/15228053.2021.1980848

Chang, C.-S., Liu, E. Z.-F., Sung, H.-Y., Lin, C.-H., Chen, N.-S., & Cheng, S.-S. (2014). Effects of online college student's Internet self-efficacy on learning motivation and performance. *Innovations in Education and Teaching International*, *51*(4), 366–377. doi:10.1080/14703297.2013.771429

Cheng, S., & Shi, Y. (2018). Thematic issue on "Brainstorm Optimization Algorithms." *Memetic Computing*, *10*(4), 351–352. doi:10.100712293-018-0276-3

Cho & Cho, Y. (2014). Instructor scaffolding for interaction and students' academic engagement in online learning: Mediating role of perceived online class goal structures. *The Internet and Higher Education*, *21*, 25–30. doi:10.1016/j.iheduc.2013.10.008

Cole, A. W., Lennon, L., & Weber, N. L. (2021). Student perceptions of online active learning practices and online learning climate predict online course engagement. *Interactive Learning Environments*, *29*(5), 866–880. doi:10.1080/10494820.2019.1619593

Draus, C. M. J., & Trempus, M. S. (2014). The Influence of Instructor-Generated Video Content on Student Satisfaction with and Engagement in Asynchronous Online Classes. *Journal of Online Learning and Teaching*, *10*(2).

Du, J., Fan, X., Xu, J., Wang, C., Sun, L., & Liu, F. (2019). Predictors for students' self-efficacy in online collaborative groupwork. *Educational Technology Research and Development*, *67*(4), 767–791. doi:10.100711423-018-9631-9

Dziuban, C., & Moskal, P. (2011). A course is a course is a course: Factor invariance in student evaluation of online, blended, and face-to-face learning environments. *The Internet and Higher Education*, *14*(4), 236–241. doi:10.1016/j.iheduc.2011.05.003

Eom, S. B., & Ashill, N. (2016). The Determinants of Students' Perceived Learning Outcomes and Satisfaction in University Online Education: An Update. *Decision Sciences Journal of Innovative Education*, *14*(2), 185–215. doi:10.1111/dsji.12097

Fitchett, P. G., Starker, T. V., & Salyers, B. (2012). Examining Culturally Responsive Teaching Self-Efficacy in a Preservice Social Studies Education Course. *Urban Education*, *47*(3), 585–611. doi:10.1177/0042085912436568

Galanis, E., Hatzigeorgiadis, A., Comoutos, N., Charachousi, F., & Sanchez, X. (2018). From the lab to the field: Effects of self-talk on task performance under distracting conditions. *The Sport Psychologist*, *32*(1), 26–3. doi:10.1123/tsp.2017-0017

Gay, G., & Kirkland, K. (2003). *Developing cultural critical consciousness and self-reflection in preservice teacher education*. Theory into Practice. doi:10.120715430421tip4203_3

Gellisch, M., Morosan-Puopolo, G., Wolf, O. T., Moser, D. A., Zaehres, H., & Brand-Saberi, B. (2023, April). Interactive teaching enhances students' physiological arousal during online learning. *Annals of Anatomy*, *247*, 152050. doi:10.1016/j.aanat.2023.152050 PMID:36693546

Glazier, R. A. (2016). Building rapport to improve retention and success in online classes. *Journal of Political Science Education*, *12*(4), 437–456. doi:10.1080/15512169.2016.1155994

Hamilton, I. (2023, September 6). By the numbers: The rise of online learning in the U.S. *Forbes*. https://www.forbes.com/advisor/education/online-learning-stats/

Hebert, C. G., Kulkin, H., & Ahn, B. (2014). Facilitating research self-efficacy through teaching strategies linked to self-efficacy theory. *American International Journal of Social Science*, *3*(1), 44–50.

Hew, K., Qiao, C., & Tang, Y. (2018). Understanding student engagement in large-scale open online courses: A machine learning facilitated analysis of student's reflections in 18 highly rated MOOCs. *International Review of Research in Open and Distance Learning*, *19*(3). Advance online publication. doi:10.19173/irrodl.v19i3.3596

Hodges, C. B. (2008). Self-efficacy in the context of online learning environments: A review of the literature and directions for research. *Performance Improvement Quarterly*, *20*(3-4), 7–25. doi:10.1002/piq.20001

Hu & Driscoll, M. P. (2013). Self-Regulation in e-Learning Environments: A Remedy for Community College? *Educational Technology & Society, 16*(4), 171–184.

Huang, X., & Mayer, R. E. (2019). Adding Self-Efficacy Features to an Online Statistics Lesson. *Journal of Educational Computing Research*, *57*(4), 1003–1037. doi:10.1177/0735633118771085

Ice, P., Curtis, R., Phillips, P., & Wells, J. (2019). Using asynchronous audio feedback to enhance teaching presence and students' sense of community. *Online Learning : the Official Journal of the Online Learning Consortium*, *11*(2). Advance online publication. doi:10.24059/olj.v11i2.1724

Jan, S. K. (2015). The Relationships Between Academic Self-Efficacy, Computer Self-Efficacy, Prior Experience, and Satisfaction With Online Learning. *American Journal of Distance Education*, *29*(1), 30–40. doi:10.1080/08923647.2015.994366

Jiang, M., & Ballenger, J. (2023). Nontraditional doctoral students' perceptions of instructional strategies used to enhance statistics self-efficacy in online learning. *The Journal of Educators Online, 20*(1). Advance online publication. doi:10.9743/JEO.2023.20.1.7

Johnston, A. N., Barton, M. J., Williams-Pritchard, G. A., & Todorovic, M. (2018). YouTube for millennial nursing students; using internet technology to support student engagement with bioscience. *Nurse Education in Practice, 31*, 151–155. doi:10.1016/j.nepr.2018.06.002 PMID:29906632

Joo, L., Lim, K. Y., & Kim, J. (2013). Locus of control, self-efficacy, and task value as predictors of learning outcome in an online university context. *Computers & Education, 62*, 149–158. doi:10.1016/j.compedu.2012.10.027

Kang, M., & Im, T. (2013). Factors of learner-instructor interaction which predict perceived learning outcomes in an online learning environment. *Journal of Computer Assisted Learning, 29*(3), 292–301. doi:10.1111/jcal.12005

Knutsson, O., Blåsjö, M., Hållsten, S., & Karlström, P. (2012). Identifying different registers of digital literacy in virtual learning environments. *The Internet and Higher Education, 15*(4), 237–246. doi:10.1016/j.iheduc.2011.11.002

Kuo, Y., & Belland, B. R. (2016). An exploratory study of adult learners' perceptions of online learning: Minority students in continuing education. *Educational Technology Research and Development, 64*(4), 661–680. doi:10.100711423-016-9442-9

Kuo, Y.-C., Walker, A. E., Schroder, K. E. E., & Belland, B. R. (2014). Interaction, Internet self-efficacy, and self-regulated learning as predictors of student satisfaction in online education courses. *The Internet and Higher Education, 20*, 35–50. doi:10.1016/j.iheduc.2013.10.001

Lee, O. E. K., Kim, S. Y., & Gezer, T. (2021). Factors Associated With Online Learning Self-Efficacy Among Students With Disabilities In Higher Education. *American Journal of Distance Education, 35*(4), 293–306. doi:10.1080/08923647.2021.1979344

Li, L. Y., & Tsai, C. C. (2017). Accessing online learning material: Quantitative behavior patterns and their effects on motivation and learning performance. *Computers & Education, 114*(1), 286-297. https://www.learntechlib.org/p/201259/

Liu, Z. Y., Lomovtseva, N., & Korobeynikova, E. (2020). Online Learning Platforms: Reconstructing Modern Higher Education. *International Journal of Emerging Technologies in Learning (iJET), 15*(13), 4-21. https://www.learntechlib.org/p/217605/

Maier, A., Schaitz, C., Kröner, J., Berger, A., Keller, F., Beschoner, P., Connemann, B., & Sosic-Vasic, Z. (2021, November 30). The Association Between Test Anxiety, Self-Efficacy, and Mental Images Among University Students: Results from an Online Survey. *Frontiers in Psychiatry, 12*, 618108. doi:10.3389/fpsyt.2021.618108 PMID:34916965

Martin, F., & Bolliger, D. U. (2018). Engagement Matters: Student Perceptions on the Importance of Engagement Strategies in the Online Learning Environment. *Online Learning : the Official Journal of the Online Learning Consortium, 22*(1), 205–222. doi:10.24059/olj.v22i1.1092

Marzano, M. S., & Allen, R. J. (2016). Online vs. face-to-face course evaluations: Considerations for administrators and faculty. *Online Journal of Distance Learning Administration, 19*(4).

Medaille, A., Beisler, M., Tokarz, R., & Bucy, R. (2022). The Role of Self-Efficacy in the Thesis-Writing Experiences of Undergraduate Honors Students. *Teaching and Learning Inquiry, 10.* doi:10.20343/teachlearninqu.10.2

Merle, P. F., & Craig, C. (2017). Be my guest: A survey of mass communication students' perception of guest speakers. *College Teaching, 65*(2), 41–49. doi:10.1080/87567555.2016.1232691

Orji, F. A., Vassileva, J., & Greer, J. E. (2018). Personalized Persuasion for Promoting Students' Engagement and Learning. *PPT@ PERSUASIVE, 18*, 77-87.

Peechapol, C., Na-Songkhla, J., Sujiva, S., & Luangsodsai, A. (2018). An exploration of factors influencing self-efficacy in online learning: A systematic review. *International Journal of Emerging Technologies in Learning, 13*(9), 64. doi:10.3991/ijet.v13i09.8351

Prior, D. D., Mazanov, J., Meacheam, D., Heaslip, G., & Hanson, J. (2016). Attitude, digital literacy, and self-efficacy: Flow-on effects for online learning behavior. *The Internet and Higher Education, 29*, 91–97. doi:10.1016/j.iheduc.2016.01.001

Pumptow, M., & Brahm, T. (2021). Students' Digital Media Self-Efficacy and Its Importance for Higher Education Institutions: Development and Validation of a Survey Instrument. *Tech Know Learn, 26*(3), 555–575. doi:10.100710758-020-09463-5

Sanders, M. J., Van Oss, T., & McGeary, S. (2016). Analyzing Reflections in Service Learning to Promote Personal Growth and Community Self-Efficacy. *Journal of Experiential Education, 39*(1), 73–88. doi:10.1177/1053825915608872

Schuessler, J. H. (2017). "Chunking" Semester Projects: Does it Enhance Student Learning? *Journal of Higher Education Theory and Practice, 17*(7). https://articlegateway.com/index.php/JHETP/article/view/1474

Schunk, D. H., & Mullen, C. A. (2012). Self-Efficacy as an Engaged Learner. In S. Christenson, A. Reschly, & C. Wylie (Eds.), *Handbook of Research on Student Engagement*. Springer. doi:10.1007/978-1-4614-2018-7_10

Smith Jaggars, S., & Xu, D. (2016). How do online course design features influence student performance? *Computers & Education, 95*, 270–284. doi:10.1016/j.compedu.2016.01.014

Stephen, J. S., & Rockinson-Szapkiw, A. J. (2021). A high-impact practice for online students: the use of a first-semester seminar course to promote self-regulation, self-direction, online learning self-efficacy. *Smart Learn. Environ., 8*, 6. 10.118640561-021-00151-0

Thomson, A., Bridgstock, R., & Willems, C. (2014). 'Teachers flipping out' beyond the online lecture: Maximising the educational potential of video. *Journal of Learning Design, 7*(3). Advance online publication. doi:10.5204/jld.v7i3.209

Vayre, E., & Vonthron, A.-M. (2017). Psychological Engagement of Students in Distance and Online Learning: Effects of Self-Efficacy and Psychosocial Processes. *Journal of Educational Computing Research, 55*(2), 197–218. doi:10.1177/0735633116656849

Wandler & Imbriale, W. J. (2017). Promoting Undergraduate Student Self-Regulation in Online Learning Environments. *Online Learning, 21*(2). doi:10.24059/olj.v21i2.881

Wang, A. Y., & Newlin, M. H. (2002). Predictors of web-student performance: The role of self-efficacy and reasons for taking an online class. *Computers in Human Behavior, 18*(2), 151–163. doi:10.1016/S0747-5632(01)00042-5

Wang, C.-H., Shannon, D. M., & Ross, M. E. (2013). Students' characteristics, self-regulated learning, technology self-efficacy, and course outcomes in online learning. *Distance Education, 34*(3), 302–323. doi:10.1080/01587919.2013.835779

Wang, S., & Wu, P. (2008). The role of feedback and self-efficacy on web-based learning: The social cognitive perspective. *Computers & Education, 51*(4), 1589-1598. doi:10.1016/j.compedu.2008.03.004

Wilde, N., & Hsu, A. (2019). The influence of general self-efficacy on the interpretation of vicarious experience information within online learning. *International Journal of Educational Technology in Higher Education, 16*(1), 26. doi:10.118641239-019-0158-x

Wolverton, C. C., Hollier, B. N. G., & Lanier, P. A. (2020). The impact of computer self-efficacy on student engagement and group satisfaction in online business courses. *Electronic Journal of e-Learning, 18*(2). Advance online publication. doi:10.34190/EJEL.20.18.2.006

Xie, K., Yu, C., & Bradshaw, A. C. (2014). Impacts of role assignment and participation in asynchronous discussions in college-level online classes. *The Internet and Higher Education, 20*, 10–19. .doi:10.1016/j.iheduc.2013.09.003

Yalcinalp, S., & Gulbahar, Y. (2010). Ontology and taxonomy design and development for personalised web-based learning systems. *British Journal of Educational Technology, 41*(6), 883–896. doi:10.1111/j.1467-8535.2009.01049.x

Yilmaz, R., & Karaoglan Yilmaz, F. G. (2019). Assigned Roles as a Structuring Tool in Online Discussion Groups: Comparison of Transactional Distance and Knowledge Sharing Behaviors. *Journal of Educational Computing Research, 57*(5), 1303–1325. doi:10.1177/0735633118786855

Yokoyama. (2019). Academic Self-Efficacy and Academic Performance in Online Learning: A Mini Review. *Frontiers in Psychology, 9*, 2794–2794. doi:10.3389/fpsyg.2018.02794

Chapter 16
Not Another Discussion Board:
One Online Instructor's Reflective Practices to Create Effective Student Engagement

Elodie J. Jones
https://orcid.org/0000-0003-4557-3710
Fort Hays State University, USA

ABSTRACT

This chapter sheds light on the journey of one online instructor's self-examination and purposeful approaches to engaging and eliciting robust student interactions in online graduate asynchronous settings. Centered on Knowles' Principles of Andragogy and Vygotsky's Social Constructivism, the researcher utilized an ongoing formal reflection process to gather student responses, alter course materials, and strived to create an environment that supported growth mindset, learner autonomy and the online graduate experience.

What immediate response(s) is conjured when "discussion board" is mentioned? Is your reaction steeped with great memories of interacting and learning from peers and instructors, or are they one of potential dread and "task" based on a class you once took or are currently teaching? In an online setting, discussion boards are a standard tool to encourage students to share their knowledge and understanding and learn from others. Discussion boards support a constructivist learning approach that aligns with andragogical theory (Knowles, 1984). However, how does an instructor illicit more profound student learning through self- and peer-constructed knowledge, collaboration, and participation by utilizing discussion boards in an online asynchronous graduate course (Lyons & Evans, 2013)?

Teaching for over 20 years in online and face-to-face settings within P12, undergraduate, and graduate environments, I had high expectations and a naive mindset regarding quality written student responses. In 2013, I entered my tenure as an Assistant Professor within a College of Education with limited experience concerning online discussion boards and student engagement. I attended graduate school face-to-face and taught undergraduate technology courses in a computer lab. A portion of my new faculty workload included online course delivery in asynchronous undergraduate teacher education courses. As a newbie, it was evident that the quintessential discussion board was a mainstay in most online curricula. The mere

DOI: 10.4018/978-1-6684-8908-6.ch016

mention of the word "discussion board" often sent my student's eyes rolling and an occasional sigh. If I told them we could skip the discussion board if they participated in round table discussions and whole group sharing, students would become engaged and chatty as if their grades depended upon it.

After several years in primarily undergraduate teacher education courses, I applied to teach online, asynchronous graduate coursework within my college. Recentering my courses on Knowles' (1984) Principles of Andragogy and Vygotsky's Social Constructivism (1978), where I expected that a portion of student learning was based on peer interactions and learning from others, I pressed on with high hopes. Based on my presumption of graduate students, why would they not naturally jump in and discuss the content with one another and be motivated by the rich experiences that their peers were sharing? Again, the thoughts regarding a naive mindset with high expectations swirled around in my head and were the basis of change. I began to reflect on my role in student learning and better understand who my students were and what they needed as learners, especially post-pandemic.

After constantly examining and observing student discussion board interactions, which contained little depth or concertedly less effort to "dig in" and engage with one another like on-campus courses made me reflect and dig deeper into soliciting the responses I knew my students were capable of as P12 classroom teachers. I wondered if meaningful human connections, peer sharing of knowledge and experiences, and genuine engagement were possible in an online asynchronous setting. What were *they* doing wrong as learners that they responded just to respond, and at best, their discussion responses or peer feedback were surface level or Recall Level per *Webb's Depth of Knowledge* (Francis, 2017)? Meaning, why were students not sharing their own application, analysis of tools they were using in my course, and applying the tools to the context of the classroom or workplace? Based on my expectations, why did I feel my students were doing the bare minimum? Societally, we have moved into a need for a workday that we have more recently coined "Bare-minimum Mondays" as a shielding act of self-care on the job (DiDonato, 2023). Were students living out the mantra of the bare minimum in my online classes?

I began to reflect on my instructional methods and expectations and re-set my courses regarding what portion of the learning I could control as the course facilitator and the "guide on the side." Self-admittedly, the change had to begin with me and how I framed the expectations and questions, thus impacting student engagement and responses. I also began to take stock of my students' course reflections and how I had utilized the use of reflection to alter my methods, materials, and overall teaching. The Transference Reflection Cycle asks students in the first stage, or the Exploration Stage, to write their initial reactions, thoughts, feelings, and biases as they enter the course (Appendix 1: *Transference Reflection Cycle*). I began having students initiate their reflection in the first week of my courses, and it proved to be very telling concerning what my students were experiencing as learners. As adult learners in an online graduate program, most of whom are full-time P12 educators, their need for support and understanding was overwhelming. After all, I was a graduate student in their first statistics course, thinking I had landed on Mars and would never understand quantitative research methods' discussions, context, or relevance. My students needed my support, encouragement, and compassion as they began their journey as online graduate students.

The changes I began to make regarding my discussion board expectations and rubric, even before COVID-19, were incremental, and it took me several semesters to notice a change in the level of students' responses, engagement, and sharing. However, the changes became evident in my student's discussion board interactions and final reflection documents as an initial and final assignment in my courses. As previously stated, I made minor changes to the standard discussion board prompts from "Respond to two peers" to "Interact with peers and engage in organic and genuine feedback, discussion, sharing, and inquiry; I do not count the number of posts." I supported my language with a developmental-based rubric explaining "organic and genuine." I pressed on and hoped for the best, only knowing that what I changed made me feel more inclusive and helped me to focus more on the qualitative versus the quantitative aspects of teaching and learning. Beyond the change in verbiage, I altered how I began my Welcome Email, or initial email each semester, with supportive autonomy-based languages, increased instructor interactions and responses, and high expectations (Cheon et al., 2020). Over the last three years, I observed significant differences in the quantity and quality of my students' interactions. I now gain student feedback regarding the value of peer interactions and the impactful learning they report carrying over into their professional lives. A simple shift in my delivery methods and language has accounted for meaningful engagement, genuine peer interaction, and impactful learning in an asynchronous setting.

Online graduate student narratives were collected through a structured reflection in the first week of a class to contain any potential bias and initial course feelings about themselves as a learner and the course in general - from materials to interface to returning to online higher education for the first time (Appendix A, *Transference Reflection Cycle*). A final course reflection takes the learner through various stages of examination, questioning, and analyzing their experience. It contains many examples demonstrating changes in instructor support, response, and overall learner experience(s). Reading and then observing students' feedback and prescriptive changes in my learner's experiences helped me to question my own methodology regarding course policies, expectations, and the words I utilized with students. This chapter explores instructor insights regarding reflective practices and realizations encompassing student interactions when prompted to engage in peer conversations and sharing genuinely. Moreover, the students' responses were far less about the quantitative response ("respond to two peers") and more about the peer interaction, sharing, and potential space of peer connection and community in an online setting. More profoundly are the shared reflections by online graduate students and how their experiences were affected by embracing a mindset for peer sharing that involved content and experiences beyond the assignment and created peer connections, resulting in the sense of camaraderie and potential safety in an online space.

BACKGROUND

Quantitative Minimum

Will students always gravitate to doing the least work for the greatest reward? I often entered my undergraduate face-to-face courses and joked with students on the first day that if I "gave them all an A right now, then can they remove all extrinsic motivation like being perfect and getting an A versus engaging in the rich experiences of failing, sharing, digging in, reflecting and growing as a learner." Most students would laugh and semi-get the drift concerning the notion that I genuinely cared about their growth and what they retained from my courses versus the grades they earned. Unfortunately, the over-testing and emphasis on P12 students' assessment scores and the battle for college entry based on standardized tests have created a mindset that rewards success. The system has created learners who strive for an "A" over truly learning and committing the content to memory, let alone recall and application (Galla et al., 2019; Long, 2023). Moreover, how can we blame P12 educators who have primarily focused on successful high-stakes test scores perpetually the loss of their jobs and focusing on tests as if their lives were dependent upon it (Barksdale-Ladd & Thomas, 2000; Baker et al., 2010; Lazarin, 2014)? I realized that the stress of testing and a no-fail mindset had created severe issues in my university course. There was no motivation for authentic learning and growth, only for the extrinsic reward of getting the A and keeping the scholarship(s).

Campbell's Law (1976) posited that "The more any quantitative social indicator is used for social decision-making, the more subject it will be to corruption pressures and the more apt it will be to distort and corrupt the social processes it is intended to monitor" (p. 34). Far before the era of online education, Campbell originally proposed the concept in response to the burgeoning field of program evaluation (Olt & Jones, 2024). Therefore, when program evaluations and standardized assessment outcomes were used for high-stakes decisions, those being measured would tailor their efforts to satisfy the quantitative metrics being applied to appear strong without necessarily being so - much like P12 teachers that taught to the test versus utilizing more robust methods to achieve enduring understandings through hands-on, project-based learning (Brown et al., 2014; PBL Works, n.d.).

Indeed, such simple, clear quantitative metrics are attractive as they provide concrete expectations for our students. However, quantity over quality does not solicit what we commonly seek from students' responses and interactions in both face-to-face and online settings. The driving force in supporting engaging and quality student responses and interaction is removing instructional verbiage and rubrics that value quantity (e.g., respond twice to your peers) versus more organic and genuine conversations. In my first five years of teaching online, I often reflected on the lack of depth regarding students' discussion(s). However, moreover, I observed that the majority followed the instructions ("Respond to two peers") and engaged in two responses at what would be considered a very "surface level" response. A colleague and I discussed the phenomenon that we were observing, and both changed our prompts regarding discussion boards, along with our rubrics, to reflect a culture that supported more interaction and true discussion ("I do not count the number of responses. Instead, I value the organic and genuine discussions you have with your peers."). Part of the shift regarding student expectations was developing a quality rubric that supports the students' understanding of what the instructor expects, combined with instructor interaction regarding feedback and praise for genuine engagement, combats the students' tendency to post surface-level responses and genuinely engage in peer sharing and interactions. The student's sense of autonomy to feel safe, the discussion becomes collaborative, and students sharing ideas in a space regarding their experiences has potentially played a large part in the overall students' experience concerning discussion boards (Hillen & Paivarinta, 2012).

Student Engagement

The word engagement is a common buzzword and is over-utilized in education, with little understanding of the facets encompassing learner engagement. In the 1930s, Tyler first focused on pioneering the construct of Time on task concerning student engagement (Koh, 2009). Engagement, or being engaged, is defined by Merriam-Webster's Dictionary (n.d.) as "emotional involvement or commitment" among the most common definitions. Within the context of student engagement, Koh (2009) defines student engagement as "the time and effort students devote to activities that are empirically linked to desired outcomes of college and what institutions do to induce students to participate in these activities" (p. 683). Researchers such as Fletcher (2015) defined student engagement as "any sustained connection a learner has towards any aspect of learning, schools or education." Engagement can be difficult to measure as it encompasses various behavioral, emotional, and cognitive components that fluctuate based on the individual and environment (Fredricks et al., 2004; Olson & Peterson, 2015). As Fredricks and colleagues (2004) report, student engagement is commonly noted when coursework encompasses some combination of the learner's behavioral, emotional, and cognitive side. Regardless of the multitude of definitions and various forms of engagement, researchers, accrediting bodies, administration, parents/guardians, educators, students, and society understand that engagement is essential when measuring learning outcomes and student achievement. What engagement components do I most commonly observe in my online graduate students based on their responses and reflections?

Commonly, my students have reported that they have not felt empowered and motivated as a learner, affecting their engagement in a course because they perceived they had little autonomy as the learner, or what I commonly refer to as choice and voice combined with instructor flexibility (Connell, 1990). One area that students commonly cite in their course reflections was the built-in flexibility and ease with which they could meet the learning objectives and frame their outcome(s) based on their individual needs as a learner. Learner autonomy or Autonomy-supportive classrooms are essential when considering learner differences regarding areas of interest or frames of reference. Moreover, in my courses, the ranges of ages and content areas my students teach as P12 educators are considered as they approach discussion contexts and individual projects. Students have reported that having the flexibility to adapt and individualize assignments based on their needs is one element that made the class enjoyable and meaningful. I purposefully created discussion boards, exploration assignments, and mini projects that are easily moldable and customizable, still meeting the same learning outcomes. Allowing students to individualize their learning or frame the learning in various contexts allows them to connect with the course, reflect on their skills or comfort level to alter their work for content areas (e.g., Math, Science, Social Studies), and choose developmentally appropriate tools and materials for their P12 learners. Recently, a Kindergarten teacher shared her experience and the built-in flexibility of an introductory masters-level technology integration course:

As the class began moving, my anxiety lowered, and my thirst for knowledge took over. Yes, I love to learn, so I am in education. It is fair to state that my fear and anxiety sometimes affect how I measure my success. When I began the first assignments, I could finally settle down and feel comfortable with technology. I loved reading classmates' posts and realizing I was not alone in my class and that others felt very similar to me. As the assignments began, they covered many specific topics. The directions were clear yet open to flexibility to allow for a broader range of learning. The assignments varied from discussion posts to mini assignments and always a response to peers. This allowed for reflection and a broader view to see the opinions of other educators in the class. When I think back to the beginning of the class, I remember being eager for the discussions because I love to be evaluated and learn. Hearing what other individuals say is a huge part of the learning process. I was apprehensive about grad-level classes and hoped they would be challenging, not just busy work. This prejudgment of the class was disproved by the involvement and the material assigned over the last 8 weeks.

The student shares the emotions related to the course, which creates potential anxiety for them, which is valid for many adult learners attending online graduate courses for the first time. There is a high level of imposter syndrome or imposter phenomenon, and the various stage of the reflection process captures the initial feelings but also captures students' initial bias, feelings, and overall mindset to their lived course experience(s) (Clance & Imes,1978; Kets de Vries, 2005). To say that the reflection stages are decisive for the learner and myself as the instructor would be an understatement. All the newness encompassed by a host of tools and directions for a 16-week course delivered in an 8-week time frame can be demanding mentally and physically for the learner. The feeling of being overwhelmed, anxious, and generalized fears of online education and using new technology(ies) are commonly reported within the first week when students complete the reflection process, or the Exploration Stage (Appendix 1). One Elementary teacher shares their initial feelings as they begin the capstone course that encompasses the development of a professional electronic portfolio (PeP) over a semester and culminates into a comprehensive interview:

The portfolio itself looks intimidating due to the length of requirements for the (web)site. I am, however, looking forward to the collaboration portion of this class. Each class I have taken in the program has us collaborating with our peers, but this time it is different. I really like the fact that I am able to work with one person and collaborate throughout the whole portfolio-building process. I think this is also a great way to gain and build professional relationships.

A fifth-grade teacher shares their final reflection stage as they circle back and address their initial thoughts in the Synthesis Stage, where students synthesize their learner experience as they close the learning loop and begin to see their experience come full circle:

I also talked about being nervous that this course was all online because I am such a people person, but now that we are finishing this course, I can say that the online community in this class is phenomenal, and all my peers helped me grow, and I learned so much from all of them. They all have so many different perspectives and have taught me to be okay with change and step out of my comfort zone when implementing technology into my classroom. After two semesters of my online master's program, I can still say that my peers listen, collaborate, and help each other reach goals and help each other become successful. We continue to be in this together and work together to better our students nationwide.

Additionally, the graduate students indicate their learning experience is flexible, thus signaling potential learner autonomy, and report overwhelming peer support. Students report various takeaways from their peers from a constructivist perspective or learning from those around them, which I highly value and align with Vygotsky's (1978) and Knowles' (1984) theories. The social component of learning and constructing knowledge through peers easily complements my courses with a high degree of social learning through various course tools and intentional peer review.

Peer Review

Peer review is a common construct in higher education associated with reviewing materials and utilizing credible sources to validate that one's work is valid and reliable. Peer review is the gold standard and seal of approval needed to move forward within higher education. It is a common practice utilized in P12 education for annual reviews. Within the context of adult learning, I once again was met with the naive realization that adult learners would automatically know how to and have the perceived authority to give their peers feedback based on the learning objectives. Once again, I was proven wrong. I decided to model peer feedback to my students within their documents (e.g., embedded comments using Google Docs). I provided students with tools concerning constructive feedback and the verbal authority to give their peers constructive feedback. As a side note, a phenomenon occurred in which I began to see my APA correction responses utilized as peer-to-peer feedback in course documents. Commonly, I refer to a formal peer review as Oreo Cookie Responses, where students are asked to "sandwich" comments beginning with something their peer did well, then perhaps an improvement or inquiry based on the stated learning objectives, followed up by an additional statement of how the student did something well. After attempting to implement peer review in my courses, it was in my first semester that I realized that students did not know how to give effective feedback, feel that they had the authority to tell their peers what to change, or even that they might be wrong, nor did they truly understand the power of peer feedback and interaction. Even though P12 teachers are observed and reviewed annually by an administration, it is expected that P12 teachers in the U.S. have little time to eat lunch or go to the bathroom; therefore, when they have time in their day to observe, share, and give feedback to a peer down the hallway (Darling-Hammond, 2003; Perna, 2022)? Once again, the students' reflections and conversations made me realize that my assumptions were severely misguided. I needed to back up and change my written instructions and model what I wanted my students to do regarding peer interaction and feedback.

To my surprise, the use of peer review as a skillset that carries over into a graduate student's professional life has become a current theme within student reflection documents. The reality is that there is little time for peer review in P12 classrooms; however, many students see the power of conferring with and gaining valuable insight, support, and examples from their peers. As a caveat, one outcome of my program is teacher leadership aligned with the ISTE Standards and future roles they see themselves in as classroom teachers. A teacher-leader could be a mentor, department chair, technology coach, or trainer during professional development. A high school Spanish teacher stated:

I enjoyed collaborating with other teachers while working on this course and felt like that aspect of the course, in particular, was one that led to growth for me. I believe that my teaching would benefit in the future from more opportunities to collaborate with my fellow teachers over the use of technology in the classroom.

A fifth-grade teacher in the capstone course that demonstrates the power of peer review and potential leadership through the development of professional electronic portfolios or PeP (e.g., student created websites) stated:

The Comprehensive Interview over Google Meet with Dr. Jones was the perfect way to wrap up the program. I enjoyed going through various aspects of my project. I appreciated the professional discourse about what worked well and what was more challenging for me. I found it very beneficial to discuss trends across my peers' PeP's, such as cyberbullying. While the content was fantastic, the best part of this experience has been the peer interactions. From discussion boards to comment sections, Flip video responses to shared Communities, I always took away something from my peers.

I would highly recommend this program to other educators. Some of my coworkers regularly joke about their Master's degrees having been busy work, but I was truly able to apply my work from every course to my 5th-grade classroom. This program made me a stronger teacher, technology user, and future trainer.

Students within the capstone course also solicit peer feedback from an internal peer (enrolled in the course) as soon as the course begins and solicit feedback from an outside source (e.g., a co-worker) before comprehensive meetings or interviews.

What is more interesting is the power that setting expectations, modeling responses, and guiding students through peer review has had on students who reregister for one of my courses and understand the purpose and power of peer interactions. Former students are comfortable and feel empowered to help their peers immediately. Peer support ranges from accessing their documents for APA or questioning their choices regarding Universal Design within a project and other vital elements regarding accessibility and technology use in P12 education. A student who enrolled back-to-back and joined my summer course shared her realization regarding the power of the Transference Reflection Cycle as a learning tool:

I love this reflection paper's process because it shows all the growth made in just one short month. I was intimidated by new technology at the beginning of this course. I had a closed-off mindset to technology like AI taking over education, and my mindset has completely changed. Through research of my own and learning from my peers, I have opened my mindset to all the possibilities technology has and will bring to the classroom. I also talked about being nervous that this course was all online because I am such a people person, but now that we are finishing this course, I can say that the online community in this class is phenomenal, and all my peers helped me grow, and I learned so much from all of them.

ISSUES/CHALLENGES

Initially, the challenges faced as an online faculty had little to do with my students and a great deal to do with how I was talking to my students, the verbiage I shared in my initial welcome email, my overall mindset, and approach as an instructor, as well as the empowerment, expectations, and modeling concerning expectations for learning and peer review. Utilizing reflection and homing in on student needs during and post-Covid changed my perspective regarding the needs of P12 teachers and the trenches they work in daily. Utilizing autonomy-supportive language, being mindful of my response to students, and utilizing a little humor made a difference.

One area I was not equipped for, as a former P12 teacher, was independent learning and the role of truly being the "guide on the side." It is commonly known in the P12 world that a teacher as a facilitator is much more powerful and learning that "sticks" when focusing on a student-centered, hands-on classroom versus a teacher-centered, lecture-based classroom (Palloff & Pratt, 2001; Brown et al., 2014). As a facilitator, I guide my students and act as a peer reviewer, a commenter, a learner right alongside, and the person who ultimately grades their work based on rubrics. Educational research preaches over and over that being a "guide on the side" and not a "sage on the stage" is a powerful and effective strategy for teaching (Woolfolk, 2020). However, I was unprepared for the overwhelming amount of learning between peers and how evident it is in student reflections. Students repeatedly cited the learning acquired from peers and mentioned my work, instructions, guidance, and hours of APA feedback as secondary. Knowing I was not at the center of their learning was difficult to swallow initially. However, now I am proud that my course(s) function independently of my teaching role and that students have the space for problem-solving, critical thinking, and being creative in an environment that supports individual learning, trials, failures, successes, reflections, playtime, and mindset focusing on "progress over perfection."

STUDENT VOICES

In my opinion, there is no more significant indicator regarding the power of classroom learning than the voice of my students' lived experiences. Student feedback that is honest, genuine, and vulnerable is applauded in my course and held in a safe and trusting space that I work to create to ensure they have a very individualized and growth-oriented experience. I opened the door in my initial email to express the notion that we are all learning and that I highly value their feedback and insight as P12 teachers and their graduate student experiences. The Transference Reflection Cycle was "just another assignment" I utilized in the first few years of university teaching. I commonly overlooked its completion as more of an APA document than the rich feedback it could provide for my instruction. Altering my teaching approaches impactfully changed the quality of reflection feedback as a student outlet for sharing their experience and ultimately changed. The reflection document was the reflective and clarifying window into my student's learning experiences. However, my teaching materials, approaches, and methods ultimately needed to be altered to manifest the best learning experience possible for my graduate students. To summarize the small yet significant changes I made and their effects on my courses, one student captures what I could not in a book chapter supported by reputable theories and credible research. The student, a high school business and computer teacher share their experiences:

Other beliefs I have after reading through the course syllabus and other provided information is that this course will indeed be more difficult than any other I've taken to this point. Dr. Jones (2023) has already stated, "Yes, I plan to challenge you. There will be rigorous reading, weekly writing assignments, reflections, peer interactions and learning, and concepts that will challenge your thinking." This tells me that it won't be a course that will have assignments that can be put together in a few minutes and submitted on Sunday evening and then ignored until the following Sunday evening. This is a course that will obviously entail some major preparation and effort in addition to time management skills. I look forward to the challenge.

After the past several weeks of this course, I have come to the conclusion that my prejudices about this course were mostly accurate in terms of the workload and the difficulty. I did spent many hours researching the various articles as with other courses I have taken at this university, but in this case, I also spent just as much time looking over the work of my peers that they submitted for each Discussion Board or Mini Assignment. I have not experienced this with other courses to this extent. I will concede I have been guilty of a few "good job," "I think you're right on track with this comment," or "I agree completely" comments to my peers in other courses. But I applaud Dr. Jones in this course for really stressing at the very beginning the belief in quality over quantity. So I definitely spent more time, quality time, looking over my peers' works and giving some genuine thought this time around in my responses. This was a great experience in the course because it gave me extra insight beyond just researching the articles and materials provided as it gave me the viewpoints of a dozen or more other peers who were contributing to my discussions and submissions. Again, this is usually done in the other courses I've taken, but it worked to a much greater and more detailed level in this course and that was greatly rewarding. It was certainly more difficult and challenging at times, but that was part of the rewarding experience.

My intent and goal after this course is to continue to strive for that knowledge through continuous research as well as maintaining contact with peers, both in my current school as well as peers from this course. I have total confidence that their shared enthusiasm and willingness to give advice and constructive criticism will go a long way toward helping me continue my development as an educator in the coming years, and I truly hope my peers in this course feel the same way about contacting me for advice as well. I cannot stress enough how valuable this course information has been and how grateful I have been to have been a part of it. With a hopeful and optimistic vision for the future, this is [insert student name], signing off for now.

As an instructor who worried about "being too nice," because universities historically focus on rigor, hard work, dedication, no boundaries, and working all hours of the night, I learned through student reflections that I can be kind, understanding, accommodating, and humorous without reducing the high expectations and quality work that I expect from students obtaining a master's degree in my program. I learned that there is space to be human and expect a great deal from my students, even if it is APA formatting and styling over and over by which I commonly joke with them and say something like, "Aren't all these APA rules fun?" and then insert a comment about their title formats, citations, or References page. The humor and statements of expectations, such as "progress over perfection," convey that mistakes are okay, corrections are expected, and there is a space for growth and learning in my courses. I also explain to students that if they "knew all the things" and had everything perfectly mapped out, why would they enroll in a master's program?

RECOMMENDATIONS AND CONCLUSIONS

The truth about our teaching is that much of what we produce and disseminate to our students begins with us as the instructor and facilitator of information in online learning environments. For ten years, I have been able to reflect on my methods, approach, and words, which have made a vast difference in getting the most out of my students and creating powerful and rewarding learning experiences for them within an online setting. The first stages of frustration with your students and the work they are producing inadvertently must begin with the gatekeeper or the instructor. What type of autonomy-based language and practices are you utilizing to support students and hold them accountable in an environment with high expectations? Second, ask yourself, why am I getting what I get? Why am I receiving surface-level responses and very little interaction from my students? Remember, students will do exactly what they are asked to do, so if you ask a low-level question, you will get a low-level response. As, well, per Campbell's Law and my own experiences, if you ask for two peer responses in a discussion board, you will get precisely two responses from many students, and again, they will more than likely be surface level because you did not guide or expect anything beyond "a response." As a side note, even P12 educators do not believe they have the authority or skill set to give peer feedback –you must model, provide insight, and praise them when engaging in insightful and powerful peer discussions. Lastly, check your words and your tone with students.

I implemented a health and wellness policy in my classes that has changed the narrative regarding my own health and wellness and that of my students (Jones & Crawford, 2023). As the semester begins and you are forming your welcome to my class post, what are my words and responses signally to students that support a safe space to grow, learn, share, fail, succeed, play, reflect, and lead? Small conscientious efforts solicit significant changes in online graduate courses, as shared by an Elementary teacher who works with students with disabilities:

In isolation, I earned my undergraduate degree and much of my studies throughout the MIT program. However, communication with my class peers via Spaces was ongoing throughout this final course of the program. The presence of a by-product of transparency, an authentic community, struck me. The day of my comp exam gives evidence of the development of such a community. While in the meeting, I received a "thinking of you" message from one of my peers. I was surprised how the three encouraging words caused me to smile and eased my nerves; I was validated and understood. Participating in and cultivating a professional culture of transparency and authentic community will be a personal goal in the future. I endeavor to "pay it forward" within my sphere of influence as I know I will benefit from the results.

REFERENCES

Baker, E. L., Barton, P. E., Darling-Hammond, L., Haertel, E., Ladd, H. F., Linn, R. L., Ravitch, D., Rothstein, R., Shavelson, R. J., & Shepard, L. A. (2010, August 29). *Problems with the use of student test scores to evaluate teachers*. Economic Policy Institute. https://files.eric.ed.gov/fulltext/ED516803.pdf

Barksdale-Ladd, M. A., & Thomas, K. F. (2000). What's at stake in high-stakes testing: Teachers and parents speak out. *Journal of Teacher Education, 51*(5), 384–397. doi:10.1177/0022487100051005006

Brown, P. C., Roediger, H. L., & McDaniel, M. A. (2014). *Make it stick: The science of successful learning*. Harvard University Press. doi:10.2307/j.ctt6wprs3

Campbell, D. T. (1976). Assessing the impact of planned social change. *Journal of Multidisciplinary Evaluation, 7*(15), 3–43. doi:10.56645/jmde.v7i15.297

Cheon, S. H., Reeve, J., & Vansteenkiste, M. (2020). When teachers learn how to provide classroom structure in an autonomy-supportive way: Benefits to teachers and their students. *Teaching and Teacher Education, 90*, 103004. Advance online publication. doi:10.1016/j.tate.2019.103004

Clance, P. R., & Imes, S. A. (1978). The imposter phenomenon in high achieving women: Dynamics and therapeutic intervention. *Psychotherapy (Chicago, Ill.), 15*(3), 241–247. doi:10.1037/h0086006

Connell, J. P. (1990). Context, self, and action: A motivational analysis of self-system processes across the lifespan. In D. Cicchetti (Ed.), *The self in transition: Infancy to childhood* (pp. 61–97). University of Chicago Press.

Darling-Hammond, L. (2003). Keeping good teachers: Why it matters, what leaders can do. *Educational Leadership, 60*(8), 6–13.

Didonato, T. E. (2023, March 1). Why "bare-minimum Mondays" can hurt a relationship. *Psychology Today*. https://www.psychologytoday.com/au/blog/meet-catch-and-keep/202303/applying-the-bare-minimum-monday-philosophy-to-relationships

Francis, E. M. (2017, May 9). *What is depth of knowledge?* ASCD. https://www.ascd.org/blogs/what-exactly-is-depth-of-knowledge-hint-its-not-a-wheel

Fredricks, J. A., Blumenfeld, P. C., & Paris, A. H. (2004). School engagement: Potential of the concept, state of the evidence. *Review of Educational Research, 74*(1), 59–109. doi:10.3102/00346543074001059

Galla, B. M., Shulman, E. P., Plummer, B. D., Gardner, M., Hutt, S. J., Goyer, J. P., D'Mello, S. K., Finn, A. S., & Duckworth, A. L. (2019). Why high school grades are better predictors of on-time college graduation than are admissions test scores: The roles of self-regulation and cognitive ability. *American Educational Research Journal*, *56*(6), 2077–2115. doi:10.3102/0002831219843292

Hillen, S. A., & Päivärinta, T. (2012). Perceived support in e-collaborative learning: An exploratory study which make use of synchronous and asynchronous online-teaching approaches. In E. Popescu, E., Q. Li, R. Klamma, H. Leung & M. Specht (Eds.), *Advances in Web-Based Learning – ICWL2012: 11th International Conference, Sinaia, Romania, September 2–4, 2012. Proceedings* (pp. 11–20). Springer.

Jones, E. J., & Crawford, B. L. (2023, January). Holding space and grace: The implementation of a health and wellness statement in graduate courses. In A. El-Amin (Ed.), *Elevating intentional education practice in graduate programs* (pp. 99–111). IGI Global. doi:10.4018/978-1-6684-4600-3.ch005

Kets de Vries, M. F. (2005). The dangers of feeling like a fake. *Harvard Business Review*, *83*, 108. https://hbr.org/2005/09/the-dangers-of-feeling-like-a-fake PMID:16171215

Knowles, M. S. (1984). *The adult learner: A neglected species*. Gulf Pub. Co., Book Division.

Long, C. (2023, March 30). *Standardized testing is still failing students*. NEA News. https://www.nea.org/advocating-for-change/new-from-nea/standardized-testing-still-failing-students

Lyons, T., & Evans, M. (2013). Blended learning to increase student satisfaction: An exploratory study. *Internet Reference Services Quarterly*, *18*(1), 43–53. doi:10.1080/10875301.2013.800626

Merriam-Webster. (n.d.). Engagement. In *Merriam-Webster.com dictionary*. Retrieved June 13, 2023, from https://www.merriam-webster.com/dictionary/engagement

Olson, A. L., & Peterson, R. L. (2015, April). *Student engagement, strategy brief*. Lincoln, NE: Student Engagement Project, University of Nebraska-Lincoln and the Nebraska Department of Education. https://k12engagement.unl.edu/student-engagement

Olt, P., & Jones, E. J. (2024). Campbell's Law and online discussion: From quantitative minima to social engagement [Manuscript unpublished]. Advanced Education Programs, Fort Hays State University.

Palloff, R. M., Pratt, K., & Stockley, D. (2001). Building learning communities in cyberspace: Effective strategies for the online classroom. *Canadian Journal of Higher Education*, *31*(3), 175–178. https://www.proquest.com/scholarly-journals/building-learning-communities-cyberspace/docview/221229996/se-2

Perna, M. C. (2022, March 28). *The life of a teacher and why it's beyond hard*. Forbes. https://www.forbes.com/sites/markcperna/2022/03/28/the-life-of-a-teacher-and-why-its-beyond-hard

Vygotsky, L. S. (1978). *Mind in society: The development of higher psychological processes*. Harvard University Press.

Woolfolk, A. (2020). *Educational psychology: Active learning edition* (14th ed.). Pearson.

Works, P. B. L. (n.d.) *What is PBL?* Buck Institute for Education. https://www.pblworks.org/what-is-pbl

ADDITIONAL READING

Reeve, J. (2016). Autonomy-supportive teaching: what it is, how to do it. In W. Liu, J. Wang, & R. Ryan (Eds.), *Building autonomous learners*. Springer. doi:10.1007/978-981-287-630-0_7

KEY TERMS AND DEFINITIONS

Asynchronous Learning: Learning in a non-traditional setting, using computer and communications technologies to work with remote learning resources, coaches, and other learners, but without the requirement to be online simultaneously.

Autonomy-Supportive Teaching: The delivery of instruction through an interpersonal tone of understanding that appreciates, supports, and vitalizes students' psychological needs (Reeves, 2016).

COVID-19 Pandemic: The widely accepted terminology for the novel coronavirus elevated to a global pandemic in March 2020.

Online Learning: Instruction delivered electronically through various multimedia and Internet platforms and applications. It is used interchangeably with other terms such as web-based learning, e-learning, computer-assisted instruction, and Internet-based learning.

P12 Educators: Individuals who educate pre-Kindergarten through 12th-grade students.

APPENDIX: TRANSFERENCE REFLECTION CYCLE

TRANSFERENCE REFLECTION: A reflection summarizes your total learning experience within the course and must include how the ISTE Standards are vital to leadership, learning, education, and student success.

This reflection should include the five stages of reflection.

Exploration Stage: You are to explicitly state your prejudgments or beliefs about your practicum/course experience (**completed in the first week**).

Explanation Stage: You are to explain how your actual experience matched or differed from the prejudgments you identified in the exploration stage.

Conjecture Stage: You are to formulate a conjecture or question that might help you resolve or at least further explore the tensions created between your presuppositions and actual experiences. Such a conjecture might resemble a thesis statement, but a conjecture preserves the exploratory purpose of the essay, an intellectual reconnoiter.

Analysis Stage: You are required to test or answer your conjecture by engaging in a more profound re-examination of your presuppositions and actual experiences. Such a reflective analysis seeks to search for truth openly rather than argue for a particular position.

Synthesis Stage: This is the crucial stage of the reflective process, in which your practices and understandings are restructured, and new actions are put forward. You are encouraged to draw out the implications of your analysis. This is an opportunity for you to say something meaningful and new towards the end of this reflective essay. This could entail explaining how your beliefs or presuppositions have changed due to your reflection on your experience. Alternatively, you could discuss how your inquiry directed you toward new goals or specific actions that apply what you learned from the reflective process.

Chapter 17
Supporting Male Students in Female-Dominated Virtual Classrooms

Daniel Bates
https://orcid.org/0000-0003-0964-4892
Truman State University, USA

ABSTRACT

In female-dominated academic disciplines, male college students face distinct challenges, such as lagging admission and graduation rates when compared to their female counterparts. To address this concerning trend and enhance support for male students, online educators should embrace a gender-adapted, culturally responsive teaching approach. This approach enables instructors to understand and support male student academic performance and tailor their educational strategies to enhance a male student's sense of belonging and engagement in the course. By adopting this approach, online educators can help male students cultivate a pro-social, strengths-based self-perception, fostering a positive sense of identity as learners, men, and future professionals. This approach emphasizes how their masculinity can be a source of strength, enabling them to derive maximum benefit from their educational journey and make meaningful contributions to their academic pursuits.

INTRODUCTION

Virtual learning offers cost-effective, convenient, flexible, and high-quality education to students (Cavinato et al., 2021; Kim & Park, 2020). However, it has also brought attention to a growing gender disparity in higher education, particularly the concerning trend of men falling behind women. Research findings indicate that men may encounter difficulties when it comes to initiating and sustaining engagement with classmates and professors in online learning environments, ultimately impacting their academic performance (Yaghmour, 2012). Male students may also find it difficult navigating online classrooms in female-dominated academic areas (e.g., nursing, education, counseling, social work). Several studies, over the last few decades, have investigated the effects and experiences of female students in male-dominated academic disciplines (Dresden et al., 2018; Steele et al., 2002), but little attention has been given to male student's experience of the converse.

Male students may experience social isolation, lack of access to academic support, including advisement and supervision (Williams, 2015), which can limit their opportunities for networking and professional development. Furthermore, male students pursuing fields of study where they are underrepresented, such as nursing, elementary education, and mental health, have faced significant challenges that have led to a higher dropout rate. These challenges include inadequate mentoring, social isolation, and the perception of discrimination (Lou et al., 2011; Severiens & ten Dam, 2012).

To address these challenges and enhance male students' learning experiences in female-dominated academic courses, virtual learning environments should be tailored to accommodate diverse learning styles among men, ways of relating to classmates, and styles of interacting with course material. This can be achieved by better equipping virtual educators to connect and support male students, and offer engaging content, and incorporating collaborative activities that may be more appealing to men's interest and learning styles.

Research examining male students and how masculinity relates to the online learning experience has been under-researched (Sbaratta & Tirpak, 2015), particularly in terms of how educators can effectively connect with and support male students. In this chapter, we will review an expanding body of research that sheds light on male students' learning outcomes and explore how educators can adapt their approach to better connect with, support, and meet the educational needs of male students in female-dominated online learning environments.

Rapid Adoption of Virtual Learning in Response to COVID-19

Before the COVID-19 pandemic, virtual education had a history spanning several decades, and distance education dating back to the late 1800s (Maeroff, 2003). However, the mandated national lockdown in the United States compelled a swift and widespread transition to online learning platforms across all educational levels. Between 2012- 2017, total enrollment in online courses in the United States jumped from 26% to 33.7% (Snyder et al., 2019). As of the latest data, approximately one-third of all college students are participating in at least one online class, with 15% of students being enrolled in fully online programs (Snyder et al., 2019). For the majority of college students, this transition was far from smooth, with learning new systems and technologies, often referred to as learning management system (LMS), becoming a significant source of stress (Aslan et al., 2020).

This unprecedented shift placed an immense burden on students, institutions, and educators alike. Educators were suddenly forced to adapt to unforeseen circumstances, primarily delivering their instruction in a virtual environment, even if they had little or no prior experience with online teaching. This adjustment often required providing instruction synchronously, asynchronously, or through a hybrid of both approaches, all while attempting to forge meaningful relationships with students.

Zamarro et al. (2022) reviewed studies that identified that teachers' attitude towards leaving their profession increased during the 2020-2021 academic year. In their analysis of a sample consisting of 1045 teachers, Zamarro and colleagues (2022) found compelling evidence of the pandemic's impact on teachers. Roughly 42% stated they considered departing or retiring from their current position during the last year, the majority of which cited stress from the pandemic being their primary reason. Relatedly, Pressley et al. (2021) found that the delivery of online teaching was a strong predictor of teacher's anxiety.

Teachers have articulated various reasons for considering leaving their profession, some of which existed prior to the pandemic, but the transition to online teaching has exacerbated stress and burnout levels (Diliberti et al., 2021). This heightened stress and burnout risk amplifying teacher turnover rates, a trend that could have detrimental effects on students (Hanushek et al., 2016). Despite the numerous challenges posed by online learning for both students and educators, recent research has suggested that online learning might represent an optimal method for delivering higher education.

Virtual Education, Participation, and Learning Outcomes

Even though quarantine measures have been lifted, the convenience and accessibility offered by online learning has prompted educational programs to reevaluate the necessity of in-person classrooms. A similar transformation in attitudes toward educational settings has been observed among students. An increasing number of students are choosing e-learning classes over traditional in-classroom options (Paul & Jeferson, 2019), including higher education (Cole et al., 2014).

For instance, Zheng et al. (2021) conducted a study among dental students who transitioned to online learning during the pandemic, yielding intriguing results. Their findings revealed that 80% of the students expressed a desire to continue online learning even after the course had ended. Moreover, academic outcomes were found to be on par with, if not better than, traditional learning methods, and there was a high level of satisfaction among students with the online learning platform. Notably, student success was strongly linked to engagement with instructors and interaction with classmates.

Numerous studies have provided valuable insights, suggesting that well-designed e-learning biology courses have the potential to be just as effective as their traditional face-to-face counterparts. For example, Biel and Brame (2016) reviewed several studies that compared the effectiveness of online learning courses to in-person biology courses. The outcomes of these studies indicate that well-designed virtual biology classes were effective in fostering student learning and comparable to in-person learning outcomes. Among engineering students, a substantial 85% reported satisfaction with their online learning experiences (Radu et al., 2020). It appears that students highly value the cost and time savings, making it difficult for them to relinquish the flexibility and accessibility offered by online learning.

Despite the overwhelming interest among students in virtual education, the shift from in-person to online learning may come with some unanticipated consequences. For example, Caspi et al. (2008) analyzed gender disparities in class participation among a sample of 1368 students enrolled in a university course in Israel that involved both in-person and distance learning components. The findings revealed that men were more active in verbal contributions during face-to-face classes, while women were more active in posting messages within the web-based conference. Caspi and colleagues (2008) suggest that the cause for these differences may be due to female preferences and sense of comfort and protection afforded by the online environment.

Price (2006) found that female students were more active in their online courses and more likely to complete them compared to male students. A more recent study also indicated that women participated to a greater extent in online courses (Morante et al., 2017). Morante and colleagues (2017) also found that female students who actively participate and engage more with their learning community tend to achieve better academic outcomes.

Virtual Learning and Student Strain

A research study found evidence linking the online learning environment with a decrease in student mental health and lowered student engagement (Akpinar, 2021). Hollister et al. (2022) found among 187 undergraduate students at a public university enrolled online themes related to struggles with attendance, engaging during live synchronous lectures, challenges with pacing and staying connected to classmates and instructor. Several studies have indicated increased rates of stress (Aslan et al., 2020), depression, anxiety and stress (Odriozola-González et al., 2020) during the lockdown, specific stress and dissatisfaction with online courses that were not effectively adapted to the platform (UNESCO, 2020).

These findings present a serious challenge for online educators in how they connect with students personally and create an active and engaged virtual learning community. There is complexity that online educators and program administrators must grapple with: providing higher education through virtual classrooms clearly is something students want, but can virtual educators manage the potential downsides effectively and deliver outcomes comparable to in-person learning experiences?

Reflecting on this question also requires that educators recognize that not every student engages with online learning in the same way and does not necessarily achieve identical outcomes from the experience. It is crucial to consider various factors such as a student's race/ethnicity, gender and gender role, socioeconomic status, and more, as significant dimensions of identity that influence learning outcomes, experiences, and expectations in the context of virtual education. This perspective aligns with an intersectional approach, recognizing that a student's experiences and outcomes in virtual education are intertwined with the complex interplay of multiple social and demographic factors, such as race/ethnicity, gender, and socioeconomic status, which cannot be understood in isolation but must be considered as interconnected aspects of their identity.

Huffman et al. (2013), for example, found among a sample of 750 undergraduate students at a mid-sized public university that gender roles, specifically masculinity, predicted self-efficacy as it relates to use of technology. Lower levels of competence and perceived self-efficacy with technology can result in increased anxiety in the workplace and in classroom settings (Shu et al., 2011) and can impact a student's academic achievement and career (Vekiri & Chronaki, 2008).

In general, male students tend to demonstrate greater comfort, positive attitudes, less anxiety and greater knowledge technology and computers compared to female students (for review, see Huffman et al., 2013). Evidence indicates that male students engage with the online learning experience in qualitatively different ways than female students (Maceli et al., 2011). These differences in engagement, class involvement and participation, relationship to classmates and professors, impact academic outcomes, student retention, and pathways to graduation. Maceli and colleagues (2011) commented that:

[G]ender differences could affect how students potentially learn and thrive in a classroom environment, and even what could potentially cause the reverse. Future success is often related to satisfaction with a classroom experience. Therefore, it is conceivable that a classroom environment could be effects by differences gender. What helps one gender may not help the other, and vice versa. (pg. 35)

Maceli et al. (2011) conducted a study with a sample of 328 students attending a mid-western university (58.1% identified themselves as business majors and 41.9% identified themselves as non-business majors). Their study found significant gender differences between male and female students in terms of overall satisfaction with the course, with the instructor, and classroom experience. Thowfeek and Jaafar

(2012) proposed that the gender dimension of learning constitutes a pivotal factor that warrants examination prior to the implementation of an e-learning system. This raises the ongoing question of whether culturally ingrained gender differences have an impact on students in the context of online learning, a question that remains unanswered.

GENDER DISPARITIES: ENROLLMENT, DEGREE COMPLETION, AND EDUCATIONAL ATTAINMENT

1981 marked the year that female students started outpacing males and has been widening every year since and is projected to continue increasing (Snyder et al., 2018). According to the National Center for Education Statistics (2022), as of fall 2020, out of the total undergraduate enrollment, females composed 58% and males made up 42% (Irwin et al., 2022). This gender disparity only widens when looking at postbaccalaureate enrollment rates. As of fall 2020, female student enrollment was 61% and increased 14% between the years of 2009 to 2020, whereas male student enrollment was 39% and only increased 4% from 2009 to 2020.

It seems the pandemic disproportionately affected male student enrollment with female enrollment decreasing by 2% compared to 2019 and male enrollment decreased by 7%. The gender disparity in enrollment is also evident in 6-year graduation rates with 60% of male students graduating compared to 67% of female students. This was true for public and private nonprofit, except for a small difference where males overtook females at private for-profit institutions.

Male students also take longer to complete their bachelor's degree. Between 2010 and 2021, educational attainment levels were generally higher for females than males. A corpus of studies reveals that decreasing levels of educational attainment among male students powerfully impacts several overall life satisfaction variables, including socioeconomic status, marriage and family structure, crime rates, health-outcomes, health-related costs (Andronie & Andronie, 2014; Debaun & Roc, 2013; Debaun et al., 2013).

Regarding higher education, there have also been significant shifts in recent years. Studies show that a higher number of women are enrolling and completing graduate level programs compared to men (Isacco & Mannarino, 2016; Aud et al., 2012). According to the Organization of Economic Cooperation and Development (OECD) has documented a growing trend predominant in most developing countries, noting greater enrollment of female students over and above male students. Additionally, they noted a greater attrition rate among male students compared to females (OECD, 2014).

In the United States, gender differences have been observed insofar as a greater proportion of female students enrolling in and completing master's degrees and doctoral degrees compared to male students (Isacco & Mannarino, 2016). Several studies have also found evidence that suggests male students have a higher attrition rate is compared to female students withing higher education programs (Michel et al., 2015; Williams, 2015). The reason for the higher attrition rate observed among male students may be due, in part, to male student's challenges they face in a female-dominated academic field (Lou et al., 2011; Severiens & ten Dam, 2012). Furthermore, masculine norms may intersect with the male student's educational experience, for instance, male students experience gender role conflict when enrolled in female-concentrated programs leading to (Dodson & Borders, 2006; Sobiraj et al., 2015). It is important for educators to be aware of the gender disparity in higher education and the role that, as more programs shift to online learning, they play in curtailing or solidifying troubling trends discussed above.

MALE EXPERIENCE IN A FEMALE-DOMINATED, RELATIONALLY ORIENTED EDUCATION

The online classroom may appeal to the strengths of female students (McKnight-Tutein & Thackaberry, 2011), and be incommensurate with typical male behavioral patterns and culturally embedded masculine norms and expectations. McKnight-Tutein and Thackaberry (2011) argued that substantial evidence indicates that women have distinct learning patterns compared to men. According to their perspective, these differences in learning styles allow women naturally more proficient in online learning settings. They contended that women possessed a distinctive advantage in the realm of effective learning due to their utilization of affective learning strategies. These strategies enabled them to engage in relational learning by tapping into various connections and associations as part of their learning process.

For example, evidence has found that women were more amenable to and well versed in navigating the online classroom experience (Selwyn, 2007), and were more likely to complete online courses (Price, 2006). The intensity or directness of the conversational/reflective learning format of the online classroom, where instructors vary lecture material with discussion-based breakout groups, reflexive journal assignments, asynchronous discussion boards, overlaps or complements with female typical approaches to learning that are heavily relational (Anderson & Haddad, 2005). Whereas male students are more active and participatory in face-to-face classroom settings (Caspi et al., 2008; Morante et al., 2017).

Female students are more likely to be collaborative in online classrooms, contribute do discussion boards and respond to peers, motivated to engage in the online classroom through communication, avoid conflict, and make appreciate statements (for review, see Yaghmour, 2012). Male students are less likely to engage in these types of behaviors (Lewis, 2007), rather men are more likely to share disagreements (Prinsen, 2007) in an effort to establish dominance, status or control (Montieth, 2002). Furthermore, men are more likely to use aggressive (Prinsen, 2007), fact oriented (Li, 2005) and authoritative statements (Prinsen, 2007).

Isacco and Mannarino (2016) briefly summarized the literature regarding male students in female-dominated academic programs and occupations, and identified studies that identified male students expressing feelings of disadvantage in their environments, citing social exclusion from predominantly female groups and a lack of connection as key issues (Chusmir, 1990; Lou et al., 2011). Men who choose nontraditional occupations have faced additional challenges, perceiving less support, social stigma, and negative stereotyping. These stereotypes include suspicions about their motives for entering such fields and fears of potential litigation (Sargent, 2001; Shen-Miller et al., 2011).

Moreover, when specifically asked about their experiences, male students have offered recommendations for additional programs to enhance their health and well-being on campus (Davies et al., 2000). Recognizing the crucial role of academic support and a sense of connection in student retention, as well as the detrimental effects of exclusion and perceived social stigma, this study examines the perceptions of male graduate students regarding their academic support systems and sense of connection in a female-concentrated university.

Morante et al. (2017), summarized their review of the literature, stating that when it comes to patterns of engagement, women tended to exhibit more personal, task-oriented, and collaborative behaviors in online learning. They were more active in posting content, used communication with peers as a source of motivation for their learning, and demonstrated higher levels of inquisitiveness by engaging in searching and asking questions. Conversely, male students demonstrated a preference for information-driven approaches to learning, were more likely to be detached in their online interactions and were interested in acquiring new skills. However, regardless of gender, students were extrinsically motivated in their studies when their efforts were rewarded through feedback and grades, as well as when their studies provided them with a sense of intrinsic satisfaction.

Relationally Oriented Pedagogical Approaches

This approach to learning and engagement to virtual education among male students may clash with pedagogical approaches and theories of learning that favor socially oriented, relationally grounded conceptualizations of the learner and the process of learning. For example, Knight (2002) views the adult learner as an agent who create knowledge through social acts of learning. According to Bandura's social learning theory (SLT), adult learners observe, model, imitate, and react to the thoughts and attitudes of other students, as they are formulating their own ideas regarding the course content (Bandura & Walters, 1977). Jaleel and Verghis (2015) view the learning process taking place through spontaneous social interactions with their peers. Research has shown that in the field of counseling, many instructors employ a "gender blind" pedagogy, that may in fact disempower male students and result in their disengagement in the classroom (Michel et al., 2013; Michel et al., 2015). Many contemporary theories of learning greatly emphasis the social, humanistic, and experiential component of education

Relationally Oriented Virtual Education

Virtual classrooms that are setup to favor relationally oriented styles of engagement may create barriers for male students. Furthermore, the fact that higher education is becoming more female-dominated may further leave male students feeling isolated from the class. The virtual platform creates distance between student and instructor, and student to student, which can lead to feelings of alienation (Rovai & Wighting, 2005), this is especially for male students.

According to Rovai and Wighting (2005), among a sample of 281 students enrolled in a graduate-level online course, female students reported significantly higher rates on every measured variable: social community, learning community, and perceived learning. Additionally, researchers identified that variables are strongly intercorrelated, suggesting that if male students do not feel connected to their classmates, then they will be less likely to engage in the learning community and will perceive having learned less. Rovai and Wighting (2005) note "Uniformly higher results demonstrated by females along the self-report variables of sense of classroom community and perceived learning suggest that the asynchronous online environment is one that can be hospitable to women" (pg. 39).

Female-Dominated Virtual Classrooms

Male students may face challenges when it comes to actively participating and engaging in online classrooms that are predominantly female-dominated. Consistent with these results, González-Gómez et al. (2012) found that female students reported higher levels of satisfaction with their online learning experience than male. Isacco and Mannarino (2016) reviewed several studies that indicated males experienced barriers in female-concentrated academic spaces such as nursing, counseling, and elementary education, which resulted in higher dropout among male students. As discussed in Morante et al. (2017), male students may want to engage in classroom discussion where aggressive, confrontational language is used, and arguments are formulated in support or in critique of viewpoints. Yet, instructors may discourage or grade against this form of communication. Furthermore, the classroom may not be structured to facilitate this type of communication as well.

Gender Differences Relative to Self-Efficacy

A study investigated a multidimensional model of online learning self-efficacy found among a sample of 406 online students (60.1% graduate degree students, and 37.2% undergraduate degree students) significant gender differences across all five self-efficacy factors (Shen et al., 2013). The body of research up to this point indicated that male students possessed greater online self-efficacy, however, those studies only examined competence with technology. Shen et al. (2013) used exploratory factor analysis to examine a more complex and multifaceted model of online self-efficacy that includes self-efficacy to: complete an online course, interact socially with classmate, handle tools in a CMS, interact with instructors in an online course, and interact with classmates for academic. Female students had significantly higher means than male students for each of the five factors, which also significantly predicted students online learning satisfaction.

Huang (2013) conducted a meta-analysis of 187 studies and found gender differences among male and female college students, specifically content domain moderated academic self-efficacy. Results demonstrated that males favored self-efficacy relative to mathematics, computer science and social science, and females favored language arts. Becker (2014) found that among the west German population, female students outperformed male students in academic attainment in higher education across all cohorts. Female students demonstrated greater self-regulation as compared to male students resulting in significantly higher positive online learning outcomes (Alghamdi et al., 2020). Yu (2021) suggests that online educators might consider differential instructional designs contingent on the gender identity of the student.

Mixed Findings

However, not all research uniformly indicates males are at a disadvantage. There are mixed findings regarding gender differences relative to attitudes and level of satisfaction among male and female students (Cuadrado-García et al., 2010), and academic outcomes (Chu, 2010). Nistor (2013) found no significant gender differences in leaning outcomes and learning styles. Also, among a sample of millennial online students, there was no significant gender differences in learning satisfaction (Harvey et al., 2017). Additionally, other research studies have reported no significant sex differences in certain contexts related to technological self-efficacy (Compton et al., 2003; Havelka, 2003), and in some cases, there have been findings indicating positive outcomes for females (Compton et al., 2003; Ray et al., 1999). However, it's important to acknowledge that such findings are less prevalent in the overall body of research, and that gender differences student experience in online classroom which should inform online educator's approach to teaching.

MASCULINITY AND EDUCATIONAL ATTAINMENT

Masculine ideals from a Western cultural milieu typically includes expectations that men should avoid appearing feminine, overtly present as heterosexual, eschew vulnerability, be adventurous, suppress and or control emotions, and make their primary pursuit about money and status (Sobiraj et al., 2015). Kahn (2011) found complex patterns of associations between the Conformity to Masculine Norms Inventory (CMNI) subscales and academic motivation. Specifically, they found a negative relationship between three CMNI subscales (primacy of work, playboy, and violence) and intrinsic motivation. Kahn (2011) also found a positive association between emotional control, disdain for homosexuality, self-reliance, and winning, and intrinsic motivation.

Furthermore, Isacco and Mannarino (2016) conducted a qualitative study with male graduate students in female-dominated academic spaces and found that male students strongly connected their academic goals with the performance of traditional gender roles. Specifically, they found that the traditional masculine ideals associated with being a hard worker and provider, as well as the ideals of pursuing of status and being achievement-oriented were closely related to male student's academic motivation.

Hallman (2020) found that male students who identify with traditional masculine characteristics or feel compelled to adhere to traditional masculinity ideals are less likely to achieve academic success. Furthermore, Hallman (2020 found that a motivation has a powerful impact on academic success in male undergraduate students. Male students tend to be more extrinsically motivated than female students (Ayub, 2010). Academic motivation, internal and external, impacts academic outcomes. Awareness of academic motivation can help online instructors better understand how to the educational experience the students' motivational drives (Taheri-Kharameh et al., 2018).

GENDER-ADAPTED TEACHING: MALE WAYS OF CONNECTING

Online educators need to be aware of the role masculinity plays in enhancing or inhibiting male students' engagement in the online classroom. Every student comes into the classroom with a base of prior knowledge (Portier & Wagemas, 1995) informed not only by their previous education but also by their culture, their family environment, their personality, their goals and vision for the future. The experiences and life history of a student are unavoidable realities that must be acknowledged and integrated into the learning process (Banks, 2013; Gay, 2000). A key part of cultural identity for male students is their understanding and experience of masculinity. Understanding the gendered lens through which students experience themselves, including learning will aid in working with gender norms to enhance the online learning experience.

Online educators need to make "meaningful cultural connections to convey academic and social knowledge and attitudes" (Vavrus, 2008, p. 49), and this also applies to masculinity. To leave these aspects of personhood aside, when embarking on the task of teaching, is to not fully accomplish the project of education. The student's whole self has to be brought to bear in education; teaching cannot simply be an intellectual exercise. Educators are encouraged in matters of identity such as race, ethnicity, and culture to broach the subjects (Bultsma, 2011) with their students and discuss how they play a role in the learning process and affect the classroom dynamic.

The idea of broaching should also extend to the topic of race and gender (Day-Vines & Holcomb-McCoy, 2013) including masculinity. By not broaching the conversation around the subject of gender norms, especially masculinity— taking a gender-blind approach (Michel et al., 2013; Michel et al., 2015)— educators may run the risk of disenfranchising male students in the classroom. This is counterproductive to the learning process and not inclusive to the diversity within the student body. Therefore, choices have to be made when designing and constructing the course— not after the course has started—

Supporting Male Students in Female-Dominated Virtual Classrooms

regarding what voices to include or exclude, and what perspectives will be surveyed (Haslerig et al., 2013). Including male student voices in the conversation, designing the course structure with men in mind, and purposefully connecting with male students at the beginning and throughout the class should not be an afterthought. It should be designed into the foundation, the core of the class itself.

Culturally Responsive Teaching With Male Students

Online educators are encouraged to utilize culturally responsive care (Garza, 2009) and culturally responsive teaching (Aronson & Laughter, 2016; Gay, 2000; 2002) with male students regarding their traditionally masculine gender identity. Online educators can make conscious decisions to include various voices and perspectives and diverse identities, including men who hold traditional ideas about masculinity in the course design (Travis et al., 2016). The gender-adapted, culturally responsive approach to online teaching pairs well with a multicultural perspective in education (Banks, 2009). Online educators can share their own process of discovering biases, understanding intersecting identities in relation to the subject matter, and discussing contextual factors that may have been historically missed during the conception and development of course subject matter.

Inevitably, discussions regarding culture and identity may introduce "hot moments" into the classroom dynamic. In order to navigate moments of tension, online educators should consider using the D.E.E.P strategy, which promotes a course climate that is conducive to healthy discourse and inclusive learning (Smith, 2016). DEEP stands for D— develop appropriate language use; E— encourage open and honest dialogue; E— empower students to share without ridicule; P— process information shared by reconnecting it to course content.

The D.E.E.P. framework serves as a valuable guide for effectively navigating inclusion and diversity within the classroom. For online educators, it offers a blueprint for demonstrating the use of appropriate language to teach students how to humanize their peers, engage in collaborative and collegial discussions, and employ emotion regulation skills when confronted with tense situations (Jiang et al., 2016). Establishing respect and open dialogue as fundamental principles in the learning environment plays a pivotal role in balancing power dynamics (Long, 2020). It also allows online instructors to immerse themselves within the classroom as fellow learners and guide discussions through active listening (Haase, 2019). Creating a space in the classroom where robust conversations are facilitated, and students feel encouraged to share diverse perspectives and relevant experiences from their own backgrounds is essential. This should be done with careful management, particularly during moments of heightened tension or conflict.

Strengths-Based Perspective

Research has identified that male students in female-dominated academic programs may encounter gender role conflict and strain, stemming from the mismatch between traditional gender roles and their chosen fields (Dodson & Borders, 2006; Sobiraj et al., 2015). With the declining enrollment and retention of male students in higher education, certain universities have proactively explored ways to enhance male student engagement through program development (Kellom & Groth, 2010). One strategy that universities and online educators may consider is a strengths-based perspective that seeks to empower and support male students facing the challenges associated with gender disparities in academic fields.

For example, Isacco and Mannarino (2016) shed light on the intriguing link between male students' embrace of traditional masculinity and their academic aspirations, goals, and motivation. Male students' academic success and motivation were tied with a vision of how their work fulfills gender norms and expectations. Similarly, Kahn's (2011) study unveiled a complex web of connections between traditional masculinity and the academic achievements of male students, implying that this relationship is not solely positive or negative. These findings offer valuable insights to educators, underscoring the need for a nuanced approach when supporting male students. This research also informs how educators may recognize and nurture the unique masculine strengths, attributes, and motivations that male students bring to their educational journey, helping them thrive and overcome gender-related barriers to success.

Educators should take a thoughtful and individualized approach to help male students identify the specific aspects of masculinity that drive their academic success. Within the field of mental health counseling, scholars, researchers, and clinicians have developed the Positive Psychology Positive Masculinity (PPPM) paradigm. This paradigm serves as a guide for clinicians, offering empowerment strategies that allow them to work with men while respecting and understanding their endorsement of traditional masculine cultural beliefs and values. Simultaneously, the PPPM framework explores how the strengths and assets inherent in traditional masculinity can contribute positively to men's mental health outcomes. Several studies by Kiselica et al. (2016), McDermott et al. (2019), and Wilson et al. (2022) have delved into this paradigm, providing valuable insights into its practical application in supporting male students in their academic pursuits and overall well-being.

Using a Positive Masculinity Framework in Online Classrooms

Wilson et al. (2022) described the PPPM as standing on two key pillars: *knowing* and *being*. Knowing relates to instilling awareness about common issues facing boys and men, understanding how gendered social development occurs, and critical appraisal of male socialization norms to enable the pursuit of an individual's own positive path. Awareness of the ways male socialization may limit men in engaging in the online classroom can help an educator encourage male students to tap into and act out their own inner sense of bravery and intellectual curiosity by discussing their point of view, asking questions and meaningfully engaging class discussions.

For example, let's consider an online psychology course where the majority of students are female, and there's a male student named Michael. Michael initially seems somewhat reserved in class discussions. The educator, having an awareness of how male socialization can influence participation, takes a proactive approach by engaging Michael privately, encouraging him to share his unique perspective during class discussions. The educator helps Michael recognize that the expression of his thoughts and questions are an expression of his intellectual curiosity and makes a contribution to the classroom. Michael finds the idea of making a contribution, i.e., being useful, motivating. As a result, Michael begins to actively participate in class discussions, sharing his insights and engaging meaningfully with his peers.

According to Wilson and colleagues' (2022) model, being is composed of three human strengths: connected (developing interpersonal relationships that are based in respect and tolerance), motivated (dedication to personal growth and better of one's community and society), and authentic (developing comfort with expressing one's true masculine identity). These three strengths also help the online educator foster healthy, prosocial and positive masculine engagement and contribution to the classroom by, first and foremost, connecting with their male student. And making it clear that being connected is not a luxury that feels good but serves a functional and logical purpose in the achievement of the male student's goals. Furthermore, making it clear how the course content will enable the male student to make a meaningful contribution to themselves, their families and their communities; they start that journey

Supporting Male Students in Female-Dominated Virtual Classrooms

of contribution and service to others in the classroom. And finally, being authentic to what they really feel and think, being congruent, even when it may lead to tension or moments of challenge. You can discuss how you plan on using the DEEP approach to navigating those hot moments, and model emotion regulation during tension moments for students to follow.

For example, let's consider an online psychology course where the majority of students are female, and there's a male student named Michael. Michael initially seems somewhat reserved in class discussions. The educator, having an awareness of how male socialization can influence participation, takes a proactive approach by engaging Michael privately, encouraging him to share his unique perspective during class discussions. The educator helps Michael recognize that the expression of his thoughts and questions are an expression of his intellectual curiosity and makes a contribution to the classroom. Michael finds the idea of making a contribution, i.e., being useful, motivating. As a result, Michael begins to actively participate in class discussions, sharing his insights and engaging meaningfully with his peers.

The goal of this framework is to "promote healthy enactments of masculinity, whilst also emphasizing a realistic understanding of the problems with traditional notions of masculinity and the breadth of change required by men" (Wilson et al., 2022, pg. 4). For a visual depiction of the model, see the table below, which was borrowed directly from Wilson and colleagues, 2022 paper.

Figure 1. Intersectional masculinities
Source: Wilson et al. (2022)

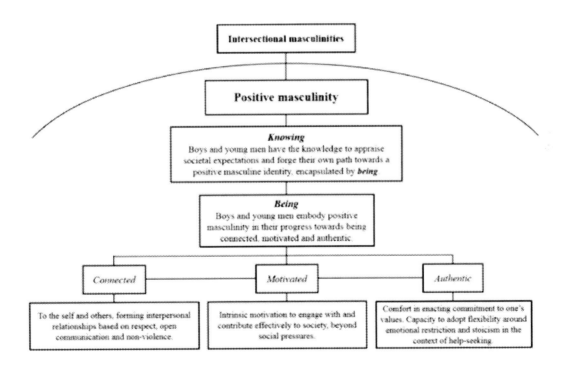

CASE EXAMPLE: JEREMY

Going back to school was not on the top of Jeremy's priority list, but since retiring from the Navy, Jeremy felt the need to find a career instead of working a "job" to make ends meet for his young family. Jeremy served as a corpsman in the United States Navy and was recently honorably discharged. Jeremy wanted to pursue his interest in medicine, so he started looking into nursing programs. One program stood out to him in particular since it was primarily online, which was a perfect fit for him being a working dad with three young kids, whose wife also worked.

Over the course of the first semester, Jeremy's initial enthusiasm quickly subsided. He found himself showing up to class late, even though "getting" to class was as simple as stepping into his private, home office. His grades started to dip, he was not turning in papers on time, his test scores were barely above passing, and he was struggling to connect with other students.

Almost all of Jeremy's classmates were female, including his professors. Jeremy found it very difficult to relate to his peers, engage in classroom discussions, and score simple participation points the teacher awarded for coming to class on time, participating in in-class discussions and posting on the weekly discussion board. When Jeremy participated in classroom discussions, he would often draw parallels between a concept they were learning in class with his previous military experience. After he made a comment, the class would typically remain silent with infrequent follow-up statements and comments from peers and teachers.

His instructors struggled to connect with Jeremy, and his reluctance to participate in class did not help. Jeremy did not like the pattern emerging, but he felt powerless to stop it. As time passed, he felt more unmotivated and disconnected from his program, which was not like him at all. In the Navy, Jeremy excelled, and often received positive commendations from his superiors and was seen as a leader among his fellow service members. But now, Jeremy was reaching a point where his dream of becoming a nurse did not seem feasible. If Jeremy enrolled in your class, what would you do as an online educator to create a meaningful and supportive connection with Jeremy? What would you do to unlock his potential and motivation?

GENDER-ADAPTED TEACHING WITH JEREMY

The story of Jeremy is becoming increasingly more common as more and more men enter into female-concentrated programs (Isacco & Mannarino, 2016; Shen-Miller & Smiler,

2015). As an online educator, it is important to note the alienating effect the virtual platform can have (Rovai & Wighting, 2005), especially for a student who does not feel as comfortable putting themselves out there amongst the classroom. Without Jeremy purposely interjecting himself by getting to know his peers and professors, he may feel distant and disconnected. These feelings can have an impact on academic outcomes and classroom engagement. Research has found a link between perceived support from classmates and instructors, including university staff and faculty, as a predictor student academic success (Sax et al., 2005; Sheard, 2009; Torres Campos et al., 2009). Absent of feeling connected and supported, it is little wonder why Jeremy's performance has surprisingly diminished over the course of his first semester. With the other demands Jeremy has on his plate, maintaining a high level of motivation is critical.

An effective online educator would take special care to form a personal connection with Jeremy and learn what his academic goals are. For male and female students, forming a personal and supportive connections with students can buffer against the natural stress that any student may face when enrolling in an online classroom where they may not know anyone else (Aslan et al., 2020). Specific to male students in female-dominated academic fields of study, research demonstrates that programs were successful in retaining male students when male-specific strategies were deployed such as focusing on financial success, male identity, and male contribution to a female-dominated space (Asakura & Watanabe, 2011).

As previously discussed, more programs are transitioning to distance education which typically favors female ways of engaging with education (Anderson & Haddad, 2005), also bearing in mind that female students are outpacing male enrollment (Aud et al., 2012; Isacco & Mannarino, 2016; Irwin et al., 2022; Snyder et al., 2018;) which culminates in male students becoming a gender minority. The gender minority role makes it challenging for male students to gain professional development and academic success (Sbaratta & Tirpak, 2015).

One response to Jeremy would be to suggest that he directly ask for support or help. Yet, Michel et al. (2013) found that male students in a different female-concentrated field, mental health counseling, struggled with voicing their perspectives in class sessions and reported that the did not feel heard. A "gender blind" teaching approach may seem admirable and conducive to creating an inclusive environment, it runs the risk of missing the role that masculinity plays in male students experience of the classroom and their perspective regarding course content (Michel et al., 2013; Michel et al., 2015), and the realities regarding male enrollment, academic success, and particular ways online education has been designed to cater to female students (Issaco & Mannarino, 2016; Shen-Miller & Smiler, 2015; Williams, 2015; Michel et al., 2013; 2015). It can be helpful to remind Jeremy that he is not alone and the stress he is feeling is real and normal (Sbaratta & Tirpak, 2015), and that he can tap into his resilience and get through the discomfort with your support.

An online educator may also want to consider using the positive masculinity framework developed by Wilson et al. (2022) with Jeremy. An instructor can help Jeremy understand that one reason he was so successful in the Navy was because he was part of something bigger than himself, he was connected, and he can capture the same power of connection in the classroom. Furthermore, you can connect the course content with Jeremy's real-world career goals and outline how the knowledge he will gain for the course will equip him to effectively serve others and contribute to his community and personal mission. And finally, you can let Jeremy know the classroom is a space where he can be his authentic self, and share his point of view, even if that point of view is not shared by other classmates.

CONCLUSION

In the virtual learning space, male students pursuing female-dominated academic disciplines encounter distinct challenges, setting them apart from their female peers. Research has begun to unveil the complexities underlying this issue, suggesting that male students may face distinct challenges when it comes to initiating and sustaining engagement with peers and professors in online learning environments, ultimately affecting their academic performance (Yaghmour, 2012). These challenges have led to disparities in admission and graduation rates, prompting a pressing need for a more nuanced approach to support these male students. While the root causes of this gender gap are multifaceted and not entirely clear, recent research has increasingly highlighted the significant influence of masculinity on the academic outcomes of male students participating in online education. To address this troubling trend, it becomes imperative for online educators to embrace a pedagogical approach that is both gender-adapted and culturally responsive.

These challenges become even more pronounced when male students find themselves navigating online classrooms within female-dominated academic areas, such as nursing, education, counseling, and social work. While numerous studies have explored the experiences of female students in male-dominated academic disciplines over the past few decades (Dresden et al., 2018; Steele et al., 2002), there has been a notable lack of attention given to the experiences of male students in female-dominated fields.

To address these obstacles and enhance the learning experiences of male students in female-dominated academic courses, virtual learning environments should be customized to accommodate diverse learning styles among male students. This includes acknowledging different ways of relating to classmates and interacting with course material. The key lies in equipping virtual educators with the tools and knowledge to connect with and support male students effectively, offering engaging content and incorporating collaborative activities that align with men's interests and learning styles.

By adopting this approach, online instructors can seek to understand and empower the strength-based aspects of male norms and masculinity to enhance academic outcomes of male students. Online educators can foster an environment that encourages male students to develop a pro-social, strengths-based, and positive self-concept in their roles as students, men, and future professionals. It is crucial to recognize the potential of masculinity as a powerful force that can empower male students to derive maximum benefit from their educational experiences. Online educators, through their understanding and support, play a pivotal role in enabling male students to unlock their potential, make meaningful contributions to their academic communities, and thrive in female-dominated academic disciplines.

REFERENCES

Akpınar, E. (2021). The effect of online learning on tertiary level students mental health during the COVID-19 lockdown. *The European Journal of Social & Behavioural Sciences*. doi:10.15405/ejsbs.288

Alghamdi, A., Karpinski, A. C., Lepp, A., & Barkley, J. (2020). Online and face-to-face classroom multitasking and academic performance: Moderated mediation with self-efficacy for self-regulated learning and gender. *Computers in Human Behavior*, *102*, 214–222. doi:10.1016/j.chb.2019.08.018

Andronie, M., & Andronie, M. (2014). Information and communication technologies (ICT) used for education and training. *Contemporary Readings in Law and Social Justice*, *6*(1), 378.

Aronson, B., & Laughter, J. (2016). The theory and practice of culturally relevant education: A synthesis of research across content areas. *Review of Educational Research*, *86*(1), 163–206. doi:10.3102/0034654315582066

Asakura, K., & Watanabe, I. (2011). Survival strategies of male nurses in rural areas of Japan. *Japan Journal of Nursing Science*, *8*(2), 194–202. doi:10.1111/j.1742-7924.2011.00176.x PMID:22117583

Aslan, I., Ochnik, D., & Çınar, O. (2020). Exploring perceived stress among students in Turkey during the covid-19 pandemic. *International Journal of Environmental Research and Public Health*, *17*(23), 8961. doi:10.3390/ijerph17238961 PMID:33276520

Aud, S., Hussar, W., Johnson, F., Kena, G., Roth, E., Manning, E., & Zhang, J. (2012). *The condition of education 2012 (NCES 20120-045). Indicator 47.* U.S. Department of Education, National Center for Education Statistics. Retrieved from https://nces.ed.gov/pubs2012/2012045.pdf

Ayub, N. (2010). Effect of intrinsic and extrinsic motivation on academic performance. *Pakistan business review, 8*(1), 363-372.

Bandura, A., & Walters, R. H. (1977). *Social learning theory* (Vol. 1). Prentice Hall.

Banks, J. A. (2013). The construction and historical development of multicultural education, 1962–2012. *Theory into Practice, 52*(sup1), 73-82. doi:10.1080/00405841.2013.795444

Bultsma, S. (2007). Broaching the subjects of race, ethnicity, and culture with students. *Colleagues, 2*(2), 11.

Caspi, A., Chajut, E., & Saporta, K. (2008). Participation in class and in online discussions: Gender differences'. *Computers & Education, 50*(3), 718–724. doi:10.1016/j.compedu.2006.08.003

Cavinato, A. G., Hunter, R. A., Ott, L. S., & Robinson, J. K. (2021). Promoting student interaction, engagement, and success in an online environment. *Analytical and Bioanalytical Chemistry, 413*(6), 1513–1520. doi:10.100700216-021-03178-x PMID:33479816

Chu, R. J. (2010). How family support and internet self-efficacy influence the effects of e-learning among higher aged adults – analyses of gender and age differences. *Computers & Education, 55*(1), 255–264. doi:10.1016/j.compedu.2010.01.011

Chusmir, L. H. (1990). Men who make nontraditional career choices. *Journal of Counseling and Development, 69*(1), 11–16. doi:10.1002/j.1556-6676.1990.tb01446.x

Cokley, K., & Moore, P. (2007). Moderating and mediating effects of gender and psychological disengagement on the academic achievement of African American college students. *The Journal of Black Psychology, 33*(2), 169–187. doi:10.1177/0095798407299512

Cole, M. T., Shelley, D. J., & Swartz, L. B. (2014). Online instruction, e-learning, and student satisfaction: A three year study. *International Review of Research in Open and Distance Learning, 15*(6), 111–131. doi:10.19173/irrodl.v15i6.1748

Compton, D. M., Burkett, W. H., & Burkett, G. G. (2003). No sex difference in perceived competence of computer use among male and female college students in 2002. *Psychological Reports, 92*(2), 503–511. doi:10.2466/pr0.2003.92.2.503 PMID:12785633

Cuadrado-García, M., Ruiz-Molina, M. E., & Montoro-Pons, J. D. (2010). Are there gender differences in e-learning use and assessment? Evidence from an interuniversity online project in Europe. *Procedia: Social and Behavioral Sciences, 2*(2), 367–371. doi:10.1016/j.sbspro.2010.03.027

Davies, J., McCrae, B. P., Frank, J., Dochnahl, A., Pickering, T., Harrison, B., Zakrzewski, M., & Wilson, K. (2000). Identifying male college students' perceived health needs, barriers to seeking help, and recommendations to help men adopt healthier lifestyles. *Journal of American College Health, 48*(6), 259–267. doi:10.1080/07448480009596267 PMID:10863869

Day-Vines, N. L., & Holcomb-McCoy, C. (2013). Broaching the subjects of race, ethnicity, and culture as a tool for addressing diversity in counselor education classes. In J. D. West, D. L. Bubenzer, J. A. Cox, & J. M. McGlothlin (Eds.), *Teaching in counselor education: Engaging students in learning* (pp. 151–166). Association for Counselor Education and Supervision.

DeBaun, B., & Roc, M. (2013). *Saving Futures, Saving Dollars: The Impact of Education on Crime Reduction and Earnings*. Alliance for Excellent Education.

DeBaun, B., Roc, M., & Muennig, P. A. (2013). *Well and well-off: Decreasing Medicaid and health-care costs by increasing educational attainment*. Academic Press.

Diliberti, M. K., Schwartz, H. L., & Grant, D. (2021). *Stress Topped the Reasons Why Public School Teachers Quit, Even Before COVID-19*. RAND Corporation. doi:10.7249/RRA1121-2

Dodson, T. A., & Borders, L. D. (2006). Men in traditional and nontraditional careers: Gender role attitudes, gender role conflict, and job satisfaction. *The Career Development Quarterly, 54*(4), 283–296. doi:10.1002/j.2161-0045.2006.tb00194.x

Dresden, B. E., Dresden, A. Y., Ridge, R. D., & Yamawaki, N. (2018). No girls allowed: Women in male-dominated majors experience increased gender harassment and bias. *Psychological Reports, 121*(3), 459–474. doi:10.1177/0033294117730357 PMID:29298544

Garza, R. (2009). Latino and white high school students' perceptions of caring behaviors: Are we culturally responsive to our students? *Urban Education, 44*(3), 297–321. doi:10.1177/0042085908318714

Gay, G. (2000). *Culturally responsive teaching: Theory, research, and practice*. Teachers College Press.

Gay, G. (2002). Preparing for culturally responsive teaching. *Journal of Teacher Education, 53*(2), 106–116. doi:10.1177/0022487102053002003

Glazier, R. A., & Harris, H. S. (2020). How teaching with rapport can improve online student success and retention: Data from two empirical studies. *Quarterly Review of Distance Education, 21*(4), 1–17.

González-Gómez, F., Guardiola, J., Martín Rodríguez, Ó., & Montero Alonso, M. Á. (2012). Gender differences in e-learning satisfaction. *Computers & Education, 58*(1), 283–290. doi:10.1016/j.compedu.2011.08.017

Haase, D. (2019). Dialogue education: A learning-centered pedagogy. *Christian Education Journal, 16*(2), 359–368. doi:10.1177/0739891319847695

Hallman, J. H. (2020). *Masculinity Perception and Motivational Influences on Male Students' Higher Education Academic Success* (Order No. 28152618). Available from GenderWatch; ProQuest Dissertations & Theses A&I; ProQuest Dissertations & Theses Global. (2466222571). https://uc.idm.oclc.org/login?qurl=https%3A%2F%2Fwww.proquest.com%2Fdissertations-theses%2Fmasculinity-perception-motivational-influences-on%2Fdocview%2F2466222571%2Fse-2%3Faccountid%3D2909

Hanushek, E. A., Rivkin, S. G., & Schiman, J. C. (2016). Dynamic effects of teacher turnover on the quality of instruction. *Economics of Education Review, 55*, 132–148. doi:10.1016/j.econedurev.2016.08.004

Harvey, H. L., Parahoo, S., & Santally, M. (2017). Should gender differences be considered when assessing student satisfaction in the online learning environment for millennials? *Higher Education Quarterly*, *71*(2), 141–158. doi:10.1111/hequ.12116

Haslerig, S., Bernhard, L. M., Fuentes, M. V., Panter, A. T., Daye, C. E., & Allen, W. R. (2013). A compelling interest: Activating the benefits of classroom-level diversity. *Journal of Diversity in Higher Education*, *6*(3), 158–173. doi:10.1037/a0034065

Havelka, D. (2003). Predicting software self-efficacy among business students: A preliminary assessment. *Journal of Information Systems Education*, *14*(2), 145.

Huang, C. (2013). Gender differences in academic self-efficacy: A meta-analysis. *European Journal of Psychology of Education*, *28*(1), 1–35. doi:10.100710212-011-0097-y

Huffman, A. H., Whetten, J., & Huffman, W. H. (2013). Using technology in higher education: The influence of gender roles on technology self-efficacy. *Computers in Human Behavior*, *29*(4), 1779–1786. doi:10.1016/j.chb.2013.02.012

Irwin, V., De La Rosa, J., Wang, K., Hein, S., Zhang, J., Burr, R., Roberts, A., Barmer, A., Bullock Mann, F., Dilig, R., & Parker, S. (2022). *Report on the Condition of Education 2022* (NCES 2022-144). U.S. Department of Education. Washington, DC: National Center for Education Statistics. Retrieved March, 21st 2023 from https://nces.ed.gov/pubsearch/pubsinfo.asp?pubid=2022144

Isacco, A., & Mannarino, M. B. (2016). "It's not like undergrad:" A qualitative study of male graduate students at an "all-women's college". *Psychology of Men & Masculinity*, *17*(3), 285–296. doi:10.1037/men0000021

Jiang, J., Vauras, M., Volet, S., & Wang, Y. (2016). Teachers' emotions and emotion regulation strategies: Self- and students' perceptions. *Teaching and Teacher Education*, *54*, 22–31. doi:10.1016/j.tate.2015.11.008

Kahn, J. S., Brett, B. L., & Holmes, J. R. (2011). Concerns with men's academic motivation in higher education: An exploratory investigation of the role of masculinity. *Journal of Men's Studies*, *19*(1), 65–82. doi:10.3149/jms.1901.65

Kegan, R. (2000). What 'Form' Transforms?: A Constructive-Developmental Perspective on Transformational Learning. In Learning as Transformation: Critical Perspectives on a Theory in Progress. San Francisco: Jossey Bass.

Kim, J., & Park, C.-Y. (2020). Education, skill training, and lifelong learning in the era of technological revolution: A review. *Asian-Pacific Economic Literature*, *34*(2), 3–19. doi:10.1111/apel.12299

Kiselica, M. S., Benton-Wright, S., & Englar-Carlson, M. (2016). Accentuating positive masculinity: A new foundation for the psychology of boys, men, and masculinity. In Y. J. Wong & S. R. Wester (Eds.), *APA handbook of men and masculinities* (pp. 123–143). American Psychological Association. doi:10.1037/14594-006

Knight, P. T. (2002). Summative assessment in higher education: Practices in disarray. *Studies in Higher Education*, *27*(3), 275–286. doi:10.1080/03075070220000662

Ladyshewsky, R. (2013). Instructor presence in online courses and student satisfaction. *International Journal for the Scholarship of Teaching and Learning, 7*(1), 1–23. doi:10.20429/ijsotl.2013.070113

Lewis, A. (2007). Australian Women's online experiences: Why e-learning doesn't necessarily guarantee an inclusive or egalitarian communication space. *International Journal of Learning, 14*(2), 81–90. doi:10.18848/1447-9494/CGP/v14i02/45195

Long, R. (2020). Dynamic Classroom Dialogue: Can Students Be Engaged Beyond Discussion? *Journal of Higher Education Theory and Practice, 20*(3), 85–92. doi:10.33423/jhetp.v20i3.2975

Lou, J. H., Li, R. H., Yu, H. Y., & Chen, S. H. (2011). Relationships among self-esteem, job adjustment and service attitude amongst male nurses: A structural equation model. *Journal of Clinical Nursing, 20*(5-6), 864–872. doi:10.1111/j.1365-2702.2010.03387.x PMID:21118324

Maceli, K. M., Fogliasso, C. E., & Baack, D. (2011). Differences of students' satisfaction with college professors: The impact of student gender on satisfaction. *Academy of Educational Leadership Journal, 15*(4), 35–45.

Maeroff, G. I. (2004). *A classroom of one: How online learning is changing our schools and colleges.* Macmillan.

McDermott, R. C., Pietrantonio, K. R., Browning, B. R., McKelvey, D. K., Jones, Z. K., Booth, N. R., & Sevig, T. D. (2019). In search of positive masculine role norms: Testing the positive psychology positive masculinity paradigm. *Psychology of Men & Masculinity, 20*(1), 12–22. doi:10.1037/men0000160

McKnight-Tutein, G., & Thackaberry, A. S. (2011). Having it all: The hybrid solution for the best of both worlds in women's postsecondary education. *Distance Learning, 8*(3), 17.

Michel, R. E., Hall, S. B., Hays, D. G., & Runyan, H. I. (2013). A mixed-methods study of male recruitment in the counseling profession. *Journal of Counseling and Development, 91*(4), 475–482. doi:10.1002/j.1556-6676.2013.00120.x

Michel, R. E., Hays, D. G., & Runyan, H. I. (2015). Faculty member attitudes and behaviors toward male counselors in training: A social cognitive career theory perspective. *Sex Roles, 72*(7-8), 308–320. doi:10.100711199-015-0473-1

Morante, A., Djenidi, V., Clark, H., & West, S. (2017). Gender differences in online participation: Examining a history and a mathematics open foundation online course. *Australian Journal of Adult Learning, 57*(2), 266–293.

Nistor, N. (2013). Stability of attitudes and participation in online university courses: Gender and location effects. *Computers & Education, 68*, 284–292. doi:10.1016/j.compedu.2013.05.016

Odriozola-González, P., Planchuelo-Gómez, Á., Irurtia, M. J., & de Luis-García, R. (2020). Psychological effects of the COVID-19 outbreak and lockdown among students and workers of a Spanish university. *Psychiatry Research, 290*, 113108. doi:10.1016/j.psychres.2020.113108 PMID:32450409

Organization for Economic Cooperation & Development. (2014). *Education at a Glance 2014: OECD Indicators.* OECD Publishing. doi:10.1787/eag-2014-

Paul, J., & Jeferson, F. (2019). A comparative analysis of student performance in an online vs. face-to-face environmental science course from 2009 to 2016. *Frontiers of Computer Science*, *1*(7), 7. Advance online publication. doi:10.3389/fcomp.2019.00007

Pressley, T., Ha, C., & Learn, E. (2021). Teacher stress and anxiety during COVID-19: An empirical study. *School Psychology*, *36*(5), 367–376. doi:10.1037pq0000468 PMID:34591587

Price, L. (2006). Gender differences and similarities in online courses: Challenging stereotypical views of women. *Journal of Computer Assisted Learning*, *22*(5), 349–359. doi:10.1111/j.1365-2729.2006.00181.x

Prinsen, F. R., Volman, M. L., & Terwel, J. (2007). Gender-related differences in computer-mediated communication and computer-supported collaborative learning. *Journal of Computer Assisted Learning*, *23*(5), 393–409. doi:10.1111/j.1365-2729.2007.00224.x

Radu, M. C., Schnakovszky, C., Herghelegiu, E., Ciubotariu, V. A., & Cristea, I. (2020). The impact of the COVID-19 pandemic on the quality of educational process: A student survey. *International Journal of Environmental Research and Public Health*, *17*(21), 7770. doi:10.3390/ijerph17217770 PMID:33114192

Ray, C. M., Sormunen, C., & Harris, T. M. (1999). Men's and women's attitudes toward computer technology: A comparison. *Office Systems Research Journal*, *17*, 1–8.

Richardson, J. T., & Woodley, A. (2003). Another look at the role of age, gender and subject as predictors of academic attainment in higher education. *Studies in Higher Education*, *28*(4), 475–493. doi:10.1080/03075070320001223305

Rovai, A. P. (2002). Development of an instrument to measure classroom community. *The Internet and Higher Education*, *5*(3), 197–211. doi:10.1016/S1096-7516(02)00102-1

Rovai, A. P., & Wighting, M. J. (2005). Feelings of alienation and community among higher education students in a virtual classroom. *The Internet and Higher Education*, *8*(2), 97–110. doi:10.1016/j.iheduc.2005.03.001

Sargent, P. (2001). *Real men or real teachers? Contradictions in the lives of men elementary school teachers*. Men's Studies Press. doi:10.1177/1097184X00002004003

Sax, L. J., Byrant, A. N., & Harper, C. E. (2005). The differential effects of student-faculty interaction on college outcomes for women and men. *Journal of College Student Development*, *46*(6), 642–657. doi:10.1353/csd.2005.0067

Sbaratta, C. A., Tirpak, D. M., & Schlosser, L. Z. (2015). Male-male advising relationships in graduate psychology: A diminishing dyad. *Sex Roles*, *72*(7-8), 335–348. Advance online publication. doi:10.100711199-015-0466-0

Selwyn, N. (2007). The use of computer technology in university teaching and learning: A critical perspective. *Journal of Computer Assisted Learning*, *23*(2), 83–94. doi:10.1111/j.1365-2729.2006.00204.x

Severiens, S., & ten Dam, G. (2012). Leaving college: A gender comparison in male and female-dominated programs. *Research in Higher Education*, *53*(4), 453–470. doi:10.100711162-011-9237-0

Sheard, M. (2009). Hardiness commitment, gender, and age differentiate university academic performance. *The British Journal of Educational Psychology, 79*(1), 189–204. doi:10.1348/000709908X304406 PMID:18466672

Shen, D. M., Cho, M. H., Tsai, C. L., & Marra, R. (2013). Unpacking online learning experiences: Online learning self-efficacy and learning satisfaction. *The Internet and Higher Education, 19*, 10–17. doi:10.1016/j.iheduc.2013.04.001

Shen-Miller, D., & Smiler, A. (2015). Men in female-dominated vocations: A rationale for academic study and introduction to the special issue. *Sex Roles, 72*(7-8), 269–276. doi:10.100711199-015-0471-3

Shen-Miller, D. S., Olson, D., & Boling, T. (2011). Masculinity in non-traditional occupations: Ecological constructions. *American. Journal of Men's Studies, 5*(1), 18–29. doi:10.1177/1557988309358443 PMID:20038508

Shu, Q., Tu, Q., & Wang, K. (2011). The impact of computer self-efficacy and technology dependence on computer-related technostress: A social cognitive theory perspective. *International Journal of Human-Computer Interaction, 27*(10), 923–939. doi:10.1080/10447318.2011.555313

Smith, K. (2016). Teaching and learning 'Respect' and 'Acceptance' in the classroom. *Faculty Focus Special Report: Diversity and Inclusion in the College Classroom*, 17-18.

Snyder, T. D., de Brey, C., & Dillow, S. A. (2018). *Digest of education statistics 2016* (52nd ed.). National Center for Education Statistics, Institute of Education Sciences, U.S. Department of Education. https://nces.ed.gov/pubs2017/2017094.pdf

Snyder, T. D., De Brey, C., & Dillow, S. A. (2019). *Digest of Education Statistics 2017, NCES 2018-070*. National Center for Education Statistics.

Sobiraj, S., Korek, S., Weseler, D., & Mohr, G. (2011). When male norms don't fit: Do traditional attitudes of female colleagues challenge men in non-traditional occupations? *Sex Roles, 65*(11-12), 798–812. doi:10.100711199-011-0057-7

Steele, J., James, J. B., & Barnett, R. C. (2002). Learning in a man's world: Examining the perceptions of undergraduate women in male-dominated academic areas. *Psychology of Women Quarterly, 26*(1), 46–50. doi:10.1111/1471-6402.00042

Torres Campos, C. M., Phinney, J. S., Perez-Brena, N., Kim, C., Ornelas, B., Nemanim, L., Padilla Kallemeyn, D. M., Mihecoby, A., & Ramirez, C. (2008). A mentor-based targeted intervention for high risk Latino college freshman: A pilot study. *Journal of Hispanic Higher Education, 8*(2), 158–178. doi:10.1177/1538192708317621

Travis, D. J., Nugent, J. S., & McCluney, C. (2016). *Engaging in Conversations About Gender, Race, and Ethnicity in the Workplace*. This product was developed as part of Catalyst's Women of Color Research Agenda: New Approaches. *New Solutions*.

UNESCO, UNICEF, & The World Bank. (2020). *What Have We Learnt? Overview of Findings from a Survey of Ministries of Education on National Responses to COVID-19*. https://openknowledge.worldbank.org/handle/10986/34700

Vavrus, M. (2008). Culturally responsive teaching. *21st century education: A reference handbook, 2*, 49-57. doi:10.4135/9781412964012.n56

Vekiri, I., & Chronaki, A. (2008). Gender issues in technology use: Perceived social support, computer self-efficacy and value beliefs, and computer use beyond school. *Computers & Education, 51*(3), 1392–1404. doi:10.1016/j.compedu.2008.01.003

Wanzer, M. B., Frymier, A. B., & Irwin, J. (2010). An explanation of the relationship between instructor humor and student learning: Instructional humor processing theory. *Communication Education, 59*(1), 1–18. doi:10.1080/03634520903367238

Williams, C. L. (2015). Crossing over: Interdisciplinary research on "men who do women's work". *Sex Roles, 72*(7-8), 390–395. doi:10.100711199-015-0477-x

Wilson, M., Gwyther, K., Swann, R., Casey, K., Featherston, R., Oliffe, J. L., Englar-Carlson, M., & Rice, S. M. (2022). Operationalizing positive masculinity: A theoretical synthesis and school-based framework to engage boys and young men. *Health Promotion International, 37*(1), daab031. Advance online publication. doi:10.1093/heapro/daab031 PMID:33842967

Yaghmour, S. (2012). Gender communication differences in synchronized distance learning lectures for users aged 18-60: A systematic literature review. *Annual Review of Education, Communication & Language Sciences, 9*, 85–90.

Yu, Z. (2021). The effects of gender, educational level, and personality on online learning outcomes during the COVID-19 pandemic. *International Journal of Educational Technology in Higher Education, 18*(1), 14. doi:10.118641239-021-00252-3 PMID:34778520

Zamarro, G., Camp, A., Fuchsman, D., & McGee, J. B. (2022). *Understanding how COVID-19 has changed teachers' chances of remaining in the classroom.* Sinquefield Center for Applied Economic Research Working Paper. doi:10.2139/ssrn.4047354

Zheng, M., Bender, D., & Lyon, C. (2021). Online learning during COVID-19 produced equivalent or better student course performance as compared with pre-pandemic: Empirical evidence from a school-wide comparative study. *BMC Medical Education, 21*(1), 495. doi:10.118612909-021-02909-z PMID:34530828

Chapter 18
The Role of the Instructor in the Online Classroom

Nurul Naimah Rose
https://orcid.org/0000-0003-3195-0685
Universiti Malaysia Perlis, Malaysia

Aida Shakila Ishak
https://orcid.org/0000-0002-8961-9154
Universiti Malaysia Perlis, Malaysia

Nazifah Hamidun
Universiti Malaysia Perlis, Malaysia

Faten Khalida Khalid
Universiti Malaysia Perlis, Malaysia

Nur Farhinaa Othman
Universiti Malaysia Perlis, Malaysia

ABSTRACT

This chapter is about the role of instructors in the online classroom particularly in Malaysian higher education. This chapter will focus on two important points, which are the redefining instructors in virtual education and the four main role of instructors in virtual education: the pedagogical role, the social role, the managerial role, and the technical role. Understanding the true role of the instructor in online classes aids in the transition between the classroom and online learning. Instructors play a more significant role in online courses than they do in traditional ones in many ways. They can adjust more easily and settle into a new environment by being aware of what the students and the online environment expect from the teachers. The requirement for instructors to facilitate an online course through a wide range of perspectives or roles is highlighted by the complexity of the online environment.

DOI: 10.4018/978-1-6684-8908-6.ch018

INTRODUCTION

The landscape of higher education in Malaysia has experienced a significant shift with the emergence of virtual education. Virtual education has made a tremendous impact on Malaysian higher education, in terms of its benefits, challenges, and the potential it holds for the future of learning in the country. Virtual education has opened doors to higher education for individuals who face geographical, financial, or physical constraints (Lee, 2017). The virtual environment promotes inclusivity and flexibility enabling students to pursue their educational aspirations regardless of their location or personal circumstances. Malaysian higher education institutions have embraced online learning platforms that offer asynchronous learning opportunities, allowing students to learn at their own pace and convenience (Mohamad Nasri et al., 2020). This flexibility empowers students to manage their schedules, balance work or other commitments, and personalize their learning journey. They can revisit lectures, access course materials, and engage in discussions according to their individual needs.

Virtual education in Malaysian higher education has redefined the concept of collaboration (De Wit & Altbach, 2021). Discussion forums, video conferencing, and virtual group projects foster interactive and collaborative learning experiences. Virtual education has compelled educators in Malaysian higher education to explore innovative teaching methods (Sia & Adamu, 2020). Lecturers leverage multimedia resources, interactive simulations, and gamification techniques to engage students and enhance their understanding of complex concepts (Donath et al., 2020). Virtual education offers cost-effective alternatives to traditional classroom-based learning (Kilag et al., 2023). Additionally, online resources and digital textbooks reduce the expenses associated with purchasing traditional learning materials. Moreover, virtual education aligns with sustainable practices by reducing carbon emissions from transportation and minimizing paper consumption (Sarkis et al., 2020). This chapter aims to provide insight into the role of instructors and lecturers in the online classroom. Information in this chapter merely focuses on Malaysian higher education institutions with a brief history of e-learning, various theories of e-learning and virtual learning as well as the four main roles of online instructors (pedagogical role, social role, managerial role, technical role).

VIRTUAL EDUCATION IN MALAYSIAN HIGHER EDUCATION INSTITUTIONS

The practices of virtual education in Malaysian higher education institutions started in the 1990s since the emergence of internet usage. The history of e-learning in Malaysia mostly influenced by technological advancements, educational policies, and a growing of digital platforms in the higher education system. Since early 2000s, the emergence of the internet and digital technologies laid the foundation for the adoption of e-learning in Malaysian universities (Nik-Ahmad-Zuky et al. 2020). Initially, universities started exploring the potential of using online platforms to complement traditional classroom and provide supplementary materials to students. Some universities began experimenting with e-learning platforms and online course offerings. These initiatives were often experimental, aiming to evaluate the possibility and acceptance of e-learning among students and educators. Universities started incorporating Learning Management Systems (LMS) to deliver course content and facilitate communication between students and faculty (Iqbal, S., 2011).

The Malaysian government recognized the importance of e-learning in enhancing the country's education system. Initiatives such as the Multimedia Super Corridor (MSC) and the MyBrain15 program were introduced to promote the integration of ICT (Information and Communication Technology) in education, including e-learning (Mustapha, 2013). Various policies and funding support were initiated to encourage universities to adopt and integrate e-learning into their curricula. In the late 2000s, several universities started establishing virtual or online-based universities (Noor et al., 2015). These virtual universities offered a wide range of degree programs and courses entirely online. They provided a flexible learning environment that allowed students to access educational materials and participate in virtual classrooms from anywhere (Abdullah et. al, 2022).

During the 2010s, universities began collaborating with international institutions and e-learning platforms to enhance the quality and diversity of online courses (Zhang et al., 2019). Partnerships with reputable global institutions allowed universities to offer joint programs and certifications through e-learning platforms, attracting a broader student base (Isa & Hashim, 2015). Then, a significant shift occurred in the mid-2010s, when universities began integrating blended learning approaches (Chew, 2009). Blended learning combines traditional face-to-face teaching with online components, offering students a more flexible and interactive learning experience (Singh et al., 2021).

E-learning continues to evolve with a strong emphasis on technological innovation and learner-centered approaches. The COVID-19 pandemic further accelerated the adoption of e-learning as universities quickly transitioned to online teaching to ensure continuity of education (Sharin, 2021). Virtual labs, augmented reality, gamification, and adaptive learning technologies are becoming more prevalent, promising an even more engaging and personalized e-learning experience for students. The history of e-learning in Malaysian universities reflects a transition from experimental adoption to a more integrated and technologically advanced approach. The government's support, technological advancements, and changing educational paradigms have collectively contributed to the growth and transformation of e-learning.

THEORIES OF E-LEARNING AND VIRTUAL LEARNING

The theoretical framework of e-learning and virtual learning provides a conceptual basis for understanding, designing, implementing, and evaluating digital education. It integrates theories from various fields such as education, psychology, technology, and instructional design to guide the development and effective use of e-learning and virtual learning platforms. Some prominent theoretical frameworks associated with e-learning and virtual learning such as Constructivist Learning Theory, Connectivism, Technology Acceptance Model (TAM), Community of Inquiry (CoI) Framework, SAMR Model (Substitution, Augmentation, Modification, Redefinition), Rogers' Diffusion of Innovations Theory and Andragogy (Adult Learning Theory).

Constructivist Learning Theory emphasizes active learning, where learners construct knowledge through interactions with their environment (Huang, 2002). In e-learning and virtual learning, creates the opportunities for learners to engage with the content, collaborate with peers, and reflect on their learning experiences. E-learning platforms should facilitate learner-centered approaches, allowing students to construct knowledge through exploration, problem-solving, and discussions. Connectivism is a contemporary learning theory that emphasizes the importance of networks and connections in the learning process (Kropf, 2013). In the context of e-learning and virtual learning, it underscores the role of online networks, social media, and collaborative tools in knowledge acquisition. Learners are encouraged to connect with diverse sources of information, engage in discussions, and participate in online communities to enhance their learning.

The Role of the Instructor in the Online Classroom

Technology Acceptance Model (TAM) explores the acceptance and adoption of technology, providing insights into users' attitudes and behaviours towards e-learning systems (Ibrahim et al., 2017). It suggests that perceived usefulness and ease of use are critical factors influencing users' acceptance of e-learning platforms. Educators should focus on creating e-learning environments that are perceived as beneficial and user-friendly to maximize engagement. Community of Inquiry (CoI) Framework is a theoretical framework that highlights the importance of social presence, cognitive presence, and teaching presence in online learning environments (Fiock, 2020). Social presence involves creating a sense of community and interpersonal interactions, cognitive presence focuses on meaningful learning through critical discourse, teaching presence emphasizes instructional design and facilitation. The CoI framework guides the design of e-learning courses to foster a supportive and intellectually stimulating online community (Garrison, 2016).

SAMR Model offers a framework for integrating technology in education (Hamilton et al., 2016). It categorizes technology use into four levels (Romrell et al., 2014); substitution, augmentation, modification, and redefinition. E-learning and virtual learning should aim to progress through these levels, ultimately transforming and redefining educational practices. Rogers' Diffusion of Innovations Theory explains how innovations, including e-learning technologies, are adopted and diffused within a social system (Jebeile & Reeve, 2003). It identifies innovators, early adopters, early majority, late majority, and laggards as categories of adopters (Kaminski, 2011). Understanding these categories helps in tailoring e-learning implementations and strategies to meet the varying needs and expectations of different learner groups.

Andragogy focuses on the unique characteristics and needs of adult learners (El-Amin, 2020). In e-learning and virtual learning, this theory suggests that adult learners prefer self-directed, problem-centered, and practical learning experiences (Ross-Gordon, 2003). Designing e-learning platforms that allow adults to take control of their learning journey, apply learning to real-world contexts, and engage in meaningful discussions is key to effective adult education. Understanding and applying these theoretical frameworks in the design, development, and implementation of e-learning and virtual learning initiatives can help optimize learning outcomes, learner engagement, and the overall educational experience in digital environments.

REDEFINING INSTRUCTOR'S ROLE IN VIRTUAL EDUCATION

The requirement for instructors to facilitate an online course through a wide range of perspectives or roles is highlighted by the complexity of the online environment. These roles can be technical, managerial, social, or educational (Easton, 2003). To effectively teach the materials to the students and foster an online learning community, an online instructor must be able to integrate all four roles. Although it may be easy to overlook or forget the fundamental differences between face-to-face and online teaching, these distinctions particularly for online classes can affect the success of both students and instructors in an online course. An instructor must be able to guide student learning, encourage students to cooperate effectively and give enough structure for students' learning while allowing for self-directed exploration in the online learning environment (Wilson, & Stacey, 2004).

Online instructors must consider a variety of roles that share some parallels with traditional classroom instruction but also differ greatly from it. The duties and competencies that go along with teaching online should be customised to the needs of the online learning environment. Online teachers may bring students together around the course material, giving them the chance to connect socially and gain new knowledge as they go. A well-organized, adaptable instructor is even more critical when managing an online course than instructing a traditional classroom. Instructors must juggle more roles than ever before when teaching online. Teachers must be able to offer coaching, a learning community, technical assistance, high-quality content, and a well-designed course all at once to their students (Baran et al., 2011). When instructors have the tools necessary to complete all these tasks, they take on a leadership role in the success of the programme as well as their students.

The role of instructors in virtual education is evolving rapidly (Yang & Cornelious, 2005). They are no longer the sole providers of information; they have become facilitators, mentors, and guides in the online learning environment. In virtual education, instructors are responsible for creating an inclusive and collaborative learning environment. They encourage active participation and engagement among students, fostering meaningful discussions, group projects, and peer learning. Instructors also play a pivotal role in cultivating critical thinking skills, fostering digital literacy, and ensuring continuous assessment and feedback. As virtual education continues to evolve, instructors must embrace this redefined role, equipping themselves with the necessary skills and qualities to excel in the digital learning environment. By doing so, they contribute to the success and growth of online education, empowering students to thrive in the digital age.

THE INSTRUCTOR'S PEDAGOGICAL ROLE

Pedagogical knowledge refers to educators' knowledge of education and learning procedures, activities, or approaches. It encompasses academic goals, values, and purposes (Zhang, 2022). This general category of information consists of overall classroom control competencies, and knowledge regarding the strategies or approaches employed in the classrooms to design lessons and evaluate students (Koehler & Mishra, 2009). To conduct online learning in a digital platform successfully, the instructors must identify their roles in pedagogy. The first role of the instructors in online classrooms is to design courses, develop the content of digital materials, develop learning activities and assessment activities according to the students' pace of learning. It consists of information about linking various beliefs depending on the material, activating students' prior knowledge and students' learning tactics. Moore et al. (2011) stated that self-paced is a descriptor used for learning environments that enable individuals to study online in their own time and at their own pace and location. This type of learning offers more autonomy to the students to proceed at their own pace, while their progress is monitored to assess their achievement (Rhode, 2009; Spector et al., 2008).

Anderson et al. (2001) also stated that instructors need to think through the process, structure, evaluation, and interaction components of the courses well before the first day of class. As regards to teaching, it is necessary to consider that the design, development, and assessment of virtual education introduce features and require specific teaching tasks (Major, 2010 & Spector, 2007). Therefore, it is necessary to assess all the changes that teaching in virtual environments entails for the instructors, both at institutional and academic levels, and this from at least a dual perspective: clarifying the profile of the instructor who is going to be acting in the virtual classroom which implies defining the roles and competencies of the teacher and establishing the training required. Therefore, it is essential for instructors to design effective lesson plans consisting of course objectives, goals, and assessment lessons using online learning platforms.

The second pedagogical role of instructors is to enhance their skills in teaching using the tools and techniques for online learning. Online learning is described by most researchers as learning experiences using the same technology (Carliner, 2002) to deliver lessons to students who are not physically in the same location (Tallent-Runnels et al., 2006). Kulal and Nayak (2020) defined an online class as a system where students can learn subjects, discuss issues with fellow students, clarify doubts with instructors share material, and check academic progress with help from internet-oriented technologies. Online learning can be classified into two modes namely asynchronous and synchronous. Asynchronous learning is temporally and geographically independent and defined as more individually based and self-paced as well as less instructor-dependent (Bernard et al., 2004; Murphy et al., 2011; Clark and Mayer, 2016; Xie et al., 2018). Another benefit of asynchronous online forums is that students mostly favour this form of online learning over face-to-face learning because it allows users to communicate at their own pace and in their own way (O'Neill et al., 2006; Wang & Woo, 2007). Asynchronous online discussion forums have the additional benefit that student participation is not limited by time (Meyer, 2003). Students can respond to a discussion prompt no matter how many students have already responded, and the discussion can continue if the students are interested in participating (Liu, 2012).

Synchronous online learning involves real-time interpersonal communication, the use of natural language, and immediate feedback (Blau et al., 2017). It has been argued that instructors need to know how to use synchronous and asynchronous communication systems (Collison et el., 2000; Guasch et al., 2010; Kearsley, 2000). Several educators have resisted integrating technology into their classes because of the failure of professional development programs to provide them with the needed competencies and knowledge to integrate technology into their classes efficiently. One of the initiatives for the instructors to equip themselves is to join the professional development classes which are known as TPACK. TPACK is an essential structure that can enhance educators in an Internet-based class. TPACK is defined as the knowledge that educators require to educate students through technology in their particular material fields and grade levels (Niess, 2008). For using the TPACK framework in technology integration, educational institutes ought to have access to technology sources, an appropriate curriculum, and experiences using technology to integrate tasks and theories into educational programs for educator training. All educators must become meta-cognitively conscious of their knowledge of technological educational knowledge, TPACK, and technological knowledge (Hughes & Scharber, 2008). It is believed that participating in these development classes can enhance the instructors' knowledge of technology.

In addition, the next pedagogical role for instructors in online learning is to provide effective feedback to the students pertaining to their learning. Feedback is defined as information given by lecturers about the performance of students (Hattie & Timperley, 2007, p. 81). Lecturers must identify which type of feedback is appropriate to be given to the students on online assignments and discussions. Since the learning is conducted on a variety of electronic devices, the instructors need to know the suitable feedback to be integrated into online learning. Some of the researchers are using technology to automate the creation and transmission of feedback information to increase the amount of individual feedback that each learner receives (Balter et al., 2013; Pardo et al., 2017). Other researchers have focussed on improving the quality and timing of feedback comments that online instructors generate, to enhance their impact (Alvarez et al., 2012; Van der Kleijet al., 2015).

Despite instructors being able to provide the feedback on a digital platform, it has been argued that the students are not receiving it because of poor internet connection and unable to comprehend the feedback given. One key barrier is that, as with face-to-face modes, online learners often do not engage with the feedback information that they receive (Mensink & King, 2020; Winstone et al., 2020). Hattie

& Timperley (2007) also highlighted that many researchers do not consider feedback as a process for learners to participate in, but information that is passed on to learners. Nevertheless, the instructors must acknowledge the importance of feedback either in online or face-to-face learning to the students. Howard (1987) addressed that the content of feedback must be correct and indicate the skills and knowledge, the degree to which feedback is individualized, the extent to which performance is to be assessed individually; and provide timely feedback as it is more effective. Furthermore, positive feedback is needed for the students as it will boost up their confidence and affect their learning. Feedback in the online learning process that should provide encouraging comments and opportunities for dialogue, as well as the possibility of commenting on feedback (Jurs & Spehte, 2021). Hyland (2001) believed that motivation may be the most important feature of effective feedback in the context of distance learning.

The other pedagogical role of instructors in online learning is to provide a positive online learning environment and facilitate the students frequently during the class. Instead of giving lectures to the students, the instructors must provide discussion activities to engage the students such as voicing out their opinions or arguing on the given topic discussed. Ong and Quek (2022) also emphasized that to boost students' engagement, instructors have to strategise in their class and provide learning experiences. Student engagement refers to students' cognitive investment, active participation in their learning and emotional commitment to it (Suharti et al., 2021; Zepke et al., 2009). Martin and Bolliger (2018) added that the more engaged the students are, the more satisfied and motivated they are to learn and improve their performance in the online learning environment. Harper (2018) and Englehart (2009) highlighted that it is important to interact and discuss as it helps the students to perform better, achieve greater academic success, feel comfortable and confident in online classrooms. Dziuban et al. (2005) identified two principal advantages from which students in online teaching can benefit, namely strengthening learning engagement and interaction. Thus, instructors and students have the equal responsibility in online learning in achieving a better performance in studies. Gopal et al. (2021) highlighted that online instructors must be enthusiastic about developing genuine instructional resources that actively connect learners and encourage them towards proficient performances. Effective online learning engagement would depend on how students interact with online courses (Lin & Hsieh, 2001). Studies have found that students with prior online learning experience tend to engage more and be satisfied with online learning (Rodriguez et al., 2005).

Moreover, the students who engage in an active discussion can stimulate their critical thinking and attract their attention in the learning process. Discussion has been recognized as a key part of active, experiential learning (Baker et al., 2005). Participation and peer-to-peer interaction contribute to critical thinking (Frijters, et al., 2008; Smith, 1977), reflection (Hara et al., 2000), and higher-order thinking (Meyer, 2003). Students who prefer more time to formulate their thoughts also benefit from online discussions (Andersen, 2009; Majid et al., 2014). In addition, the instructors must also guide and facilitate the students during the discussion by providing the new directions of discussion. To conclude, instructors' pedagogical role is vital to create a positive learning environment which can enhance students' thinking skill and confidence.

THE INSTRUCTOR'S SOCIAL ROLE

Online teaching and learning continue to grow and play an important role in education in Malaysia (Gunawan et al., 2020). Shirley (2019) defines online teaching and learning as face-to-face learning that uses the medium of computer equipment where students can see and hear other students from a distance. Muhammad et al. (2016) stated that online teaching and learning is the use of various web-based technology tools for education. Therefore, online teaching and learning have grown rapidly because there are many advantages such as flexibility, internet accessibility, and cost-effectiveness (Naveed et al., 2018). This advantage can change education towards a lifelong learning process that encourages students to be more creative in accessing various sources of knowledge. Online learning is more affordable as students can earn as they learn, and travel costs are reduced. For these reasons, online learning is important in supporting access to higher education for disadvantaged groups (Castaño-Muñoz et al., 2018). However, there are some challenges faced by the instructors and students in conducting teaching and learning online (Losius et al., 2020).

Social role explains that the instructor must foster a friendly social environment to promote learning and sharing by focus on student participation. Instructors need to be precise about what type and level of participation this should be. Online student engagement is affected by several interrelated psychosocial influences such as teaching support, motivation, skills, and self-efficacy. Teaching support plays a critical role in online courses, with instructor engagement and connection having a positive effect on online student retention (Stone & O'Shea, 2019). Effective online instructors support their students through timely, proactive, embedded support which establishes their personal presence and actively engages students through synchronous and asynchronous methods (Rose, 2018; Stone & O'Shea, 2019). Kahu et al. (2019) found that student self-efficacy influenced interest and enjoyment, and behavioural engagement with learning. Online student engagement is particularly influenced by a sense of belonging where the lesson needs deliberately orchestrated to compensate the physical presence (Delahunty et al., 2014).

Besides that, the instructor also needs to integrate online discussions, topics, and responses as much as possible in the course content. For online students, structural influences such as course design significantly impact on their learning experiences. Online student engagement can be supported by a well-designed course which promotes interaction and social presence and creates a clear purposeful learning journey, efficient use of students' limited time, linking learning activities, addressing gaps in understandings, and providing immersive real-world experiences (Buck, 2016; Frey, 2015). Inappropriately designed online courses and delivery can negatively impact on online student engagement (Stone & O'Shea, 2019).

There are no nonverbal or social cues of student learning or cognitive involvement in the online classroom. For instructors, students must interact with the course material in a way that leaves observable traces in the online classroom for instructors to know that they are present. This is typically accomplished through threaded discussions, tests, activities, or written assignments. Credit is then given for meeting each condition to encourage students' participation in lessons and homework. Since the objective is to encourage student learning, each of these task needs to be graded and given personalised feedback. The social role of an instructor is to promote community building within the learning environment. A community is a supportive social group in which members feel a sense of belonging and share a common interest, experience, or goals (Berry, 2017; Brown, 2001; McMillan & Chavis, 1986; Rovai, 2003). Particularly in a learning community, both students and instructors engage in collective inquiry and provide each other with academic and social support (Lai, 2015; Shrivastava, 1999).

Community building is about creating a space in which students and instructors are committed to a shared learning goal and achieve learning through frequent collaboration and social interaction (Adams & Wilson, 2020). With intentional planning and deliberate pedagogical choices, cultivating and reinforcing positive interactions among classroom participants becomes an essential component of building a classroom community. Instructor can build community through group activities that help students feel comfortable with each other. These activities can even accelerate the forming process in a group. Community building in the classroom is important because of many benefits. For one, it helps create a sense of belonging and connection among students. This can lead to increase social interaction and engagement, as well as making them feel welcomed. Additionally, a close-knit community can be a great resource for information and help. Lecturers may get to know their students, know their names, and determine their skills and knowledge. Understanding students' interests will help in providing the quality of learning opportunities. The more opportunity given to explore areas they are interested in will encourage them to be more engaged with the learning process.

According to Hassan et al. (2020), the learning environment began to be one of the main topics in educational study only after Lewin (1936); Murray (1938) created the concept of the learning environment. It implies a variety of elements including educational, physical, psychological, emotional, and social, that affect students' intellectual growth (Afari et al., 2013). The way students approach their studies and potential learning results are positively impacted by the learning environment that is within the control of the instructor. The learning environment, which determines what, how, and why students learn, has a significant impact on students' learning experiences and outcomes. The instructor can create a welcoming learning environment to influence the behaviour of all students. Three themes that can be considered when working to create a welcoming learning environment include the development of a positive relationship between students and teachers, the implementation of effective teaching strategies, and the effective resolution of conflict in the classroom. Research shows students value an instructor's willingness to give them attention, respect, and time. Students also express preferences for instructors who share opinions, share personal experiences, make eye contact, have good posture, and show students recognition regarding their thoughts and opinions (Schrader, 2004). Basically, when students have positive interactions among peers inside and outside of class and when they feel accepted their learning is enhanced even in an online classroom (Evans, 2000).

The social role of an instructor is to set and communicate expectations. Setting expectations is crucial for guiding students through the learning environment and ensuring that they are aware of the requirements for online learning. Early expectation establishes the guidelines for how students should communicate with one another. Set clear expectations for students and the instructors such as what they will accomplish each week. Lecturers may initially interpret the social role as one that requires them to provide and support opportunities for students to build social and emotional attachments to increase pleasure and motivation. The importance of the social role extends beyond the cognitive domain but is frequently linked to the emotive area of learning. The learning environment becomes one that engages students with the learning outcomes, gives them the chance to ask questions, and gives them the space to co-construct knowledge when they feel like they are a part of the learning community and feel a sense of connection with each other and their instructors (Aragon, 2003; Liu et al., 2005).

THE INSTRUCTOR'S MANAGERIAL ROLE

The word 'managerial role' has been interrelatedly defined by several authors. Berge (1995, cited in Berge, 2008) identified managerial role as one of the categories for instructor's functions. He describes the roles involving the set-up of the agenda for the course, objectives of the discussion, the timetable, procedural rules, and decision-making norms. Qiang (2018) defined managerial roles as instructor behaviors related to course planning, organizing, leading, and controlling. While Dennen & Jones (2022) alternately referred to managerial roles as administrative roles related to course supervision. These roles can be associated with managing objectives, time, and structural components of learning activities. In online learning, instructors engage in tasks such as determining the class schedule and deadlines, planning, and assigning groups, evaluating, and revisiting part of the course, and providing regular announcements and updates. Managerial roles include the organizational, procedural, and administrative tasks associated with the learning environment. The tasks involve coordinating assignments, managing online discussion forums, and handling overall course structure. Online instructors take strong leadership in shaping online interaction by setting clear agendas and objectives for online conferences and establishing procedural rules and decision-making norms.

Managerial roles usually begin at earlier stages of online courses before new instructors gain extensive online experience. With respect to managerial roles, instructors are first seen as the managers of online learning. Chang et al (2008) mentioned that managerial competencies are the most important competence instructors should possess. For the instructor to be effective, there is a need for careful planning, detailed preparations, and mastery of the basic teaching competencies considering using instructional technology (Arah, 2012). To ensure the quality of online education, instructors should take active roles in planning and managing online courses. McKenzie et al. (2005, cited in Yi,2010) mentioned that to make distance education programs successful, areas in planning, implementation, and quality control are important for instructors to consider. When planning and managing online programs, instructors should use techniques aligned with quality online learning. Alley (2001, cited by Yi, 2010) pointed out that to ensure the quality of online education, instructors should take active roles in planning and managing online courses. When planning and managing the course, they need to develop a more detailed course syllabus by including a timetable, learning tasks, and learning outcomes.

As online instructors, their responsibility is to come up with clearly stated learning goals and course objectives and then decide on the instructional methods that will enable learners to achieve the learning outcomes of the course. Instructors need some level of competence and mastery to support and respond to learners' needs. Besides, learners will have an expectation that the instructors are able to deal with any issues or problems and be confident in leading and directing the course. Apart from that, instructors are expected to be knowledgeable about the subject matter, to conduct and manage online learning comfortably. They should also be able to direct and control students' behaviors by providing constructive feedback. This managerial role includes ensuring equity in online discussion. Instructors should provide guidelines to ensure students are given equal opportunities to contribute to the discussion. Setting up rules or guidelines can also prevent students from giving extensive redundant information during the online learning session. Some online instructors created specific rules related to not repeating previous comments or ideas. Arbaugh (2010) supported these decisions as they allow instructors to fully grasp on engaging the students and focus on their pedagogical role. The next role of the online instructors is that they should be the organizer or planner of online learning. All instructions given must be clear to ensure students' comprehension and efficiency of the learning process. Aside from that, the course itself must be properly organized and structured so that learners would be able to engage themselves with the learning. An instructor's flexibility can help accommodate a student's schedule. For example, they are changing the assignment due date.

Gomez-Rey et al. (2018) stated that managerial roles should be included in the list of the most important roles. Several studies from the literature claim that effective classroom management is one of the most important responsibilities assumed by educators. For instance, providing the syllabus to the students at the beginning of the class or semester would give them not only educational information but also all detailed forms that will make learning more transparent. Providing a clear syllabus design will give more time for instructors to focus on other tasks. Keengwe & Kidd (2010) asserted that managerial roles are usually related to classroom and course management. Developing and teaching online courses requires specific sets of skills that instructors must acquire to be successful in this new paradigm of learning and teaching. Managerial tasks during the delivery of the course include getting students into the learning as well as motivating and coordinating students to participate and monitoring their learning outcomes. Therefore, it is important for instructors to keep a record of students' exercises in online learning as it is the most distinct aspect of the managerial role in online learning.

Other items of the managerial role are developing lesson plans, teaching schedules, setting up rules, and disciplining the class. The lesson plan is an essential part of teaching. It elaborated on the goals, objectives, activities, and assessments of a course. Instructors will use lesson plans to interpret them as a guide to what learners need to do and do it successfully through class instruction. Thus, instructors are obliged to develop a complete and systematic lesson plan to ensure that learning will take place in an interactive way and motivate learners to actively participate. The use of a well-tailored course syllabus with clearly stated learning outcomes is seen as helping the instructors to minimize his or her social presence without interrupting learners' active learning. Instructions should be carefully planned to prevent unnecessary monitoring, clearly stating what is required for the learners to complete the learning at the end of the course, and allowing students to interact with the course content itself concomitantly so they can monitor their own learning.

In online classrooms, the managerial roles of the instructors will gradually be decreased as the responsibilities of learning are being passed to the learners. Nevertheless, instructors still play a greater role across different aspects of classroom management ranging from discipline, recordkeeping, rules, and regulations. Such monitoring by the instructors is supposed to help learners enrolled in online learning and prevent them from dropping out of the course. The role of the instructors is primary in education. It is not just limited to engaging in teaching but also performing other roles. Planning is defined as the process of determining goals for the future and the approach means to achieve those goals. Instructors must plan carefully in designing the course content relate the classroom activities appropriately and ensure that the resources are made available for students to engage themselves in learning activities.

THE INSTRUCTOR'S TECHNICAL ROLE

The ability of the instructors to transfer their level of comfort with the technology being used to their students depends on their technical role (Keengwe & Kidd, 2010). This is in line with the claim by Liu et al. (2005) that students should be able to feel at ease when using the system and software for online courses with the technical assistance by instructors during online learning. Technical tasks cover a wide range of responsibilities including technological issues, identifying, and explaining technical issues encountered, and giving them enough time to master new programmes and online platforms. Learning digital skills requires time and space, so students should be given time to learn and adapt just like the instructors. Since technical abilities are required to design online learning settings and technical tools that may be utilised effectively in those contexts, the technical role addresses the instructor's capacity to use media effectively (Sason et al., 2022).

The instructor's responsibility is to ensure that the students are at ease with the information and communication technology hardware, software, and resources used in the online learning environment as possible (Berge, 2008). This is because the instructors' main objective when performing their technical duties is to make technology transparent to students. The more this objective is accomplished, the more the students will be able to focus on the academic task and other activities required for effective learning. This is just one of the essential factors for educators to become proficient in their technical roles. It is important to highlight that as online education develops and matures, more of this technical role is handled by support staff instead of the instructor. This is more easily seen in higher education institutions, where technical-related work such as projectors and laptops are usually managed by technicians. This is in line with a study by Conrad (2004) that mentioned some of the technical roles of a university instructor could be handed off to an audio-visual assistant.

However, even though there are other staff who can help in handling equipment such as projectors and laptops, instructors who teach in higher education institutions still need to have knowledge of operating the tools and should be able to solve issues related to chosen online platforms for the learning sessions to become smoother and more effective. In the current state of the digital world, technical glitches such as re-installation fixes, updates and reboots may occur frequently. Instructors should have a backup plan in case anything goes wrong during online lessons (Berge, 2008). The most common issue would be the Internet connection. Instructors need to always be prepared if the system goes down during lessons. Waiting for a technician or for the system to be restored will result in time wasting, hence, technical expertise is important for instructors in the current education era.

Moreover, the instructor is often the first person whom students seek help when a technical issue interferes with their learning. When a technical problem hinders students' learning process, the instructor is frequently the first person they contact for assistance. It is to be expected since an instructor is the go-to person if students encounter any difficulties or concerns. This is in line with research by Kanuka et al. (2002) that to ensure effective and successful online learning, instructors must have a basic understanding of Internet communication tools and productivity applications. Kanuka et al. (2002) also mentioned that many students ask their instructors for advice on how to use online communication platforms efficiently for online lessons. In connection with that, instructors consider technical support and material development assistance to be an important factor when deciding whether they are interested in teaching online or not (Marek, 2009). Hence, for students to learn effectively, instructors must have a basic grasp of how to use online communication platforms and have great instructional design skills to boost students' interest in online learning at the same time.

One of the numerous problems of online learning that require technical knowledge to resolve is inadequate hardware and software, slow internet connection, and students' attitude, especially the problem of procrastination. Lack of technical expertise among the instructors is also a problem, especially during the COVID-19 pandemic since online learning is the only way to continue teaching and learning. Another technical issue is the lack of release time for instructors to build and develop their online courses and it has been cited as a barriers in developing and teaching online courses (Nkonge & Gueldenzoph, 2006). The researchers suggested that instructors should receive adequate support and training. The students will be able to focus on the academic task when the instructor is able to facilitate a smooth use of technology during online lessons (Liu et al., 2005). However, there is not much consensus in the research regarding the significance of technical roles, in part because technical support can be given in several different ways and in part because online courses use various levels of technology expertise.

Anderson et al. (2001) stated that as students and instructors gain more online learning experience, and as the instruments of online learning become more convenient, the significance of the technical role declines. Evolution of technology and recent events concurrently impact the technical tasks of instructors in online learning. The spread of COVID-19 is an example of how current events can affect the technical role of instructors. The pandemic posed a threat to humanity and forced the closure of numerous global operations including education (Abdesalam et al., 2022). To reduce the spread of the virus, education institutions were forced to switch to e-learning using available educational platforms, despite the challenges facing this sudden transformation. According to de Vries (2021), the sudden implementation shows that online teaching strategies are promptly adopted by instructors worldwide. Surveys on teacher readiness confirm the low level of preparedness at the beginning of the pandemic (Scherer et al., 2021). Instructors must prepare themselves with the knowledge of online teaching and learning in a short period of time, and need to master how to use the internet technology tools competently to ensure that the teaching process is not affected.

It was also noted by Kanuka et al. (2002) that many of the teachers concurred that to facilitate effective online learning, one must be proficient with a variety of software programs and technical processes, including virus checking, online editing tools, and file attachment. Although it seems trivial, these basic skills are also important before the instructors learn to operate and integrate more complicated tools in their teaching and learning. Many instructors noted that students look for them to learn how to use online communication tools, so it is important that the instructor knows how to operate the tools effectively. Technical proficiency with internet communication tools is necessary for this. It is interesting that Kanuka et al. (2002) concluded that these technical issues are the easiest to overcome while other issues, such as creating and sustaining a collegial relationship, continue to be challenging. This shows that although learning how to operate ICT tools and other technical tasks is challenging, it is also the easiest to complete compared to the other three instructor roles listed by Berge (2008). The findings in the technical category corroborate writers' claims that in online learning, technological skills are the most easily surmounted and are less important than well-developed learning goals and objectives (Berge, 2008).

While the studies above found that technical issues are not a big challenge to instructors as some instructors claim that it is the easiest to overcome, there are studies that prove otherwise. Condie and Livingston (2007) suggested that many instructors are not so confident in the online technology used for instruction when teaching. The findings of this study are the opposite compared to those discussed earlier as the instructors showed a lack of interest in learning how to use online tools effectively to advance students' learning in addition to criticising its purported benefits. Effective use of technology is one aspect of the successful and effective implementations of online learning (Bailey & Card, 2009). While online learning may be an option, there are occasions where mastering it is a must. During crucial times like the COVID-19 pandemic, instructors need to make sure the learning process is effective, whether the lesson is conducted online or in a conventional way. According to Sason et al. (2022), students who find technology to be a barrier will steer clear of online classes, as well as instructors who are uncomfortable creating online learning platforms. However, the pandemic provided no other option and forced everyone to take online courses.

It is important to know the students' perceptions of instructors' technical role in online learning as they are a part of the teaching and learning process. In a study by Roby et al. (2008), it was mentioned that students still regarded having a range of delivery methods for the content and the availability of technical support like teaching assistant support and helpdesk, as critical and extremely important. Although the students identified themselves as tech-savvy, they also stated that they needed access to technical support while taking an online course. Similarly, a study by Sason et al. (2022) revealed how much of a challenge this is for the students as well, as how much more technical support they anticipate from the instructors. Not only students, but there are also instructors who find technical roles challenging. Roby et al. (2013) studied the instructors' perceptions, and it was found that technical assistance, which includes assistance with supplying students with accessible materials, received the highest rating from the instructors. The study also reported that instructors' incompetence over the technology tools utilized in the course will affect how well they will be evaluated by students.

Similarly, a study by Orr et al. (2009) asserted that instructors should receive assistance with technical support because they are experts in their fields, not necessarily in technology. To relieve instructors from the need to provide technical assistance on top of their numerous duties while facilitating the course, it is important to provide support for those technologies to the students who are utilising the corresponding hardware or software. These findings about instructors needing assistance for technical support show that it is a difficult role for them. It is obvious that in an online lesson, technical support is important for both students and instructors to ensure the lesson is effective. It can be concluded that the instructor's technical role is important to ensure an effective online learning environment. This is further supported by Sason et al. (2022) in their studies as they mentioned investment in technical skills is necessary, especially in times of emergency, and does not come second to investment in pedagogy. This proves that while teaching pedagogy is important, technical support is as important as well. Sason et al. (2022) also mentioned that technical support aids in reducing students' stress levels and will help them succeed in their studies. It is crucial for the instructor to have a firm grasp of how to use Internet communication tools for effective learning and to boost students' interest in online learning. This is because the instructor is frequently the first person that students turn to for assistance when a technical problem interferes with their learning.

CONCLUSION

Instructors play crucial roles in facilitating learning and creating a conducive online learning environment in Malaysian higher education. Their roles extend beyond traditional classroom teaching and encompass various responsibilities in the virtual setting. Instructors guide and support students' learning experiences via online platforms. They design and organize online courses, develop learning materials, and provide clear instructions to help students navigate the virtual environment effectively. They deliver online lectures, conduct discussions, and provide explanations to ensure students understand the subject matter. Instructors are responsible for developing appropriate assessment methods, such as quizzes, assignments, and exams, to evaluate students' knowledge and skills. They provide timely and constructive feedback to students, helping them understand their strengths and areas for improvement.

Instructors offer guidance and social support to students throughout their virtual learning journey. They provide academic advice, clarify doubts, and address students' concerns via online platforms, email, or virtual office hours. They also serve as mentors, offering personalized assistance and helping students navigate challenges they may encounter. In addition, instructors have a technical role and are expected to be proficient in utilizing the learning management system (LMS) and other virtual tools required for online instruction. They troubleshoot technical issues, provide guidance on accessing and using online resources, and ensure students have a smooth learning experience. In conclusion, instructors in virtual education in higher education in Malaysia play multifaceted roles as pedagogy experts, social facilitators, content managers, and technical experts. Their expertise and efforts contribute to creating an engaging, interactive, and effective virtual learning environment, enabling students to achieve their learning goals and succeed academically.

REFERENCES

Abdullah, S. I. N. W., Arokiyasamy, K., Goh, S. L., Culas, A. J., & Manaf, N. M. A. (2022). University students' satisfaction and future outlook towards forced remote learning during a global pandemic. *Smart Learning Environments*, *9*(1), 1–21. doi:10.118640561-022-00197-8

Adams, B., & Wilson, N. S. (2020). Building community in asynchronous online higher education courses through collaborative annotation. *Journal of Educational Technology Systems*, *49*(2), 250–261. doi:10.1177/0047239520946422

Afari, E., Aldridge, J. M., Fraser, B. J., & Khine, M. S. (2013). Students' perceptions of the learning environment and attitudes in game-based mathematics classrooms. *Learning Environments Research*, *16*(1), 131–150. doi:10.100710984-012-9122-6

Anderson, T., Liam, R., Garrison, D. R., & Archer, W. (2001). Assessing teaching presence in a computer conferencing context. *Journal of Asynchronous Learning Networks*, *5*(2), 1–17.

Aragon, S. R. (2003). Creating social presence in online environments. *New Directions for Adult and Continuing Education*, *100*(100), 57–68. doi:10.1002/ace.119

Arah, B.O. (2012). The competencies, preparations, and challenging (new) roles of online instructors. *US-China Education Review*, A10.

Baker, A. C., Jensen, P. J., & Kolb, D. A. (2005). Conversation as experiential learning. *Management Learning*, *36*(4), 411–427. doi:10.1177/1350507605058130

Baran, E., Correia, A. P., & Thompson, A. (2011). Transforming online teaching practice: Critical analysis of the literature on the roles and competencies of online teachers. *Distance Education*, *32*(3), 421–439. doi:10.1080/01587919.2011.610293

Berge, Z. L. (2008). Changing instructor's roles in virtual worlds. *Quarterly Review of Distance Education*, *9*(4), 407–414.

Berry, S. (2017). Building community in online doctoral classrooms: Instructor practices that support community. *Online Learning : the Official Journal of the Online Learning Consortium*, *21*(2), 42–63. doi:10.24059/olj.v21i2.875

Brown, R. E. (2001). The process of community-building in distance learning classes. *Journal of Asynchronous Learning Networks*, *5*(2), 18–35.

Buck, S. (2016). In their own voices: Study habits of distance education students. *Journal of Library & Information Services in Distance Learning*, *10*(3-4), 137–173. doi:10.1080/1533290X.2016.1206781

Castaño-Muñoz, J., Colucci, E., & Smidt, H. (2018). Free digital Learning for inclusion of migrants and refugees in Europe: A qualitative analysis of three types of learning purposes. *International Review of Research in Open and Distance Learning*, *19*(2), 1–21. doi:10.19173/irrodl.v19i2.3382

Chew, E. (2009). *A blended learning model in higher education: A comparative study of blended learning in UK and Malaysia*. University of South Wales.

Conrad, D. (2004). University instructors' reflections on their first online teaching experiences. *Journal of Asynchronous Learning Networks*, *8*(2), 31–44.

de Vries, T. J. (2021). The pandemic that has forced teachers to go online. Zooming in on tips for online teaching. In *Frontiers in Education* (p. 105). Frontiers. doi:10.3389/feduc.2021.647445

De Wit, H., & Altbach, P. G. (2021). Internationalization in higher education: Global trends and recommendations for its future. In *Higher Education in the Next Decade* (pp. 303–325). Brill. doi:10.1163/9789004462717_016

Delahunty, J., Verenikina, I., & Jones, P. (2014). Socio-emotional connections: Identity, belonging and learning in online interactions. A literature review. *Technology, Pedagogy and Education*, *23*(2), 243–265. doi:10.1080/1475939X.2013.813405

Dennen, V. P., & Jones, M. K. (2015). The role of the online instructor: A nexus of skills, activities, and values that support online learning. In O. Zawacki-Smith & I. Jung (Eds.), *The handbook of open, distance, and distributed education*. Springer.

Donath, L., Mircea, G., & Rozman, T. (2020). E-learning platforms as leverage for education for sustainable development. *European Journal of Sustainable Development*, *9*(2), 1–1. doi:10.14207/ejsd.2020.v9n2p1

El-Amin, A. (2020). Andragogy: A theory in practice in higher education. *Journal of Research in Higher Education*, *4*(2).

Englehart, J. M. (2009). Teacher–student interaction. In L. J. Saha & A. G. Dworkin (Eds.), *International handbook of research on teachers and teaching* (pp. 711–722). Springer. doi:10.1007/978-0-387-73317-3_44

Evans, N. J. (2000). Creating a positive learning environment for gay, lesbian, and bisexual students. *New Directions for Teaching and Learning*, *2000*(82), 81–87. doi:10.1002/tl.8208

Fabriz, S., Mendzheritskaya, J., & Stehle, S. (2021). Impact of synchronous and asynchronous settings of online teaching and learning in higher education on students' learning experience during COVID-19. *Frontiers in Psychology*, *12*, 733554. doi:10.3389/fpsyg.2021.733554 PMID:34707542

Frijters, S., ten Dam, G., & Rijlaarsdam, G. (2008). Effects of dialogic learning on value-loaded critical thinking. *Learning and Instruction*, *18*(1), 66–82. doi:10.1016/j.learninstruc.2006.11.001

Goliong, L., Kasin, A., Johnny, M., & Yulip, N. G. (2020). *Cabaran pelaksanaan pengajaran dan pembelajaran jarak jauh semasa Perintah Kawalan Pergerakan*. Pejabat Pendidikan Daerah Ranau.

Gomez-Rey, P., Barbera, E., & Fernandez-Navarro, F. (2018). Students' perceptions about online teaching effectiveness: A bottom-up approach for identifying online instructors' roles. *Australasian Journal of Educational Technology*, *34*(1). Advance online publication. doi:10.14742/ajet.3437

Gopal, R., Singh, V., & Aggarwal, A. (2021). Impact of online classes on the satisfaction and performance of students during the pandemic period of COVID 19. *Education and Information Technologies*, *26*(6), 6923–6947. doi:10.100710639-021-10523-1 PMID:33903795

Gunawan, G., Suranti, N. M. Y., & Fathoroni, F. (2020). Variations of models and learning platforms for prospective teachers during the COVID-19 pandemic period. *Indonesian Journal of Teacher Education*, *1*(2).

Hamilton, E. R., Rosenberg, J. M., & Akcaoglu, M. (2016). The substitution augmentation modification redefinition (SAMR) model: A critical review and suggestions for its use. *TechTrends*, *60*(5), 433–441. doi:10.100711528-016-0091-y

Harper, B. (2018). Technology and teacher–student interactions: A review of empirical research. *Journal of Research on Technology in Education*, *50*(3), 214–225. doi:10.1080/15391523.2018.1450690

Hassan, N. M., Majid, N. A., & Hassan, N. K. A. (2020). Validation of learning environment inventory for secondary school contexts. *International Journal of Evaluation and Research in Education*, *9*(2), 379–384. doi:10.11591/ijere.v9i2.20444

Hattie, J., & Timperley, H. (2007). The power of feedback. *Review of Educational Research*, *77*(1), 81–112. doi:10.3102/003465430298487

Huang, H. M. (2002). Toward constructivism for adult learners in online learning environments. *British Journal of Educational Technology*, *33*(1), 27–37. doi:10.1111/1467-8535.00236

Hyland, K. (2001). Bringing in the reader: Addressee features in academic writing. *Written Communication*, *18*(4), 549–574. doi:10.1177/0741088301018004005

Ibrahim, R., Leng, N. S., Yusoff, R. C. M., Samy, G. N., Masrom, S., & Rizman, Z. I. (2017). E-learning acceptance based on technology acceptance model (TAM). *Revue des Sciences Fondamentales et Appliquées*, *9*(4S), 871–889. doi:10.4314/jfas.v9i4S.50

Iqbal, S. (2011). Learning management systems (LMS): Inside matters. *Information Management and Business Review*, *3*(4), 206–216. doi:10.22610/imbr.v3i4.935

Isa, P. M., & Hashim, R. (2015). *Issues and challenges of e-learning in higher education: A Malaysian perspective*. Academic Press.

Jebeile, S., & Reeve, R. (2003). The diffusion of e-learning innovations in an Australian secondary college: Strategies and tactics for educational leaders. *Innovation*, *8*(4).

Jurs, P., & Špehte, E. (2021). The Role of Feedback in the Distance Learning Process. *Journal of Teacher Education for Sustainability.*, *23*(2), 91–105. doi:10.2478/jtes-2021-0019

Kahu, E. R., Stephens, C., Zepke, N., & Leach, L. (2014). Space and time to engage: Mature-aged distance students learn to fit study into their lives. *International Journal of Lifelong Education*, *33*(4), 523–540. doi:10.1080/02601370.2014.884177

Kaminski, J. (2011). Diffusion of innovation theory. *Canadian Journal of Nursing Informatics*, *6*(2), 1–6.

Kanuka, H., Collett, D., & Caswell, C. (2002). University instructor perceptions of the use of asynchronous text-based discussion in distance courses. *American Journal of Distance Education*, *16*(3), 151–167. doi:10.1207/S15389286AJDE1603_3

Keengwe, J., & Kidd, T. T. (2010). Towards best practices in online learning and teaching in higher education. *Journal of Online Learning and Teaching, 6*(2), 533–541.

Kilag, O. K. T., del Socorro, A. S., Largo, J. L., Peras, C. C., Book, J. F. P., & Abendan, C. F. K. (2023). Perspectives and experiences in online teaching and learning. *Science and Education, 4*(6), 561–571.

Koehler, M. J., & Mishra, P. (2006). Technological pedagogical content knowledge: A framework for teacher knowledge. *Teachers College Record, 108*(6), 1017–1054. doi:10.1111/j.1467-9620.2006.00684.x

Kropf, D. C. (2013). Connectivism: 21st Century's New Learning Theory. *European Journal of Open. Distance and E-Learning, 16*(2), 13–24.

Lai, K. W. (2015). Knowledge construction in online learning communities: A case study of a doctoral course. *Studies in Higher Education, 40*(4), 561–579. doi:10.1080/03075079.2013.831402

Lee, K. (2017). Rethinking the accessibility of online higher education: A historical review. *The Internet and Higher Education, 33*, 15–23. doi:10.1016/j.iheduc.2017.01.001

Lin, B., & Hsieh, C. T. (2001). Web-based teaching and learner control: A research review. *Computers & Education, 37*(3), 377–386. doi:10.1016/S0360-1315(01)00060-4

Liu, O. L. (2012). Student Evaluation of Instruction: In the new paradigm of distance education. *Research in Higher Education, 53*(4), 471–486. doi:10.100711162-011-9236-1

Liu, X., Bonk, C. J., Magjuka, R. J., Lee, S. H., & Su, B. (2005). Exploring four dimensions of online instructor roles: A program level case study. *Journal of Asynchronous Learning Networks, 9*(4), 29–48.

Majid, S., Yang, P., Lei, H., & Haoran, G. (2014). Knowledge sharing by students: Preference for online discussion board vs face-to-face class participation. In *The Emergence of Digital Libraries–Research and Practices* (pp. 149–159). Springer International Publishing. doi:10.1007/978-3-319-12823-8_16

Marek, K. (2009). Learning to teach online: Creating a culture of support for faculty. *Journal of Education for Library and Information Science, 50*(4), 275–292.

Martin, F., & Bolliger, D. U. (2018). Engagement matters: Student perceptions on the importance of engagement strategies in the online learning environment. *Online Learning : the Official Journal of the Online Learning Consortium, 22*(1), 205–222. doi:10.24059/olj.v22i1.1092

McMillan, D. W., & Chavis, D. M. (1986). Sense of community: A definition and theory. *Journal of Community Psychology, 14*(1), 6–23. doi:10.1002/1520-6629(198601)14:1<6::AID-JCOP2290140103>3.0.CO;2-I

Meyer, K. A. (2003). Face-to-face versus threaded discussions: The role of time and higher-order thinking. *Journal of Asynchronous Learning Networks, 7*(3), 55–65.

Mohamad Nasri, N., Husnin, H., Mahmud, S. N. D., & Halim, L. (2020). Mitigating the COVID-19 pandemic: A snapshot from Malaysia into the coping strategies for pre-service teachers' education. *Journal of Education for Teaching, 46*(4), 546–553. doi:10.1080/02607476.2020.1802582

Murray, H. A. (1938). *Explorations in personality*. Oxford University Press.

Mustapha, R. (2013). Transforming education toward K-economy in Malaysia. *Educare (San José), 6*(1).

Nik-Ahmad-Zuky, N. L., Baharuddin, K. A., & Rahim, A. A. (2020). Online clinical teaching and learning for medical undergraduates during the COVID-19 pandemic: The Universiti Sains Malaysia (USM) experience. *Education in Medicine Journal*, *12*(2), 75–80. doi:10.21315/eimj2020.12.2.8

Nkonge, B., & Geuldenzolph, L. (2006). Best practices in online education: Implications for policy and practice. *Business Education Digest*, *15*, 42–53.

Noor, A. M., Attaran, M., & Alias, N. (2015). Students' experiences in using spectrum: Textbook or classroom? *Procedia: Social and Behavioral Sciences*, *176*, 667–673. doi:10.1016/j.sbspro.2015.01.525

O'Neill, P., Duplock, A., & Willis, S. (2006). Using clinical experience in discussion with problem-based learning groups. *Advances in Health Sciences Education : Theory and Practice*, *11*(4), 349–363. doi:10.100710459-006-9014-6 PMID:16937238

Ong, S. G. T., & Quek, G. C. L. (2023). Enhancing teacher–student interactions and student online engagement in an online learning environment. *Learning Environments Research*, *26*(3), 681–707. doi:10.100710984-022-09447-5 PMID:36685638

Orr, R., Williams, M. R., & Pennington, K. (2009). Institutional efforts to support faculty in online teaching. *Innovative Higher Education*, *34*(4), 257–268. doi:10.100710755-009-9111-6

Qiang, H. (2018). Teachers' roles in online learning: The student perspective. *Irish Journal of Academic Practice.*, *7*(1).

Roby, T., Ashe, S., Singh, N., & Clark, C. (2013). Shaping the online experience: How administrators can influence student and instructor perceptions through policy and practice. *The Internet and Higher Education*, *17*, 29–37. doi:10.1016/j.iheduc.2012.09.004

Rodriguez, M. C., Ooms, A., Montanez, M., & Yan, Y. L. (2005). *Perceptions of online learning quality given comfort with technology, motivation to learn technology skills, satisfaction, and online learning experience*. Paper presented at the Annual meeting of the American Educational Research Association, Montreal.

Romrell, D., Kidder, L., & Wood, E. (2014). The SAMR model as a framework for evaluating mLearning. *Online Learning Journal*, *18*(2).

Rose, M. (2018). What are some key attributes of effective online teachers? *Journal of Open. Flexible and Distance Learning*, *22*(2), 32–48. doi:10.61468/jofdl.v22i2.336

Ross-Gordon, J. M. (2003). Adult learners in the classroom. *New Directions for Student Services*, *2003*(102), 43–52. doi:10.1002s.88

Sarkis, J., Cohen, M. J., Dewick, P., & Schröder, P. (2020). A brave new world: Lessons from the COVID-19 pandemic for transitioning to sustainable supply and production. *Resources, Conservation and Recycling*, *159*, 104894. doi:10.1016/j.resconrec.2020.104894 PMID:32313383

Sason, H., Wasserman, E., Safrai, M. Z., & Romi, S. (2022). Students' perception of the role of online teachers: Comparing routine and emergency times. *Frontiers in Education*, *6*, 569. doi:10.3389/feduc.2021.767700

Scherer, A. M., Gedlinske, A. M., Parker, A. M., Gidengil, C. A., Askelson, N. M., Petersen, C. A., & Lindley, M. C. (2021). Acceptability of adolescent COVID-19 vaccination among adolescents and parents of adolescents—United States, April 15–23, 2021. *Morbidity and Mortality Weekly Report, 70*(28), 997. doi:10.15585/mmwr.mm7028e1 PMID:34264908

Schrader, D. E. (2004). Intellectual safety, moral atmosphere, and epistemology in college classrooms. *Journal of Adult Development, 11*(2), 87–101. doi:10.1023/B:JADE.0000024542.67919.55

Sharin, A. N. (2021). E-learning during COVID-19: A review of literature. *Journal Pengajian Media Malaysia, 23*(1), 15–28. doi:10.22452/jpmm.vol23no1.2

Shirley, A. S., Paul, A. S., Hart, P., Augustin, L., Clarke, P. J., & Pike, M. (2020). Parents perspectives on home-based character education activities. *Journal of Family Studies*, •••, 1–23.

Shrivastava, P. (1999). Management classes as online learning communities. *Journal of Management Education, 23*(6), 691–702. doi:10.1177/105256299902300607

Sia, J. K. M., & Adamu, A. A. (2020). Facing the unknown: Pandemic and higher education in Malaysia. *Asian Education and Development Studies, 10*(2), 263–275. doi:10.1108/AEDS-05-2020-0114

Singh, J., Steele, K., & Singh, L. (2021). Combining the best of online and face-to-face learning: Hybrid and blended learning approach for COVID-19, post vaccine, & post-pandemic world. *Journal of Educational Technology Systems, 50*(2), 140–171. doi:10.1177/00472395211047865

Stone, C., & O'Shea, S. (2019). Older, online and first: Recommendations for retention and success. *Australasian Journal of Educational Technology, 35*(1), 57–69. doi:10.14742/ajet.3913

Tallent-Runnels, M., Thomas, J., Lan, W., Cooper, S., Ahern, T., Shaw, S., & Liu, X. (2006). Teaching Courses Online: *A Review of the Research. Review of Educational Research, 76*(1), 93–135. doi:10.3102/00346543076001093

Wang, Q., & Woo, H. L. (2007). Systematic Planning for ICT Integration in Topic Learning. *Journal of Educational Technology & Society, 10*(1), 148–156.

Wilson, G., & Stacey, E. (2004). Online interaction impacts on learning: Teaching the teachers to teach online. *Australasian Journal of Educational Technology, 20*(1). Advance online publication. doi:10.14742/ajet.1366

Yang, Y., & Cornelious, L. F. (2005). Preparing instructors for quality online instruction. *Online Journal of Distance Learning Administration, 8*(1), 1–16.

Yi, Y. (2010). Roles of Administrators in Ensuring the Quality of Online Programs. *Knowledge Management & E-Learning. International Journal (Toronto, Ont.), 2*(4).

Zhang, K., Bonk, C. J., Reeves, T. C., & Reynolds, T. H. (Eds.). (2019). *MOOCs and open education in the Global South: Challenges, successes, and opportunities*. Routledge. doi:10.4324/9780429398919

Zhang, Y. (2022). Developing EFL teachers' technological pedagogical knowledge through practices in virtual platform. *Frontiers in Psychology, 13*, 916060. Advance online publication. doi:10.3389/fpsyg.2022.916060 PMID:35712156

Compilation of References

Abbas, J., Aman, J., Nurunnabi, M., & Bano, S. (2019). The impact of social media on learning behavior for sustainable education: Evidence of students from selected universities in Pakistan. *Sustainability (Basel)*, *11*(6), 1683. Advance online publication. doi:10.3390u11061683

Abbott, D. M., Pelc, N., & Mercier, C. (2019). Cultural humility and the teaching of psychology. *Scholarship of Teaching and Learning in Psychology*, *5*(2), 169–181. doi:10.1037tl0000144

Abbott, H. P. (2020). *The Cambridge introduction to narrative*. Cambridge University Press. doi:10.1017/9781108913928

Abdolrezapour, P., Jahanbakhsh Ganjeh, S., & Ghanbari, N. (2023). Self-efficacy and resilience as predictors of students' academic motivation in online education. *PLoS One*, *18*(5), e0285984–e0285984. doi:10.1371/journal.pone.0285984 PMID:37220147

Abdullah, S. I. N. W., Arokiyasamy, K., Goh, S. L., Culas, A. J., & Manaf, N. M. A. (2022). University students' satisfaction and future outlook towards forced remote learning during a global pandemic. *Smart Learning Environments*, *9*(1), 1–21. doi:10.118640561-022-00197-8

Abedini, A., Abedin, B., & Zowgi, D. (2021). Adult learning in online communities of practice: A systematic review. *British Journal of Educational Technology*, *52*(4), 1663–1694. doi:10.1111/bjet.13120

Abrahim, M., & Suhara, M. (2019). Structural equation modeling and confirmatory factor analysis of social media use and education. *International Journal of Educational Technology in Higher Education*, *16*(1), 32. doi:10.118641239-019-0157-y

Abutiheen, Z. A., Abdulmunem, A. A., & Harjan, Z. A. (2022). Assessment Online Platforms During COVID-19 Pandemic. In Advances in Intelligent Computing and Communication *Proceedings of ICAC*, *2021*, 519–527.

Achor, S. (2010). *The happiness advantage: the seven principles that fuel success and performance at work*. Virgin.

ADA Amendments Act of 2008, H.R.3195 - 110th Congress (2007-2008). (2008, June 27). https://www.congress.gov/bill/110th-congress/house-bill/3195/text

ADA.gov. (2022, March 18). *Guidance on web accessibility and the ADA*. https://www.ada.gov/resources/web-guidance/

Adaji, I., Oyibo, K., & Vassileva, J. (2018). Shopper types and the influence of persuasive strategies in E-commerce. *Proceedings of the Personalization in Persuasive Technology Workshop, Persuasive Technology*, *2089*, 58–67.

Adams, B., & Wilson, N. S. (2020). Building Community in Asynchronous Online Higher Education Courses Through Collaborative Annotation. *Journal of Educational Technology Systems*, *49*(2), 250–261. doi:10.1177/0047239520946422

Adams, C., & Rose, E. (2014). Will I ever connect with the students?" Online teaching and the pedagogy of care. *Phenomenology & Practice*, *8*(1), 5–16. doi:10.29173/pandpr20637

Compilation of References

Admon, A. J., Kaul, V., Cribbs, S. K., Guzman, E., Jiminez, O., & Richards, J. B. (2020). Twelve tips for developing and implementing a medical education X chat. *Medical Teacher*, *42*(5), 500–506. doi:10.1080/0142159X.2019.1598553 PMID:30999789

Afari, E., Aldridge, J. M., Fraser, B. J., & Khine, M. S. (2013). Students' perceptions of the learning environment and attitudes in game-based mathematics classrooms. *Learning Environments Research*, *16*(1), 131–150. doi:10.100710984-012-9122-6

Aghaee & Keller, C. (2016). ICT-supported peer interaction among learners in Bachelor's and Master's thesis courses. *Computers and Education*, *94*, 276–297. doi:10.1016/j.compedu.2015.11.006

Aichner, T., Grunfelder, M., Maurer, O., & Jegeni, D. (2021). Twenty-five years of social media: A review of social media applications and definitions from 1994 to 2019. *Cyberpsychology, Behavior, and Social Networking*, *24*(4), 215–222. doi:10.1089/cyber.2020.0134 PMID:33847527

Aitken, G., & Hayes, S. (2021). Online Postgraduate Teaching: Re-Discovering Human Agency. In T. Fawns, G. Aitken, & D. Jones (Eds.), *Online Postgraduate Education in a Postdigital World. Postdigital Science and Education*. Springer. doi:10.1007/978-3-030-77673-2_8

Ajmal, M., & Ahmad, S. (2019). Exploration of anxiety factors among students of distance learning: A case study of Allama Iqbal Open University. *Bulletin of Education and Research August*, *41*(2), 67–78.

Akcaoglu, M., & Lee, E. (2018). Using facebook groups to support social presence in online learning. *Distance Education*, *39*(3), 334–352. doi:10.1080/01587919.2018.1476842

Akpınar, E. (2021). The effect of online learning on tertiary level students mental health during the COVID-19 lockdown. *The European Journal of Social & Behavioural Sciences*. doi:10.15405/ejsbs.288

Alalwan, N. (2022). Actual use of social media for engagement to enhance students' learning. *Education and Information Technologies*, *27*(7), 9767–9789. doi:10.100710639-022-11014-7 PMID:35399784

Aldosari, A. M., Alramthi, S. M., & Eid, H. F. (2022). Improving social presence in online higher education: Using live virtual classroom to confront learning challenges during COVID-19 pandemic. *Frontiers in Psychology*, *13*, 994403. Advance online publication. doi:10.3389/fpsyg.2022.994403 PMID:36467142

Alghamdi, A., Karpinski, A. C., Lepp, A., & Barkley, J. (2020). Online and face-to-face classroom multitasking and academic performance: Moderated mediation with self-efficacy for self-regulated learning and gender. *Computers in Human Behavior*, *102*, 214–222. doi:10.1016/j.chb.2019.08.018

Alkış, N., & Temizel, T. T. (2018). The Impact of Motivation and Personality on Academic Performance in Online and Blended Learning Environments. *Journal of Educational Technology & Society*, *21*(3), 35–47. https://www.jstor.org/stable/26458505

Allen, C. (2019). Calling all the sisters: The Impact of sister circles on the retention and experiences of Black womyn collegians at predominantly White institutions. *All Dissertations*, 2374. https://tigerprints.clemson.edu/all_dissertations/2374

Allen, I. E., & Seaman, J. (2017). *Digital Compass Learning: Distance Education Enrollment Report 2017*. Babson Survey Research Group.

Allen, I. E., & Seaman, J. (2011). *Going the distance: Online education in the United States*. Sloan Consortium.

Allodi, M. W. (2010). The meaning of social climate of learning environments: Some reasons why we do not care enough about it. *Learning Environments Research*, *13*(2), 89–104. doi:10.100710984-010-9072-9

Almazova, N., Krylova, E., Rubtsova, A., & Odinokaya, M. (2020). Challenges and opportunities for Russian higher education amid COVID-19. *Education Sciences*, *10*(12), 368. doi:10.3390/educsci10120368

Almedom, A. M. (2005). Social capital and mental health: An interdisciplinary review of primary evidence. *Social Science & Medicine*, *61*(5), 943–964. doi:10.1016/j.socscimed.2004.12.025 PMID:15955397

Alonso-Tapia, J., & Nieto, C. (2019). Classroom emotional climate: Nature, measurement, effects and implications for education. Revista de Psicodidáctica (English ed.), 24(2), 79-87.

Alonso-Tapia, J., Ruiz, M. Á., Huertas, J. A. (2020). Differences in classroom motivational climate: Causes, effects and implications for teacher education. A multilevel study. *Anales De Psicología/Annals of Psychology, 36*(1), 122-133.

Alonso-Tapia, J., & Ruiz-Díaz, M. (2022). Student, teacher, and school factors predicting differences in classroom climate: A multilevel analysis. *Learning and Individual Differences*, *94*, 102115. doi:10.1016/j.lindif.2022.102115

Alqurashi. (2016). Self-Efficacy In Online Learning Environments: A Literature Review. *Contemporary Issues in Education Research, 9*(1), 45–52. doi:10.19030/cier.v9i1.9549

Alshammari, T., Alseraye, S., Alqasim, R., Rogowska, A., Alrasheed, N., & Alshammari, M. (2022). Examining anxiety and stress regarding virtual learning in colleges of health sciences: A cross-sectional study in the era of the COVID-19 pandemic in Saudi Arabia. *Saudi Pharmaceutical Journal*, *30*(3), 256–264. doi:10.1016/j.jsps.2022.01.010 PMID:35498216

Alton, L. (2023). *How X chats can improve your audience engagement strategy*. https://business.X.com/en/blog/how-to-promote-your-X-chat.html

Alvarez VazquezE.Cortes-MendezM.StrikerR.SingelmannL.PearsonM.SwartzE.

American Psychiatric Association. (2022). *Diagnostic and statistical manual of mental disorders* (5th ed., text rev.). doi:10.1176/appi.books.9780890425787

Analytics, B. (2021). *Digital Learning Pulse Survey: Pandemic-Era Report Card Students, Faculty and Administrators Reflect Upon the Academic Year*. https://cengage.widen.net/view/pdf/ilw9jvg8hs/pandemic-era-report-card-digital-learning-pulse-survey-infographic-1649584.pdf?t.download=true&u=lpaabn

Anderson, B. (2023). *Sharpen your axe: A leadership lesson*. NetGain Technologies. https://www.netgainit.com/blogs/sharpen-your-axe/

Anderson, C. S. (1982). The Search for School Climate: A Review of the Research. *Review of Educational Research*, *52*(3), 368–420. doi:10.3102/00346543052003368

Anderson, T., Liam, R., Garrison, D. R., & Archer, W. (2001). Assessing teaching presence in a computer conferencing context. *Journal of Asynchronous Learning Networks*, *5*(2), 1–17.

Andronie, M., & Andronie, M. (2014). Information and communication technologies (ICT) used for education and training. *Contemporary Readings in Law and Social Justice*, *6*(1), 378.

Angelino, L. M., Williams, F. K., & Natvig, D. (2007). Strategies to engage online students and reduce attrition rates. *The Journal of Educators Online*, *4*(2). doi:10.9743/JEO.2007.2.1

Arachchige, P., & Wijesekara, D. S. N. (2022). A study in University of Ruhuna for investigating prevalence, risk factors and remedies for psychiatric illnesses among students. *Scientific Reports*, 12. PMID:35896566

Aragon, S. R. (2003). Creating social presence in online environments. *New Directions for Adult and Continuing Education*, *100*(100), 57–68. doi:10.1002/ace.119

Aragon, S. R., & Johnson, E. S. (2008). Factors influencing completion and noncompletion of community college online courses. *American Journal of Distance Education, 22*(3), 146–158. doi:10.1080/08923640802239962

Arah, B.O. (2012). The competencies, preparations, and challenging (new) roles of online instructors. *US-China Education Review,* A10.

Araka, E., Maina, E., Gitonga, R., & Oboko, R. (2020). Research trends in measurement and intervention tools for self-regulated learning for e-learning environments—Systematic review (2008–2018). *Research and Practice in Technology Enhanced Learning, 15*(1), 1–21. doi:10.118641039-020-00129-5

Arao, B., & Clemens, K. (2023). From safe spaces to brave spaces: A new way to frame dialogue around diversity and social justice. In L. M. Landreman (Ed.), The Art of Effective Facilitation: Reflections from Social Justice Educators. Stylus Publishing LLC.

Arnold & Paulus. (2010). Using a social networking site for experiential learning: Appropriating, lurking, modeling and community building. *The Internet and Higher Education, 13*(4), 188-196.

Aronson, B., & Laughter, J. (2016). The theory and practice of culturally relevant education: A synthesis of research across content areas. *Review of Educational Research, 86*(1), 163–206. doi:10.3102/0034654315582066

Asakura, K., & Watanabe, I. (2011). Survival strategies of male nurses in rural areas of Japan. *Japan Journal of Nursing Science, 8*(2), 194–202. doi:10.1111/j.1742-7924.2011.00176.x PMID:22117583

Ashar, H., & Skenes, R. (1993). Can Tinto's student departure model be applied to nontraditional students? *Adult Education Quarterly, 43*(2), 90–100. doi:10.1177/0741713693043002003

Ashforth, B. E., & Mael, F. (2004). Social identity theory and the organization. *Organizational identity. REAd (Porto Alegre),* 134–160.

Aslan, I., Ochnik, D., & Çınar, O. (2020). Exploring perceived stress among students in Turkey during the covid-19 pandemic. *International Journal of Environmental Research and Public Health, 17*(23), 8961. doi:10.3390/ijerph17238961 PMID:33276520

Aslanian, C., & Fischer, S. (2021). *Online College Students 2021 Meeting Online Student Demands and Preferences in a Reshaped World.* EducationDynamics.

Association for Multicultural Counseling and Development (AMCD). (2023). *Multicultural and social justice counseling competencies.* https://www.multiculturalcounselingdevelopment.org/competencies

Attilee, S. (2019). Multicultural competency in online counseling courses: Before and after a multicultural counseling course. *Walden Dissertations and Doctoral Studies.* https://scholarworks.waldenu.edu/dissertations/6302

Au, C. H., Ho, K. K. W., & Chiu, D. K. W. (2021). Does political extremity harm the ability to identify online information validity? Testing the impact of polarisation through online experiments. *Government Information Quarterly, 38*(4), 101602. Advance online publication. doi:10.1016/j.giq.2021.101602

Au, C. H., Ho, K. K. W., & Chiu, D. K. W. (2022). Managing users' behaviors on open content crowdsourcing platform. *Journal of Computer Information Systems, 62*(2), 1125–1135. doi:10.1080/08874417.2021.1983487

Aud, S., Hussar, W., Johnson, F., Kena, G., Roth, E., Manning, E., & Zhang, J. (2012). *The condition of education 2012 (NCES 20120-045). Indicator 47.* U.S. Department of Education, National Center for Education Statistics. Retrieved from https://nces.ed.gov/pubs2012/2012045.pdf

Ayala, M. I., & Chalupa Young, D. (2022). Racial microaggressions and coping mechanisms among Latina/o college students. *Sociological Forum*, *37*(1), 200–221. doi:10.1111ocf.12785

Ayllón, S., Alsina, Á., & Colomer, J. (2019). Teachers' involvement and students' self-efficacy: Keys to achievement in higher education. *PLoS One*, *14*(5), e0216865–e0216865. doi:10.1371/journal.pone.0216865 PMID:31125346

Ayub, N. (2010). Effect of intrinsic and extrinsic motivation on academic performance. *Pakistan business review*, *8*(1), 363-372.

Bada, S. O., & Olusegun, S. (2015). Constructivism learning theory: A paradigm for teaching and learning. *Journal of Research & Method in Education*, *5*(6), 66–70.

Bahula, T., & Kay, R. (2021). Exploring student perceptions of video-based feedback in higher education: A systematic review of the literature. *Journal of Higher Education Theory and Practice*, *21*(4), 248–258. doi:10.33423/jhetp.v21i4.4224

Baker, E. L., Barton, P. E., Darling-Hammond, L., Haertel, E., Ladd, H. F., Linn, R. L., Ravitch, D., Rothstein, R., Shavelson, R. J., & Shepard, L. A. (2010, August 29). *Problems with the use of student test scores to evaluate teachers*. Economic Policy Institute. https://files.eric.ed.gov/fulltext/ED516803.pdf

Baker, A. C., Jensen, P. J., & Kolb, D. A. (2005). Conversation as experiential learning. *Management Learning*, *36*(4), 411–427. doi:10.1177/1350507605058130

Baldwin, S., & Ching, Y. H. (2017). Interactive storytelling: Opportunities for online course design. *TechTrends*, *61*(2), 179–186. doi:10.100711528-016-0136-2

Bal, M., & Van Boheemen, C. (2009). *Narratology: Introduction to the theory of narrative*. University of Toronto Press.

Bandura, A. (1986). *Social foundations of thought and action: A social cognitive theory*. Prentice Hall.

Bandura, A. (1997). *Self-efficacy: The exercise of control*. Freeman.

Bandura, A. (2012). On the Functional Properties of Perceived Self-Efficacy Revisited. *Journal of Management*, *38*(1), 9–44. doi:10.1177/0149206311410606

Bandura, A., & Walters, R. H. (1977). *Social learning theory* (Vol. 1). Prentice Hall.

Banks, J. A. (2013). The construction and historical development of multicultural education, 1962–2012. *Theory into Practice*, *52*(sup1), 73-82. doi:10.1080/00405841.2013.795444

Banks, B. M., & Landau, S. (2022). Take a deep breath: Coping and the cognitive consequences of racial microaggression among Black college women. *Journal of College Student Psychotherapy*, 1–20. doi:10.1080/87568225.2022.2100855

Banna, J., Grace Lin, M. F., Stewart, M., & Fialkowski, M. K. (2015). Interaction matters: Strategies to promote engaged learning in an online introductory nutrition course. *Journal of Online Learning and Teaching*, *11*(2), 249–261. PMID:27441032

Baran, E., Correia, A. P., & Thompson, A. (2011). Transforming online teaching practice: Critical analysis of the literature on the roles and competencies of online teachers. *Distance Education*, *32*(3), 421–439. doi:10.1080/01587919.2011.610293

Barbera, E., & Linder-VanBerschot, J. A. (2011). Systemic multicultural model for online education: Tracing connections among learner inputs, instructional processes, and outcomes. *Quarterly Review of Distance Education*, *12*(3), 167–180.

Barber, W., King, S., & Buchanan, S. (2015). Problem Based Learning and Authentic Assessment in Digital Pedagogy: Embracing the Role of Collaborative Communities. *Electronic Journal of e-Learning*, *13*(2), 59–64.

Compilation of References

Barbetta, P. M. (2023). Technologies as tools to increase active learning during online higher-education instruction. *Journal of Educational Technology Systems*, *51*(3), 317–339. doi:10.1177/00472395221143969

Barker, M. J. (2016). The Doctorate in Black and White: Exploring the engagement of black doctoral students in cross-race advising relationships with White faculty. *The Western Journal of Black Studies*, *40*(2), 126–140.

Barksdale-Ladd, M. A., & Thomas, K. F. (2000). What's at stake in high-stakes testing: Teachers and parents speak out. *Journal of Teacher Education*, *51*(5), 384–397. doi:10.1177/0022487100051005006

Barnard-Brak, L., & Sulak, T. (2012). The relationship of institutional distance education goals and students requests for accommodations. *Journal of Postsecondary Education and Disability*, *25*(1), 5–19.

Barnard-Brak, L., Sulak, T., Tate, A., & Lechtenberger, D. (2010). Measuring college students' attitudes toward requesting accommodations: A national multi-institutional study. *Assessment for Effective Intervention*, *35*(3), 141–147. doi:10.1177/1534508409358900

Barnett, B. G., Basom, M. R., Yerkes, D. M., & Norris, C. J. (2000). Cohorts in educational leadership programs: Benefits, difficulties, and the potential for developing school leaders. *Educational Administration Quarterly*, *36*(2), 255–282. doi:10.1177/0013161X00362005

Barnett, B. G., & Muse, I. D. (1993). Cohort groups in educational administration: Promises and challenges. *Journal of School Leadership*, *3*(4), 400–415. doi:10.1177/105268469300300405

Barnett, J. E., & Johnson, W. B. (2015). *EthicsDesk reference for counselors* (2nd ed.). American Counseling Association. doi:10.1002/9781119221555

Barnett, R. M. (2020). Leading with meaning: Why diversity, equity, and inclusion matters in US higher education. *Perspectives in Education*, *38*(2), 20–35. doi:10.18820/2519593X/pie.v38.i2.02

Barrio Minton, C. A., Morris, C. W., & Bruner, S. L. (2018). Pedagogy in counselor education: 2011-2015 update. *Counselor Education and Supervision*, *57*(3), 227–236. doi:10.1002/ceas.12112

Barr, J. J. (2016). *Developing a Positive Classroom Climate. IDEA Paper# 61*. IDEA Center, Inc.

Barry, A. E., Whiteman, S. D., & MacDermid Wadsworth, S. M. (2012). Implications of posttraumatic stress among military-affiliated and civilian students. *Journal of American College Health*, *60*(8), 562–573. doi:10.1080/07448481.2012.721427 PMID:23157198

Basch, C. H., Hillyer, G. C., & Jaime, C. (2020). COVID-19 on TikTok: Harnessing an emerging social media platform to convey important public health messages. *International Journal of Adolescent Medicine and Health*, *34*(5), 367–369. doi:10.1515/ijamh-2020-0111 PMID:32776899

Bates, R., & Khasawneh, S. (2004). Self-efficacy and college students' perceptions and use of online learning systems. *Computers in Human Behavior*, *23*(1). doi:10.1016/j.chb.2004.04.004

Bates, A. T., & Sangra, A. (2011). *Managing technology in higher education: Strategies for transforming teaching and learning*. John Wiley & Sons.

Bean, J., & Eaton, S. (2000). A psychological model of college student retention. In J. Braxton (Ed.), *Rethinking the departure puzzle: New theory and research Tinto 265 on college student retention* (pp. 48–62). Vanderbilt University Press.

Becker, C., Cooper, N., Atkins, K., & Martin, S. (2009). What helps students thrive? An investigation of student engagement and performance. *Recreational Sports Journal*, *33*(2), 139–149. doi:10.1123/rsj.33.2.139

Becker, J. D., & Schad, M. (2022). Understanding the lived experience of online learners: Towards a framework for phenomenological research on distance education. *Online Learning : the Official Journal of the Online Learning Consortium, 26*(2), 296–322. doi:10.24059/olj.v26i2.2642

Beemyn, G. (2013). A presence in the past: A transgender historiography. *Journal of Women's History, 25*(4), 113–121. doi:10.1353/jowh.2013.0062

Beer, M. (2022, December 2). *Honest transformative conversations: The key to successful change.* Udemy Blog. https://blog.udemy.com/keys-to-honest-transformative-conversations-workplace/

Bennett-Levy, J., Hawkins, R., Perry, H., Cromarty, P., & Mills, J. (2012). Online cognitive behavioural therapy training for therapists: Outcomes, acceptability, and impact of support. *Australian Psychologist, 47*(3), 174–182. doi:10.1111/j.1742-9544.2012.00089.x

Benshoff, J. M., & Gibbons, M. M. (2011). Bringing life to e-learning: Incorporating a synchronous approach to online teaching in counselor education. *The Professional Counselor, 1*(1), 21–28.

Benshoff, J. M., & Gibbons, M. M. (2011). Bringing life to e-learning: Incorporating a synchronous approach to online teaching in counselor education. *The Professional Counselor, 1*(1), 21–28. doi:10.15241/jmb.1.1.21

Benson, O. M., & Whitson, M. L. (2022). The protective role of sense of community and access to resources on college student stress and COVID-19-related daily life disruptions. *Journal of Community Psychology, 50*(6), 2746–2764. doi:10.1002/jcop.22817 PMID:35142379

Bentrim, E. M., Grygier, J., Ralicki, J., Schiller, J., & Widenhorn, M. (2022). *Nationwide student survey: Opportunities to grow student success and career preparation.* https://thestacks.anthology.com/wp-content/uploads/2022/05/WhitePaper_Student-Success-and-Career-Preparation.pdf?_ga=2.15546033.643518578.1652197075-1075087224.1652197075

Bequette, J. W., & Bequette, M. B. (2012). A place for ART and DESIGN education in the STEM conversation. *Art Education, 65*(2), 40–47. doi:10.1080/00043125.2012.11519167

Berge, Z. L. (2008). Changing instructor's roles in virtual worlds. *Quarterly Review of Distance Education, 9*(4), 407–414.

Bernieri, F. J. (1988). Coordinated movement and rapport in teacher-student interactions. *Journal of Nonverbal Behavior, 12*(2), 120–138. doi:10.1007/BF00986930

Berry, S. (2017). Building community in online doctoral classrooms: Instructor practices that support community. *Online Learning : the Official Journal of the Online Learning Consortium, 21*(2), n2. doi:10.24059/olj.v21i2.875

Berry, S. (2019). Faculty perspectives on online learning: The instructor's role in creating community. *Online Learning : the Official Journal of the Online Learning Consortium, 23*(4), 181–191. doi:10.24059/olj.v23i4.2038

Berry, S. (2019). Teaching to connect: Community-building strategies for the virtual classroom. *Online Learning : the Official Journal of the Online Learning Consortium, 23*(1), 164–183. doi:10.24059/olj.v23i1.1425

Best Colleges. (2022). *Online Education Trends Report.* https://www.bestcolleges.com/research/annual-trends-in-online-education/

Bethell, S., & Morgan, K. (2011). Problem-based and experiential learning: Engaging students in an undergraduate physical education module. *Journal of Hospitality, Leisure, Sport and Tourism Education, 10*(1), 128–134. doi:10.3794/johlste.101.365

Compilation of References

Betts, K. (2013). National perspective: Q&A with national federation of the blind & association of Higher education and disability. *Online Learning : the Official Journal of the Online Learning Consortium, 17*(3). Advance online publication. doi:10.24059/olj.v17i3.379

Betts, K., Welsh, B., Pruitt, C., Hermann, K., Dietrich, G., Trevino, J. G., ... Coombs, N. (2013b). Understanding disabilities & online student success. *Online Learning : the Official Journal of the Online Learning Consortium, 17*(3), 15–48. doi:10.24059/olj.v17i3.388

Bialowas, A., & Steimel, S. (2019). Less is more: Use of video to address the problem of teacher immediacy and presence in online courses. *International Journal on Teaching and Learning in Higher Education, 31*(2), 354–364. https://eric.ed.gov/?id=EJ1224346

Bielefeldt, A. R., Dewoolkar, M. M., Caves, K. M., Berdanier, B. W., & Paterson, K. G. (2011). Diverse models for incorporating service projects into engineering capstone design courses. *International Journal of Engineering Education, 27*(6), 1206–1220.

Bista, K. (2015). Examining the role of multicultural competence in online teaching. *International Journal of Online Pedagogy and Course Design, 5*(2), 17–30. doi:10.4018/IJOPCD.2015040102

Black, J. B., & Bower, G. H. (1979). Episodes as chunks in narrative memory. *Journal of Verbal Learning and Verbal Behavior, 18*(3), 309–318. doi:10.1016/S0022-5371(79)90173-7

Blickle, G., Witzki, A. H., & Schneider, P. B. (2009). Mentoring support and power: A three year predictive field study on protege networking and career success. *Journal of Vocational Behavior, 74*(2), 181–189. doi:10.1016/j.jvb.2008.12.008

Boerngen, M. A., & Rickard, J. W. (2021). To zoom or not to zoom: The impact of rural broadband on online learning. *Natural Sciences Education, 50*(1), e20044. Advance online publication. doi:10.1002/nse2.20044

Boettcher, J. V. (2011). *Ten best practices for teaching online*. Designing for Learning. http://www.designingforlearning.info/services/writing/ecoach/tenbest.html

Boettcher, J. V. (2018). ECoaching tip 2 online discussions – Why and how of using discussion forums. *Designing for Learning*. http://designingforlearning.info/ecoachingtips/e-coaching-tip-2/

Bolliger, D. U., Shepherd, C. E., & Bryant, H. V. (2019, October 31). Faculty members' perceptions of the online program community and their efforts to sustain it. *British Journal of Educational Technology*. https://eric.ed.gov/?id=EJ1232104

Bonilla-Silva, E. (2014). *Racism without racists: Color-blind racism and the persistence of racial inequality in the United States*. Rowman & Littlefield Publishers.

Bonk, C. J., & Khoo, E. (2014). Adding some TEC-VARIETY: 100+ activities for motivating and retaining learners online. OpenWorldBooks. com and Amazon CreateSpace.

Borup, J., Graham, C. R., West, R. E., Archambault, L., & Spring, K. J. (2020). Academic communities of engagement: An expansive lens for examining support structures in blended and online learning. *Educational Technology Research and Development, 68*(2), 807–832. doi:10.100711423-020-09744-x

Bouchrika, I. (2022, August 23). *Best Digital Learning Platforms for 2023*. Research.Com. https://research.com/software/best-digital-learning-platforms

Bouchrika, I. (2023, May 22). *50 online education statistics: 2023 data on Higher Learning & Corporate training*. https://research.com/education/online-education-statistics#:~:text=Moreover%2C%20findings%20from%20a%20survey,female%20(Duffin%2C%202019)

Boyd, B. (2009). *On the Origin of Stories: Evolution, Cognition, and Fiction.* Harvard University Press. doi:10.4159/9780674053595

Brackett, M. (2019). *Permission to feel: Unlocking the power of emotions to help our kids, ourselves, and our society thrive.* Celadon Books.

Brame, C. (2013). *Flipping the classroom.* Vanderbilt University Center for Teaching. Retrieved 06/1/23 from http://cft.vanderbilt.edu/guides-sub-pages/flipping-the-classroom/

Brancati, G. E., Perugi, G., Milone, A., Masi, G., & Sesso, G. (2021). Development of bipolar disorder in patients with attention-deficit/hyperactivity disorder: A systematic review and meta-analysis of prospective studies. *Journal of Affective Disorders, 293,* 186–196. doi:10.1016/j.jad.2021.06.033 PMID:34217137

Brandes, A. H. (1998). *Assessment of the validity of the Adult Classroom Environment Scale.* Rutgers The State University of New Jersey, School of Graduate Studies.

Bransford, J. D., Brown, A. L., & Cocking, R. R. (2000). *How people learn* (Vol. 11). National academy press.

Brashear, C. A., & Thomas, N. (2020). Core competencies for combatting crisis: Fusing ethics, cultural competence, and cognitive flexibility in counseling. *Counselling Psychology Quarterly, 35*(1), 1–15. doi:10.1080/09515070.2020.1768362

Bratlien, M. J., Genzer, S. M., Hoyle, J. R., & Oates, A. D. (1992). The professional studies doctorate: Leaders for learning. *Journal of School Leadership, 2*(1), 75–89. doi:10.1177/105268469200200107

Bridges, C. W., & Frazier, W. (2019). Teaching across settings. In L. Haddock & J. Whitman (Eds.), Preparing the educator in counselor education: A comprehensive guide to building knowledge and developing skills (pp. 190-212). Routledge.

Brindley, J., Walti, C., & Blaschke, L. (2009). Creating effective collaborative learning groups in an online environment. *International Review of Research in Open and Distance Learning, 10*(3), •••. doi:10.19173/irrodl.v10i3.675

Brissett, N. (2020). Inequitable rewards: Experiences of faculty of color mentoring students of color. *Mentoring & Tutoring, 28*(5), 556–577. doi:10.1080/13611267.2020.1859327

Brookfield, S. D. (1987). *Developing Critical Thinkers.* Jossey-Bass.

Brooks, S. K., Webster, R. K., Smith, L. E., Woodland, L., Wessely, S., Greenberg, N., & Rubin, G. J. (2020). The psychological impact of quarantine and how to reduce it: Rapid review of the evidence. SSRN *Electronic Journal.* doi:10.2139/ssrn.3532534

Brooks, D. (1997). *Web-Teaching: A guide to interactive teaching for the World Wide Web.* Plenum Press.

Brooms, D. R., & Davis, A. R. (2017). Staying focused on the goal: Peer bonding and faculty mentors supporting Black males' persistence in college. *Journal of Black Studies, 48*(3), 305–326. doi:10.1177/0021934717692520

Brower, H. H. (2011). Sustainable development through service learning: A pedagogical framework and case example in a third world context. *Academy of Management Learning & Education, 10*(1), 58–76. doi:10.5465/amle.10.1.zqr58

Brown, I., & Inouye, D. K. (1978). Learned helplessness through modeling: The role of perceived similarity in competence. *Journal of Personality and Social Psychology, 36*(8), 900–908. doi:10.1037/0022-3514.36.8.900

Brown, P. C., Roediger, H. L., & McDaniel, M. A. (2014). *Make it stick: The science of successful learning.* Harvard University Press. doi:10.2307/j.ctt6wprs3

Brown, R. E. (2001). The process of community-building in distance learning classes. *Journal of Asynchronous Learning Networks, 5*(2), 18–35.

Buck, S. (2016). In their own voices: Study habits of distance education students. *Journal of Library & Information Services in Distance Learning*, *10*(3–4), 137–173. doi:10.1080/1533290X.2016.1206781

Budiman, A. (2020). *Key findings about U.S. immigrants*. Pew Research Center. Retrieved May 26, 2023, from https://www.pewresearch.org/short-reads/2020/08/20/key-findings-about-u-s-immigrants/

Bultsma, S. (2007). Broaching the subjects of race, ethnicity, and culture with students. *Colleagues*, *2*(2), 11.

Bureau of Labor Statistics. (2019, October 29). *Employment characteristics of people with a disability in 2018*. https://www.bls.gov/opub/ted/2019/employment-characteristics-of-people-with-a-disability-in-2018.htm

Burke, D. D., Clapper, D., & McRae, D. (2016). Accessible online instruction for students with disabilities: Federal imperatives and the challenge of compliance. *Journal of Law & Education*, *45*(2), 135–180.

Buskirk-Cohen, A. A., & Plants, A. (2019). Caring about success: Students' perceptions of professors' caring matters more than grit. *International Journal on Teaching and Learning in Higher Education*, *31*(1), 108–114. https://files.eric.ed.gov/fulltext/EJ1206948.pdf

Bussing, R., & Gary, F. A. (2012). Eliminating mental health disparities by 2020: Everyone's actions matter. *Journal of the American Academy of Child and Adolescent Psychiatry*, *51*(7), 663–666. doi:10.1016/j.jaac.2012.04.005 PMID:22721587

Butnaru, G. I., Haller, A.-P., Dragolea, L.-L., Anichiti, A., & Tacu Hârşan, G.-D. (2021). Students' well-being during the transition from onsite to online education: Are there risks arising from social isolation? *International Journal of Environmental Research and Public Health*, *18*(18), 9665. doi:10.3390/ijerph18189665 PMID:34574589

Cacioppo, J. T., & Patrick, W. (2009). *Loneliness: Human nature and the need for social connection*. W. W. Norton & Company.

Caffarella, R. S., & Merriam, S. B. (1999). *Perspectives on adult learning: Framing our research*. Academic Press.

Cai, H., & King, I. (2020). Education technology for online learning in times of crisis. *2020 IEEE International Conference on Teaching, Assessment, and Learning for Engineering (TALE), Teaching, Assessment, and Learning for Engineering (TALE), 2020 IEEE International Conference*, 758–763. 10.1109/TALE48869.2020.9368387

Campante, F., Durante, R., & Tesei, A. (2022). Media and social capital. *Annual Review of Economics*, *14*(1), 69–91. doi:10.1146/annurev-economics-083121-050914

Campbell, S. (2023). *How many people use Facebook in 2023?* https://thesmallbusinessblog.net/facebook-statistics/

Campbell, D. T. (1976). Assessing the impact of planned social change. *Journal of Multidisciplinary Evaluation*, *7*(15), 3–43. doi:10.56645/jmde.v7i15.297

Candy, P. C. (1991). *Self-Direction for Lifelong Learning*. Jossey-Bass.

Cannon, Y., Haiyasoso, M., & Tello, A. (2020). Relational aspects in research mentoring of women doctoral counseling students. *Journal of Creativity in Mental Health*, *15*(3), 278–291. doi:10.1080/15401383.2019.1689213

Canty, A. J., Chase, J., Hingston, M., Greenwood, M., Mainsbridge, C. P., & Skalicky, J. (2020). Addressing student attrition within higher education online programs through a collaborative community of practice. *Journal of Applied Learning and Teaching*, *3*(Special Issue), 1–12. doi:10.37074/jalt.2020.3.s1.3

Carey-Butler, S., & Myrick-Harris, C. (2008, November 21-22). *Faculty's role in student success: Engagement in and outside of the classroom* [Conference presentation]. Defining and Promoting Student Success: A National Symposium, San Francisco, CA.

Carmack, H. J., & Heiss, S. N. (2018). Using the theory of planned behavior to predict college students' intent to use LinkedIn for job searches and professional networking. *Communication Studies*, *69*(2), 145–160. doi:10.1080/10510974.2018.1424003

Carpenter, J. P., & Krutka, D. G. (2014). How and why educators use X: A survey of the field. *Journal of Research on Technology in Education*, *46*(4), 414–434. doi:10.1080/15391523.2014.925701

Carrell, S. E., & Kurlaender, M. (2020). *My professor cares: Experimental evidence on the role of faculty engagement* (Working Paper Series No. w27312). National Bureau of Economic Research. https://www.nber.org/system/files/working_papers/w27312/w27312.pdf

Casañ-Núñez, J. C. (2021). Creating a Positive Learning Environment in the Online Classroom with Flipgrid. *The EuroCALL Review*, *29*(2), 22–32. doi:10.4995/eurocall.2021.15347

Case, K. A. (2017). Toward an intersectional pedagogy model: Engaged learning for social justice. In K. A. Case (Ed.), *Intersectional pedagogy: Complicating identity and social justice* (pp. 1–24). Routledge.

Casey, G., & Wells, M. (2015). Remixing to design learning: Social media and peer-to-peer interaction. *Journal of Learning Design*, *8*(1). Advance online publication. doi:10.5204/jld.v8i1.225

Cashion, J., & Palmieri, P. (2002). *'The secret is the teacher': the learner's view of online learning*. NCVER.

Caspi, A., Chajut, E., & Saporta, K. (2008). Participation in class and in online discussions: Gender differences'. *Computers & Education*, *50*(3), 718–724. doi:10.1016/j.compedu.2006.08.003

CAST. (2018). *Universal Design for Learning guidelines version 2.2*. http://udlguidelines.cast.org

CAST. (2023). *About Universal Design for Learning*. https://www.cast.org/impact/universal-design-for-learning-udl

Castaño-Muñoz, J., Colucci, E., & Smidt, H. (2018). Free digital Learning for inclusion of migrants and refugees in Europe: A qualitative analysis of three types of learning purposes. *International Review of Research in Open and Distance Learning*, *19*(2), 1–21. doi:10.19173/irrodl.v19i2.3382

Castro, M. D. B., & Tumibay, G. M. (2021). A literature review: Efficacy of online learning courses for higher education institutions using meta-analysis. *Education and Information Technologies*, *26*(2), 1367–1385. doi:10.100710639-019-10027-z

Caulfield, J. (2011). *How to Design and Teach a Hybrid Course. Sterling*. Stylus Publishing.

Cavanagh, S. R. (2020). *The online class: Empathy, equity, and the future of education*. Harvard University Press.

Cavinato, A. G., Hunter, R. A., Ott, L. S., & Robinson, J. K. (2021). Promoting student interaction, engagement, and success in an online environment. *Analytical and Bioanalytical Chemistry*, *413*(6), 1513–1520. doi:10.100700216-021-03178-x PMID:33479816

Cela, K., Silcilia, M., & Sanches-Alonso, S. (2016). Influence of learning styles on social structures in online learning environments. *British Journal of Educational Technology*, *47*(6), 1065–1082. doi:10.1111/bjet.12267

Celuch, K., Milewicz, C., & Saxby, C. (2021). Student and faculty interaction in motivated learning for face-to-face and online marketing classes. *Journal of Education for Business*, *96*(6), 366–372. doi:10.1080/08832323.2020.1848767

Center for Universal Design. (1997). *Center for Universal Design*. North Carolina State University. https://design.ncsu.edu/research/center-for-universal-design/

Compilation of References

Cercone, K. (2008). Characteristics of adult learners with implications for online learning design. AACE review (formerly. *AACE Journal*, *16*(2), 137–159.

Chadha, A. (2017). Comparing student reflectiveness in online discussion forums across modes of instruction and levels of courses. *The Journal of Educators Online*, *14*(2). Advance online publication. doi:10.9743/jeo.2017.14.2.8

Champion, K., & Gunnlaugson, O. (2017). Fostering generative conversation in higher education course discussion boards. *Innovations in Education and Teaching International*, 1–9. doi:10.1080/14703297.2017.1279069

Chan, A. W. Y., Chiu, D. K. W., & Ho, K. K. W. (2022). Workforce information needs for vocational guidance system design. *International Journal of Systems and Service-Oriented Engineering*, *12*(1), 34. doi:10.4018/IJSSOE.297134

Chan, A. W. Y., Chiu, D. K. W., Ho, K. K. W., & Wang, M. (2019). Information needs of vocational training from training providers' perspectives. *International Journal of Systems and Service-Oriented Engineering*, *8*(4), 26–42. doi:10.4018/IJSSOE.2018100102

Chandra, S., & Palvia, S. (2021). Online education next wave: Peer to peer learning. *Journal of Information Technology Case and Application Research*, *23*(3), 157–172. doi:10.1080/15228053.2021.1980848

Chang, C.-S., Liu, E. Z.-F., Sung, H.-Y., Lin, C.-H., Chen, N.-S., & Cheng, S.-S. (2014). Effects of online college student's Internet self-efficacy on learning motivation and performance. *Innovations in Education and Teaching International*, *51*(4), 366–377. doi:10.1080/14703297.2013.771429

Chang, V., Chiu, D. K. W., Ramachandran, M., & Li, C.-S. (2018). Internet of Things, Big Data and Complex Information Systems: Challenges, solutions and outputs from IoTBD 2016, COMPLEXIS 2016 and CLOSER 2016 selected papers and CLOSER 2015 keynote. *Future Generation Computer Systems*, *79*(3), 973–974. doi:10.1016/j.future.2017.09.013

Chan, M. K. Y., Chiu, D. K. W., & Lam, E. T. H. (2020). Effectiveness of overnight learning commons: A comparative study. *Journal of Academic Librarianship*, *46*(6), 102253. Advance online publication. doi:10.1016/j.acalib.2020.102253 PMID:34173399

Chan, M. M. W., & Chiu, D. K. W. (2022). Alert driven customer relationship management in online travel agencies: Event-condition-actions rules and key performance indicators. In A. Naim & S. K. Kautish (Eds.), *Building a brand image through electronic customer relationship management* (pp. 286–303). IGI Global. doi:10.4018/978-1-6684-5386-5.ch012

Chan, T. T. W., Lam, A. H. C., & Chiu, D. K. W. (2020). From Facebook to Instagram: Exploring user engagement in an academic library. *Journal of Academic Librarianship*, *46*(6), 102229. Advance online publication. doi:10.1016/j.acalib.2020.102229 PMID:34173399

Chan, V. H. Y., Chiu, D. K. W., & Ho, K. K. W. (2022). Mediating effects on the relationship between perceived service quality and public library app loyalty during the COVID-19 era. *Journal of Retailing and Consumer Services*, *67*, 102960. Advance online publication. doi:10.1016/j.jretconser.2022.102960

Chapman, R. N. (2018). The Thrive Mosaic developmental framework: A systems activist approach to marginalized STEM Scholar success. *The American Behavioral Scientist*, *62*(5), 600–611. doi:10.1177/0002764218768859

Chaudhury, P. K., Deka, K., & Chetia, D. (2006). Disability associated with mental disorders. *Indian Journal of Psychiatry*, *48*(2), 95–101. doi:10.4103/0019-5545.31597 PMID:20703393

Chayka, K. (2021). *Facebook wants us to live in the metaverse*. https://www.newyorker.com/culture/infinite-scroll/facebook-wants-us-to-live-in-the-metaverse

Chen, R., & Bennett, S. (2012). When Chinese learners meet constructivist pedagogy online. *Higher Education*, *64*(5), 677–691. 10.100710734-012-9520-9

Chen, F., & Cui, X. (2022). Teaching controversial issues online: Exploring college professors' risk appraisals and coping strategies in the US. *Teaching and Teacher Education*, *115*, 1–9. doi:10.1016/j.tate.2022.103728

Cheng, S., & Shi, Y. (2018). Thematic issue on "Brainstorm Optimization Algorithms." *Memetic Computing*, *10*(4), 351–352. doi:10.100712293-018-0276-3

Cheng, W. W. H., Lam, E. T. H., & Chiu, D. K. W. (2020). Social media as a platform in academic library marketing: A comparative study. *Journal of Academic Librarianship*, *46*(5), 102188. Advance online publication. doi:10.1016/j.acalib.2020.102188

Cheng, W., Tian, R., & Chiu, D. K. W. (2023). Travel vlogs influencing tourist decisions: Information preferences and gender differences. *Aslib Journal of Information Management*. Advance online publication. doi:10.1108/AJIM-05-2022-0261

Chen, S. Y., Basma, D., Ju, J., & Ng, K. M. (2020). Opportunities and challenges of multicultural and international online education. *The Professional Counselor*, *10*(1), 120–132. doi:10.15241yc.10.1.120

Cheon, S. H., Reeve, J., & Vansteenkiste, M. (2020). When teachers learn how to provide classroom structure in an autonomy-supportive way: Benefits to teachers and their students. *Teaching and Teacher Education*, *90*, 103004. Advance online publication. doi:10.1016/j.tate.2019.103004

Cheung, K.-y., Lam, A. H. C., & Chiu, D. K. W. (2023). Using YouTube and Facebook as German Language Learning Aids: A pilot study in Hong Kong. *German as a Foreign Language*, *2023*(1), 146–168.

Cheung, T. Y., Ye, Z., & Chiu, D. K. W. (2021). Value chain analysis of information services for the visually impaired: A case study of contemporary technological solutions. *Library Hi Tech*, *39*(2), 625–642. doi:10.1108/LHT-08-2020-0185

Cheung, V. S. Y., Lo, J. C. Y., Chiu, D. K. W., & Ho, K. K. W. (2023). Evaluating social media's communication effectiveness on travel product promotion: Facebook for college students in Hong Kong. *Information Discovery and Delivery*, *51*(1), 66–73. doi:10.1108/IDD-10-2021-0117

Chew, E. (2009). *A blended learning model in higher education: A comparative study of blended learning in UK and Malaysia*. University of South Wales.

Chin, G. Y. L., & Chiu, D. K. W. (2023). RFID-based robotic process automation for smart museums with an alert-driven approach. In R. K. Tailor (Ed.), *Application and adoption of robotic process automation for smart cities*. IGI. Global. doi:10.4018/978-1-6684-7193-7.ch001

Chirikov, I., Soria, K. M., Horgos, B., & Jones-White, D. (2020). *Undergraduate and graduate students' mental health during the COVID-19 pandemic*. UC Berkeley: Center for Studies in Higher Education. Retrieved from https://escholarship.org/uc/item/80k5d5hw

Chiu, D. K. W., & Ho, K. K. W. (2022a). Editorial: Special selection on bibliometrics and literature review. *Library Hi Tech*, *40*(3), 589–593. doi:10.1108/LHT-06-2022-510

Chiu, D. K. W., & Ho, K. K. W. (2022b). Editorial: Special selection on contemporary digital culture and reading. *Library Hi Tech*, *40*(5), 1204–1209. doi:10.1108/LHT-10-2022-516

Chiu, D. K. W., & Ho, K. K. W. (2022c). Editorial: 40th anniversary: Contemporary library research. *Library Hi Tech*, *40*(6), 1525–1531. doi:10.1108/LHT-12-2022-517

Chiu, D. K. W., & Ho, K. K. W. (2023). Editorial: Special selection on contemporary bibliometric analytics. *Library Hi Tech*, *41*(2), 277–286. doi:10.1108/LHT-04-2023-586

Chiu, D. K. W., Leung, H.-F., & Lam, K.-M. (2009). On the making of service recommendations: An action theory based on utility, reputation, and risk attitude. *Expert Systems with Applications*, *36*(2), 3293–3301. doi:10.1016/j.eswa.2008.01.055

Chiu, D. K. W., & Wong, S. W. S. (2023). Reevaluating remote library storage in the digital age: A comparative study. portal. *Portal (Baltimore, Md.)*, *23*(1), 89–109. doi:10.1353/pla.2023.0009

Chizmar, J. F., & Walbert, M. S. (1999). Web-based learning environments guided by principles of good teaching practice. *The Journal of Economic Education*, *30*(3), 248–264. doi:10.1080/00220489909595985

Cho & Cho, Y. (2014). Instructor scaffolding for interaction and students' academic engagement in online learning: Mediating role of perceived online class goal structures. *The Internet and Higher Education, 21*, 25–30. doi:10.1016/j.iheduc.2013.10.008

Choi, K. W., Chen, C. Y., Ursano, R. J., Sun, X., Jain, S., Kessler, R. C., Koenen, K. C., Wang, M. J., Wynn, G. H., Campbell-Sills, L., Stein, M. B., & Smoller, J. W. (2019). Prospective study of polygenic risk, protective factors, and incident depression following combat deployment in US Army soldiers. *Psychological Medicine*, *50*(5), 737–745. doi:10.1017/S0033291719000527 PMID:30982473

Cho, M. H., & Heron, M. L. (2015). Self-regulated learning: The role of motivation, emotion, and use of learning strategies in students' learning experiences in a self-paced online mathematics course. *Distance Education*, *36*(1), 80–99. doi:10.1080/01587919.2015.1019963

Christian, D. D., McCarty, D. L., & Brown, C. L. (2020). Experiential education during the COVID-19 pandemic: A reflective process. *Journal of Constructivist Psychology*, 1–14. doi:10.1080/10720537.2020.1813666

Chung, C., Chiu, D. K. W., Ho, K. K. W., & Au, C. H. (2020). Applying social media to environmental education: Is it more impactful than traditional media? *Information Discovery and Delivery*, *48*(4), 255–266. doi:10.1108/IDD-04-2020-0047

Chu, R. J. (2010). How family support and internet self-efficacy influence the effects of e-learning among higher aged adults – analyses of gender and age differences. *Computers & Education*, *55*(1), 255–264. doi:10.1016/j.compedu.2010.01.011

Chusmir, L. H. (1990). Men who make nontraditional career choices. *Journal of Counseling and Development*, *69*(1), 11–16. doi:10.1002/j.1556-6676.1990.tb01446.x

Cisneros, D., Anandavalli, S., Brown, E. M., Whitman, J. S., & Chaney, M. P. (2022). Anti-racist mentorship: A multicultural and social justice approach to mentoring students identifying as Black, Indigenous, and persons of color in counselor education. *Journal of Counselor Leadership & Advocacy*, 1–13. doi:10.1080/2326716X.2022.2162462

Clance, P. R., & Imes, S. A. (1978). The imposter phenomenon in high achieving women: Dynamics and therapeutic intervention. *Psychotherapy (Chicago, Ill.)*, *15*(3), 241–247. doi:10.1037/h0086006

Clark, M. C., & Rossiter, M. (2008). *Narrative learning in the adult classroom*. https://newprairiepress.org/cgi/viewcontent.cgi?article=2897&context=aerc

Clarke, R., & Davison, R. M. (2020). Through whose eyes? The critical concept of researcher perspective. *Journal of the Association for Information Systems*, *21*(2), 483–501. doi:10.17705/1jais.00609

Cokley, K., & Moore, P. (2007). Moderating and mediating effects of gender and psychological disengagement on the academic achievement of African American college students. *The Journal of Black Psychology*, *33*(2), 169–187. doi:10.1177/0095798407299512

Colby, S. A., Ort, S. W., Pearson, C. S., & Conway, M. (2018). Seeing possibility through a new lens: An exploratory study of teachers' perspective taking. *Teaching and Teacher Education*, *73*, 87–97.

Cole, A. W., Lennon, L., & Weber, N. L. (2021). Student perceptions of online active learning practices and online learning climate predict online course engagement. *Interactive Learning Environments*, *29*(5), 866–880. doi:10.1080/10494820.2019.1619593

Cole, M. T., Shelley, D. J., & Swartz, L. B. (2014). Online instruction, e-learning, and student satisfaction: A three year study. *International Review of Research in Open and Distance Learning*, *15*(6), 111–131. doi:10.19173/irrodl.v15i6.1748

Coleman, J. S. (1988). Social capital in the creation of human capital. *American Journal of Sociology*, *94*, S95–S120. doi:10.1086/228943

Compton, D. M., Burkett, W. H., & Burkett, G. G. (2003). No sex difference in perceived competence of computer use among male and female college students in 2002. *Psychological Reports*, *92*(2), 503–511. doi:10.2466/pr0.2003.92.2.503 PMID:12785633

Connell, J. P. (1990). Context, self, and action: A motivational analysis of self-system processes across the lifespan. In D. Cicchetti (Ed.), *The self in transition: Infancy to childhood* (pp. 61–97). University of Chicago Press.

Conrad, R.-M., & Donaldson, J. A. (2011). Engaging the online learner: Activities and resources for creative instruction. Jossey-Bass.

Conrad, D. (2004). University instructors' reflections on their first online teaching experiences. *Journal of Asynchronous Learning Networks*, *8*(2), 31–44.

Conrad, D. (2005). Building and maintaining community in cohort-based online learning. *Journal of Distance Education*, *20*(1), 1–20.

Cornell, H. R., Sayman, D., & Herron, J. (2019). Sense of community in an online graduate program. *Journal of Effective Teaching in Higher Education*, *2*(2), 117–132. doi:10.36021/jethe.v2i2.52

Correia, H. M., & Strehlow, K. (2018). Mindful care and compassion in higher education: Cultivating communities of practice. In N. Lemon & S. McDonough (Eds.), *Mindfulness in the academy: Practices and perspectives from scholars* (pp. 189–202). Springer. doi:10.1007/978-981-13-2143-6_12

Corwin Visible Learning Plus. (2023, June). *Visible learning metax*. Visible Learning. https://www.visiblelearningmetax.com/

Cory, R. C. (2011). Disability services offices for students with disabilities: A campus resource. *New Directions for Higher Education*, *154*(154), 27–36. doi:10.1002/he.431

Coupland, J. (2003). Small talk: Social functions. *Research on Language and Social Interaction*, *36*(1), 16. doi:10.1207/S15327973RLSI3601_1

Cox, J. (n.d.). *How to build trust with students*. Western Governors University. https://www.wgu.edu/heyteach/article/how-build-trust-students1808.html

Cox, B. E., Reason, R. D., Nix, S., & Gillman, M. (2016). Life happens (outside of college): Non-college life-events and students' likelihood of graduation. *Research in Higher Education*, *57*(7), 823–844. doi:10.100711162-016-9409-z

Cuadrado-García, M., Ruiz-Molina, M. E., & Montoro-Pons, J. D. (2010). Are there gender differences in e-learning use and assessment? Evidence from an interuniversity online project in Europe. *Procedia: Social and Behavioral Sciences*, *2*(2), 367–371. doi:10.1016/j.sbspro.2010.03.027

Cuijpers, P., Smit, F., Aalten, P., Batelaan, N., Klein, A., Salemink, E., Spinhoven, P., Struijs, S., Vonk, P., Wiers, R. W., deWit, L., Gentili, C., Ebert, D. D., Bruffaerts, R., Kessler, R. C., & Karyotaki, E. (2021). The associations of common psychological problems with mental disorders among college students. *Frontiers in Psychiatry*, *12*, 573637. Advance online publication. doi:10.3389/fpsyt.2021.573637 PMID:34646167

Cvorovic, J., & Coe, K. (2022). *Storytelling around the World: Folktales, Narrative Rituals, and Oral Traditions*. Bloomsbury Publishing USA. doi:10.5040/9798216019398

Dabbagh, N., & Kitsantas, A. (2012). Personal Learning Environments, social media, and self-regulated learning: A natural formula for connecting formal and informal learning. *The Internet and Higher Education*, *15*(1), 3–8. doi:10.1016/j.iheduc.2011.06.002

Dai, C., & Chiu, D. K. W. (2023). Impact of COVID-19 on reading behaviors and preferences: Investigating high school students and parents with the 5E instructional model. *Library Hi Tech*, *41*(6), 1631–1657. Advance online publication. doi:10.1108/LHT-10-2022-0472

Dallimore, E. J., Hertenstein, J. H., & Platt, M. B. (2004). Classroom participation and discussion effectiveness: Student-generated strategies. *Communication Education*, *53*(1), 103–115. doi:10.1080/0363452032000135805

Darkenwald, G. G. (1987). Assessing the Social Environment of Adult Classes. *Studies in the Education of Adults*, *19*(2), 127–136. doi:10.1080/02660830.1987.11730484

Darkenwald, G. G. (1989). Enhancing the adult classroom environment. *New Directions for Adult and Continuing Education*, *1989*(43), 67–75. doi:10.1002/ace.36719894308

Darling-Hammond, L. (2003). Keeping good teachers: Why it matters, what leaders can do. *Educational Leadership*, *60*(8), 6–13.

Davies, D. J., & Forsey, M. (2019). *Making sense of the modern world: An anthropological perspective*. Oxford University Press.

Davies, J., McCrae, B. P., Frank, J., Dochnahl, A., Pickering, T., Harrison, B., Zakrzewski, M., & Wilson, K. (2000). Identifying male college students' perceived health needs, barriers to seeking help, and recommendations to help men adopt healthier lifestyles. *Journal of American College Health*, *48*(6), 259–267. doi:10.1080/07448480009596267 PMID:10863869

Davis, B., & Korpi, S. (2022). Authentic human connection: Coaching with care to promote student perceptions of belonging. *UAGC Chronicle*, (Winter Issue), 2022.

Davis, E. B., Plante, T. G., Grey, M. J., Kim, C. L., Freeman-Coppadge, D., Lefevor, G. T., Paulez, J. A., Giwa, S., Lasser, J., Stratton, S. P., Deneke, E., & Glowiak, K. J. (2021). The role of civility and cultural humility in navigating controversial areas in psychology. *Spirituality in Clinical Practice*, *8*(2), 79–97. doi:10.1037cp0000236

Davis, J., Wolff, H. G., Forret, M. L., & Sullivan, S. E. (2020). Networking via LinkedIn: An examination of usage and career benefits. *Journal of Vocational Behavior*, *118*, 103396. doi:10.1016/j.jvb.2020.103396

Day-Vines, N. L., & Holcomb-McCoy, C. (2013). Broaching the subjects of race, ethnicity, and culture as a tool for addressing diversity in counselor education classes. In J. D. West, D. L. Bubenzer, J. A. Cox, & J. M. McGlothlin (Eds.), *Teaching in counselor education: Engaging students in learning* (pp. 151–166). Association for Counselor Education and Supervision.

De Gagne, A. C., Cho, E., Park, H. K., Nam, J. D., & Jung, D. (2021). A qualitative analysis of nursing students' tweets during the COVID-19 pandemic. *Nursing & Health Sciences*, *23*(1), 273–278. doi:10.1111/nhs.12809 PMID:33404157 de Hei, M., Tabacaru, C., Sjoer, E., Rippe, R., & Walenkamp, J. (2020). Developing Intercultural Competence Through Collaborative Learning in International Higher Education. *Journal of Studies in International Education*, *24*(2), 190–211. doi:10.1177/1028315319826226

de Vries, T. J. (2021). The pandemic that has forced teachers to go online. Zooming in on tips for online teaching. In *Frontiers in Education* (p. 105). Frontiers. doi:10.3389/feduc.2021.647445

De Wit, H., & Altbach, P. G. (2021). Internationalization in higher education: Global trends and recommendations for its future. In *Higher Education in the Next Decade* (pp. 303–325). Brill. doi:10.1163/9789004462717_016

Deardorff, D. K. (2019). *Manual for developing intercultural competencies: Story circles*. Routledge. doi:10.4324/9780429244612

Deardorff, D. K., & Jones, E. (2009). Intercultural Competence. In V. Savicki (Ed.), *Developing Intercultural Competence and Transformation* (pp. 32–52). Stylus Pub. doi:10.4135/9781071872987.n28

DeBaun, B., Roc, M., & Muennig, P. A. (2013). *Well and well-off: Decreasing Medicaid and health-care costs by increasing educational attainment*. Academic Press.

DeBaun, B., & Roc, M. (2013). *Saving Futures, Saving Dollars: The Impact of Education on Crime Reduction and Earnings*. Alliance for Excellent Education.

Delahunty, J., Verenikina, I., & Jones, P. (2014). Socio-emotional connections: Identity, belonging and learning in online interactions. A literature review. *Technology, Pedagogy and Education*, *23*(2), 243–265. doi:10.1080/1475939X.2013.813405

Deng, J., Zhou, F., Hou, W., Silver, Z., Wong, C. Y., Chang, O., Drakos, A., Zuo, Q. K., & Huang, E. (2021). The prevalence of depressive symptoms, anxiety symptoms and sleep disturbance in higher education students during the COVID-19 pandemic: A systematic review and meta-analysis. *Psychiatry Research*, *301*, 113863. doi:10.1016/j.psychres.2021.113863 PMID:33984824

Deng, Q., Allard, B., Lo, P., Chiu, D. K. W., See-To, E. W. K., & Bao, A. Z. R. (2019). The role of the library café as a learning space: A comparative analysis of three universities. *Journal of Librarianship and Information Science*, *51*(3), 823–842. doi:10.1177/0961000617742469

Deng, S., & Chiu, D. K. W. (2023). Analyzing the Hong Kong Philharmonic Orchestra's Facebook community engagement with the Honeycomb Model. In M. Dennis & J. Halbert (Eds.), *Community engagement in the online space* (pp. 31–47). IGI. Global. doi:10.4018/978-1-6684-5190-8.ch003

Dennen, V. P., & Burner, K. J. (2020). Creative engagement in online learning environments. In *Learning Online: The Student Experience* (2nd ed., pp. 193–211). Routledge.

Dennen, V. P., & Jones, M. K. (2015). The role of the online instructor: A nexus of skills, activities, and values that support online learning. In O. Zawacki-Smith & I. Jung (Eds.), *The handbook of open, distance, and distributed education*. Springer.

Dennen, V. P., & Wieland, K. (2007). From interaction to intersubjectivity: Facilitating online group discourse processes. *Distance Education*, *28*(3), 281–297. doi:10.1080/01587910701611328

Dewaele, J. M., Albakistani, A., & Ahmed, I. K. (2022a). Levels of foreign language enjoyment, anxiety and boredom in emergency remote teaching and in-person classes. *Language Learning Journal*, •••, 1–14. doi:10.1080/09571736.2022.2110607

Di Malta, G., Bond, J., Conroy, D., Smith, K., & Moller, N. (2022). Distance education students' mental health, connectedness and academic performance during COVID-19: A mixed methods study. *Distance Education*, *43*(1), 97–118. doi:10.1080/01587919.2022.2029352

Didonato, T. E. (2023, March 1). Why "bare-minimum Mondays" can hurt a relationship. *Psychology Today*. https://www.psychologytoday.com/au/blog/meet-catch-and-keep/202303/applying-the-bare-minimum-monday-philosophy-to-relationships

Diener, E., & Seligman, M. E. P. (2002). Very happy people. *Psychological Science*, *13*(1), 81–84. doi:10.1111/1467-9280.00415 PMID:11894851

Diep, N. A., Cocquyt, C., Zhu, C., & Vanwing, T. (2017). Online Interaction Quality among Adult Learners: The Role of Sense of Belonging and Perceived Learning Benefits. *Turkish Online Journal of Educational Technology-TOJET*, *16*(2), 71–78.

Diliberti, M. K., Schwartz, H. L., & Grant, D. (2021). *Stress Topped the Reasons Why Public School Teachers Quit, Even Before COVID-19*. RAND Corporation. doi:10.7249/RRA1121-2

Dingel, M., & Punti, G. (2023). Building faculty-student relationships in higher education. *Mentoring & Tutoring*, *31*(1), 61–82. Advance online publication. doi:10.1080/13611267.2023.2164976

Ding, S. J., Lam, E. T. H., Chiu, D. K. W., Lung, M. M., & Ho, K. K. W. (2021). Changes in reading behavior of periodicals on mobile devices: A comparative study. *Journal of Librarianship and Information Science*, *53*(2), 233–244. doi:10.1177/0961000620938119

Dixon-Saxon, S., & Buckley, M. R. (2020). Student selection, development, and retention: A commentary on supporting student success in distance counselor education. *The Professional Counselor*, *10*(1), 57–77. doi:10.15241ds.10.1.57

Dodgen-Magee, D. (2020, April 17). *Why video chats are so exhausting*. Psychology Today. https://www.psychologytoday.com/blog/deviced/202004/why-video-chats-are-so-exhausting

Dodson, T. A., & Borders, L. D. (2006). Men in traditional and nontraditional careers: Gender role attitudes, gender role conflict, and job satisfaction. *The Career Development Quarterly*, *54*(4), 283–296. doi:10.1002/j.2161-0045.2006.tb00194.x

Donath, L., Mircea, G., & Rozman, T. (2020). E-learning platforms as leverage for education for sustainable development. *European Journal of Sustainable Development*, *9*(2), 1–1. doi:10.14207/ejsd.2020.v9n2p1

Dong, G., Chiu, D. K. W., Huang, P.-S., Ho, K. K. W., Lung, M. M., & Geng, Y. (2021). Relationships between research supervisors and students from coursework-based Master's degrees: Information usage under social media. *Information Discovery and Delivery*, *49*(4), 319–327. doi:10.1108/IDD-08-2020-0100

Dooly, M., & Tudini, V. (2022). 'I Remember When I Was in Spain': Student-Teacher Storytelling in Online Collaborative Task Accomplishment. In A. Filipi, B. T. Ta, & M. Theobald (Eds.), *Storytelling Practices in Home and Educational Contexts*. Springer. doi:10.1007/978-981-16-9955-9_15

Draus, C. M. J., & Trempus, M. S. (2014). The Influence of Instructor-Generated Video Content on Student Satisfaction with and Engagement in Asynchronous Online Classes. *Journal of Online Learning and Teaching*, *10*(2).

Drescher, J. (2015). Out of DSM: Depathologizing homosexuality. *Behavioral Sciences (Basel, Switzerland)*, *5*(4), 565–575. doi:10.3390/bs5040565 PMID:26690228

Dresden, B. E., Dresden, A. Y., Ridge, R. D., & Yamawaki, N. (2018). No girls allowed: Women in male-dominated majors experience increased gender harassment and bias. *Psychological Reports*, *121*(3), 459–474. doi:10.1177/0033294117730357 PMID:29298544

Drezner, N. D., & Pizmony-Levy, O. (2021). I Belong, Therefore, I Give? The Impact of Sense of Belonging on Graduate Student Alumni Engagement. *Nonprofit and Voluntary Sector Quarterly*, *50*(4), 753–777. doi:10.1177/0899764020977687

du Toit-Brits, C. (2019). A focus on self-directed learning: The role that educators' expectations play in the enhancement of students' self-directedness. *South African Journal of Education*, *39*(2), 1–11. doi:10.15700aje.v39n2a1645

Duenyas, D. L., & Perkins, R. (2021). Making space for a makerspace in counselor education: The creative experiences of counseling graduate students. *Journal of Creativity in Mental Health*, *16*(4), 537–547. doi:10.1080/15401383.2020.1790456

Du, J., Fan, X., Xu, J., Wang, C., Sun, L., & Liu, F. (2019). Predictors for students' self-efficacy in online collaborative groupwork. *Educational Technology Research and Development*, *67*(4), 767–791. doi:10.100711423-018-9631-9

Dukic, Z., Chiu, D. K. W., & Lo, P. (2015). How useful are smartphones for learning? Perceptions and practices of Library and Information Science students from Hong Kong and Japan. *Library Hi Tech*, *33*(4), 545–561. doi:10.1108/LHT-02-2015-0015

Dunning, D., Fetchenhauer, D., & Schlösser, T. (2019). Why people trust: Solved puzzles and open mysteries. *Current Directions in Psychological Science*, *28*(4), 366–371. doi:10.1177/0963721419838255

Duraku, Z. H., & Hoxha, L. (2021). The impact of COVID-19 on higher education: A study of interaction among Kosovar students' mental health, attitudes toward online learning, study skills, and lifestyle changes. In Z.H. Duraku (Ed.) Impact of the COVID-19 pandemic on education and wellbeing: Implications for practice and lessons for the future (pp. 46-63). University of Prishtina "Hasan Prishtina" Faculty of Philosophy, Department of Psychology.

Dutta, A. (2020). Impact of digital social media on Indian higher education: Alternative approaches of online learning during COVID-19 pandemic crisis. *International Journal of Scientific and Research Publications*, *10*(5), 604–611. doi:10.29322/IJSRP.10.05.2020.p10169

Dwyer, K. K., Bingham, S. G., Carlson, R. E., Prisbell, M., Cruz, A. M., & Fus, D. A. (2004). Communication and connectedness in the classroom: Development of the connected classroom climate inventory. *Communication Research Reports*, *21*(3), 264–272. doi:10.1080/08824090409359988

Dziuban, C., & Moskal, P. (2011). A course is a course is a course: Factor invariance in student evaluation of online, blended, and face-to-face learning environments. *The Internet and Higher Education*, *14*(4), 236–241. doi:10.1016/j.iheduc.2011.05.003

Edmiston, W. F. (1989). Focalization and the first-person narrator: A revision of the theory. *Poetics Today*, *10*(4), 729–744. doi:10.2307/1772808

Educationdata.org. (2022). *College graduation statistics*. https://educationdata.org/number-of-college-graduates

Edwards, M., & Perry, B. (2005). Exemplary online educators: Creating a community of inquiry. *Turkish Online Journal of Distance Education*, *6*(2), 45–54.

Edwards, M., Poes, S., Al-Nawab, H., & Penna, O. (2022). Academic accommodations for university students living with disability and the potential of universal design to address their needs. *Higher Education*, *84*(4), 779–799. doi:10.100710734-021-00800-w PMID:35079174

Ehlinger, E., & Ropers, R. (2020). "It's all about learning as as community": Facilitating the learning of students with disabilities in higher education classrooms. *Journal of College Student Development*, *61*(3), 333–349. doi:10.1353/csd.2020.0031

El-Amin, A. (2020). Andragogy: A theory in practice in higher education. *Journal of Research in Higher Education*, *4*(2).

Elliott, M., Rhoades, N., Jackson, C. M., & Mandernach, B. J. (2015). Professional development: Designing initiatives to meet the needs of online faculty. *The Journal of Educators Online*, *12*(1), n1. doi:10.9743/JEO.2015.1.2

Ellis, K. (2000). Perceived teacher confirmation: The development and validation of an instrument and two studies of the relationship to cognitive and affective learning. *Human Communication Research*, *26*(2), 264291. doi:10.1111/j.1468-2958.2000.tb00758.x

Ellison, N. B., Steinfield, C., & Lampe, C. (2007). The benefits of Facebook "Friends:" Social capital and college students' use of online social network sites. *Journal of Computer-Mediated Communication*, *12*(4), 1143–1168. doi:10.1111/j.1083-6101.2007.00367.x

Elshami, W., Taha, M. H., Abdalla, M. E., Abuzaid, M., Saravanan, C., & Al Kawas, S. (2022). Factors that affect student engagement in online learning in health professions education. *Nurse Education Today*, *110*, 105261. doi:10.1016/j.nedt.2021.105261 PMID:35152148

Englehart, J. M. (2009). Teacher–student interaction. In L. J. Saha & A. G. Dworkin (Eds.), *International handbook of research on teachers and teaching* (pp. 711–722). Springer. doi:10.1007/978-0-387-73317-3_44

Eom, S. B., & Ashill, N. (2016). The Determinants of Students' Perceived Learning Outcomes and Satisfaction in University Online Education: An Update. *Decision Sciences Journal of Innovative Education*, *14*(2), 185–215. doi:10.1111/dsji.12097

Escamilla-Fajardo, P., Alguacil, M., & Lopez-Carril, S. (2021). Incorporating TikTok in higher education: Pedagogical perspectives from a corporal expression sport sciences course. *Journal of Hospitality, Leisure, Sport and Tourism Education*, *28*, 100302. Advance online publication. doi:10.1016/j.jhlste.2021.100302

Eschenbacher, S. (2020). Transformative learning theory and migration: Having transformative and edifying conversations. *European Journal for Research on the Education and Learning of Adults*, *11*(3), 367–381. doi:10.3384/2000-7426.ojs1678

Esposito, J., Lee, T., Limes-Taylor, H. K., Mason, A., Outler, A., Rodriguez Jackson, J., ... Whitaker-Lea, L. (2017). Doctoral students' experiences with pedagogies of the home, pedagogies of love, and mentoring in the academy. *Educational Studies (Ames)*, *53*(2), 155–177. doi:10.1080/00131946.2017.1286589

Evans, I. M., Harvey, S. T., Buckley, L., & Yan, E. (2009). Differentiating classroom climate concepts: Academic, management, and emotional environments. *Kotuitui*, *4*(2), 131–146. doi:10.1080/1177083X.2009.9522449

Evans, N. J. (2000). Creating a positive learning environment for gay, lesbian, and bisexual students. *New Directions for Teaching and Learning*, *2000*(82), 81–87. doi:10.1002/tl.8208

Evans, N. J., Broido, E. M., Brown, K. R., Wilke, A. K., & Herriott, T. K. (2017). *Disability in higher education: A social justice approach*. John Wiley & Sons, Incorporated.

Evans, N. J., Forney, D. S., Guido, F. M., Patton, L. D., & Renn, K. A. (2010). *Student development in college. Theory, research, and practice* (2nd ed.). Jossey-Bass.

Ezeamuzie, N. M., Rhim, A. H. R., Chiu, D. K. W., & Lung, M. M. (2022). (in press). Exploring gender differences in foreign domestic helpers' mobile information usage. *Library Hi Tech*. Advance online publication. doi:10.1108/LHT-07-2022-0350

Fabriz, S., Mendzheritskaya, J., & Stehle, S. (2021). Impact of synchronous and asynchronous settings of online teaching and learning in higher education on students' learning experience during COVID-19. *Frontiers in Psychology*, *12*, 733554. doi:10.3389/fpsyg.2021.733554 PMID:34707542

Facebook. (2023). *Differences between profiles, groups, and pages on Facebook.* https://www.facebook.com/help/337881706729661

Fang, F., Ying, J., Chen, Y., Qiu, X., Hou, X., & Zhang, Y. (2017). Practical exploration of resource co-construction and sharing alliance of medical libraries in Fudan University. *Chinese Journal of Medical Library and Information*, *26*(6), 30–32.

Fan, K. Y. K., Lo, P., Ho, K. K. W., So, S., Chiu, D. K. W., & Ko, K. H. T. (2020). Exploring the mobile learning needs amongst performing arts students. *Information Discovery and Delivery*, *48*(2), 103–112. doi:10.1108/IDD-12-2019-0085

Farr, J. (2004). Social capital. *Political Theory*, *32*(1), 6–33. doi:10.1177/0090591703254978

FauvilleG.LuoM.Muller QueirozA. C.BailensonJ. N.HancockJ. (2021). Nonverbal mechanisms predict zoom fatigue and explain why women experience higher levels than men. SSRN, 1–18. https://doi.org/ doi:10.2139/ssrn.3820035

Finney, J., & Moos, R. (1986). Matching patients with treatments: Conceptual and methodological issues. *Journal of Studies on Alcohol*, *47*(2), 122–134. doi:10.15288/jsa.1986.47.122 PMID:3713174

Fisher, W. R. (1985). The narrative paradigm: In the beginning. *Journal of Communication*, *35*(4), 74–89. doi:10.1111/j.1460-2466.1985.tb02974.x

Fitchett, P. G., Starker, T. V., & Salyers, B. (2012). Examining Culturally Responsive Teaching Self-Efficacy in a Preservice Social Studies Education Course. *Urban Education*, *47*(3), 585–611. doi:10.1177/0042085912436568

Flaherty, C. (2023, March 23) What students want (and don't) from their professors. *Inside Higher Ed College Pulse*. https://www.insidehighered.com/news/2023/03/24/survey-faculty-teaching-style-impedes-academic-success-students-say

Flanigan, A. E., Akcaoglu, M., & Ray, E. (2022). Initiating and maintaining student-instructor rapport in online classes. *The Internet and Higher Education*, *53*, 100844. doi:10.1016/j.iheduc.2021.100844

Flock, H. (2020). Designing a community of inquiry in online courses. *International Review of Research in Open and Distance Learning*, *21*(1), 135–153. doi:10.19173/irrodl.v20i5.3985

Fong, K. C. H., Au, C. H., Lam, E. T. H., & Chiu, D. K. W. (2020). Social network services for academic libraries: A study based on social capital and social proof. *Journal of Academic Librarianship*, *46*(1), 102091. Advance online publication. doi:10.1016/j.acalib.2019.102091

Fontichiaro, K. (2019). What I've learned from 7 years of the maker movement in schools and libraries. *Teacher Librarian*, *46*(4), 51.

Foronda, C., Prather, S., Baptiste, D. L., & Luctkar-Flude, M. (2022). Cultural humility toolkit. *Nurse Educator*, *47*(5), 267–271. doi:10.1097/NNE.0000000000001182 PMID:35324491

Fowler, P. R., & Boylan, H. R. (2010). Increasing student success and retention: A multidimensional approach. *Journal of Developmental Education*, *34*(2), 2. https://files.eric.ed.gov/fulltext/EJ986268.pdf

Francis, E. M. (2017, May 9). *What is depth of knowledge?* ASCD. https://www.ascd.org/blogs/what-exactly-is-depth-of-knowledge-hint-its-not-a-wheel

Francis, B., Mills, M., & Lupton, R. (2017). Towards social justice in education: Contradictions and dilemmas. *Journal of Education Policy*, *32*(4), 414–431. doi:10.1080/02680939.2016.1276218

Franklin, T., & Peat, M. (2018). Beyond passive consumption: Encouraging active participation in online learning. *EDUCAUSE Review*. Retrieved from https://er.educause.edu/articles/2018/10/beyond-passive-consumption-encouraging-active-participation-in-online-learning

Fraser, B. J. (2002). Learning environments research: Yesterday, today and tomorrow. In *Studies in educational learning environments: An international perspective* (pp. 1-25). Academic Press.

Fraser, B. (2002). Research involving classroom environmental instruments. Learning Environments Research: Yesterday, Today and Tomorrow. In *Studies In Educational Learning Environments: An International Perspective*. World Scientific Publishing Company. doi:10.1142/9789812777133_0001

Fraser, B. J. (1986). *Classroom environment* (Vol. 234). Routledge.

Fraser, B. J. (1998). Classroom environment instruments: Development, validity and applications. *Learning Environments Research*, *1*(1), 7–34. doi:10.1023/A:1009932514731

Fraser, B. J., & Treagust, D. F. (1986). Validity and use of an instrument for assessing classroom psychological environment in higher education. *Higher Education*, *15*(1-2), 37–57. doi:10.1007/BF00138091

Fredricks, J. A., Blumenfeld, P. C., & Paris, A. H. (2004). School engagement: Potential of the concept, state of the evidence. *Review of Educational Research*, *74*(1), 59–109. doi:10.3102/00346543074001059

Fredrickson, B. L. (2001). The role of positive emotions in positive psychology. The broaden-and-build theory of positive emotions. *The American Psychologist*, *56*(3), 218–226. doi:10.1037/0003-066X.56.3.218 PMID:11315248

Freeman, S., Eddy, S. L., McDonough, M., Smith, M. K., Okoroafor, N., Jordt, H., & Wenderoth, M. P. (2014). Active learning increases student performance in science, engineering, and mathematics. *Proceedings of the National Academy of Sciences of the United States of America*, *111*(23), 8410–8415. doi:10.1073/pnas.1319030111 PMID:24821756

Freire, C., Ferradás, M. D. M., Regueiro, B., Rodríguez, S., Valle, A., & Núñez, J. C. (2020). Coping strategies and self-efficacy in university students: A person-centered approach. *Frontiers in Psychology*, *11*, 841. doi:10.3389/fpsyg.2020.00841 PMID:32508707

Frijters, S., ten Dam, G., & Rijlaarsdam, G. (2008). Effects of dialogic learning on value-loaded critical thinking. *Learning and Instruction*, *18*(1), 66–82. doi:10.1016/j.learninstruc.2006.11.001

Frisby, B. N., & Martin, M. M. (2010). Instructor–student and student–student rapport in the classroom. *Communication Education*, *59*(2), 146–164. doi:10.1080/03634520903564362

Frisby, B. N., & Myers, S. A. (2008). The relationships among perceived instructor rapport, student participation, and student learning outcomes. *Texas Speech Communication Journal*, *33*, 2734.

Froyd, J. (2008, June). *White paper on promising practices in undergraduate STEM education*. Academic Press.

Frymier, A. B., & Houser, M. L. (2000). The teacher-student relationship as an interpersonal relationship. *Communication Education*, *49*(3), 207–219. doi:10.1080/03634520009379209

Fuhrmann, B. S., & Grasha, A. F. (1983). *A practical handbook for college teachers*. Little Brown.

Fung, R. H. Y., Chiu, D. K. W., Ko, E. H. T., Ho, K. K. W., & Lo, P. (2016). Heuristic usability evaluation of University of Hong Kong Libraries' mobile website. *Journal of Academic Librarianship*, *42*(5), 581–594. doi:10.1016/j.acalib.2016.06.004

Gait, S., & Halewood, A. (2019). Developing countertransference awareness as a therapist in training: The role of containing contexts. *Psychodynamic Practice*, *25*(3), 256–272. doi:10.1080/14753634.2019.1643961

Galanis, E., Hatzigeorgiadis, A., Comoutos, N., Charachousi, F., & Sanchez, X. (2018). From the lab to the field: Effects of self-talk on task performance under distracting conditions. *The Sport Psychologist*, *32*(1), 26–3. doi:10.1123/tsp.2017-0017

Galla, B. M., Shulman, E. P., Plummer, B. D., Gardner, M., Hutt, S. J., Goyer, J. P., D'Mello, S. K., Finn, A. S., & Duckworth, A. L. (2019). Why high school grades are better predictors of on-time college graduation than are admissions test scores: The roles of self-regulation and cognitive ability. *American Educational Research Journal*, *56*(6), 2077–2115. doi:10.3102/0002831219843292

Gallagher, M. W., Zvolensky, M. J., Long, L. J., Rogers, A. H., & Garey, L. (2020). The impact of Covid-19 experiences and associated stress on anxiety, depression, and functional impairment in American adults. *Cognitive Therapy and Research*, *44*(6), 1043–1051. doi:10.100710608-020-10143-y PMID:32904454

Gamage, K. A., Wijesuriya, D. I., Ekanayake, S. Y., Rennie, A. E., Lambert, C. G., Futch, L. S., DeNoyelles, A., Thompson, K., & Howard, W. (2016). Comfort" as a Critical Success Factor in Blended Learning Courses. *Online Learning : the Official Journal of the Online Learning Consortium*, *20*(3), 140–158.

Garber, S. (2007). *The fabric of faithfulness: Weaving together belief and behavior* (Expanded edition). IVP.

Gardner, H. (2011). Frames of mind: The theory of multiple intelligences. Hachette. In R. J. Sternberg & W. M. Williams (Eds.), *Theory Instruction, and Assessment: Theory Into Practice* (pp. 17–42). Lawrence Erlbaum Associates.

Gares, S. L., Kariuki, J. K., & Rempel, R. P. (2020). Community matters: Student-instructor relationships foster student motivation and engagement in an emergency remote teaching environment. *Journal of Chemical Education*, *97*(9), 3332–3335. doi:10.1021/acs.jchemed.0c00635

Garner, J., Wakeling, S., Hider, P., Jamali, H. R., Kennan, M. A., Mansourian, Y., & Randell-Moon, H. (2022). The lived experience of Australian public library staff during the COVID-19 library closures. *Library Management*, *43*(6/7), 427–438. doi:10.1108/LM-04-2022-0028

Garrett, S. D., Williams, M. S., & Carr, A. M. (2022). Finding their way: Exploring the experiences of tenured Black women faculty. *Journal of Diversity in Higher Education*, *16*(5), 527–538. doi:10.1037/dhe0000213

Garrison, R., Anderson, T., & Archer, W. (2021). *The Community of Inquiry model. The Community of Inquiry.* Athabasca University, Mount Royal University, KTH Royal Institute of Technology, Canadian Journal of Learning and Technology. Retrieved June 26, 2023, from https://creativecommons.org/licenses/by-sa/4.0/

Garrison, D. R. (2009). Communities of inquiry in online learning. In *Encyclopedia of distance learning* (2nd ed., pp. 352–355). IGI Global. doi:10.4018/978-1-60566-198-8.ch052

Garrison, D. R., Anderson, T., & Archer, W. (2001). Critical thinking, cognitive presence, and computer conferencing in distance education. *American Journal of Distance Education*, *15*(1), 7–23. doi:10.1080/08923640109527071

Garrison, D. R., Anderson, T., & Archer, W. (2010). The first decade of the community of inquiry framework: A retrospective. *The Internet and Higher Education*, *13*(1), 5–9. doi:10.1016/j.iheduc.2009.10.003

Garrison, D. R., & Arbaugh, J. B. (2007). Researching the community of inquiry framework: Review, issues, and future directions. *The Internet and Higher Education*, *10*(3), 157–172. doi:10.1016/j.iheduc.2007.04.001

Garza, R. (2009). Latino and white high school students' perceptions of caring behaviors: Are we culturally responsive to our students? *Urban Education*, *44*(3), 297–321. doi:10.1177/0042085908318714

Gay, G. (2010). Culturally responsive teaching: Theory, research, and practice (2nd ed.) (Multicultural education series). Teachers College.

Gay, G. (2000). *Culturally responsive teaching: Theory, research, and practice.* Teachers College Press.

Gay, G. (2002). Preparing for culturally responsive teaching. *Journal of Teacher Education*, *53*(2), 106–116. doi:10.1177/0022487102053002003

Gay, G., & Kirkland, K. (2003). *Developing cultural critical consciousness and self-reflection in preservice teacher education*. Theory into Practice. doi:10.120715430421tip4203_3

Gellisch, M., Morosan-Puopolo, G., Wolf, O. T., Moser, D. A., Zaehres, H., & Brand-Saberi, B. (2023, April). Interactive teaching enhances students' physiological arousal during online learning. *Annals of Anatomy*, *247*, 152050. doi:10.1016/j.aanat.2023.152050 PMID:36693546

Ghaderizefreh, S., & Hoover, M. L. (2018). Student satisfaction with online learning in a blended course. *Int. J. Digit. Soc*, *9*(3), 1393–1398. doi:10.20533/ijds.2040.2570.2018.0172

Gibson, C., Hardy, J. H., & Buckley, M. R. (2014). Understanding the role of networking in organizations. *Career Development International*, *19*(2), 146–161. doi:10.1108/CDI-09-2013-0111

Gigone, D., & Hastie, R. (1997). The impact of information on small group choice. *Journal of Personality and Social Psychology*, *72*(1), 132–140. doi:10.1037/0022-3514.72.1.132

Gin, L. E., Wiesenthal, N. J., Ferreira, I., & Cooper, K. M. (2021). PhDepression: Examining how graduate research and teaching affect depression in life sciences PhD students. *CBE Life Sciences Education*, *20*(3), ar41. Advance online publication. doi:10.1187/cbe.21-03-0077 PMID:34309412

Giuri, P., Munari, F., Scandura, A., & Toschi, L. (2019). The strategic orientation of universities in knowledge transfer activities. *Technological Forecasting and Social Change*, *138*, 261–278. doi:10.1016/j.techfore.2018.09.030

Givens Rolland, R. (2012). Synthesizing the evidence on classroom goal structures in middle and secondary schools: A meta-analysis and narrative review. *Review of Educational Research*, *82*(4), 396–435. doi:10.3102/0034654312464909

Glazier, R. A. (2016). Building rapport to improve retention and success in online classes. *Journal of Political Science Education*, *12*(4), 437–456. doi:10.1080/15512169.2016.1155994

Glazier, R. A., & Harris, H. S. (2020). How teaching with rapport can improve online student success and retention: Data from two empirical studies. *Quarterly Review of Distance Education*, *21*(4), 1–17.

Gokcora, D. (1989, November). *A descriptive study of communication and teaching strategies used by two types of international teaching assistants at the University of Minnesota, and their cultural perceptions of teaching and teachers*. Paper presented at the meeting of the National Conference on Training and Employment of Teaching Assistants, Seattle, WA. (ERIC Document Reproduction Service No. ED351730)

Goliong, L., Kasin, A., Johnny, M., & Yulip, N. G. (2020). *Cabaran pelaksanaan pengajaran dan pembelajaran jarak jauh semasa Perintah Kawalan Pergerakan*. Pejabat Pendidikan Daerah Ranau.

Gomez-Rey, P., Barbera, E., & Fernandez-Navarro, F. (2018). Students' perceptions about online teaching effectiveness: A bottom-up approach for identifying online instructors' roles. *Australasian Journal of Educational Technology*, *34*(1). Advance online publication. doi:10.14742/ajet.3437

Gong, J. Y., Schumann, F., Chiu, D. K. W., & Ho, K. K. W. (2017). Tourists' mobile information seeking behavior: An investigation on China's youth. *International Journal of Systems and Service-Oriented Engineering*, *7*(1), 58–76. doi:10.4018/IJSSOE.2017010104

González-Gómez, F., Guardiola, J., Martín Rodríguez, Ó., & Montero Alonso, M. Á. (2012). Gender differences in e-learning satisfaction. *Computers & Education*, *58*(1), 283–290. doi:10.1016/j.compedu.2011.08.017

Gooden, M. A., Devereaux, C. A., & Hulse, N. E. (2020). #BlackintheIvory: Culturally responsive mentoring with Black women doctoral students and a Black male mentor. *Mentoring & Tutoring*, *28*(4), 392–415. doi:10.1080/13611267.2020.1793083

Goodman, L. A., Liang, B., Helms, J. E., Latta, R. E., Sparks, E., & Weintraub, S. R. (2004). Training counseling psychologists as social justice agents: Feminist and multicultural principles in action. *The Counseling Psychologist*, *32*(6), 793–836. doi:10.1177/0011000004268802

Goodyear, P. (2002). Psychological foundations for networked learning. In C. Steeples & C. Jones (Eds.), *Networked Learning: Perspectives and Issues* (pp. 49–75). Springer London. doi:10.1007/978-1-4471-0181-9_4

Google. (2023). *Google Meet*. https://apps.google.com/meet/

Gopalan, M., & Brady, S. T. (2020). College Students' Sense of Belonging: A National Perspective. *Educational Researcher*, *49*(2), 134–137. doi:10.3102/0013189X19897622

Gopalan, M., Linden-Carmichael, A., & Lanza, S. (2022). College Students' Sense of Belonging and Mental Health Amidst the COVID-19 Pandemic. *The Journal of Adolescent Health*, *70*(2), 228–233. doi:10.1016/j.jadohealth.2021.10.010 PMID:34893423

Gopal, R., Singh, V., & Aggarwal, A. (2021). Impact of online classes on the satisfaction and performance of students during the pandemic period of COVID 19. *Education and Information Technologies*, *26*(6), 6923–6947. doi:10.100710639-021-10523-1 PMID:33903795

Gordon, G., & Whitchurch, C. (2010). *Academic and professional identities in higher education*. Routledge.

Goulding, A. (2004). Libraries and social capital. *Journal of Librarianship and Information Science*, *36*(1), 3–6. doi:10.1177/0961000604042965

Graham, C. (2023). *The History of the Black Student Union*. https://www.bestcolleges.com/blog/history-of-black-student-union/

Graham, S. W., & Gisi, S. L. (2000). The effects of instructional climate and student affairs services on college outcomes and satisfaction. *Journal of College Student Development*, *41*, 279–291.

Granitz, N. A., Koernig, S. K., & Harich, K. R. (2009). Now it's personal: Antecedents and outcomes of rapport between business faculty and their students. *Journal of Marketing Education*, *31*(1), 52–65. doi:10.1177/0273475308326408

Granovetter, M. (1985). Economic action and social structure: The problem of Embeddedness. *American Journal of Sociology*, *91*(3), 481–510. doi:10.1086/228311

Greenhow, C., & Galvin, S. (2020). Teaching with social media: Evidence-based strategies for making remote higher education less remote. *Information and Learning Science*, *121*(7-8), 513–524. doi:10.1108/ILS-04-2020-0138

Guilbaud, T. C., Marin, F., & Newton, X. (2021). Faculty perception on accessibility in online learning: Knowledge, practice and professional development. *Online Learning : the Official Journal of the Online Learning Consortium*, *25*(12), 6–35. doi:10.24059/olj.v25i2.2233

Gunawan, G., Suranti, N. M. Y., & Fathoroni, F. (2020). Variations of models and learning platforms for prospective teachers during the COVID-19 pandemic period. *Indonesian Journal of Teacher Education*, *1*(2).

Gunawardena, C. N., & Zittle, F. J. (1997). Social presence as a predictor of satisfaction within a computer-mediated conferencing environment. *American Journal of Distance Education*, *11*(3), 8–26. doi:10.1080/08923649709526970

Gunawardena, M., & Brown, B. (2021). Fostering Values Through Authentic Storytelling. *The Australian Journal of Teacher Education*, *46*(6), 36–53. Advance online publication. doi:10.14221/ajte.2021v46n6.3

Gunawardhana, N. (2020). Online delivery of teaching and laboratory practices: Continuity of university programmes during COVID-19 pandemic. *Education Sciences*, *10*(10), 291. doi:10.3390/educsci10100291

Guo, Y., Lam, A. H. C., Chiu, D. K. W., & Ho, K. K. W. (2022). Perceived quality of reference service with WhatsApp: A quantitative study from user perspectives. *Information Technology and Libraries*, *41*(3). Advance online publication. doi:10.6017/ital.v41i3.14325

Guzzardo, M. T., Khosla, N., Adams, A. L., Bussman, J. D., Engelman, A., Ingraham, N., Gamba, R., Jones-Bey, A., Moore, M. D., Toosi, N. R., & Taylor, S. (2021). "The ones that care make all the difference:" Perspectives on student-faculty relationships. *Innovative Higher Education*, *46*(1), 41–58. doi:10.100710755-020-09522-w PMID:33012971

Haase, D. (2019). Dialogue education: A learning-centered pedagogy. *Christian Education Journal*, *16*(2), 359–368. doi:10.1177/0739891319847695

Haddock, L., Cannon, K., & Grey, E. (2020). A comparative analysis of traditional and online counselor training program delivery and instruction. *The Professional Counselor*, *10*(1), 92–105. doi:10.15241/lh.10.1.92

Hagenauer, G., Muehlbacher, F., & Ivanova, M. (2023). "It's where learning and teaching begins- is this relationship" - insights on the teacher-student relationship at university from the teachers' perspective. *Higher Education*, *85*(4), 819–835. doi:10.100710734-022-00867-z PMID:37128236

Ha, J., & Shin, D. H. (2013). Facebook in a standard college class: An alternative conduit for promoting teacher-student interaction. *American Communication Journal*, *16*(1), 36–52.

Hall, S. (Ed.). (1997). Representation: Cultural representations and signifying practices. Sage Publications, Inc.

Hallman, J. H. (2020). *Masculinity Perception and Motivational Influences on Male Students' Higher Education Academic Success* (Order No. 28152618). Available from GenderWatch; ProQuest Dissertations & Theses A&I; ProQuest Dissertations & Theses Global. (2466222571). https://uc.idm.oclc.org/login?qurl=https%3A%2F%2Fwww.proquest.com%2Fdissertations-theses%2Fmasculinity-perception-motivational-influences-on%2Fdocview%2F2466222571%2Fse-2%3Faccountid%3D2909

Hamann, K., Glazier, R. A., Wilson, B. M., & Pollock, P. H. (2021). Online teaching, student success, and retention in political science courses. *European Political Science*, *20*(3), 427–439. doi:10.105741304-020-00282-x

Hamilton, I. (2023, September 6). By the numbers: The rise of online learning in the U.S. *Forbes*. https://www.forbes.com/advisor/education/online-learning-stats/

Hamilton, E. R., Rosenberg, J. M., & Akcaoglu, M. (2016). The substitution augmentation modification redefinition (SAMR) model: A critical review and suggestions for its use. *TechTrends*, *60*(5), 433–441. doi:10.100711528-016-0091-y

Hansen, B., & Gray, E. (2018). Creating boundaries within the ubiquitous online classroom. *The Journal of Educators Online*, *15*(3), 1–21. doi:10.9743/jeo.2018.15.3.2

Hanushek, E. A., Rivkin, S. G., & Schiman, J. C. (2016). Dynamic effects of teacher turnover on the quality of instruction. *Economics of Education Review*, *55*, 132–148. doi:10.1016/j.econedurev.2016.08.004

Harasim, L. H., Hiltz, R., Teles, L., & Turoff, M. (1996). *Learning networks: A field guide to teaching and learning online*. MIT Press.

Harper, B. (2018). Technology and teacher–student interactions: A review of empirical research. *Journal of Research on Technology in Education*, *50*(3), 214–225. doi:10.1080/15391523.2018.1450690

Harrison, A. (2022). 10 tips for navigating online graduate school: A Guide for single parents & primary caretakers. Author.

Harrison, K. L. (2021). A call to action: Online learning and distance education in the training of couple and family therapists. *Journal of Marital and Family Therapy*, *47*(2), 408–423. doi:10.1111/jmft.12512 PMID:33755219

Harris, T. M., & Lee, C. N. (2019). Advocate-mentoring: A communicative response to diversity in higher education. *Communication Education*, *68*(1), 103–113. doi:10.1080/03634523.2018.1536272

Hartley, K., & Bendixen, L. D. (2001). Educational research in the Internet age: Examining the role of individual characteristics. *Educational Researcher*, *30*(9), 22–26. doi:10.3102/0013189X030009022

Harvey, H. L., Parahoo, S., & Santally, M. (2017). Should gender differences be considered when assessing student satisfaction in the online learning environment for millennials? *Higher Education Quarterly*, *71*(2), 141–158. doi:10.1111/hequ.12116

Hash, K. M., & Rogers, A. (2013). Clinical practice with older LGBT clients: Overcoming lifelong stigma through strength and resilience. *Clinical Social Work Journal*, *41*(3), 249–257. doi:10.100710615-013-0437-2

Haskins, N. H., & Singh, A. (2015). Critical race theory and counselor education pedagogy: Creating equitable training. *Counselor Education and Supervision*, *54*(4), 288–301. doi:10.1002/ceas.12027

Haslerig, S., Bernhard, L. M., Fuentes, M. V., Panter, A. T., Daye, C. E., & Allen, W. R. (2013). A compelling interest: Activating the benefits of classroom-level diversity. *Journal of Diversity in Higher Education*, *6*(3), 158–173. doi:10.1037/a0034065

Hassan, N. M., Majid, N. A., & Hassan, N. K. A. (2020). Validation of learning environment inventory for secondary school contexts. *International Journal of Evaluation and Research in Education*, *9*(2), 379–384. doi:10.11591/ijere.v9i2.20444

Hattie, J. A. C. (2009). *Visible learning: A synthesis of over 800 meta-analyses relating to achievement*. Routledge.

Hattie, J., & Timperley, H. (2007). The power of feedback. *Review of Educational Research*, *77*(1), 81–112. doi:10.3102/003465430298487

Havelka, D. (2003). Predicting software self-efficacy among business students: A preliminary assessment. *Journal of Information Systems Education*, *14*(2), 145.

Hayes, C., Stott, K., Lamb, K. J., & Hurst, G. A. (2020). "Making every second count:" Utilizing TikTok and systems thinking to facilitate scientific public engagement and contextualization of chemistry at home. *Journal of Chemical Education*, *97*(10), 3858–3866. doi:10.1021/acs.jchemed.0c00511

Hebert, C. G., Kulkin, H., & Ahn, B. (2014). Facilitating research self-efficacy through teaching strategies linked to self-efficacy theory. *American International Journal of Social Science*, *3*(1), 44–50.

Hebert, H. S., Dye, C. K., Lauber, D. E., Roy, D. P., Harden, V., Wrye, B. A., Harris, A., Hendrix, S. P., Sheehan-Smith, L., & Zhang, H. (2023). Connecting online graduate students to the university community. *Journal of Higher Education Theory and Practice*, *23*(2), 190–201. doi:10.33423/jhetp.v23i2.5815

Helvacioglu, E., & Karamanoglu, N. N. (2012). Awareness of the concept of universal design in design education. *Procedia: Social and Behavioral Sciences*, *51*, 99–103. doi:10.1016/j.sbspro.2012.08.125

Hennein, R., Ggita, J. M., Turimumahoro, P., Ochom, E., Gupta, A. J., Katamba, A., Armstrong-Hough, M., & Davis, J. L. (2022). Core components of a community of practice to improve community health worker performance: A qualitative study. *Implementation Science Communications*, *3*(1), 27. Advance online publication. doi:10.118643058-022-00279-1 PMID:35272705

Herbert, M. (2006). Staying the course: A study in online student satisfaction and retention. *Online Journal of Distance Learning Administration*, 9.

Herman, D., Phelan, J., Rabinowitz, P. J., Richardson, B., & Warhol, R. (2012). *Narrative theory: Core concepts and critical debates*. The Ohio State University Press.

Hernandez Rivera, S. (2020). A space of our own: Examining a womxn of color retreat as a counterspace. *Journal of Women and Gender in Higher Education*, *13*(3), 327–347. doi:10.1080/26379112.2020.1844220

Herrington, J., Reeves, T. C., & Oliver, R. (2010). *A guide to authentic e-learning*. Routledge.

Herrman, J. (2019). *How TikTok is rewriting the world*. https://www.nytimes.com/2019/03/10/style/what-is-tik-tok.html

Hewitt, J. (2003). How habitual online practices affect the development of asynchronous discussion threads. *Journal of Educational Computing Research*, *28*(1), 31–45. doi:10.2190/PMG8-A05J-CUH1-DK14

Hew, K., Qiao, C., & Tang, Y. (2018). Understanding student engagement in large-scale open online courses: A machine learning facilitated analysis of student's reflections in 18 highly rated MOOCs. *International Review of Research in Open and Distance Learning*, *19*(3). Advance online publication. doi:10.19173/irrodl.v19i3.3596

He, Z., Chiu, D. K. W., & Ho, K. K. W. (2022). Weibo analysis on Chinese cultural knowledge for gaming. In Z. Sun & Z. Wu (Eds.), *Handbook of research on foundations and applications of intelligent business analytics* (pp. 320–349). IGI Global. doi:10.4018/978-1-7998-9016-4.ch015

Hillen, S. A., & Päivärinta, T. (2012). Perceived support in e-collaborative learning: An exploratory study which make use of synchronous and asynchronous online-teaching approaches. In E. Popescu, E., Q. Li, R. Klamma, H. Leung & M. Specht (Eds.), *Advances in Web-Based Learning – ICWL2012: 11th International Conference*, Sinaia, Romania, September 2–4, 2012. Proceedings (pp. 11–20). Springer.

Hillenbrand, C. (2005). A place for all: Social capital at the Mount Barker Community Library, South Australia. *Australasian Public Libraries and Information Services*, *18*(2), 41–58.

Hill, M. S. (1995). Educational leadership cohort models: Changing the talk to change the walk. *Planning and Changing*, *26*(3/4), 179–189.

Hirschy, A. S., & Wilson, M. E. (2002). The sociology of the classroom and its influence on student learning. *Peabody Journal of Education*, *77*(3), 85–100. doi:10.1207/S15327930PJE7703_5

Hirvonen, N. (2022). Nameless strangers, similar others: The affordances of a young people's anonymous online forum for health information practices. *The Journal of Documentation*, *78*(7), 506–527. doi:10.1108/JD-09-2021-0192

Ho, K. K. W., Takagi, T., Ye, S., Au, C. K., & Chiu, D. K. W. (2018). The use of social media for engaging people with environmentally friendly lifestyle – A conceptual model. *Pre-ICIS Workshop Proceedings 2018*, Article 2. https://aisel.aisnet.org/sprouts_proceedings_siggreen_2018/2/

Ho, C. Y., Chiu, D. K. W., & Ho, K. K. W. (2022). Green space development in academic libraries: A case study in Hong Kong. In V. Okojie & M. O. Igbinovia (Eds.), *Global perspectives on sustainable library practices* (pp. 142–156). IGI Global. doi:10.4018/978-1-6684-5964-5.ch010

Hodges, C. B. (2008). Self-efficacy in the context of online learning environments: A review of the literature and directions for research. *Performance Improvement Quarterly, 20*(3-4), 7–25. doi:10.1002/piq.20001

Ho, K. K. W., Chan, J. Y., & Chiu, D. K. W. (2022). Fake news and misinformation during the pandemic: What we know, and what we don't know. *IT Professional, 24*(2), 19–24. doi:10.1109/MITP.2022.3142814

Ho, K. K. W., Chiu, D. K. W., & Sayama, K. L. C. (2023). When privacy, distrust, and misinformation cause worry about using COVID-19 contact-tracing apps. *IEEE Internet Computing, 27*(2), 7–12. doi:10.1109/MIC.2022.3225568

Hokanson, S. C., Grannan, S., Greenler, R., Gillian-Daniel, D. L., Campa, H. III, & Goldberg, B. B. (2019). A study of synchronous, online professional development workshops for graduate students and postdocs reveals the value of reflection and community building. *Innovative Higher Education, 44*(5), 385–398. doi:10.100710755-019-9470-6

Holmes, A. F., & Rasmussen, S. J. (2018). Using Pinterest to stimulate student engagement, interest, and learning in managerial accounting courses. *Journal of Accounting Education, 43*, 43–56. doi:10.1016/j.jaccedu.2018.03.001

Holt, K. (2012). *Teachers Pin With Their Students.* https://mashable.com/2012/03/22/teachers-using-pinterest/

Hong, B. (2015). Qualitative analysis of barriers college students with disabilities experience in higher education. *Journal of College Student Development, 56*(3), 209–226. doi:10.1353/csd.2015.0032

Hong, F.-Y., Shao-I., C., Huang, D.-H., & Chiu, S.-L. (2021). Correlations among classroom emotional climate, social self-efficacy, and psychological health of university students in Taiwan. *Education and Urban Society, 53*(4), 446–468. doi:10.1177/0013124520931458

Horn, R. A. (2000). Providing leadership for the new millennium. *Journal of the Intermountain Center for Education Effectiveness, 1*(1), 1–6.

Horn, R. A. Jr. (2001). Promoting social justice and caring in schools and communities: The unrealized potential of the cohort model. *Journal of School Leadership, 11*(4), 313–334. doi:10.1177/105268460101100404

How Has Online Education Evolved. (n.d.). https://learn.org/articles/How_Has_Online_Education_Evolved.html

Hoxha, E., Sahiti, N., Fetaji, M., & Berisha-Shaqiri, A. (2020). Virtual laboratories in engineering education: A systematic literature review. *IEEE Access : Practical Innovations, Open Solutions, 8*, 176000–176014.

Hradilová, A., & Chovancová, B. (2023). *Visual representations as a means to motivate students and curb feelings of isolation in distance learning.* https://www.hltmag.co.uk/feb23/visual-representations

Hsiao, F., Burgstahler, S., Johnson, T., Nuss, D., & Doherty, M. (2019). Promoting an accessible learning environment for students with disabilities via faculty development. *Journal of Postsecondary Education and Disability, 32*(1), 91–99.

Hsu, Y. C., & Ching, Y. H. (2012). Mobile micoblogging: Using X and mobile devices in an online course to promote learning in authentic contexts. *International Review of Research in Open and Distance Learning, 13*(4), 211–227. doi:10.19173/irrodl.v13i4.1222

Hu & Driscoll, M. P. (2013). Self-Regulation in e-Learning Environments: A Remedy for Community College? *Educational Technology & Society, 16*(4), 171–184.

Huang, C. (2013). Gender differences in academic self-efficacy: A meta-analysis. *European Journal of Psychology of Education, 28*(1), 1–35. doi:10.100710212-011-0097-y

Huang, H. M. (2002). Toward constructivism for adult learners in online learning environments. *British Journal of Educational Technology, 33*(1), 27–37. doi:10.1111/1467-8535.00236

Compilation of References

Huang, P.-S., Paulino, Y. C., So, S., Chiu, D. K. W., & Ho, K. K. W. (2021). Editorial. *Library Hi Tech*, *39*(3), 693–695. doi:10.1108/LHT-09-2021-324

Huang, P.-S., Paulino, Y. C., So, S., Chiu, D. K. W., & Ho, K. K. W. (2022). Guest editorial: COVID-19 pandemic and health informatics part 2. *Library Hi Tech*, *40*(2), 281–285. doi:10.1108/LHT-04-2022-447

Huang, P.-S., Paulino, Y. C., So, S., Chiu, D. K. W., & Ho, K. K. W. (2023). Guest editorial: COVID-19 pandemic and health informatics part 3. *Library Hi Tech*, *41*(1), 1–6. doi:10.1108/LHT-02-2023-585

Huang, X., & Mayer, R. E. (2019). Adding Self-Efficacy Features to an Online Statistics Lesson. *Journal of Educational Computing Research*, *57*(4), 1003–1037. doi:10.1177/0735633118771085

Huffman, A. H., Whetten, J., & Huffman, W. H. (2013). Using technology in higher education: The influence of gender roles on technology self-efficacy. *Computers in Human Behavior*, *29*(4), 1779–1786. doi:10.1016/j.chb.2013.02.012

Hui, S. C., Kwok, M. Y., Kong, E. W. S., & Chiu, D. K. W. (2023). (in press). Information security and technical issues of cloud storage services: A qualitative study on university students in Hong Kong. *Library Hi Tech*. Advance online publication. doi:10.1108/LHT-11-2022-0533

Hurtado, S. (2019). Making higher education more inclusive. *Journal of Diversity in Higher Education*, *12*(3), 147–155.

Huss, J. A., & Eastep, S. (2016). Okay, our courses are online, but are they ADA compliant? An investigation of faculty awareness of accessibility at a Midwestern university. *Inquiry in Education*, *8*(2). https://eric.ed.gov/?id=EJ1171774

Hutchins, D., & Goldstein Hode, M. (2021). Exploring faculty and staff development of cultural competence through communicative learning in an online diversity course. *Journal of Diversity in Higher Education*, *14*(4), 468–479. doi:10.1037/dhe0000162

Hwang, W. Y., & Nurtantyana, R. (2022). X-Education: Education of all things with AI and edge computing—one case study for EFL learning. *Sustainability (Basel)*, *14*(12533), 12533. doi:10.3390u141912533

Hyland, K. (2001). Bringing in the reader: Addressee features in academic writing. *Written Communication*, *18*(4), 549–574. doi:10.1177/0741088301018004005

Ibrahim, R., Leng, N. S., Yusoff, R. C. M., Samy, G. N., Masrom, S., & Rizman, Z. I. (2017). E-learning acceptance based on technology acceptance model (TAM). *Revue des Sciences Fondamentales et Appliquées*, *9*(4S), 871–889. doi:10.4314/jfas.v9i4S.50

Ice, P., Curtis, R., Phillips, P., & Wells, J. (2019). Using asynchronous audio feedback to enhance teaching presence and students' sense of community. *Online Learning : the Official Journal of the Online Learning Consortium*, *11*(2). Advance online publication. doi:10.24059/olj.v11i2.1724

Imad, M. (2020, April 25). *10 strategies to support students and help them learn during the coronavirus crisis*. Google Docs. https://drive.google.com/file/d/1X63HVRzxHd41ZmlOZPxZ_UCC9QtgNMmf/view?usp=sharing&usp=embed_facebook

Iqbal, S. (2011). Learning management systems (LMS): Inside matters. *Information Management and Business Review*, *3*(4), 206–216. doi:10.22610/imbr.v3i4.935

Irwin, V., De La Rosa, J., Wang, K., Hein, S., Zhang, J., Burr, R., Roberts, A., Barmer, A., Bullock Mann, F., Dilig, R., & Parker, S. (2022). *Report on the Condition of Education 2022* (NCES 2022-144). U.S. Department of Education. Washington, DC: National Center for Education Statistics. Retrieved March, 21st 2023 from https://nces.ed.gov/pubsearch/pubsinfo.asp?pubid=2022144

Isa, P. M., & Hashim, R. (2015). *Issues and challenges of e-learning in higher education: A Malaysian perspective.* Academic Press.

Isacco, A., & Mannarino, M. B. (2016). "It's not like undergrad:" A qualitative study of male graduate students at an "all-women's college". *Psychology of Men & Masculinity, 17*(3), 285–296. doi:10.1037/men0000021

Izzo, M. V., & Horne, L. R. (2016). *Empowering students with hidden disabilities: A path to pride and success.* Brookes Publishing.

Jack, B. M., Lin, H. S., & Yore, L. D. (2014). The synergistic effect of affective factors on student learning outcomes. *Journal of Research in Science Teaching, 51*(8), 1084–1101. doi:10.1002/tea.21153

Jackson, D. (2016). Re-conceptualising graduate employability: The importance of pre-professional identity. *Higher Education Research & Development, 35*(5), 925–939. doi:10.1080/07294360.2016.1139551

Jacobs, J., & Archie, T. (2008). Investigating sense of community in first-year college students. *Journal of Experiential Education, 30*(3), 282–285. doi:10.1177/105382590703000312

Jaggars, S. S., & Xu, D. (2016). How do online course design features influence student performance? *Computers & Education, 95,* 270–284. doi:10.1016/j.compedu.2016.01.014

Jan, S. K. (2015). The Relationships Between Academic Self-Efficacy, Computer Self-Efficacy, Prior Experience, and Satisfaction With Online Learning. *American Journal of Distance Education, 29*(1), 30–40. doi:10.1080/08923647.2015.994366

Jebeile, S., & Reeve, R. (2003). The diffusion of e-learning innovations in an Australian secondary college: Strategies and tactics for educational leaders. *Innovation, 8*(4).

Jiang, T., Lo, P., Cheuk, M. K., Chiu, D. K. W., Chu, M. Y., Zhang, X., Zhou, Q., Liu, Q., Tang, J., Zhang, X., Sun, X., Ye, Z., Yang, M., & Lam, S. K. (2019). 文化新語:兩岸四地傑出圖書館、檔案館及博物館傑出工作者訪談 [New cultural dialog: Interviews with outstanding librarians, archivists, and curators in Greater China]. Systech Publications.

Jiang, J., Vauras, M., Volet, S., & Wang, Y. (2016). Teachers' emotions and emotion regulation strategies: Self-and students' perceptions. *Teaching and Teacher Education, 54,* 22–31. doi:10.1016/j.tate.2015.11.008

Jiang, M., & Ballenger, J. (2023). Nontraditional doctoral students' perceptions of instructional strategies used to enhance statistics self-efficacy in online learning. *The Journal of Educators Online, 20*(1). Advance online publication. doi:10.9743/JEO.2023.20.1.7

Jiang, M., & Koo, K. (2020). Emotional presence in building an online learning community among non-traditional graduate students. *Online Learning : the Official Journal of the Online Learning Consortium, 24*(4), 93–111. doi:10.24059/olj.v24i4.2307

Jiang, M., Lam, A. H. C., Chiu, D. K. W., & Ho, K. K. W. (2023). Social media aids for business learning: A quantitative evaluation with the 5E instructional model. *Education and Information Technologies, 28*(9), 12269–12291. doi:10.100710639-023-11690-z PMID:37361768

Jiang, X., Chiu, D. K. W., & Chan, C. T. (2023). Application of the AIDA model in social media promotion and community engagement for small cultural organizations: A case study of the Choi Chang Sau Qin Society. In M. Dennis & J. Halbert (Eds.), *Community engagement in the online space* (pp. 48–70). IGI Global. doi:10.4018/978-1-6684-5190-8.ch004

Johnson, L., Adams Becker, S., Estrada, V., & Freeman, A. (2015a). *NMC/CoSN Horizon Report: 2015 K-12 Edition.* The New Media Consortium. Retrieved from https://www.learntechlib.org/p/152103/

Johnson, R. D., Adams Becker, S., Estrada, V., & Freeman, A. (2015b). *NMC/CoSN Horizon Report: 2015 Higher Education Edition*. The New Media Consortium. Retrieved from https://www.learntechlib.org/p/152102/

Johnson, C. A. (2010). Do public libraries contribute to social capital? *Library & Information Science Research*, *32*(2), 147–155. doi:10.1016/j.lisr.2009.12.006

Johnson, E., Morwane, R., Dada, S., Pretorius, G., & Lotriet, M. (2018). Adult Learners' Perspectives on Their Engagement in a Hybrid Learning Postgraduate Programme. *The Journal of Continuing Higher Education*, *66*(2), 88–105. doi:10.1080/07377363.2018.1469071

Johnston, A. N., Barton, M. J., Williams-Pritchard, G. A., & Todorovic, M. (2018). YouTube for millennial nursing students; using internet technology to support student engagement with bioscience. *Nurse Education in Practice*, *31*, 151–155. doi:10.1016/j.nepr.2018.06.002 PMID:29906632

Johnston, J. P. (2020). Creating better definitions of distance education. *Online Journal of Distance Learning Administration*, *23*(2).

Joksimovic, S., Gaševic, D., Kovanovic, V., Riecke, B. E., & Hatala, M. (2015). Social presence in online discussions as a process predictor of academic performance. *Journal of Computer Assisted Learning*, *31*(6), 638–654. doi:10.1111/jcal.12107

Jonassen, D., & Reeves, T. C. (2001). Learning with technology: Using computers as cognitive tools. In D. H. Jonassen (Ed.), *The handbook of research for educational communications and technology*. Lawrence Earlbaum.

Jones, E. J., & Crawford, B. L. (2023, January). Holding space and grace: The implementation of a health and wellness statement in graduate courses. In A. El-Amin (Ed.), *Elevating intentional education practice in graduate programs* (pp. 99–111). IGI Global. doi:10.4018/978-1-6684-4600-3.ch005

Jones, S. R., & Wijeyesinghe, C. L. (2011). The promises and challenges of teaching from an intersectional perspective: Core components and applied strategies. *New Directions for Teaching and Learning*, *2011*(125), 11–20. doi:10.1002/tl.429

Joo, L., Lim, K. Y., & Kim, J. (2013). Locus of control, self-efficacy, and task value as predictors of learning outcome in an online university context. *Computers & Education*, *62*, 149–158. doi:10.1016/j.compedu.2012.10.027

Jorgenson, J. (1992). Social approaches: Communication, rapport, and the interview: A social perspective. *Communication Theory*, *2*(2), 148156. doi:10.1111/j.1468-2885.1992.tb00034.x

Joyner, D. A., & Isbell, C. (2019, June). Master's at scale: Five years in a scalable online graduate degree. In *Proceedings of the Sixth ACM Conference on Learning@ Scale* (pp. 1-10). Academic Press.

Junco, R., Heibergert, G., & Loken, E. (2011). The effect of X on college student engagement and grades. *Journal of Computer Assisted Learning*, *27*(2), 119–132. doi:10.1111/j.1365-2729.2010.00387.x

Junco, R., & Mastrodicasa, J. (2007). *Connecting to the Net.Generation: What higher education professionals need to know about today's students* (1st ed.). National Association of Student Personnel Administrators.

Jurs, P., & Špehte, E. (2021). The Role of Feedback in the Distance Learning Process. *Journal of Teacher Education for Sustainability.*, *23*(2), 91–105. doi:10.2478/jtes-2021-0019

Kahn, J. S., Brett, B. L., & Holmes, J. R. (2011). Concerns with men's academic motivation in higher education: An exploratory investigation of the role of masculinity. *Journal of Men's Studies*, *19*(1), 65–82. doi:10.3149/jms.1901.65

Kahu, E. R., Stephens, C., Zepke, N., & Leach, L. (2014). Space and time to engage: Mature-aged distance students learn to fit study into their lives. *International Journal of Lifelong Education*, *33*(4), 523–540. doi:10.1080/02601370.2014.884177

Kaminski, J. (2011). Diffusion of innovation theory. *Canadian Journal of Nursing Informatics*, *6*(2), 1–6.

Kang, M., & Im, T. (2013). Factors of learner-instructor interaction which predict perceived learning outcomes in an online learning environment. *Journal of Computer Assisted Learning*, *29*(3), 292–301. doi:10.1111/jcal.12005

Kanter, R. (2007). *Enduring principles for changing times*. Long Now Foundation. https://www.youtube.com/watch?v=ga0VXYlbK7M

Kantor, D. (2012). *Reading the room: Group dynamics for coaches and leaders*. Jossey-Bass.

Kanuka, H., Collett, D., & Caswell, C. (2002). University instructor perceptions of the use of asynchronous text-based discussion in distance courses. *American Journal of Distance Education*, *16*(3), 151–167. doi:10.1207/S15389286AJDE1603_3

Kara, M., Erdogdu, F., Kokoc, M., & Cagiltay, K. (2019). Challenges faced by adult learners in online distance education: A literature review. *Open Praxis*, *11*(1), 5–22. https://search.informit.org/doi/10.3316/informit.234110355704611

Karaahmetoglu, K., & Korkmaz, Ö. (2019). The Effect of project-based Arduino educational robot applications on students' computational thinking skills and their perception of basic STEM skill levels. *Online Submission*, *6*(2), 1–14. doi:10.17275/per.19.8.6.2

Karatekin, C., & Ahluwalia, R. (2020). Effects of adverse childhood experiences, stress, and social support on the health of college students. *Journal of Interpersonal Violence*, *35*(1-2), 150–172. doi:10.1177/0886260516681880 PMID:27920360

Kauffman, H. (2015). A review of predictive factors of student success in and satisfaction with online learning. *Research in Learning Technology*, *23*, 23. doi:10.3402/rlt.v23.26507

Kaufman, T. (n.d.). Building positive relationships with students: What brain science says. *Understood*. https://www.understood.org/en/articles/brain-science-says-4-reasons-to-build-positive-relationships-with-students

Kaufmann, R., Sellnow, D. D., & Frisby, B. N. (2016). The development and validation of the online learning climate scale (OLCS). *Communication Education*, *65*(3), 307–321. doi:10.1080/03634523.2015.1101778

Keegan, D. (1980). On defining distance education. *Distance Education*, *1*(1), 13–36. doi:10.1080/0158791800010102

Kee, H. C., Chan, M. M., & Chiu, D. K. W. (2023). Building social capital in contemporary major U.S. public libraries: Leading Information services and beyond. In D. K. W. Chiu & K. K. W. Ho (Eds.), *Emerging technology-based services and systems in libraries, educational institutions, and non-profit organizations* (pp. 239–269). IGI Global. doi:10.4018/978-1-6684-8671-9.ch010

Keehn, M. G. (2015). "When You Tell a Personal Story, I Kind of Perk up a Little Bit More": An Examination of Student Learning From Listening to Personal Stories in Two Social Diversity Courses. *Equity & Excellence in Education*, *48*(3), 373–391. doi:10.1080/10665684.2015.1056712

Keels, M. (2020). *Campus counter spaces: Black and Latinx Students' search for the community at historically White Universities*. Cornell University Press. doi:10.7591/cornell/9781501746888.001.0001

Keengwe, J., & Kidd, T. T. (2010). Towards best practices in online learning and teaching in higher education. *Journal of Online Learning and Teaching*, *6*(2), 533–541.

Kegan, R. (2000). What 'Form' Transforms?: A Constructive-Developmental Perspective on Transformational Learning. In Learning as Transformation: Critical Perspectives on a Theory in Progress. San Francisco: Jossey Bass.

Kelly, K., & Zakrajsek, T. D. (2023). *Advancing online teaching: Creating equity-based digital learning environments.* Taylor & Francis.

Kemp, S. K. (2019). In that dimension grossly clad": Transgender rhetoric, representation, and Shakespeare. *Shakespeare Studies, 47*, 120–13.

Kennedy, B. A., & Arthur, N. (2014). Social justice and counselling psychology: Recommitment through action. *Canadian Journal of Counselling and Psychotherapy, 48*(3).

Kentnor, H. E. (2015). Distance education and the evolution of online learning in the United States. *Curriculum and Teaching Dialogue, 17*(1), 21–34.

Kets de Vries, M. F. (2005). The dangers of feeling like a fake. *Harvard Business Review, 83*, 108. https://hbr.org/2005/09/the-dangers-of-feeling-like-a-fake PMID:16171215

Khamis, T., Naseem, A., Khamis, A., & Petrucka, P. (2021). The COVID-19 pandemic: A catalyst for creativity and collaboration for online learning and work-based higher education systems and processes. *Journal of Work-Applied Management, 13*(2), 184–196. doi:10.1108/JWAM-01-2021-0010

Khudhair, A., Khudhair, M., Jaber, M., Awreed, Y., Ali, M., AL-Hameed, M., Jassim, M., Malik, R., Alkhayyat, A., & Hameed, A. (2023). Impact on Higher Education and College Students in Dijlah University after COVID through E-learning. *Computer-Aided Design and Applications*, 104–115. doi:10.14733/cadaps.2023.S12.104-115

Kilag, O. K. T., del Socorro, A. S., Largo, J. L., Peras, C. C., Book, J. F. P., & Abendan, C. F. K. (2023). Perspectives and experiences in online teaching and learning. *Science and Education, 4*(6), 561–571.

Kim, B., & Kim, Y. (2017). College students' social media use and communication network heterogeneity: Implications for social capital and subjective well-being. *Computers in Human Behavior, 73*, 620–628. doi:10.1016/j.chb.2017.03.033

Kim, J., & Park, C.-Y. (2020). Education, skill training, and lifelong learning in the era of technological revolution: A review. *Asian-Pacific Economic Literature, 34*(2), 3–19. doi:10.1111/apel.12299

Kim, M., Jun, M., & Han, J. (2023). The relationship between needs, motivation, and information sharing behaviors on social media: Focus on the self-connection and social connection. *Asia Pacific Journal of Marketing and Logistics, 35*(1), 1–16. doi:10.1108/APJML-01-2021-0066

Kimmel, S. C., Burns, E., & DiScala, J. (2019). Community at a distance: Employing a community of practice framework in online learning for rural students. *Journal of Education for Library and Information Science, 60*(4), 265–284. doi:10.3138/jelis.2018-0056

Kim, Y. K., & Lundberg, C. A. (2015). A structural model of the relationship between student-faculty interaction and cognitive skills development among college students. *Research in Higher Education, 57*(3), 288–309. doi:10.100711162-015-9387-6

King, C., & Piotrowski, C. (2021). Navigating the ADA accessibility requirements and legal pitfalls in online education. *College Student Journal, 55*(2), 127–134.

King, K. M., & Summers, L. (2020). Predictors of broaching: Multicultural competence, racial color blindness, and interpersonal communication. *Counselor Education and Supervision, 59*(3), 216–230. doi:10.1002/ceas.12185

King, R. B., & Datu, J. A. (2017). Happy classes make happy students: Classmates' well-being predicts individual student well-being. *Journal of School Psychology, 65*, 116–128. doi:10.1016/j.jsp.2017.07.004 PMID:29145940

Kiselica, M. S., Benton-Wright, S., & Englar-Carlson, M. (2016). Accentuating positive masculinity: A new foundation for the psychology of boys, men, and masculinity. In Y. J. Wong & S. R. Wester (Eds.), *APA handbook of men and masculinities* (pp. 123–143). American Psychological Association. doi:10.1037/14594-006

Klem, A. M., & Connell, J. P. (2004). Relationships matter: Linking teacher support to student engagement and achievement. *The Journal of School Health*, *74*(7), 262–273. doi:10.1111/j.1746-1561.2004.tb08283.x PMID:15493703

Knight, P. T. (2002). Summative assessment in higher education: Practices in disarray. *Studies in Higher Education*, *27*(3), 275–286. doi:10.1080/03075070220000662

Knowles, M. S. (1984). *Andragogy in action*. Academic Press.

Knowles, M. S. (1980). *The modern practice of adult education: From pedagogy to andragogy* (2nd ed.). Association Press.

Knowles, M. S. (1990). *The adult learner: A neglected species* (4th ed.). Gulf Publishing Company.

Knutsson, O., Blåsjö, M., Hållsten, S., & Karlström, P. (2012). Identifying different registers of digital literacy in virtual learning environments. *The Internet and Higher Education*, *15*(4), 237–246. doi:10.1016/j.iheduc.2011.11.002

Koehler, M. J., & Mishra, P. (2006). Technological pedagogical content knowledge: A framework for teacher knowledge. *Teachers College Record*, *108*(6), 1017–1054. doi:10.1111/j.1467-9620.2006.00684.x

Kolb, A. Y., & Kolb, D. A. (2017). The experiential educator: Principles and practices of experiential learning. EBLS Press.

Kolb, D. (1984). *Experiential Learning: Experience as the Source of Learning and Development*. Prentice Hall.

Kolb, D. A. (1984). *Experiential learning: Experience as the source of learning and development*. Prentice Hall.

Kordrostami, M., & Seitz, V. (2022). Faculty online competence and student affective engagement in online learning. *Marketing Education Review*, *32*(3), 240–254. doi:10.1080/10528008.2021.1965891

Kornbluh, M., Bell, S., Vierra, K., & Herrnstadt, Z. (2022). Resistance capital: Cultural activism as a gateway to college persistence for minority and first-generation students. *Journal of Adolescent Research*, *37*(4), 501–540. doi:10.1177/07435584211006920

Kourea, L., Christodoulidou, P., & Fella, A. (2021). Voices of undergraduate students with disabilities during the COVID-19 pandemic: A pilot study. *European Journal of Psychology Open*, *80*(3), 111–124. doi:10.1024/2673-8627/a000011

Kramarczuk, K., Atchison, K., Plane, J., & Narayanasamy, M. (2021). The Power of mentoring programs in retaining women and Black, Indigenous, and students of color in undergraduate computing majors. *2021 International Conference on Computational Science and Computational Intelligence (CSCI), Computational Science and Computational Intelligence (CSCI), 2021 International Conference on CSCI*, 1125–1128. 10.1109/CSCI54926.2021.00237

Krizek, R. L. (2017). Narrative and storytelling. The International Encyclopedia of Organizational Communication, 1-17. doi:10.1002/9781118955567.wbieoc146

Kropf, D. C. (2013). Connectivism: 21st Century's New Learning Theory. *European Journal of Open. Distance and E-Learning*, *16*(2), 13–24.

Kuhfeld, M., Soland, J., Tarasawa, B., Johnson, A., Ruzek, E., & Liu, J. (2020). Projecting the potential impact of COVID-19 school closures on academic achievement. *Educational Researcher*, *49*(8), 549–565. doi:10.3102/0013189X20965918

Kumi-Yeboah, A., Dogbey, J., Yuan, G., & Smith, P. (2020). Cultural diversity in online education: An exploration of instructors' perceptions and challenges. *Teachers College Record*, *122*(7), 1–46. doi:10.1177/016146812012200708

Kumi-Yeboah, A., Yuan, G., & Dogbey, J. (2017). Online collaborative learning activities: The perceptions of culturally diverse graduate students. *Online Learning : the Official Journal of the Online Learning Consortium, 21*(4), 5–28. doi:10.24059/olj.v21i4.1277

Kung, M. (2017). Methods and strategies for working with international students learning online in the U.S. *TechTrends, 61*(5), 479–485. doi:10.100711528-017-0209-x

Kuo, Y., & Belland, B. R. (2016). An exploratory study of adult learners' perceptions of online learning: Minority students in continuing education. *Educational Technology Research and Development, 64*(4), 661–680. doi:10.100711423-016-9442-9

Kuo, Y.-C., Walker, A. E., Schroder, K. E. E., & Belland, B. R. (2014). Interaction, Internet self-efficacy, and self-regulated learning as predictors of student satisfaction in online education courses. *The Internet and Higher Education, 20*, 35–50. doi:10.1016/j.iheduc.2013.10.001

Kurt, Y., Özkan, Ç. G., & Öztürk, H. (2022). Nursing students' classroom climate perceptions: A longitudinal study. *Nurse Education Today, 111*, 105311. doi:10.1016/j.nedt.2022.105311 PMID:35240399

Kwan, Y. K. C., Chan, M. W., & Chiu, D. K. W. (2023). (in press). Youth Marketing Development of Special Libraries in the Digital Era: Viewpoint from the Taste Library with 7Ps Marketing Mix. *Library Hi Tech*. Advance online publication. doi:10.1108/LHT-03-2023-0129

Ladyshewsky, R. (2013). Instructor presence in online courses and student satisfaction. *International Journal for the Scholarship of Teaching and Learning, 7*(1), 1–23. doi:10.20429/ijsotl.2013.070113

Lai, K. W. (2015). Knowledge construction in online learning communities: A case study of a doctoral course. *Studies in Higher Education, 40*(4), 561–579. doi:10.1080/03075079.2013.831402

Laird-Magee, T. (2013). Teams build a wiki to teach each other four social media platforms. *Journal of Advertising Education, 17*(1), 46–54. doi:10.1177/109804821301700107

Lam, A. H. C., Ho, K. K. W., & Chiu, D. K. W. (2023). Instagram for student learning and library promotions? A quantitative study using the 5E Instructional Model. *Aslib Journal of Information Management, 75*(1), 112–130. doi:10.1108/AJIM-12-2021-0389

Lam, E. T. H., Au, C. H., & Chiu, D. K. W. (2019). Analyzing the use of Facebook among university libraries in Hong Kong. *Journal of Academic Librarianship, 45*(3), 175–183. doi:10.1016/j.acalib.2019.02.007

Lampe, N. M. (2023, October). (online first 2023). Teaching with TikTok in online sociology of sex and gender courses. *Teaching Sociology, 51*(4), 323–335. Advance online publication. doi:10.1177/0092055X231159091

Lancaster, M., & Arango, E. (2021). Health and emotional well-being of urban university students in the era of COVID-19. *Traumatology, 27*(1), 107–117. doi:10.1037/trm0000308

Landrum, R. E., Brakke, K., & McCarthy, M. A. (2019). The pedagogical power of storytelling. *Scholarship of Teaching and Learning in Psychology, 5*(3), 247–253. doi:10.1037tl0000152

Land, S. M., & Greene, B. A. (2000). Projectbased learning with the World Wide Web: A qualitative study of resource integration. *Educational Technology Research and Development, 48*(1), 45–68. doi:10.1007/BF02313485

LaPointe, L., & Reisetter, M. (2008). Belonging online: Students' perceptions of the value and efficacy of an online learning community. *International Journal on E-Learning, 7*(4), 641–665.

Lau, K. P., Chiu, D. K. W., Ho, K. K. W., Lo, P., & See-To, E. W. K. (2017). Educational usage of mobile devices: Differences between postgraduate and undergraduate students. *Journal of Academic Librarianship*, *43*(3), 201–208. doi:10.1016/j.acalib.2017.03.004

Lau, K. S. N., Lo, P., Chiu, D. K. W., Ho, K. K. W., Jiang, T., Zhou, Q., Percy, P., & Allard, B. (2020). Library and learning experiences turned mobile: A comparative study between LIS and non-LIS students. *Journal of Academic Librarianship*, *46*(2), 102103. Advance online publication. doi:10.1016/j.acalib.2019.102103

Lawrence, A. (2020). Teaching as Dialogue: Toward Culturally Responsive Online Pedagogy. *Journal of Online Learning Research*, *6*, 5–33. https://www.learntechlib.org/primary/p/210657/

Law, T. Y., Leung, F. C. W., Chiu, D. K. W., Lo, P., Lung, M. M.-W., Zhou, Q., Xu, Y., Lu, Y., & Ho, K. K. W. (2019). Mobile learning usage of LIS students in Mainland China. *International Journal of Systems and Service-Oriented Engineering*, *9*(2), 12–34. doi:10.4018/IJSSOE.2019040102

Lazzara, J., & Clinton-Lisell, V. (2022). Using social annotation to enhance student engagement in psychology courses. *Scholarship of Teaching and Learning in Psychology*, 1–7. Advance online publication. doi:10.1037tl0000335

Ledford, H. (2021). How severe are Omicron infections. *Nature*, *600*(7890), 577–578. doi:10.1038/d41586-021-03794-8 PMID:34934198

Lee, A., & Gage, N. A. (2020). Updating and expanding systematic reviews and meta-analyses on the effects of school-wide positive behavior interventions and supports. *Psychology in the Schools*, *57*(5), 783–804. doi:10.1002/pits.22336

Lee, E., & Bertera, E. (2007). Teaching diversity by using instructional technology: Application of self-efficacy and cultural competence. *Multicultural Education & Technology Journal*, *1*(2), 112–125. doi:10.1108/17504970710759602

Lee, E.-K. O., Brown, M., & Bertera, E. M. (2010). The use of an online diversity forum to facilitate social work students' dialogue on sensitive issues: A quasi-experimental design. *Journal of Teaching in Social Work*, *30*(3), 272–287. doi:10.1080/08841233.2010.499066

Lee, K. (2017). Rethinking the accessibility of online higher education: A historical review. *The Internet and Higher Education*, *33*, 15–23. doi:10.1016/j.iheduc.2017.01.001

Lee, O. E. K., Kim, S. Y., & Gezer, T. (2021). Factors Associated With Online Learning Self-Efficacy Among Students With Disabilities In Higher Education. *American Journal of Distance Education*, *35*(4), 293–306. doi:10.1080/08923647.2021.1979344

Lefler, E. K., Sacchetti, G. M., & Del Carlo, D. I. (2016). ADHD in college: A qualitative analysis. *Attention Deficit and Hyperactivity Disorders*, *8*(2), 79–93. doi:10.100712402-016-0190-9 PMID:26825556

Lei, S. Y., Chiu, D. K. W., Lung, M. M., & Chan, C. T. (2021). Exploring the aids of social media for musical instrument education. *International Journal of Music Education*, *39*(2), 187–201. doi:10.1177/0255761420986217

Leithwood, K., Jantzi, D., & Coffin, G. (1995). *Preparing school leaders: What works*. Ontario Institute for Studies in Education.

Lertora, I. M., Croffie, A., Dorn-Medeiros, C., & Christensen, J. (2020). Using relational cultural theory as a pedagogical approach for counselor education. *Journal of Creativity in Mental Health*, *15*(2), 265–276. doi:10.1080/15401383.2019.1687059

Leung, T. N., Chiu, D. K. W., Ho, K. K. W., & Luk, C. K. L. (2022). User perceptions, academic library usage, and social capital: A correlation analysis under COVID-19 after library renovation. *Library Hi Tech*, *40*(2), 304–322. doi:10.1108/LHT-04-2021-0122

Leung, T. N., Hui, Y. M., Luk, C. K. L., Chiu, D. K. W., & Ho, K. K. W. (2022). (in press). Evaluating Facebook as aids for learning Japanese: Learners' perspectives. *Library Hi Tech*. Advance online publication. doi:10.1108/LHT-11-2021-0400

Lewin, K. (1935). *A dynamic theory of personality: Selected papers*. McGraw-Hill.

Lewis, A. (2007). Australian Women's online experiences: Why e-learning doesn't necessarily guarantee an inclusive or egalitarian communication space. *International Journal of Learning*, *14*(2), 81–90. doi:10.18848/1447-9494/CGP/v14i02/45195

Lewis, K. G. (2001). Using midsemester student feedback and responding to it. *New Directions for Teaching and Learning*, *2001*(87), 33–44. doi:10.1002/tl.26

Lewis, K. R., & Shah, P. P. (2021). Black students' narratives of diversity and inclusion initiatives and the campus racial climate: An interest-convergence analysis. *Journal of Diversity in Higher Education*, *14*(2), 189–202. doi:10.1037/dhe0000147

Li, L. Y., & Tsai, C. C. (2017). Accessing online learning material: Quantitative behavior patterns and their effects on motivation and learning performance. *Computers & Education*, *114*(1), 286-297. https://www.learntechlib.org/p/201259/

Li, S. M., Lam, A. H. C., & Chiu, D. K. W. (2023). Digital transformation of ticketing services: A value chain analysis of POPTICKET in Hong Kong. In J. Santos, I. Pereira, & P. Pires (Eds.), Management and marketing for improved retail competitiveness and performance (pp. 156-179). IGI Global. doi:10.4018/978-1-6684-8574-3.ch008

Lien, B. (2020). *Why understanding channel types makes using Slack more awesome*. https://uit.stanford.edu/blog/why-understanding-channel-types-makes-using-slack-more-awesome

Lien, C., Cao, Y., & Zhou, X. (2017). Service quality, satisfaction, stickiness, and usage intentions: An exploratory evaluation in the context of WeChat services. *Computers in Human Behavior*, *68*, 403–410. doi:10.1016/j.chb.2016.11.061

Li, K. K., & Chiu, D. K. W. (2022). A worldwide quantitative review of the iSchools' archival education. *Library Hi Tech*, *40*(5), 1497–1518. doi:10.1108/LHT-09-2021-0311

Li, L., Chiu, D. K. W., & Ho, K. K. W. (2023). How important is it to be beautiful?: The effect of beauty premium on wages. In Z. Sun (Ed.), *Handbook of Research on driving socioeconomic development with big data* (pp. 320–340). IGI Global. doi:10.4018/978-1-6684-5959-1.ch015

Lim, H. L. (2007). Community of inquiry in an online undergraduate information technology course. *Journal of Information Technology Education*, *6*(1), 153–168. doi:10.28945/207

Lin, B., & Hsieh, C. T. (2001). Web-based teaching and learner control: A research review. *Computers & Education*, *37*(3), 377–386. doi:10.1016/S0360-1315(01)00060-4

Lin, C.-H., Chiu, D. K. W., & Lam, K. T. (2022). (in press). Hong Kong academic librarians' attitudes towards robotic process automation. *Library Hi Tech*. Advance online publication. doi:10.1108/LHT-03-2022-0141

LinkedIn. (2023). *What is LinkedIn and how can I use it?* https://www.linkedin.com/help/linkedin/answer/a548441/what-is-linkedin-and-how-can-i-use-it-?lang=en

Lin, X., & Gao, L. (2020). Students' sense of community and perspectives of taking synchronous and asynchronous online courses. *Asian Journal of Distance Education*, *15*(1), 169–179.

Lipka, O., Khouri, M., & Shecter-Lerner, M. (2019). University faculty attitudes and knowledge about learning disabilities. *Higher Education Research & Development*, 1–15. doi:10.1080/07294360.2019.1695750

Li, Q., Wong, J., & Chiu, D. K. W. (2023). School library reading support for students with dyslexia: A qualitative study in the digital age. *Library Hi Tech*. Advance online publication. doi:10.1108/LHT-03-2023-0086

Li, S., Chiu, D. K. W., Kafeza, E., & Ho, K. K. W. (2023). Social media analytics for non-governmental organizations: A case study of Hong Kong Next Generation Arts. In Z. Sun (Ed.), *Handbook of research on driving socioeconomic development with big data* (pp. 277–295). IGI Global. doi:10.4018/978-1-6684-5959-1.ch013

Li, S., Xie, Z., Chiu, D. K. W., & Ho, K. K. W. (2023). Sentiment analysis and topic modeling regarding online classes on the Reddit Platform: Educators versus learners. *Applied Sciences (Basel, Switzerland)*, *13*(4), 2250. Advance online publication. doi:10.3390/app13042250

Liston, D. D. (1994). *Storytelling and narrative: A neurophilosophical perspective*. Retrieved from https://files.eric.ed.gov/fulltext/ED372092.pdf

Littlefield, M. B., & Bertera, E. M. (2004). A discourse analysis of online dialogs in social work diversity courses: Topical themes, depth, and tone. *Journal of Teaching in Social Work*, *24*(3-4), 131–146. doi:10.1300/J067v24n03_09

Liu, Q., Lo, P., Zhou, Q., Chiu, D. K. W., & Cheuk, M. K. (2022). 走進大專院校圖書館: 圖書館員視角下的大中華區高等教育 [Why the Library? The Role of Librarians in the Higher Education Systems of Greater China]. City University Press.

Liu, T. (2021). *Relationships among mentoring support and student success in a Chinese first-year experience program* [Doctoral dissertation, Chapman University]. Chapman University Digital Commons. doi:10.36837/chapman.000329

Liu, Z. Y., Lomovtseva, N., & Korobeynikova, E. (2020). Online Learning Platforms: Reconstructing Modern Higher Education. *International Journal of Emerging Technologies in Learning (iJET)*, *15*(13), 4-21. https://www.learntechlib.org/p/217605/

Liu, O. L. (2012). Student Evaluation of Instruction: In the new paradigm of distance education. *Research in Higher Education*, *53*(4), 471–486. doi:10.100711162-011-9236-1

Liu, X., Bonk, C. J., Magjuka, R. J., Lee, S. H., & Su, B. (2005). Exploring four dimensions of online instructor roles: A program level case study. *Journal of Asynchronous Learning Networks*, *9*(4), 29–48.

Liu, Y. (2010). Social media tools as a learning resource. *Journal of Educational Technology Development and Exchange*, *3*(1), 8. Advance online publication. doi:10.18785/jetde.0301.08

Liu, Y., Chiu, D. K. W., & Ho, K. K. W. (2023). Short-form videos for public library marketing: Performance analytics of Douyin in China. *Applied Sciences (Basel, Switzerland)*, *13*(6), 3386. Advance online publication. doi:10.3390/app13063386

Liu, Y., Lei, J., Chiu, D. K. W., & Xie, Z. (2023). Adult learners' perception of online language English learning in China. In A. Garcés-Manzanera & M. E. C. García (Eds.), *New approaches to the investigation of language teaching and literature* (pp. 123–140). IGI Global. doi:10.4018/978-1-6684-6020-7.ch007

Lively, C. L., Blevins, B., Talbert, S., & Cooper, S. (2021). Building community in online professional practice doctoral programs. *Impacting Education: Journal on Transforming Professional Practice*, *6*(3), 21–29. doi:10.5195/ie.2021.187

Li, X., & Pei, Z. (2023). Improving effectiveness of online learning for higher education students during the COVID-19 pandemic. *Frontiers in Psychology*, *13*, 1111028. doi:10.3389/fpsyg.2022.1111028 PMID:36726501

Lockman, A., & Schirmer, B. (2020). Online instruction in Higher Education: Promising, research-based, and evidence-based practices. *Journal of Education and e-learning Research*, *7*(2), 130–152. doi:10.20448/journal.509.2020.72.130.152

Loeng, S. (2020). Self-directed learning: A core concept in adult education. *Education Research International*, *2020*, 1–12. doi:10.1155/2020/3816132

Long, C. (2023, March 30). *Standardized testing is still failing students*. NEA News. https://www.nea.org/advocating-for-change/new-from-nea/standardized-testing-still-failing-students

Long, R. (2020). Dynamic Classroom Dialogue: Can Students Be Engaged Beyond Discussion? *Journal of Higher Education Theory and Practice*, *20*(3), 85–92. doi:10.33423/jhetp.v20i3.2975

Lo, P., Allard, B., Anghelescu, H. G. B., Xin, Y., Chiu, D. K. W., & Stark, A. J. (2020). Transformational leadership practice in the world's leading academic libraries. *Journal of Librarianship and Information Science*, *52*(4), 972–999. doi:10.1177/0961000619897991

Lo, P., Allard, B., Wang, N., & Chiu, D. K. W. (2020). Servant leadership theory in practice: North America's leading public libraries. *Journal of Librarianship and Information Science*, *52*(1), 249–270. doi:10.1177/0961000618792387

Lo, P., Chan, H. H. Y., Tang, A. W. M., Chiu, D. K. W., Cho, A., See-To, E., Ho, K. K. W., He, M., Kenderdine, S., & Shaw, J. (2019). Visualising and revitalising traditional Chinese martial arts: Visitors' engagement and learning experience at the 300 years of Hakka KungFu. *Library Hi Tech*, *37*(2), 269–288. doi:10.1108/LHT-05-2018-0071

Lo, P., & Chiu, D. K. W. (2015). Enhanced and changing roles of school librarians under the digital age. *New Library World*, *116*(11/12), 696–710. doi:10.1108/NLW-05-2015-0037

Lo, P., Chiu, D. K. W., Cho, A., & Allard, B. (2018). *Conversations with leading academic and research library directors: International perspectives on library management*. Chandos Publishing.

Lo, P., Chiu, D. K. W., & Chu, W. (2013). Modeling your college library after a commercial bookstore? The Hong Kong Design Institute Library experience. *Community & Junior College Libraries*, *19*(3-4), 59–76. doi:10.1080/02763915.2014.915186

Lo, P., Cho, A., Law, B. K.-K., Chiu, D. K. W., & Allard, B. (2017). Progressive trends in electronic resources management among academic libraries in Hong Kong. *Library Collections, Acquisitions & Technical Services*, *40*(1-2), 28–37. doi:10.1080/14649055.2017.1291243

Lo, P., Yu, K., & Chiu, D. K. W. (2015). A research agenda for enhancing teacher librarians' roles and practice in Hong Kong's 21st century learning environments. *School Libraries Worldwide*, *21*(1), 19–37. doi:10.29173lw6881

Lou, J. H., Li, R. H., Yu, H. Y., & Chen, S. H. (2011). Relationships among self-esteem, job adjustment and service attitude amongst male nurses: A structural equation model. *Journal of Clinical Nursing*, *20*(5-6), 864–872. doi:10.1111/j.1365-2702.2010.03387.x PMID:21118324

Lovett, J. T., Munawar, K., Mohammed, S., & Prabhu, V. (2021). Radiology content on TikTok: Current use of a novel video-based social media platform and opportunities for radiology. *Current Problems in Diagnostic Radiology*, *50*(2), 125–131. doi:10.1067/j.cpradiol.2020.10.004 PMID:33250298

Lovitts, B. E. (2001). *Leaving the Ivory Tower: The causes and consequences of departure from doctoral study*. Rowman & Littlefield.

Lowenthal, P. R., Humphrey, M., Conley, Q., Dunlap, J. C., Greear, K., Lowenthal, A., & Giacumo, L. A. (2020). Creating accessible and inclusive online learning: Moving beyond compliance and broadening the discussion. *Quarterly Review of Distance Education*, *21*(2), 1–21.

Lu, S. S., Tian, R., & Chiu, D. K. W. (2023). (in press). Why do people not attend public library programs in the current digital age? A mix method study in Hong Kong. *Library Hi Tech*. Advance online publication. doi:10.1108/LHT-04-2022-0217

Lu, W. (2023). Socrates on Slack: Text-based persistent-chat platforms as an alternative to "Zoom classes" in synchronous online learning. *Communication Teacher*, *37*(2), 141–150. doi:10.1080/17404622.2022.2117395

Lyn, A. E., Broderick, M., & Spranger, E. (2023). Student well-being and empowerment: SEL in online graduate education. In *Exploring Social Emotional Learning in Diverse Academic Settings* (pp. 312–336). IGI Global. doi:10.4018/978-1-6684-7227-9.ch016

Lyons, T., & Evans, M. (2013). Blended learning to increase student satisfaction: An exploratory study. *Internet Reference Services Quarterly*, *18*(1), 43–53. doi:10.1080/10875301.2013.800626

M. (2020). *Lessons learned using Slack in engineering education: An innovation-based learning approach*. Paper presented at 2020 ASEE Virtual Annual Conference. https://peer.asee.org/34916

Maceli, K. M., Fogliasso, C. E., & Baack, D. (2011). Differences of students' satisfaction with college professors: The impact of student gender on satisfaction. *Academy of Educational Leadership Journal*, *15*(4), 35–45.

Macready, H. (2022). *How to use hashtags in 2023: A guide for every network*. https://blog.hootsuite.com/how-to-use-hashtags/

Macready, H. (2023). *47 LinkedIn Statistics you need to know in 2023*. https://blog.hootsuite.com/linkedin-statistics-business/

Mael, F., & Ashforth, B. E. (1992). Alumni and their alma mater: A partial test of the reformulated model of organizational identification. *Journal of Organizational Behavior*, *13*(2), 103–123. doi:10.1002/job.4030130202

Maeroff, G. I. (2004). *A classroom of one: How online learning is changing our schools and colleges*. Macmillan.

Maheu, M. (2020, June 11). Zoom fatigue: What can you do about it. *TBH Institute Blog*. https://telehealth.org/blog/zoom-fatigue-what-it-is-what-you-can-do/

Maier, A., Schaitz, C., Kröner, J., Berger, A., Keller, F., Beschoner, P., Connemann, B., & Sosic-Vasic, Z. (2021, November 30). The Association Between Test Anxiety, Self-Efficacy, and Mental Images Among University Students: Results from an Online Survey. *Frontiers in Psychiatry*, *12*, 618108. doi:10.3389/fpsyt.2021.618108 PMID:34916965

Majid, S., Yang, P., Lei, H., & Haoran, G. (2014). Knowledge sharing by students: Preference for online discussion board vs face-to-face class participation. In *The Emergence of Digital Libraries–Research and Practices* (pp. 149–159). Springer International Publishing. doi:10.1007/978-3-319-12823-8_16

Mak, M. Y. C., Poon, A. Y. M., & Chiu, D. K. W. (2022). Using social media as learning aids and preservation: Chinese martial arts in Hong Kong. In S. Papadakis & A. Kapaniaris (Eds.), *The digital folklore of cyberculture and digital humanities* (pp. 171–185). IGI Global. doi:10.4018/978-1-6684-4461-0.ch010

Malott, K. M., Hall, K. H., Sheely-Moore, A., Krell, M. M., & Cardaciotto, L. (2014). Evidence based teaching in higher education: Application to counselor education. *Counselor Education and Supervision*, *53*(4), 294–305. doi:10.1002/j.1556-6978.2014.00064.x

Mandernach, B. J. (March 2009). Three ways to improve student engagement in the online classroom. *Online Cl@ssroom: Ideas for Effective Online Instruction*. 1-2.

Mann, G. (2022). Allies as guides in the borderlands: The development of an online ally program to foster belonging for LGBTIQ+ students and staff at a regional university. *Journal of University Teaching & Learning Practice*, *19*(4), 1–18.

Maor, D. (2008). Changing relationship: Who is the learner and who is the teacher in the online educational landscape? *Australasian Journal of Educational Technology*, *24*(5), 627–638. doi:10.14742/ajet.1195

Marek, K. (2009). Learning to teach online: Creating a culture of support for faculty. *Journal of Education for Library and Information Science*, *50*(4), 275–292.

Marszalek, M. A., Faksvåg, H., Frøystadvåg, T. H., Ness, O., & Veseth, M. (2021). A mismatch between what is happening on the inside and going on, on the outside: A qualitative study of therapists' perspectives on student mental health. *International Journal of Mental Health Systems*, *15*(1), 87. doi:10.118613033-021-00508-5 PMID:34930381

Martin, F., & Bolliger, D. U. (2018). Engagement Matters: Student Perceptions on the Importance of Engagement Strategies in the Online Learning Environment. *Online Learning : the Official Journal of the Online Learning Consortium*, *22*(1), 205–222. doi:10.24059/olj.v22i1.1092

Martin, F., Ritzhaupt, A., Kumar, S., & Budhrani, K. (2019). Award-winning faculty online teaching practices: Course design, assessment and evaluation, and facilitation. *The Internet and Higher Education*, *42*, 34–43. doi:10.1016/j.iheduc.2019.04.001

Martin, F., Xie, K., & Bolliger, D. U. (2022). Engaging learners in the emergency transition to online learning during the COVID-19 pandemic. *Journal of Research on Technology in Education*, *54*(sup1), S1–S13. doi:10.1080/15391523.2021.1991703

Martin, J. (2019). Building relationships and increasing engagement in the virtual classroom: Practical tools for the online instructor. *The Journal of Educators Online*, *16*(1), n1–n8. doi:10.9743/jeo.2019.16.1.9

Marzano, M. S., & Allen, R. J. (2016). Online vs. face-to-face course evaluations: Considerations for administrators and faculty. *Online Journal of Distance Learning Administration*, *19*(4).

Maslow, A. H. (1943). A theory of human motivation. *Psychological Review*, *50*(4), 370–396. doi:10.1037/h0054346

Maulana, A. E., Patterson, P. G., Satria, A., & Pradipta, I. A. (2023). Alumni connectedness and its role in intention to contribute to higher education institutions. *Journal of Marketing for Higher Education*, 1–22. doi:10.1080/08841241.2023.2186560

Maunder, R. E. (2018). Students' peer relationships and their contribution to university adjustment: The need to belong in the university community. *Journal of Further and Higher Education*, *42*(6), 756–768. doi:10.1080/0309877X.2017.1311996

Mayer, R. E. (2014). Incorporating motivation into multimedia learning. *Learning and Instruction*, *29*, 171–173. doi:10.1016/j.learninstruc.2013.04.003

Mazer, J. P., Murphy, R. E., & Simonds, C. J. (2007). I'll see you on "Facebook": The effects of computer-mediated teacher self-disclosure on student motivation, affective learning, and classroom climate. *Communication Education*, *56*(1), 1–17. doi:10.1080/03634520601009710

McAuliffe, D. (2019). Challenges for best practice in online social work education. *Australian Social Work*, *72*(1), 110–112. doi:10.1080/0312407X.2018.1534982

McCavanagh, T. M., & Cadaret, M. C. (2022). Creating safe spaces for lesbian, gay, bisexual, transgender, and queer (LGBTQ+) student–athletes. In Affirming LGBTQ+ students in higher education. (pp. 141–159). American Psychological Association. doi:10.1037/0000281-009

McCombs, B. L. (1997). Self-assessment and reflection: Tools for promoting teacher changes toward learner-centered practices. *NASSP Bulletin*, *81*(587), 1–14. doi:10.1177/019263659708158702

McCorkle, D. E., & McCorkle, Y. L. (2012). Using LinkedIn in the marketing classroom: Exploratory insights and recommendations for teaching social media/networking. *Marketing Education Review*, *22*(2), 157–166. doi:10.2753/MER1052-8008220205

McDermott, R. C., Pietrantonio, K. R., Browning, B. R., McKelvey, D. K., Jones, Z. K., Booth, N. R., & Sevig, T. D. (2019). In search of positive masculine role norms: Testing the positive psychology positive masculinity paradigm. *Psychology of Men & Masculinity*, *20*(1), 12–22. doi:10.1037/men0000160

McEwan, R. C., & Downie, R. (2013). College success of students with psychiatric disabilities: Barriers of access and distraction. *Journal of Postsecondary Education and Disability*, *26*(3), 233–248.

McFarland, J., Hussar, B., De Brey, C., Snyder, T., Wang, X., Wilkinson-Flicker, S., ... & Hinz, S. (2017). *The Condition of Education 2017*. NCES 2017-144. National Center for Education Statistics.

McInnerney, J. M., & Roberts, T. S. (2004). Online learning: Social interaction and the creation of a sense of community. *Journal of Educational Technology & Society*, *7*(3), 73–81.

McKean, C., Law, J., Laing, K., Cockerill, M., Allon-Smith, J., McCartney, E., & Forbes, J. (2016). A qualitative case study in the social capital of Co-professional collaborative Co-practice for children with speech, language and communication needs. *International Journal of Language & Communication Disorders*, *52*(4), 514–527. doi:10.1111/1460-6984.12296 PMID:27813256

McKenna, T., & Woods, D. B. (2012). Using psychotherapeutic arts to decolonise counselling for Indigenous peoples. *Asia Pacific Journal of Counselling and Psychotherapy*, *3*(1), 29–40. doi:10.1080/21507686.2011.631145

McKnight-Tutein, G., & Thackaberry, A. S. (2011). Having it all: The hybrid solution for the best of both worlds in women's postsecondary education. *Distance Learning*, *8*(3), 17.

McManus, D., Dryer, R., & Henning, M. (2017). Barriers to learning online experienced by students with a mental health disability. *Distance Education*, *38*(3), 336–352. doi:10.1080/01587919.2017.1369348

McMillan, D. W., & Chavis, D. M. (1986). Sense of Community: A definition and theory. *Journal of Community Psychology*, *14*(1), 6–23. doi:10.1002/1520-6629(198601)14:1<6::AID-JCOP2290140103>3.0.CO;2-I

McPhail, C. J. (2000). *Transforming Community College Leadership Preparation: A Cohort Leadership Learning Model*. Academic Press.

Means, Toyama, Murphy, Bakia, & Jones. (2010). Department of Education, Office of Planning, Evaluation, and Policy Development. *Evaluation of evidence-based practices in online learning*.

Medaille, A., Beisler, M., Tokarz, R., & Bucy, R. (2022). The Role of Self-Efficacy in the Thesis-Writing Experiences of Undergraduate Honors Students. *Teaching and Learning Inquiry*, *10*. doi:10.20343/teachlearninqu.10.2

Mehta, D., & Wang, X. (2020). COVID-19 and digital library services – A case study of a university library. *Digital Library Perspectives*, *36*(4), 351–363. doi:10.1108/DLP-05-2020-0030

Meletiou-Mavrotheris, M., Eteokleoius, N., & Stylianou-Georgiou, A. (2022). Emergency remote learning in higher education in Cyprus during COVID-19 lockdown: A zoom-out view of challenges and opportunities for quality online learning. *Education Sciences*, *12*(477), 477. Advance online publication. doi:10.3390/educsci12070477

Meng, Y., Chu, M. Y., & Chiu, D. K. W. (2023). The impact of COVID-19 on museums in the digital era: Practices and challenges in Hong Kong. *Library Hi Tech*, *41*(1), 130–151. doi:10.1108/LHT-05-2022-0273

Merle, P. F., & Craig, C. (2017). Be my guest: A survey of mass communication students' perception of guest speakers. *College Teaching*, *65*(2), 41–49. doi:10.1080/87567555.2016.1232691

Merriam, S. B. (2001). Andragogy and self-directed learning: Pillars of adult learning theory. *New Directions for Adult and Continuing Education*, *2001*(89), 3–14. doi:10.1002/ace.3

Merriam, S. B., & Caffarella, R. S. (1999). *Learning in Adulthood* (2nd ed.). Jossey-Bass.

Merriam, S. B., Cafferella, R. C., & Baumgartner, L. M. (2007). *Learning in adulthood* (3rd ed.). Jossey-Bass.

Merriam-Webster Dictionary. (2023). *Social media*. https://www.merriam-webster.com/dictionary/social%20media

Merriam-Webster. (n.d.). Engagement. In *Merriam-Webster.com dictionary*. Retrieved June 13, 2023, from https://www.merriam-webster.com/dictionary/engagement

Merriweather, L. R., Howell, C. D., & Gnanadass, E. (2022). Cross-cultural mentorships with Black and Brown US STEM Doctoral Students: Unpacking the perceptions of International faculty. *2022 IEEE Frontiers in Education Conference (FIE), Frontiers in Education Conference (FIE), 2022 IEEE*, 1–9. 10.1109/FIE56618.2022.9962715

Meyer, K. A. (2003). Face-to-face versus threaded discussions: The role of time and higher-order thinking. *Journal of Asynchronous Learning Networks*, *7*(3), 55–65.

Mezirow, J. (1981). A critical theory of adult learning and education. *Adult Education*, *32*(1), 3–24. doi:10.1177/074171368103200101

Mezirow, J. (1997). Transformative learning. *New Directions for Adult and Continuing Education*, *74*(74), 5–12. doi:10.1002/ace.7401

Michel, R. E., Hall, S. B., Hays, D. G., & Runyan, H. I. (2013). A mixed-methods study of male recruitment in the counseling profession. *Journal of Counseling and Development*, *91*(4), 475–482. doi:10.1002/j.1556-6676.2013.00120.x

Michel, R. E., Hays, D. G., & Runyan, H. I. (2015). Faculty member attitudes and behaviors toward male counselors in training: A social cognitive career theory perspective. *Sex Roles*, *72*(7-8), 308–320. doi:10.100711199-015-0473-1

Miller, A. S. (2007). *Students that persist: Caring relationships that make a difference in higher education*. https://files.eric.ed.gov/fulltext/ED497500.pdf

Miller, W. (2023, May 25). Maslow's hierarchy in action: How student affairs can use the framework for better assessment of well-being. *Student Affairs Assessment Leaders*. http://studentaffairsassessment.org/entries/announcements/maslow-s-hierarchy-in-action-how-student-affairs-can-use-the-framework-for-better-assessment-of-wellbeing

Moen, T. (2006). Reflections on the narrative research approach. *International Journal of Qualitative Methods*, *5*(4), 56–69. doi:10.1177/160940690600500405

Moessenlechner, C., Obexer, R., Sixl-Daniell, K., & Seeler, J. M. (2015). E-learning degree programs: A better way to balance work and education? *Studies*, *23*(24), 25. http://learningideasconf.s3.amazonaws.com/Docs/Past/2015/Papers/Moessenlechner_Obexer_et_al.pdf

Mohamad Nasri, N., Husnin, H., Mahmud, S. N. D., & Halim, L. (2020). Mitigating the COVID-19 pandemic: A snapshot from Malaysia into the coping strategies for pre-service teachers' education. *Journal of Education for Teaching*, *46*(4), 546–553. doi:10.1080/02607476.2020.1802582

Mohammed, T. F., Gin, L. E., Wiesenthal, N. J., & Cooper, K. M. (2022). The experiences of undergraduates with depression in online science learning environments. *CME – Life. CBE Life Sciences Education*, *21*(2), ar18. Advance online publication. doi:10.1187/cbe.21-09-0228 PMID:35294254

Mohammed, T. F., Nadile, E. M., Busch, C. A., Brister, D., Brownell, S. E., Claiborne, C. T., Edwards, B. A., Wolf, J. G., Lunt, C., Tran, M., Vargas, C., Walker, K. M., Warkina, T. D., Witt, M., Zheng, Y., & Cooper, K. M. (2021). Aspects of large-enrollment online college science courses that exacerbate and alleviate student anxiety. *CBE Life Sciences Education*, *20*(4), ar69. Advance online publication. doi:10.1187/cbe.21-05-0132 PMID:34806910

Montag, C., Yang, H., & Elhai, J. D. (2021). On the psychology of TikTok use: A first glimpse from empirical findings. *Frontiers in Public Health*, *9*, 641673. Advance online publication. doi:10.3389/fpubh.2021.641673 PMID:33816425

Moore, M. G. (1997). Theory of transactional distance. In D. Keegan (Ed.), *Theoretical principles of distance education* (pp. 22–38). Routledge.

Moorfield-Lang, H., Copeland, C. A., & Haynes, A. (2016). Accessing abilities: Creating innovative accessible online learning environments and putting quality into practice. *Education for Information*, *32*(1), 27–33. doi:10.3233/EFI-150966

Moos, R. H., Trickett, E. (1974). *Classroom environment scale*. Academic Press.

Moos, R. H. (1979). *Evaluating educational environments*. Jossey-Bass.

Moos, R. H. (1984). Context and coping: Toward a unifying conceptual framework. *American Journal of Community Psychology*, *12*(1), 5–36. doi:10.1007/BF00896933 PMID:6711492

Moos, R. H. (1987). Person-environment congruence in work, school, and health care settings. *Journal of Vocational Behavior*, *31*(3), 231–247. doi:10.1016/0001-8791(87)90041-8

Moos, R. H., & Holahan, C. J. (2017). Environmental Assessment. In *Reference Module in Neuroscience and Biobehavioral Psychology*. Elsevier Inc. doi:10.1016/B978-0-12-809324-5.05552-8

Morante, A., Djenidi, V., Clark, H., & West, S. (2017). Gender differences in online participation: Examining a history and a mathematics open foundation online course. *Australian Journal of Adult Learning*, *57*(2), 266–293.

Morgan, H., & Houghton, A. (2011). *Inclusive curriculum design in higher education: Considerations for effective practice across and within subject areas*. The Higher Education Academy.

Moriña, A. (2019). The keys to learning for university students with disabilities: Motivation, emotion and faculty-student relationships. *PLoS One*, *14*(5), e0215249. doi:10.1371/journal.pone.0215249 PMID:31116748

Morissette, S. B., Ryan-Gonzalez, C., Yufik, T., DeBeer, B. B., Kimbrel, N. A., Sorrells, A. M., Holleran-Steiker, L., Penk, W. E., Gulliver, S. B., & Meyer, E. C. (2021). The effects of posttraumatic stress disorder symptoms on educational functioning in student veterans. *Psychological Services*, *18*(1), 124–133. doi:10.1037er0000356 PMID:31192672

Morris, C. C. (2006). *Narrative theory: A culturally sensitive counseling and research framework*. http://www.counselingoutfitters.com/Morris.htm

Motulsky, S. L., Gere, S. H., Saleem, R., & Trantham, S. M. (2014). Teaching social justice in counseling psychology. *The Counseling Psychologist*, *42*(8), 1058–1083. doi:10.1177/0011000014553855

Moustakas, C. (1994). *Phenomenological research methods*. Sage Publications. doi:10.4135/9781412995658

Mouw, T. (2006). Estimating the causal effect of social capital: A review of recent research. *Annual Review of Sociology*, *32*(1), 79–102. doi:10.1146/annurev.soc.32.061604.123150

Mrvova, K. (2022, July 28). *35 icebreakers perfect for virtual and hybrid meetings*. Slido Blog. https://blog.slido.com/virtual-icebreakers/

Mulenga, E. M., & Marban, J. M. (2020). Is COVID-19 the gateway for digital learning in mathematics education? *Contemporary Educational Technology*, *12*(2), 269. Advance online publication. doi:10.30935/cedtech/7949

Müller, S. (2023). How Slack Facilitates Communication and Collaboration in Seminars and Project-Based Courses. *Journal of Educational Technology Systems*, *51*(3), 303–316. doi:10.1177/00472395231151910

Munshi, K. (2003). Networks in the modern economy: Mexican migrants in the U. S. labor market. *The Quarterly Journal of Economics*, *118*(2), 549–599. doi:10.1162/003355303321675455

Murphy, M. C. (2022). How Social Belonging Impacts Retention at Broad-Access Colleges. *Academic Upshot*. https://www.thirdway.org/report/how-social-belonging-impacts-retention-at-broad-access-colleges

Murphy, E., & Rodriguez, A. M. (2012). Rapport in distance education. *International Review of Research in Open and Distance Learning*, *13*(1), 167–190. doi:10.19173/irrodl.v13i1.1057

Murphy, P. K., Wilkinson, I. A. G., Soter, A. O., Hennessey, M. N., & Alexander, J. F. (2009). Examining the effects of classroom discussion on students' comprehension of text: A meta-analysis. *Journal of Educational Psychology*, *101*(3), 740–764. doi:10.1037/a0015576

Murray, H. A. (1938). *Explorations in personality*. Oxford University Press.

Mustapha, R. (2013). Transforming education toward K-economy in Malaysia. *Educare (San José)*, *6*(1).

Mustika, Yo, Faruqi, & Zhuhra. (n.d.). *Evaluating the Relationship Between Online Learning Environment and Medical Students' Wellbeing During COVID-19 Pandemic*. Academic Press.

Mustika, R., Yo, E. C., Faruqi, M., & Zhuhra, R. T. (2021, October). Evaluating the Relationship Between Online Learning Environment and Medical Students' Wellbeing During COVID-19 Pandemic. *The Malaysian Journal of Medical Sciences : MJMS*, *28*(5), 108–117. doi:10.21315/mjms2021.28.5.11 PMID:35115893

Myers, S. A. (1995). Student perceptions of teacher affinity-seeking and classroom climate. *Communication Research Reports*, *12*(2), 192–199. doi:10.1080/08824099509362056

Myers, S. A., & Rocca, K. A. (2001). Perceived instructor argumentativeness and verbal aggressiveness in the college classroom: Effects on student perceptions of climate, apprehension, and state motivation. *Western Journal of Communication*, *65*(2), 113–137. doi:10.1080/10570310109374696

Nacu, D. C., Martin, C. K., Pinkard, N., & Gray, T. (2016). Analyzing educators' online interactions: A framework of online learning support roles. *Learning, Media and Technology*, *41*(2), 283–305. doi:10.1080/17439884.2015.975722

Nadal, K. L. (2021). *Why representation matters and why it's still not enough: Reflections on growing up brown, queer, and Asian American*. https://www.psychologytoday.com/us/blog/psychology-the-people/202112/why-representation-matters-and-why-it-s-still-not-enough

Nadal, K. L., Wong, Y., Griffin, K. E., Davidoff, K., & Sriken, J. (2014). The adverse impact of racial microaggressions on college students' self-esteem. *Journal of College Student Development*, *55*(5), 461–474. doi:10.1353/csd.2014.0051

Nájera, J. R. (2020). Creating safe space for undocumented students: Building on politically unstable ground. *Anthropology & Education Quarterly*, *51*(3), 341–358. doi:10.1111/aeq.12339

National Center for Education Statistics | U.S. Department of Education. (2023). https://www.ed.gov/category/keyword/national-center-education-statistics

National Center for Education Statistics. (2018, May). *Digest of education statistics.* https://nces.ed.gov/programs/digest/d20/tables/dt20_311.10.asp

National Center for Education Statistics. (2022). *Race/ethnicity of college faculty.* https://nces.ed.gov/fastfacts/display.asp?id=61

National Center for Education Statistics. (2022). *Undergraduate Enrollment. Condition of Education.* https://nces.ed.gov/programs/coe/indicator/cha

National Center for Education Statistics. (2022, April 26). *A majority of college students with disabilities do not inform school, new NCES data shows.* https://nces.ed.gov/whatsnew/press_releases/4_26_2022.asp

National Center for Education Statistics. (2023). Undergraduate Enrollment. In *Condition of Education.* U.S. Department of Education, Institute of Education Sciences. https://nces.ed.gov/programs/coe/indicator/cha

National Center for Education Statistics. (n.d.). *Beginning postsecondary students: 2012/2017 (BPS).* https://nces.ed.gov/datalab/powerstats/71-beginning-postsecondary-students-2012-2017/percentage-distribution

Ness, B. M., & Vroman, K. (2014). Preliminary examination of the impact of traumatic brain injury and posttraumatic stress disorder on self-regulated learning and academic achievement among military service members enrolled in postsecondary education. *The Journal of Head Trauma Rehabilitation*, 29(1), 33–43. doi:10.1097/HTR.0b013e3182a1cd4e PMID:23982790

Ng, T. C. W., Chiu, D. K. W., & Li, K. K. (2022). Motivations of choosing archival studies as major in the i-Schools: Viewpoint between two universities across the Pacific Ocean. *Library Hi Tech*, 40(5), 1483–1496. doi:10.1108/LHT-07-2021-0230

Ni, A. Y. (2013). Comparing the effectiveness of classroom and online learning: Teaching research methods. *Journal of Public Affairs Education*, 19(2), 199–215. doi:10.1080/15236803.2013.12001730

Niazov, Z., Hen, M., & Ferrari, J. R. (2022). Online and academic procrastination in students with learning disabilities: The impact of academic stress and self-efficacy. *Psychological Reports*, 125(2), 890–912. doi:10.1177/0033294120988113 PMID:33573501

Ni, J., Rhim, A. H. R., Chiu, D. K. W., & Ho, K. K. W. (2022). Information search behavior among Chinese self-drive tourists in the smartphone era. *Information Discovery and Delivery*, 50(3), 285–296. doi:10.1108/IDD-05-2020-0054

Nik-Ahmad-Zuky, N. L., Baharuddin, K. A., & Rahim, A. A. (2020). Online clinical teaching and learning for medical undergraduates during the COVID-19 pandemic: The Universiti Sains Malaysia (USM) experience. *Education in Medicine Journal*, 12(2), 75–80. doi:10.21315/eimj2020.12.2.8

Nistor, N. (2013). Stability of attitudes and participation in online university courses: Gender and location effects. *Computers & Education*, 68, 284–292. doi:10.1016/j.compedu.2013.05.016

Nitzburg, G. C., Russo, M., Cuesta-Diaz, A., Ospina, L., Shanahan, M., Perez-Rodriguez, M., McGrath, M., & Burdick, K. E. (2016). Coping strategies and real-world functioning in bipolar disorder. *Journal of Affective Disorders*, 198, 185–188. doi:10.1016/j.jad.2016.03.028 PMID:27017375

Nkonge, B., & Geuldenzolph, L. (2006). Best practices in online education: Implications for policy and practice. *Business Education Digest*, 15, 42–53.

Noor, A. M., Attaran, M., & Alias, N. (2015). Students' experiences in using spectrum: Textbook or classroom? *Procedia: Social and Behavioral Sciences*, 176, 667–673. doi:10.1016/j.sbspro.2015.01.525

O'Neill, P., Duplock, A., & Willis, S. (2006). Using clinical experience in discussion with problem-based learning groups. *Advances in Health Sciences Education : Theory and Practice*, *11*(4), 349–363. doi:10.100710459-006-9014-6 PMID:16937238

Ockerman, M., & Adams, B. (2019). Teaching across settings. In L. Haddock & J. Whitman (Eds.), Preparing the educator in counselor education: A comprehensive guide to building knowledge and developing skills (pp. 190-212). Routledge.

Odriozola-González, P., Planchuelo-Gómez, Á., Irurtia, M. J., & de Luis-García, R. (2020). Psychological effects of the COVID-19 outbreak and lockdown among students and workers of a Spanish university. *Psychiatry Research*, *290*, 113108. doi:10.1016/j.psychres.2020.113108 PMID:32450409

Okechukwu, A. (2019). *To fulfill these rights: Political struggle over affirmative action and open admissions*. Columbia University Press. doi:10.7312/okec18308

Olson, A. L., & Peterson, R. L. (2015, April). *Student engagement, strategy brief*. Lincoln, NE: Student Engagement Project, University of Nebraska-Lincoln and the Nebraska Department of Education. https://k12engagement.unl.edu/student-engagement

Olson, J. N., & Carter, J. A. (2014). Caring and the college professor. *National Forum Journals: Focus on Colleges, Universities, and Schools*, *8*(1), 1-9. http://www.nationalforum.com/Electronic%20Journal%20Volumes/Olson,%20James%20Caring%20and%20the%20College%20Professor%20FOCUS%20V8%20N1%202014.pdf

Olt, P., & Jones, E. J. (2024). Campbell's Law and online discussion: From quantitative minima to social engagement [Manuscript unpublished]. Advanced Education Programs, Fort Hays State University.

Ong, S. G. T., & Quek, G. C. L. (2023). Enhancing teacher–student interactions and student online engagement in an online learning environment. *Learning Environments Research*, *26*(3), 681–707. doi:10.100710984-022-09447-5 PMID:36685638

Oren, A., Mioduser, D., & Nachmias, R. (2002). The development of social climate in virtual learning discussion groups. *International Review of Research in Open and Distance Learning*, *3*(1), 1–19. doi:10.19173/irrodl.v3i1.80

Organisation for Economic Co-operation and Development. (2020). *The potential of online learning for adults: Early lessons from the COVID-19 crisis*. OECD Publishing.

Organization for Economic Cooperation & Development. (2014). *Education at a Glance 2014: OECD Indicators*. OECD Publishing. doi:10.1787/eag-2014-

Orji, F. A., Vassileva, J., & Greer, J. E. (2018). Personalized Persuasion for Promoting Students' Engagement and Learning. *PPT@ PERSUASIVE*, *18*, 77-87.

Orr, R., Williams, M. R., & Pennington, K. (2009). Institutional efforts to support faculty in online teaching. *Innovative Higher Education*, *34*(4), 257–268. doi:10.100710755-009-9111-6

Otchie, W. O., & Pedaste, M. (2020). Using social media for learning in high schools: A systematic literature review. *European Journal of Educational Research*, *9*(2), 889–903. doi:10.12973/eu-jer.9.2.889

Ouled Salem, F. (2023). *Faculty-student and student-student connections amidst the COVID-19 pandemic* (Order No. 30527974). Available from Dissertations & Theses @ Walden University. (2827837803). https://www.proquest.com/dissertations-theses/faculty-student-connections-amidst-covid-19/docview/2827837803/se-2

Oxford Concise English Dictionary. (2011). Adaptability. In Oxford Concise English Dictionary (12th ed., p.16). Academic Press.

Pacansky-Brock, M. (2013). *Best practices for teaching with emerging technologies*. Routledge.

Pacansky-Brock, M., Smedshammer, M., & Vincent-Layton, K. (2020). Humanizing online teaching to equitize higher education. *Current Issues in Education (Tempe, Ariz.), 21*(2).

Pace, J. L. (2022). Learning to teach controversial issues in a divided society: Adaptive appropriation of pedagogical tools. *Democracy & Education, 30*(1), 1–11.

Padilla, A. M. (1994). Research news and comment: Ethnic minority scholars; research, and mentoring: Current and future issues. *Educational Researcher, 23*(4), 24–27. doi:10.3102/0013189X023004024

Painter, C., Coffin, C., & Hewings, A. (2003). Impacts of directed tutorial activities in computer conferencing: A case study. *Distance Education, 24*(2), 159–173. doi:10.1080/0158791032000127455

Paldam, M. (2000). Social capital: One or many? Definition and measurement. *Journal of Economic Surveys, 14*(5), 629–653. doi:10.1111/1467-6419.00127

Palloff, R. M., & Pratt, K. (1999). *Building learning communitities in cyberspace: Effective strategies for the online classroom*. Jossey-Bass.

Palloff, R. M., & Pratt, K. (2007). *Building online learning communities: Effective strategies for the virtual classroom*. John Wiley & Sons.

Palloff, R. M., & Pratt, K. (2013). *Lessons from the Virtual Classroom* (2nd ed.). Jossey-Bass.

Palloff, R. M., & Pratt, K. (2013). *Lessons from the virtual classroom: The realities of online teaching*. John Wiley & Sons.

Palloff, R. M., Pratt, K., & Stockley, D. (2001). Building learning communities in cyberspace: Effective strategies for the online classroom. *Canadian Journal of Higher Education, 31*(3), 175–178. https://www.proquest.com/scholarly-journals/building-learning-communities-cyberspace/docview/221229996/se-2

Parizeau, K. (2022). Instructor perspectives on student mental health. *Canadian Journal of Higher Education, 52*(2), 67–80. doi:10.47678/cjhe.v52i2.189391

Parker, J., & Herrington, J. (2015). *Setting the Climate in an Authentic Online Community of Learning*. Australian Association for Research in Education.

Parsazadeh, N., Cheng, P.-Y., Wu, T.-T., & Huang, Y.-M. (2021). Integrating Computational Thinking Concept Into Digital Storytelling to Improve Learners' Motivation and Performance. *Journal of Educational Computing Research, 59*(3), 470–495. doi:10.1177/0735633120967315

Paudel, P. (2021). Online education: Benefits, challenges and strategies during and after COVID-19 in higher education. *International Journal on Studies in Education, 3*(2), 70–85. doi:10.46328/ijonse.32

Paul, J. D., & Maranto, R. (2023). Elite schools lead an empirical examination of diversity requirements in higher education job markets. *Studies in Higher Education, 48*(2), 314–328. doi:10.1080/03075079.2022.2134334

Paul, J., & Jeferson, F. (2019). A comparative analysis of student performance in an online vs. face-to-face environmental science course from 2009 to 2016. *Frontiers of Computer Science, 1*(7), 7. Advance online publication. doi:10.3389/fcomp.2019.00007

Pawlak, M., Derakhshan, A., Mehdizadeh, M., & Kruk, M. (2022). Boredom in online English language classes: Mediating variables and coping strategies. *Language Teaching Research*. Advance online publication. doi:10.1177/13621688211064944

Payne, R., Harrison, A., & Griffin, M. (2020, September). *Mentorship and African American women: Exploring topics that arise in safe spaces* [Presentation]. Walden University National Faculty Meeting, Virtual.

Payne, R., Harrison, A., & Griffin, M. (2021, August 19). *Confronting integration, belonging and isolation of graduate students of color* [Presentation]. Walden University Real-World Solutions to Real-World Problems: Expanding the Women-in-Leadership Advantage, Virtual.

Payne, R., Harrison, A., & Griffin, M. (2023). *"Safe spaces are built": How African American women discuss personal and professional connectedness in online doctoral program* [Manuscript submitted for publication].

Payne, M. (2020). *The origins of social work: Continuity and change*. Bloomsbury Publishing.

Pearce, N., & Learmonth, S. (2013). Learning beyond the classroom: Evaluating the use of Pinterest in learning and teaching in an introductory anthropology class. *Journal of Interactive Media in Education*, *2*(2), 12. Advance online publication. doi:10.5334/2013-12

Pedersen, D. E. (2020). Bipolar disorder and the college student: A review and implications for universities. *Journal of American College Health*, *68*(4), 341–346. doi:10.1080/07448481.2019.1573173 PMID:30908152

Peechapol, C., Na-Songkhla, J., Sujiva, S., & Luangsodsai, A. (2018). An exploration of factors influencing self-efficacy in online learning: A systematic review. *International Journal of Emerging Technologies in Learning*, *13*(9), 64. doi:10.3991/ijet.v13i09.8351

Pemberton, C. L. A., & Akkary, R. K. (2010). A cohort, is a cohort, is a cohort… or is it? *Journal of Research on Leadership Education*, *5*(5), 179–208. doi:10.1177/194277511000500501

Perera-Diltz, D. M., & Greenidge, W. L. (2018). Mindfulness techniques to promote culturally appropriate engagement. *Journal of Creativity in Mental Health*, *13*(4), 490–504. doi:10.1080/15401383.2018.1459215

Perna, M. C. (2022, March 28). *The life of a teacher and why it's beyond hard*. Forbes. https://www.forbes.com/sites/markcperna/2022/03/28/the-life-of-a-teacher-and-why-its-beyond-hard

Petts, A. L. (2022). Attitudes about affirmative action in higher education admissions. *The Sociological Quarterly*, *63*(4), 711–732. doi:10.1080/00380253.2021.1951627

Pew Research Center. (2021). *Social Media Fact Sheet*. https://www.pewresearch.org/internet/fact-sheet/social-media/

Phirangee, K., Epp, C. D., & Hewitt, J. (2016). Exploring the relationships between facilitation methods, students' sense of community, and their online behaviors. *Online Learning : the Official Journal of the Online Learning Consortium*, *20*(2), 134–154. doi:10.24059/olj.v20i2.775

Phirangee, K., & Malec, A. (2017). Othering in online learning: An examination of social presence, identity, and sense of community. *Distance Education*, *38*(2), 160–172. doi:10.1080/01587919.2017.1322457

Pike, G. R., Kuh, G. D., & McCormick, A. C. (2011). An investigation of the contingent relationships between learning community participation and student engagement. *Research in Higher Education*, *52*(3), 300–322. doi:10.100711162-010-9192-1

Pinterest. (2023a). *All about Pinterest*. https://help.pinterest.com/en/guide/all-about-pinterest

Pinterest. (2023b). *Why Pinterest*. https://business.pinterest.com/

Platz, M., Platz, M. (2021). Trust in the Teacher-Student Relationship. *Good Relationships in Schools: Teachers, Students, and the Epistemic Aims of Education*, 65-81.

Pollard, R., & Kumar, S. (2021). Mentoring graduate students online: Strategies and challenges. *International Review of Research in Open and Distance Learning, 22*(2), 267–284. doi:10.19173/irrodl.v22i2.5093

Poole, D. M. (2000). Student participation in a discussion-oriented online course: A case study. *Journal of Research on Computing in Education, 33*(2), 162–177. doi:10.1080/08886504.2000.10782307

Pophal, L. (2023). ChatGPT: Opportunities and Risks Related to AI-Generated Content. *Information Today, 40*(2), 36–38.

PopoloM. (2013). *How to use Pinterest for beginners.* https://www.pcmag.com/news/how-to-use-pinterest-for-beginners

Porter, C. M., Woo, S. E., & Campion, M. A. (2016). Internal and external networking differentially predict turnover through job embeddedness and job offers. *Personnel Psychology, 69*(3), 635–672. doi:10.1111/peps.12121

Prakash, J., Chatterjee, K., Guha, S., Srivastava, K., & Chauhan, V. S. (2021). Adult attention-deficit hyperactivity disorder: From clinical reality toward conceptual clarity. *Industrial Psychiatry Journal, 30*(1), 23–28. doi:10.4103/ipj.ipj_7_21 PMID:34483520

Prashantham, S. (2010). Social capital and Indian Micromultinationals. *British Journal of Management, 22*(1), 4–20. doi:10.1111/j.1467-8551.2010.00720.x

Pressley, T., Ha, C., & Learn, E. (2021). Teacher stress and anxiety during COVID-19: An empirical study. *School Psychology, 36*(5), 367–376. doi:10.1037pq0000468 PMID:34591587

Preston, D. (2017). *Untold barriers for Black students in higher education: Placing race at the center of developmental education.* https://southerneducation.org/wp-content/uploads/untold-barriers-for-black-students-in-higher-ed.pdf

Price, E., Lau, A. C., Goldberg, F., Turpen, C., Smith, P. S., Dancy, M., & Robinson, S. (2021). Analyzing a faculty online learning community as a mechanism for supporting faculty implementation of a guided-inquiry curriculum. *International Journal of STEM Education, 8*(1), 1–26. doi:10.118640594-020-00268-7 PMID:33643775

Price, L. (2006). Gender differences and similarities in online courses: Challenging stereotypical views of women. *Journal of Computer Assisted Learning, 22*(5), 349–359. doi:10.1111/j.1365-2729.2006.00181.x

Prinsen, F. R., Volman, M. L., & Terwel, J. (2007). Gender-related differences in computer-mediated communication and computer-supported collaborative learning. *Journal of Computer Assisted Learning, 23*(5), 393–409. doi:10.1111/j.1365-2729.2007.00224.x

Prior, D. D., Mazanov, J., Meacheam, D., Heaslip, G., & Hanson, J. (2016). Attitude, digital literacy, and self-efficacy: Flow-on effects for online learning behavior. *The Internet and Higher Education, 29*, 91–97. doi:10.1016/j.iheduc.2016.01.001

Prochaska, J. O., & Norcross, J. C. (2018). *Systems of psychotherapy: A transtheoretical analysis.* Oxford University Press.

Puhy, C., Prakash, N., Lacson, C., & Bradt, J. (2021). Multicultural teaching competence among undergraduate faculty: A convergent mixed methods study. *Journal for Multicultural Education, 15*(4), 459–473. doi:10.1108/JME-05-2021-0059

Pumptow, M., & Brahm, T. (2021). Students' Digital Media Self-Efficacy and Its Importance for Higher Education Institutions: Development and Validation of a Survey Instrument. *Tech Know Learn, 26*(3), 555–575. doi:10.100710758-020-09463-5

Putnam, R. D. (1995). Bowling alone: America's declining social capital. *Journal of Democracy, 6*(1), 65–78. doi:10.1353/jod.1995.0002

Qiang, H. (2018). Teachers' roles in online learning: The student perspective. *Irish Journal of Academic Practice., 7*(1).

Qiu, F. (2022, October 21). Reviewing the role of positive classroom climate in improving English as a foreign language students' social interactions in the online classroom. *Frontiers in Psychology, 13*, 1012524. doi:10.3389/fpsyg.2022.1012524 PMID:36337469

Radu, M. C., Schnakovszky, C., Herghelegiu, E., Ciubotariu, V. A., & Cristea, I. (2020). The impact of the COVID-19 pandemic on the quality of educational process: A student survey. *International Journal of Environmental Research and Public Health, 17*(21), 7770. doi:10.3390/ijerph17217770 PMID:33114192

Ragusa, A. T., & Crampton, A. (2018). Sense of connection, identity and academic success in distance education: Sociologically exploring online learning environments. *Rural Society, 27*(2), 125–142. doi:10.1080/10371656.2018.1472914

Ramos-Morcillo, A. J., Leal-Costa, C., Moral-García, J. E., & Ruzafa-Martínez, M. (2020). Experiences of nursing students during the abrupt change from face-to-face to e-learning education during the first month of confinement due to COVID-19 in Spain. *International Journal of Environmental Research and Public Health, 17*(15), 5519. doi:10.3390/ijerph17155519 PMID:32751660

Rania, N., Siri, A., Bagnasco, A., Aleo, G., & Sasso, L. (2014). Academic climate, well-being and academic performance in a university degree course. *Journal of Nursing Management, 22*(6), 751–760. doi:10.1111/j.1365-2834.2012.01471.x PMID:23617787

Rapanta, C., Botturi, L., Goodyear, P., Guàrdia, L., & Koole, M. (2021). Balancing technology, pedagogy and the new normal: Post-pandemic challenges for higher education. *Postdigital Science and Education, 3*(3), 715–742. doi:10.100742438-021-00249-1

Raposa, E. B., Hagler, M., Liu, D., & Rhodes, J. E. (2021). Predictors of close faculty-student relationships and mentorship in higher education: Findings from the Gallup-Purdue Index. *Annals of the New York Academy of Sciences, 1483*(1), 36–49. doi:10.1111/nyas.14342 PMID:32242962

Raskin, J. D. (2008). The evolution of constructivism. *Journal of Constructivist Psychology, 21*(1), 1–24. doi:10.1080/10720530701734331

Ratcliff, J. J., Minster, K. I., & Monheim, C. (2021). Engaging students in an online format during the COVID-19 pandemic: A jury voir dire activity. *Scholarship of Teaching and Learning in Psychology*. Advance online publication. doi:10.1037tl0000246

Ratts, M. J., Singh, A. A., Nassar-McMillan, S., Butler, S. K., & McCullough, J. R. (2017). Multicultural and Social Justice Counseling Competencies: A leadership framework for professional school counselors. *Professional School Counseling, 21*(1b). doi:10.1177/2156759X18773582

Ratts, M. J., Singh, A. A., Nassar-McMillan, S., Butler, S. K., & McCullough, J. R. (2016). Multicultural and social justice counseling competencies: Guidelines for the counseling profession. *Journal of Multicultural Counseling and Development, 44*(1), 28–48. doi:10.1002/jmcd.12035

Ray, C. M., Sormunen, C., & Harris, T. M. (1999). Men's and women's attitudes toward computer technology: A comparison. *Office Systems Research Journal, 17*, 1–8.

Raymundo, M. R. D. R. (2020). Fostering creativity through online creative collaborative group projects. *Asian Association of Open Universities Journal, 15*(1), 97–113. doi:10.1108/AAOUJ-10-2019-0048

Raza, S. H., & Reddy, E. (2021). Intentionality and players of effective online courses in mathematics. *Frontiers in Applied Mathematics and Statistics, 7*, 612327. Advance online publication. doi:10.3389/fams.2021.612327

Read, J. P., Ouimette, P., White, J., Colder, C., & Farrow, S. (2011). Rates of *DSM–IV–TR* trauma exposure and post-traumatic stress disorder among newly matriculated college students. *Psychological Trauma: Theory, Research, Practice, and Policy*, *3*(2), 148–156. doi:10.1037/a0021260 PMID:25621098

Reddick, R. J. (2015). Of feral faculty and magisterial Mowgli: The domestication of junior faculty. In C. Turner (Ed.), *New directions for higher education* (pp. 43–51). Jossey-Bass., doi:10.1002/he.20141

Reeve, J. (2016). Autonomy-supportive teaching: What is is, how to do it. In *Building autonomous learners: Perspectives from research and practice using self-determination theory* (pp. 129–152). Springer Singapore. doi:10.1007/978-981-287-630-0_7

Reeves, A., & Stewart, S. L. (2015). Exploring the integration of Indigenous healing and western psychotherapy for sexual trauma survivors who use mental health services at Anishnawbe Health Toronto. *Canadian Journal of Counselling and Psychotherapy*, *49*(1).

Reid, L. D., & Radhakrishnan, P. (2003). Race matters: The relation between race and general campus climate. *Cultural Diversity & Ethnic Minority Psychology*, *9*(3), 263–275. doi:10.1037/1099-9809.9.3.263 PMID:12971093

Reyes, M. R. (2020). The role of empathy in creating a sense of belonging in online learning environments. *The Journal of Scholarship of Teaching and Learning*, *20*(3), 1–12.

Rhoades, G. (2012). *Faculty engagement to enhance student attainment* [White paper]. National Commission on Higher Education Attainment. https://www.acenet.edu/news-room/Documents/Faculty-Engagement-to-EnhanceStudent-Attainment--Rhoades.pdf

Richards, J., & Schubert-Irastorza, C. (2013). Valuing creativity in online teaching. *Journal of Research in Innovative Teaching*, *6*(1), 68–79.

Richardson, C., Mishra, P., & Henriksen, D. (2021). Creativity in online learning and teacher education: An interview with Leanna Archambault. *TechTrends*, *65*(6), 914–918. doi:10.100711528-021-00669-7

Richardson, J. T., & Woodley, A. (2003). Another look at the role of age, gender and subject as predictors of academic attainment in higher education. *Studies in Higher Education*, *28*(4), 475–493. doi:10.1080/0307507032000122305

Rigamonti, L., Dolci, A., Galetta, F., Stefanelli, C., Hughes, M., Bartsch, M., Seidelmeier, I., Bonaventura, K., & Back, D. A. (2020). Social media and e-learning use among European exercise science students. *Health Promotion International*, *35*(3), 470–477. doi:10.1093/heapro/daz046 PMID:31071200

Rinke, C. R., Williams, S. A. S., Conlin, V., & Coshal, S. (2021). Shaping an inclusive higher education curriculum: Building capacity for transformational change. *School Psychology Training & Pedagogy*, *38*(1), 24–36.

Rios, T., Elliot, M., & Mandernach, B. J. (2008). Efficient instructional strategies for maximizing online student satisfaction. *The Journal of Educators Online*, *15*(3). Advance online publication. doi:10.9743/jeo.2018.15.3.7

Robb, M., & Spadaro, K. (2022). Exploration of online doctor of nursing practice students' perceptions of effective teaching methods using the critical incident technique. *Nurse Educator*, *47*(6), 328–331. doi:10.1097/NNE.0000000000001217 PMID:35503108

Robinson, C., & Taylor, C. (2007). Theorizing student voice: Values and perspectives. *Improving Schools*, *10*(1), 5–17. doi:10.1177/1365480207073702

Robison, L. J., Schmid, A. A., & Siles, M. E. (2002). Is social capital really capital? *Review of Social Economy*, *60*(1), 1–21. doi:10.1080/00346760110127074

Roblyer, M. D., McDaniel, M., Webb, M., Herman, J., & Witty, J. V. (2010). Findings on Facebook in higher education: A comparison of college faculty and student uses and perceptions of social networking sites. *The Internet and Higher Education*, *13*(3), 134–140. doi:10.1016/j.iheduc.2010.03.002

Roby, T., Ashe, S., Singh, N., & Clark, C. (2013). Shaping the online experience: How administrators can influence student and instructor perceptions through policy and practice. *The Internet and Higher Education*, *17*, 29–37. doi:10.1016/j.iheduc.2012.09.004

Rodriguez, M. C., Ooms, A., Montanez, M., & Yan, Y. L. (2005). *Perceptions of online learning quality given comfort with technology, motivation to learn technology skills, satisfaction, and online learning experience*. Paper presented at the Annual meeting of the American Educational Research Association, Montreal.

Rogers, C. R. (1961). *On becoming a person: A therapist's view of psychotherapy*. Robinson.

Rogers, S., Aytur, S., Gardner, K., & Carlson, C. (2012). Measuring community sustainability: Exploring the intersection of the built environment & social capital with a participatory case study. *Journal of Environmental Studies and Sciences*, *2*(2), 143–153. doi:10.100713412-012-0068-x

Rohr, L., Squires, L., & Peters, A. (2022). Examining the use of X in online classes: Can X improve interaction and engagement? *The Canadian Journal for the Scholarship of Teaching and Learning*, *13*(1), 9. Advance online publication. doi:10.5206/cjsotlrcacea.2022.1.10892

Romrell, D., Kidder, L., & Wood, E. (2014). The SAMR model as a framework for evaluating mLearning. *Online Learning Journal*, *18*(2).

Rose, M. (2018). What are some key attributes of effective online teachers? *Journal of Open. Flexible and Distance Learning*, *22*(2), 32–48. doi:10.61468/jofdl.v22i2.336

Ross-Gordon, J. M. (2003). Adult learners in the classroom. *New Directions for Student Services*, *2003*(102), 43–52. doi:10.1002s.88

Ross, S. M. (2019). Slack it to me: Complementing LMS with student-centric communications for the millenial/post-millenial student. *Journal of Marketing Education*, *41*(2), 91–108. doi:10.1177/0273475319833113

Rovai, A. (2002). Building Sense of Community at a Distance. *International Review of Research in Open and Distance Learning*, *3*(1), 1–16. doi:10.19173/irrodl.v3i1.79

Rovai, A. (2007). Facilitating online discussions effectively. *The Internet and Higher Education*, *1*(1), 77–88. doi:10.1016/j.iheduc.2006.10.001

Rovai, A. P. (2002). Development of an instrument to measure classroom community. *The Internet and Higher Education*, *5*(3), 197–211. doi:10.1016/S1096-7516(02)00102-1

Rovai, A. P., & Downey, J. R. (2010). Why some distance education programs fail while others succeed in a global environment. *The Internet and Higher Education*, *13*(3), 141–147. doi:10.1016/j.iheduc.2009.07.001

Rovai, A. P., & Wighting, M. J. (2005). Feelings of alienation and community among higher education students in a virtual classroom. *The Internet and Higher Education*, *8*(2), 97–110. doi:10.1016/j.iheduc.2005.03.001

Rovai, A., & Jordan, H. (2004). Blended Learning and Sense of Community: A comparative analysis with traditional and fully online graduate courses. *International Review of Research in Open and Distance Learning*, *5*(2), 1–13. doi:10.19173/irrodl.v5i2.192

Ruey, S. (2010). A case study of constructivist instructional strategies for adult online learning. *British Journal of Educational Technology*, *41*(5), 706720. doi:10.1111/j.1467-8535.2009.00965.x

Rutter, M. (2000). School effects on pupil progress: Research findings and policy implications. In Psychology of education: Major themes (Vol. 1, pp. 3–50). London: Falmer Press.

Ruus, V. R., Veisson, M., Leino, M., Ots, L., Pallas, L., Sarv, E. S., & Veisson, A. (2007). Students well-being, coping, academic success, and school climate. *Social Behavior and Personality*, *35*(7), 919–936. doi:10.2224bp.2007.35.7.919

Saadé, R. G., Kira, D., Mak, T., & Nebebe, F. (2017). *Anxiety and performance in online learning. In Proceedings of the Informing Science and Information Technology Education Conference*. Informing Science Institute. https://www.informingscience.org/Publications/3736

Sabin, J., & Olive, A. (2018). Slack: Adopting social-networking platforms for active learning. *PS, Political Science & Politics*, *51*(1), 183–189. doi:10.1017/S1049096517001913

Sabolović-Krajina, D. (2021). Društveni utjecaj narodnih knjižnica tijekom pandemije COVID-19 u kontekstu koncepta pametnih gradova – komparacija Singapura I Hrvatske [The social impact of public libraries during the COVID-19 pandemic in the context of the concept of the smart cities – Comparison of Singapore and Croatia]. *Vjesnik bibliotekara Hrvatske, 64*(1), 250-278. doi:10.30754/vbh.64.1.853

Sadeghi, M. (2019). A shift from classroom to distance learning: Advantages and limitations. *International Journal of Research in English Education*, *4*(1), 80–88. doi:10.29252/ijree.4.1.80

Sadera, W. A., Robertson, J., Song, L., & Midon, M. N. (2009). The role of community in online learning success. *Journal of Online Learning and Teaching*, *5*(2), 277–284.

Salim, J., Tandy, S., Arnindita, J. N., Wibisono, J. J., Haryanto, M. R., & Wibisono, M. G. (2022). Zoom fatigue and its risk factors in online during the COVID-19 pandemic. *Medical Journal of Indonesia*, *31*(1), 13–19. doi:10.13181/mji.oa.225703

Salim, N., Gere, B., Talley, W., & Irioogbe, B. (2023). College students mental health challenges: Concerns and considerations in the COVID-19 pandemic. *Journal of College Student Psychotherapy*, *37*(1), 39–51. doi:10.1080/87568225.2021.1890298

Sanders, M. J., Van Oss, T., & McGeary, S. (2016). Analyzing Reflections in Service Learning to Promote Personal Growth and Community Self-Efficacy. *Journal of Experiential Education*, *39*(1), 73–88. doi:10.1177/1053825915608872

Sangaramoorthy, T., & Richardson, B. J. (2020). *Black lives matter without Black people?* https://www.insidehighered.com/advice/2020/10/16/many-people-deny-how-pervasive-racism-higher-ed-and-how-its-often-reproduced

Santa-Ramirez, S. (2022). Sink or swim: The mentoring experiences of Latinx PhD students with faculty of color. *Journal of Diversity in Higher Education*, *15*(1), 124–134. doi:10.1037/dhe0000335

Santa-Ramirez, S., Block, S., Vargas, A., Muralidhar, K., & Ikegwuonu, C. (2022). "It was rough": The experiences of first-generation collegians transitioning into higher education amid COVID-19. *New Directions for Higher Education*, *2022*(199), 41–56. doi:10.1002/he.20451

Sargent, A. G., & Schlossberg, N. K. (1988). Managing Adult Transitions. *Training and Development Journal*, *42*(12), 58–60.

Sargent, P. (2001). *Real men or real teachers? Contradictions in the lives of men elementary school teachers*. Men's Studies Press. doi:10.1177/1097184X00002004003

Sarkis, J., Cohen, M. J., Dewick, P., & Schröder, P. (2020). A brave new world: Lessons from the COVID-19 pandemic for transitioning to sustainable supply and production. *Resources, Conservation and Recycling*, *159*, 104894. doi:10.1016/j.resconrec.2020.104894 PMID:32313383

Sason, H., Wasserman, E., Safrai, M. Z., & Romi, S. (2022). Students' perception of the role of online teachers: Comparing routine and emergency times. *Frontiers in Education*, *6*, 569. doi:10.3389/feduc.2021.767700

Sax, L. J., Byrant, A. N., & Harper, C. E. (2005). The differential effects of student-faculty interaction on college outcomes for women and men. *Journal of College Student Development*, *46*(6), 642–657. doi:10.1353/csd.2005.0067

Sbaratta, C. A., Tirpak, D. M., & Schlosser, L. Z. (2015). Male-male advising relationships in graduate psychology: A diminishing dyad. *Sex Roles*, *72*(7-8), 335–348. Advance online publication. doi:10.100711199-015-0466-0

Scarpena, K., Riley, M., & Keathley, M. (2018). Creating successful professional development activities for online faculty: A reorganized framework. *Online Journal of Distance Learning Administration*, *21*(1), 1–8.

Scharmer, O. (2015, February 17). U.Lab: Seven principles for revolutionizing higher ed. *HuffPost*. https://www.huffpost.com/entry/ulab-seven-principles-for_b_6697584

Scherer, A. M., Gedlinske, A. M., Parker, A. M., Gidengil, C. A., Askelson, N. M., Petersen, C. A., & Lindley, M. C. (2021). Acceptability of adolescent COVID-19 vaccination among adolescents and parents of adolescents—United States, April 15–23, 2021. *Morbidity and Mortality Weekly Report*, *70*(28), 997. doi:10.15585/mmwr.mm7028e1 PMID:34264908

Schlossberg, N. K. (1981). Adult Transitions. *The Counseling Psychologist*, *9*(2), 2–18. doi:10.1177/001100008100900202

Schlossberg, N. K. (1989). Marginality and mattering: Key issues in building community. *New Directions for Student Services*, *48*(1), 5–15. doi:10.1002s.37119894803

Schlossberg, N. K., Waters, E. B., & Goodman, J. (1995). *Counseling adults in transition* (2nd ed.). Springer.

Schmidt, S. W., Hodge, E. M., & Tschida, C. M. (2013). How university faculty members developed their online teaching skills. *Quarterly Review of Distance Education*, *14*(3), 131–140.

Schneider, M., & Yin, L. (2011). *The high cost of low graduation rates: How much does dropping out of college really cost?* American Institutes for Research. https://files.eric.ed.gov/fulltext/ED523102.pdf

Schrader, D. E. (2004). Intellectual safety, moral atmosphere, and epistemology in college classrooms. *Journal of Adult Development*, *11*(2), 87–101. doi:10.1023/B:JADE.0000024542.67919.55

Schuessler, J. H. (2017). "Chunking" Semester Projects: Does it Enhance Student Learning? *Journal of Higher Education Theory and Practice*, *17*(7). https://articlegateway.com/index.php/JHETP/article/view/1474

Schunk, D. H., & Mullen, C. A. (2012). Self-Efficacy as an Engaged Learner. In S. Christenson, A. Reschly, & C. Wylie (Eds.), *Handbook of Research on Student Engagement*. Springer. doi:10.1007/978-1-4614-2018-7_10

Schwartz, H. L. (2019). *Connected teaching: Relationship, power, and mattering in higher education*. Stylus Publishing.

Schwartz, H. L. (2019). Connected teaching: Relationships, power, and mattering in higher education. *Stylus (Rio de Janeiro)*.

Scott, B. L., Muñoz, S. M., & Scott, S. B. (2022). How whiteness operates at a Hispanic serving institution: A qualitative case study of faculty, staff, and administrators. *Journal of Diversity in Higher Education*. Advance online publication. doi:10.1037/dhe0000438

Scott, L., & Sharp, L. A. (2019). Black males who hold advanced degrees: Critical factors that preclude and promote success. *The Journal of Negro Education*, *88*(1), 44–61. doi:10.7709/jnegroeducation.88.1.0044

Seaman, J. E., Allen, I. E., & Seaman, J. (2018). *Grade increase: Tracking distance education in the United States*. https://www.bayviewanalytics.com/reports/gradeincrease.pdf

Seaman, J. E., Allen, I. E., & Seaman, J. (2018). *Grade increase: Tracking distance education in the United States*. Babson Survey Research Group.

Seay, A. K. M., Benavides, M. T., Eddington, S. M., & Coleman, J. A. (2022). Beyond perspective taking: Fostering equity through critical empathy and intercultural listening. In A. M. Seay, M. T. Benavides, S. M. Eddington, & J. A. Coleman (Eds.), *Achieving equity in higher education using empathy as a guiding principle* (pp. 141–171). IGI Global. doi:10.4018/978-1-7998-9746-0.ch007

Seery, K., Barreda, A. A., Hein, S. G., & Hiller, J. K. (2021). Retention strategies for online students: A systematic literature review. *Journal of Global Education and Research*, *5*(1), 72–84. doi:10.5038/2577-509X.5.1.1105

Seif, H. (2009). *The Civic education and engagement of Latina/o immigrant youth: Challenging boundaries and creating safe spaces*. Research Paper Series on Latino Immigrant Civic and Political Participation, no 5. University of Illinois.

Seligman, M. E. (2011). *Flourish: A visionary new understanding of happiness and well-being*. Simon and Schuster.

Seligman, M. E., Ernst, R. M., Gillham, J., Reivich, K., & Linkins, M. (2009). Positive education: Positive psychology and classroom interventions. *Oxford Review of Education*, *35*(3), 293–311. doi:10.1080/03054980902934563

Sells, J., Tan, A., Brogan, J., Dahlen, U., & Stupart, Y. (2012). Preparing international counselor educators through online distance learning. *International Journal for the Advancement of Counseling*, *34*(1), 39–54. doi:10.100710447-011-9126-4

Selwyn, N. (2007). The use of computer technology in university teaching and learning: A critical perspective. *Journal of Computer Assisted Learning*, *23*(2), 83–94. doi:10.1111/j.1365-2729.2006.00204.x

Severiens, S., & ten Dam, G. (2012). Leaving college: A gender comparison in male and female-dominated programs. *Research in Higher Education*, *53*(4), 453–470. doi:10.100711162-011-9237-0

Seymour, G. (2016). The compassionate makerspace: Grief and healing in a high school library makerspace. *Teacher Librarian*, *43*(5), 28.

Shahnama, M., Yazdanmehr, E., & Elahi Shirvan, M. (2021). Challenges of online language teaching during the COVID-19 pandemic: A process tracing approach. *Teaching English as a Second Language*, *40*(3), 159–195.

Shapiro, S. (2020). Fostering online learning communities: Strategies to support collaboration and interaction in virtual classrooms. *EDUCAUSE Review*. Retrieved from https://er.educause.edu/articles/2020/10/fostering-online-learning-communities-strategies-to-support-collaboration-and-interaction-in-virtual-classrooms

Sharin, A. N. (2021). E-learning during COVID-19: A review of literature. *Journal Pengajian Media Malaysia*, *23*(1), 15–28. doi:10.22452/jpmm.vol23no1.2

Sharoff, L. (2019). Creative and innovative online teaching strategies: Facilitation for active participation. *The Journal of Educators Online*, *16*(2). Advance online publication. doi:10.9743/JEO.2019.16.2.9

Shavers, M. C., & Moore, J. L. III. (2014). Black female voices: Self-presentation strategies in doctoral programs at predominately White institutions. *Journal of College Student Development*, *55*(4), 391–407. doi:10.1353/csd.2014.0040

Shea, P., Li, C. S., Swan, K., & Pickett, A. (2005). Developing learning community in online asynchronous college courses: The role of teaching presence. *Journal of Asynchronous Learning Networks*, *9*(4), 59–82.

Shea, P., Swan, K., Fredericksen, E., & Pickett, A. (2002). Student satisfaction and reported learning in the SUNY learning network. *Elements of Quality Online Education*, *3*, 145–156.

Sheard, M. (2009). Hardiness commitment, gender, and age differentiate university academic performance. *The British Journal of Educational Psychology*, *79*(1), 189–204. doi:10.1348/000709908X304406 PMID:18466672

She, L., & Martin, F. (2022). Systematic review (2000 to 2021) of online accessibility research in higher education. *American Journal of Distance Education*, *36*(4), 327–346. doi:10.1080/08923647.2022.2081438

Shen, D. M., Cho, M. H., Tsai, C. L., & Marra, R. (2013). Unpacking online learning experiences: Online learning self-efficacy and learning satisfaction. *The Internet and Higher Education*, *19*, 10–17. doi:10.1016/j.iheduc.2013.04.001

Shen-Miller, D. S., Olson, D., & Boling, T. (2011). Masculinity in non-traditional occupations: Ecological constructions. *American. Journal of Men's Studies*, *5*(1), 18–29. doi:10.1177/1557988309358443 PMID:20038508

Shen-Miller, D., & Smiler, A. (2015). Men in female-dominated vocations: A rationale for academic study and introduction to the special issue. *Sex Roles*, *72*(7-8), 269–276. doi:10.100711199-015-0471-3

Shepherd, J. (2023). *21 Essential TikTok statistics you need to know in 2023*. https://thesocialshepherd.com/blog/tiktok-statistics#:~:text=Most%20of%20the%20Platform's%20Users,600%20million%20daily%20active%20users.

Sherry, J., Warner, L., & Kitchenham, A. (2021). What's Bred in the Bone: Transference and Countertransference in Teachers. *Brock Journal of Education*, *30*(1), 136–154. doi:10.26522/brocked.v30i1.859

Shiri, A., Howard, D., & Farnel, S. (2022). Indigenous digital storytelling: Digital interfaces supporting cultural heritage preservation and access. *The International Information & Library Review*, *54*(2), 93–114. doi:10.1080/10572317.2021.1946748

Shirley, A. S., Paul, A. S., Hart, P., Augustin, L., Clarke, P. J., & Pike, M. (2020). Parents perspectives on home-based character education activities. *Journal of Family Studies*, •••, 1–23.

Shockley, K. M., Gabriel, A. S., Robertson, D., Rosen, C. C., Chawla, N., Ganster, M. L., & Ezerins, M. E. (2021). The fatiguing effects of camera use in virtual meetings: A within-person field experiment. *The Journal of Applied Psychology*, *106*(8), 1137–1155. doi:10.1037/apl0000948 PMID:34423999

Shoet, R., & Shoet, J. (2020). *In love with supervision: Creating transformative conversations*. PCCS Books Ltd.

Shrivastava, P. (1999). Management classes as online learning communities. *Journal of Management Education*, *23*(6), 691–702. doi:10.1177/105256299902300607

Shu, Q., Tu, Q., & Wang, K. (2011). The impact of computer self-efficacy and technology dependence on computer-related technostress: A social cognitive theory perspective. *International Journal of Human-Computer Interaction*, *27*(10), 923–939. doi:10.1080/10447318.2011.555313

Sia, J. K. M., & Adamu, A. A. (2020). Facing the unknown: Pandemic and higher education in Malaysia. *Asian Education and Development Studies*, *10*(2), 263–275. doi:10.1108/AEDS-05-2020-0114

Sidelinger, R. J., & Booth-Butterfield, M. (2010). Co-constructing student involvement: An examination of teacher confirmation and student-to-student connectedness in the college classroom. *Communication Education*, *59*(2), 165–184. doi:10.1080/03634520903390867

Silverstein, M. W., Fix, R. L., Nuhu, N., & Kaslow, N. J. (2023). Disseminating a mentoring program for undergraduates of color: Lessons learned. *Scholarship of Teaching and Learning in Psychology*, *9*(1), 38–49. doi:10.1037tl0000224

Silverstein, M. W., Miller, M., Rivet, J., & Nuhu, N. (2022). Program evaluation of a virtual mentoring program for BIPOC undergraduates in psychology. *Scholarship of Teaching and Learning in Psychology*. Advance online publication. doi:10.1037tl0000322

Simón, C., & Alonso-Tapia, J. (2016). Positive Classroom Management: Effects of Disruption Management Climate on Behaviour and Satisfaction with Teacher//Clima positivo de gestión del aula: efectos del clima de gestión de la disrupción en el comportamiento y en la satisfacción con el pro. *Revista de Psicodidáctica*, *21*(1), 65–86. doi:10.1387/RevPsicodidact.13202

Sinek, S. (2011). *Start with why: How great leaders inspire everyone to take action*. Penguin.

Singh, A. A., Appling, B., & Trepal, H. (2020). Using the multicultural and social justice counseling competencies to decolonize counseling practice: The important roles of theory, power, and action. *Journal of Counseling and Development*, *98*(3), 261–271. doi:10.1002/jcad.12321

Singh, A. A., Nassar, S. C., Arredondo, P., & Toporek, R. (2020). The past guides the future: Implementing the multicultural and social justice counseling competencies. *Journal of Counseling and Development*, *98*(3), 238–252. doi:10.1002/jcad.12319

Singh, J., Singh, L., & Matthees, B. (2022). Establishing social, cognitive, and teaching presence in online learning—A panacea in covid-19 pandemic, post vaccine and Post Pandemic Times. *Journal of Educational Technology Systems*, *51*(1), 28–45. doi:10.1177/00472395221095169

Singh, J., Steele, K., & Singh, L. (2021). Combining the best of online and face-to-face learning: Hybrid and blended learning approach for COVID-19, post vaccine, & post-pandemic world. *Journal of Educational Technology Systems*, *50*(2), 140–171. doi:10.1177/00472395211047865

Singleton, G. E. (2015). Courageous conversations about race: A field guide for achieving equity in schools. SAGE Publications Ltd.

Sithole, A., Mupinga, D. M., Kibirige, J., Manyanga, F., & Bucklein, B. K. (2019). Expectations, challenges and suggestions for faculty teaching online courses in higher education. *International Journal of Online Pedagogy and Course Design*, *9*(1), 62–77. doi:10.4018/IJOPCD.2019010105

Sitzman, K. L. (2016). What student cues prompt online instructors to offer caring interventions? *Nursing Education Perspectives*, *37*(2), 61–71. doi:10.5480/14-1542 PMID:27209863

Slack Technologies. (2023). *What is Slack?* https://slack.com/help/articles/115004071768-What-is-Slack-

Sloan Consortium. (2004). *Entering the mainstream: The quality and extent of online education in the United States, 2003 and 2004*. Retrieved March 10, 2005, from http://www.sloan-c.org/resources/

Slone, A. R., & Gaffney, A. L. H. (2016). Assessing students' use of LinkedIn in a business and professional communication course. *Communication Teacher*, *30*(4), 206–214. doi:10.1080/17404622.2016.1219043

Smith, K. (2016). Teaching and learning 'Respect' and 'Acceptance' in the classroom. *Faculty Focus Special Report: Diversity and Inclusion in the College Classroom*, 17-18.

Smith, D., Leonis, T., & Anandavalli, S. (2021). Belonging and loneliness in cyberspace: Impacts of social media on adolescents' well-being. *Australian Journal of Psychology*, *73*(1), 12–23. doi:10.1080/00049530.2021.1898914

Smith, J. G., Vilhauer, R. P., & Chafos, V. (2017). Do military veteran and civilian students function differently in college? *Journal of American College Health*, *65*(1), 76–79. doi:10.1080/07448481.2016.1245193 PMID:27723430

Sniatecki, J. L., Perry, H. B., & Snell, L. H. (2015). Faculty attitudes and knowledge regarding college students with disabilities. *Journal of Postsecondary Education and Disability, 28*(3), 259–275.

Snijders, I., Wijnia, L., Rikers, R. M. J. P., & Loyens, S. M. M. (2020). Building bridges in higher education: Student-faculty relationship quality, student engagement, and student loyalty. *International Journal of Educational Research, 100*, 101538. Advance online publication. doi:10.1016/j.ijer.2020.101538

Snow, W. H., & Coker, J. K. (2020). Distance counselor education: Past, present, future. *The Professional Counselor, 10*(1), 40–56. doi:10.15241/whs.10.1.40

Snyder, T. D., De Brey, C., & Dillow, S. A. (2019). *Digest of Education Statistics 2017, NCES 2018-070*. National Center for Education Statistics.

Snyder, C. R., Shorey, H. S., Cheavens, J., Pulvers, K. M., Adams, V. H., & Wiklund, C. (2002). Hope and academic success in college. *Journal of Educational Psychology, 94*(4), 820–826. doi:10.1037/0022-0663.94.4.820

Snyder, T. D., de Brey, C., & Dillow, S. A. (2018). *Digest of education statistics 2016* (52nd ed.). National Center for Education Statistics, Institute of Education Sciences, U.S. Department of Education. https://nces.ed.gov/pubs2017/2017094.pdf

Sobaih, A. E., Hasanein, A. M., & Abu Elnasr, A. E. (2020). Responses to COVID-19 in higher education: Social media usage for sustaining formal academic communication in developing countries. *Sustainability (Basel), 12*(16), 6520. Advance online publication. doi:10.3390u12166520

Sobiraj, S., Korek, S., Weseler, D., & Mohr, G. (2011). When male norms don't fit: Do traditional attitudes of female colleagues challenge men in non-traditional occupations? *Sex Roles, 65*(11-12), 798–812. doi:10.100711199-011-0057-7

Solórzano, D. G., & Pérez Huber, L. (2020). *Racial microaggressions: Using critical race theory to respond to everyday racism*. Teachers College Press.

Song, L. (2005). *Adult learners' self-directed learning in online environments: Process, personal attribute, and context* [Unpublished Dissertation]. The University of Georgia, Athens, GA.

Song, H., Kim, J., & Park, N. (2019). I know my professor: Teacher self-disclosure in online education and a mediating role of social presence. *International Journal of Human-Computer Interaction, 35*(6), 448–455. doi:10.1080/10447318.2018.1455126

Song, L., & Hill, J. R. (2007). A conceptual model for understanding self-directed learning in online environments. *Journal of Interactive Online Learning, 6*(1), 27–42.

Song, L., Singleton, E. S., Hill, J. R., & Koh, M. H. (2004). Improving online learning: Student perceptions of useful and challenging characteristics. *The Internet and Higher Education, 7*(1), 59–70. doi:10.1016/j.iheduc.2003.11.003

Sponcil, M., & Gitimu, P. (2013). Use of social media by college students: Relationship to communication and self-concept. *Journal of Technology Research, 4*, 1–13.

Sriharan, A. (2020, October 14). Teaching Online: Tips for Engaging Students in Virtual Classrooms. *Medical Science Educator, 30*(4), 1673–1675. doi:10.100740670-020-01116-7 PMID:33078083

Staff, T. B. S. (2022, August 30). *The ultimate guide to campus clubs and organizations*. https://thebestschools.org/magazine/popular-college-clubs/

Staudt Willet, K. B. (2019). Revisiting how and why educators use X: Tweet types and purposes in #Edchat. *Journal of Research on Technology in Education, 51*(3), 273–289. doi:10.1080/15391523.2019.1611507

Stebleton, M., Soria, K., Huesman, R. Jr, & Torres, V. (2014). Recent immigrant students at research universities: The relationship between campus climate and sense of belonging. *Journal of College Student Development*, *55*(2), 196–202. doi:10.1353/csd.2014.0019

Steele, J., James, J. B., & Barnett, R. C. (2002). Learning in a man's world: Examining the perceptions of undergraduate women in male-dominated academic areas. *Psychology of Women Quarterly*, *26*(1), 46–50. doi:10.1111/1471-6402.00042

Stephen, J. S., & Rockinson-Szapkiw, A. J. (2021). A high-impact practice for online students: the use of a first-semester seminar course to promote self-regulation, self-direction, online learning self-efficacy. *Smart Learn. Environ.*, *8*, 6. 10.118640561-021-00151-0

Stevens, C. M., Schneider, E., & Bederman-Miller, P. (2018). Identifying faculty perceptions of awareness and preparedness relating to ADA compliance at a small, private college in NE PA. *American Journal of Business Education*, *11*(2), 27–40. doi:10.19030/ajbe.v11i2.10142

Stinson, D. W., & Liu, Y. (2019). The influence of teacher empathy on collective teacher efficacy: Examining the mediating role of teacher-student relationships. *Teaching and Teacher Education*, *85*, 215–225.

Stone, C., & O'Shea, S. (2019). Older, online and first: Recommendations for retention and success. *Australasian Journal of Educational Technology*, *35*(1), 57–69. doi:10.14742/ajet.3913

Strayhorn, T. (2008). Fittin' in: Do diverse interactions with peers affect sense of belonging for black men at predominantly white institutions? *Journal of Student Affairs Research and Practice*, *45*(4), 953–979.

Strayhorn, T. (2012). *College students' sense of belonging*. Routledge. doi:10.4324/9780203118924

Substance Abuse and Mental Health Services Administration. (2021). *Key substance use and mental health indicators in the United States: Results from the 2020 National Survey on Drug Use and Health* (HHS Publication No. PEP21-07-01-003, NSDUH Series H-56). Rockville, MD: Center for Behavioral Health Statistics and Quality, Substance Abuse and Mental Health Services Administration. Retrieved from https://www.samhsa.gov/data/

Suen, R. L. T., Chiu, D. K. W., & Tang, J. K. T. (2020). Virtual reality services in academic libraries: Deployment experience in Hong Kong. *The Electronic Library*, *38*(4), 843–858. doi:10.1108/EL-05-2020-0116

Sue, S. (1998). In search of cultural competence in psychotherapy and counseling. *The American Psychologist*, *53*(4), 440–448. doi:10.1037/0003-066X.53.4.440 PMID:9572007

Sung, Y. Y. C., & Chiu, D. K. W. (2022). E-book or print book: Parents' current view in Hong Kong. *Library Hi Tech*, *40*(5), 1289–1304. doi:10.1108/LHT-09-2020-0230

Sun, X., Chiu, D. K. W., & Chan, C. T. (2022). Recent digitalization development of buddhist libraries: A comparative case study. In S. Papadakis & A. Kapaniaris (Eds.), *The digital folklore of cyberculture and digital humanities* (pp. 251–266). IGI Global. doi:10.4018/978-1-6684-4461-0.ch014

Supiano, B. (2022, March 29). The redefinition of rigor. *The Chronicle of Higher Education*. https://www.chronicle.com/article/the-redefinition-of-rigor

Suriel, R. L., Martinez, J., & Evans-Winters, V. (2018). A Critical co-constructed autoethnography of a gendered cross-cultural mentoring between two early career Latin@ scholars working in the deep South. *Educational Studies (Ames)*, *54*(2), 165–182. doi:10.1080/00131946.2017.1356308

Swan, K. (2002). Building learning communities in online courses: The importance of interaction. *Education Communication and Information*, *2*(1), 23–49. doi:10.1080/1463631022000005016

Compilation of References

Sweller, J., Ayres, P., & Kalyuga, S. (2011). *Cognitive load theory*. Springer. doi:10.1007/978-1-4419-8126-4

Tackie, H. N. (2022). (Dis) Connected: Establishing social presence and intimacy in teacher–student relationships during emergency remote learning. *AERA Open*, *8*, 1–14. doi:10.1177/23328584211069525

Tajfel, H. (1974). Social identity and intergroup behaviour. *Social Sciences Information. Information Sur les Sciences Sociales*, *13*(2), 65–93. doi:10.1177/053901847401300204

Tajfel, H., & Turner, J. C. (2004). The social identity theory of intergroup behavior. In *Political psychology* (pp. 276–293). Psychology Press. doi:10.4324/9780203505984-16

Tallent-Runnels, M., Thomas, J., Lan, W., Cooper, S., Ahern, T., Shaw, S., & Liu, X. (2006). Teaching Courses Online: A Review of the Research. *Review of Educational Research*, *76*(1), 93–135. doi:10.3102/00346543076001093

Tam, M. (2000). Constructivism, Instructional Design, and Technology: Implications for Transforming Distance Learning. *Journal of Educational Technology & Society*, *3*(2).

Tanis, C. J. (2020). The seven principles of online learning: Feedback from faculty and alumni on its importance for teaching and learning. *Research in Learning Technology*, *28*(0). Advance online publication. doi:10.25304/rlt.v28.2319

Tareen, H., & Haand, M. T. (2020). A case study of UiTM post-graduate students' perceptions on online learning: Benefits challenges. *International Journal of Advanced Research and Publications*, *4*(6), 86–94.

Tatman, A. W. (2004). Hmong history, culture, and acculturation: Implications for counseling the Hmong. *Journal of Multicultural Counseling and Development*, *32*(4), 222–233. doi:10.1002/j.2161-1912.2004.tb00629.x

Tatum, A. L., & McBride, R. (2021). Creating inclusive online classrooms through intentional course design. *Online Learning Journal*, *25*(2), 74–90. doi:10.24059/olj.v25i2.2467Thompson, J., & Bridges, C. W. (2019). Intersectionality pedagogy in the classroom: Experiences of counselor educators. *Teaching and Supervision in Counseling*, *1*(2), 98–112. doi:10.7290/tsc010207

Taylor, J. (2019). *Perception is not reality*. https://www.psychologytoday.com/us/blog/the-power-prime/201908/perception-is-not-reality

Teitel, L. (1997). Understanding and harnessing the power of the cohort model in preparing educational leaders. *Peabody Journal of Education*, *72*(2), 66–85. doi:10.120715327930pje7202_4

Terras, K., Phillips, A., & Leggio, J. (2015). Disability accommodations in online courses: The graduate student experience. *Journal of Postsecondary Education and Disability*, *28*(3), 329–340.

The University of Arizona Global Campus. (2023a). *About UAGC*. https://www.uagc.edu/about

The University of Arizona Global Campus. (2023b). *Academic Resolution*. https://www.uagc.edu/catalog/student-rights-responsibilities/academic-resolution

The University of Arizona Global Campus. (2023c). *Student Rights and Responsibilities*. https://www.uagc.edu/student-experience/rights-responsibilities

The University of Arizona Global Campus. (2023d). *Institutional Data at UAGC*. https://www.uagc.edu/institutional-data

The University of Arizona. (2023a) *Interactive Factbook: Enrollment*. https://uair.arizona.edu/content/enrollment

The University of Arizona. (2023b). *Interactive Factbook: Academic College Diversity*. https://uair.arizona.edu/content/academic-college-diversity

Thomas, L., Herbert, J., & Teras, M. (2014). A sense of belonging to enhance participation, success and retention in online programs. *The International Journal of the First Year in Higher Education, 5*(2), 69–80. doi:10.5204/intjfyhe.v5i2.233

Thompson, J., Porto, S. (2014). *Supporting wellness in adult online education*. Academic Press.

Thompson, J. J., & Porto, S. C. (2014). Supporting wellness in adult online education. *Open Praxis, 6*(1), 17–28. doi:10.5944/openpraxis.6.1.100

Thompson, J. T. (2006). Best practices in asynchronous online course discussions. *Journal of College Teaching and Learning, 3*(7), 7. Advance online publication. doi:10.19030/tlc.v3i7.1698

Thoms, B., Garrett, N., Herrera, J. C., & Ryan, T. (2008). Understanding the Roles of Knowledge Sharing and Trust in Online Learning Communities. *Proceedings of the 41st Annual Hawaii International Conference on System Sciences (HICSS 2008)*. 10.1109/HICSS.2008.481

Thomson, A., Bridgstock, R., & Willems, C. (2014). 'Teachers flipping out' beyond the online lecture: Maximising the educational potential of video. *Journal of Learning Design, 7*(3). Advance online publication. doi:10.5204/jld.v7i3.209

Tik Tok. (2023). *About Tik Tok*. https://www.tiktok.com/about?lang=en

Tillman, L. C. (1998). The mentoring of African American faculty: Scaling the promotion and tenure mountain. In H. T. Frierson (Ed.), *Diversity in Higher Education* (pp. 141–155). JAI Press.

Tillman, L. C. (2001). Mentoring African-American faculty in predominantly White institutions. *Research in Higher Education, 42*(3), 295–325. doi:10.1023/A:1018822006485

Tinto, V. (1987). *Leaving college: Rethinking the causes and cures of student attrition*. The University of Chicago Press.

Tinto, V. (1993). Building community. *Liberal Education, 79*(4), 16–21.

Tinto, V. (2017). Reflections on student persistence. *Student Success., 8*(2), 1–8. doi:10.5204sj.v8i2.376

Tinto, V. (2017). Through the eyes of students. *Journal of College Student Retention, 19*(3), 254–269. doi:10.1177/1521025115621917

Tobin. (2014). Increase online student retention with universal design for learning. *The Quarterly Review of Distance Education, 15*(3), 13-24.

Tomlinson, M., & Jackson, D. (2021). Professional identity formation in contemporary higher education students. *Studies in Higher Education, 46*(4), 885–900. doi:10.1080/03075079.2019.1659763

Toney, S., Light, J., & Urbaczewski, A. (2021). Fighting Zoom fatigue: Keeping the zoombies at bay. *Communications of the Association for Information Systems, 48*(1), 10. doi:10.17705/1CAIS.04806

Toolan, M. J. (1994). Narrative: Linguistic and structural theories. In R. E. Asher & J. M. Y. Simpson (Eds.), *The Encyclopedia of Language and Linguistics* (Vol. 6, pp. 2679–2696). Pergamont Press.

Tormey, R. (2021). Rethinking student-teacher relationships in higher education: a multidimensional approach. *Higher Education, 82*(5), 993–1011. doi:10.1007/s10734-021-00711-w

Torres Campos, C. M., Phinney, J. S., Perez-Brena, N., Kim, C., Ornelas, B., Nemanim, L., Padilla Kallemeyn, D. M., Mihecoby, A., & Ramirez, C. (2008). A mentor-based targeted intervention for high risk Latino college freshman: A pilot study. *Journal of Hispanic Higher Education, 8*(2), 158–178. doi:10.1177/1538192708317621

Compilation of References

Travis, D. J., Nugent, J. S., & McCluney, C. (2016). *Engaging in Conversations About Gender, Race, and Ethnicity in the Workplace*. This product was developed as part of Catalyst's Women of Color Research Agenda: New Approaches. *New Solutions*.

Trickett, E. J., Leone, P. E., Fink, C. M., & Braaten, S. L. (1993). The perceived environment of special education classrooms for adolescents: A revision of the classroom environment scale. *Exceptional Children*, *59*(5), 411–420. doi:10.1177/001440299305900504 PMID:8440299

Trickett, E. J., & Moos, R. H. (1973). Assessment of the psychosocial environment of the high school classroom. *Journal of Educational Psychology*, *65*, 93–102. doi:10.1037/h0034823

Trifu, A. (2021). Can we talk of empathy in online communication in education and business? *Anuarul Universitatii "Petre Andrei" Din Iasi - Fascicula: Drept, Stiinte Economice. Stiinte Politice*, *28*, 300–305. doi:10.18662/upalaw/83

Trust, T., & Goodman, L. (2023, May 03). (online first 2023). Cameras optional?: Examining student camera use from a learner-centered perspective. *TechTrends*. Advance online publication. doi:10.100711528-023-00855-9 PMID:37362589

Tsang, A. L. Y., & Chiu, D. K. W. (2022). Effectiveness of virtual reference services in academic libraries: A qualitative study based on the 5E Learning Model. *Journal of Academic Librarianship*, *48*(4), 102533. Advance online publication. doi:10.1016/j.acalib.2022.102533

Tse, C. T., Scholz, K. W., & Lithgow, K. (2018). Beliefs or intentionality? Instructor approaches to ePortfolio pedagogy. *The Canadian Journal for the Scholarship of Teaching and Learning*, *9*(3). Advance online publication. doi:10.5206/cjsotl-rcacea.2018.3.10

Tse, H. L. T., Chiu, D. K. W., & Lam, A. H. C. (2022). From reading promotion to digital literacy: An analysis of digitalizing mobile library services with the 5E Instructional Model. In A. P. Almeida & S. Esteves (Eds.), *Modern reading practices and collaboration between schools, family, and community* (pp. 239–256). IGI Global. doi:10.4018/978-1-7998-9750-7.ch011

Tu, C. H. (2002). The measurement of social presence in an online learning environment. International *Journal of eLearning, Corporate, Government, Healthcare*, *2*, 34–45.

Tuitt, F. (2012). Black like me: Graduate students' perceptions of their pedagogical experiences in classes taught by Black faculty in a predominantly White institution. *Journal of Black Studies*, *43*(2), 186–206. doi:10.1177/0021934711413271

Turan, Z., Kucuk, S., & Cilligol Karabey, S. (2022). The university students' self-regulated effort, flexibility and satisfaction in distance education. *International Journal of Educational Technology in Higher Education*, *19*(35), 1–19. doi:10.118641239-022-00342-w PMID:35891707

Tygret, J., Green, P., & Mendez, S. (2022). Promoting faculty-student relationships. *Journal of College Orientation, Transition, and Retention*, *29*(1), 6. https://pubs.lib.umn.edu/index.php/jcotr/article/view/4873

U.S. Department of Health and Human Services. (2006, June). *Your Rights Under Section 504 of the Rehabilitation Act (H-8/June 2000 – revised June 2006 - English)*. https://www.hhs.gov/sites/default/files/ocr/civilrights/resources/factsheets/504.pdf

U.S. Department of Health and Human Services. (n.d.). *Introduction to Section 508 Compliance and Accessibility*. https://www.hhs.gov/sites/default/files/Intro%20to%20Accessibility%20and%20508.pdf

Undergraduate enrollment. (2022). National Center for Education Statistics. https://nces.ed.gov/programs/coe/indicator/cha

UNESCO, UNICEF, & The World Bank. (2020). *What Have We Learnt? Overview of Findings from a Survey of Ministries of Education on National Responses to COVID-19*. https://openknowledge.worldbank.org/handle/10986/34700

UNESCO. (2020). *Policy brief: Education during COVID-19 and beyond.* United Nations. https://www.un.org/development/desa/dspd/wp-content/uploads/sites/22/2020/08/sg_policy_brief_covid-19_and_education_august_2020.pdf

United States Census Bureau. (2022). *Educational attainment in the United States: 2021.* Author.

University of Michigan Center for Academic Innovation. (2020). *Asynchronous tools and how to use them.* https://onlineteaching.umich.edu/asynchronous-tools-and-how-to-use-them/

Urdaneta-Ponte, M. C., Oleagoria-Ruiz, I., & Mendez-Zorrilla, A. (2022). Using LinkedIn endorsements to reinforce an ontology and machine learning-based recommender system to improve professional skills. *Electronics (Basel), 11*(8), 1190. doi:10.3390/electronics11081190

Vagos, P., & Carvalhais, L. (2022). Online versus classroom teaching: Impact on teacher and student relationship quality and quality of life. *Frontiers in Psychology, 13,* 13. doi:10.3389/fpsyg.2022.828774 PMID:35250769

Van Roekel, N. P. D. (2008). *Promoting educators' cultural competence to better serve culturally diverse students.* National Education Agency.

Van Soest, D., Canon, R., & Grant, D. (2000). Using an interactive website to educate about cultural diversity and societal oppression. *Journal of Social Work Education, 36*(3), 463–479. doi:10.1080/10437797.2000.10779022

Vårheim, A. (2007). Social capital and public libraries: The need for research. *Library & Information Science Research, 29*(3), 416–428. doi:10.1016/j.lisr.2007.04.009

Vårheim, A., Steinmo, S., & Ide, E. (2008). Do libraries matter? Public libraries and the creation of social capital. *The Journal of Documentation, 64*(6), 877–892. doi:10.1108/00220410810912433

Vavrus, M. (2008). Culturally responsive teaching. *21st century education: A reference handbook, 2,* 49-57. doi:10.4135/9781412964012.n56

Vayre, E., & Vonthron, A.-M. (2017). Psychological Engagement of Students in Distance and Online Learning: Effects of Self-Efficacy and Psychosocial Processes. *Journal of Educational Computing Research, 55*(2), 197–218. doi:10.1177/0735633116656849

Vekiri, I., & Chronaki, A. (2008). Gender issues in technology use: Perceived social support, computer self-efficacy and value beliefs, and computer use beyond school. *Computers & Education, 51*(3), 1392–1404. doi:10.1016/j.compedu.2008.01.003

Verma, P. (2023, May 18). A professor accused his class of using ChatGPT, putting diplomas in jeopardy. *The Washington Post.* https://www.washingtonpost.com/technology/2023/05/18/texas-professor-threatened-fail-class-chatgpt-cheating/

Vygotsky, L. (1962). *Thought and language.* MIT Press. doi:10.1037/11193-000

Vygotsky, L. S. (1978). *Mind in society: The development of higher psychological processes.* Harvard University Press.

W3C. (2017, April 12). *Tips and tricks.* https://www.w3.org/WAI/tutorials/images/tips/

W3C. (2018, June 5). *Web Content Accessibility Guidelines (WCAG) 2.1.* https://www.w3.org/TR/WCAG21/

W3C. (2022, January 17). *Complex images.* https://www.w3.org/WAI/tutorials/images/complex/

Wai, I. S. H., Ng, S. S. Y., Chiu, D. K. W., Ho, K. K. W., & Lo, P. (2018). Exploring undergraduate students' usage pattern of mobile apps for education. *Journal of Librarianship and Information Science, 50*(1), 34–47. doi:10.1177/0961000616662699

Compilation of References

Walker-Gleaves, C. (2019). Is caring pedagogy really so progressive? Exploring the conceptual and practical impediments to operationalizing care in higher education. In P. Gibbs & A. Peterson (Eds.), *Higher Education and Hope* (pp. 93–112). Palgrave Macmillan. doi:10.1007/978-3-030-13566-9_5

Walter, S., Lorcher, I., & Bruggemann, M. (2019). Scientific networks on X: Analyzing scientists' interactions in the climate change debate. *Public Understanding of Science (Bristol, England)*, 28(6), 696–712. doi:10.1177/0963662519844131 PMID:31027461

Wandler & Imbriale, W. J. (2017). Promoting Undergraduate Student Self-Regulation in Online Learning Environments. *Online Learning, 21*(2). doi:10.24059/olj.v21i2.881

Wang, S., & Wu, P. (2008). The role of feedback and self-efficacy on web-based learning: The social cognitive perspective. *Computers & Education, 51*(4), 1589-1598. doi:10.1016/j.compedu.2008.03.004

Wang, A. Y., & Newlin, M. H. (2002). Predictors of web-student performance: The role of self-efficacy and reasons for taking an online class. *Computers in Human Behavior, 18*(2), 151–163. doi:10.1016/S0747-5632(01)00042-5

Wang, C.-H., Shannon, D. M., & Ross, M. E. (2013). Students' characteristics, self-regulated learning, technology self-efficacy, and course outcomes in online learning. *Distance Education, 34*(3), 302–323. doi:10.1080/01587919.2013.835779

Wang, J., Deng, S., Chiu, D. K. W., & Chan, C. T. (2022). Social network customer relationship management for orchestras: A case study on Hong Kong Philharmonic Orchestra. In N. B. Ammari (Ed.), *Social customer relationship management (Social-CRM) in the era of Web 4.0* (pp. 250–268). IGI Global. doi:10.4018/978-1-7998-9553-4.ch012

Wang, M. T., Degol, J. L., Amemiya, J., Parr, A., & Guo, J. (2020). Classroom climate and children's academic and psychological well being: A systematic review and meta-analysis. *Developmental Review, 57*, 100912. doi:10.1016/j.dr.2020.100912

Wang, M. T., & Eccles, J. S. (2012). Social support matters: Longitudinal effects of social support on three dimensions of school engagement from middle to high school. *Child Development, 83*(3), 877–895. doi:10.1111/j.1467-8624.2012.01745.x PMID:22506836

Wang, P., Chiu, D. K. W., Ho, K. K. W., & Lo, P. (2016). Why read it on your mobile device? Change in reading habit of electronic magazines for university students. *Journal of Academic Librarianship, 42*(6), 664–669. doi:10.1016/j.acalib.2016.08.007

Wang, Q., & Woo, H. L. (2007). Systematic Planning for ICT Integration in Topic Learning. *Journal of Educational Technology & Society, 10*(1), 148–156.

Wang, V., & Edwards, S. (2016). Strangers are friends I haven't met yet: A positive approach to young people's use of social media. *Journal of Youth Studies, 19*(9), 1204–1219. doi:10.1080/13676261.2016.1154933

Wang, W., Guo, L., He, L., & Wu, Y. J. (2019). Effects of social-interactive engagement on the dropout ratio in online learning: Insights from MOOC. *Behaviour & Information Technology, 38*(6), 621–636. doi:10.1080/0144929X.2018.1549595

Wang, W., Lam, E. T. H., Chiu, D. K. W., Lung, M. M., & Ho, K. K. W. (2021). Supporting higher education with social networks: Trust and privacy vs perceived effectiveness. *Online Information Review, 45*(1), 207–219. doi:10.1108/OIR-02-2020-0042

Wang, Y. (2020). Humor and camera view on mobile short-form video apps influence user experience and technology-adoption intent, an example of TikTok. *Computers in Human Behavior, 110*, 106373. Advance online publication. doi:10.1016/j.chb.2020.106373

Wanzer, M. B., Frymier, A. B., & Irwin, J. (2010). An explanation of the relationship between instructor humor and student learning: Instructional humor processing theory. *Communication Education*, *59*(1), 1–18. doi:10.1080/03634520903367238

Waters, J. M., Gantt, A. C., Worth, A., Duyile, B., Johnson, K., & Mariotti, D. (2022). Motivated but challenged: Counselor educators' experiences teaching about social determinants of health. *The Journal of Counselor Preparation and Supervisor*, *15*(2), 1–32.

Watson, J. (2008). *Blended Learning: The Convergence of online and face-to-face education. Promising practices in online learning*. North American Council for Online Learning.

Webb, E., Jones, A., Barker, P., & van Schaik, P. (2004). Using e-learning dialogues in higher education. *Innovations in Education and Teaching International*, *41*(1), 93–103. doi:10.1080/1470329032000172748

Wei, C. W., Chen, N. S., & Kinshuk. (2012). A model for social presence in online classrooms. *Educational Technology Research and Development*, *60*(3), 529–545. doi:10.100711423-012-9234-9

Weintraub, K. (2021). New coronavirus variants aren't cause for alarm yet, but mutations could make COVID-19 harder to fght, experts say. *USA Today*. Retrieved January 22, 2021, from https://www.usatoday.com/story/news/health/2021/01/09/new-coronavirus-strains-variants-not-yet-cause-formore-covid-vaccine-concerns-experts-say/6575267002/

Westbrook, T. P. (2014). Global contexts for learning: Exploring the relationship between low-context online learning and high-context learners. *Christian Higher Education*, *13*(4), 281–294. doi:10.1080/15363759.2014.924888

Whittaker, A. L., Haworth, G. S., & Lymn, K. A. (2014). Evaluation of Facebook to create an online learning community in an undergraduate animal science course. *Educational Media International*, *51*(2), 135–145. doi:10.1080/09523987.2014.924664

Wilde, N., & Hsu, A. (2019). The influence of general self-efficacy on the interpretation of vicarious experience information within online learning. *International Journal of Educational Technology in Higher Education*, *16*(1), 26. doi:10.118641239-019-0158-x

Williams, C. L. (2015). Crossing over: Interdisciplinary research on "men who do women's work". *Sex Roles*, *72*(7-8), 390–395. doi:10.100711199-015-0477-x

Williams, J. M., Byrd, J. A., & Washington, A. R. (2021). Challenges in implementing antiracist pedagogy into counselor education programs: A collective self-study. *Counselor Education and Supervision*, *60*(4), 254–273. doi:10.1002/ceas.12215

Williams, M. T. (2020). Microaggressions: Clarification, evidence, and impact. *Perspectives on Psychological Science*, *15*(1), 3–26. doi:10.1177/1745691619827499 PMID:31418642

Wilson, G., & Stacey, E. (2004). Online interaction impacts on learning: Teaching the teachers to teach online. *Australasian Journal of Educational Technology*, *20*(1). Advance online publication. doi:10.14742/ajet.1366

Wilson, M., Gwyther, K., Swann, R., Casey, K., Featherston, R., Oliffe, J. L., Englar-Carlson, M., & Rice, S. M. (2022). Operationalizing positive masculinity: A theoretical synthesis and school-based framework to engage boys and young men. *Health Promotion International*, *37*(1), daab031. Advance online publication. doi:10.1093/heapro/daab031 PMID:33842967

Wlodkowski, R. J., & Ginsberg, M. B. (2017). *Enhancing adult motivation to learn: A comprehensive guide for teaching all adults*. John Wiley & Sons.

Wojciechowska, M. (2019). *Kształtowanie kapitału społecznego - ujęcie z perspektywy bibliotekoznawczej* [Shaping social capital. A view from the library science perspective]. Difin.

Compilation of References

Wojciechowska, M. D. (2021). The role of public libraries in the development of social capital in local communities – A theoretical study. *Library Management*, *42*(3), 184–196. doi:10.1108/LM-10-2020-0139

Wojciechowska, M., & Topolska, K. (2021). Social and cultural capital in public libraries and its impact on the organization of new forms of services and implementation of social projects. *Journal of Library Administration*, *61*(6), 627–643. doi:10.1080/01930826.2021.1947053

Wolverton, C. C., Hollier, B. N. G., & Lanier, P. A. (2020). The impact of computer self-efficacy on student engagement and group satisfaction in online business courses. *Electronic Journal of e-Learning*, *18*(2). Advance online publication. doi:10.34190/EJEL.20.18.2.006

Wong, A. K.-k., & Chiu, D. K. W. (2023). Digital transformation of museum conservation practices: A value chain analysis of public museums in Hong Kong. In R. Pettinger, B. B. Gupta, A. Roja, & D. Cozmiuc (Eds.), *Handbook of research on the digital transformation digitalization solutions for social and economic needs* (pp. 226–242). IGI. Global. doi:10.4018/978-1-6684-4102-2.ch010

Wong, I. H. S., Fan, C. H., Chiu, D. K. W., & Ho, K. K. W. (2023). (in press). Social media celebrities' influence on youths' diet behaviors: A gender study based on the AIDA marketing communication model. *Aslib Journal of Information Management*. Advance online publication. doi:10.1108/AJIM-11-2022-0495

Wong, J., Baars, M., Davis, D., Van Der Zee, T., Houben, G. J., & Paas, F. (2019). Supporting self-regulated learning in online learning environments and MOOCs: A systematic review. *International Journal of Human-Computer Interaction*, *35*(4-5), 356–373. doi:10.1080/10447318.2018.1543084

Wong, J., Ho, K. K. W., Leung, T. N., & Chiu, D. K. W. (2023). Exploring the associations of youth Facebook addiction with social capital perceptions. *Online Information Review*, *47*(2), 283–298. doi:10.1108/OIR-06-2021-0300

Wong, K. C., & Chiu, D. K. W. (2023). Promoting the use of electronic resources of international schools: A case study of ESF King George V School in Hong Kong. In E. Meletiadou (Ed.), *Handbook of research on redesigning teaching, learning, and assessment in the digital era* (pp. 123–143). IGI Global. doi:10.4018/978-1-6684-8292-6.ch007

Wood, J. (2022, January 27). *These 3 charts show the global growth in online learning*. World Economic Forum. https://www.weforum.org/agenda/2022/01/online-learning-courses-reskill-skills-gap

Woodley, X., Hernandez, C., Parra, J., & Negash, B. (2017). Celebrating difference: Best practices in culturally responsive teaching online. *TechTrends*, *61*(5), 470–478. doi:10.100711528-017-0207-z

Woods, R., & Ebersole, S. (2003). Using non-subject-matter discussion boards to build connectedness in online learning. *American Journal of Distance Education*, *17*(2), 99–118. doi:10.1207/S15389286AJDE1702_3

Woolfolk, A. (2020). *Educational psychology: Active learning edition* (14th ed.). Pearson.

Works, P. B. L. (n.d.) *What is PBL?* Buck Institute for Education. https://www.pblworks.org/what-is-pbl

Wu, M., Lam, A. H. C., & Chiu, D. K. W. (2023). Transforming and promoting reference services with digital technologies: A case study on Hong Kong Baptist University Library. In B. Holland (Ed.), Handbook of research on advancements of contactless technology and service innovation in library and information science (pp. 128 – 145). IGI Global. doi:10.4018/978-1-6684-7693-2.ch007

Wu, Y., & Cheng, Z. (2019). Formation of user stickiness in an online knowledge community in China. *Social Behavior and Personality*, *47*(9), 1–14. doi:10.2224bp.8292

X. (2023). *New user FAQ*. https://help.X.com/en/resources/new-user-faq

Xiao, J. (2018). On the margins or at the center? Distance education in higher education. *Distance Education*, *39*(2), 259–274. doi:10.1080/01587919.2018.1429213

Xie, K., Yu, C., & Bradshaw, A. C. (2014). Impacts of role assignment and participation in asynchronous discussions in college-level online classes. *The Internet and Higher Education*, *20*, 10–19. . doi:10.1016/j.iheduc.2013.09.003

Xie, Z., Chiu, D. K. W., & Ho, K. K. W. (2023). (in press). The role of social media as aids for accounting education and knowledge sharing: Learning effectiveness and knowledge management perspectives in Mainland China. *Journal of the Knowledge Economy*. Advance online publication. doi:10.100713132-023-01262-4

Xie, Z., Wong, G. K. W., Chiu, D. K. W., & Lei, J. (2023). Bridging K-12 Mathematics and computational thinking in the Scratch community: Implications drawn from a creative learning context. *IT Professional*, *25*(2), 64–70. doi:10.1109/MITP.2023.3243393

Xue, B., Lam, A. H. C., & Chiu, D. K. W. (2023). Redesigning library information literacy education with the BOPPPS Model: A case study of the HKUST. In R. Taiwo, B. Idowu-Faith, & S. Ajiboye (Eds.), *Transformation of higher education through institutional online spaces*. IGI Global. doi:10.4018/978-1-6684-8122-6.ch017

Yaghmour, S. (2012). Gender communication differences in synchronized distance learning lectures for users aged 18-60: A systematic literature review. *Annual Review of Education, Communication & Language Sciences*, *9*, 85–90.

Yalcinalp, S., & Gulbahar, Y. (2010). Ontology and taxonomy design and development for personalised web-based learning systems. *British Journal of Educational Technology*, *41*(6), 883–896. doi:10.1111/j.1467-8535.2009.01049.x

Yamauchi, L. A., Taira, K., & Trevorrow, T. (2016). Effective instruction for engaging culturally diverse students in higher education. *International Journal on Teaching and Learning in Higher Education*, *28*(3), 460–470.

Yang, Y., & Cornelious, L. F. (2005). Preparing instructors for quality online instruction. *Online Journal of Distance Learning Administration*, *8*(1), 1–16.

Yang, Z., Zhou, Q., Chiu, D. K. W., & Wang, Y. (2022). Exploring the factors influencing continuance usage intention of academic social network sites. *Online Information Review*, *46*(7), 1225–1241. doi:10.1108/OIR-01-2021-0015

Yew, A., Chiu, D. K. W., Nakamura, Y., & Li, K. K. (2022). A quantitative review of LIS programs accredited by ALA and CILIP under contemporary technology advancement. *Library Hi Tech*, *40*(6), 1721–1745. doi:10.1108/LHT-12-2021-0442

Yilmaz, R., & Karaoglan Yilmaz, F. G. (2019). Assigned Roles as a Structuring Tool in Online Discussion Groups: Comparison of Transactional Distance and Knowledge Sharing Behaviors. *Journal of Educational Computing Research*, *57*(5), 1303–1325. doi:10.1177/0735633118786855

Yi, P. (2022). Teachers' communities of practice in response to the COVID-19 pandemic: Will innovation in teaching practices persist and prosper? *Journal of Curriculum and Teaching*, *11*(5), 241–251. doi:10.5430/jct.v11n5p241

Yip, K. H. T., Lo, P., Ho, K. K. W., & Chiu, D. K. W. (2021). Adoption of mobile library apps as learning tools in higher education: A tale between Hong Kong and Japan. *Online Information Review*, *45*(2), 389–405. doi:10.1108/OIR-07-2020-0287

Yip, T., Chiu, D. K. W., Cho, A., & Lo, P. (2019). Behavior and informal learning at night in a 24-hour space: A case study of the Hong Kong Design Institute Library. *Journal of Librarianship and Information Science*, *51*(1), 171–179. doi:10.1177/0961000617726120

Yi, Y. (2010). Roles of Administrators in Ensuring the Quality of Online Programs. *Knowledge Management & E-Learning. International Journal (Toronto, Ont.)*, *2*(4).

Compilation of References

Yi, Y., & Chiu, D. K. W. (2023). Public information needs during the COVID-19 outbreak: A qualitative study in mainland China. *Library Hi Tech*, *41*(1), 248–274. doi:10.1108/LHT-08-2022-0398

Yokoyama. (2019). Academic Self-Efficacy and Academic Performance in Online Learning: A Mini Review. *Frontiers in Psychology*, *9*, 2794–2794. doi:10.3389/fpsyg.2018.02794

Yosso, T., Smith, W., Ceja, M., & Solarzano, D. (2009). Critical race theory, microaggressions, and campus racial climate for Latina/o undergraduates. *Harvard Educational Review*, *79*(4), 659–690.

Young, S., & Hockfield, B. (2019). Bringing the curtain down on affinity groups: Cultural equity teams wait in the wings. *Profiles in Diversity Journal*, 66–69.

Yu, H. H. K., Chiu, D. K. W., & Chan, C. T. (2022). Resilience of symphony orchestras to challenges in the COVID-19 era: Analyzing the Hong Kong Philharmonic Orchestra with Porter's five force model. In W. J. Aloulou (Ed.), *Handbook of research on entrepreneurship and organizational resilience during unprecedented times* (pp. 586–601). IGI Global. doi:10.4018/978-1-6684-4605-8.ch026

Yu, H. Y., Tsoi, Y. Y., Rhim, A. H. R., Chiu, D. K. W., & Lung, M. M.-W. (2022). Changes in habits of electronic news usage on mobile devices in university students: A comparative survey. *Library Hi Tech*, *40*(5), 1322–1336. doi:10.1108/LHT-03-2021-0085

Yu, P. Y., Lam, E. T. H., & Chiu, D. K. W. (2023). Operation management of academic libraries in Hong Kong under COVID-19. *Library Hi Tech*, *41*(1), 108–129. doi:10.1108/LHT-10-2021-0342

Yu, Z. (2021). The effects of gender, educational level, and personality on online learning outcomes during the COVID-19 pandemic. *International Journal of Educational Technology in Higher Education*, *18*(1), 14. doi:10.118641239-021-00252-3 PMID:34778520

Zajac, C. (2020). *Outstanding first year teacher perceptions*. Northeastern University Library. doi:10.17760/D20350267

Zamarro, G., Camp, A., Fuchsman, D., & McGee, J. B. (2022). *Understanding how COVID-19 has changed teachers' chances of remaining in the classroom*. Sinquefield Center for Applied Economic Research Working Paper. doi:10.2139/ssrn.4047354

Zhang, H., Watkins, C. E. Jr, Hook, J. N., Hodge, A. S., Davis, C. W., Norton, J., Wilcox, M., Davis, D., DeBlaere, C., & Owen, J. (2022). Cultural humility in psychotherapy and clinical supervision: A research review. *Counselling & Psychotherapy Research*, *22*(3), 548–557. doi:10.1002/capr.12481

Zhang, K., Bonk, C. J., Reeves, T. C., & Reynolds, T. H. (Eds.). (2019). *MOOCs and open education in the Global South: Challenges, successes, and opportunities*. Routledge. doi:10.4324/9780429398919

Zhang, X., Lo, P., So, S., Chiu, D. K. W., Leung, T. N., Ho, K. K. W., & Stark, A. (2021). Medical students' attitudes and perceptions towards the effectiveness of mobile learning: A comparative information-need perspective. *Journal of Librarianship and Information Science*, *53*(1), 116–129. doi:10.1177/0961000620925547

Zhang, Y. (2022). Developing EFL teachers' technological pedagogical knowledge through practices in virtual platform. *Frontiers in Psychology*, *13*, 916060. Advance online publication. doi:10.3389/fpsyg.2022.916060 PMID:35712156

Zhang, Y., Lo, P., So, S., & Chiu, D. K. W. (2020). Relating library user education to business students' information needs and learning practices: A comparative study. *RSR. Reference Services Review*, *48*(4), 537–558. doi:10.1108/RSR-12-2019-0084

Zheng, B., & Beck Dallaghan, G. (2022). A X-facilitated professional learning community: Online participation, connectedness, and satisfaction. *BMC Medical Education*, *22*(1), 577. Advance online publication. doi:10.118612909-022-03639-6 PMID:35897094

Zheng, J., Lam, A. H. C., & Chiu, D. K. W. (2023). Evaluating the effectiveness of learning commons as third spaces with the 5Es usability model: The case of Hong Kong University of Science and Technology Library. In C. Kaye & J. Haynes Writer (Eds.), *Third-space exploration in education* (pp. 123–143). IGI Global. doi:10.4018/978-1-6684-8402-9.ch007

Zheng, M., Bender, D., & Lyon, C. (2021). Online learning during COVID-19 produced equivalent or better student course performance as compared with pre-pandemic: Empirical evidence from a school-wide comparative study. *BMC Medical Education*, *21*(1), 495. doi:10.118612909-021-02909-z PMID:34530828

Zhou, J., Lam, E., Au, C. H., Lo, P., & Chiu, D. K. W. (2022). Library café or elsewhere: Usage of study space by different majors under contemporary technological environment. *Library Hi Tech*, *40*(6), 1567–1581. doi:10.1108/LHT-03-2021-0103

Zigelman, I. (2018). Constructivism and the Community of Inquiry. *Technology and the Curriculum: Summer 2018*.

Zimmerle, J. (2020). Nice to Tweet you: Supporting rural preservice teachers through X chats. *SRATE Journal*, *29*(2), Article 10. https://www.srate.org/z_journal_archive_29_2.html

Zoom. (2022). *What is Zoom video conferencing?* https://support.zoom.us/hc/en-us/articles/4420426401037-What-is-Zoom-Video-Conferencing-

Zuo, Y., Lam, A. H. C., & Chiu, D. K. W. (2023). Digital protection of traditional villages for sustainable heritage tourism: A case study on Qiqiao Ancient Village, China. In A. Masouras, C. Papademetriou, D. Belias, & S. Anastasiadou (Eds.), *Sustainable growth strategies for entrepreneurial venture tourism and regional development* (pp. 129–151). IGI Global. doi:10.4018/978-1-6684-6055-9.ch009

About the Contributors

Sarah Jarvie is an Associate Professor at Colorado Christian University. She has been a full-time counselor educator since 2015. She has a background in community mental health and private practice with clients of all ages from children to adults. Dr. Jarvie enjoys infusing connections between clinical practice and the classroom. Her research interests include person-centered education, teaching applications to counseling, and counselor and counselor educator wellness.

Cara Metz is a Program Chair and Professor in the College of Art & Sciences at the University of Arizona Global Campus. She received a master's degree in Clinical Mental Health Counseling and a doctorate in Counselor Education and Supervision from the University of Cincinnati. She also holds a bachelor's degree in Psychology and Economics from Ohio University. Dr. Metz has been licensed as a counselor since 2006. She started her practicum in an elementary school setting, then moved into the community mental health setting, where she worked with adults. Then she moved into a private practice setting, where she worked as a counselor and supervisor, seeing clients from ages 8-80, focusing on transitional aged youth from 14 to 22. In her practice, she has worked with individuals, couples, families, and groups. Dr. Metz really enjoys the counseling process and getting to know her clients. In 2013, she moved into teaching full-time, working with master's- and doctoral-level students studying counseling, where she earned an award for Outstanding Faculty of the Year in 2016. She began working at the University of Arizona Global Campus in 2017, where she works in the human services and psychology programs. Dr. Metz's research interests include wellness, burnout, humanistic theories and education, online education, and job satisfaction in counselors and educators. She has presented on these topics at state, regional, national, and international conferences. Dr. Metz's professional memberships include American Counseling Association, Association for Counselor Education and Supervision, Association for Humanistic Counseling, National Organization for Human Services, and Tau Upsilon Alpha.

***

Daniel Bates earned his Ph.D. in Counselor Education from the University of Cincinnati and holds professional licenses in several states. Daniel is also a nationally board-certified counselor. His research, advocacy, and published work explores the intersection between men's mental health, access to services and masculine norms.

Kathleen A. Boothe is an Associate Professor and Program Coordinator of Special Education at Southeastern Oklahoma State University in Durant, OK, where she teaches graduate students in a fully online program. Dr. Boothe is an active member of the Council for Exceptional Children Teacher Education Division. Additionally, Dr. Boothe serves on the executive board of the Small Special Education Programs Caucus. Dr. Boothe's research interests include improving the online education for pre and in-service teachers, with a focus on universal design for learning (UDL). Dr. Boothe has taught asynchronous online teacher education courses since 2015 averaging approximately 12 courses per academic year. In 2020, Dr. Boothe received the Faculty Senate Recognition Award for Outstanding Research and Scholarly Activity.

Crystal Brashear, LPC-S, is a counselor educator and clinician who trusts in the creative power each person carries inside to facilitate growing awareness and self-compassion. As an Assistant Professor for Colorado Christian University, she favors an experiential approach to counselor education. Crystal believes that cognitive flexibility helps her meet clients' here-and-now needs as they emerge in session. She is the proud recipient of the Association for Counselor Education and Supervision (ACES) Counseling Vision and Innovation Award (2021). Her doctoral dissertation explored the effectiveness of creative online group supervision. Crystal has spoken at numerous state, national, and international professional counseling conferences, and she is a part of a research team who have received multiple grants to study the perceptions of telehealth counseling that people who identify as BIPOC hold. She is a published author.

Corinne W. Bridges, LPC, BC-TMH, NCC, AAT-I is a full-time core faculty member of the Counselor Education and Supervision PhD program at Walden University and a contributing faculty member at Buena Vista University. As a faculty member and dissertation chair, Dr. Bridges emphasizes the need for collaboration and mutual respect to explore cultural awareness with students while modeling empathy and reflection of intersecting identities. In January of 2020, she was the recipient of the Walden University Faculty Excellence Award which honors faculty that exemplify the values of quality, integrity, and student centeredness and in 2019 and 2020 the Outstanding Adjunct Faculty certificate from Southern New Hampshire University which recognizes instructors who exceed expectations in personal, intellectual, and instructor presence in the classroom. Dr. Bridges has experience presenting and publishing both qualitative and quantitative work relative to her research interests which include ecological and rural counseling; multicultural and LGBTQ counseling; online education, gender, and relationship building. Additionally, Dr. Bridges serves as an editorial reviewer for the Journal of Counseling Sexology and Sexual Wellness: Research, Practice, and Education and for the Journal of Counselor Preparation and Supervision NARACES, as well as for Adoption Quarterly.

Dickson K.W. Chiu received the B.Sc. (Hons.) degree in Computer Studies from the University of Hong Kong in 1987. He received the M.Sc. (1994) and Ph.D. (2000) degrees in Computer Science from the Hong Kong University of Science and Technology (HKUST). He started his own computer consultant company while studying part-time. He has also taught at several universities in Hong Kong. His teaching and research interest is in Library & Information Management, Service Computing, and E-learning with a cross-disciplinary approach involving library and information management, e-learning, e-business, service sciences, and databases. The results have been widely published in over 300 international publications (most of them have been indexed by SCI/-E, SSCI, and EI, such as top journals MIS Quarterly, Computer & Education, Government Information Quarterly, Decision Support Systems, Information Sciences, Knowledge-Based Systems, Expert Systems with Application, Information Systems Frontiers,

About the Contributors

IEEE Transactions, including many taught master and undergraduate project results and around 20 edited books. He received a best paper award at the 37th Hawaii International Conference on System Sciences in 2004. He is an Editor (-in-chief) of Library Hi Tech, a prestigious journal indexed by SSCI. He is the Editor-in-chief Emeritus of the International Journal on Systems and Service-Oriented0 Engineering (founding) and International Journal of Organizational and Collective Intelligence, and serves on the editorial boards of several international journals. He co-founded several international workshops and co-edited several journal special issues. He also served as a program committee member for around 300 international conferences and workshops. Dr. Chiu is a Senior Member of both the ACM and the IEEE and a life member of the Hong Kong Computer Society. According to Google Scholar, he has over 8,200 citations, h-index=47, i-10 index=187, and ranked worldwide 1st in "LIS," "m-learning," and "e-services." He received nearly 1,000 citations in 2022 and over 2,000 in 2023.

Kim Cowan is the Student Rights and Responsibilities Manager in Student Affairs for the University of Arizona Global Campus (UAGC). She graduated from California State University, San Marcos where she received a BA in Literature and Writing and completed her MA in English at National University. She was a professional soccer coach in San Diego for twelve years, coaching children under eight to adults at Palomar Community College. After four years at Palomar she began working for Ashford University as an Instructional Specialist, finding her passion for education and the adult student experience. She became a Manager in the Center for Excellence in Teaching and Learning supporting and coaching online faculty. Within that role she collaborated with Student Conduct and the Behavioral Intervention Team and when an opportunity opened to continue her growth within Student Affairs, she pursued it. In her current role, she oversees Student Conduct, Academic Resolution, and Co-Chairs the Behavioral Intervention Team. Throughout her time in Student Affairs, she has helped revamp processes to focus on the student's individual experience and more on student development and support. She believes that there are multiple ways to support our students and it takes meaningful interactions, supportive communication, and a community approach to help adult learners navigate a successful student experience.

Bill Davis has extensive experience and education in all aspects of business: consultant, management, leadership, sales, marketing, strategic planning, human resources, and organizational change. He has over three decades of experience working in the beverage industry, specifically in the PepsiCo system, a Fortune 500 company, serving in front, middle management, and executive level leadership positions. Bill is a pracademic who successfully transitioned his highly successful career into academia. He has taught over 300+ courses in higher education in online and on ground modalities and has over 18 years of extensive academic experience, serving as a program chair, lead faculty, assistant professor, core faculty, instructor, instructional specialist, instructional specialist manager, and associate faculty. Bill loves furthering student success, and empowering, enriching, supporting and graduating UAGC students, seeing them achieve their purpose and their academic, personal, and career goals. Bill has received numerous local and national awards for excellence in teaching, leadership, management, community service, scholarship, sales, and marketing. Bill has published and presented at numerous academic conferences nationally and internationally and to several businesses, community organizations, and Fortune 500 companies. Bill has published 160+ articles on business, strategic planning, marketing, management, leadership, organizational change, and adult learning and development. In 2019, he coauthored "Staying Engaged It's Essential – Leadership Principles for Success," and is coauthor of "Learning in Practice," a collaboration of several short articles written for students.

About the Contributors

Carrie Grimes is an Assistant Professor of the Practice in the department of Leadership, Policy and Organizations at Vanderbilt University's Peabody College of Education and Human Development. She also serves as the Director of the Independent School Leadership Master's program. She completed her Ed.D. in Leadership and Learning in Organizations at Vanderbilt University, where her research focuses on community in educational settings.

Nazifah Hamidun is a senior lecturer in the Department of Language & General Studies, Faculty of Business & Communication. Her research interests are in the area of TESL, pedagogy, assessment and curriculum.

Ariel Harrison, Ph.D., LPC, LSC, NCC is a licensed school counselor in Virginia, a certified school counselor in Georgia, and a licensed professional counselor in Georgia. She worked as a school counselor for 13 years in elementary, middle, and high school settings that include private, public, charter, and online schools. Ariel is currently the Academic Program Coordinator and Core Faculty in the School Counseling masters program at Walden University and the owner of Ariel Harrison Consulting.

Donna Hickman is an Assistant Professor and coordinator of the school counseling program at Texas A&M University-Commerce. She is also a Licensed Professional Counselor and certified school counselor in the state of Texas. Donna has 22 years of experience in Texas public schools as an elementary school teacher and counselor. She has also worked with children, adolescents, and adults in private practice. Her dissertation research examined the impact of role ambiguity on stress and burnout in elementary school counselors. She is an active member of several professional counseling associations with presentations on topics such as school counselor supervision, research methods and statistics, sandtray therapy, counselor self-care, and counseling ethics. Her research interest areas include professional school counselor advocacy and counselor self-care and wellness.

Aida Shakila Ishak is a Senior Lecturer at the Faculty of Business and Communication, Universiti Malaysia Perlis. Her area of expertise is counseling psychology and her sub-field expertise is related to drug abuse. She has served in the field of Education since 2019 until now. After being awarded a Doctor of Philosophy Degree from Universiti Malaysia Perlis, she actively continued to contribute in terms of scholarly writing, namely papers in national and international journals.

Elodie Jones is an Associate Professor at Fort Hays State University in the Department of Advanced Education Programs. She received her Ph.D. from the University of Kansas, where her research interests include instructional technology and message design, experiential learning and accreditation, and program development. She facilitates courses in both face-to-face and online settings at the graduate and undergraduate levels for in-service and pre-service educators. Elodie is active on several community-based boards that promote relations between the university and the area communities.

Faten Khalida Khalid is a language instructor at the Department of Languages & General Studies, Faculty of Business and Communication. Her research interests are in the area of applied linguistics, technical communication and education.

About the Contributors

Apple Hiu Ching Lam obtained her degree of Bachelor of Business Administration (Honours) in International Business from City University of Hong Kong (2016) and degree of Master of Science in Library and Information Management with distinction from the University of Hong Kong (2020). She is a doctoral candidate in Education at the University of Hong Kong. Her current research interests are social media in library, user education, and the 5E Instructional Model.

Marla J. Lohmann is an Associate Professor of Special Education at Colorado Christian University, where she teaches both special education alternative certification and master's degree students in fully online programs. Dr. Lohmann is an active member of the Council for Exceptional Children Teacher Education Division (TED) at both the state and national levels. Dr. Lohmann is passionate about offering high quality teacher preparation and ongoing training for in-service teachers in the remote classroom. Dr. Lohmann has taught more than 100 asynchronous online graduate-level teacher education courses and is passionate about supporting community-building in the online classroom.

Shalini Mathew, Ph.D is an Assistant Professor and Practicum-Internship coordinator in the Counseling Department at Northern State University. Dr. Mathew is a Nationally Certified Counselor through NBCC. Dr. Mathew has a PHD in Counselor Education & Supervision from North Carolina Agricultural and Technical State University, an MPhil in School Counseling, and an MS in Behavior Science from India. She also holds a B.S. in Family & Community Science from Mahatma Gandhi University in Kerala, India. For the last three years Dr. Mathew taught different counseling classes and supervised practicum and internship students. She has also served as an Assessment coordinator and practiced as a School Counselor and Child psychologist at a psychiatric setting in India for twelve years. Dr. Mathew's research interests include Children with specific learning disabilities, Complementary and alternative therapies in counseling, Counselor wellness, Trauma-Informed Care, and Counselor Education, Assessment and evaluation, Counseling immigrants and refugees, Experiences of international students and Cross-cultural counseling.

Rebecca Mathews, a Clinical Assistant Professor at the University of North Carolina at Greensboro, is a Licensed Professional Counselor and Board-Approved Supervisor who has provided mental health care for 15 years. Her clinical and research interests include suicide prevention, child & adolescent counseling, the therapeutic relationship, trauma, and counselor development. Dr. Mathews works to bridge the scientist-practitioner gap by providing supervision and training to counselors, medical personnel (psychiatry fellows, medical students), school personnel, and legal professionals.

Paula McMahon is the Chair and an Assistant Professor at the Department of Rehabilitation and Human Services at Montana State University, Billings (MSUB). Paula joined the faculty of MSUB in July 2017 after a 5 ½-year career with Virginia Commonwealth University. She teaches medical and psychosocial aspects of disability, individual and family response to disability, ethics, and psychiatric rehabilitation. She has served on several campus wide committees as well as engaging in community service. She has presented numerous times at the national, state, and local level on topics related to Rehabilitation Counseling and the Americans with Disabilities Act. Her research interests include transition services for students with disabilities, social justice and advocacy, professional development and identity, community accessibility and integrated academic and employment practices.

About the Contributors

Rosina Mete is the Director of Faculty within the Department of Behavioural Sciences at Yorkville University in Canada. She is a Registered Psychotherapist (Ontario) and a Canadian Certified Counsellor with the Canadian Counselling and Psychotherapy Association (CCPA). Dr. Mete joined Yorkville University in 2022 as the Course Lead for Assessment and continues contributing to other areas within the academic milieu. Before joining the Yorkville team, she worked in community health, hospital, academic, and private practice settings. She also has experience as an adjunct professor at other educational institutions. Dr. Mete has won awards for her academic and clinical work. Her research and publications include equity and access to mental health care, stress management, problem-solving and decision-making, and technology in education. She recently published a chapter, Conquering Mental Health Stigma and Developing Strategies to Reduce Workplace Stress: The CALM Model within the Handbook of Research on Dissecting and Dismantling Occupational Stress in Modern Organizations. Dr. Mete is on the Board Executive for the CCPA Counsellor Educator & Supervisors Chapter and a member of the CCPA and ACA. Her educational credentials include a BSc in Psychology from Carleton University, a MSc in Clinical Mental Health Counselling and a PhD in Leadership and Policy both from Niagara University.

Yuanjun Ni received the bachelor degree in Information Management and Information System at the Nanjing Normal University and the MSc in Library and Information Management from the University of Hong Kong. Her research interest is in social media and information system management.

Nur Farhinaa Othman received her bachelor degree (Bachelor of Human Sciences in English Language and Literature) from the International Islamic University Malaysia (IIUM) in 2011. Since 2011 to this day, she is with Universiti Malaysia Perlis (UniMAP) as a language instructor. She loves to incorporate technology into her lessons and is constantly seeking new and innovative ways to engage her students. Her research interest includes online learning, teaching and learning, tertiary level education, and TESL (teaching English as a second language).

Fatma Ouled Salem has a PhD in Counselor Education and Supervision from Walden University, a Master's degree in Clinical Mental Health Counseling from Southern New Hampshire University, and a Bachelor's degree in Applied Behavioral Science from Arizona State University. Currently, Dr. Fatma Ouled Salem is a Licensed Clinical Mental Health Counselor working in private practice and offering services to a variety of clients focusing on anxiety disorders and trauma and stressor related disorders. Dr. Fatma Ouled Salem is also an Adjunct Professor, currently teaching at Fisher College.

Heather Pederson is an Associate Professor in the Doctor of Psychology Program, Department of Behavioral Sciences at the University of Arizona Global Campus. In her role, she supports doctoral students, instructors, and Doctoral Chairs, and serves as a lead in the proactive advancement of Applied Doctoral Project courses, focusing on improved resources, clarity, and purposeful activities with intentional attention to improving student success.

Selin Philip is the director of Colorado Christian University's Ph.D. in Counselor Education and Supervision program and an Associate Professor of Counseling at the School of Counseling. She is a Licensed Professional Counselor in Michigan and a National Board-Certified Counselor. Dr. Philip's research interests cover a wide range of topics, including multicultural counseling, religious and spiritual

About the Contributors

integration in mental health, mentorship in counselor education and supervision, and mental health advocacy for South Asian communities. Outside of her professional endeavors, Dr. Philip finds fulfillment in her family life, enjoying the company of her husband, two daughters, and a beloved teddy bear dog.

Alyssa Weiss, PhD, MS.Ed, LMFT, CCTP, Approved Supervisor for AAMFT is a fulltime Professor within the Masters of Counselling Psychology (MACP) Program at Yorkville. She is a Licensed Marriage and Family Therapist in the state of Florida. Outside of academia Dr. Weiss has served in a variety of functions supporting mental health including private practice, program development, and program consultation. She has presented at a local, regional, national and international level, as well as, been published on myriad topics, including the therapeutic process. She holds advanced training in Traumatology, certification in Hypnotherapy and she is Level 1 IFS trained. She is a column editor for the Humanistic Counselor, the Therapeutic Speakeasy and serves on the editorial boards for Journal of Human Services, Journal of Adolescent and Family Health, and Counseling Outcome Research and Evaluation. Her educational credentials include a Bachelor of Arts in Sociology from Brandeis University, Masters in Special Education from the University of Miami and a PhD in Marriage and Family Therapy from Nova Southeastern University.

Nurul Naimah Rose is a Senior Lecturer at the Faculty of Business and Communication, Universiti Malaysia Perlis. Her area of expertise is guidance and counseling, and her sub-field expertise is related to mental health counseling, teaching, and learning. After being awarded a Doctor of Philosophy Degree (Counseling) from University Science Malaysia, she actively continued to contribute in terms of scholarly writing, namely papers in national and international journals.

Stephanie Stubbs is the Associate Director of Graduate Studies and Research at the University of Arizona Global Campus. She earned her B.A. in psychology and sociology at the University of Nebraska at Kearney and her M.A. and Ph.D. in (social) psychology at the University of Kansas. Dr. Stubbs is passionate about teaching and learning, toward which she devotes her research efforts.

Nancy Thomas has her PhD in Counselor Education and Supervision and MA in Counseling. She works as the Program Director and an Assistant Professor at Colorado Christian University's Master of Arts in Clinical Mental Health Counseling program. She is also a Licensed Professional Counselor and Supervisor in Texas. She is an active advocate for the mental health needs of the Asian community, providing resources through her counseling services, teaching, podcasts, workshops, and trainings. She is also a researcher, supervisor, presenter at a number of state, national, and international conferences, and the winner of the 2021 AHC Humanistic Advocacy and Social Justice Award.

Whitney Walters-Sachs is an experienced K-12 school administrator and lifelong learner. In her current role on the senior leadership team at Pine Crest School as the Vice President of School and Legal Affairs, Dr. Walters-Sachs serves as an educational thought leader, school administrator, and trusted advisor to the school's President and Board of Trustees. She works collaboratively with colleagues school-wide to advance the school's mission, support student learning, promote team development, communicate internally and externally, continuously improve processes, and strategically plan for the future. Outside of Pine Crest, Dr. Walters-Sachs is an Adjunct Professor in the Department of Leadership,

Policy, and Organizations at Vanderbilt's Peabody College, where she teaches courses in independent school leadership, action-based research, and the fiscal and legal dimensions of independent schools.

Index

4-Dimension Library Social Capital Assessment 288

A

Academic Achievement 13, 44, 182, 212, 299, 304, 328, 331, 343
Academic Resolution 90, 100-101, 104, 109
Accessibility 22, 26-27, 29, 81, 87, 193-194, 198, 206-209, 227, 252-258, 261-265, 301, 321, 330, 357, 367
Accommodation 257-258
ADA 252-256, 258, 261-264
Adjunct Faculty 93, 102-103, 107, 109
Adult Learners 16-21, 23-25, 27-30, 36, 43-46, 48, 50, 57, 91-94, 99-101, 103, 107, 164-167, 170-171, 173-176, 178-182, 184, 187, 191, 237, 283, 311, 315, 318-319, 334, 353, 366, 368
Adult Learning Theory 188, 314, 352
Adult Online Learner 46, 90-91, 93, 100, 102-103, 106, 109
Americans With Disabilities Act 252-254, 264
Anxiety 1-2, 4-5, 7-15, 86, 106, 142, 185, 204, 221, 254, 294-295, 299-300, 302, 304, 311, 318, 329, 331, 347
Assistive Technology 252, 254, 261, 264
Asynchronous Discussion 49, 55, 62-65, 67, 158, 186, 237-238, 333
Asynchronous Learning 35-36, 51, 53, 181, 190, 235, 326, 351, 355, 364-365, 367
Asynchronous Online Discussion 55, 61-62, 64, 69, 72, 355
Attention Deficit Hyperactivity Disorder (ADHD) 7, 15
Autonomy-Supportive Teaching 52, 326
Awareness 21, 29, 44, 66, 74-75, 77, 81-82, 84-85, 95, 114-115, 120, 123, 134, 137-139, 149, 152-154, 178, 194-195, 198, 201, 203-204, 258, 261, 263-264, 305, 336, 338-339

B

Belonging 16-17, 19-21, 25, 27-29, 31, 33, 35-36, 38, 40-41, 44, 48-50, 53, 90-91, 93, 104, 106, 108, 111-113, 118, 123-125, 128-130, 134-135, 138-140, 142, 145-146, 156, 165-167, 171, 177, 182, 185, 191-193, 197, 203, 205, 207, 212, 220, 240, 276, 285, 328, 357-358, 365
BIPOC Students 128-131, 133-140, 142
Bipolar 1-2, 5, 11, 13, 15
Black, Indigenous, and People of Color (BIPOC) 128-129, 148
Boundaries 8, 10, 74, 79-82, 86, 147, 323
Bracketing 121, 125
Building Community 29, 34, 42, 47, 53, 63, 108, 192, 237-238, 249-250, 364
Building Relationships 8-9, 38, 79, 87, 124, 215, 217, 222-224, 227, 237, 241-243, 246, 250, 252-253, 259, 267

C

Caring 44, 49, 90-94, 102-103, 106-109, 160, 220, 237-241, 243, 246-247, 300, 344
Case Study 16, 26, 34, 36-37, 43-44, 46, 50-51, 53, 72, 111, 119, 142, 146, 189-191, 211, 266, 277-278, 281, 283-288, 367
Climate 16, 30-31, 35, 44-45, 53, 78, 121, 124, 135, 148, 164-165, 167-183, 185-192, 234, 240, 303, 309, 337
College Teaching 72, 214, 312
Communication 5, 8, 18, 24, 46-47, 53, 65-66, 78-79, 90, 93-94, 96-97, 102-106, 113-115, 117, 120, 122-123, 136, 139-142, 144, 148, 152, 156, 161-162, 168-171, 173, 175, 177-179, 184-191, 193, 197-198, 205-207, 209, 213-215, 222, 224, 229-232, 234, 238-245, 248, 256, 259-260, 270-271,

274-275, 277-279, 284-285, 287, 296, 298, 301, 312, 324, 333, 335, 342, 346-347, 349, 351-352, 355, 360-363, 366

Community 16-22, 24-54, 58, 60, 63-70, 72, 78-79, 87, 90, 93-94, 100, 104-108, 111-114, 116, 118, 125, 129, 137, 144, 146, 156, 165-167, 170-172, 174-180, 182-184, 188-190, 192, 200, 204-205, 207, 209, 214-216, 223-224, 227-231, 233, 235-241, 243-246, 248-250, 262, 267-269, 271, 273-276, 279-281, 284-287, 289, 298-300, 305, 308, 310, 312, 316, 319, 321, 324, 330-331, 334, 338, 341, 347, 352-354, 357-358, 364, 367

Compliance 12, 152, 252, 254, 256-258, 261-264

Connection 8, 10-11, 16, 19-21, 24-26, 28-29, 32, 34, 38, 41, 55-56, 64-65, 69, 77, 79, 90-93, 102, 106, 108, 119, 128-129, 131, 134-137, 139-142, 148, 150-152, 157-159, 162, 165-167, 170-171, 173, 176-179, 181, 193, 195-196, 202, 208-209, 215-217, 220, 223, 227-228, 231, 236, 238-244, 247, 259, 276, 290, 298-299, 316-317, 333, 340-341, 355, 357-358, 361

Constructive Feedback 64-65, 119, 197, 208, 305, 314, 319, 359, 363

Core Components 50, 149, 152, 154, 230

Counselor Educator 74-75, 82, 84

Countertransference 120, 123-125

Courageous Conversations 59-60, 72

COVID-19 Pandemic 1, 10-12, 14, 47, 51, 70, 72, 78, 123, 150, 154, 186, 189-190, 194-195, 198, 203-204, 210-212, 218, 224, 228-229, 233, 235, 251, 263, 267, 272-273, 281, 285, 326, 329, 342, 347, 349, 352, 361-362, 366-368

Creativity 61, 63, 68, 70-71, 119, 155, 162, 193-194, 197, 199-201, 203, 209, 211-212

Cultural and Ethnic Representation 131-132, 134, 137, 139-140, 148

Cultural Belonging 128

Cultural Competence 111-115, 119-121, 123, 125, 134, 147, 153, 161, 206

Cultural Competency 114, 121, 125, 128-129, 135, 142, 150

Culture 31, 39, 44, 77, 88, 90-91, 93, 98, 102, 105-107, 109, 119-121, 125, 130-131, 133-134, 138, 152, 158, 209, 229, 254, 278, 305, 317, 324, 336-337, 343-344, 367

Culture of Care 90, 98, 102, 105, 107, 109

D

Depression 1-6, 8, 12-13, 15, 86, 254, 331
Disability 2-3, 7, 10-14, 252-254, 257-265

Diversity 17, 22-23, 27, 31, 59, 62, 69, 81, 84, 99, 109, 114-116, 119, 123-126, 131-134, 139, 143-151, 153, 158, 162, 180, 190, 203, 206, 211, 241, 253, 299-300, 307, 336-337, 344-345, 348, 352

Diversity, Equity, and Inclusion 132-133, 143, 148

E

Empathy 2, 8-10, 59, 64, 66, 92-93, 102-107, 111, 113-118, 120, 124, 193-194, 199, 203-206, 209-210, 212-213, 220, 239, 243, 245-246, 248, 252, 268

Engagement 9, 16, 19-21, 23-24, 28, 30-32, 34-35, 37, 39, 43-45, 48-50, 55, 64, 66-68, 71, 79, 81, 87, 90, 98, 102-104, 106-109, 113, 118-119, 124, 134-135, 137, 143, 147, 151, 153, 156-158, 161-162, 165-167, 169-174, 176-177, 180-182, 185, 187, 192-195, 197-199, 203-211, 213, 215, 217, 219, 221, 223-224, 226, 228-231, 233-234, 238, 240, 246, 248, 250, 271, 278-279, 281, 284, 290, 294-298, 302-304, 309-318, 324-325, 328, 330-331, 333-334, 336-338, 340-341, 343, 353-354, 356-358, 367-368

Ethics 76, 149, 161

Experiential Learning 23-24, 30, 32, 50, 63, 65, 67, 70-71, 156, 160, 174, 198, 211, 228, 356, 364

F

Facilitator 24, 39, 174, 204, 315, 321, 323
Faculty-Student Connections 195
FUML 266-267, 270-277, 289

G

Gaming 67, 72, 280
Gender Adapted Strategies 328
Graduate Online Learning 314

H

Hardship(s) 110
Higher Education 1-5, 10-14, 17, 19, 21-23, 47-52, 54-56, 58-59, 65, 67-70, 72, 74-75, 78, 80, 87, 89-95, 102-103, 106-109, 113-115, 117, 122-124, 129-130, 132-133, 136, 140, 142-147, 151, 158, 162-164, 169, 180, 182, 184-185, 187, 189-192, 199, 203-204, 210-211, 213-214, 227-235, 249-250, 252-254, 257-258, 261-264, 283, 285-287, 299-302, 306, 308-309, 311-313, 316, 319, 325, 328, 330-332, 334-335, 337, 344-351, 357, 361, 363-369

450

Index

Hybrid Learning 50, 187

I

Intentionality 38, 58, 132, 134-135, 153, 170, 177, 193-195, 198-199, 209, 212-213

L

Learning 1-3, 7, 11-14, 16-37, 39, 41, 43-54, 56-59, 63, 65-72, 74-75, 78-81, 83-90, 92, 100-101, 103-105, 107, 111-123, 125, 128-131, 136, 141-142, 144-147, 149-153, 155-201, 203-217, 219-222, 224, 226-240, 242-249, 251-257, 259-265, 267, 269-271, 273, 277-284, 286-337, 340-369

Learning Communities 22, 24, 43, 50, 52-53, 57, 75, 164, 168, 171, 173, 176, 178-180, 182-183, 189, 191-192, 213, 216, 236, 248, 325, 367, 369

Learning Community 16-17, 20-22, 24, 26, 28, 32, 34, 43-45, 49-50, 52-53, 156, 164-167, 174, 176-178, 190, 205, 207, 230, 233, 235, 300, 305, 330-331, 334, 353-354, 357-358

Learning Environment 19-20, 25, 29-31, 34, 37, 39, 41, 44, 46, 57, 67, 75, 79, 104, 112-117, 119-121, 125, 151-152, 155-157, 160-161, 164, 166-167, 170-171, 176-180, 184, 189, 192-195, 197-198, 203, 205-209, 245, 247, 252-254, 261, 263, 291, 294, 300, 303, 311, 331, 337, 345, 352-354, 356-360, 363-368

Learning Management System (LMS) 24, 28, 43, 174, 222, 236, 304, 329, 363

Learning Outcomes 17-18, 20, 25, 45, 67-68, 90, 101, 151, 164, 166, 180, 186-187, 194-195, 204, 206, 208, 290, 296, 304, 310-311, 318, 329-331, 335, 349, 353, 358-360

M

Malaysian Higher Education 350-351, 363

Male Students 328-338, 341-342, 344

Meaningful Bonds or Connections 125

Meaningful Connections 10, 44, 111-114, 117, 119-121, 193-194

Mental Health 1-3, 6, 8-15, 70-71, 76-77, 88, 92, 94, 104, 113, 123, 130, 137, 160, 162, 202, 253, 268, 277, 329, 331, 338, 341-342

Mentorship 128-129, 135-143, 146, 148, 153-154, 233

Multicultural Sensitivity 149, 152

N

Narrative Approach 111, 113, 120, 125

Narrative Theory 111-112, 115-117, 119-121, 123-124, 126

Non-College Life Events 100-103, 106, 110

O

Online Classroom 1-2, 4, 8-9, 16, 24, 45, 56, 67, 72, 74-75, 79, 85-86, 90-91, 93-94, 102, 104, 111, 116, 120-121, 125, 151-152, 155, 157-158, 164, 170, 174, 184, 189, 193-194, 196, 202, 207-209, 214-215, 219, 237-241, 243, 245-248, 250, 252, 255-256, 260-261, 325, 333, 335-336, 338, 341, 350-351, 357-358

Online Discussion 7, 55, 57-58, 60-65, 67-70, 72-73, 80, 114, 117-118, 156, 201, 298, 313-314, 325, 355, 359, 367

Online Education 2, 10-11, 21, 23-24, 48, 53, 57, 74, 78, 86, 88, 91, 94, 111-114, 121, 128-129, 136, 139, 143, 151, 161-162, 165, 172-173, 178, 181, 183, 189-194, 198-200, 203-204, 206, 209, 214, 228, 237-238, 243, 245, 248, 250, 253-254, 263, 290, 298-301, 304-305, 308-311, 317, 319, 341-342, 354, 359, 361, 368

Online Educational Programs 148, 199

Online Engagement 31, 55, 79, 368

Online Instructor 24, 30, 35-36, 51, 68-69, 87, 119, 124, 174, 207-208, 237-238, 314, 353, 365, 367

Online Learning 12, 14, 16, 19-23, 25-26, 28, 32, 41, 43-45, 48-54, 57, 69, 75, 79, 81, 87, 89, 103, 113-114, 118, 120-123, 125, 130, 145-146, 151, 155-156, 162-166, 169-175, 177-184, 186-187, 189-195, 197, 199-200, 203-205, 207, 210-214, 216, 220, 227-232, 234-237, 239, 245, 247, 249, 251, 254, 261-263, 290-304, 307-314, 323, 326, 328-336, 341-342, 345-346, 348-351, 353-369

P

P12 Educators 315-316, 318, 323, 326

Peer Review 305, 314, 319-321

Pell Grant Recipients 99, 110

Post-Traumatic Stress Disorder 1-2, 6

Problem-Based Learning 65-66, 72, 368

Professional Identity 149-150, 152, 154, 157, 160, 223, 234

Professional Networks 225-226, 236

R

Racial Microaggressions 130, 143, 145, 147-148
Recognition 21, 90, 94, 103, 131, 134, 138, 140, 148, 246, 358
Relationship 8, 10, 14, 21, 32, 46, 53, 55, 57, 76, 78-79, 82, 88, 91, 103-104, 106, 133, 135, 137-138, 157-158, 160, 163, 167-168, 176-178, 185-186, 188-189, 191, 207, 213-216, 222, 227, 230-231, 234, 239, 241-242, 244-245, 248, 258-262, 264, 266-269, 277-278, 286, 291-292, 299, 301, 324, 331, 336, 338, 349, 358, 362
Relationships 2, 8-9, 11, 18, 21, 29, 31, 35-36, 38, 51, 59, 78-79, 82-84, 87-88, 90-94, 100, 102, 104-108, 112-114, 117, 120-121, 124, 128-129, 134-138, 141-143, 145, 152, 156, 167-168, 170-171, 175-179, 183, 186, 189, 193-194, 197-198, 204, 210, 213-225, 227, 229-230, 233-234, 236-253, 259-261, 263, 267-268, 270-273, 277, 279, 289, 296, 299, 301, 310, 319, 329, 338, 346-347

S

Safe Spaces 42, 69, 128, 135-139, 142, 145-148, 195, 247
Satisfaction 8, 14, 20-21, 35, 49-50, 79, 113, 123, 163, 165-167, 171, 173, 186-187, 190, 193-195, 197, 200, 207, 216, 235, 237-239, 241, 245-250, 283, 295-297, 303-304, 306, 309-311, 313, 325, 330-332, 334-335, 343-346, 348, 364-365, 368
Self-Efficacy 7, 9, 12-13, 25, 79, 83, 91, 104, 106, 110, 123, 142, 169, 173, 176, 182, 187, 199, 243, 247, 290-305, 307-313, 331, 335, 342-343, 345, 348-349, 357
Sensitivity 66, 74-75, 77, 85, 125, 149-150, 152, 161, 195
Service Learning 66-67, 70, 72, 312
Simulation Activities 55, 67, 73
Skill Building 290
Social Annotation 55, 67-68, 71, 73
Social Capital 223, 231, 266-277, 279-282, 284-289
Social Climate Theory 164, 167-170, 172, 174, 181-182
Social Media 29, 48, 61, 184, 214-220, 222-225, 227-236, 244, 266, 270, 274-279, 281-285, 287, 289, 309, 352
Storytelling 111-113, 115-120, 122-125, 201
Student Connection 129, 137, 193
Student Engagement 28, 30, 71, 90, 104, 119, 156, 161, 169-170, 177, 193-195, 197, 203, 206-208, 210, 213-214, 219, 221, 224, 230-231, 233, 238, 240, 250, 290, 295-296, 298, 310-315, 317-318, 325, 331, 337, 356-357
Student Mattering 90-91, 93, 104, 106
Student Persistence 20, 90-91, 93-94, 106, 109, 121, 167, 170, 219
Student Voices 29, 104, 322, 337
Students 1-14, 16, 20-27, 29-47, 49-56, 58-76, 78-81, 84, 87, 90-121, 123-125, 128-147, 149-150, 152-174, 176-179, 181-187, 189-209, 212, 214-216, 218-231, 233-244, 246-248, 250, 252-264, 266-267, 271-273, 275-276, 278-283, 286, 288, 290-303, 305-326, 328-347, 350-356, 358-368
Support 8-12, 17, 20, 23, 25, 27, 33, 44-46, 48, 58-59, 61-62, 66-67, 71, 82-85, 91-95, 97, 99-107, 114, 117, 121, 125, 128-131, 133-142, 145, 148, 151-153, 155-158, 161, 166, 168-169, 173, 175-178, 181, 192, 194, 198, 205, 207-208, 212-216, 220, 222-228, 235, 237-250, 252-253, 258-260, 270, 283, 289, 291, 297, 300-302, 304-305, 311, 314-316, 319-321, 323, 325, 328-329, 333-334, 337, 340-343, 349, 352, 357-359, 361-365, 367-368
SWOT Analysis 266, 270-271, 289
Synchronous Discussion 55, 60-63, 73, 159
Synchronous Learning 22, 24, 128, 174, 221, 236
Synchronous Online Discussion 60-61, 63, 73

T

Technology 14, 21, 24, 43-44, 47-51, 53-54, 68, 77, 85, 87, 91, 95, 103, 109, 112, 114, 121-123, 140, 142, 163, 174, 178, 180, 187-188, 190, 195-196, 199-200, 202-203, 209-210, 212-213, 227, 229, 231-232, 234, 236, 238, 241, 246-247, 249, 251-256, 261, 264-265, 267-268, 270, 276, 280, 287-288, 290, 292, 294-295, 299, 301, 304-306, 308-311, 313-314, 318-321, 331, 335, 345, 347-349, 352-353, 355, 357, 359-366, 368-369
The Managerial Role 350, 360
The Pedagogical Role 350
The Social Role 350, 357-358
The Technical Role 350, 360-362
The University of Arizona Global Campus 1, 90, 99-100, 105, 109, 237, 252
Training 27, 46, 48, 76, 81, 86, 88, 102, 107, 114, 123, 128, 138, 141, 146, 148-154, 160-161, 181, 183, 186, 211, 237, 254, 261, 266, 271, 276-277, 292,

Index

298, 306, 342, 345-346, 354-355, 361
Transformative Conversation 55, 57, 73

U

Understanding 1-2, 8-9, 11, 17, 19-20, 23, 53, 56, 59, 64-66, 68, 75-79, 84-85, 91-94, 99-100, 102-104, 106-107, 111-119, 129, 134-135, 137-139, 142, 150-151, 165, 167-168, 172, 176, 180, 190-192, 197-199, 202-208, 210, 227, 229, 231, 234, 238-239, 243, 245, 255, 259-260, 262, 272, 291, 295, 299-300, 303-304, 306, 310, 314-315, 317, 323, 326, 336-339, 342, 349-353, 358, 361
Universal Design 12, 252, 254-255, 261-265, 321
Universal Design for Learning 254, 261-262, 264-265
University 1, 9, 11-12, 14, 16-17, 19-21, 23, 26-29, 31, 34-35, 48-51, 53, 55, 74, 78, 81-82, 87, 90-91, 93-94, 99-105, 107-111, 117-118, 121-125, 128, 130, 132, 134, 136, 142, 144-147, 149, 157, 163-164, 166-167, 181-184, 186-188, 190-193, 203, 209-210, 212, 214-216, 219-221, 223-226, 230, 237, 243, 246, 251-252, 254, 256-258, 262-263, 265-267, 269-272, 274-276, 280-284, 286-292, 295-296, 304-305, 310-311, 314, 317, 322, 324-325, 328, 330-331, 333, 340, 346-348, 361, 364-367
University Libraries 266-267, 269-272, 274-276, 282, 289
University Library 109, 266-267, 271, 284, 287, 289

V

Video Chat Exhaustion (i.e., Zoom Fatigue) 60, 73
Vincent Tinto 90-91
Virtual Classroom 8, 24, 31-32, 44, 46, 48, 52, 87, 111, 113-114, 117-121, 124-125, 151, 159, 165, 171, 174, 183, 189, 197, 210, 214-215, 228, 250, 301, 347, 354
Virtual Classroom and Online Classroom 125
Virtual Cultural Affinity Groups 140, 148
Virtual Education 113, 329-331, 334, 350-351, 353-354, 363
Virtual Learning 11, 17, 21, 24, 26, 33-34, 41, 45, 112, 114, 117, 119-121, 174, 176, 189, 219, 311, 328-329, 331, 341-342, 351-353, 363
Virtual Makerspace 68, 73
Virtual Spaces 32, 128, 142

Recommended Reference Books

IGI Global's reference books are available in three unique pricing formats:
Print Only, E-Book Only, or Print + E-Book.

Order direct through IGI Global's Online Bookstore at
www.igi-global.com or through your preferred provider.

ISBN: 9781799897064
EISBN: 9781799897088
© 2022; 302 pp.
List Price: US$ **215**

ISBN: 9781799889854
EISBN: 9781799889878
© 2022; 383 pp.
List Price: US$ **215**

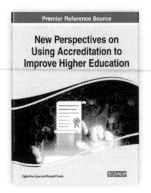

ISBN: 9781668451953
EISBN: 9781668451960
© 2022; 300 pp.
List Price: US$ **195**

ISBN: 9781799852001
EISBN: 9781799852018
© 2022; 355 pp.
List Price: US$ **215**

ISBN: 9781799897507
EISBN: 9781799897521
© 2022; 304 pp.
List Price: US$ **215**

ISBN: 9781799868293
EISBN: 9781799868316
© 2022; 389 pp.
List Price: US$ **215**

Do you want to stay current on the latest research trends, product announcements, news, and special offers?
Join IGI Global's mailing list to receive customized recommendations, exclusive discounts, and more.
Sign up at: **www.igi-global.com/newsletters**.

Publisher of Timely, Peer-Reviewed Inclusive Research Since 1988

www.igi-global.com   Sign up at www.igi-global.com/newsletters   facebook.com/igiglobal   twitter.com/igiglobal   linkedin.com/igiglobal

Ensure Quality Research is Introduced to the Academic Community

Become an Evaluator for IGI Global Authored Book Projects

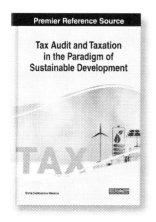   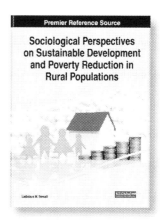

The overall success of an authored book project is dependent on quality and timely manuscript evaluations.

Applications and Inquiries may be sent to:
development@igi-global.com

Applicants must have a doctorate (or equivalent degree) as well as publishing, research, and reviewing experience. Authored Book Evaluators are appointed for one-year terms and are expected to complete at least three evaluations per term. Upon successful completion of this term, evaluators can be considered for an additional term.

If you have a colleague that may be interested in this opportunity, we encourage you to share this information with them.

Easily Identify, Acquire, and Utilize Published Peer-Reviewed Findings in Support of Your Current Research

IGI Global OnDemand

Purchase Individual IGI Global OnDemand Book Chapters and Journal Articles

For More Information:
www.igi-global.com/e-resources/ondemand/

Browse through 150,000+ Articles and Chapters!

Find specific research related to your current studies and projects that have been contributed by international researchers from prestigious institutions, including:

- Accurate and Advanced Search
- Affordably Acquire Research
- Instantly Access Your Content
- Benefit from the InfoSci Platform Features

"It really provides an excellent entry into the research literature of the field. It presents a manageable number of highly relevant sources on topics of interest to a wide range of researchers. The sources are scholarly, but also accessible to 'practitioners'."

- Ms. Lisa Stimatz, MLS, University of North Carolina at Chapel Hill, USA

Interested in Additional Savings?

Subscribe to
IGI Global OnDemand *Plus*

Learn More

Acquire content from over 128,000+ research-focused book chapters and 33,000+ scholarly journal articles for as low as US$ 5 per article/chapter (original retail price for an article/chapter: US$ 37.50).

7,300+ E-BOOKS.
ADVANCED RESEARCH.
INCLUSIVE & AFFORDABLE.

IGI Global e-Book Collection

- Flexible Purchasing Options (Perpetual, Subscription, EBA, etc.)
- Multi-Year Agreements with No Price Increases Guaranteed
- No Additional Charge for Multi-User Licensing
- No Maintenance, Hosting, or Archiving Fees
- Continually Enhanced & Innovated Accessibility Compliance Features (WCAG)

Handbook of Research on Digital Transformation, Industry Use Cases, and the Impact of Disruptive Technologies
ISBN: 9781799877127
EISBN: 9781799877141

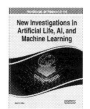

Handbook of Research on New Investigations in Artificial Life, AI, and Machine Learning
ISBN: 9781799886860
EISBN: 9781799886877

Handbook of Research on Future of Work and Education
ISBN: 9781799882756
EISBN: 9781799882770

Research Anthology on Physical and Intellectual Disabilities in an Inclusive Society (4 Vols.)
ISBN: 9781668435427
EISBN: 9781668435434

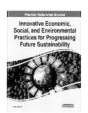

Innovative Economic, Social, and Environmental Practices for Progressing Future Sustainability
ISBN: 9781799895909
EISBN: 9781799895923

Applied Guide for Event Study Research in Supply Chain Management
ISBN: 9781799889694
EISBN: 9781799889717

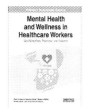

Mental Health and Wellness in Healthcare Workers
ISBN: 9781799888130
EISBN: 9781799888147

Clean Technologies and Sustainable Development in Civil Engineering
ISBN: 9781799898108
EISBN: 9781799898122

Request More Information, or Recommend the IGI Global e-Book Collection to Your Institution's Librarian

For More Information or to Request a Free Trial, Contact IGI Global's e-Collections Team: eresources@igi-global.com | 1-866-342-6657 ext. 100 | 717-533-8845 ext. 100

Are You Ready to Publish Your Research?

IGI Global — PUBLISHER of TIMELY KNOWLEDGE

IGI Global offers book authorship and editorship opportunities across 11 subject areas, including business, computer science, education, science and engineering, social sciences, and more!

Benefits of Publishing with IGI Global:

- Free one-on-one editorial and promotional support.
- Expedited publishing timelines that can take your book from start to finish in less than one (1) year.
- Choose from a variety of formats, including Edited and Authored References, Handbooks of Research, Encyclopedias, and Research Insights.
- Utilize IGI Global's eEditorial Discovery® submission system in support of conducting the submission and double-blind peer review process.
- IGI Global maintains a strict adherence to ethical practices due in part to our full membership with the Committee on Publication Ethics (COPE).
- Indexing potential in prestigious indices such as Scopus®, Web of Science™, PsycINFO®, and ERIC – Education Resources Information Center.
- Ability to connect your ORCID iD to your IGI Global publications.
- Earn honorariums and royalties on your full book publications as well as complimentary content and exclusive discounts.

Join Your Colleagues from Prestigious Institutions, Including:

- Australian National University
- Massachusetts Institute of Technology
- Johns Hopkins University
- Harvard University
- Tsinghua University
- Columbia University in the City of New York

Learn More at: www.igi-global.com/publish
or Contact IGI Global's Aquisitions Team at: acquisition@igi-global.com

Individual Article & Chapter Downloads
US$ 29.50/each

Easily Identify, Acquire, and Utilize Published Peer-Reviewed Findings in Support of Your Current Research

- Browse Over **170,000+ Articles & Chapters**
- **Accurate & Advanced** Search
- Affordably Acquire **International Research**
- **Instantly Access** Your Content
- Benefit from the **InfoSci® Platform Features**

THE UNIVERSITY of NORTH CAROLINA at CHAPEL HILL

It really provides an excellent entry into the research literature of the field. *It presents a manageable number of* highly relevant sources *on topics of interest to a wide range of researchers. The sources are* scholarly, but also accessible *to 'practitioners'.*

- Ms. Lisa Stimatz, MLS, University of North Carolina at Chapel Hill, USA

Interested in Additional Savings?

Subscribe to

Learn More

Acquire content from over 137,000+ research-focused book chapters and 33,000+ scholarly journal articles for as low as US$ 5 per article/chapter (original retail price for an article/chapter: US$ 29.50).